# Aging
## IN MASS SOCIETY
*Myths and Realities*

# Aging

## IN MASS SOCIETY
## *Myths and Realities*
### THIRD EDITION

**Jon Hendricks**
University of Kentucky

**C. Davis Hendricks**

LITTLE, BROWN and COMPANY
Boston   Toronto

Library of Congress Cataloging-in-Publication Data

Hendricks, Jon, 1943–
    Aging in mass society.

    Bibliography: p.
    Includes index.
    1. Aged—United States.  2. Aging.  3. Gerontology.
I. Hendricks, C. Davis, 1948–    . II. Title.
HQ1064.U5H44   1986        305.2'6'0973        85-24075
ISBN 0-316-35634-4

Library of Congress Catalog Card No. 85-24075

ISBN 0-316-35634-4

9  8  7  6  5  4  3  2  1

ALP

Published simultaneously in Canada by Little, Brown & Company (Canada) Limited

Printed in the United States of America

*Credits*

    *Figure 1.1:* Reprinted from *Population Bulletin* by permission of the Population Reference Bureau, Inc.
    *Table 2.1:* Reprinted by permission of the National Council on Aging. *Figures 2.2 and 2.3:* Reprinted by permission of the American Philosophical Society. *Table 2.2:* Reprinted by permission of Biometrika Trustees. *Table 2.3:* Reprinted from *Population Studies* by permission of the Population Investigation Committee, London School of Economics. *Table 2.4:* Reprinted by permission of John P. Demos, Brandeis University. *Figures 2.4 and 2.5:* Reprinted from *Population Studies* by permission of the Population Investigation Committee, London School of Economics. *Figure 2.7:* Reprinted from *Population Bulletin* by permission of the Population Reference Bureau, Inc.
    *Figure 3.1:* From K. A. McClelland, "Self-Conception and Life-Satisfaction: Integrating Aged Subculture and Activity Theory," *Journal of Gerontology* 37, 6 (1982): 723. Reprinted by permission of the *Journal of Gerontology. Figure 3.2:* "Processes related to structural elements," Fig. 1-2 in *Aging and Society,* Vol. 3: A Sociology of Age Stratification by M. W. Riley, M. Johnson, and A. Foner. © 1972 by Russell Sage Foundation, Basic Books, Inc., Publishers, New York. *Figure 3.3:* From Donald O. Cowgill, "Aging and Modernization: A Revision of the Theory," in Jon Hendricks and C. Davis Hendricks, eds., *Dimensions of Aging: Readings,* p. 64. Copyright © 1979 by Winthrop Publishers, Inc. Reprinted by permission of Little, Brown and Company. *Figure 3.5:* Reprinted from *Human Development* by permission of S. Karger AG, Basel.
    *Figure 4.2:* From B. L. Strehler et al., "Rate and Magnitude of Age Pigment Accumulation in the Human Myocardium," *Journal of Gerontology* 14, 4 (1959): 433. Reprinted by permission of the *Journal of Gerontology. Figure 4.3:* From G. A. Borkan and A. H. Norris, "Assessment of Biological Age Using a Profile of Physical Parameters," *Journal of Gerontology* 35, 2 (1980): 180. Reprinted by permission of the *Journal of Gerontology. Table 4.1:* Courtesy of Charles C Thomas, Publishers, Springfield, Illinois. *Figure 4.4:* Reprinted by permission of N. W. Schock. *Figure 4.5 and Table 4.2:* Reprinted by permission of W. H. Freeman & Company, Publishers.
    *Figure 5.1:* Reprinted from *Federation Proceedings* by permission of the Federation of American Societies for Experimental Biology.
    *Figure 6.1:* Reprinted by permission of Raven Press, Publishers. *Figure 6.2:* From K. Warner Schaie and James Geiwitz, *Adult Development and Aging,* p. 309. Copyright © 1982 by K. Warner Schaie and James Geiwitz. Reprinted by permission of Little, Brown and Company. *Figure 6.4:* Reprinted by permission of Guilford Press. *Figure 6.5:* From E. W. Busse and D. G. Blazer, eds., *Handbook of Geriatric Psychiatry,* p. 209. Copyright © 1980 by E. W. Busse and D. G. Blazer. Reprinted by permission of Van Nostrand Reinhold Company. *Figure 6.6:* Reprinted from *Human Development* by permission of S. Karger AG, Basel.
    *Table 7.2:* Reprinted by permission of the *American Journal of Psychiatry* and Eric Pfeiffer. *Figure 7.5:* From Theodore H. Koff, *Long-Term Care: An Approach to Serving the Frail Elderly,* p. 93. Copyright © 1982 by Little, Brown and Company. Reprinted by permission. *Figure 7.6:* Reprinted from *Aging and Work* by permission of the National Council on Aging.
    *Table 8.2:* Reprinted by permission of William Heinemann Ltd., London.
    *Table 9.4:* Reprinted by permission of *Ageing and Society.*
    *Figures 10.1 and 10.2:* Reprinted by permission of *Public Opinion.*
    *Figure 12.2:* Reprinted by permission of *Public Opinion.*

**For our Parents**
and in memory of
**Don Kent** — *still*

# PREFACE

In the nine years since our first edition appeared, the field of gerontology has undergone many changes. It no longer offers the heady promise of growth it did then — the political winds having shifted — nevertheless, the need for serious study and research remain. During the past decade gerontology has become considerably more sophisticated. It is our intent to communicate these changes, to offer a comprehensive review of the current state of the elderly, to sensitize our readers to the essence of aging in today's world, and to suggest prospects for the future.

At the time our second edition was published we noted that there still existed a number of myths about what it is like to grow old. Today these myths are mostly perpetuated by the popular press. The best way to stop the proliferation of misinformation is through education, specifically in courses on gerontology. While many students using this text may not enter the field as professionals, they will nonetheless supply a much needed corrective balance to uninformed views. It is to this goal that this book is dedicated. Take whatever lessons it has to teach into the world. Do not stand silent as the elderly or the process of growing old are subjected to the stereotypical thinking that seems to take place whenever events are not well understood.

The past few years have witnessed widespread acceptance of gerontology, even if political forces have not always been hospitable to its recommendations. As a result of the diversity of the aging population and because aging is a dynamic process involving the physiological, social, and psychological facets of our existence, generalizations about growing and being old are difficult to support. Often the answers offered to the multitude of questions raised are as varied as the questions themselves. There are no easy answers to why people age as they do, but what has become apparent is that some type of unifying conceptual framework enables students and researchers to make sense of the diversity of facts that underpin our lives.

The present edition is intended to provide a comprehensive description of the dimensions of aging. It takes as its point of departure the proposition that it is meaningless to talk about any element of aging without having a grasp of the others as well. Our goal is to provide a holistic view of aging and to point to the ways in which the personal, social, and structural levels of the process interact to shape our daily lives.

To appreciate the relative character of aging in modern mass societies, it is prudent if not essential to have some grasp of where the elderly stand in other places and in other times. This will also allow us to understand how the relationship of older persons to the rest of their society is colored by the society's internal structure and how in turn each society is affected by the principal powers influencing world affairs today.

Finally, to describe or interpret the assumed facts about aging, it is necessary to understand the conceptual frameworks employed in gathering those facts. It is only in this way that change or accommodation can be forthcoming. There is no denying that an interdisciplinary approach to the study of aging may be a monumental task: to recognize, collect, and collate all the loose ends. Although we know that our efforts cannot yield definitive conclusions, we hope they will encourage further inquiry.

This edition is markedly different from the two previous ones: there have been sizable deletions, much reorganization, and the addition of a new chapter. The vast majority of the material in the present text is new: four chapters have been combined into two and a new section on policy formation has been added (Chapter 11). We have given long and careful consideration to the diverse recommendations of users and reviewers and believe the suggestions we have incorporated have noticeably improved this edition. Moreover, the typeface and graphics have been redesigned to change the entire appearance of the text. The production staff at Little, Brown listened to the concerns of scholars and students and have provided the extremely competent assistance necessary to make the text more accessible to readers. We welcome the input of new or renewed readers; without their comments and support our task is immeasurably more difficult.

Part One, comprising the first three chapters, offers an introduction to the field of social gerontology and the necessary conceptual tools for interpreting what happens as people age. It furnishes a working vocabulary, some idea of the fluid boundaries of aging, an overview of the demographic facts of life, and an indication of the relative meaning we attach to growing old. Part Two, with its four chapters, summarizes what we know of the lifeworld of the aging person. It begins with explanatory frameworks in physiology and continues with an overview of the health-related declines accompanying aging (including the pattern of health care services) and what they mean. The focus then shifts to psychological factors of interest to gerontologists. Part Three contains a broader, societal view of aging: the ways social context affect the individual. A key component of this section is the relevance of policy issues for individual functioning. Part Four attempts to forecast the future, both for the elderly themselves and for those who might be interested in gerontology as a vocation.

The words set in **boldface** type in the text are terms used in a technical sense, and are listed in the glossary. The meaning of words in *italics*, while they may be used in a technical or special sense, should be clear from the context in which they appear in the chapter. At the end of each chapter is a list of pertinent readings.

Many friends and colleagues have aided our efforts over the years, and it is impossible to cite the numerous ways in which we are indebted to them. We hope it will be sufficient to say we recognize we are who we are because they have touched and reached us.

There are a number of individuals who gave invaluable assistance to this third edition. Leonard Cain, William Rakowski, Harold Sheppard, Joseph Tindale, and Wen-hui Tsai made initial suggestions for revisions, and in some instances they also commented on the working manuscript. While we did not follow all their suggestions, their insights and efforts made our job easier. At Little, Brown the production personnel, coordinated by Phyllis Mitzman, as well as the efforts of Carolita Deter and her staff are evident in the physical product you now read. Manuscript preparation at the University of Kentucky was done by Marlene Pettit, who continues to amaze us by her speed, concern, and ability to render textual hieroglyphics into legible copy. The instructor's manual was typed by Wendy Price. There are also three very special people who made inestimable contributions to this third edition. They are true professionals and valuable colleagues; they have treated this project as if it were their own, performing all manner of tasks willingly, quickly, and unflinchingly. Toni Calasanti has offered criticisms on two editions now, and as always, her editorial suggestions are right on target. Howard Turner helped keep everything in perspective and was always available for any task. Cynthia Leedham made substantial contributions from start to finish. Without the efforts and support of these colleagues, the end result would have suffered.

While we are sincerely grateful for the invaluable assistance we have been fortunate to have, any mistakes in this edition are our own. We remain convinced that you, the reader, are embarking on the study of a fascinating, provocative, and complex topic. Welcome to a most rewarding field.

# CONTENTS

**PART ONE**
## Making Sense of Aging in the Modern World   1

**1**   **THE AGE-OLD QUESTION OF OLD AGE**   3

Making Sense of Aging: The Perspective of This Book   4

   The Many Levels of Aging   4

   Approaching the Multifaceted Nature of Aging   5

   Our Framework for Looking at Old Age   6

   Interpreting Data on Aging   7

Gerontology: The Study of Aging   14

   Incentives for the Development of Gerontology as a Field of Study   14

   The Depression and Concern for the Elderly   15

   Development and Scope of Gerontology   17

Summary   23

Discussion Questions   24

Pertinent Readings   26

**2**   **AGING IN THE MODERN WORLD**   28

Some Key Concepts in Social Gerontology   29

   Nature of Aging   29

   Age Grading   30

   Age-Appropriate Behavior   31

   Rites of Passage   33

   Ageism: Stereotyping the Elderly   34

   Age Structure of the Population   38

Aging in Historical Context   44

   Population Trends and Age Structure in History   44

   Attitudes Toward Aging in History   53

Aging in Advanced Industrial Society   57

   Population Age Structures   57

   Age-Dependent Populations   65

Increases in Life Expectancy    67

Expansion of the Elderly Population    69

Aging in the Third World    70

Population Structure    70

Quality of Life    70

Summary    72

Discussion Questions    74

Pertinent Readings    76

**3    THEORIES OF SOCIAL GERONTOLOGY**    80

The Role of Theory in Social Gerontology    81

The Relevance of Theory    81

How Theories Make Sense of Aging    82

Evaluating Theories    82

The Focus of Social Gerontology    83

Explaining the Aging Experience    84

Early Theoretical Developments    87

Disengagement Theory    87

Activity Theory    89

Subcultural Theory    90

Continuity Theory    92

Second Generation Theoretical Developments    94

Age Stratification Theory    95

Modernization Theory    100

Emergent Theories in Social Gerontology    103

Social Environmental Theories    103

Political Economy    108

Summary    114

Discussion Questions    116

Pertinent Readings    118

**PART TWO**

**The Lifeworld of the Aging Person**    123

**4    THE PHYSIOLOGY OF AGING**    125

The Relevance of Physiology to Social Gerontology    126

The Impact of Early Physiological Theories    126

The Effect of Sociological Factors on Physiology    126

Physiology as Part of the Social Context    128

Early Biological Theories    129

The Rate of Living Theory    130

The Stress Theory    131
Recent Biological Theories    131
    Cellular Theories    132
    Molecular Theories    135
    Immunological Theory    137
    Neuroendocrine Theory    137
    Free Radical and Waste Product Theories    138
    Cross-Linkage Theory    140
    Implications of Physiological Theories of Aging    140
Functional Capacity and Age    141
    Functional Variability Within Age Categories    141
    The Picture of Function    144
    Life-Style Factors and Functional Variability    144
Summary    147
Discussion Questions    148
Pertinent Readings    150


**5**    **HEALTH STATUS IN THE LATER YEARS**    152
Dimensions of Health    153
    Definitions of Health    153
    The Meaning of Health for the Elderly    156
Health Problems of the Later Years    158
    Health and the Rectangularization of the Life Curve    158
    Patterns of Mortality and Morbidity Among the Elderly    160
The Diseases of Later Life    165
    Cardiovascular Diseases    166
    Cancer    172
    Arthritis and Rheumatism    174
    Diabetes Mellitus    174
    Oral and Dental Problems    175
Life-Style and Health in the Later Years    176
    The Sociocultural Context and Health    176
    Control and Longevity    178
    Life-Style Factors Affecting Health and Longevity    179
Health Care Services for the Elderly    187
    Cost Effectiveness in Health Services for the Elderly    187
    Cost Containment and Health Expenditures    188
    Appropriate Levels of Care for the Elderly    192
Summary    193
Discussion Questions    195
Pertinent Readings    196

**6** **PSYCHOLOGICAL FACTORS IN ADULT LIFE** 201

Multiple Facets of the Psychology of Aging 202

Sensory and Cognitive Functioning 203

Sensory Modalities 203

Reaction Time and Psychomotor Response 208

Learning, Remembering, and Forgetting 209

Intelligence and Creativity 213

Stability and Change Over the Life Cycle 221

Stage Theories of Development in Adulthood 221

Alternatives to Developmental Models 223

Sex Roles and Adult Life 224

Psychological Disorders in the Later Years 225

Mental Health and Mental Disorders 225

Mental Health in Later Life 227

Mental Disorders Among the Elderly 229

Psychogenic Disorders 230

Organic Brain Syndromes 237

Treatment and Intervention 241

Summary 244

Discussion Questions 246

Pertinent Readings 248

**7** **EVERYDAY WORLD OF THE ELDERLY** 253

Key Questions 254

Family Relations in Later Life 254

The Nature of Family Ties 254

Structural Factors and Family Relations 266

Abuse and Conflict in Families 269

The Meaning of Sexuality 270

Living Arrangements 276

The Elderly in the Community 276

Congregate Living Facilities 280

Issues of Daily Life 288

Leisure, Diversions, and Time 289

Issues for Thought 294

Concerns About Crime 294

The Role of Religion 297

Anticipating Death 299

Temporal Orientation 300

Summary 302

Discussion Questions 305

Pertinent Readings 306

**PART THREE**

# Aging in Social Context: Social Policy, Structural Factors, and the Aging   315

**8**    **WORK, FINANCES, AND THE GOLDEN YEARS**   317

Work and Aging in Mass Society   318
   Changes in the Economy, Labor Patterns, and Retirement   318
   Two Perspectives on Work and Retirement   320
Work Patterns and the Life Cycle   322
   Social Construction of Careers   322
   Models of Career Development   323
The Meaning of Work   326
   Worker Stereotypes   326
   Status Displacement   328
   Age Discrimination   329
   Work and Self-Image   332
   Anticipating Retirement   335
Working Around the World   338
   Trends in Western Countries   338
   Countries in Transition: Japan and the Soviet Union   341
   Working Women   343
   Minorities and the Labor Market   347
Finances in the Later Years   350
   Income During the Golden Years   350
   Expenditures During the Golden Years   359
Summary   360
Discussion Questions   362
Pertinent Readings   363

**9**    **AGING AT THE MARGINS OF SOCIETY**   369

Minority Aging   370
   Aging at the Margins   370
   The Minority Experience   371
   The Logic of This Chapter   372
Aging and Minorities in the United States   372
   Multiple Jeopardy: The Minority Experience   372
   Aged Black Americans   380
   Aged Hispanic Americans   386
   Older Native Americans   392
   Aged Asian Americans   397
   Ramifications of Ethnicity   407
Aging in the Third World   407

Summary   412
Discussion Questions   414
Pertinent Readings   415

**10   THE AGED AND THE POLITICAL ARENA**   420
The Nature and Structure of Politics   421
   The Nature of Politics   421
   The Structure of Politics   421
The Elderly as a Social Movement   422
   Age Groups in the Political Arena   423
   The Advent of Age-Based Social Movements   425
   The Second Coming: Developments Since the 1950s   426
   Age Group Identification   430
Political Attitudes and Opinions   431
   Aging and Sociopolitical Attitudes   431
   Party Affiliation   435
   Taking a Stance on Social Issues   435
Political Participation   438
   Voting and Participation in the Political Process   438
   Other Political Behavior   442
The Political Future of the Elderly   443
   A Generational Alliance   444
   Politics of Tomorrow   445
Summary   446
Discussion Questions   448
Pertinent Readings   449

**11   SOCIAL POLICY AND AGING**   453
The Nature of Social Policy   454
   The Multiple Levels of Social Policy   454
   The Relationship Between the Individual and Society   455
   Unidimensional vs Multidimensional Approaches   456
Social Policy for the Elderly   456
   Social Policy in Relation to Problems of the Elderly   456
   Policy as Social Construction: Constituency Concerns   457
   Social Policy as Formative of the Lifeworld of the Elderly   458
   Metapolicy and the Elderly   459
Fiscal Policies and the Elderly   462
   Social Security   462
   The Future of Social Security   469
   Supplemental Security Income   472
   Private Pension Provisions   472

Individual Retirement Accounts 474

Age Discrimination and Employment 474

Health Care Policies and the Elderly 476

Development of Health Care for the Aged 476

Medicare and Medicaid 479

The Issue of Cost 483

Medicare: A Broken Promise? 487

Private Health Policy Options 490

Additional Social Service Policies for the Elderly 491

Death with Dignity 491

Legal Services 492

Social Services 492

Housing 493

The Metapolicy of Aging: Issues for the Future 494

Intergenerational Equity vs Societal Equity 494

The Issue of Financial Feasibility 495

Summary 496

Discussion Questions 497

Pertinent Readings 499


**PART FOUR**

# Looking Ahead   503

**12**   **THE PROSPECTS OF AGING**   505

The Future of Aging: The Issues 506

The Elderly of Tomorrow 507

General Projections 507

Interpersonal Relations and the Prospect of Aging 511

Preparing the Way — Social Policy Issues 514

Social Security 515

Working Ahead 517

Making Room for the Future: The Prognosis on Health 520

The Response 531

Gerontology as a Vocation 531

Careers in Aging 532

Training and Course Work 536

The Challenge 538

Summary 538

Discussion Questions 540

Pertinent Readings 541

**GLOSSARY** 545

**INDEX** 551

# PART ONE

# MAKING SENSE
# OF AGING IN
# THE MODERN WORLD

# 1

# THE AGE-OLD QUESTION OF OLD AGE

**MAKING SENSE OF AGING: THE PERSPECTIVE OF THIS BOOK**
The Many Levels of Aging
Approaching the Multifaceted Nature of Aging
Our Framework for Looking at Old Age
Interpreting Data on Aging
  *Collecting Data*
  *The Use of Statistics in Assessing the Situation of the Elderly*
  *The Adequacy of Statistics*
  *The Claims of Statistics as a Method*
  *Methodological and Conceptual Impediments*
  *Conceptual Hurdles*
  *The Meaning of Generalizability*

**GERONTOLOGY: THE STUDY OF AGING**
Incentives for the Development of Gerontology as a Field of Study
The Depression and Concern for the Elderly
Development and Scope of Gerontology
  *Historical Foundations*
  *Advancement of Gerontology*
  *The Focus of Gerontological Study*

**SUMMARY**

**DISCUSSION QUESTIONS**

**PERTINENT READINGS**

**W**hat is it like to grow old? If a young person could stand in the shoes of an old person for even a single day, many misconceptions could be swept away. We all think we have some notion of what life is like in the later years, but if we look at life closely, many wrong-headed notions become apparent. How many of us realize that the process has already begun? In fact, with the possible exception of a few precocious readers, the rest of you are well along in life. With so many years behind us, it seems reasonable to expect we would know what old is. Unfortunately, stereotypes may stand in the way both for the uninitiated and the professional. There are theories supporting the essential similarity between old and young people, and there are theories that refute this. One thing is certain, however; the complexity of change precludes any easy answers; further questions are the most frequent result of our inquiries (Borgatta and Loeb, 1979). One of the major purposes of this book is to help the reader develop perspectives for making sense of the process of aging.

## Making Sense of Aging: The Perspective of This Book

### THE MANY LEVELS OF AGING

The research on aging brings up many questions. Is aging a universal phenomenon that follows rather uniform, well-defined stages in all times and places, or is aging different in diverse cultures and societies? Do all individuals within a particular society age in the same way, or are there individual differences? In speaking of aging are we thinking primarily of a physiological process, or are we looking at the whole person, including psychological development and changes in the ways people relate to the culture and social structure of which they are part? Do people's personalities and worldviews change as they age, or are they congruent with their earlier personalities? What kinds of differences exist between old people as a group and younger people in the same society? How radical are the differences that do appear? Are any differences that exist a result of aging, or is it that successive generations of people mature at different ages under different historical conditions? To what extent are the differences among old people and their life-styles associated with physiological factors, cultural value systems for interpreting and dealing with situations, and the availability of economic resources, support systems, and social structural factors and policies? How can we best improve the lot of the elderly? Should we change social policy, develop the potential of the individual, or perform scientific research designed to produce better medical care and technical aids for the elderly? What do we want to change about the conditions that constrain their lives? Are these the same things the elderly themselves would wish to see changed? How do we regard the elderly? Do we see them as an economically unproductive drain on an overburdened economy? Do we view them as resource persons with much to offer, both in problem-solving skills and in experience gained through surviving the vicissitudes of changing historical circumstances? Or do we see them as people who have put a great deal into society, who have supported their elders during their own working lives and are therefore entitled to something during their own later years?

There are no easy answers to these questions, and we are not going to try to offer any. Rather, our aim is to raise questions, to suggest perspectives for considering such questions, and to relate them to currently available data and social policies on aging. We use these perspectives to analyze the current data, and we hope that the student will acquire the analytic skills necessary to examine new developments and new data critically.

## APPROACHING THE MULTIFACETED NATURE OF AGING

The kinds of questions raised clearly call for an interdisciplinary approach involving sociology, anthropology, psychology, medicine, physiology, political science, and others. When a researcher or practitioner of a particular discipline is working on multidisciplinary problems, two broad approaches are possible. The first of these may be characterized as a limited focus, single discipline; that is, the researcher or practitioner remains within his or her own field of study and does not try to become familiar with the approaches of other disciplines. Other approaches may be recognized but not pursued. The second approach may be characterized as truly interdisciplinary. An open dialogue exists between members of different disciplines; they discuss issues and share insights, and they practice their own discipline bearing in mind the other facets to the problem. In this way people arrive at a deeper understanding than would be possible if they had used any one particular discipline. This kind of interdisciplinary approach is needed to answer the key questions concerning aging — it is the perspective of this book.

The limited approach may not raise as many questions, but it can lead to a number of problems. Important elements of a situation may be totally ignored in addressing an issue because they fall outside the scope of a particular researcher's discipline. The problems of the elderly may be treated as either exclusively structural or personal, cultural or economic, physical or psychological, according to the researcher's approach. This may mean that problems which have their roots in the social structure may be treated as purely personal problems and personal problems as arising from the social structure. As C. S. Lewis once noted, people have a decided tendency to rush about with fire extinguishers when there is a flood (Lewis, 1965). When faced with a sense of personal inadequacy, we tend to blame structural factors. When faced with problems created by structural factors, we decry the lack of willpower and spirit on the part of those who are implicated by those factors.

As noted, the thesis of this book is that our lives, and the lives of the elderly, are created through a complex interweaving of structural, cultural, historical, and personal variables. We are constrained by circumstances, but there are varying possibilities within those constraints. When dealing with structural factors we should look for ways in which we can modify those factors to enlarge our options for intervention and emancipation. When dealing with our reaction to circumstances, we should look for ways in which we can realize and choose between options that are not always readily apparent. Knowledge without action is unacceptable. The reverse is no better.

The goal of this book is to distinguish between levels of analysis (for instance, structural vs individual) and to pose appropriate questions at appropriate levels. Having attempted that, we aim to link the levels and make apparent the interaction that continually goes on between the various dimensions as they affect the course of aging in modern industrial societies.

Throughout the discussion the primary focus will be on aging in mass societies: those characterized as urban and complex, with a large-scale organization modeled on an ethos of instrumental and economic rationality. In such societies many areas of our lives become separated from other spheres and much interaction is based on superficial evidence. According to sociologists who have attempted to unravel the workings of these mass, or postindustrial, societies, the impersonal and often commercialized basis of interaction rests on **achieved status,** the status accorded to those who contribute directly to the needs of bureaucratic systems, in which a person's usefulness too frequently forms the basis of his or her identity. Clearly, under these circumstances the pattern of aging will reflect an interweaving of factors not necessarily found in all societies. To help highlight these differences we will provide both historical and cross-cultural information for purposes of illustration. In this way we hope to make the features of aging in mass societies more apparent. We also hope to show how a dialectical process is affecting the development of Third World countries through their interaction with societies that have already undergone modernization. The point in both cases is that the life of an elderly person is determined not only by structural arrangements and policies in the society in which that person lives but also by cultural, political, and economic relations among all societies.

## OUR FRAMEWORK FOR LOOKING AT OLD AGE

There are four major sections in this book. Part I is an introductory outline. Chapter 1 deals with what gerontology is, how to approach it, and why it is important in our society. We have already suggested some perspectives with which to approach the study of aging: these themes will be discussed throughout the book. In the following section we consider the interpretation and uses of statistical and other data. The reader should find the points made in this section useful in dealing both with the data in this book and with outside sources. Next we look at why the study of aging has become important in the United States, and we briefly review the history of gerontology and its current scope. Chapter 2 is a survey of the population of the elderly today. To provide a meaningful context the first section introduces some basic terms used in social gerontology. In the rest of the chapter we look at aging in three sociocultural contexts: aging in history, aging in advanced industrial societies, and aging in the Third World. Chapter 3 explores major theories of social gerontology, their relationship to the perspectives on aging developed in Chapter 1, and the types of research they spawn.

Part II looks at aging from the inside out. We take factors that are generally thought of as operating at the individual, personal level, and, although acknowledging the personal aspects of these phenomena, we demonstrate how they also reflect social structural and cultural factors. Four aspects of the lifeworld of the elderly will be dealt with: physiological change over time (Chapter 4); health status in the later years (Chapter 5); psychological processes in later life (Chapter 6); and everyday concerns of the elderly (Chapter 7).

Part III, by contrast, looks at aging from the outside in. We take components usually thought to have their existence at the structural level and show how these affect — and can be affected by — people as individuals. Chapters 8 and 9 look at some ways in which structural variables influence particular facets of the lives of the elderly: finances (Chapter 8) and place in the social structure (Chapter 9 — which deals with aging among minority groups and those outside the mainstream of society). Chapter 10 looks at the elderly as a political force and shows the ways people may shape and change social policies. Chapter 11 outlines current social policies, the debates surrounding them, and analyzes suggestions for linking these issues to the everyday concerns of the elderly.

Part IV turns toward the future. In our final chapter we consider where present trends might lead us; we look at dilemmas, possible options, and research questions for the future, and we give some information regarding possible careers in aging for those who may want to become actively involved.

## INTERPRETING DATA ON AGING

Much data concerning the elderly, taken from a variety of sources, will be offered in this book. In analyzing the data, however, the reader should bear in mind four questions:

- To what extent is our thinking about aging shaped by the way we collect information?
- What is an appropriate use of statistics in assessing the situation of the elderly?
- How well can statistics be expected to describe the situation of the elderly?
- What does it mean to make generalizations?

These questions will prove useful not only with regard to the data presented in the book, but the reader should find them helpful in analyzing other sources of information about the elderly as well.

**Collecting Data.** The methodological techniques employed by social gerontologists have undoubtedly contributed in part to the clouding of what are age-related characteristics and what are artifacts. Traditionally, researchers have most often relied on cross-sectional survey methods, that is, drawing a sample of older and younger respondents, and then providing a descriptive comparison of the ways in which the elderly differ from their younger counterparts. The validity of **age differences** discovered in this manner is beyond question; however, the conclusion that such differences are a consequence of aging is now recognized as untenable. Actually, the discrepancies between the age groups may be caused by the effects of a particular historical and social milieu on the respondents. Observed differences in the number of years of school for older and younger people can in no way be construed to be an indication that a person's educational attainment declines with age. On the contrary, all it implies is that at the time the respondents in the older generation were of school age, educational opportunities that have subsequently become the norm were unavailable. It would not be any more appropriate to evaluate a group of eighty-year-olds to predict what life will be like twenty years hence for those who are now in their early sixties. In other words, cross-sectional analyses cannot distinguish between changes occurring because of age and those growing out of **cohort** or generational differences in experiences or any of a wide range of other external factors. Longitudinal research, such as the studies conducted since the mid-1950s at Duke University and elsewhere around the country, is one means of avoiding the pitfalls of cross-sectional techniques, but it too has its limitations. Following the same individual or group of people over a period of time permits gerontologists to identify more closely developmental age changes, yet it is still possible to confound the results with environmental changes between the times the evaluations are made. As gerontologists have become more theoretically and methodologically concerned, alternative research strategies have evolved that offset some of these problems. In the course of the next few years gerontological research is likely to take yet another turn as it incorporates new data-gathering perspectives (Schaie and Geiwitz, 1982; Palmore, 1978).

**The Use of Statistics in Assessing the Situation of the Elderly.** The **ecological fallacy** is a prime example of an inappropriate use of statistical data. It is a misuse of generalizations drawn from large-scale statistical studies to predict the situation and behavior of individuals. An example of an ecological fallacy would be to conclude from a statistical report that shows the annual per capita income of people over sixty-five as $10,000 that this figure gives a picture of the actual income of particular people. Another example would be to suppose that because American Cancer Society statistics show one in eleven women in the United States will be affected by breast cancer at some time in their lives, Mary Smith, as an individual woman, has a one in eleven chance of developing breast cancer (American Cancer Society, 1985). A number of problems result from this type of assumption. At best, assuming the study is methodologically sound, all that an estimate of annual per capita income provides is precisely what it says: an estimate of the average or mean income per person, or, in the case of the breast cancer statistics, the general probability of developing breast cancer for all members of a group. Because the mean is derived from a composite statistical process, no actual person may have the average income, the average risk of developing cancer, or anything else.

In a country in which the majority of the population is involved in subsistence agriculture an average annual per capita income of $10,000 may reflect a combination of a very rich elite who, for instance, might control the oil industry, with a vast majority of the population having only minimal incomes. Significant variations within the population under consideration, or the presence or absence of risk factors, may result in significant differences regarding any variable. Using the hypothetical Mary Smith as an example, if her grandmother, mother, and sisters all had breast cancer, her risk of developing it will be considerably higher than one in eleven. If she has smoked heavily for forty years, her risk of dying of lung cancer will be significantly higher than that of the general population.

The incidence and death rates for particular diseases also vary according to the area of the country. For instance, age-adjusted cancer death rates for 1970–1979 were 233.5 per 100,000 population in the District of Columbia, as opposed to 122.0 per 100,000 population in Utah (American Cancer Society, 1985). Incidence rates for the whole country obscure variations in regional incidence rates and individual risk factors. They may be useful for national planning, but when the concern is with a particular individual, a number of environmental, structural, genetic, and life-style factors need to be taken into account in assessing risk (Robinson, 1950; Gore and Hughes, 1980).

The **individual fallacy** is an unwarranted assumption that everyone else's situation is just like one's own. Older people whose opportunities have allowed them to attain a certain level of education or to amass a certain amount of financial resources may have a hard time understanding why problem-solving techniques that work for them simply will not work for those with fewer resources at their disposal. Carefully designed and reported statistical studies, which aim to report variability within the population and general trends, may be useful for making us aware of what a variety of other people have to deal with as they get older. Ideally, this disparity of circumstances will also help us realize that many people's lives can be improved.

*Planning* is one of the major uses of statistics at the local, regional, and national levels. To have an accurate idea of the number of people likely to be depending on social services, their access to other resources, and the cost of living will aid the planner in deciding the amount of revenue required to meet social service needs in that year and the measures necessary to generate it.

And only with a reasonably sound idea of the health needs and health facility use patterns in a particular area, can there be an adequate basis for deciding which parts of the health care system need more funding in the future.

**The Adequacy of Statistics.** We should remember that the best conducted studies cannot give a truly complete picture of a situation; furthermore, not all studies are equally well conducted. Factors that limit the comprehensiveness of the picture given by statistical data are:

- The way in which the questions are framed
- The limited claims of statistics as a method of study
- Methodological problems

Framing the research questions asked, the terms used, and the factors taken into account in trying to answer them will, to a large extent, be shaped by the frame of reference and interests of those who commission and conduct the study. Certain questions may not be asked. Those that are asked may be posed in a way that influences how they are answered. While the factors taken into account by the investigation may be pertinent to the matter at hand, other, equally pertinent factors may be overlooked or ignored. One reason for this may be the social situation of the researcher: it may never occur to the researcher to ask certain questions. Or the researcher's personal history or current situation may also make it difficult to investigate certain issues. Possibly political pressures and interests within the society may discourage certain lines of investigation.

To take a seemingly absurd example: set up a cost-benefit analysis of the economics of television watching in the United States. If the minimum hourly wages for each person for all the hours spent watching television were figured as part of the cost, and added to this was the cost of the electricity, depreciation on the television sets, and the cost of production of the shows, would the benefits be worth the input? And how would we measure them? Although this idea may seem ridiculous to the reader, is it really so very different from assessing the benefits or costs of health care in terms of the economic outcomes it allows those who receive it? Or to those who administer it? Investigations regarding cost effectiveness in health care will have very different results depending on whether the intent is (1) to decrease per capita expense by whatever means necessary to keep spending within certain limits, (2) to maximize the quality of life with the resources available, (3) to distribute health care to maximize economic productivity, (4) to make a minimum of care available to as many people as possible, (5) to limit health care expenditures to those who need them because they are threatened by disability or death, or (6) to promote medical research and advances.

In interpreting the studies cited in this book the reader is encouraged to look for unasked questions, for unaddressed aspects of the questions asked, and for who benefits and at what cost. Some of these issues will be raised in the course of the analysis; undoubtedly the reader will come up with others.

**The Claims of Statistics as a Method.** A good statistician will not claim to give us the facts; rather he or she will give an educated assessment about certain aspects of a situation. While there is always the temptation to simplify in the interests of making things easy to understand, one should remember that the claims of statistics are strictly limited. There is always an error factor in reported results. In attempting to estimate the mean income of a population, for instance, a statistician will not simply take a scientific sample and then report the sample mean as the mean income for the population. Rather, on the basis of a statistical method, he or she will state that, from the data in the sample, he or she is 90 or 95 percent sure that the mean income for the population falls within a particular range (called a confidence interval). One might then say the sample allows for a 95 percent certainty that the mean income is $10,000 ($\pm$ $1000).

When in statistics we talk about using changes in one factor, or variable, to predict changes in another variable, we are using the term "variable" in a specialized sense that does not necessarily have anything to do with causality or with predicting the future. All we are implying is that if two variables are directly associated, when the values of one tend to rise, the values of the other also tend to rise. For example, ice cream sales tend to rise when the temperature rises. Similarly, when the values of one variable decrease, the values of the other also decrease. For example, ice cream sales tend to fall off as the weather becomes colder. If two variables are negatively correlated, as the values of one rise, the values of the other tend to fall. We are only certain about this relationship being true for the range of values for which we have data available. Thus, if our evidence showed ice cream sales continued to increase until the temperature rose to 100°F, but we had no data for higher temperatures, we could not be sure that they would continue to rise as it got hotter. People might find it too hot outside to go to the stores. Furthermore, we only claim that the relationship holds for the population of interest, all other things being equal; a change in circumstances might lead to a change in the relationship.

The proviso of all things being equal is also fundamental to attempts to predict future trends from the present. In trying to predict the age distribution of the population in the future, if we assume that birth and death rates continue as they have over the past decade or so, we can have a fairly good idea of the age distribution of the population of the United States in the year 2050. If however, we were to have a baby boom in the next few years, there would be a considerably higher proportion of young people than we would now anticipate. If, on the other hand, we found a cure for cancer and birth rates remained constant or fell, there might be a considerably higher proportion of older people. When gerontologists calculate dependency ratios, as will be discussed in Chapter 2, they attempt to take these variables into account.

**Methodological and Conceptual Impediments.** In interpreting and using the results of studies, we also need to be aware of other potential problems. We should look carefully at the way in which variables are conceptualized and measured. In dealing with "life satisfaction among the elderly," a number of important conceptual decisions have been made. To *operationalize* such an imponderable term as "life satisfaction" so it can be measured is difficult. We should be aware that there may be technical problems with recording and coding data and calculating statistics. Census data, disease incidence, and mortality rates are notoriously inaccurate in developing countries where there are high illiteracy rates, limited access to medical care, underdeveloped transportation systems, and not much in the way of formal recording systems. There are also political problems, which are not limited to underdeveloped countries; many questions exist concerning the reliability of the data in the United States census. For example, the 1950 census counted more people in the sixty-five to seventy age group than the 1940 census recorded for the fifty-five to sixty age group. The difference could not be accounted for in terms of immigration, and it has been surmised that the discrepancy might have been the result of large-scale falsifying of ages by people who wished to collect Social Security payments (Huff, 1957). When we are dealing with a sample survey, we should look at how the sample was selected and be aware that it may not represent the population. Because of convenience, time, and cost constraints, people may use an expediency sample rather than selecting representative samples by scientific methods.

These qualifications do not make statistical studies worthless, although we should be cautious in the way we interpret and apply them. They may be valid for demonstrating general trends, but they may also contain a certain margin of error. We should be careful not to apply conclusions drawn from them outside their range of applicability, and we should look for unanswered questions and neglected points of view. Statistical and other data should be tools for gaining insight into the situation and concerns of the elderly; they should not be viewed as a final description of reality that prevents us from being sensitive to variations and changes in actual situations.

**Conceptual Hurdles.** The increasing attention being paid to the aging process by lay people, politicians, and scholars must be seen as something of a mixed blessing. On the one hand, it ensures continuing support for research and practical intervention; on the other hand, it has the potential of introducing biases that are difficult if not impossible to overcome. Knowledge is always a matter of interpretation and perspective — as anyone who has been embroiled in a disagreement can readily testify. Despite our willingness to turn to the "facts" to settle questions about aging or anything else, facts can never speak for themselves. The ways in which the inquiry is phrased always influence in advance several features of the answer supplied. They determine, for instance, which dimensions of the situation will be included as significant variables, ruling out others as unimportant or irrelevant. Since gerontology is both a cultural and a scientific enterprise, its focus necessarily reflects the society in which it takes root. Professionals, whatever their discipline, bring with them to their work in gerontology some elements of attitudes learned long before their scholarly interests in aging developed. An example drawn specifically in terms of aging research can amply illustrate the point. Because the dominant stereotypes of older people emphasized the darker side of aging, early social gerontology tended to concentrate on those things that are difficult for the elderly. Thus, instead of looking for attributes that could conceivably be enhanced by age, earlier studies examined almost exclusively the disadvantages assumed to be inherent in the aging process. Between those whose emphasis on the negative aspects of aging reinforced society's preconceptions and those who were content simply to accumulate descriptive statistics about the elderly, it has taken the last two decades to show that a great number of what were once taken to be characteristics of aging may actually stem from a combination of physical, social, and individual variables not causally linked to age.

Another major hurdle gerontologists must face if they are to provide a reliable and meaningful picture of aging involves providing unifying conceptual frameworks. If the data collected in the many aging studies are to be in any sense cumulative, rather than merely expanding our store of descriptive details, it is necessary to go beyond the facts and to trace the links between various facets of aging. Thus far those working in the field have been slow to act on the need for an integrative overview, whether out of expediency because of the fervor generated by short-run pragmatic accomplishments or because of the nature of their training in a single academic discipline. Consequently, research findings are too often noncomparable, and the impact of the work falls short of its potential (Seltzer, 1975). With the flourish in theoretical activity in the last few years, integrative perspectives capable of lending some order to the disparate findings of the field may not be too far in the future. Although there are no straightforward avenues to so complex a goal as explaining why men and women age the way they do, recognizing the importance of interdisciplinary training and the pointlessness of concentrating on any isolated aspect of aging without making reference to others will go a long way toward resolving the lack of a holistic grasp of the issues. So, too, will an appreciation of historical and cross-cultural variables in terms of their influence on individual, cohort, and societal aging help enhance the explanatory power of gerontology (Philibert, 1979).

**The Meaning of Generalizability.** Are quantitative methods the only tools for studying the social situation of the elderly, or is there a place for qualitative methods? Advocates of the exclusive use of quantitative methods sometimes criticize qualitative studies because their findings are not generalizable. This contention rests on a confusion between two meanings of the term "generalizable," and once this is clarified, quantitative and qualitative methods can be complementary.

Generalizability in statistics refers to whether a relationship or trait is characteristic of a population as a whole, or whether it is particular to some part of it. If the evidence indicates that the relationship between two variables is characteristic of the population as a whole, then conclusions about that relationship drawn from a sample will be considered to be generalizable to the population as a whole. We noted earlier that a particular relationship between two variables is likely to be true only if all other things are equal. In concluding that a relationship is generalizable to a population, we are assuming all other things are equal, at least as far as they affect the nature of the relationship.

Generalizability in qualitative research should be considered differently. Rather than dealing with what is generally the case, we are looking at what might more generally be the case. Qualitative research explores the ways in which people interpret and negotiate the circumstances in which they find themselves; it seeks to penetrate the causal web and see just what it is that makes a situation or event as it is and not otherwise. It may thus uncover a variety of understandings of and reactions to essentially similar circumstances. In some cases these understandings and reactions may lead to consequences that are considered desirable by the people involved; in other cases it may lead to consequences considered undesirable. In saying that an approach to a problem is generalizable, we are saying that an approach may be applied, perhaps with some modifications, in circumstances other than the ones where we found it. Thus, quantitative methods might be used to identify widespread conditions (the structural constraints) that impinge on the lives of the elderly; qualitative methods may be used to identify creative and varied approaches to those conditions. Both approaches can shed light on the ways in which people age.

# Gerontology: The Study of Aging

Having offered these caveats, it is time to begin the study of aging. Old people have existed in every society. What has changed is the socially ascribed definition of the term "old." Those who were thought of as elderly at thirty-five some 2000 years ago would today be thought of quite differently. A range of issues is implicit in defining a person as "old." Underlying this determination are a number of normative expectations reflecting what the group making the definition value. Age borders are never static—neither in our lifetimes, nor historically (Keith, 1982).

## INCENTIVES FOR THE DEVELOPMENT
## OF GERONTOLOGY AS A FIELD OF STUDY

It was not until the dawn of the modern era that the **age distribution** of most societies began to reflect a significant aggregation of older people. As a consequence of medical, technological, and economic advances, a decline in mortality occurred in industrially developed countries, so that for the first time sizable numbers of people were living into their sixth decade or beyond. Gradually technology spread into a variety of productive realms, making it possible for people to spend less time engaged in various kinds of work with no reduction in per capita output. Yet these very innovations carried with them a demand for workers with new skills and capacities that in effect helped establish a surplus of older workers and eventually led to the institution of retirement policies as we know them today.

Prior to the end of the nineteenth century the increasing proportion of the elderly, along with their pressing needs, had awakened the social consciousness of several European governments. By the 1880s social service programs had been inaugurated in Germany and Denmark, and by the early decades of the present century, similar schemes had spread across the continent and to as far away as New Zealand. While each country openly acknowledged societal responsibility for providing a basic economic security for older people, both the content and extent of the support varied widely. In many instances health insurance was included as an integral component of the package, although in the United States few people were willing to admit the need for such services until quite recently. Older people had a long time to wait before becoming a truly visible component of the American scene. Even though the federal government had already begun to assume a protective role over the rights of children, calls made in the political campaigns of 1900 by the Social Democrats and again in 1912 by the Progressives for similar federal responsibility on behalf of the elderly apparently fell on deaf ears. At the time America was in the midst of an expansionist era and its priorities lay elsewhere. Successive political debates failed to incorporate or even to consider humanitarian principles regarding older people for three decades into the twentieth century.

## THE DEPRESSION AND CONCERN FOR THE ELDERLY

The beginnings of publicly supported old age assistance programs occurred later in the United States than in most European countries. What finally propelled the federal government into action was the Depression of the 1930s. Faced with economic hardships, a decline in productivity, and what was viewed as a stagnating labor force, the first national legislation addressing the elderly was passed in 1935. The Social Security Act as originally passed and as revised in the first few years represented a critical juncture in the development of categorical programs for the elderly. It established a new and dynamic relationship among public, private, and individual welfare (Achenbaum, 1983). People were immediately provided with a goal toward which they could dedicate their working lives, something they were entitled to by right. At the same time employers were relieved of any possible responsibilities for the economic well-being of workers released because of their age. At a time when the United States had more workers than jobs, while industry was in major need of development capital and a stable labor force, no better solution could have been found.

Traditionally, families had been expected to come to the aid of their elderly, but with double digit unemployment rampant during the 1930s it was beyond the capacities of ever greater numbers of families to provide for their aged relatives. It was not that a whole new range of difficulties suddenly emerged; rather, problems previously defined largely in personal terms were now redefined as consequences of events over which individuals had little or no personal control. Although medicine and technology were beginning to prolong life, social change was effectively undermining whatever advances had been made. Under the circumstances it was perhaps only just that old people should have taken their place alongside children and adolescents as an age group with particular needs deserving special attention (Achenbaum, 1983).

In analyzing the forces that have focused attention on the problematic aspects of aging and the enactment of protective legislation for older people, several authorities have suggested these resulted from a combination of ideological factors brought to the public's awareness by the practical realities of the years preceding the collapse of 1929 and the Depression. Spengler (1969), for example, highlights the spread of a kind of collectivistic redistributive ideology during the first three decades of the century that supported public assistance programs for various indigent groups, the elderly included. Added to this was a transformation of conventional religious injunctions of charitable deeds toward the less fortunate into a kind of secularized belief that gradually came to be translated into a political doctrine. Still further support came in the form of an espousal of Keynesian fiscal principles by New Deal programs advocating expanded public spending to prime the pumps of private enterprise to reestablish fiscal and social stability. These same principles also lent credibility to the notion of providing for the economic well-being of older people. Supplementing these three value shifts was a variety of very real conditions, including the undeniable hardships of the Depression and the heightened visibility of the elderly. Part of that visibility arose from the growing number of older Americans.

Another facet of the conspicuousness of older people's economic difficulties revolves around the process of urbanization. At the turn of the century the United States was still predominantly rural, with the bulk of the population living on or near the country's farms. By 1920, however, a change had occurred. America had become an urbanized nation, with a majority of its people now concentrated in cities of at least 2500. Because the younger segments of the population were both more willing and able to relocate, the obvious population movement for younger people was to the cities. Indeed, for the elderly who found themselves living out their later years in urban areas, there was a preponderance of financial and personal difficulties. This is not to say rural environments did not pose their own risks; it is merely to note that because of their dependence on salaried employment, with the concurrent adoption of formal retirement policies, urban residents were more aware of the problems associated with growing old in a rapidly changing society.

Rounding out the list of actual conditions that played an important role in highlighting the plight of older people, Spengler points to three complementary economic trends. As the burgeoning wartime economy of the early 1940s returned disposable per capita income to pre-Depression levels and beyond, there was relatively little opposition to expanding the Social Security taxes first imposed in 1935. Consequently, payments to retired workers were allowed to increase, while current wage earners saw visions of substantial benefits awaiting them on their own retirement. As the federal government became more intricately involved in public assistance programs, and as poverty guidelines were developed, it also became evident that older people were not only more likely to have incomes below established subsistence levels, but were also overrepresented among the long-term unemployed. Finally, the effects of the inflation that has plagued the country since World War II have obviously eroded the buying power of those on fixed incomes to a greater extent than those who were or are in a position to negotiate their financial situations. Spengler and others suggest that all these forces are probably sufficient in themselves to ensure continuing attention to the needs of the elderly.

Even though older persons were disproportionately represented among those hardest hit by the Depression, it was their sheer numbers that accounted for increased public awareness. **Birth cohorts** comprised of all those born in a given period move through life as a gradually decreasing group. What they encounter along the way depends on time, size, and individual attributes.

The "graying of America" in the years ahead will be reflected by shifts in the age distribution of the population. In Figure 1.1 we show the progression of three distinct cohorts through life. By 1960 the United States could no longer be characterized as having a predominantly young population. The expansionist phase was over, and we were now moving toward a slow-growth pattern. By the end of the 1980s we will be in what demographers call a no-growth stage — a fairly equal distribution of people of all ages. Fewer children will be born, but most of these will survive until they reach their seventies at least. In Chapter 2 we will look at the questions raised by shifting age and sex structures; suffice it to say at this point that the passage of birth cohorts through the life cycle has an effect across all of society.

## DEVELOPMENT AND SCOPE OF GERONTOLOGY

Lying as it does on the borders of many disciplines *gerontology*, the systematic exploration of the aging process, encompasses a broad territory. Its practitioners include scientists who prefer to focus their attention on plants and animals, as well as those who are concerned with the aging of human beings. Not all areas of interest have proceeded apace; research in the biological or clinical aspects of aging has had a longer history than studies of behavioral and social factors. "Social gerontology," a term coined around 1950 to describe the study of the ways in which social and cultural factors enter into the aging process, is perhaps the most recent of the subspecialties to have achieved widespread recognition. Still, it has only been within the past three decades that all areas have flourished and become firmly established as academic disciplines. Because the mission of gerontology is not simply concerned with advancing our understanding of the ways in which people age, it cannot confine itself within the walls of our colleges and universities. Gerontology is also an applied disci-

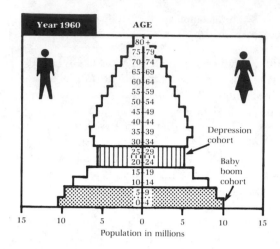

Year 1960 · AGE · Population in millions

80+, 75-79, 70-74, 65-69, 60-64, 55-59, 50-54, 45-49, 40-44, 35-39, 30-34, 25-29, 20-24, 15-19, 10-14, 5-9, 0-4

Depression cohort

Baby boom cohort

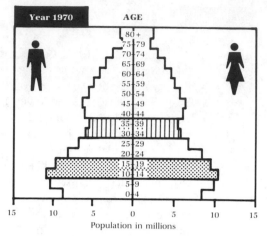

Year 1970 · AGE · Population in millions

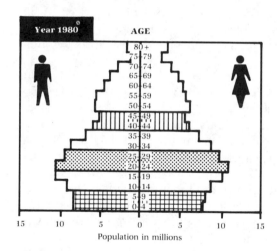

Year 1980 · AGE · Population in millions

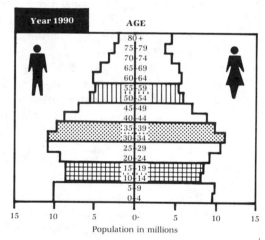

Year 1990 · AGE · Population in millions

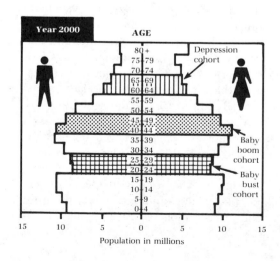

Year 2000 · AGE · Population in millions

Depression cohort

Baby boom cohort

Baby bust cohort

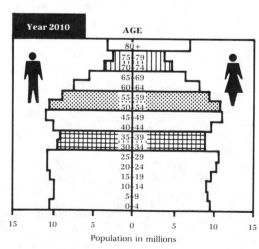

Year 2010 · AGE · Population in millions

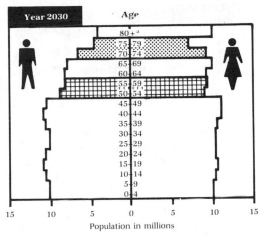

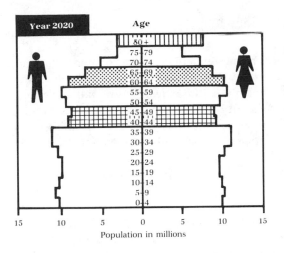

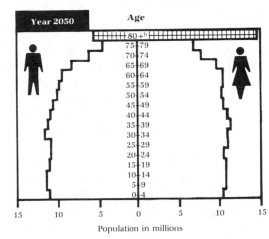

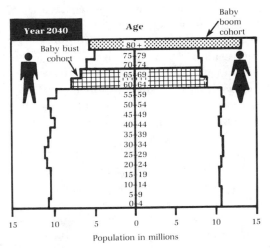

Depression cohort
persons born
1930–1939

Baby boom cohort
persons born
1950–1959

Baby bust cohort
persons born
1970–1979

Compilations: 1960–1970 U.S. Bureau of the Census, 1970 *U.S. Census of Population: General Population Characteristics, United States Summary*, Vol. 1, PC(1)-B1, 1972, Table 52; and 1980–2050: Special unpublished tabulations prepared by Leon F. Bouvier for the Select Commission on Immigration and Refugee Policy, 1980.

[a] Includes survivors of Depression cohort.

[b] Includes survivors of baby boom cohort.

Note: 1980–2050 projections assume a total fertility rate rising to 2.0 births per woman by 1985 and constant thereafter; life expectancy at birth rising to 72.8 years for males and 82.9 years for females by 2050; net immigration constant at 750,000 persons per year.

## FIGURE 1.1

Progress of Depression cohort, baby boom cohort, and baby bust cohort through United States population age-sex pyramid, 1960–2050. (*Source:* "America's Baby Boom Generation: The Fateful Bulge." *Population Bulletin* 35, 1 [1980]: 18–19.)

pline addressing itself to the practical and immediate effects of aging. Its practitioners attempt both to counsel those who are encountering difficulties and to forestall maladjustments for the bulk of the elderly. Although gerontologists are fully aware that aging does not begin when people pass some magic point, they do tend to confine their focus to changes occurring in the second half of life — if only because the complexities preclude an adequate grasp even of that period. Perhaps because the physical manifestations of aging are the most obvious, it was inevitable that they were the first to attract the attention of early gerontologists.

**Historical Foundations.** As an analytical science, the study of aging is still young — barely out of adolescence. But from time immemorial, oracles, pundits, and philosophers alike have puzzled over the secrets of prolonging life, and by the thirteenth century the body of humanist literature on the subject was sizable, though repetitious. One of the most astute of the early views of aging and one that stood out from the rest was propounded by Roger Bacon. Writing in the thirteenth century, Bacon explicitly acknowledged the interaction of heredity with physical health, resulting in the increasing vulnerability of the organism over time. With the popularization of scientific analysis in the seventeenth century, systematic inquiry into the process of growing old began to quicken. Yet what little information was collected for the most part resulted as a byproduct of other studies. Even so eminent a scholar as Francis Bacon, responsible for proposing what is still regarded as the scientific method of inquiry, paused in the midst of his many intellectual pursuits to write *The History of Life and Death*, dwelling on the possible causes of aging. Bacon suggested that hygienic practices were likely to be a major contributing factor; thus, by improving the citizenry's hygiene, significant advances in life expectancy would be forthcoming (Freeman, 1979). His prominence undoubtedly spurred the interests of other scientists, and it was not long before Halley, the noted astronomer, began collecting actuarial statistics to construct the first scientific analysis of life expectancy. Within the century others joined their ranks. Foremost among them was the Belgian astronomer-mathematician Quetelet. Curious about what he perceived to be the normal distribution of various human characteristics, Quetelet compiled a list of the ways in which a wide range of abilities, skills and strengths varied by ages. While his judgments were occasionally farfetched by contemporary standards, his attention to changing physical capacities was the forerunner of the kinds of physiological analyses discussed in the second half of Chapter 4. Meanwhile, a Russian physician, I. Fisher, was also seeking answers to questions of longevity by investigating the importance of physical attributes, mental status, and environmental factors. Both Fisher and a younger colleague, P. Yengalytchev, concluded that exercise, hygiene, diet, and timely medical attention were essential to survive to an advanced age (Birren and Clayton, 1975; Chebotarev and Duplenko, 1972).

The first of the large-scale surveys assessing differences in age-related abilities was undertaken near the end of the last century. In the 1880s Francis Galton collected data on seventeen physical measures from a sampling of 9000 visitors to the International Health Exhibition in London. With his findings on the reaction time, visual and auditory acuity, grip strength, and so on for individuals ranging in age from five to eighty, Galton was able to demonstrate rather conclusively that physical characteristics do differ by age. At roughly the same time another Russian scientist, S. P. Botkin, conducted a mass examination of almshouse residents in St. Petersburg. Based on a sample of nearly 3000 of the city's poor, 85 percent of whom were over sixty-five, Botkin sought to discriminate normal from pathological aging. The guiding premise was unique in itself, but, even further, Botkin and his colleagues included data on marital status, number of children, hereditary factors, use of alcohol, and other social variables that might conceivably influence longevity. Among his findings, which have been verified many times, Botkin noted older men had a higher incidence of atherosclerosis than older women, women tended to live longer, heavy alcohol use inhibited longevity, and married people outlived their single cohorts. Perhaps most important, Botkin drew the initial distinction between chronological and biological age (Birren and Clayton, 1975; Chebotarev and Duplenko, 1972).

**Advancement of Gerontology.** During the early years of the twentieth century, multidisciplinary interest in aging continued to spread at a gradual but ever increasing rate. Beginning in the early 1900s, Elie Metchnikoff, a transplanted Russian, began to publish his research concerning the role of intestinal bacteria. On the basis of work he conducted in England, Metchnikoff concluded — incorrectly, it might be noted — that autotoxicity of the lower intestinal tract was a cause of foreshortened life expectancy; therefore, purging the bowels of all bacteria should lengthen life. We now know the alimentary bacteria that Metchnikoff saw as so detrimental perform an important function in the assimilation of nutrients. Nevertheless, his studies were not entirely in vain, because they awakened further interest and eventually led to establishing the International Club for Research on Aging. Founded by Lord Nuffield and one of Metchnikoff's students, V. Korenchevsky, the Club sought to attract the attention of the worldwide scientific community to the study of aging. By the 1920s Americans were also becoming active in the study of aging. G. Stanley Hall's *Senescence, the Last Half of Life* (1922) was a pioneering effort in which he presented his own views on old age supported by analyzing a questionnaire he had administered to a sample of older people. Before the decade was out several other innovative books also appeared, and, in San Francisco, Lillian Martin set up the first Old Age Counseling Center to advise people on how to age successfully.

By the time the Club dispatched Korenchevsky to the United States in 1939 to create a North American branch, his efforts were almost anticlimactic.

Prior to his arrival the cause of gerontology had already become somewhat of a social movement, gaining adherents among both laypeople and scientists. The 1930s witnessed popular campaigns that helped pave the way for the Social Security Act, the initiation of occasional course offerings in major universities, and the publication of a number of landmark treatises. Among these E. V. Cowdry's edited volume *Problems of Ageing* (1939) caused quite a stir, bringing together as it did the most creative thinkers of the time and setting the stage for the rapid growth of gerontology over the course of the next two decades. During the 1940s activity in gerontology increased dramatically. The war years interrupted a series of innovative, highly publicized conferences that gave scientific respectability to the field, but within a year of the war's end, the Gerontological Society was founded and the first issue of the *Journal of Gerontology* made its appearance. Responding to increasing attention and pressure, even the federal government became involved, launching the first of a series of agencies that culminated nearly thirty years later in the 1974 birth of The National Institute of Aging.

The development of gerontology has been exponential. What was a trickle of five or six books augmented by some 100 articles in 1940 has since turned into an enormous flood of scores of books and well over 5000 articles yearly (Kent, 1972). So extensive has the bibliography become that an attempt a few years ago to compile a listing of the titles published during the period 1954–1974 resulted in approximately 50,000 entries, certainly too many for any one student to ever assimilate and a number exceeding the literature of all previous years combined (Woodruff, 1975; Birren and Clayton, 1975). According to an article in the 1983 *Annual Review of Psychology*, over 4000 additions to the literature of that discipline alone appeared in the six-year period ending in 1981 (Birren et al., 1983).

The availability of social services and practical programs designed for the elderly has also undergone a remarkable period of expansion. Unfortunately, both of these, as well as funding for research in gerontology, appear to be entering a period of retrenchment. In the late 1970s and early 1980s many types of programs, facilities, and services provided to the elderly expanded enormously. Over 500,000 people were involved in delivering direct service, more than 800 colleges and universities listed some kind of educational program for older adults, and vocational programs were offered across the country. But in the mid-1980s freezes of existing appropriations and recessions threaten to reduce funds already allocated to support programs under the 1984 revisions of the Older Americans Act. Cutbacks being proposed range from modest curtailments to the total elimination of crucial services. Although there is no denying the severity of federal budget deficits, the politics of determining just what type of cuts will be made would appear to leave services for the elderly at serious risk.

**The Focus of Gerontological Study.** Experts in the field are not in agreement when it comes to deciding what all who call themselves gerontologists should know. Old academic boundaries and petty disputes too often inhibit the development of a real understanding of the aging process. As a consequence, those who are new to the study of aging may not get the full picture. Imagine, if you will, a person standing on the edge of a tall building threatening to jump while a biochemist, a psychologist, and a sociologist stand and argue over the cause of this "craziness." Likely as not the formula for the acceleration of a falling body will win out. Ridiculous as such a scenario sounds it is not too far from an accurate description of the internecine disagreements among some gerontologists. It would be far more productive to forget what they call themselves and get on with the business at hand. Later on, once certain core information is available, there will be plenty of time for narrow specialization.

In a joint undertaking the Association for Gerontology in Higher Education and the Gerontological Society attempted to identify what, if anything, constitutes core knowledge expected of all gerontologists. Although no complete agreement emerged, there is a consensus that a common body of knowledge exists and that it is multidisciplinary in nature. Depending on the focus of one's interest, curriculum content clusters into three basic areas: biomedical, psychological, and socioeconomic-environmental (Foundations Project, 1980). Within each cluster a number of key topics are specified both in terms of general knowledge and career preparation.

Here, as in our previous editions, we use an interdisciplinary approach to cover crucial issues in the structuring of later life. The foundation of a meaningful and personally relevant approach to growing old begins with an appreciation of the intertwining of physiological, psychological, and social dimensions of the process we call aging.

## Summary

Growing old is a dynamic process encompassing complex body changes, redefinitions of social identities, and adjustments in psychological functioning. By itself chronological age has little meaning, although it is a convenient indicator not only of physiological change but also of social status. It is not likely that any appreciation of what it means to age can be complete if analysis is focused on only a given individual or social group. If students of gerontology are to offer an explanation of why aging occurs the way it does, they must be willing to adopt a broad perspective, one that cuts across time, space, and academic boundaries. Throughout history there have been a few concerned people and scholars who attempted to intervene in the lives of the elderly and to improve their lot relative to the rest of the population. However, it was not until late in the nineteenth century that societal concern began to grow in Europe, and not until the 1930s that Americans began to acknowledge that the situations in which the elderly were involved were not entirely of their own making. Out of the pattern of shifting values and practical questions, gerontology has emerged as something of a social movement, as well as a systematic area of inquiry.

All societies use age as a social variable by which they prescribe and evaluate what they consider to be appropriate behavior. Because of this universal tendency for age status systems to develop, most of our social interaction takes place within homogeneous age categories. People move through the life cycle adopting and abandoning one set of roles after another, preparing at each step for what is to follow and learning the cues about how to act in the process. Gradually they pass into the nebulous era of old age. Unlike all previous transitions, this one is seldom anticipated, not in the sense that it always spells difficulty, rather because little of what has gone before prepares people for what it is like to be old. Partially because it represents something most people view as alien to their ideas and values, old age is surrounded by a series of inappropriate stereotypes. Unfortunately, these sometimes carry over into the realm of scientific inquiry, as the negative conclusions of early gerontological research so readily point out.

As long as there have been old people there has been speculation about aging, but in terms of systematic codification, gerontology is still a relatively young field. Its forerunners can be traced back through the centuries, though it is only in the last hundred years that the problems of the aged have been addressed as legitimate in their own right. Although academic interest in the United States dates from within a decade or two of the enactment of the Social Security Act, it is only in the last few years that research has developed at an ever accelerating pace. Social gerontology is conceptually an even more recent arrival than is an interest in the physical aspects of aging; many of its founders are still living and actively contributing to its nurturance. The growth and expansion of the study of aging has not been without its problems, however. Theoretically and methodologically it has taken a number of years to recognize that many of what were once defined as age-related declines may have been artifacts of particular historical times or research procedures. To overcome the hurdles that have impeded gerontologists of the past, many of whose judgments came close to being canonized as inevitable truths, contemporary students of aging must take a more holistic approach to the process. Of necessity then we must turn our attention not only to social and cultural variables, but also to the physiological and psychological factors impinging on all humans traveling the paths of growth, development, and aging.

# Discussion Questions

**Making Sense of Aging**

1. Do you think the elderly are very different from younger people? (Think about particular old people you know or have heard about in the news and how their attitudes differ from your own.)

2. Is there anything you think should be changed about the living conditions of the elderly?

3. What means would you use to make these changes?

**The Multifaceted
Nature of Aging**

4. Choose one of the problems you listed in question 2 above and think about:
   a. In what ways might this problem result from:
      - The behavior of particular old people
      - Their personal situation
      - The beliefs and practices prevalent in the culture
      - Economic factors and social policy
   b. How might people from different professions or disciplines try to deal with these problems without communicating with each other (multidisciplinary approach)? What problems might be caused by their lack of communication?
   c. How could these same people work together on the problem (interdisciplinary approach)? (For example, you might take the problem of poor nutrition among the elderly and think about how a nutritionist, a medical doctor, a psychologist, an anthropologist, a social worker, and a congressional representative would deal with it.)

5. A study shows that a certain percent of people over fifty have three chronic illnesses. Does this mean that you will have three or more chronic illnesses when you are over fifty?

6. What do you expect your life to be like when you are in your sixties? What advantages do you expect to have that other people will not? What problems that other people do not? How will your old age be different from that of your parents?

7. How could statistics be used in planning so that the elderly will get an appropriate amount of health care? Can statistics be used in deciding what is an appropriate amount of health care or do we need to take other considerations into account?

8. We want to know whether a national pension plan is working well. Think of as many questions as possible that could be asked in a study on this issue. In asking your questions, try to put yourself in the place of a number of different kinds of people (for instance, taxpayers, pension recipients, or elected officials).

9. Imagine you were living in the late 1940s or early 1950s when birth rates were increasing. What would you expect the age distribution of the population of the United States to be like in the year 2000?

10. A study of the major causes of death in a developing country lists "old age" as one of the most frequent causes of death. Do you think this is accurate?

11. How would you go about identifying generalizable causes for nutritional problems in old people? How would you go about searching for generalizable solutions to these?

12. Why do you think people and governments might be willing or unwilling to develop programs for the elderly?

**Depression and Concern for the Elderly**

13. Why do you think the Depression led to an increased concern with the needs of the elderly?

14. Do you think that government-sponsored assistance programs are a good solution to the problems of the elderly? (Refer to some of the things you listed in question 2 you would like to change about the living conditions of the elderly in this country.) What form should they take?

**Scope of Gerontology**

15. Think of the range of questions studied by gerontology. How are they interrelated? What disciplines are represented?

# Pertinent Readings

Achenbaum, W. A. *Shades of Gray: Old Age, American Values, and Federal Policies Since 1920.* Boston: Little, Brown & Company, 1983.

American Cancer Society. *1985 Cancer Facts and Figures.* New York: American Cancer Society, 1985.

Birren, J., and V. Clayton. "History of Gerontology." In *Aging: Scientific Perspectives and Social Issues,* eds. D. S. Woodruff and J. E. Birren, pp. 15–27. New York: D. Van Nostrand Company, 1975.

———, Cunningham, W. R., and K. Yamamoto. "The Psychology of Adult Development and Aging." *Annual Review of Psychology* 33 (1983): 543–75.

Borgatta, E. F., and M. B. Loeb. "Research on Aging." *Research on Aging* 1 (1979): 3–9.

Breytspraak, L. M. *Development of the Self in the Later Years.* Boston: Little, Brown & Company, 1984.

Chebotarev, D. F., and Y. K. Duplenko. "On the History of the Home Gerontology Movement." In *The Main Problems of Soviet Gerontology,* ed. D. F. Chebotarev, pp. 3–40. Kiev: U.S.S.R. Academy of Social Sciences, 1972.

Clark, M., and B. G. Anderson. *Culture and Aging.* Springfield, Ill.: Charles C Thomas, Publisher, 1967.

Conover, W. F. *Practical Nonparametric Statistics,* 2nd ed. New York: John Wiley and Sons, Inc., 1980.

Eisenstadt, S. N. *From Generation to Generation.* New York: The Free Press, 1956.

Foundations Project. "Foundations for Gerontological Education." *The Gerontologist* 20, 3, Pt. II (1980).

Freeman, J. T. *Aging: Its History and Literature.* New York: Human Sciences Press, 1979.

Gore, W. R., and M. Hughes. "Reexamining the Ecological Fallacy: A Study in Which Aggregate Data are Critical in Investigating the Pathological Effects of Living Alone." *Social Forces* 58, 4 (1980): 1157–77.

Huff, D. *How To Lie with Statistics.* New York: W. W. Norton & Company, Inc., 1957.

Keith, J. *Old People as People: Social and Cultural Influences on Aging and Old Age.* Boston: Little, Brown & Company, 1982.

Kent, D. P. "Social Policy and Program Considerations in Planning for the Aging." In *Research Planning and Action for the Elderly,* eds. D. P. Kent, R. Kastenbaum, and S. Sherwood, pp. 3–19. New York: Behavioral Publications, Inc., 1972.

Kogan, N. "Beliefs, Attitudes and Stereotypes about Old People." *Research on Aging* 1 (1979):11–36.

Levin, J., and W. C. Levin. *Ageism: Prejudice and Discrimination against the Elderly.* Belmont, Calif.: Wadsworth Publishing Company, 1980.

Lewis, C. S. *The Screwtape Letters.* London: Fontana, 1965.

Palmore, E. "When Can Age, Period and Cohort Be Separated?" *Social Forces* 57, 1 (1978): 282–95.

Philibert, M. "Philosophical Approaches to Gerontology." In *Dimensions of Aging,* eds. J. Hendricks and C. D. Hendricks, pp. 379–94. Cambridge, Mass.: Winthrop Publishers, Inc., 1979.

Robinson, W. S. "Ecological Correlations and the Behavior of Individuals." *American Sociological Review* 15, 4 (June 1950): 351–57.

Schaie, K. W., and J. Geiwitz. *Adult Development and Aging.* Boston: Little, Brown & Company, 1982.

Scheaffer, R. L., Mendenhall, W., and L. Ott. *Elementary Survey Sampling,* 2nd ed. Boston: Duxbury Press, 1979.

Seltzer, M. M. "The Quality of Research Is Strained." *The Gerontologist* 15, 6 (1975): 503–07.

Spengler, J. J. "The Aging and Public Policy." In *Behavior and Adaptation in Late Life,* eds. E. W. Busse and E. Pfeiffer, pp. 367–83. Boston: Little, Brown & Company, 1969.

Woodruff, D. S. "Introduction: Multidisciplinary Perspectives of Aging." In *Aging: Scientific Perspectives and Social Issues,* eds. D. S. Woodruff and J. E. Birren, pp. 3–14. New York: D. Van Nostrand Company, 1975.

Younger, M. S. *Handbook for Linear Regression.* Boston: Duxbury Press, 1979.

# 2

# AGING IN THE MODERN WORLD

**SOME KEY CONCEPTS IN SOCIAL GERONTOLOGY**

Nature of Aging
Age Grading
Age-Appropriate Behavior
Rites of Passage
Ageism: Stereotyping the Elderly
Age Structure of the Population
  *The Number of Elderly and*
    *What it Means*
  *Aging of the Population vs the Aging*
    *of Individuals*
  *Life Expectancy vs Life Span*
  *Cross-Sectional vs Cohort Analysis*
  *Dependency Ratios*

**AGING IN HISTORICAL CONTEXT**

Population Trends and Age Structure
  in History
  *Aging in the Prehistoric Period*
  *Classical Antiquity*
  *The Middle Ages and the Renaissance*
  *Colonial America*
  *The Modern Era*
Attitudes Toward Aging in History

**AGING IN ADVANCED INDUSTRIAL SOCIETY**

Population Age Structures
Age-Dependent Populations
Increases in Life Expectancy
Expansion of the Elderly Population

**AGING IN THE THIRD WORLD**

Population Structure
Quality of Life

**SUMMARY**

**DISCUSSION QUESTIONS**

**PERTINENT READINGS**

Having looked at the nature, scope, and roots of gerontology in the previous chapter, it is time now to turn to a closer examination of the broad spectrum of social gerontology. The first task will be to introduce some key concepts. We will then look at aging in its historical context. Apart from the intrinsic interest in the history of aging, a grasp of the historical perspective will help us more deeply appreciate the elderly in the modern world. In the third section we will review various demographic aspects of aging in advanced industrial societies, particularly the United States. Finally, for purposes of comparison we will give a brief overview of aging in Third World countries and how it differs from aging in mass societies.

## Some Key Concepts in Social Gerontology

### NATURE OF AGING

**Senescence** refers to the increasing vulnerability of an organism progressing through life. Although the term "aging" is often used to refer to changes in later life following the reproductive period (U.S. Census, 1984a), the aging process begins at birth and progresses throughout life. It is a multidimensional process involving a complex interplay of physiological, psychological, cultural, and social structural factors. Thus, while one of the first classic texts in gerontology was primarily composed of biological and medical articles, almost one-fifth of its chapters were devoted to locating aging and the aged in their psychological, social, and historical environments (Cowdry, 1942). Yet, despite our early cognizance of the interdisciplinary character of gerontology, it remains true that gerontologists often neglect the fundamental, dynamic interplay of various analytic levels in their day-to-day research and writing. Although it is, of course, very difficult to adopt a truly interdisciplinary focus in ongoing research, we continually need to be reminded of the importance of striving for such an approach if we are to have any grasp of the phenomenon of aging in all of its complexity.

If we think of the aging process as encompassing the whole of life, it becomes readily apparent that aging is not exclusively a process of decline. While people experience a greater or lesser degree of decline in their physical and, in some instances, mental powers as they age, the aging process may also be one of attaining greater maturity: the development of coping skills and increased insight into the human condition. This aspect of aging is, with rare exceptions, often neglected. While **senile dementia** — an organic disorder of the brain — is a tragic problem for those who are affected by it, old age is not inevitably associated with a loss of mental powers. Even when dementia is present, it may be progressive, static, or remitting. Estimates for the 1976–1979 period indicated that from 15 to 25 percent of the elderly in the community may have significant symptoms of mental illness. These symptoms are thought to be caused by senile dementia in only 5 to 6 percent of the population. In about 10 percent they are thought to be caused by depression, which is a potentially treatable condition. In other words, 75 to 85 percent of the elderly in the community are thought to be free of symptoms of mental deterioration, and a further 10 percent are believed to be suffering from a reversible condition (U.S. Census, 1983a). These rates are really not very different from the rest of the population.

Because aging involves so many facets of life and because it is affected by so many factors, it proceeds at different rates for different individuals (see Chapter 4). Individuals of the same age may differ markedly with respect to any standard for their particular age cohort. We shall see as we explore the various aspects of aging in the course of this book that differences in the rate of aging between individuals may be partly a matter of heredity, of life-style, of nutrition and the availability of medical care, of the cultural options open to the individual, of the historical events in which he or she participates, of social class, and of the social structural factors that encompass his or her life. These variations in the rate of aging have led gerontologists to distinguish between **chronological age,** which is simply the number of years since an individual's birth, and **functional age,** which compares the individual's level of functioning to ideal typical levels of functioning for particular age cohorts. Thus, for instance, a forty-year-old who is affected by a chronic disability may have the physical strength of a typical seventy-year-old. Alternately, another forty-year-old may have the kidney function of someone much younger. Regardless of these incongruities, age is universally used in the assignment of social standing.

## AGE GRADING

Age is so pervasive an element of social organization that anthropologists are convinced it is a universal feature in the assignment of social roles, rights, and responsibilities. That is to say, age is never merely a biological fact of life; everywhere it takes on cultural meanings that color the social definitions of people and the things they do. Some societies have only two grades: boys and men, girls and women. Others have up to eight or more, but all differentiate roles by age (Keith, 1982). The nature of the criteria may change, but modern and traditional societies alike distribute valued social responsibilities on the basis of age. In traditional, less modern societies, functional age or performance capacities and social definitions were closely aligned because of the relatively homogeneous structure of opportunity. With the increasing complexity of modern mass societies, the functional determination of age group membership has been replaced by more formal criteria. Nonetheless, whatever system is used, it ensures a continuous progression of individuals through socially valued roles.

In modern and preindustrial societies **age norms,** however they are derived, considerably constrain members of various age grades. In advanced industrial societies the age-related criteria for role assignment may appear more arbitrary because various segments of the population are characterized by differential access to medical care, education, and other valued resources. In fact, those who have access to more resources may be functionally younger. Yet age norms do establish widely accepted boundaries that people recognize and use to anticipate the broad contours of their lives (Keith, 1982; Bengtson and Haber, 1975).

## AGE-APPROPRIATE BEHAVIOR

If asked to provide a list of our friends, most of us would find on inspection that the ages of those people whose names we wrote down cluster fairly close around our own age. That this should be the case for young as well as for old ought not to come as a surprise, because the greatest proportion of interaction takes place among individuals from socially homogeneous groups who share a comparable position vis-à-vis the larger social system (Rosow, 1967). As we move through life, this tendency to associate most with those who are approximately our age and of similar circumstances is one of the means by which we all learn what is expected of us. These age norms, as they are called by social scientists, have an inexorable influence on how individuals behave. For the most part they do not designate in detail how a person is to carry out a particular social role; instead they provide a general definition of acceptable behavior within a given complex of roles. For example, norms regarding parental conduct do not specify an exact manner for discharging the responsibilities of being a parent, though they do prescribe what we usually consider suitable responses. It ought to be emphasized, however, that expectations of age-appropriate behavior are seldom formulated in isolation — that is, without reference to earlier and later age grades or reciprocal roles. Continuing with the parental example, anticipations of how the parents of young children will act are based in part on the relative youthfulness of the parents themselves, plus the dependent position of their offspring. At a later time, when both parents and children are more mature, slightly different behaviors are expected, until finally each child becomes an adult and still further redefinitions take place. At each juncture, both parents and offspring find themselves interacting most with others who are at a like stage in the life cycle, taking cues from one another as to what are acceptable attitudes and actions. It is only when the entire process is viewed as lasting throughout life that the meaningfulness of age-graded expectations becomes apparent (Eisenstadt, 1956).

Although age norms circumscribe the implicit boundaries of desirable conduct, and hence are most noticeable in their transgression, researchers have found a marked consensus in people's conceptions of appropriate behavior (Breytspraak, 1984). This is not to claim that everyone moves through life locked into an invariable chronological timetable in which there are no opportunities for individual description or modification. Indeed, there is a whole array of social factors, many of which are seemingly endemic to the social order, that play a part in the timing of the life cycle. At the outset, socioeconomic status has a profound effect on considerations of social age. Generally speaking, members of disadvantaged socioeconomic classes pass what most people view as life's transition points at earlier chronological ages than their counterparts in more affluent social classes. Thus, they establish independent households, marry, have children, cease having children, and so on at relatively earlier ages. Similarly they see themselves as middle-aged or old a few years in advance of men and women in the upper socioeconomic categories.

Patterns of education and labor force participation also have an effect on determinations of social age; for example, students nearing their late twenties who are still enrolled in school are often thought of as younger, by themselves and by others, than their age mates who terminated their education earlier and have since established families or careers. In addition, there are indications that sex, ethnicity, and racial background are contributing factors in the timing of the aging process. As will be seen in Chapter 9, members of various minority groups in the United States do not necessarily age the same way as the majority white population. Among the most commonly observed differences are perceptions of the chronological age at which people undergo various changes in social age (Bengtson and Haber, 1975; Drevenstedt, 1976).

Despite the significant effects these variables have on assessments of social age, their impact, at least singly, does not preclude individual variations. As one concomitant of the pluralistic nature of modern life and the numerous institutional spheres in which we participate, each with its own timetable, the succession of people through a well-regulated age-status system is not nearly as coordinated as it may have been in less complex societies. Today, because of fairly distinct boundaries, perhaps basic to the various spheres of life, it is entirely conceivable for many people to experience a kind of asynchronous movement through the life cycle. This process is by no means as mysterious as it may at first sound. Returning again to the earlier example of parenthood may be a useful way to clarify **age-status asynchronization.** Since most people marry for the first time in their early twenties, it is not at all unusual for them to have completed the procreative phase of the family life cycle before their occupational careers have taken root. Hence, in terms of family life, they are at a later stage of development than they are in their work lives. Likewise, for those women who do not work outside the home, family responsibilities may be essentially complete at an age when their husbands are considered to be too young for certain executive positions. Or, alternatively, both partners may find themselves grandparents when they themselves have barely crossed the threshold of middle age. Of course, these are not the only examples of asynchronization. Equally valid illustrations arise in the cases of those who delay starting their families, remarry and begin another set of family relationships, or embark on a second career at a point in life later than is customary (Cain, 1964).

Interestingly enough, people are often fully aware of subtle variations in age-appropriate behavior and if asked can provide a reasonably accurate assessment of their own adherence to the norm. Neugarten and her associates have used the concept of *social clocks* to describe the marking off of various units of the life cycle. They have found that in most instances people recognize whether they are passing some transition point ahead of or behind schedule and, depending on their timing, often modify subsequent behavior to bring themselves closer to what they see as typically the case (Neugarten, 1979; Neugarten and Datan, 1973). While they may desire to approximate the norms with regard to certain aspects of aging, it appears most people feel somehow exempt from strict adherence to the general normative patterns of aging. In a sense age norms are conceived by most of us as compelling strictures for others but lacking in any specific hegemony over our own lives. Why this should be the case is one of those paradoxes gerontologists have so far been unable to resolve. Nevertheless, it may be an age-related phenomenon, since, in comparison to middle-aged or older people, younger age groups often see themselves as more at variance with what they think of as the norm (Bengtson and Haber, 1975).

## RITES OF PASSAGE

As people encounter the sequence of age-graded roles, **rites of passage** are one of the mechanisms used by society to denote their movement from one phase of the life cycle to the next. Originally such rites were celebrated by highly ritualized ceremonies and provided an institutionalized means for ending certain behaviors and introducing a new set of expectations. Readily familiar examples are the use among certain tribal peoples of circumcision or clitorectomy rites to initiate young males and females to adult status, or of Bar Mitzvahs, debutante balls, high school graduations, formal inaugurations, and so on in modern social systems to indicate the transition to new statuses. In fact, rites of passage need not be so formalized to qualify, exclude, or limit what is expected within particular age-related roles. Advancing through grades in school, joining new clubs or associations, or even buying a house can be seen as ways in which people are socially redefined, though these latter forms obviously lack much of the symbolic significance of ceremonial transitions. Usually such status shifts imply increasing maturity and responsibility, each helping in its own way to prepare the person for still later transitions, thereby ensuring some semblance of continuity to the passage through life's stages without the distraction of major disjunctures (Van Gennep, 1960; Rosow, 1974).

Becoming socially defined as an "older person" presents something of an exception to the foregoing pattern of rites and transitions. As with all changes, the movement into old age entails delicate alterations in social relationships, but these are much more nebulous. Formal rites of passage, the occasional retirement dinner notwithstanding, are seldom features of the initial phases of the later years, since this period is most often experienced as an unscheduled gradual passage. Although today reaching one's sixty-fifth birthday is in a sense a rite, in many respects a redefinition is likely to have been imminent for a number of years. It should also be noted at this point that one reason the specter of institutionalization is so emotionally potent among older people might well be because it signifies so clearly what most perceive to be the final transition in the life cycle. Unlike all previous transitions, instead of expanding alternatives, old age tends to have a constricting influence over the structure of opportunities and causes some people to feel alienated from important social roles. Part of this explanation is simply that the institutional supports implicit in all previous transitions are lacking in the passage into old age. For what is often the first time in their lives, people are confronted by the attrition or absence of predetermined institutional alternatives so integral to their sense of self-worth.

Historically, men may have experienced greater degrees of role discontinuity than women as they moved into old age, since little or nothing in their backgrounds prepared them for what life in the later years would be like. In contrast, women have traditionally had far more experience in adapting to role redefinition, while the gradual alterations in domestic chores allows them more time to adapt to the changing expectations of later life. With the increasing participation of women in the work force, perhaps they too will come to experience the disjunctures of role loss through retirement. In the case of men who have been the head of a single parent family, they may have more emotional and personal resources to draw on as they enter retirement. Clearly, the pattern of role involvement is an undeniable aspect of adapting to changes brought on by progressing through life. Rather than being simply a matter of the old being expected to disengage from society, the problem may also be a question of the young and the middle-aged being overly dependent on institutional involvements, of a failure to develop a sense of self-worth based on the knowledge and development of one's own particular attributes and abilities and on meaningful personal relationships rather than on the ability to fulfill a prescribed role (Rosow, 1974).

## AGEISM: STEREOTYPING THE ELDERLY

Gerontologists have coined the term **ageism** to refer to the pejorative image of someone who is old simply because of his or her age. Like racism or sexism, it connotes wholesale discrimination against all members of a category, though usually it appears more covertly. Threatened cutbacks in Social Security, failure to provide meaningful outlets or activities, or the belief that those in their sixties and beyond do not benefit from psychotherapy are all examples of subtle, or in some cases not so subtle, appraisals of the old. Part of the myth, a fundamental if implicit element of ageism, is the view that the elderly are somehow different from our present *and* future selves and therefore not subject to the same desires, concerns, or fears. Even our attempts at humor, though more complex than is often thought (Richland, 1977; Seltzer, 1986), reveal the existence of largely negative attitudes about the elderly, with those referring to older women suggesting a particularly pernicious "double standard" (Davies, 1977). Why should ageism have become a national prejudice? Probably because of the emphasis on productive capacity and technological expertise, or perhaps out of a thinly veiled attempt to avoid the reality that we will all one day grow old and die. Not to be dismissed is the early gerontological research that filtered into the public consciousness and reinforced existing misconceptions based largely on institutionalized older people who, however important they may have been in their own right, were still a scant minority among the elderly (Butler and Lewis, 1977). According to the best estimates, only about 5 percent of the elderly live in nursing homes on any given day. The population of nursing homes turns over regularly; some move in, some move out, others die. But it is not until people are well into their seventies that the prospect of institutionalization increases appreciably (Eustis et al., 1984; U.S. Census, 1983a).

Indicative of the range of commonly held stereotypes about the elderly are the beliefs that most older people are living isolated lives beset by serious health problems, causing them to be emotionally distraught. Just as widespread are the ideas that women experience psychological trauma with the onset of the so-called empty nest years and that retirement causes certain morale problems for men. That older people are no longer sexually active, that they are no longer even interested, is another generally held view unsupported by the facts. Surely some or all of these themes can be observed among those over sixty-five, but they can also be found in any other age group. The realities of aging simply do not fit the stereotypes; however, despite the accumulation of new information, the myths continue to thrive. Again, even older people who may not be experiencing the difficulties attributed to old age see themselves as exceptions to an otherwise dreary picture. Because of our misconceptions, we do the elderly a great disservice by regarding them as just another problem rather than as a potential resource for resolving society's dilemmas (Levin and Levin, 1980; NCOA, 1981).

Either because of a lack of information or the absence of **anticipatory socialization**, old age occupies a unique place in the life cycle, at least insofar as it is surrounded by more misconceptions than any other phase. The tendency to develop *stereotypes*, oversimplified and often erroneous generalizations about various groups or categories of people, is apparently very common. If nothing else, it protects us from being overwhelmed by too many particulars. However, such categorizations form the basis of stereotypes that are frequently derived from limited knowledge and allow no room for individual variation. Americans, or members of any modern society, are not distinctive in their systematic denigration of certain classes of people. Nor is youth atypical in its perception of old age as a time of feared changes. Unfortunately, even the elderly themselves are influenced by the characteristically unfavorable image of older people. Not only are the phrases and adjectives they use to describe their contemporaries generally deprecating, but their own self-concepts reflect the very ambivalence they perceive in the attitudes of those with whom they interact. In every instance the views people have toward both minority groups and specific age stages are shaped by the ideals of the culture in which they live and the stigmatizing of that which is at odds with those ideals. In an era that eschews traditional authority and values youth, freedom, and the rapid dissemination of new ideas, old age is unlikely to be accorded very high prestige (Kogan, 1979).

To try to gauge the public's attitudes toward aging, The National Council on the Aging commissioned what may be the most extensive study of its **type**, which was conducted by Louis Harris and Associates. In 1974 and again in 1981 the Harris polling organization asked a representative cross section of adult Americans what it is like to grow old in the United States. They found that some major changes had taken place over the seven years between the polls, but a pattern of stereotypes continued nonetheless. Among the 4250 interviewed in 1977 and the 3427 polled in 1981, marked disparities existed between younger adult expectations and the actual experiences of those over sixty-five. In nearly all cases the younger respondents held exaggerated views of the isolation and problems encountered in old age (NCOA, 1981). As Table 2.1 makes clear, misconceptions about the plight of the elderly are rampant. By way of illustration, 74 percent of the general population (eighteen to sixty-four) viewed the fear of crime as a serious problem for those over sixty-five, while only 25 percent of the elderly actually held the same view.

Despite the dire expectations about what life is going to be like, Harris and his associates found that for every older person who feels life to be worse than he or she thought it was going to be, there are at least three age mates who claim they are pleasantly surprised. Of course, there are some in every age category who are dismayed that things are not working out as they had hoped; the elderly can hardly be considered an exception. On the whole, income and racial background have been identified as having a greater impact on life satisfaction than age. The more affluent respondents were not only more likely to express satisfaction with their current situation, but they were more positively disposed toward the prospect of growing old. Though the sample does not differentiate among racial or ethnic groups other than between black and white, it appears there is a paradox among minority respondents about rising expectations. Older blacks feel more satisfied with their lives than do their younger counterparts, though a similar pattern tends to emerge among all respondents who are at the bottom end of the lower income scale. Regardless of financial levels, the black respondents felt less adequately prepared for old age than did the white, yet, racial characteristics aside, most people over sixty-five express regrets for not having planned better for their later lives (Harris, 1975; NCOA 1981). Had they been more aware of what they would face and less insulated from the facts by the common tendency to shut

**TABLE 2.1**

Differences Between Personal Experience of Americans Sixty-five and Over and Expectations of Other Adults About Those Experiences

| Rank As Actual Very Serious Problem for 65 and Over (No.) | | 1981 | | | 1974 | | |
|---|---|---|---|---|---|---|---|
| | | Personal Experience "Very Serious" Problems Felt Personally | Public Expectation "Very Serious" Problems Attributed to Most People Over 65 | | Personal Experience "Very Serious" Problems Felt Personally | Public Expectation "Very Serious" Problems Attributed to Most People Over 65 | |
| | | By Public 65 and Over (%) | By Public 18–64 (%) | By Public 65 and Over (%) | By Public 65 and Over (%) | By Public 18–64 (%) | By Public 65 and Over (%) |
| 4 | Not having enough money to live on | 17 | 68 | 50 | 15 | 63 | 59 |
| 3 | Poor health | 21 | 47 | 40 | 21 | 50 | 53 |
| 6 | Loneliness | 13 | 65 | 45 | 12 | 61 | 56 |
| 9 | Poor housing | 5 | 43 | 30 | 4 | 35 | 34 |
| 2 | Fear of crime | 25 | 74 | 58 | 23 | 50 | 51 |
| 8 | Not enough education | 6 | 21 | 17 | 8 | 19 | 25 |
| 9 | Not enough job opportunities | 6 | 51 | 24 | 5 | 47 | 32 |
| 7 | Not enough medical care | 9 | 45 | 34 | 10 | 45 | 36 |
| 1 | High cost of energy such as heating oil, gas, and electricity | 42 | 81 | 72 | x | x | x |
| 5 | Getting transportation to stores, to doctors, to places of recreation, and so forth | 14 | 58 | 43 | x | x | x |

x = not asked.

*Source:* NCOA. *Aging in the Eighties: America In Transition.* Washington, D.C.: The National Council on the Aging, Inc., 1981.

the later years off from the rest of the life cycle, the problems they encounter might have been gradually ameliorated.

## AGE STRUCTURE OF THE POPULATION

In demographic studies aging is defined essentially in terms of chronological age. Demographers justify this approach on the assumption that for large populations the aging process, functional age, and physiological age follow chronological age closely; this approach avoids the problem of fixing the onset of aging in individual cases, and it permits the use of statistical tabulations from censuses and population surveys for conventional age groups (U.S. Census, 1984a). Although it is indeed true that demographic studies have an important part to play in understanding aging in a social context, they do not tell the entire story.

Demographic studies of chronological age in particular societies are useful in a number of important ways. In advanced industrial societies, where transitions such as entry into the work force, retirement, and eligibility for Social Security payments are regulated largely on the basis of chronological age, information about the numbers of people in particular age groups has important implications for social policy and planning. Knowledge regarding average life expectancies is a vital component of projections of overall population growth, which in itself has social policy implications. A comparison of life expectancies at birth (which reveals, for instance, that the life expectancy at birth in Ethiopia for 1975–1980 was 37.5 years for males and 40.6 years for females, as opposed to a life expectancy of 70.0 years for males and 77.8 for females in the United States in 1979) provides a striking indicator of differences in conditions of life in different countries (United Nations, 1984a). Knowledge of the age composition of a society can also enable us to identify different segments of the population with regard to the important historical events that have shaped their lives. Figure 2.1 is an example of how historical events and birth cohorts are interrelated.

Conclusions drawn from demographic studies can, however, be misleading. For example, the assumption that old people are extremely rare in preindustrial societies is not necessarily true (Stearns, 1982). This conclusion involves the use of two problematic assumptions in interpreting the data: (1) a generalization about the age distribution of the population based exclusively on **life expectancies** at birth and (2) that a chronological age of, for example, forty in a preindustrial society is functionally equivalent to forty in an advanced industrial society.

---

**FIGURE 2.1**
Relationship between historical events, year of birth, and age in 1983. (*Source:* U.S. Bureau of the Census. *Estimates of the Population of the United States by Age, Sex and Race: 1980 to 1983,* p. 3. Current Population Reports, P-25, No. 979. Washington, D.C.: U.S. Government Printing Office, 1983.)

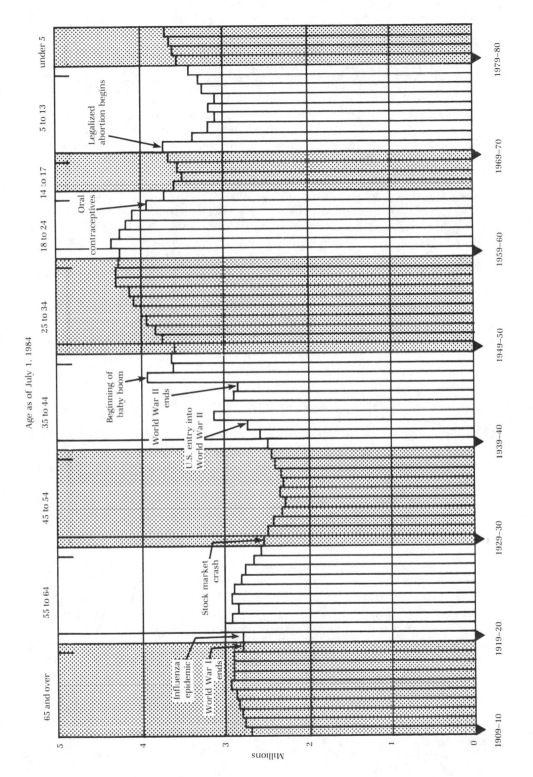

Age as of July 1, 1984

under 5

5 to 13

14 to 17

18 to 24

25 to 34

35 to 44

45 to 54

55 to 64

65 and over

Legalized
abortion begins

Oral
contraceptives

Beginning of baby boom

World War II
ends

U.S. entry into
World War II

Stock market
crash

Influenza
epidemic

World War I
ends

Millions

5

4

3

2

1

0

1909–10

1919–20

1929–30

1939–40

1949–50

1959–60

1969–70

1979–80

Year of birth (July 1–June 30)

As has often been noted, low life expectancy at birth may be accounted for in large part by high infant and childhood mortality rates. By adulthood, life expectancy rates in preindustrial and Third World countries may be much more comparable to those in advanced industrial societies. Thus, in preindustrial Europe, life expectancy at birth was around twenty-eight years; twenty-year-olds, however, could expect to live into their later fifties on the average (Stearns, 1982; Yin and Shine, 1985). We therefore need to find some way of ascertaining the distribution of mortality over a lifetime before we draw conclusions about the age distribution of a society. Furthermore, a chronological age of forty in one society may not be functionally equivalent to a chronological age of forty in another society. A Nicaraguan woman of twenty-five who has been married since fifteen, had five pregnancies, virtually no access to medical care, and a diet consisting mainly of rice and beans is likely to be functionally much older than an American woman of twenty-five who has just completed graduate school. Thus, although a society may not contain cohorts of comparable chronological age to those found in advanced industrial societies, it may contain cohorts that are perceived as being old. Old age is always contextually determined. It is the adult frame of reference that really determines attitudes toward and treatment of the elderly (Stearns, 1982). To assess the functioning of the elderly in a society we need to know not only the age distribution of the population but also the functional age of various cohorts and societal attitudes toward aging.

Too frequently life expectancy at birth has been taken as indicative of overall improvements in how long people can expect to live. The changes observed over the course of the twentieth century have been the result primarily of changes in infant mortality and secondarily of cures for the infectious diseases of middle age. Only recently has medicine begun to make inroads against the chronic diseases of old age (Fries, 1984). As a consequence, an interesting controversy has arisen about improvements in *age-specific life expectancy* and *morbidity*, or the departure from well-being, among the *old-old*—those over seventy-five.

For years gerontologists contended that rectangularization of the human survival curve — from relatively low death rates until late in life — meant the healthy period of middle-aged people would be stretched out into the later years. In other words, the period of diminished vigor thought to characterize old age would be compressed into the very furthest reaches of life expectancy (Fries, 1983, 1984). The logic is that for 150 years improving housing, nutrition, sanitation, medical practices, and so on have added years to our lives and therefore expanded the number of healthy years we experience. As Strehler (1979) points out, and as we will see in Chapter 4, the advances have come about because of the control of various causes of death that express themselves during specific periods of life. The question is, however, does the downward shift in exponential mortality rates in the later decades of life portend a similar pattern for nonterminal morbidity? There is little agreement as yet whether this will indeed be the case. Some have suggested that the number of years of ill-health will be expanded, while others argue just the opposite (Schneider and Brody, 1983; Myers and Manton, 1984). All agree that the resolution lies in primary prevention and not patch-up medical attention. The significance of the issue is that the outcome will constitute an important dimension in the criteria for age differentiation.

**The Number of Elderly and What it Means.** Why is it not sufficient simply to note that there are many old people (over 25.5 million) and that life expectancy is going up? First, these 25.5 million are not all alike. They differ by sex, racial and social characteristics, economic position, and so on. A little over 16.1 million fall into the *young-old* bracket, or those between sixty-five and seventy-four, and another 8.2 million are between seventy-five and eighty-four; further, there are roughly 33,000 Americans now living who were born over a century ago. Some important questions are:

- Why is it that 60 percent of all the aged are women?
- Why is the difference between the sexes in life expectancy growing wider?
- Why do we find blacks and other minorities are underrepresented at first, but that after seventy-five blacks have longer remaining life expectancies?

Second, the demographics are important because they point to the changing nature of the aging process. If the longer living are better off in many ways, the implication is that improvement is possible for those who fall into less advantaged categories. In other words, if there is something about being wealthy, white, or female that promotes greater life expectancy, then once that something is identified it may be possible to improve everyone's chances of living a longer time.

To help make sense of the data the demographers use to talk about age and to decipher the meanings of changes over time in what age itself means, it is necessary to become familiar with the underpinnings of what the demographers point to when they are making projections about age structures. We will briefly review a few key points and then look at historical change and what the future may hold.

**Aging of the Population vs the Aging of Individuals.** Demographers distinguish between two areas of study: the aging of individuals and the aging of populations. Their concern with the aging of individuals focuses on the aggregate experience of individuals in various population groups with respect to aging; mostly they address questions of survival and longevity. Such measures include life expectancy at birth, age-specific life expectancy at sixty-five, the probability of survival from one age to another, person-years lived in an age interval, and total life expectancy. Aging of this type reflects changes in death rates, which are themselves the result of a variety of medical, social, and other factors (U.S. Census, 1984a).

The aging of populations refers to the relative age of the entire population. Is it getting older or getting younger? The answer to such a question may be phrased in terms of the mean age, the median age, the percentage of people sixty-five and over, the ratio of people sixty-five and over to children under fifteen, the proportion of the population above the age corresponding to a given life expectancy, or some other agreed-on indicator of age structure. Depending on which index is adopted, a range of possible answers may describe a given time period. Then again, if both the proportion of children and the proportion of elderly people are increasing, the population may be said to be getting younger or older, depending on which measure is employed. Clearly a variety of measures may be used to assess the aging patterns of a population. Adopting one or the other demographic measure is a reflection of the information communicated, as well as the political realities of policy makers. At base, whether a population is aging or not is a function of changes in its mortality, fertility, and migration rates, with fertility rates being especially germane (U.S. Census, 1984a).

**Life Expectancy vs Life Span.** The **life span** is the maximum length of life potentially attainable. The human life span appears to be somewhat over 100 years, with little evidence to suggest the maximum has changed much over recorded history (U.S. Census, 1984a; Comfort, 1979; Kent, 1980). A measure of far greater interest to students of gerontology is life expectancy, the average number of years lived by any **cohort** of individuals born in the same period. At any given age, remaining life expectancy is determined by demographers from a mathematical model called a *life table*, which specifies the probability of surviving from one age to another. Life tables are calculated on the basis of *age-specific death rates* operative at a particular time; these in turn are based on *crude death rates* compiled for each age group in the population (Yin and Shine, 1985; Havighurst and Sacher, 1977).

**Cross-Sectional vs Cohort Analysis.** Two major methods are used by demographers in their study of aging and the older population: cohort analysis and cross-sectional or period analysis. *Birth cohorts* are groups of people born in the same years who, in the process of **cohort analysis,** may be followed analytically through their lives with respect to some event or other characteristic, such as marital status. **Cross-sectional** or **period analysis** is based on an examination of the status of different age groups at a given point in time.

Because cohort analysis follows the evolution of some characteristic, be it a demographic or socioeconomic event, over the life of a cohort, and because it is based on data for the actual years through which the cohort lives, it gives a more realistic picture of age variation in demographic events or characteristics than does cross-sectional analysis. Cohort analysis also avoids certain absurd conclusions or gross distortions of interpretations that might occur with cross-sectional analysis, such as educational attainment declining with age. It is based on the assumption that the demographic events in people's lives are influenced by their previous demographic experience and by the historical circumstances through which they live. It has disadvantages, however, in that a large number of years have to pass before a record of experience over the life course can be established.

In cross-sectional demographic analysis, data for a relatively brief period are used to project changes over the life cycle. By creating a hypothetical or synthetic cohort from a number of real cohorts, a lifetime evolution of an event or characteristic may be projected. Of course, all these cohorts share common sociocultural, environmental, and historical events in a given year. The theory is that the impact of some external events, such as an economic depression or a major war, tends to be pervasive over the age span, even though the events do not affect all ages equally. Undoubtedly, their effects vary with the previous cohort experience of each age group, but for purposes of projection these are assumed to have minimal influence.

According to standard U.S. Bureau of the Census interpretations, the variation with respect to age of a given event or characteristic in any year may be viewed as a consequence of three general factors: (1) the general (cohort) pattern of the age cycle of a particular event or characteristic for a given population in a given era *(age cycle effect)*, (2) the changing historical-sociocultural conditions to which the various cohorts involved are exposed as they move through the age cycle *(period effect)*, and (3) the properties of specific birth cohorts under consideration *(cohort effect)*. The age cycle effect refers to the general succession of events characterizing the life course as members of a cohort grow older (for instance, the rise, leveling off, and decline of labor force participation). The period effect includes such historical conditions as the level of technology, the state of the economy, and the social norms prevalent in a particular period. The cohort effect refers to such properties of a cohort as its relative size and structure (large cohorts, such as the baby boom cohort, for example, tend to have very different experiences from small cohorts). As will be seen in Chapter 3, several of these components are taken into consideration in the theoretical formulations used to explain the aging experience.

**Dependency Ratios.** Dependency ratios are designed to measure the ratio of the economically dependent members of society to the economically productive members of society (people in the work force). There are two basic types of dependency ratios: **age-dependency ratios** and **economic-dependency ratios.**

*Age-dependency ratios* relate the number of people of dependent ages to the number of people of productive ages and are designed to show how the age composition contributes to economic dependency in a given population. Traditionally, the dependent population was calculated as including young people under fifteen and those over sixty-five. In more recent estimates the child-dependency ratio has been calculated to include young people under eighteen. In examining the impact of the rising proportion of those over sixty-five, it is important to balance this increase against falling child-dependency ratios; part of the funding that had formerly been used for financial support for the young might thus be transferred to support for the elderly. Age-dependency ratios are important in policy formulation. There are a number of conceptual problems with age-dependency ratios because a considerable number of those counted within the dependent age categories may actually be working, and many of those within the productive age group may not. Age-dependency ratios do not show the impact on the dependency ratio of the increasing entry of women into the work force. Though they are widely used for that purpose, age-dependency ratios are not a very useful tool for cross-cultural comparison, since patterns of entry into and exit from the work force vary between societies, and large numbers of young children may be working in Third World countries (Myles, 1984; U.S. Census, 1984a; Walker, 1982).

*Economic-dependency ratios* reflect the ratio of noninstitutionalized non-workers over sixty to workers from twenty to fifty-nine. They thus take account of the fact that many of the people in the productive age group may not be working and that some older people may be working. Economic-dependency ratios do not, however, consider several other factors affecting the economic surplus available for supporting the dependent population, particularly whether those who are employed work full- or part-time and the number of weeks worked in a year. They also do not take into account the contribution to the economy by homemakers and by volunteer workers, many of whom may fall into older age groups. Neither do they take into account the large number of older people who are economically independent, who do not depend on benefit packages from public revenues (U.S. Census, 1984). The **index of aging** (Valoras, 1950) is still another measure: it contrasts the number of persons on either end of the life course. By comparing the number of people sixty-five and over with those under fifteen, demographers are able to assess the extent to which the entire population is aging. It is also a viable way to compare populations of widely diverse geographic regions.

Having briefly introduced the tools employed in demographic analysis, it is time to turn to a consideration of changing age structures in both historical and contemporary contexts.

# Aging in Historical Context

An understanding of aging in history is necessary to evaluate the position of the elderly in the modern world. Some sense of how the position of elderly people in society evolved is important to assess their position today. Furthermore, an understanding of the intricacies and ambiguities of everyday life for the elderly in history may make us sensitive to some of the complexities and potential roles of the elderly in contemporary society.

## POPULATION TRENDS AND AGE STRUCTURE IN HISTORY

There has been an enormous increase in the world population and in human longevity since 1650. This is partly because of advances in sanitation, health practices, medical science, and improvements in nutrition and the general quality of life that has accompanied modernization. As we shall see in the section on the Third World later in this chapter, these advances have not been uniform for all countries and classes.

Demographic data regarding aging in history should be approached with caution. Systematic, accurate, and reliable data are not readily available, and for preliterate societies, assessments of life expectancy are based largely on archaeological evidence and conjecture. In literate societies the knowledge we have is generally about the upper classes, who probably fared rather better than their lower-class counterparts with regard to living conditions and longevity. Generally speaking, available information relates to individual aging (such as life expectancy at birth), rather than the age structure of the population. Because of high infant and childhood mortality, and because people may have been regarded as old at a younger age than today, old people may not have been nearly so rare as one would expect, even in societies with relatively low life expectancies at birth. In fourteenth-century Italy, for example, the apparent average life expectancy was twenty-eight years (Herlihy, 1982), yet Dante distinguished four stages of life: adolescence (birth to twenty-five years), full manhood (twenty-five to forty-five years), old age (forty-five to seventy years), and decrepitude, which began at seventy and typically lasted for ten or fewer years. Trexler (1982) cites evidence indicating that the life expectancy for women who survived the childbearing years in sixteenth-century Florence was approximately forty-two years, yet a number of the matrons of the Orbatello (an asylum for widows) were well over sixty. Life expectancies in England seem to have been about the same. Smith (1982) reports that life expectancy at birth in late seventeenth-century England was somewhere in the late twenties or early thirties. Yet he also notes that the best estimates indicate that many people actually lived to be sixty or more. Thus, Gregory Kind, a pioneer demographer, on the basis of a survey conducted in 1695, estimated that about one in every ten people was sixty or older. Compilation of statistics for Chilvers Coton in 1684 indicates that 6.7 percent of its population were sixty or older, and for Litchfield in 1695, 8.1 percent. E. A. Wrigley's study of Colyton, Devonshire, indicated that approximately half of those who lived to twenty-five and married lived to the age of sixty, and about one-fourth survived to the age of seventy (Smith, 1982). Thus, it may be that the gains in longevity we will describe had an impact in the increase in the number of middle-aged people as well as the increase in the proportion of elderly. In looking at the demography of aging in history, it is interesting to note the effect of social and natural occurrences on population structure (for example, the wars of the Middle Ages or the Black Death). Population structures in the modern world are subject to similar contingencies.

**Aging in the Prehistoric Period.** The very early period of human life on earth is thought to have been characterized exclusively by small, nomadic populations, which eked out an existence by means of hunting and gathering.

These societies were seldom able to accumulate any surplus, requiring large amounts of land to support small numbers of people, and consequently could not sustain any noticeable population growth. Survival was fraught with risk and danger because any natural disaster, be it drought or epidemic, carried with it the potential decimation of the group. Our prehistoric predecessors probably had a life span of forty years, though the average life expectancy was undoubtedly less. According to analyses of the skeletal remains of several African tribes, the normal length of life was approximately eighteen years (Lerner, 1970). Anyone managing to live beyond twenty-five may well have boasted of a greater than average degree of wisdom, charm, or both, perhaps rightfully so. Other calculations suggest ordinary Neanderthals roaming the earth 150,000 to 100,000 years ago might have lived into their late twenties, whereas 95 percent of their comrades died before forty (Thomlinson, 1965). It has been hypothesized that as climatic conditions stabilized, longevity improved somewhat; though an estimated 90 percent of those living from 35,000 to 8000 years ago still died before the age of forty, with the remainder succumbing by fifty. One of the major drawbacks in using data from these historical periods is that analyses of skeletal remains and burial inscriptions rarely reveal population boundaries, the nature or extent of the particular sample under examination, or the societal factors that may have affected burial practices (Dublin et al., 1949; Richardson, 1933).

**Classical Antiquity.** Evidence derived from a compilation of available sources indicates an increment in life expectancy between 3000 B.C. and 1300 A.D. of roughly eight years for men and four years for women. Studies of skeletons excavated from Greek tombs suggest an increase in body size, a decline in arthritic debilities, and an improvement of dental conditions took place during the same period. Many factors, such as nutrition, living conditions, and medical practices, must have evolved considerably for these advances to have come about. Although gathering historical evidence from graveyards is at best difficult, sepulcher inscriptions from burial sites laid down about 400 B.C. suggest the average length of life was around 30 years. Extrapolations from these and other sources point to a survival curve approximating that shown in Figure 2.2, where less than half of the Greek population during the Hellenistic and Roman eras reached what we would today consider young adulthood.

As a consequence of the extremely high infant mortality rates throughout all but our most recent history, life expectancy at birth has always been somewhat less, proportionately, than during adolescence. If a person managed to survive the innumerable diseases of childhood, he or she could expect to reach life's peak during the teenage years. Accordingly, Figure 2.3 demonstrates graphically the approximate life expectancy of a fifteen-year-old during various historical periods. The fluctuations are caused by many events that have an impact on life expectancy, perhaps the most important being infectious diseases. Historical accounts are replete with descriptions of the havoc

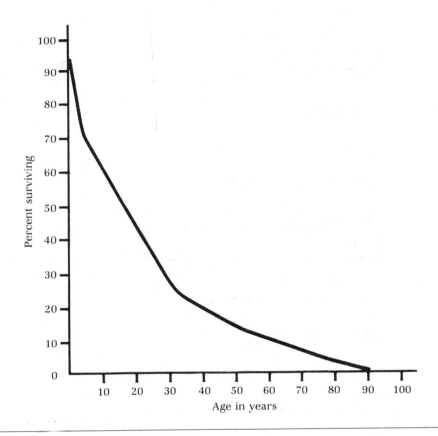

**FIGURE 2.2**
Survivorship curve for the Greek population of the Hellenistic and Roman periods. (*Source:*
Angel, J. L. "Human Biology, Health, and History in Greece from the First Settlement Until Now."
*American Philosophical Society Yearbook* [1954]: 171–72 [adapted from numeric data].)

wrought by pestilence, plagues, and wars on societies around the world. For
illustration we need only recall the pestilences chronicled in the notes of Marcus Aurelius during the second century after Christ; Justinian's plague, which
raged for more than half of the sixth century after Christ; and the Crusades of
the twelfth and thirteenth centuries. Interestingly enough, the twelfth century is sometimes referred to as the "savage twelfth," not because of the wars
waged but because of the deadly plagues that swept over Europe. More lives
were claimed by disease than by the combined forces of the human combat-
ants. Indeed, pestilence rendered life so precarious in the Middle Ages that
"soul and body" poems, depicting the grisliness of slow death, were commonplace. These poems, with their graphic descriptions of putrefactive processes,
survive as some of the most insightful annals of an era when death was never
far removed.

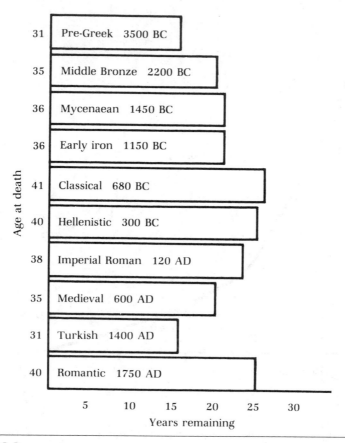

| | | |
|---|---|---|
| 31 | Pre-Greek   3500 BC | |
| 35 | Middle Bronze   2200 BC | |
| 36 | Mycenaean   1450 BC | |
| 36 | Early iron   1150 BC | |
| 41 | Classical   680 BC | |
| 40 | Hellenistic   300 BC | |
| 38 | Imperial Roman   120 AD | |
| 35 | Medieval   600 AD | |
| 31 | Turkish   1400 AD | |
| 40 | Romantic   1750 AD | |

Age at death

5    10    15    20    25    30

Years remaining

**FIGURE 2.3**

Expectation of life at age fifteen for various historical eras. (*Source:* Angel, J. L. "Human Biology, Health, and History in Greece from the First Settlement Until Now." *American Philosophical Society Yearbook* [1954]: 171.)

Like their earlier Greek counterparts, the ruins of Roman burial sites prove useful in collecting mortality estimates, especially for males. Roman inscriptions are similarly uninformative about the deaths of children, women, and old people in all but the higher social classes. As with the Greeks, ages from Roman monuments are prone to slight exaggeration since they too were recorded in multiples of five. Following the death of Christ, life expectancy remained rather low for the next 400 years. The results of one study indicate the citizens of Rome experienced a shorter life expectancy on the average than did their provincial brethren (Nordberg, 1963). Approximate longevity for residents of Rome and three of the provinces is presented in Table 2.2. The colonists in Africa apparently far outlived the other groups, possibly a consequence of a self-selecting process — that is, only the hardiest migrated to the

**TABLE 2.2**
Expectation of Life in Years at Specified Ages for Three Roman Areas, 1–400 A.D.

| Specified Ages | Rome | | Hispania and Lusitania | | Africa | |
|---|---|---|---|---|---|---|
| | Male | Female | Male | Female | Male | Female |
| Birth | 22 | 21 | 40 | 34 | 48 | 46 |
| 5 | 22 | 19 | 36 | 30 | 45 | 43 |
| 20 | 20 | 14 | 26 | 21 | 36 | 33 |
| 40 | 18 | 15 | 21 | 17 | 28 | 26 |

Note: All values approximate; data converted from graphic representation.
*Source:* Macdonell, W. R. "On the Expectation of Life in Ancient Rome, and in the Provinces of Hispania and Lusitania, and Africa." *Biometrika* 9 (1913): 370, 373, 376.

strenuous agricultural outposts in northern Africa. Assuming the data for Rome are accurate, the high mortality rates, stemming in part from problems with sanitation and food supplies, paralleled those reported for urban areas during the Middle Ages and early industrial periods in Europe.

Examination of early Egyptian mummies furnishes additional support for the conclusions regarding Roman life expectancy. However, since children and lower-class adults were seldom given this form of burial, there is once again a dearth of information on which to base generalizations about their life expectancies. Nonetheless, we do have a fairly complete picture of longevity for upper-class adults. At birth a male could expect roughly twenty-two years of life, but if he survived infancy for five years, at least another twenty-five or twenty-six years stretched ahead of him. The Egyptian man who attained age twenty-five would be likely to live to the ripe old age of forty-eight. Further corroboration is lent these figures by anthropological reports of modern day aboriginal tribes, provided we are willing to grant their comparability with ancient Greek, Roman, or Egyptian societies (Cook, 1947).

**The Middle Ages and the Renaissance.** By the thirteenth century estimates of male life expectancy at birth in England range from a high of 35.3 years to a low of approximately 33 years in the second quarter of the fourteenth century (Russell, 1948). However, as was the case with the historical documents and artifacts previously considered, generally only the upper social classes are represented in the records. Another factor to be taken into account is that, because of high childhood mortality, the records usually available describe only those who managed to survive childhood. Such diverse resources as family archives, official registers, and legal documents dealing with inheritance have yielded valuable information about both the social and health situations of the elderly.

The contemporary literature also provides a glimpse of the most pervasive themes on aging. An examination of the secular peerage from 1350 to 1500 reveals that at least one-fifth of every twenty-five-year cohort born after 1350 died by violence, with slightly less than one-quarter of those who actively engaged in battle living to celebrate age fifty. By comparison, the remaining nobles, whose deaths were attributed to natural causes, fared considerably better; over half lived beyond fifty. These rates are probably inflated above the norms likely to be representative of the general populace, since to have been included on the rolls, peers must have reached twenty-one. Approximate life expectancies may be calculated for each successive decade: life expectancy was estimated to be 29.3 years at twenty, 23.8 at thirty, and to reach nearly ten years for those who survived to sixty (Rosenthal, 1973). In addition, persons of noble birth nearly always experienced greater longevity, partly because of better food, living conditions, and personal health. And, unlike the rest of society, the aristocracy presumably had the mobility to flee if contagion or wars should suddenly threaten. They also had the resources to escape periodic malnutrition, the effects of inclement weather, and the chronic problems of insufficient heating or inadequate clothing.

Throughout history we find evidence of the complex interplay between longevity and various characteristics of societal organization. For instance, potential members of the ranks of nobility, the peerage described above, were mandated by law to be at least twenty-one years of age. This custom was associated with high fertility among the eligible families, since without a son who survived adolescence, the title together with all its privileges had to be passed to collateral relatives. Losing the peerage entailed not simply a loss of status, but, of at least equal significance, the accoutrements so important for living a comfortable and long life. In all likelihood many of the religious practices observed in the preindustrial era were designed to offer strength to the multitudes who were confronted with high rates of child mortality and the inexorable experience of early and frequent death. It appears that every society demarks certain age cohorts for which death is always premature and, thus, always a tragedy (Nash, 1978).

These statistics begin to reflect a brighter picture as humankind experienced continuing gains in life expectancy in the centuries following the Renaissance. Mortality among those fifty to seventy years of age has declined by half during the modern era. Much of the evidence examined for the past two centuries is derived from census or parish records, yet even if we assume earlier mortality rates are calculated from data for aristocratic classes, the declining rate portended a pattern that gradually spread to the whole of Western societies (Achenbaum, 1978; Peller, 1948; Stearns, 1976). The proportion of people dying under fifty has steadily decreased in recent centuries, while the expectation of life for those already fifty years old has improved at a corresponding rate over the years, as is shown in Table 2.3. Upper-class men who reached fifty in the sixteenth century might expect to live twelve years longer to age sixty-two; by the nineteenth century their descendants could anticipate an additional 18.7 years of life after age fifty. Life expectancy for women has shown a similar upswing; the 14.6 years remaining for fifty-year-old women in the sixteenth century increased to twenty-one years by the nineteenth. Interestingly enough, however, the declining mortality rates over the past several centuries have been observed primarily in the early years of life; mortality has

**TABLE 2.3**

Percentage of Individuals Dying Between the Ages of Fifty and Seventy in the European Ruling Classes

| Century | Male | Female |
|---------|------|--------|
| 16th | 82.5 | 69.1 |
| 17th | 72.4 | 70.7 |
| 18th | 65.9 | 56.3 |
| 19th | 56.1 | 45.7 |

*Source:* Peller, S. "Mortality, Past and Future." *Population Studies* 1, 4 (1948): 439.

been cut by as much as 90 percent for those under fifteen, 85 percent for those under forty-four, yet only 35 percent for the ages above sixty-five (Bogue, 1969). Infant and child mortality had traditionally been extremely high primarily because medical techniques were inadequate for dealing with infectious diseases. The dramatic reductions in fatalities beginning shortly after the industrial era occurred as a consequence of the inroads against these, rather than the degenerative diseases to which the aged succumbed. As will be seen in Chapter 5, the situation today is not markedly different. The elderly continue to die as a result of chronic conditions not yet within the reach of advanced medical techniques. In the sixteenth and seventeenth centuries the risk of dying increased greatly with each succeeding decade of life; however, from the seventeenth century onward life chances began to improve throughout middle age, even for women in their childbearing years.

**Colonial America.** It is often assumed that the European colonists who set out for distant corners of the earth were hardy but short-lived pioneers. An interesting challenge to this assumption has been offered by research focused on the Plymouth Colony in America (Demos, 1970). The figures on longevity from 600 residents of the seventeenth-century settlement presented in Table 2.4 disclose a quite considerable life expectancy for men reaching their

**TABLE 2.4**

Average Life Expectancy and Percentage Dying During Subsequent Decade for Specified Ages in Plymouth Colony

| Age | Male | (Percent Deceased) | Female | (Percent Deceased) |
|-----|------|--------------------|--------|--------------------|
| 21 | 48.2 | (1.6) | 41.4 | (5.9) |
| 30 | 40.0 | (3.6) | 34.7 | (12.0) |
| 40 | 31.2 | (7.8) | 29.7 | (12.0) |
| 50 | 23.7 | (10.2) | 23.4 | (10.9) |
| 60 | 16.3 | (18.0) | 16.8 | (14.9) |
| 70 | 9.9 | (30.5) | 10.7 | (20.7) |
| 80 | 5.1 | (22.4) | 6.7 | (16.0) |
| 90+ | — | (5.9) | — | (7.6) |

*Source:* Demos, J. "Notes on Life in Plymouth Colony." *The William and Mary Quarterly* 22, 2 (1965): 271.

twenty-first birthday. At twenty-one a man might expect to live to 69.2 years, nearly equivalent to twentieth-century expectations. A woman could look forward to 62.4 years of life, unusually high considering the hazards attendant with childbirth during the sixteenth and seventeenth centuries. Of those in the Plymouth sample, a third of the women and one-tenth of the men died between twenty and fifty. Subsequent investigations of other colonies in New England lend some support to the notion that the pilgrims were indeed long-lived (Demos, 1979; Greven, 1970). Despite such an improvement in life chances, the endless process of migration and expansion continued to take a toll on both social structures and personal relationships, especially family ties.

**The Modern Era.** With the rise of science during the later Renaissance and early Enlightenment, a greater emphasis on record keeping brought about a closer scrutiny of life expectancy. The well-known English astronomer Halley constructed what is believed to be the first scientific life table. Halley's careful

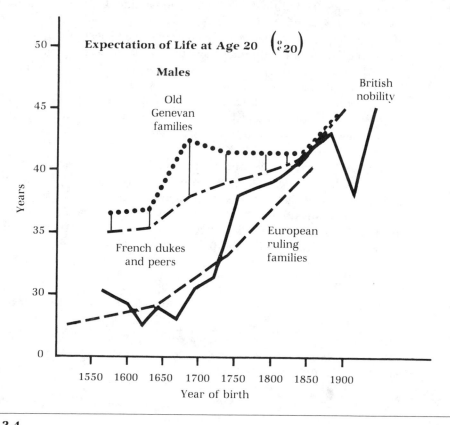

**FIGURE 2.4**

Expectation of life at age twenty for European aristocratic males between 1550 and 1900. (*Source:* Hollingsworth, T. H. "The Demography of the British Peerage." *Population Studies*, Supplement, 28, 2 [1965]: 68.)

study of the actuarial records compiled in the industrial city of Breslaw in southern Poland revealed normal life expectancy for late seventeenth-century residents to be somewhat more than 33 years. Demographic investigations of other European cities supported Halley's findings, demonstrating the similarity of longevity patterns across the continent. By the turn of the twentieth century careful recording of vital statistics disclosed that ten or more years had been added to the general life expectancy. By the turn of this century Swedish males enjoyed the greatest life expectancy at birth, nearly 51 years.

Prolongation of life was fostered in large measure by the complex changes accompanying the Industrial Revolution. Yet, there are frequent condemnations of early industrial societies because it is assumed that initially industrialization contributed to earlier individual mortality (Stearns, 1976). No doubt evidence can be adduced to support both positions, since in either case urbanization played an influential role in the higher death rates of industrial areas (Wrigley, 1969). True, contagion raged in densely populated urban slum areas just as had occurred prior to the presence of factories. However, in rural areas and smaller towns, even those undergoing rapid industrialization, mortality statistics were appreciably lower (Dubos, 1959). In keeping with our supposition about the quality of life, Figures 2.4 and 2.5 reveal that old Genevan families consistently fared better than their aristocratic peers elsewhere in Europe. Throughout modern history, citizens of Switzerland have experienced a general standard of living unmatched by neighbors. The figures also illustrate the steady upward trend in life expectancy for all aristocratic families from 1550 to 1900. The increase was much less rapid in those countries not yet undergoing industrialization.

## ATTITUDES TOWARD AGING IN HISTORY

Stearns (1982) identifies three stages in the study of the place of the elderly in history and of attitudes toward them. In the first stage, the "golden age of age" theory, gerontologists idealized the role of the elderly in historical times. They saw the elderly in history as being relatively few, having supportive family networks, and having a control of resources and of traditional knowledge that was regarded as valuable. They believed that the prestige of the elderly has declined in contemporary society because of the rise in their numbers, the fragmentation of family networks, and the replacement of traditional knowledge and values with new, ever-changing technical knowledge and an emphasis on practical efficiency. Cowgill (1972) put the issue most succinctly when he noted: "the status of the aged . . . is inversely proportional to the degree of modernization of the society."

The second stage in the discipline consisted of a revision of the golden age theory. The focus shifted to the bleaker side of the treatment of the elderly in historical times: the number of poor and abandoned older people in almshouses and city hospitals, the absence of any policy to deal with old people, and the tensions between adult generations as younger adults rebelled against the control of their older, propertied parents. To support this view they cited

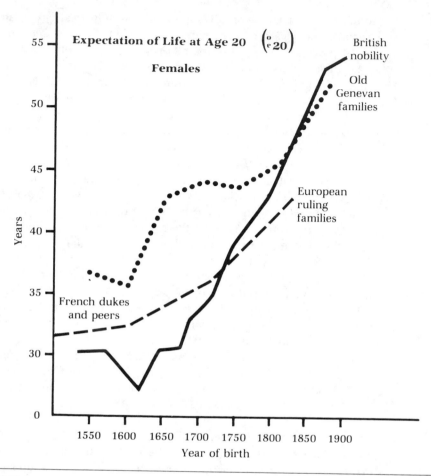

**FIGURE 2.5**
Expectation of life at age twenty for European aristocratic females between 1550 and 1900.
(*Source:* T. H. Hollingsworth, "The Demography of the British Peerage." *Population Studies,* Supplement, 28, 2 [1965]: 68.)

detailed contracts in which old people who could no longer work their property stipulated the support their children would provide in return for rights to the property. These were taken as evidence of the need to ensure care that would not otherwise have been forthcoming.

Stearns notes a third stage in the discipline in which the contrast between preindustrial and modern societies would be de-emphasized to favor a more subtle balance to understand the distinctions in the status of the elderly in historical times. If we are to get an idea of the richness, complexity, diversity, and ambivalence of attitudes toward aging in history, we must look at the total picture and take account of the changes in treatment of the elderly that resulted from differences between historical periods, cultures and subcultures, social class, and the relationship of the elderly to the economic system.

Allusions to aging in literature reveal both negative and positive attitudes going back to classical antiquity. Aristotle saw old age as a time of conservatism and small-mindedness. In his *Treatise on Rhetoric* he remarks that the elderly err

> . . . in everything more on the side of defect than they ought. And they always *"suppose,"* but never *"know"* certainly; and questioning everything, they always subjoin a *"perhaps,"* or a *"possibly."* And they talk of everything in this undecisive tone, asserting nothing decisively . . . moreover they are apt to be suspicious from distrust, and they are distrustful from their experience. And on this account they neither love nor hate with great earnestness . . . they both love as though about to hate, and hate as though about to love . . . men of this age appear to be naturally temperate, for both their desires have relaxed, and they are enslaved to gain. And they live more by calculation than by moral feeling; for calculation is of expediency, but moral feeling is of virtue (Bk. II, ch. XIII).

Plato's view of old age was somewhat better, as was that of the Roman scholar Cicero. Cicero saw the way in which the individual aged as resulting from the development of character in earlier life. The shortcomings of the later years are nothing more than those of a lifetime writ large. Certain facets of an individual's character, however, such as intellectual or moral qualities, were also enhanced by age. He stated:

> It is not by muscle, speed, or physical dexterity that great things are achieved, but by reflection, force of character, and judgment; in these qualities old age is usually not only not poorer, but is even richer . . . the crowning glory of old age is influence . . . when the preceding part of life has been nobly spent, old age gathers the fruits of influence at the last (VI.17. XVII.61, XVIII.62, 1923).

In looking at portrayals of aging in literature, we should remember that they are literary: the portrayal may be designed to create a particular impression on the reader or audience, rather than to give a lifelike view of aging. Furthermore, portrayals of old people as people may be very different from portrayals of old people as examples of old age, both in history and in literature. One of the most frequently quoted negative pictures of aging in literature is found in Jacques' description of the seven ages of man in Shakespeare's *As You Like It:*

> . . . The sixth age shifts
> Into the lean and slippered pantaloon,
> With spectacles on nose and pouch on side,
> His youthful hose, well saved, a world too wide
> For his shrunk shank, and his big manly voice,
> Turning again toward childish treble, pipes

And whistles in his sound.
Last scene of all,
That ends this strange eventful history,
Is second childishness, and mere oblivion,
Sans teeth, sans eyes, sans taste, sans everything (2.7.160–61).

It should be noted that these lines form part of the speech beginning "All the world's a stage," which is a satirical outcry against the vicissitudes of life and the foibles of mankind spoken by a world-weary libertine turned philosopher. The portrayals of the other ages of man, including youth and maturity, are hardly more flattering than those of old age. Shakespeare's Old Adam in the same play is a relatively sympathetic portrait of an old man. Macbeth speaks of "that which should accompany old age" as "honour, love, obedience and troops of friends" (Shakespeare, *Macbeth*, 5.3.25). Shakespeare does give vivid descriptions of the physical ravages that old age can cause. He also, however, returns to the theme of the constancy of the human spirit in the face of the vicissitudes of life.

In looking at aging as it is portrayed in the historical literature, we find a wide gamut of attitudes toward the elderly associated with a variety of cultural systems and varying with the relationship of the particular old people to the structures of society. Aging in history, as well as in modern society, is a complex phenomenon. The position of the elderly and the attitudes toward them are shaped by their relationship to the political, economic, and cultural configurations of the society of which they are a part. In the works of the authors in the German Enlightenment, such as Schopenhauer, Stifter, and Hesse, we see examples of a culture that emphasizes wisdom and insight and views old age as a time when one is freed from the passions of youth to gain a maturity for seeing life more objectively. Goethe asserted that the immortality of the soul is accorded only to those who remain active into old age. Brecht rendered two of the most life-affirming portraits of old women in literature (Schneider, in press). Francois Villon, the poet, was a kind of vagabond, who lived on the fringes of fifteenth-century French courtly society. His "belle Healmière" (beautiful helmet seller), lamenting her present ugliness and the loss of the physical charms of her youth, is an example of an aging woman at the periphery of society. Once the mistress of Nicolas d'Orgemont, the archdeacon of Paris, she was a courtesan whose fortunes in youth had depended on trading her charms to men of position. Her physical beauty gone, what was left to her? At one level her lament might be taken as an expression of the plight of women who, without resources of their own, are treated as sexual objects and then abandoned. Brecht's old women, by contrast, have resources of their own and are engaged in activities and social networks. In contrast, the *Pillow Book* of Sei Shonagon, a Japanese woman, is expressive of a subculture that values youth and elegance and scorns the elderly who put creature comforts before the rules of court etiquette (Helm, in press). This is particularly interesting, as Japan is generally thought of as a culture in which there is a long tradition of respect for the elderly based on the precepts of Confucianism.

Rather than looking for any simple sweeping generalizations, the student of aging in history should be prepared for a complex picture. An understanding of this picture may enrich the approach to aging in the modern world in two ways: by developing sensitivity to the ways in which structural and cultural factors shape patterns and interpretations of aging and by allowing the exploration of a variety of approaches to aging, some of which might teach us how aging in the modern world can be a creative experience.

# Aging in Advanced Industrial Society

Having taken a brief look at aging in a historical perspective, we will now examine some of the demographic parameters of aging in advanced industrial societies, particularly the United States. In the next section these are briefly contrasted with the Third World, or developing countries. The following tables and figures give the reader a more vivid idea of the contrasts between the two regions. There are, of course, significant variations within and between particular countries in both the industrialized nations and in the Third World (Table 2.5). A comparison does, however, suggest some of the distinctive features of broad demographic patterns of aging and the ways in which they influence and are influenced by sociopolitical and scientific factors.

In the sociopolitical area older populations challenge the structuring of social organizations to provide acceptable living conditions for the increasing proportion of the elderly. The major problem for medicine is embodied in the chronic diseases characteristic of those in their later years. It has two facets that will be explored further in the chapter on health: the contribution of the life-style in advanced industrial society to the etiology and aggravation of these diseases, plus the relative lack of medical knowledge in the treatment of chronic conditions. Although the number of elderly in Third World countries is increasing, the population structure of the least developed countries is still relatively young. While knowledge about managing the infectious diseases characteristic of Third World countries exists (largely through research conducted in advanced industrial societies), they remain major killers in developing regions, because of inadequate sanitation, nutrition, medical care, and political factors. The most significant issue facing these countries is the need for education and economic and sociopolitical changes if the lives of their citizens are to improve. As improvements in mortality rates are made, the high fertility rates in these countries will cause population pressures from increasing proportions first of middle-aged then of elderly citizens as the cohorts that escape the devastating levels of infant and child mortality survive to maturity and old age.

## POPULATION AGE STRUCTURES

Demographers often classify populations on the basis of the percentage of people sixty-five and over. Thus, a young population is usually considered to be one in which those sixty-five or over constitute less than 4 percent of the

**TABLE 2.5**

Life Expectancy at Birth for Selected Industrialized Countries and for Regions of the World

| Life Expectancy at Birth for Selected Industrialized Countries | | | | Life Expectancy at Birth for Regions of the World, 1980–1985 | |
| --- | --- | --- | --- | --- | --- |
| | | Years | | | |
| Date[a] | Country | Male | Female | Area | Years |
| 1980 | Austria | 69.0 | 76.2 | World total | 58.9 |
| 1979 | Canada | 71.1 | 78.5 | More developed regions | 73.1 |
| 1975–1980 | China | 62.1 | 65.9 | Less developed regions | 56.6 |
| 1980–1981 | Denmark | 71.1 | 77.2 | Eastern Africa | 48.8 |
| 1980 | Finland | 69.2 | 77.6 | Ethiopia | 42.9 |
| 1980 (provisional) | France | 70.2 | 78.4 | Mauritius | 66.7 |
| | | | | Latin America | 64.1 |
| 1980 | Fed. Rep. Germany | 69.6 | 76.4 | Bolivia | 50.7 |
| 1980 | German Democ. Repub. | 68.7 | 74.6 | Cuba | 74.3 |
| | | | | Northern America | 74.3 |
| 1979–1980 | Iceland | 73.7 | 79.7 | Canada | 74.5 |
| 1981 | Israel | 72.7 | 75.9 | U.S.A. | 74.2 |
| 1981 | Japan | 73.8 | 79.1 | East Asia | 68.0 |
| 1980 | Netherlands | 72.4 | 79.2 | South Asia | 53.6 |
| 1979–1980 | Norway | 72.3 | 79.0 | Europe | 72.9 |
| 1980 | Sweden | 72.8 | 78.8 | Iceland | 76.5 |
| 1971–1972 | U.S.S.R. | 64.0 | 74.0 | Hungary | 70.6 |
| 1980 | U.K.: England and Wales | 70.4 | 76.5 | Oceania | 67.6 |
| 1979 | U.S.A. | 74.7 | 77.7 | U.S.S.R. | 71.3 |

[a]Latest available figures.

*Sources:* Adapted from United Nations. *Concise Report on the World Population Situation in 1983*, pp. 101–08. Population Studies, No. 85. New York: United Nations, 1984; and United Nations, *Demographic Yearbook, 1982*. New York: United Nations. 1984.

total population. Similarly, a mature population has between 4 and 7 percent of its members in this age group, while an aged population has over 7 percent sixty-five or older (United Nations, 1975, 1956). The age structure of population is an important indicator of many societal patterns. Demographers have found those countries in the world with young populations are characterized by economic underdevelopment, are often agricultural, and have relatively high birth and death rates combined with comparatively short life expectancies. Nations with mature age structures include those undergoing rapid industrial transition and those experiencing high birth rates, declining death rates, and gradually increasing longevity. Typically, many Eastern European countries fall into this category. To date, countries with aged populations still account for only a small proportion of the world population. Generally speaking, these countries demonstrate the lowest birth rates, lower death rates, and greater longevity than the rest of the world. The most aged populations are found in the advanced industrialized societies of Northern and Western Europe.

The population of the United States is somewhat younger than those of these Northern European countries, as can be seen from Figure 2.6. Figure 2.7 depicts composite population pyramids for contemporary developed, under-developed, and a hypothetical postindustrial society of Western Europe in the next century. As can be seen, the distribution of the population changes dra-

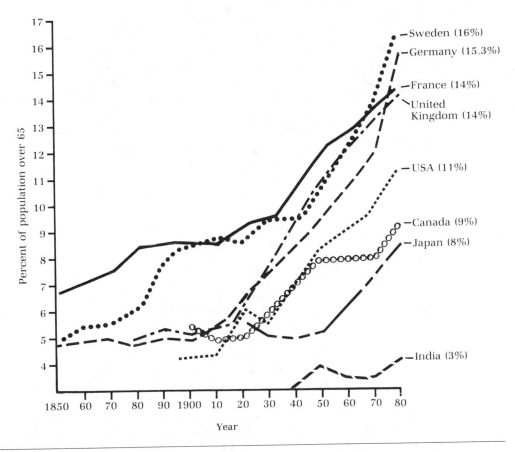

**FIGURE 2.6**

Percentage of the population age sixty-five and over for selected countries. (*Sources:* Population Reference Bureau, Inc. *1980 World Population Data Sheet.* Washington, D.C.: Population Reference Bureau, Inc., 1980; *1981 World Population Data Sheet;* United Nations. *The Aging of Populations and Its Economic and Social Implications.* Population Studies, No. 26. New York: United Nations, 1956; United Nations, *Demographic Yearbook, 1977,* 29th ed. New York: United Nations, 1978 [adapted from numeric data]; and United Nations, *Demographic Yearbook, 1982,* 34th ed. New York: United Nations, 1984.)

matically in the three instances. Still further worldwide comparisons are contained in Table 2.6, where changing dependency ratios, indexes of aging, and median age of populations are shown for the period between 1950 and 2025. To help see what the future holds in the United States in terms of changing age compositions, the reader is referred to Figure 2.8. These figures will be discussed throughout the remainder of the book.

As should already be evident, the aging of populations is a relatively recent phenomenon associated primarily with the growth of industrialism and the facilities available in technologically sophisticated societies. Although the rapid expansion of the proportion of the population sixty-five or over began in the mid-nineteenth century for Sweden and France, the remaining countries illustrated in Figure 2.6 did not display such patterns until the present century.

One might easily assume populations age because of declining death rates, but this is not necessarily the case. For example, despite the fact French mortality rates have not been reduced to the level of the Netherlands, France nevertheless has an older population. Why should this be so? Contrary to popular expectations, declining mortality is not sufficient in itself to bring about an aged population. In the last chapter it was noted that a lower birth rate does not necessarily follow a decline in mortality. In industrializing countries,

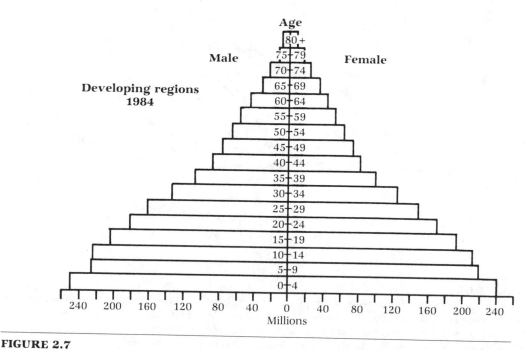

**FIGURE 2.7**

Population pyramids for contemporary underdeveloped, developed, and a hypothetical Western European country in the twenty-first century. (*Source:* Adapted from Bouvier, L. F. "Planet Earth 1984–2034: A Demographic Vision." *Population Bulletin* 39, No. 1 [1984].)

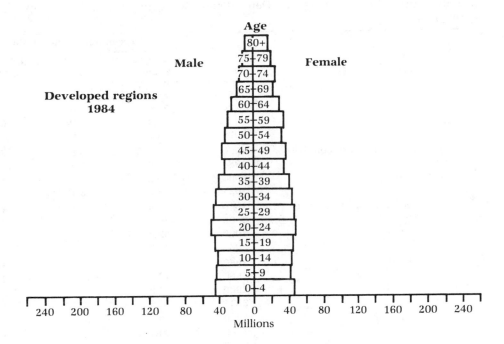

Developed regions
1984

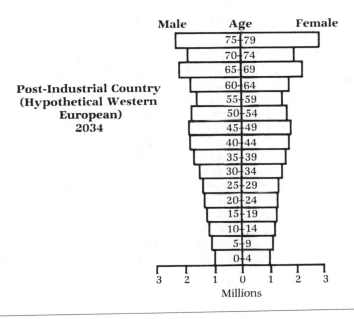

Post-Industrial Country
(Hypothetical Western
European)
2034

**FIGURE 2.7, cont'd**

**TABLE 2.6**

Age Structure, Index of Aging, and Dependency Ratios for Various Regions of the World, 1950–2025

| Area | Year | Percentage of Population | | |
|------|------|--------------------------|---|---|
| | | Under 15 Years | 15–64 Years | 65 Years and Over |
| World | 1950 | 35.1 | 59.6 | 5.3 |
| | 1980 | 35.6 | 58.6 | 5.7 |
| | 2000 | 30.4 | 63.0 | 6.6 |
| | 2025 | 24.7 | 65.9 | 9.4 |
| More developed countries | 1950 | 27.8 | 64.6 | 7.6 |
| | 1980 | 23.0 | 65.6 | 11.4 |
| | 2000 | 20.8 | 66.0 | 13.2 |
| | 2025 | 19.9 | 63.1 | 17.0 |
| Less developed countries | 1950 | 38.8 | 57.1 | 4.1 |
| | 1980 | 40.0 | 56.2 | 3.8 |
| | 2000 | 32.9 | 62.2 | 4.9 |
| | 2025 | 25.7 | 66.4 | 7.8 |
| Africa | 1950 | 42.2 | 54.2 | 3.6 |
| | 1980 | 45.2 | 51.7 | 3.1 |
| | 2000 | 45.2 | 51.8 | 3.0 |
| | 2025 | 35.5 | 60.7 | 3.8 |
| Latin America | 1950 | 40.5 | 56.2 | 3.3 |
| | 1980 | 39.4 | 56.3 | 4.3 |
| | 2000 | 33.4 | 61.5 | 5.2 |
| | 2025 | 26.1 | 65.7 | 8.2 |
| Northern America | 1950 | 27.2 | 64.7 | 8.1 |
| | 1980 | 22.6 | 66.3 | 11.1 |
| | 2000 | 21.6 | 66.7 | 11.8 |
| | 2025 | 20.1 | 62.6 | 17.3 |
| East Asia | 1950 | 35.4 | 61.0 | 3.6 |
| | 1980 | 35.5 | 59.5 | 5.1 |
| | 2000 | 23.6 | 68.9 | 7.5 |
| | 2025 | 18.4 | 68.3 | 13.2 |
| South Asia | 1950 | 40.2 | 54.8 | 5.0 |
| | 1980 | 40.8 | 55.9 | 3.3 |
| | 2000 | 33.2 | 62.4 | 4.3 |
| | 2025 | 23.9 | 68.7 | 7.4 |
| Europe | 1950 | 25.4 | 65.9 | 8.7 |
| | 1980 | 22.3 | 64.7 | 13.0 |
| | 2000 | 19.4 | 66.2 | 14.4 |
| | 2025 | 18.6 | 63.5 | 17.8 |
| Oceania | 1950 | 29.8 | 62.8 | 7.4 |
| | 1980 | 29.5 | 62.6 | 7.9 |
| | 2000 | 26.2 | 64.7 | 9.1 |
| | 2025 | 23.0 | 64.6 | 12.4 |
| USSR | 1950 | 30.1 | 63.8 | 6.1 |
| | 1980 | 24.3 | 65.6 | 10.0 |
| | 2000 | 23.8 | 64.2 | 12.1 |
| | 2025 | 22.2 | 63.3 | 14.5 |

*Source:* Adapted from United Nations. *Concise Report on the World Population Situation in 1983*, pp. 56–57. New York: United Nations, 1984.

| | | Dependency Ratio | | |
|---|---|---|---|---|
| Index of Aging | Total Dependency | Under 15 Years | 65 Years and Over | Median Age |
| 15.1 | 67.9 | 59.0 | 8.9 | 22.9 |
| 16.0 | 70.6 | 60.8 | 9.8 | 22.4 |
| 21.7 | 58.8 | 48.3 | 10.5 | 26.3 |
| 38.1 | 51.5 | 37.5 | 14.3 | 31.0 |
| 27.3 | 54.8 | 43.0 | 11.8 | 28.2 |
| 48.2 | 52.6 | 35.1 | 17.4 | 31.4 |
| 15.8 | 51.6 | 31.6 | 20.0 | 36.0 |
| 85.2 | 58.4 | 31.5 | 27.0 | 38.4 |
| 10.6 | 75.2 | 68.0 | 7.2 | 20.5 |
| 9.5 | 77.8 | 71.1 | 6.8 | 19.8 |
| 14.9 | 60.8 | 52.9 | 7.8 | 24.3 |
| 30.3 | 50.5 | 38.7 | 11.8 | 29.7 |
| 8.5 | 84.7 | 77.9 | 6.7 | 18.9 |
| 6.8 | 93.4 | 87.5 | 5.9 | 17.3 |
| 6.6 | 93.1 | 87.3 | 5.9 | 17.3 |
| 10.7 | 64.9 | 58.6 | 6.3 | 21.8 |
| 8.1 | 78.1 | 72.1 | 6.0 | 19.7 |
| 10.9 | 77.5 | 69.9 | 7.6 | 19.8 |
| 15.5 | 62.7 | 54.3 | 8.4 | 23.7 |
| 31.4 | 52.2 | 39.7 | 12.4 | 29.8 |
| 29.8 | 54.4 | 41.9 | 12.5 | 30.0 |
| 49.1 | 50.7 | 34.0 | 16.7 | 29.9 |
| 54.5 | 50.0 | 32.3 | 17.7 | 35.7 |
| 86.1 | 59.9 | 32.1 | 27.7 | 38.1 |
| 10.2 | 63.9 | 58.0 | 5.9 | 22.4 |
| 14.4 | 68.2 | 59.6 | 8.5 | 22.6 |
| 31.8 | 45.2 | 34.3 | 10.9 | 30.6 |
| 71.7 | 46.3 | 27.0 | 19.4 | 38.4 |
| 12.4 | 82.6 | 73.4 | 9.2 | 19.7 |
| 8.1 | 78.8 | 72.9 | 5.9 | 19.3 |
| 13.0 | 60.2 | 53.2 | 7.0 | 23.5 |
| 31.0 | 45.5 | 34.7 | 10.8 | 31.2 |
| 34.2 | 51.7 | 38.5 | 13.2 | 30.5 |
| 58.3 | 54.6 | 34.5 | 20.1 | 33.0 |
| 74.2 | 51.0 | 29.3 | 21.7 | 37.1 |
| 95.7 | 57.4 | 29.3 | 28.0 | 40.2 |
| 24.8 | 59.2 | 47.4 | 11.9 | 27.9 |
| 26.8 | 59.8 | 47.2 | 12.7 | 26.4 |
| 34.7 | 54.5 | 40.5 | 14.0 | 30.0 |
| 53.9 | 54.9 | 35.7 | 19.2 | 33.6 |
| 20.3 | 56.7 | 47.1 | 9.5 | 24.7 |
| 41.2 | 52.4 | 37.1 | 15.3 | 29.4 |
| 50.8 | 55.8 | 37.0 | 18.8 | 33.5 |
| 65.3 | 57.9 | 35.0 | 22.8 | 35.2 |

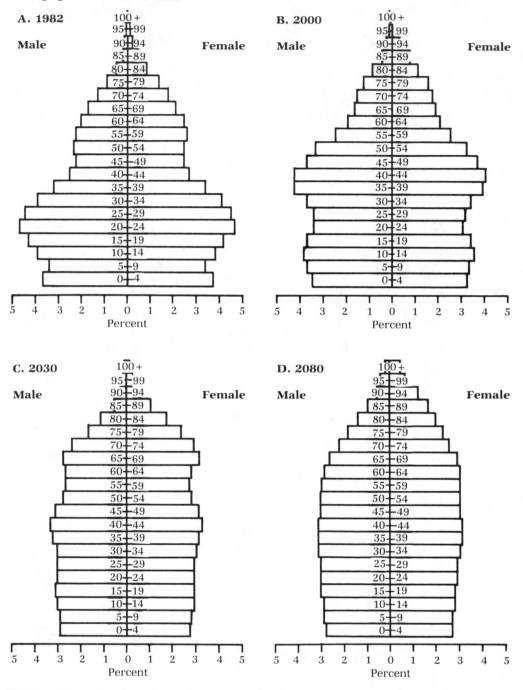

**FIGURE 2.8**

Population pyramids for the United States, 1982–2080. (*Source:* U.S. Bureau of the Census. *Projections of the Population of the United States by Age, Sex, and Race: 1982–2080*, p. 5. Washington, D.C.: U.S. Government Printing Office, 1984.)

reductions of fertility lag behind those of mortality, creating in the interval something resembling a baby boom. The reasons for this are twofold: first, and perhaps most significant, improvements in medical technology have been most successful in combating infectious diseases. Older people, however, are more likely to succumb as a consequence of the debilitating effects of chronic illnesses that sap their strength. Children on the other hand are more susceptible to the acute conditions of infectious diseases; hence medical advances initially inhibit aging of the entire population by swelling the numbers of the very young. Only after larger cohorts of children survive to adulthood does the age structure begin to shift upward. In all circumstances the crucial variable is a declining fertility rate (United Nations, 1975, 1956). Since fertility is so closely tied to a host of social practices, demographic data must be considered with an eye to the intricate association of biological, psychological, and social factors. By looking back at Figure 2.1 the reader can observe the relationship between significant events and changing **fertility rates** in the United States.

A variable of considerable importance, but one beyond the scope of the present discussion, is migration. Migratory movements can alter the population age structure in a variety of ways. Large-scale international migrations, generally of less importance to today's industrialized countries, have, as recent years demonstrated for the United States and other receiver countries, a significant impact on societies that encourage or allow the resettlement of a large group of mobile individuals from other cultures. Whether we select the colonization process by European powers, the influx of settlers to nineteenth-century America, movement among or from Third World nations, or the recent exodus from Cuba, Vietnam, and Latin American countries makes little difference. The crucial fact that must be assessed for each population in question is the intensity of the migratory movement, both for sender and receiver societies. Intensity must of necessity include consideration of age and sex distribution. However, the interaction of migration with fertility and mortality involves even more complex and less certain relationships than the latter have with population age structures.

## AGE-DEPENDENT POPULATIONS

As previously pointed out, age-dependency ratios in current U.S. Census data are calculated to include children under eighteen and people over sixty-four in the age-dependent population. International statistics are still calculated to include children under fifteen and people over sixty-four in the dependent population. Estimated and predicted age-dependency ratios and the index of aging for the major areas of the world are given in Table 2.6. Table 2.7 provides a breakdown of estimated and predicted dependency ratios in the United States for the years 1950–2080. As is evident from both tables, the social responsibilities for children and for older people are moving in opposite directions, so that overall dependency shows only modest changes.

In considering these tables the reader should remember the warnings at the beginning of this chapter regarding the politics of demography. The ratios

**TABLE 2.7**

Dependency Rates for Young and Old in The United States to the Year 2080

| Year | Total | Under Age 18 | Aged 65 Years and Over |
|---|---|---|---|
| **Estimates** | | | |
| 1950 | 64.4 | 51.0 | 13.3 |
| 1955 | 73.5 | 58.3 | 15.2 |
| 1960 | 81.6 | 64.9 | 16.8 |
| 1965 | 83.1 | 65.7 | 17.4 |
| 1970 | 78.0 | 60.6 | 17.5 |
| 1975 | 71.3 | 53.3 | 18.0 |
| 1980 | 64.6 | 46.0 | 18.6 |
| 1985 | 62.9 | 44.1 | 18.8 |
| **Projections** | | | |
| 1985 | 62.1 | 42.7 | 19.4 |
| 1990 | 62.5 | 41.9 | 20.6 |
| 1995 | 63.7 | 42.3 | 21.4 |
| 2000 | 61.8 | 40.7 | 21.1 |
| 2010 | 58.1 | 36.2 | 21.9 |
| 2020 | 65.6 | 36.9 | 28.7 |
| 2030 | 74.8 | 37.8 | 37.0 |
| 2050 | 74.6 | 36.6 | 38.0 |
| 2080 | 78.1 | 36.2 | 41.9 |

**Young and Elderly Support Ratios: 1900–2050**

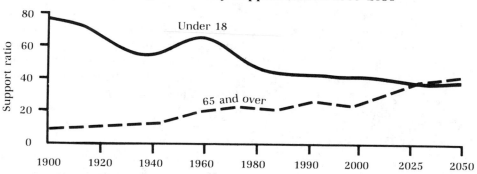

*Sources:* Adapted from U.S. Bureau of the Census. *Projections of the Population of the United States by Age, Sex and Race: 1983–2080*, p. 6. Current Population Reports, P-25, No. 952. Washington, D.C.: U.S. Government Printing Office, 1984; and U.S. Bureau of the Census, *America in Transition: An Aging Society*, p. 6. Current Population Reports, P-23, No. 128. Washington, D.C.: U.S. Government Printing Office, 1983.

for the United States, for instance, do not take into account that many people under eighteen and over sixty-four may be active in the labor force, whereas many, because of disability or unemployment, may not. This becomes even more important when considering recent actions against mandatory retirement. Nor do the ratios consider changing rates of women in the labor force.

International comparisons are even more problematic because customs and legislation regarding entry into and exit from the labor force may vary significantly between countries. How these factors are used in the political decision-making process will be explored further in Chapter 11 in the discussion of social policy.

Age-dependency ratios do, however, give an idea of the proportions of the population at the extreme ends of the life cycle which are more likely to be in need of economic assistance than those in the middle years, although with teenagers and the very recently retired (the young-old) this is more a matter of social custom and legislation than of anything else. These figures are important for social planning and legislation because estimated and projected age distributions and age-dependency ratios can give at least some idea of the anticipated consequences of the impact of policies such as compulsory retirement at a given age (the allocation of old age pensions) or even changes in the minimum age for entry into the labor force. Although Table 2.7 reports that the proportion of the population under eighteen is expected to decrease from 1985–2080, a fairly abrupt increase in the proportion of persons over sixty-five is projected as the baby-boom generation ages. This will result in a higher proportion of older people with relation to younger people in the year 2080. The overall anticipated increase in the dependency ratio from 1950–2080 is 13.7 percent, with a decrease of 14.8 percent in dependents under eighteen, and an increase of 28.6 percent in dependents over sixty-five. In actuality, the decrease in the number of child dependents is probably slightly higher than shown in this projection because of a pattern of earlier entry into the work force in the 1950s. Thus, there is a very real possibility that some of the needs for increased funding for the elderly might be counterbalanced by decreased needs for funding for the young. Table 2.6 suggests there is a worldwide trend toward equalizing the proportion of young and old persons. Though it is relatively minimal in the developing countries, it is much more dramatic in the industrialized nations, particularly in Northern Europe.

## INCREASES IN LIFE EXPECTANCY

As can be seen in Table 2.5, throughout the industrialized world women live longer than men. Since the 1900s the gap has been widening, and by the end of the present century it will amount to some ten years or more. A male born in the United States today can expect to live an average of 71 years; a female can expect to live 78.3 years. For a man who is now sixty-five, an average of slightly more than 14 years of life remain; a woman of the same age has approximately 18.5 years left to live. The reasons are complicated; there may be a genetic basis, but it is undeniably compounded by social factors, regional differences, racial background, and other factors. In the United States both white and black females generally live longer than their male counterparts. Whatever the causes may be, mortality rates for men over sixty-five declined an average of 1.5 percent in the ten-year period after 1968; for women the decline was 2.3 percent. Differential mortality for women has improved threefold over that for men in the last forty years. The result? More women are living longer. There are now three women for every two men at age sixty-five; by age seventy-five there are 66 percent more women; after age eighty-five there are 224 women for every 100 men. In Canada, Europe, and Japan, in fact in all industrialized societies, the sex ratio after sixty-five is very much the same. In Canada there are 78 older men per 100 older women; in Denmark the ratio is 73; in Japan 74, while France, the United Kingdom, and the two Germanies all range around 63. Projections through 2020 suggest no appreciable alterations will occur.

With life expectancy in the years after sixty-five continuing to increase, a white woman has a one in three chance of living to eighty-five; a nonwhite woman has a 28 percent chance of reaching eighty-five. Unfortunately, regardless of race, men's chances of celebrating their eighty-fifth birthday is no better than one in six. With the percentage of women in the labor force now equal to that of men, it will be interesting to see if health patterns and life expectancies converge. By 1990, when it is projected that 61.5 percent of all women will be working, as opposed to 52.5 percent of men, the situation may well change. The beginnings of the trend may already be seen. According to recently released figures, the rate of increase in white women's life expectancy since 1970 is now equal to, or perhaps slightly below, that observed for white men (U.S. Census, 1985a). For the time being, however, it is no wonder gerontologists sometimes say the problems of old age are women's problems.

In large measure the literature on old age is most typically representative of whites because almost 90 percent of the aged fall into that category. Of the remainder, 8.2 percent are black, with about 2 percent being labeled of Hispanic origin. In actual numbers these figures break down to over 21 million blacks, roughly 540,000 Hispanics, 212,000 Asians, and 175,000 Native Americans. The numbers are important, as we will see in Chapter 9, because many of these subpopulations are particularly at risk. Not only do they have shorter life expectancies and higher age-specific mortality and morbidity rates, but they also have become old following generally hard lives. Most have experienced the results of years of depressed earnings, fewer educational opportunities, and a higher prevalence of serious illnesses. The disadvantages become apparent when we examine some of the particulars.

First, life expectancy at birth has traditionally been far more favorable for whites. But in the last four decades the percentage increase in life expectancy for nonwhites has been dramatic. The differential has been reduced by over half, so that today an average of only five years separates whites from blacks. By sixty-five the differential has all but disappeared and, as mentioned earlier, after seventy-five blacks have a better chance of survival. Although there is still a gap between the two groups, blacks are making greater inroads, experiencing a one-third gain in the number over sixty-five compared to a 23 percent gain for whites. While overall patterns are difficult to interpret, most experts contend higher nonwhite fertility rates have combined with improved health care opportunities and supportive legislation ensuring economic and physical well-being. In all likelihood, differences would disappear altogether if socioeconomic status were comparable between the two races throughout life (U.S. Census, 1983a; Kitagawa and Hauser, 1973). Figure 2.9 illustrates the "best guess" projections the U.S. Bureau of the Census is able to make for sex and racial differences in the aged population. Despite improvements, the differential between the races is expected to continue for the foreseeable future.

## EXPANSION OF THE ELDERLY POPULATION

If there seem to be more older people around, it is because their numbers have grown twice as fast as the rest of the population over the past twenty-five years. Between 1980 and 2020 their number will double again, with those over eighty-five growing nearly twice as fast. As is clear from these figures, the percentage increase of the elderly in the total population may amount to a veritable explosion before the middle of the next century.

What is true for the United States is also true for other industrialized countries. In the United Kingdom the percentage of the elderly in the population has tripled during the same period to reach approximately 14 percent in

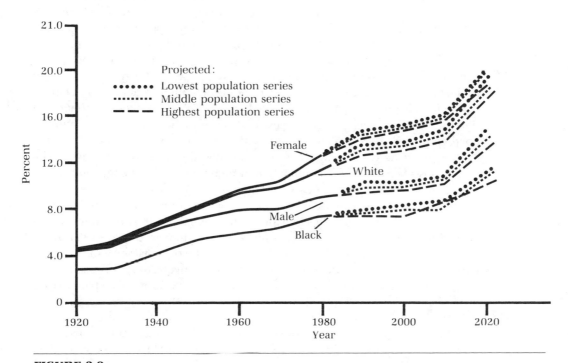

**FIGURE 2.9**

Percent distribution of population over sixty-five: by sex and race, 1920–2020. (*Source:* U.S. Bureau of the Census. *Demographic and Socioeconomic Aspects of Aging in the United States*, p. 21. Current Population Reports, P-23, No. 138. Washington, D.C.: U.S. Government Printing Office, 1984.)

1981. The percentage of older people in West Germany has also tripled. In France and Sweden it has doubled, and in Canada it has almost doubled during this century. Despite these changes, only France and Sweden had a large enough proportion of their populations over sixty-five to exhibit aged population structures before 1900. Currently, each of the countries shown in Figure 2.6, except India, has an aged population structure, with 7 percent or more of its citizens sixty-five or older. Unless there is a highly unusual and as yet unpredicted change in the current birth rates, it is unlikely that any reversal will take place in the near future.

# Aging in the Third World

## POPULATION STRUCTURE

For comparison let us look more closely at aging in Third World countries. As was shown earlier in Figure 2.7, the population structure of the developing regions of the world is very different from that of the advanced industrialized societies. It should be apparent that there is a tremendous amount of variability within the Third World. Drought-stricken East Africa is presently one of the most severely underdeveloped areas, while Latin America has a relatively high level of development in comparison. Yet regardless of these differences, the populations of Third World countries are young populations, with high percentages of infants, children, and young adults and low percentages of the elderly. In Ethiopia those over sixty-five represent only approximately 3.5 percent of the total population and in Zaire only 2.5 percent. Unless she lives in India, Bangladesh, Nepal, Pakistan, or Ethiopia, a woman generally lives longer than a man (United Nations, 1984a). As shown in Table 2.6, age-dependency ratios for the less developed countries tend to be higher than those for developed countries (77.8 vs 52.6 in 1980, with a high of 93.4 for parts of Africa); caution must be used so as not to misconstrue these figures, however. The high ratios are caused by a combination of high youth-dependency figures and low age-dependency ones, and even then many of those on the far reaches of the life cycle do participate in the subsistence economy. Returning again to Table 2.5, it can be seen that life expectancy at birth is generally much shorter. In Ethiopia, for example, it was only 42.9 for the period 1980–1985. Bearing in mind what has been said about birth rates being a prime factor in determining age composition, it is possible to see in Figure 2.10 that reproduction rates show wide variability, resulting in markedly different age structures.

## QUALITY OF LIFE

Still, there are people considered old in all countries. What is it like to age in a Third World country? Those who emphasize the "world we have lost" view see less developed societies as holding old people in greater esteem, in part because there are so few of them. We need to remember, however, that the majority of those who would have been old by the standards of advanced industrial societies are dead in less developed societies. Although cultural and

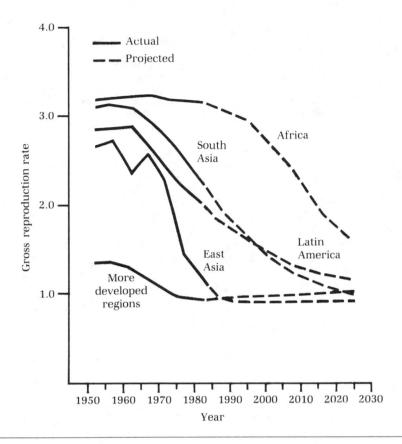

**FIGURE 2.10**

1982 gross reproduction rates: various regions of the world. (*Source:* United Nations. *Concise Report on the World Population Situation in 1983.* Population Studies, No. 85. New York: United Nations, 1984.)

psychological aspects of aging are important to the well-being of the elderly, certain physical amenities are necessary for any decent quality of life for the entire population, let alone old people. As mentioned before, infectious and parasitic diseases are still major killers in Third World countries. Many thousands of people starve to death each year in East Africa. Of those who grow to adulthood and old age, many are impaired because of earlier nutritional deficiencies. To cite just one example, 9 percent of the people in Nepal and 12 percent of the people in Indonesia had access to safe water in the period 1974–1978 (Durch, 1980). Table 2.8 includes a number of items relevant to a discussion of quality of life. A glance at the differences points up the reason why the "necessities" in some parts of the world are viewed as amenities in the developed market economies in others. As can be seen, medical care is minimal or nonexistent in many developing areas. There was only one doctor for every 14,517 people in Africa, as opposed to one per 663 people in developed market

**TABLE 2.8**

Distribution of Key Amenities by Societal Development Status, 1975 Comparisons

| Country Groups | Energy Consumption (Equivalent to Kilograms of Coal) | Proportion of Urban Population | Primary and Secondary School Enrollment (Percentage) | Persons per Physician | Persons per Nurse | Radio Receivers per 1000 Persons |
|---|---|---|---|---|---|---|
| 116 countries | 2038 | 39 | 70 | 4615 | 7904 | 322 |
| Developed market economies | 6207 | 72 | 89 | 663 | 257 | 814 |
| Centrally planned economies of Eastern Europe and U.S.S.R. | 5444 | 60 | 90 | 415 | 324 | 412 |
| Developing economies | 470 | 28 | 57 | 7061 | 9878 | 86 |
| Geographical area | | | | | | |
| Africa | 214 | 25 | 49 | 14517 | 3250 | 74 |
| Latin America | 934 | 61 | 78 | 1897 | 2828 | 249 |
| East Asia | 654 | 25 | 80 | 2000 | 1506 | 192 |
| South Asia | 270 | 23 | 55 | 7012 | 12402 | 39 |
| Oceania | 335 | 21 | 45 | 9721 | . . . | 524 |
| Type of economy | | | | | | |
| Petroleum-exporting countries | 541 | 30 | 22 | 13377 | 6402 | 79 |
| Non–petroleum-exporting countries | 462 | 28 | 29 | 5921 | 10556 | 87 |

*Source:* United Nations. *Concise Report on the World Population Situation in 1983*, p. 69. Population Series, No. 85. New York: United Nations, 1984.

economies in the mid-1970s. The use of energy in the less developed countries is a fraction of that used in the developed countries. The consequence is that physical labor is used instead of coal or other power sources, and what we would regard as necessary amenities are largely lacking. For many years it was maintained that, given time, Third World countries would develop and attain a standard of living comparable to that of the developed countries. It has become apparent, however, that there are major obstacles and problems to be negotiated if such a pattern of modernization is to take place. As we shall see in the chapters on theory, social policy, and aging in the periphery, major policy changes will be necessary if such an optimistic goal is to be achieved.

# Summary

Having acquired some familiarity with the conceptual tools of social gerontology, it should be possible to review relevant data critically. Underlying the whole process of aging are broad structural features of a culture or society. To make sense of what it means to grow old it is necessary to bear in mind the interaction among the various levels.

Historically, until 1650, societies experienced sporadic, at best gradual, population expansion. Those conditions inimical to the aggregation of people contributed likewise to foreshorten life expectancies. A combination of uncontrollable infectious diseases, poor nutrition and the unreliability of available food supplies, and inadequate health and medical knowledge effectively operated to suppress even the potential for attaining a ripe old age among most peoples. The normal duration of life hovered around thirty-five years until after the Middle Ages, though this figure must be offered hesitantly because of the often incomplete and speculative data. Life chances among the upper classes provide a partial glimpse of the patterns of fertility and morality found later among the rest of society. It is perhaps surprising in light of the brevity of life that prevailing literary references to old age echo Aristotle's critique of the conservativeness and calculating greed of old men. Cicero is one of the few who maintained that old age is not indisputably linked to particular character flaws. Rather, if anything, a good person will achieve a measure of wisdom, tolerance, grace, and influence rarely found in youth. Interestingly, the dominant imagery of old age appropriated from the past by lay people and scientists alike is closer to the view of Aristotle than to Cicero.

The Renaissance, heralding the inauguration of the modern era in Europe, also marks the beginning of vast changes in population structure. The rise of science and the spread of industrialization were to revolutionize societies. The earliest manifestation of the new order was a diminishing death rate. Since birth rates declined much more gradually, populations expanded rapidly. The initial beneficiaries of lower mortality rates were children and women of childbearing age; hence some years elapsed before a significant proportion of the population attained what we now regard as old age. The combination of lowered death and birth rates brought about the eventual aging of entire populations in industrialized societies.

The twentieth century has witnessed an astounding growth of the elderly population in the industrialized societies of the world. This aging of populations generally occurred after 1920, as the proportion of individuals sixty-five and over doubled or in some cases tripled. The sizable numbers of elderly today owe their existence to a period of fairly high birth rates coupled with declining death rates. Life expectancy has increased in a corresponding manner in this century; on the average, gains are in the neighborhood of twenty years. Today most men can look forward to at least seventy years of life and women to seventy-eight or more years. Many observers view enhanced longevity as one index of social progress, leading them to conclude the fate of humankind has generally improved. In a sense it provides a measure of our mastery over the ever-present forces of nature that eventually terminate life. These factors alone create a range of health, economic, and social issues confronting both individuals and institutions concerned with the well-being of the elderly. It was noted, however, that the expansion of elderly populations and the average duration of life signals only the beginning of changes in contemporary industrialized societies. Mortality rates have improved differentially, to the extent that elderly women outlive men by seven or eight years. In addition, modifications in sex ratios in the later years have implications for the living arrangements and family status of older men and women alike.

Third World or developing countries have a far different age structure. The question is whether modernization is likely to alter their life expectancy. Judging by the distribution of goods and services currently available, drastic changes are not likely to occur in the near future.

## Discussion Questions

**Nature of Aging**

1. How many positive and negative features associated with aging can you list?

2. Think of some people who seem younger or older than they are in years. (Choose either famous people or people you know.) What makes them seem younger or older? Can you think of anything in their past history, life-style, or situation that has made them "younger" or "older?"

**Age Grading**

3. How many age grades do you think there are in the United States? What distinguishes these age grades from each other? Give some examples of behavior appropriate for people of each age grade.

4. Do you think that you are on time, ahead, or behind normal patterns in your progress through the various stages of your life? Why?

**Rites of Passage**

5. Try to invent some rites of passage that might be useful in helping people adjust to old age. Can you think of examples of rites of passage in the middle years?

**Ageism**

6. Interview some elderly people you know. How does their situation correspond to the stereotypes revealed in the Harris polls? Do they have any age biases themselves?

**Age Structure of the Population**

7. Population projections made by different agencies or in different years tend to yield slightly different results. Why might this be the case?

8. The life expectancy at birth for women in the United States in 1979 was 77.7 years. Therefore, Sue assumes that she will die when she is seventy-seven. What kind of fallacy is she falling into? List some factors that might influence how long she lives.

9. Imagine you are in charge of the Department of Health and Human Services. How could information regarding life expectancies and the age structure of the population be useful to you? (Contrast the ways in which you would use the two types of information.)

10. You have to do a study of the health status of the middle-aged and elderly in the United States. What would be the advantages and disadvantages of using cross-sectional analysis in such a study? What would be the advantages and disadvantages of using cohort analysis?

11. Think of some ways in which people's income is affected by age cycle effect, period effect, and cohort effect, respectively.

12. You are a consultant to a congressional committee concerned with long-range planning of the budget for social needs. Discuss the advantages and disadvantages of age-dependency ratios, economic-dependency ratios, and the index of aging in making long-range plans that take into account the needs of the elderly, the disabled, the unemployed, and of youth.

**Aging in Historical Context**

13. Pick a specific place during a particular historical period you know something about. Do you think that the situation of the elderly might have been better or worse at that time?

14. Reread the sections on statistical and qualitative generalizability in Chapter 1. Do you think we are more likely to be able to make statistical or qualitative generalizations about aging from studying history? Why?

15. Describe something you have learned in studying history or reading literature that might be useful to you as you age.

**Aging in Advanced Industrial Society**

16. On the basis of the material contained in this section, what do you think will be the major problems with regard to aging facing advanced industrial societies in the next fifty years? Compare these problems with the list of things that you would like to see changed about the situation of the elderly (from Chapter 1).

**Aging in the Third World**

17. What do you think are likely to be the major population and social problems facing the developing countries in the next fifty years?

# Pertinent Readings

Achenbaum, W. A. *Old Age in the New Land: The American Experience Since 1790.* Baltimore: The Johns Hopkins University Press, 1978.

Angel, J. L. "The Length of Life in Ancient Greece." *Journal of Gerontology* 2, 1 (1947): 18–24.

———. "Human Biology, Health, and History in Greece from the First Settlement Until Now." *American Philosophical Society Yearbook*, 1954.

Aristotle. *Treatise on Rhetoric.* Trans. Theodore Buckley. London: George Bell and Sons, 1883.

Bengtson, V. L., and D. A. Haber. "Sociological Approaches to Aging." In *Aging: Scientific Perspectives and Social Issues*, eds. D. S. Woodruff and J. E. Birren, pp. 70–91. New York: D. Van Nostrand Company, 1975.

Bogue, D. J. *Principles of Demography.* New York: John Wiley and Sons, Inc., 1969.

Bouvier, L. F. "Planet Earth 1984–2034: A Demographic Vision." *Population Bulletin* 39, No. 1 (1984).

Breytspraak, L. M. *The Development of Self in Later Life.* Boston: Little, Brown & Company, 1984.

Butler, R. N., and M. I. Lewis. *Aging and Mental Health.* St. Louis: The C. V. Mosby Company, 1977.

Cain, L. D. "Life Course and Social Structure." In *Handbook of Modern Sociology*, ed. R. E. L. Farris, pp. 272–309. Chicago: Rand McNally & Company, 1964.

Cicero. *De Senectute, De Amicitia, De Divinatione.* Trans. William Armistead Falconer. London: William Heinemann, 1923.

Comfort, A. *The Biology of Senescence*, 3rd ed. New York: Elsevier Science Publishing Co., Inc., 1979.

Cook, S. F. "Survivorship in Aboriginal Population." *Human Biology* 19, 2 (1947): 83–89.

Cowdry, E. V., ed. *Problems of Ageing: Biological and Medical Aspects*, 2nd ed. Baltimore: The Williams & Wilkins Company, 1942.

Cowgill, D. O. "A Theory of Aging in Cross-Cultural Perspective." In *Aging and Modernization*, eds. D. O. Cowgill and L. D. Holmes, pp. 1–13. New York: Appleton-Century-Crofts, 1979.

———, and L. D. Holmes, eds. *Aging and Modernization.* New York: Appleton-Century-Crofts, 1972.

Davies, L. J. "Attitudes Toward Old Age and Aging as Shown by Humor." *The Gerontologist* 17, 3 (1977): 220–26.

Demos, J. "Notes on Life in Plymouth Colony." *The William and Mary Quarterly* 22, 2 (1964): 271.

———. *A Little Commonwealth: Family Life in Plymouth Colony.* New York: Oxford University Press, 1970.

———. "Old Age in Early New England." In *Aging, Death, and the Completion of Being*, ed. D. D. Van Tassel, pp. 115–64. Philadelphia: University of Pennsylvania Press, 1979.

Drevenstedt, J. "Perceptions of Onsets of Young Adulthood, Middle Age, and Old Age." *Journal of Gerontology* 31, 1 (1976): 53–57.

Dublin, L. I., A. J. Lotka, and M. Spiegelman. *Length of Life: A Study of the Life Table*, rev. ed. New York: Ronald Press Company, 1949.

Dubos, R. *Mirage of Health: Utopias, Progress, and Biological Change.* Garden City, N.Y.: Anchor-Doubleday and Company, 1959.

Durch, J. S. *Nuptiality Patterns in Developing Countries: Applications for Fertility.* Washington, D.C.: Population Reference Bureau, Inc., 1980.

Eisenstadt, S. N. *From Generation to Generation.* New York: The Free Press, 1956.

Eustis, N., J. Greenberg, and S. Patten. *Long-Term Care for Older Persons: A Policy Perspective.* Monterey, Calif.: Brooks/Cole Publishing Company, 1984.

Falls, J. F. "The Compression of Morbidity." *Milbank Memorial Fund Quarterly* 61 (1983): 397–419.

Fries, J. F. "The Compression of Morbidity." *Milbank Memorial Fund Quarterly* 61 (1983): 397–419.

———. "The Compression of Morbidity: Miscellaneous Comments About a Theme." *The Gerontologist* 24 (1984): 354–59.

Greven, P. J., Jr. *Four Generations: Population, Land, and Family in Colonial Andover, Massachusetts.* Ithaca, N.Y.: Cornell University Press, 1970.

Harris, L., et al. *The Myth and Reality of Aging in America.* Washington, D.C.: The National Council on the Aging, Inc., 1975.

Havighurst, R. J., and G. A. Sacher. "Prospects of Lengthening Life and Vigor." In *Extending the Human Life Span: Social Policy and Social Ethics*, eds. B. L. Neugarten and R. J. Havighurst, pp. 13–18. Washington, D.C.: National Science Foundation, 1977.

Helm, V. "Japanese Literature." In *Old Age in Literature*, ed. Von Dorotka Bagnell. New York: Syracuse University Press (in press).

Herlihy, D. "Growing Old in the Quattrocento." In *Old Age in Preindustrial Society*, ed. P. N. Stearns, 104–118. New York: Holmes & Meier, 1982.

Hollingsworth, T. H. "The Demography of the British Peerage." *Population Studies* 38, 2 (1965): iv–108.

Keith, J. *Old People as People: Social Cultural Influences on Aging and Old Age.* Boston: Little, Brown & Company, 1982.

Kent, S. "The Evolution of Longevity." *Geriatrics* 35 (1980): 98–104.

Kitagawa, E. M., and P. M. Hauser. *Differential Mortality in the United States: A Study in Socioeconomic Epidemiology.* Cambridge, Mass.: Harvard University Press, 1973.

Kogan, N. "Beliefs, Attitudes and Stereotypes About Old People." *Research on Aging* 1 (1979): 11–36.

Levin, J., and W. C. Levin. *Ageism: Prejudice and Discrimination Against the Elderly.* Belmont, Calif.: Wadsworth Publishing Company, 1980.

Lerner, M. "When, Why and Where People Die." In *The Dying Patient*, eds. O. G. Brim Jr., H. E. Freeman, S. Levine, and N. A. Scotch. New York: Russell Sage Foundation, 1970.

Macdonell, W. R. "On the Expectation of Life in Ancient Rome, and in the Provinces of Hispania and Lusitania, and Africa." *Biometrika* 9 (1913): 370–76.

Myers, G. C., and K. G. Manton. "Recent Changes in the U.S. Age at Death Distribution: Further Observations." *The Gerontologist* 24 (1984): 572–75.

Myles, J. *Old Age in the Welfare State: The Political Economy of Public Pensions.* Boston: Little, Brown & Company, 1984.

Nash, L. L. "Concepts of Existence: Greek Origins of Generational Thought." *Daedalus* (Fall 1978): 1–21.

National Council on the Aging. *Aging in the Eighties: America in Transition.* Washington, D.C.: NCOA, 1981.

Neugarten, B. L. "Personality and Aging." In *Handbook of the Psychology of Aging*, eds. J. E. Birren and K. W. Schaie, pp. 626–49. New York: Van Nostrand Reinhold Company, 1979.

———, and N. Datan. "Sociological Perspectives on the Life Cycle." In *Life Span Developmental Psychology*, eds. P. Baltes and K. W. Schaie, pp. 53–69. New York: Academic Press, Inc., 1973.

Nordberg, H. "Biometrical Notes: The Information on Ancient Christian Inscriptions From Rome Concerning the Duration of Life and the Dates of Birth and Death." *Acta Instituti Romani Finlandiae* 2, 2 (1963).

Peller, S. "Mortality, Past and Future." *Population Studies* 1, 4 (1948): 405–56.

Population Reference Bureau, Inc. *1981 World Population Data Sheet*. Washington, D.C.: Population Reference Bureau, Inc., 1981.

Richardson, B. E. *Old Age Among the Ancient Greeks: The Greek Portrayal of Old Age in Literature, Art, and Inscriptions*. Baltimore: The Johns Hopkins Press, 1933.

Richland, J. "The Foolishness and Wisdom of Age: Attitudes Toward the Elderly as Reflected in Jokes." *The Gerontologist* 17, 3 (1977): 210–19.

Rosenthal, J. T. "Mediaeval Longevity and the Secular Peerage, 1350–1500." *Population Studies* 27, 2 (1973): 287–93.

Rosow, I. *Social Integration of the Aged*. New York: The Free Press, 1967.

———. *Socialization to Old Age*. Berkeley: University of California Press, 1974.

Russell, J. C. *British Medieval Population*. Albuquerque: University of New Mexico Press, 1948.

Seltzer, M. M. "Timing: The Significant Common Variable in Both Humor and Aging." In *Humor and Aging: A New Field of Inquiry*, eds. L. N. Nakemow and K. McClusky. New York: Academic Press, Inc., 1986.

Schneider, E. L., and J. A. Brody. "Aging, Natural Death, and the Compression of Morbidity: Another View." *New England Journal of Medicine* 309 (1983): 854–56.

Schneider, G. "Austrian and German Literature." In *Old Age in Literature*, ed. Von Dorotka Bagnell. New York: Syracuse University Press (in press).

Shakespeare, W. *Complete Works*. London: Collins, 1959.

Smith, S. R. "Growing Old in an Age of Transition." In *Old Age in Preindustrial Society*, ed. P. N. Stearns. New York: Holmes & Meier, 1982.

Stearns, P. N., ed. *Old Age in European Society: The Use of France*. New York: Holmes & Meier, 1976.

———. *Old Age in Preindustrial Society*. New York: Holmes & Meier, 1982.

Strehler, B. L. "Implications of Aging Research for Society." In *Dimensions of Aging*, eds. J. Hendricks and C. D. Hendricks. Cambridge, Mass.: Winthrop Publishers, Inc., 1979.

Thomlinson, R. *Population Dynamics: Causes and Consequences of World Demographic Change*. New York: Random House, Inc., 1965.

Trexler, R. C. "A Widows' Asylum of the Renaissance: The Orbatollo of Florence." In *Old Age in Preindustrial Society*, ed. P. N. Stearns. New York: Holmes & Meier, 1982.

United Nations. *The Aging of Populations and Its Economic and Social Implications*. Population Studies, No. 26. New York: United Nations, 1956.

———. *Economic Survey of Europe in 1974, Part II: Post-War Demographic Trends in Europe and the Outlook Until the Year 2000*. New York: United Nations, 1975.

———. *Demographic Yearbook, 1982*, 34th ed. New York: United Nations, 1984a.

———. *Mortality and Health Policy: Proceedings of the Expert Group on Mortality and Health Policy, Rome 30 May to 3 June, 1983*. New York: United Nations, 1984b.

———. *Concise Report on the World Population Situation in 1983*. Population Series, No. 85. New York: United Nations, 1984c.

U.S. Bureau of the Census. *America in Transition: An Aging Society*. Current Population Reports, Series P-23, No. 128. Washington, D.C.: U.S. Government Printing Office, 1983a.

————. *World Population, 1983. Recent Demographic Estimates for the Countries and Regions of the World.* Washington, D.C.: U.S. Government Printing Office, 1983b.

————. *Demographic and Socioeconomic Aspects of Aging in the United States.* Current Population Reports, P-23, No. 138. Washington, D.C.: U.S. Government Printing Office, 1984a.

————. *Estimates of the Population of the United States by Age, Sex, and Race: 1980 to 1983.* Current Population Reports, P-25, No. 949. Washington, D.C.: U.S. Government Printing Office, 1984b.

————. *Projections of the Population of the United States by Age, Sex, and Race: 1983–2080.* Current Population Reports, P-25, No. 952. Washington, D.C.: U.S. Government Printing Office, 1984c.

————. *Statistical Abstract of the United States, 1985,* 105th ed. Washington, D.C.: U.S. Government Printing Office, 1985a.

————. *Estimates of the Population of the United States, by Age, Sex, and Race: 1980 to 1984.* Washington, D.C.: U.S. Government Printing Office, 1985b.

Valaoras, V. G. "Patterns of Aging of Human Populations." In *The Social and Biological Challenge of Our Aging Population.* Proceedings of the Eastern States Health Education Conference. New York: Columbia University Press, 1950.

Van Gennep, A. *The Rites of Passage.* Chicago: University of Chicago Press, 1960.

Von Dorotka Bagnell, P., ed. *Old Age in Literature: A Cross-Cultural Review.* New York: Syracuse University Press (in press).

Walker, A. "Dependency and Old Age?" *Social Policy and Administration* 16, 2 (1982): 115–135.

Wrigley, E. A. *Population and History.* New York: McGraw-Hill Book Company, 1969.

Yin, P., and M. Shine. "Misinterpretation of the Increases in Life Expectancy in Gerontology Textbooks." *The Gerontologist* 25, 1 (1985): 78–82.

# 3

# THEORIES OF SOCIAL GERONTOLOGY

**THE ROLE OF THEORY IN SOCIAL GERONTOLOGY**

The Relevance of Theory
How Theories Make Sense of Aging
Evaluating Theories
The Focus of Social Gerontology
Explaining the Aging Experience

**EARLY THEORETICAL DEVELOPMENTS**

Disengagement Theory
Activity Theory
Subcultural Theory
Continuity Theory

**SECOND GENERATION THEORETICAL DEVELOPMENTS**

Age Stratification Theory
Modernization Theory

**EMERGENT THEORIES IN SOCIAL GERONTOLOGY**

Social Environmental Theories
Political Economy
  *Dependency Theory*
  *Internal Colonialism*
  *Dual Economy Models*

**SUMMARY**

**DISCUSSION QUESTIONS**

**PERTINENT READINGS**

# The Role of Theory in Social Gerontology

## THE RELEVANCE OF THEORY

Conceptual and theoretical development is central to gerontology. Too frequently the uninformed shun theory in favor of quick answers to pressing issues. The result has been a proliferation of stopgap measures that may have some short-term benefits but seldom address the underlying mechanisms that created the problems in the first place. The evolution of age segregation in which the opposite ends of life are defined in terms of the separateness from and dependency on the young and middle adult years is a contingent event. This separation is not inevitable; rather it stems from the normative sequencing of events in our lives.

Society and culture prescribe certain general patterns within which people age. The effect of social, historical, and psychological influences is not ironclad. It is interactive, always a matter of degree. Life is a transactional process determined by a mixture of personal attributes and structural constraints that circumscribe how any one person experiences the aging process.

Although it is true that we will all become old, there are many routes people follow. Earlier we asked why some people seem younger than their years and why some seem older? In attempting to answer those questions we did some basic gerontological theorizing. In a number of important respects the theories formulated by social gerontologists can be viewed as extensions of just such theorizing carried out in everyday life. That little bit of reflection could conceivably have a profound impact on the readers' lives. Why? Because the way we reckon our life's script will surely influence the way we live it. What if we could extend this logic? What if it were possible to look at whole collections of people, some of whom were doing very well and others very poorly, and what if we could pinpoint the reasons for the variance? If we could identify what those who were doing well had that the others did not, we might be able to intervene. Aging is not a common lot; differences between people mean different old ages. The goal of theorizing in gerontology is to identify, describe, classify, explain, and ultimately understand the social dimensions of the aging process.

But this will take some time. To begin with the questions are complicated. Also, not everyone agrees on the agenda. What if the solution involved a major shift of national priorities? What if it meant a fundamental redistribution of something important to us all? Would people give something up to ensure that others had a more fulfilling old age? What if it meant a deliberate decision to limit the life-styles of all older citizens? Is their well-being less important than ours? Although it is not within the purview of this text to deal with the ethics involved — tinkering with values is as dangerous as tinkering with dynamite — we can address the question of explanation. Why do some people fare better than others? In this chapter and the rest of the text we will try to point the way to some of the intriguing models formulated by gerontologists.

## HOW THEORIES MAKE SENSE OF AGING

Theory in social gerontology was initially inherited from its parent disciplines of psychology and sociology. The principal developmental models will not be discussed until Chapter 6; this chapter will be confined to the more sociological points of view. By and large the focus of gerontological theories is a spin-off of primary paradigms in the parent disciplines. The first explicit conceptual model formulated by sociologists studying aging grew out of a functionalist orientation. It stressed the maintenance of social equilibrium. Accordingly, gerontologists sought clues to both personal and social stability through a disengagement model thought to be mutually advantageous to both individuals and groups. When functionalism in sociology gave way to newer theories, so too did disengagement in gerontology. The same happened with later models, but they all have contributed to the cumulative theoretical perspective in the aging literature.

It is not that theories are only fads. They are more sophisticated than that. The point is that in making sense of aging the knowledge used necessarily has ties to what has gone before. Furthermore, gerontology theorizers are themselves socially situated. They receive their training, their salaries, and their orientations through concrete entities from which they assimilate points of view. These may be in the form of an explicit ideology, a level or technique of analysis, or perhaps only a vague orientation; whichever is the case, it influences the way they write theory.

## EVALUATING THEORIES

If theory in social gerontology is constructed out of so many relative factors, how does one distinguish those that are worthwhile? Is it merely a matter of personal preference, of picking the one best suited to whatever one wants to assert? Or are there criteria for judging how good a theory is? Philosophers of science have pondered these questions for generations. Rather than enumerate the various formal criteria they employ for sifting the wheat from the chaff, we will give a few summary rules of thumb that should be adequate for this discussion. First, a theory should explain what it claims to explain; it should be relevant to the subject at hand and the types of problems identified.

That a theory does so may not be immediately apparent. It may be necessary to learn a specialized language or something about the discipline of which it is a part before making a judgment. No one expects to grasp the explanation of the laws of thermodynamics the first time they encounter them, and every student who delves into sociological theory must also work hard to master the concepts. In gerontology the same is true; some specialization is required.

Second, theories must be internally consistent. Once set up the constituent elements of the model must be interconnected without great leaps in logic to explain unanticipated contingencies. Sloppy thinking and ill-conceived paradigms are best abandoned rather than patched together to retain a model once conceived. Before rejecting a model, however, the critic must understand its internal logic. Equally, it is important that the rejection is not based upon personal bias.

Third, systematically ignoring relevant components of the object of study because they cannot be incorporated into the explanatory model is also grounds for discarding a theory. In the case of nutrition, for instance, if an explanation of suitable nutrition ignored loss of teeth it would be inadequate. So, too, if less directly relevant components are ignored, this can also diminish a theory's explanatory power. Using the same example again: if a model of nutritional behavior in the elderly does not take account of the relevance of the social, cultural, and psychological ramifications of eating meals, it would not fulfill its proclaimed goal.

Social scientists looking at aging may focus on individual, structural, national, or even international factors affecting the lives of old people. They must also bear in mind, however, the relevance of other levels. The gerontological focus has many frames of reference and levels of analysis. A theory cannot and probably should not try to explain everything. Its scope should be well defined but not so constricted that accepting it precludes considering other points of view. Hence the importance of the interdisciplinary focus called for at the beginning of this book. Above all it must be stressed that the way an issue is posed delimits its possible solutions. The models developed by gerontologists grow out of the same cultural matrix as the problems they study. While there may be no other recourse, it is necessary to bear this relationship in mind. Those models that explicitly recognize the problematic nature of the common roots of their science and their subject matter are often better rounded.

## THE FOCUS OF SOCIAL GERONTOLOGY

Social gerontologists are confronted with many conceptual problems not faced by their biologically oriented colleagues. In physiological processes at least the objects of study are not likely to change their minds. Those who work in the realm of conscious behavior have no such luxury. For thirty years social gerontologists have worked alongside their colleagues in the health sciences trying to formulate explanations that have both substance and predictive value. During several decades before that they proceeded in piecemeal fashion, focusing attention on those issues society defined as important without any overriding concern for theoretical modeling. Once a foothold was gained, concern for prediction demanded a broader and long-range perspective, one that would help explain why some people experienced problems in their later years and others did not.

The analysis of human behavior is infinitely complex and requires its own particular approach. Over and above any disciplinary orientation or field of investigation, all theoretical explanations share the common objective of making explicit the order behind what often appear as chaotic or isolated events. By developing a logical and verifiable system of interrelated propositions, gerontologists subscribe to a similar goal of producing an integrative framework capable of providing a coherent explanation of why people age the way they do. To begin with, an awareness of the *normative* character of aging in a sociocultural context brings about a broad appreciation of individual situations and the patterning fixed on them by the institutional order in a given society. Once we have an impression of the relative nature of age-related norms, we should then recognize their malleability. The realization that aging does not necessarily have to be the way it is justifies interceding in what is often taken to be a predetermined natural process. As Brim (1972) points out, the possibility for changing the manner in which we age has the potential of enhancing not only our personal lives but also the general welfare of society.

## EXPLAINING THE AGING EXPERIENCE

Before discussing the theories themselves, let us touch on some of the difficulties involved in accounting for the social patterns of aging. Not the least of these has to do with the validity of a theory applicable only to the later years. There is less than complete agreement among gerontologists themselves that the social nature of aging requires its own explanation. Granted, theories have a significant heuristic value, aiding collection of data and organization of existing information, as well as giving direction for the implementation of policy changes. Still, the question remains as to *why* old age should demand its own, perhaps singular, interpretation.

By the time people reach their later years, have they not already weathered innumerable personal changes and life crises which ought to leave them well prepared to face whatever ambiguities or anxieties they might encounter in their postretirement years? In one respect, no. For nearly every other age-related transformation in life, most people undergo what social psychologists call **anticipatory socialization**, the learning of a new role before actually assuming it. In addition, while it is true that adapting to change is a lifelong process, the adjustments made after sixty or sixty-five are carried out against a backdrop of involutional physical and social changes. Whether it is essential or even possible to devise theoretical explanations is an issue that cannot be resolved here. Let us merely caution that some social scientists have noted the fallacy of inferring that each new social problem demands a novel description.

With regard to aging, some have suggested that a perspective focusing on the nature of readjustments following transitional episodes throughout life may be sufficient to account for those changes associated with old age. Such a model might well examine the matrix of personal resources individuals can call on to maximize their fulfillment. In all fairness it must be pointed out that during the early phases of theorizing most gerontologists looked almost exclusively to the role of personal attributes to explain adjustment. True to their functionalist heritage, many of the early models stressed modes of fitting into ongoing structural arrangements, never seriously contemplating the possibility of individuals being more than mere reactors to social conditions (Marshall and Tindale, 1978–1979; Dowd, 1980; Estes et al., 1982).

In constructing their explanations, social scientists are forced to treat all members of a category as though they are nearly identical. It is the only way in which any useful generalizations can be made, although in the case of human beings, they recognize the risks involved in making such an assumption. The aged are not, however, a homogeneous aggregate: the same factors that differentiate people at the earlier stages of life continue to operate unabated through the later phases. To adequately discuss the social and sociopsychological processes integral to the way older people adjust to their situations, it is necessary to distinguish the consequences of aging per se from those more appropriately attributed to discontinuities in personal life-style or to situational constraints and generational effects. While there is no denying the importance of the latter, they do not actually reflect maturational age changes as much as they do differences among cohorts or individuals (Maddox and Wiley, 1976).

In tracing the growth of theoretical development in social gerontology, two related issues are immediately apparent. First, even though explicitly stated models are not as numerous as in biological investigations, they are present and operational nonetheless. The selection of study areas, variables, methodologies, explanations, and so on are always influenced by a tacit theoretical model. Second, several formative periods of theory construction can be identified. Initially there was a long latent period during which no clearly defined models reached the literature and a "problems" orientation served as a guide for research. During the 1960s the first theoretical frameworks were expressed and debated. The ideology of a problems approach was dominant, and explanations were couched in terms of disengagement, activity, and subcultural orientations.

Generally the points of view developed during the first wave of theorizing can be seen as complementary. Each focused on declines and losses and drew from the symbolic interactionist or the role theory traditions of sociology. Furthermore, all of the early models were cast in individualistic terms, looking at age-related alterations in the basis of identity for the older person. Roles, norms, and reference groups were relevant, all reconciled with assumed declines in individual competencies or attributes. The negotiated basis of identity was recognized, but the negotiations that took place were *ex parte*, calling for adjustments on the part of the aging person with each new situation.

In the 1970s two parallel theoretical developments attempted to challenge some of the givens accepted by the first generation. The emphasis shifted to a somewhat broader focus on the structural separation of the elderly from the rest of society. Together, the age stratification and modernization models offered a more inclusive perspective. While both led to a spate of scholarly articles, the age stratification approach has received the most attention. It stresses the dynamic interplay between individual aging processes and societal transformations. Regardless of its shortcomings, one of the key contributions the model makes is that relativity is important: aging and social change are interdependent and reciprocal. Modernization theory furthered the attention to historical and dynamic influences. By adopting a cross-cultural point of view, those who used this perspective sought to identify the impact of societal development on individual role allocation in the later years. Now, some fifteen years after its appearance in gerontology, it seems trite to say that modernization theory reminded gerontologists that the situation of the elderly they saw in their own countries was not necessarily the same throughout the world.

As though the theoretical microscope in social gerontology had been turned to a different power, theory building at the end of the 1970s and early 1980s gave even more attention to variations in social settings and their effect on aging. Attributes of aging individuals were still important, but they were seen as bartering mechanisms within contextual and structural constraints. This most recent theoretical phase marks a more or less radical departure from much that had gone before. Proponents of a political economy approach do not take the situation older people find themselves in as given but as a deliberate creation of interest group politics. The experiences of the elderly may be constructed in the world of everyday life, but they did not happen by chance. As before, there is an attempt to tie micro- and macro-level processes together, but the emphasis is on who benefits and not merely on the accommodations that must be made.

The explicit explanatory models have come a long way since the 1961 publication of Cumming and Henry's *Growing Old*. In the following section we will review each of their contributions and the different phases. As should be evident from this review, the thrust has turned from just looking at older persons to the interactive and correlative quality of individual aging. As one model transcended another, a gradual reconstruction of the paradigms in use by the field's leading theoreticians becomes apparent. Over the years the ecology of human aging (Bronfenbrenner, 1979) has moved to center stage and will likely be in the spotlight throughout the remainder of the decade. Although we cannot predict what theories will emerge in the last years of the 1980s, it seems likely they will integrate processual age changes with alterations in economics, politics, and services.

# Early Theoretical Developments

## DISENGAGEMENT THEORY

Disengagement represents the first major theoretical system attempted by social gerontologists. It was originally based on a cross-sectional survey analysis of 275 people ranging in age from fifty to ninety, all of whom resided in Kansas City and were physically and financially self-sufficient. Reflecting the common sense observation that older people are more subject to ill-health and to the probability of death than their younger counterparts, Cumming and Henry (1961) assert that a process of mutual withdrawal normally occurs to ensure both an optimum level of personal gratification and an uninterrupted continuation of the social system. Since disengagement is thought to be a normatively governed phenomenon woven into the social fabric of mass society, they conceive of it as quite beyond individual whim or fancy, excepting some limited input into its timing. In setting forth the basic tenets of their theory, the authors refer to the aging process as:

> . . . an inevitable mutual withdrawal or disengagement, resulting in decreased interaction between the aging person and others in the social system he belongs to. The process may be initiated by the individual or by others in the situation. The aging person may withdraw more markedly from some classes of people while remaining relatively close to others. His withdrawal may be accompanied from the outset by a preoccupation with himself; certain institutions in society may make this withdrawal easy for him. When the aging process is complete, the equilibrium which existed in middle life between the individual and his society has given way to a new equilibrium characterized by a greater distance and an altered type of relationship.

In spelling out the details of disengagement, Cumming and Henry clearly enunciate the inevitability and universality of the process. Society retracts because of the need to fit younger people into the slots once occupied by older people, no longer as useful or dependable as they were, and to maintain the equilibrium of the system. Individuals, on the other hand, choose to retreat because of an awareness of their diminishing capacities and the short time left to them before death. Although individual or cultural factors may alter the configuration of withdrawal, it is thought that older people everywhere will ultimately experience a severing of their social ties. As the number, nature, and diversity of the older person's contacts with the rest of the world contract, he or she will in effect become the sole judge of what is appropriate, freed as it were from normative control over commonplace behavior. Consequently, with the narrowing of the social life space, disengagement becomes a circular or self-perpetuating process in which there is a continuing shrinkage of interactional opportunities.

A disjuncture may occur when either the individual or society is not yet ready to begin disengagement, although in most cases societal needs will take priority in initiating the process. When older people suffer severe adjustment problems, it usually implies a lack of synchronization between individual readiness and societal demands. However, as a corollary to the postulate of mutuality, Cumming and Henry did concede the possibility of reengagement should the individual choose to cultivate a new set of valued skills. Morale will obviously suffer as the disengagement process gains momentum because of the gaps between opportunities and orientation to previous roles, but once the elderly person is able to carve out new concerns and rearrange his or her priorities to fit the new station in life, high morale can conceivably be reestablished (Cumming and Henry, 1961).

Almost from its inception disengagement theory engendered a running controversy among social gerontologists. For the most part, criticisms tended to converge on the presumed inevitability and inherent nature of the process. Questions were also posed about the functionality of withdrawal from either the individual or societal standpoint and the apparent lack of attention to personality factors and their effect on the whole process (Maddox, 1964; Atchley, 1971). Even Cumming and Henry have expressed misgivings in separate revisions of their original formulation. In her further thoughts on disengagement theory, Cumming (1963) backed away from an emphasis on societal equilibrium and prescribed behavior to concentrate instead on the role of innate biological and personality differences as distinct from externally imposed withdrawal. She no longer viewed societal pressures as sufficient to account for disengagement. Responding to the theory's critics, Cumming added a caveat regarding what she termed the *appearance,* contrasted to the *experience,* of engagement. To those who would look simply at activity levels Cumming suggested it is possible for disengaged people to appear involved, when in fact they are merely going through the motions of interaction, remaining oblivious to or simply shrugging off social sanctions on their behavior. The psychologically engaged, on the other hand, engrossed as they are in social intercourse, would still be responsive to feedback from others. At the same time Cumming indicated a nascent attitudinal detachment, akin to a desocialization, may begin in middle age, far in advance of actual withdrawal and in the midst of what may for all intents and purposes look like the height of engagement.

Cumming repeatedly distinguished men and women along a social dimension, not necessarily related to personality attributes as much as socialization, with men being the more ill-prepared to accommodate themselves to compensating forms of sociability in their later years because of the instrumental nature of their previous roles. In either case the remaining socioemotional roles assume added importance in maintaining self-conceptions or stimulation, helping both men and women resist shrinkage throughout much of the rest of life. Subsequent research has affirmed Cumming's emphasis on differential disengagement as an avenue for maximizing adjustment in various relationships (Williams and Wirths, 1965; Strieb and Schneider, 1971; Cumming, 1975).

Finally, Cumming repeated her original contention of the interest mass society has in controlling its vital affairs by removing crucial functions from the role repertoires of older people, though she does not explicitly address the part played by structural conditions.

Henry (1965) also amended his initial view of the disengagement model to lay greater stress on psychological dynamics. In essence, Henry's later statement is practically synonymous with the position propounded by Havighurst et al. (1968), who also worked with the Kansas City data but arrived at a somewhat different conclusion from that originally drawn by Cumming and Henry. In Henry's restatement the character of personality coping mechanisms and a focus on interiority are derived from previous experiences that determine the level of engagement or disengagement during subsequent stages of the life cycle. Those people who have customarily dealt with stress by turning inward and insulating themselves from the world will probably continue to withdraw. At the same time those who remain engaged are likely to have been similarly predisposed over the course of their lives. For this latter group the nature of activities may change, but generally they will rely on their interaction to resist the centripetal movement inherent in the disengagement model.

## ACTIVITY THEORY

The activity perspective posits that in the course of maturing children gain a sense of themselves through their socializing experiences and via responses of significant others to various identities tried on in much the same way adults try on clothing. As adults, people continue to refine and refurbish their self-concepts in their performance of socially valued, or at least legitimated, actions, seeking out what is sometimes referred to as **consensual validation,** the affirmation of their personal sense of worth and integrity. Upon reaching that socially prescribed stage of life when they are commonly divested of many of the roles that have been so central to their lives for years, older people experience a narrowing of their social radius, a reduction in activity levels, and, consequently, a loss or confusion in their sense of who they are. To offset these losses, to preserve morale, and to sustain self-concepts, the activity theory of aging presumes almost the converse of disengagement, that restitution, in the form of compensatory activities, must take place. By keeping active it is presumed people will remain socially and psychologically fit. In the words of one researcher: "the greater the number of optional role resources with which the individual enters old age, the better he or she will withstand the demoralizing effects of exit from the obligatory roles ordinarily given priority in adulthood" (Blau, 1973).

The proponents of activity theory assert that the disengagement theory may be applicable to a small minority of the elderly, usually the very old, but for the vast bulk of older people, the continuance of a moderately active life-style will have a marked preservative effect on their sense of well-being (Havighurst and Albrecht, 1953; Maddox, 1970). Despite recognizing that not all activities provide sustenance for self-concept, little attention has been directed to the differences between types of activity or an individual's ability to exert any significant control over either the roles themselves or the performance of those roles. As a result, the theory has received only limited empirical support and has been criticized as an oversimplification of the questions involved. It may hardly be appropriate merely to substitute pastimes, geared to what is thought to be older people's interests and abilities, for those roles they surrendered as they moved beyond middle age. Busying one's self with enterprises meaningless in terms of dominant cultural values, presumably still subscribed to by older people, may not in itself contribute to adjustment (Phillips, 1957; Gubrium, 1973). On the other hand, both longitudinal and cross-cultural investigations of old age have repeatedly found a positive, but by no means incontrovertible, association among morale, personal adjustment, and activity levels (Havighurst et al., 1969; Palmore, 1970).

The first full-bodied, systematic statement of activity theory did not appear until over a decade after the disengagement theory caused such a furor in gerontological circles, and even then its validation was somewhat problematic. Following an explicit definition of the concepts implied, four postulates central to activity theory have been stipulated. First, the greater the role loss, the less the participation in activity. Second, as activity levels remain high, the greater the availability of role support for role identities claimed by the older person. Third, the stability of role supports ensures a stable self-concept. Fourth, the more positive one's self-concept, the greater the degree of life satisfaction. From these four propositions six theorems were deduced that specify in detail the relationships implied by the theory (Lemon et al., 1972). Unfortunately, methodological difficulties precluded verifying the model in the first full-scale attempt to test its value in aging research (Lemon et al., 1972). In a later replicative study Longino and Kart (1982) were able to specify the nature of activities more fully and discovered that different types of activities had profoundly different effects. Informal interaction activity prompted expressions of well-being, while formal, highly structured activity had exactly the opposite impact. Solitary pursuits, on the other hand, seem to have little if any effect either way. The obvious implication is that it is meaningful interaction with others and not merely activity that makes a difference. Another team of investigators arrived at a similar conclusion, labeling the key factor subjective integration, as opposed to objective integration in which the participant merely went through the motions (Liang et al., 1980).

## SUBCULTURAL THEORY

Social integration on an individual level is also the focus of the subcultural model. Drawing on a long sociological tradition called symbolic interactionism, the subcultural perspective maintains simply that the crucial features of one's self-concept derive from interpersonal relationships. Positive interaction results in positive self-definition, and negative interaction leads to a disrupted sense of self. Like the activity theory, the emphasis is on social roles, social identities, and maintaining self-concepts. The difference centers on whether the norms and expectations of the middle years should be carried over into later life or whether old age should carry with it its own standards as to what is appropriate (McClelland, 1982). If the latter, then the model contends that older persons will fare better psychologically by interacting most with people like themselves.

As conceived by Rose (1965), the initial advocate of this perspective, whenever members of one category interact more among themselves than with people from other categories, a subculture will be generated. In addition, he suggested that a variety of demographic and social trends contribute to the genesis of an identifiable aged subculture that effectively cuts across all previous statuses to impart to the elderly a sense of group identity over and above earlier memberships. Among the specific factors mentioned by Rose are the sheer numbers of individuals beyond sixty-five who are still healthy and mobile enough to interact. With the growth of what some have termed aged ghettos, retirement communities, inner city neighborhoods, or residual rural congregations created when younger people migrate to urban areas, older people live in close proximity to one another. Legally established retirement policies now common in most industrialized societies have blocked major avenues for many older people to retain their integration with the larger society, thereby promoting a greater identification with an aged peer group. Social services designed to assist older people also tend to prompt recognition of their common situation at a time when many have an opportunity to engage in wide-ranging, nonwork-related activities for the first time. Rose also notes that many attributes of an aged subculture may stem from biological changes, normative expectations and perceptions of older people held by the general population, or from generational differences in socialization, each making its own contribution to an age-graded segregation.

As Rose outlines it, individual involvement in an aged subculture depends on the solidarity of the age group itself, plus the nature and extent of contacts retained with the total society through families, the media, employment, or the older person's own resistance to aging. In many instances the statuses previously so important are not nearly as meaningful in the world of the older person, who is isolated from the spheres of life that imparted the status originally. Good health and physical mobility confer status within the aged subculture, while occupational, educational, or economic prestige tend to be redefined as less influential than they were during earlier years. Commenting on the development of an aging self-concept, Rose avers that societal institutions, especially formalized retirement, have imposed an artificial boundary on what is socially recognized as old age. Concomitantly, an aging group consciousness has arisen, fostering an awareness of belonging to a particular group and not simply a chronological category. Participation in voluntary associations has also been a primary mechanism in the development of group self-consciousness, as has the greater publicity given to the elderly's common predicament or occasional victories. Although many disagree with the idea of an aged subculture, claiming for instance that the elderly do not fit traditional definitions or minority groups, there is an accumulating body of evidence to indicate many of the elements in Rose's framework are indeed extremely powerful factors in delineating associational patterns sponsoring a communal consciousness (Streib, 1965; Rosow, 1967, 1974; Hochschild, 1973; Allen and von de Vliert, 1984).

Whether the social stigma attached to being old or the elderly's own affinity for people their age provides sufficient grounds for a subculture to evolve to the point where older people become a voting bloc as Rose envisions is a question that presently cannot be answered, despite the admitted increase in militancy among older people. It is agreed, however, that there is certainly a strong relationship between peer group participation rates and the adjustment process of the elderly. From the standpoint of activity theory, the occasional person who expresses high morale but low activity levels is a deviant, while from a subcultural perspective he or she may simply be listening to an older drummer. If by engaging in activities governed by performance standards not suitable to their capabilities older people perceive the possibility of failure, they will in all likelihood readjust their interests to reflect their current status, joining with their age peers (Miller, 1965). Neither the disengagement model, the activity theory, nor the idea of an aged subculture has so far proven to be as useful a predictive tool as social gerontologists are searching for, although their underlying use as heuristic aids remains unquestioned.

In keeping with the social psychological traditions from which they both draw, there may be considerable overlap between the activity and the subcultural models. As shown in Figure 3.1, each assumes that interaction affects the sense of self and life satisfaction. The feedback that stems from participation in meaningful activities with those who reinforce one's personal identity is crucial in affirming personal identities. Just how important association with age peers is for psychological and emotional well-being remains a topic of debate. What does appear certain, however, is that it plays a valuable role in disseminating knowledge that can then be used to maximize opportunities for buttressing one's sense of worth (Sherman et al., 1985).

## CONTINUITY THEORY

The debate over the need for or applicability of monolithic theoretical frameworks to explain what happens late in life is by no means resolved. A sizable contingent of social gerontologists claim, within certain limits, that characteristic coping strategies are in place long before a person is defined as old. How we appear to those who have contact with us is a reflection of the interplay of biological, psychological, and social factors that we usually refer to as a *personality*. Beginning in childhood and continuing until the day we die, we use what seems to us through trial and error to be our own best way of adapting to new situations and problems. While these features of ourselves are stable, recognizable from one time to the next as the same, they are also dynamic, perpetually evolving to accommodate to new demands (Havighurst, 1968).

There is another side to the notion of continuity over the life course. Once

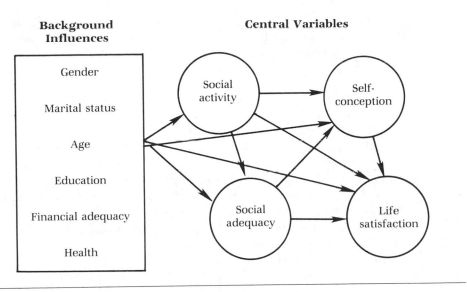

**Background
Influences**

**Central Variables**

Gender

Marital status

Age

Education

Financial adequacy

Health

Social
activity

Self-
conception

Social
adequacy

Life
satisfaction

**FIGURE 3.1**
Causal path connections in activity and subcultural theory. (*Source:* McClelland, K. A. "Self-Conception and Life-Satisfaction: Integrating Aged Subculture and Activity Theory." *Journal of Gerontology* 37, 6 [1982]: 723.)

again drawing from the same pool of social and psychological traditions, role theorists looking at individual adjustment to old age concentrate on maintaining nonwork roles, relationships, and orientations into the later years (Fox, 1981–1982). Personal stability is thought to be a consequence of enduring ties in the face of the emerging social realities of being old. Surely no one retires and suddenly becomes a blank slate: people have biographies, traits, personalities, and, above all, relationships that carry over from one age to the next. They live in environments that, while they may evolve, do not usually show radical disjunctures. This being the case, why should an older person demonstrate or require different coping mechanisms than a middle-aged person? People are not ahistorical nor do they become strangers in a totally new land (Rosenmayr, 1981).

As far as the adaptability of older people to the situations confronted in later life is concerned, those who focus on the persistence of personality traits assert:

There is considerable evidence that, in normal men and women, there is no sharp discontinuity of personality with age, but instead an increasing consistency. Those characteristics that have been central to the personality seem to become even more clearly delineated, and those values the individual has been cherishing become even more salient. In the personality that remains integrated — and in the environment that permits — patterns of overt behavior are likely to become increasingly consonant with the individual's underlying personality needs and his desires (Neugarten et al., 1968).

To help shed light on the continuous, dynamic, yet self-determining nature of personalities, Back (1976) used the notion of the *chreod*. Passed from the Greeks to modern theoretical biology via the eighteenth-century metaphysics of Leibniza, chreod may be thought of as a self-maintaining feature of an individual — a constitutional pattern that once acquired will resist disruption. As applied to behavioral aspects of life, even in the wake of wrenching experiences, previous traits will come through to shape subsequent action because of built-in tendencies toward homeostasis. Whether one refers to chreods or merely consistency, personality models dealing with the later years of life claim that whatever configuration of behaviors may be manifested, such are the outgrowths of long-standing characteristics. In looking at adjustment or any other facet of life, personality is thought to be highly predictive of who will experience difficulties. Indeed, empirical studies that have used adequate typologies to determine personal traits have been reasonably successful in pointing to events that have yet to occur (George, 1980; McCrae and Costa, 1984).

Similarly, those who prefer to concentrate on the importance of social roles refer to the structural model of participation in life learned through lifelong engagements. Social identities once learned or reinforced are not forgotten, abandoned, or deemed irrelevant as one moves from one context to another. Whether there is an analytical difference between *roles* and *personalities* is not the crucial issue; it is that coping strategies remain pretty much the same in the circumstances most of us find ourselves in during our daily lives. Of course, not everyone has an equal opportunity to continue in valued social roles. The ability to do so varies with an individual's social resources, the importance of certain roles to that individual, and the opportunities afforded by the social system. As will be discussed later, control over valued resources itself is a negotiated process that goes beyond psychological needs to retain personal identity. The primary importance of the continuity model is that stability acquired tends to be stability retained regardless of the roles lost or gained (Covey, 1981; Breytspraak, 1984; McCrae and Costa, 1984).

## Second Generation Theoretical Developments

Second generation theoretical developments are an attempt to go beyond the strictly individual aspects of socialization and to look at the structural factors affecting aging. Age stratification theory views aging itself as a social structural factor, whereas modernization theory focuses on the effects of modernization on the situation of the elderly. Although there have been some attempts by age stratification theorists to broaden the perspective to include issues of individual variation and the differential allocation of power and resources, these theories, particularly modernization theory, tend to focus on structural factors at the expense of individual intentions and issues of power allocation.

## AGE STRATIFICATION THEORY

Age stratification theory has preoccupied social gerontologists from its initial presentation in the early 1970s. It seeks a somewhat broader stance than any of the foregoing explanations in its efforts to unravel the linkages among age, personality, social structure, valued resources, and late life involvements. Proponents of an age stratification model start with the seemingly straightforward observation that societies arrange themselves into a hierarchy of socially defined *age grades* or *strata* complete with obligations and prerogatives assigned to members as they move from one stratum to the next. As such, societies intrinsically involve structured inequalities; some have more, others less of nearly all valued qualities. Transitions between strata are one-way, may vary in timing, and may involve marked discontinuities in expected behavior. The perpetual flow of cohorts makes both necessary and crucial the fitting together of people and available roles — thus opening the door to potential conflicts.

The particular configuration of one's social roles is dependent on individual attributes; yet at the same time it reflects certain parameters imposed by structural factors and by the composition of successive biological cohorts. Since each age stratum develops its own characteristic subculture as it moves through time, and because history itself presents subsequent cohorts with their own unique conditions, sequential generations manifest distinctive patterns of aging (Riley et al., 1972; Foner and Kertzer, 1979).

The notion that "age orders both people and roles" is a familiar concept in the anthropological literature but only infrequently has it been applied to modern mass societies. As a fundamental component of social structure, social definitions of age reflect perceived functional requisites seen as essential for maintaining viable social systems. Accordingly, all roles are viewed as having built-in definitions independent of their occupants (Foner, 1975). The question of course is whether all age-related changes operate uniformly for all social classes in a given society. Might not some variation be a result of differential opportunities quite distinct from those associated with aging itself? In fact, there may well be a multifaceted hierarchy wherein age is merely added to ethnicity, sex, socioeconomic status, and so on (Ragan and Wales, 1980).

As shown in Figure 3.2, the age structure of a society is constructed from four primary elements. The first requirement is a population of disparate individuals who can be grouped together on the basis of chronological age or other developmental criteria into a series of *age strata*, a good analogy being seen in the levels of the population pyramids presented in Chapter 1. As these cohorts move through life, innumerable forces impinge on them to alter the overall size and composition of each stratum and, indirectly, the population as a whole. Second, each stratum, because of actual physical, social, or psychological factors, differs from the others in the contributions it makes to ongoing

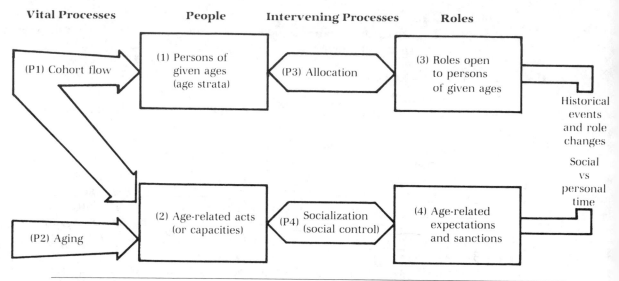

**FIGURE 3.2**

Elements and processes in age stratification theory. (*Source:* Riley, M. W., M. Johnson, and A. Foner. *Aging and Society*, vol. 3: *A Sociology of Age Stratification.* New York: Russell Sage Foundation, Basic Books, Inc., 1972.)

societal needs. *Age-related capacities* of successive strata might vary as a result of the impact of cultural values on the definition of childhood and old age, technological change, or the influence of health factors on physical performance throughout life. Consequently, aging can be viewed either as a movement from one stratum to the next or as an indicator of physical abilities or motivations in other areas of life.

The third ingredient of the model is the patterning and distribution of *social roles*. Age may be a direct linkage — as when biological constraints limit when women may be pregnant, or when age criteria are legally established for voting, holding certain public offices, retirement, and so on. It may also operate indirectly — as when there are socially prescribed parameters for given roles. Examples of these might include the sanctions regarding the appropriate age for high school students or for those desiring to enter medical school or the appropriate age for a junior executive. Most often, age-graded roles appear as sets or constellations of roles simultaneously accessible to people within a certain flexible time; for instance, parents of preschool children are not usually found among the retired or those ensconced in the upper echelons of their occupations. In a general but very real sense the criteria used in establishing the distribution of age-related roles provide a reliable guide to societal priorities and values. Finally there is an element of *age-related expectations* intrinsic to the ways in which people react in the roles they perform. Even when a role may not be closed to a person on the basis of age, age nevertheless influences the perceptions of competence and the finer shadings of performance. What is considered suitable behavior ranges along a sliding scale within the larger definition of the role, thereby allowing people to continue in roles for some time without experiencing serious disjunctures or incongruities.

As originally formulated, the age stratification model also posits a series of interrelated processes affecting the degree of articulation between the structural elements and the rhythm or patterning of individual lives. The two most basic and vital processes are said to be cohort flow and aging. Cohort flow refers to all those factors that contribute to the shaping of the age strata; foremost would of course be fertility, mortality, and migration. Perhaps the best way to illustrate the process of cohort flow is the metaphor used by the authors themselves of people stepping on a conveyor belt at birth. How many and what types of people get on at any two points are never identical, although in every instance those arriving at the bottom at the same time move along collectively. However, they do not remain a completely stable group as they move: some get off by leaving the area (particularly men, by dying; hence proportionately more women continue along after early adulthood). As they move along, some acquire social attributes that come to distinguish them from others, either enhancing or impeding their likelihood of staying on the conveyor belt for the full ride. Eventually, fewer and fewer people are left on the belt, until all of those who began together are dead. As successive cohorts pass by, they alter conditions to such a degree that later groups never encounter the world in exactly the same way.

Interrelating the ideas of age strata and cohort flow provides a means of conceptualizing the dynamic nature of age in determining social location, but it does not explicitly account for individual exceptions or for how mobility from one stratum to the next occurs. For this purpose the age stratification model incorporates the concept of aging as an endemic process taking place on two levels. As we will see in Chapter 4, physiological aging, although fundamental, does not occur in a vacuum; rather, it is influenced by many exogenous factors. Some of these are already apparent, and more will be discussed later as we address the question of health among the elderly. It should be sufficient at this point to note that physical aging is by no means an isolated experience. At the same time aging can be seen as a maturational phenomenon, a measure of acquired experience or knowledge, reflecting the extent of whatever personal resources are available to bolster and guide a person. According to age stratification theory, the nature of aging is inextricably bound

> . . . by the individual's characteristics and dispositions, by the modifications of these characteristics through socialization, by the particular role sequences in which he participates, and by the particular social situations and environmental events he encounters. Hence, it follows that patterns of aging can differ, not only from one society to another and from one country to another, but also among successive cohorts in a single society (Riley et al., 1972).

It is not possible to explain the multifarious differences between strata by referring to age alone; therefore, the age stratification model proposes the intervening processes of allocation and socialization to account for the disparities that arise. *Allocation* refers to the process of assigning and reassigning people of various ages to suitable roles. Although the size and compositions of successive cohorts may change, the functional needs of society evolve at a different rate, necessitating occasional redefinitions of age-appropriate or essential positions to redistribute people in the system's role structure. As people age, they also adopt and abandon a sequence of roles. The process of deciding which people will fill what roles is not, however, always conscious, deliberate, or immutable. Among the examples of allocative processes we could mention are the number of students admitted to college as determined by age, sex, income levels, race, and so on, or the size of the faculty responsible for their instruction. Similarly, age is an important consideration in apportioning the role of parents for those who wish to adopt a child, in filling an executive position, or even for securing certain kinds of fairly menial positions such as a stock clerk in a grocery store. In the case of adoption the age criterion for allocation is often abandoned when the number of children grows too large; or, in the case of new industries, executives may be appreciably younger than in more established spheres. Overall, the criteria used for allocating particular roles or role complexes reflect both social values and the vital processes inherent in aging.

*Socialization,* the other intervening process included in the theory, is a means of ensuring a smooth transition of individuals from one age status to the next. Sociologists previously discussed socialization almost exclusively within the context of childhood, though it has been widely accepted for a number of years that it is a never-ending process, operating throughout life for every role assumed. The age stratification model views individuals as well as entire cohorts as molded by socializing agencies independently and together. Some researchers have suggested that in complex industrial societies, the criteria for role assignments have become increasingly ambiguous, and socialization processes have been weakened to the point of being inoperative. As a consequence, there is an undercurrent of asynchronization, sometimes called role strain or simply personal stress, built into the movement between age strata that requires special attention (Cain, 1964). An obvious example is the need for preretirement counseling to help older workers adjust to their future and to the new roles that present themselves. Preretirement programs are reciprocal, not only in helping a person socialize out of the work role in anticipation of future roles, but at the same time having a latent socializing influence on company policies regarding older workers.

Finally, age stratification theory includes, but does not deal extensively with, a set of exogenous processes not directly linked to age structures, but that nonetheless influences the role available. Some role changes may reflect historical events, as in the relatively few blacksmith positions currently available. Similarly, differences in timing between the life span of a social order and the timetables of individuals are thought to add to the strains experienced as part of aging. Although these external factors impinge on the way people age, they are not explicitly considered by the model. They do, however, remind us that the age-specific elements in society never constitute a complete system, nor can any aspect of aging be adequately understood without referring to the complicated interplay among the factors involved. In spite of the numerous aspects of aging left untouched, the age stratification model offers the most comprehensive theoretical perspective yet developed. Perhaps one of the more significant omissions is any serious discussion of an actor's intentional participation in a process that cannot be mandated entirely by societal constraints. Further, while the authors assert that generations are not limited to mere chronological age groups — that they can be defined by attitudinal variation or perceptual factors — little is made of this important distinction. These unresolved questions do not negate the importance of the age stratification model for greatly expanding the scope of theories and their practical applications in social gerontology.

In light of the difficulties inherent in validating such a global theoretical model it is not surprising that the legacy has been more mundane than originally hoped (Dowd, 1980). A number of commentaries have appeared criticizing the model for its conceptual structure. The notion of age as a hierarchy has been challenged, as has the analogy of age to a status variable such as sex or ethnicity (Cain, 1982). Yet age stratification theory does stress that variable roles undergo historical change, thereby affecting life as it is experienced. Proponents of the model have continued to refine it over the years in response to their own and other's criticisms. Riley (1982), for example, has explicated the intrinsic imbalance between people and roles and has addressed some of the thorny policy issues raised by the model.

Many of the recent theoretical statements in the age stratification perspective have focused on the need to deal more explicitly with the interplay between social change and the relationship of individuals to roles, rights, and responsibilities as these reflect transformations in concepts about human nature. While Riley (1982) alludes to the inherent imbalance contained in the process of role allocation, she skirts the issue of power and its effect on both access and risk taking. Nancy Foner (1982), on the other hand, moves closer to such an examination when she contends that age systems in themselves breed inequality because of their function in the distribution of opportunity structures. Consequently, intergenerational conflict is endemic. Another dimension of Foner's argument is that old age must be removed from its insulated position at the far end of the life cycle and returned to the natural flow of life. If our analyses are to amount to anything, it is time to realize that the continuum runs unbroken. In short, social relations, the division of labor, and the distribution of rights and resources shape and color the content of old age — in fact every age. Certainly this is true at the social level. Here prescriptive practices, based on the control of qualifications and credentials and abetted by a manipulation of essential resources and statutory provisions, determine who will be considered old.

Advocates of age stratification appear keenly aware of the need to give a full and particular account of the mechanisms linking the components of the model together. They are also aware of the criticisms made of the global nature of their theoretical orientation. Perhaps the most influential result has been the development of **cohort analysis** — indexing individual aging and historical change together through the identification of distinct *aging, period,* and **cohort** effects. These have led in turn to a new phase of specification and testing in the quest, now asking "what is it about age that is relevant for understanding some particular age-related phenomenon?" The future of the age stratification model lies in detailed analyses of the processual nature of life course sequences relating individuals to specific dimensions of societal structures (Riley and Campbell, 1979).

## MODERNIZATION THEORY

Modernization theory represents yet another attempt to broaden the horizons of gerontologists by laying the conceptual groundwork for cross-cultural and historical comparisons of the status of the elderly. Together with the age stratification paradigm, it has shown researchers the importance of structural arrangements in the daily lives of older people.

What is called modernization theory had become a central feature of the vocabulary of international social science by the time aging research was beginning to fashion its own theories. It began as a theoretical perspective from an attempt to analyze social evolution as a dynamic process based on certain universal patterns and from the assumption that structural differentiation develops distinctively regardless of context (Parsons, 1964). With each successive phase of development, all aspects of a society were thought to move away from diffused activities based on closed, **ascriptive status** systems with extended kinship networks to technologically intensive, industrial economies based on **achieved status.** Because modernization is a "package," changes begun in one sphere will, through what the language of functionalism termed "eurhythmic changes," spread across all others irreversibly and in short order. Part of the hypothesized reason for a convergence of modern structural characteristics is a need for integration bringing forth administrative bureaucracies, money market economies, rational scientific worldviews, and so on. By means of secondary carriers of modernization, language, religion, and other belief systems, new cultural values appear to justify the emergent dimensions of the human condition. At each stage these values increasingly stress secular, instrumental rationality and contractual relationships (Hendricks, 1982).

Focusing on nation-states and other well-defined geographic units, the modernization paradigm defines all such changes as interrelated, making instrumental or economic rationality the defining criterion for all events. Inevitably, then, similar arrangements will evolve and revise the bases of personal identity (Eisenstadt, 1974). Within gerontology, the focus has been on the ways these transformations affect the roles and statuses accorded to the elderly. Empirical surveys and case studies of societal change seemingly indicate support for the notion that modernization marked the beginning of the end for old people. Most of the research takes as a given Simmons' (1945) early claim that the assets and resources of the elderly were more highly valued in primitive and stable agrarian economies. Simmons' conclusions, based on his analysis of seventy-one preliterate societies, demonstrated that old people were better off before modernization. The bases of their security resided in their traditional skills, control of knowledge, civic and political power, property rights, and the performance of mundane maintenance activities. With rapid social change, the structured framework that favored the elderly, ensured their power, and buttressed their seniority rights disappeared as their roles are usurped and allocated to the young (Simmons, 1960).

In an effort to specify further the role of social change in undermining the position of old people, Cowgill and Holmes (1972), asked contributors to their study to provide information about fifteen societies that would speak of the question of universals accompanying modernization (Shanas, 1963). Consistent with earlier formulations, they maintained there is an inverse relationship between the demographic distribution of the elderly, the rate of social change per se, changes in other related institutional patterns, and the prestige of older people. In thirteen of the original twenty-two orienting propositions, modernization was cast as the independent variable. In another eight the notion was not explicit but was assumed to provide the underpinning. Only one hypothesis, dealing with individual value systems, was disparate with the model. In every instance the factors of modernization, *inter alia*, were found to be inimical to the status of the elderly.

In his later refinement, Cowgill (1979) gives an insightful account of the casual links involved. While contending that it is a complex process, priority is given to scientific technology as it affects economics, urbanization, literacy and mass education, and health technology, which promotes an intergenerational competition for jobs and other roles. In what is surely the most concise exposition in the aging literature, Cowgill elaborates the broad range of changes that accompany primary factors. For example, retirement is institutionalized as a mechanism to ensure a smooth allocation of occupational opportunities to alleviate generational competition. At the same time a consequence of urbanization is mobility and the geographic separation of families that not only relegates the old to the periphery of family life, but also inverts their status (Figure 3.3). Summarizing the chain of events, Cowgill contends it is a functional relationship that converges to depreciate late life.

Many case studies could be cited to sustain the claim, but there is little point in doing so here. More relevant is the fact that numerous indicators of modernity have been used, all with the same result. Indicative of the trend, Palmore and Manton (1974) used the gross national product (GNP), the proportion of workers in agriculture, literacy rates, the percentage of the population in school, and several other related measures to rank thirty-one countries in terms of "development." They found a significant inverse correlation with

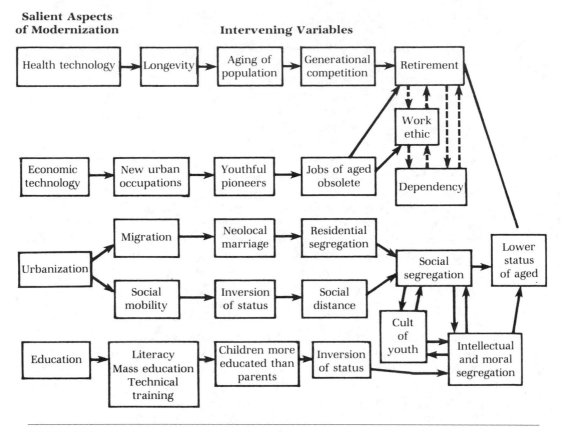

**FIGURE 3.3**

Societal modernization and its impact on the elderly. (*Source:* Cowgill, D. O. "Aging and Modernization: A Revision of the Theory." In *Dimensions of Aging,* eds. J. Hendricks and C. D. Hendricks, pp. 54–67. Cambridge, Mass.: Winthrop Publishers, Inc., 1979.)

relative status for older people throughout. Maxwell and Silverman (1980) developed modernity protocols and applied them to their own selection of twenty-six societies drawn from the Human Relations Area Files. They found information control to be a highly relevant factor for veneration of the elderly, but it was inversely related to modernization. In looking at the esteem of aged Samoans, Maxwell (1980) further noted that as contact with the industrial world increases, bringing about market and exchange relations modeled along western lines, older people are deprived of their central importance in the affairs of daily life, thereby relinquishing their authority and control. Press and McKool (1980) identified the same disruptive factors in Mesolithic American cultures. Correlating six structural components with four role sets, they conclude that the heterogeneity accompanying economic, industrial, and social development is antithetical to a favorable valuation of old people.

As is the case with all attempts to develop explanatory frameworks, criticism and commentaries were forthcoming. All too frequently those who adopt modernization theory cast traditional societies as ideal types, merely as the converse of societies today. While many of the assumptions could be investigated empirically, because the emphasis is elsewhere, they are left as unquestioned assertions. It is crucial to remember, however, that current preindustrial societies may bear little resemblance to their historical counterparts. While each may be said to be moving toward industrial or postindustrial social systems — the fact that the latter already exist and exert influence over the former may be the decisive factor.

The modernization perspective has also been criticized for its tendency to simply dichotomize societal types and ascribe characteristics solely on this basis. As Laslett (1976) has pointed out, gerontology has accepted the proposition of an historical *before/after* bifurcation marked by the onset of industrialization and modernization. As far as old people are concerned, the preexisting form of stratification is assumed to be more favorable because it is thought to incorporate those things that accrete with age. So persuasive is this belief that Laslett terms it "the world we have lost" syndrome. By this he means gerontology has uncritically accepted the idea that prior to the modern era the elderly had valued economic and emotional roles in an extended family setting, thus ensuring that they were accorded universal respect. In the *after* phase values and role definitions have changed, leading to an erosion of the position of the elderly as society develops in a manner in which old people have no valued function at all. As pointed out in Chapter 2, historians are beginning to reanalyze our conception of historical societies and are finding as many exceptions as rules. The result has been a realization that personal lives and structural level factors work together to influence the meaning of old age.

# Emergent Theories in Social Gerontology

Since the mid-1970s theory in social gerontology has become more dynamic, considering structure and people but with people being seen as more intentional and less passive in creating their lives. Exchange theory, again as a spin-off of sociological traditions, was adopted by some theorists as a viable mechanism for explaining how personal resources are used to exercise control over interpersonal relationships and environmental constraints. A new wave of theorizing — political economy — is a radical departure, attempting to identify the roots of varying situations individuals encounter by examining the nature of social structures. Particular attention is paid to the economic and political underpinnings of the arenas within which older people find themselves.

## SOCIAL ENVIRONMENTAL THEORIES

Spurred on by the lucidity of the age stratification paradigm, one approach taken in the latest wave of theorizing has tended to concentrate on the processual nature of all age-related changes. Concerned that it would not be possible to develop predictive models without closer attention to the interaction between people and the context in which they seek fulfillment, recent efforts among social gerontologists have focused on person/environment transactional processes. As Schwartz (1974) points out, the concept of environmental interaction with behavior is well entrenched in human studies. In light of the increasing interdependence between people and their environment with age, it is unfortunate that developments in gerontology have not kept pace, reflecting instead a normative bias in which people are expected to adjust to ongoing societal requirements. The *social environmental* perspective emphasizes the functional context surrounding the daily lives of the elderly. In essence, it is asserted that the values and beliefs generated in particular situations exert an undeniable degree of control over individuals insofar as they constitute the cultural backdrop in which the elderly test their adaptability and personal worth. Adaptation, self-fulfillment, and so on are seen as both active and reactive, negotiated by people in their efforts to master a situation while extracting from it what they need to retain a positive self-concept (Huyck, 1979; Marshall, 1980).

Today variants of the social environmental perspective are being developed to explain both micro (individual level) factors and macro (structural) dimensions of personal well-being. On an individual level one's ability to exert some control over his or her social surroundings may be thought of as a system of exchange. For an older person, or anyone else, to participate satisfactorily in social interaction, there must be a sufficient personal resource inventory. Three basic premises are implicit in nearly all social environmental models: an emphasis on normative expectations derived from particular contexts, attention to individual capacities for interaction, and a focus on the subjectively evaluated correspondence between ability and what is expected in a particular situation. If all three components are reasonably consonant, older people are much more likely to feel a sense of well-being. Yet since each is constantly changing at its own unique rate, adjustment is always contingent on maintaining supportive environments and individual resources for manipulating unfavorable situations (Gubrium, 1973, 1974; Lawton, 1983).

For those who stress individual adaptability, aging is conceived as involving a rebalancing of exchange relationships. The thrust of the exchange model is relatively simple: interaction is predicated on all parties maximizing the rewards to be had from their association while minimizing the costs. In other words, people continue to trade in personal exchange only so long as the benefits of their interaction outweigh the costs. Should the rewards, whether material or nonmaterial, be devalued relative to what must be undergone or foregone to achieve them, social contact will subsequently cease. Naturally an assessment of the costs entailed depends on an appraisal of alternatives for reaching the same goal or a viable substitute (Emerson, 1972). In terms of the interaction of older people, exchange theory explains their shrinking social networks as a realignment of their personal relationships brought about by a debasing of the influence that they are able to exercise over their environments. Without valued skills and finding themselves more often recipients than initiators of personal bonds, the only commodity older people have to bargain with in the social marketplace to win acceptance and support from others is compliance. Hence, for example, they may cultivate the appearance of "mellowness" to avoid alienating the affections of those on whom they depend for their interpersonal ties (Blau, 1973). The link between the ability to control one's environment and a whole gamut of physiological and social factors needs to be specified in far greater detail; however, the exchange paradigm at least permits a consideration of these in the adjustment process of the elderly (Dowd, 1980; Bengtson and Dowd, 1980).

As shown in Figure 3.4, three overlapping dimensions of personal resources are necessary to enable individuals to maximize satisfaction and retain a viable position as creative agents in the exchange process. *Personal-physiological* resources are essential both for bodily and psychological integrity and for active participation in one's environment. In cases of extreme illness or the incapacity of sensory or psychological capabilities, opportunities will be curtailed. The *social-familial* dimension refers to interaction partners, those to whom one turns, whether it is through attempts to influence or for positive reinforcement, to affirm self-concepts. The *fiduciary* dimension reflects what-

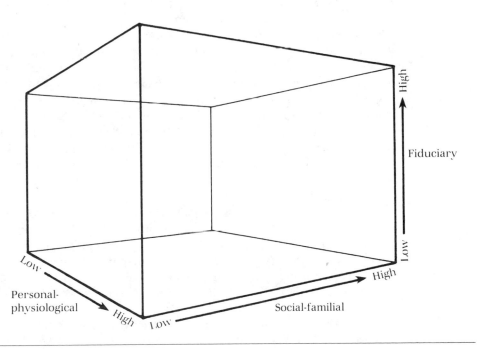

**FIGURE 3.4**
Personal resource dimensions of social life space.

ever the "coin of the realm" is in a particular context. Money is the most familiar example, but goods and services such as information, personal perquisites of many types, privileges, and other barterable items are also included. To participate, to exert one's self through mastery to give what Marshall (1980) refers to as a "sense and semblance of order" to one's *lifescript*, adequate resources must be available. Yet this is exactly the problem for those old people who encounter difficulties in their later years; their power or their resources have diminished. While the exact increments in any of these dimensions cannot be determined apart from the context in which behavior takes place, in an abstract sense they cut across all social and cultural situations.

For purposes of discussion we may refer to the volume of the cube shown in Figure 3.4 as the social life space of older people — defined by the power they can exert over whatever situation they find themselves in. At the same time we may use the volume graphically to represent adjustment. Optimum control of resources, high ratings on all three dimensions, would place an individual in the front upper-right quadrant while a low rating would result in placement in the opposite rear corner. Not only does such a pictorial representation help in conceptualizing the relative resources found in an aggregation of older people, but it also suggests appropriate intervention strategies. Seen in this fashion it is evident that older people's resources must be defined in a context-specific fashion and that their relationships are dependent on negotiations derived from those resources. Adaptability is a dual-edged process of adjusting to and influencing one's environment.

What has been labeled the *social breakdown* theory provides a general but systematic statement of the interdependence between older people and their social world. As initially drafted, the social breakdown syndrome referred to the negative feedback generated by a person already susceptible to psychological problems. Once the cycle is initiated it reinforces everyone's conception of incompetence, thereby ensuring even further difficulties (Zusman, 1966). A parallel is assumed by some gerontologists to exist among older people who encounter societal prejudices about aging. As is the case with anyone else surrounded by unfamiliar circumstances, role loss, or drastic change without adequate preparation, older people reach out for some concrete cues to advise them how they should react. That they must reach out at all is then taken by all parties as an indication of failing capacity, a cause for concern. To elicit further interaction, older persons gradually, almost inadvertently, adopt some of the negative characteristics ascribed to them, thus slipping deeper into a dependent status as the cycle is repeated. In adapting the social breakdown model to explain aging in modern societies, as illustrated in Figure 3.5, Kuypers and Bengtson (1973) assert the continuing adherence to the middle-age values of visible productivity, so prevalent in American society, practically assures an invitation to involvement in the breakdown syndrome.

There are, however, alternatives available that might lessen the probability of social breakdown. Intervention in the cycle through providing opportunities for older people to enhance their sense of competence in appropriate-

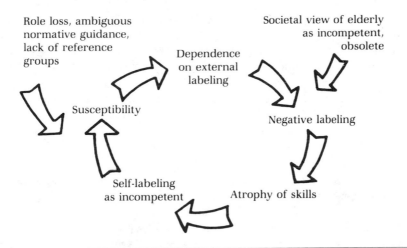

**FIGURE 3.5**

The social breakdown cycle in old age. (*Source:* Kuypers, J. A., and V. R. Bengtson. "Social Break-down and Competence: A Model of Normal Aging." *Human Development* 26, 3 [1973]: 190.)

ly structured environments free from the dominance of general societal values engenders the possibility of breaking the spiral, or of replacing it with what Kuypers and Bengtson term a "reconstruction syndrome." By improving environmental supports while facilitating an expression of personal strengths, if in no other way than recognizing the tendency toward inferiority or allow-ing older people to make independent decisions, the forces leading to break-down could be ameliorated within a positive interactive environment (Figure 6.6). Shifting the focus from general theoretical explanations or the narrow emphasis on the continuity of personality traits to one that attempts to align personal factors, including self-labeling, with a fluid responsive world will, ac-cording to those espousing a social environmental model, allow for effective participation by older people. In the view of Kuypers and Bengtson the place to begin is with a model having practical applicability at the individual level, since it is unlikely the larger society will furnish alternative environments when dominant values are what brought about the situation in the first place. Restructuring the environment will be by no means simple, as all sponsors of an environmental approach realize, but even small gains will improve our chances for ensuring a satisfying life among the elderly, paving the way for the eventual acknowledgment of the potential inhumanity of unresponsive societal institutions (Lawton, 1983).

A second facet of a social environmental approach concentrates on differ-ential resource allocation and access as influenced by the nature of social class or other structural factors. Although these theories share the same premise that behavior is inevitably embedded in the social world, there is a significant difference in their assumptions about the nature of structural components shaping the lives of individuals. Most explanatory frameworks, at least as they are formulated by social scientists in North America, tend to reflect an incrementalist and individualistic approach to the analysis of social problems of old people. That is, while these theories attempt to combine structural and micro-level variables, factors such as "social class" become a characteristic of the individual, something to be noted when delineating attributes that contribute to such things as self-esteem. Essentially the structure of society itself is taken as a given, and the focus is on how individuals vary within that system.

## POLITICAL ECONOMY

A new orientation in theorizing attempts to tie individual experiences to macro-level structural factors by investigating the nature of the structure itself. Although differences among individuals are not ignored, these variations are linked to the location of older persons within particular types and sub-types of social systems. Supposed deficiencies (or the opposite) in human attributes cannot be used as the sole explanatory variable in predicting such things as life satisfaction; the nature of the distinctive qualities of the social relations growing out of the organization of different social systems must also be taken into account (Estes et al., 1982).

Without meaning to oversimplify or state a one-to-one correspondence between the following approaches, it is useful for conceptual purposes to subsume these theories under the general rubric "political economy." Usually taken to imply a more radical framework, the starting point for these analyses is the relationship between the distribution of power and the form of economic organization. There is nothing static about this relation; while the mode of production in many countries could be characterized as capitalistic — based on free market economies — the mode of organization in such markets themselves is in flux. The simple observation that the economy in the colonial United States or in the 1800s was quite different from today's is indicative of the kind of change discussed. Similarly, there is no unified group that dominates all others; rather, while power may be intimately tied to position in the socioeconomic structure, it is something that cannot be taken for granted and must be constantly reasserted (Hendricks and Calasanti, 1986). Hence no one structure is taken as a given; in explaining the life of older people, the particular political economic context at the time of interest must be carefully specified and examined. Thus, changes that have come about over time are viewed not as evolutionary concomitants of modernization but as shifts in the relations between individuals and groups as socioeconomic beings. Because power is vested in one broad age category after another, as is suggested by the age stratification paradigm, the lives of those beyond the boundaries of the category are structured by those who hold the power. As a consequence, retirement problems, for example, do not simply revolve around socialization to new roles, but involve the process of allocating the roles themselves. Why are proportionately fewer people in their sixties in the labor force in 1986 than in

1946? How does this reflect and reshape the political economic context? Each of the following models attempts, albeit at times somewhat differently, to formulate concepts that in one way or another acknowledge the association between power differentials and economic organization, even though these perspectives differ in terms of the unit of analysis. While all are concerned with the overarching context, some comparisons are made on a global level, and others use smaller geographical units, such as nations, or focus on one particular mode of economic organization.

**Dependency Theory.** Dependency theory uses an adapted version of the world systems perspective (Langholm, 1971; Wallerstein, 1974) for cross-cultural comparisons. The unit of analysis is not particular nations but the interaction between advantaged core areas and peripheral locales. In the beginning some particular locale may have a wealth of resources: it is a port of call, a communications hub, has an abundance of material resources, is occupied by an elite group, or is otherwise advantaged. It is a nucleus, a core or central place from which innovations emerge. Beyond the center is a peripheral region less advantaged and perhaps set apart by distinct language, government, agricultural production, religion, and related social patterns. A symbiotic relationship develops because each region has something to offer the other, be it raw materials or markets for finished products. This interaction does not bring commonality as the modernization perspective would have it, but a lopsided duality by which the dominant core grows more complex while the periphery becomes a satellite.

It is not that the outlying area is totally vanquished. This would not be in the best long-run interests of the core. Development is encouraged, but the forms of urbanization, industrialization, commercialization of agriculture, political reform, and so on are designed to ensure the continuing benefit of the core. With those benefits, the core is able to expand its catchment area, thereby fostering a specialized regional development that will assure its ascendancy. There is no doubt the standard of living rises in the periphery, but cash crops replace subsistence agriculture, and the growth of the production of material goods is concentrated on those produced, designed, and destined for the core. Per capita income may well increase, but growth in real earnings is likely to be confined to a small minority in the employ of core interests. Finally, other indicators of modernization may likewise increase. Railway lines, roads, communication, and social services are improved but primarily in central enclaves or along supply corridors (Hechter, 1975; Hoogvelt, 1977).

As technology is imported and development induced, entrenched hierarchies based on old-line subsistence activities will be restructured to reflect the dominant influence of the export economy. There will probably be unequal pockets of surplus labor, and state, local, and other public services will be channeled to fit the image of the future held by the new elite bourgeoisie. As it gains momentum, the decisions made by the new agencies will acquire the power of normative accord. The impact of this changeover includes a complete restructuring of domestic social orders together with the demise of pre-contact relations of production (Portes, 1976).

From the standpoint of the dependency theorist, the interaction between core and peripheral regions and the differential location of older persons within this area circumscribe the experiences of aging individuals. While in agreement that the status of older people has been debased in the process of industrialization, gerontologists who advocate this alternative interpretation focus on the political economy as it influences the definition of what it means to be old. The "structured dependency of the elderly" (Townsend, 1981) comes about because of changes in their relative abilities or "use value." Such an assertion is based on the supposition that economic systems set the broad parameters of all social organization. By focusing on the relations of production, a dependency/world systems theorist examines the situation of the elderly in terms of the interactive process that depreciates the old not merely because they are elderly, but because they also embody values or behaviors that may be inimical to core interests. Thus, modernization is seen not as a broad-ranging process wherein inequalities are an unintended and unfortunate consequence. Rather, disadvantages for the elderly stem from interest group politics and deliberate structural arrangements brought about by those who control new components of industrial production (Myles, 1980; Dowd, 1980; Neysmith and Edwardh, 1984; Tigges and Cowgill, 1981). Such politics cause problems for the elderly in the periphery, but not necessarily for those in the core.

Looking at the membership in either the core or the periphery may shed a new light on old age inequalities not disclosed by simple neoclassical economic models or modernization perspectives. Core membership may carry with it certain advantages making for a more satisfying old age not available to those in the periphery. For example, in an early effort to identify actual policy outcomes of structured dependency, Neysmith and Edwardh (1984) refer to the widening income gap between those working for the interests of developed countries and the residual population left behind in subsistence agriculture. In their opinion the pattern of health insurance, pension programs, unemployment, job security, the status accorded to women, and so on all reflect core-periphery distinctions. In each instance a disproportionate share of surplus economic fringe benefits will be given those affiliated with core interests, while those functioning in the periphery economy will be left out to a greater or lesser extent. Furthermore, as the gains of the core are solidified, social policies increasingly stress the assumption of individual or private responsibility during times of need. If the elderly are indigent, this is attributed to personal or familial shortcomings rather than a reflection of state intervention, manipulation, or policies. If market economies are fostered and cost-benefit ratios stressed at the expense of humanitarian values, then old people are bound to be challenged as to whether they are entitled to a share of the accumulated wealth.

**Internal Colonialism.** Internal colonialism is another model similar to the dependency perspective, but the unit of analysis is more circumscribed, relating to unequal development within a single set of national boundaries. Seen in basic geographic terms, a *polis* and the bureaucratic apparatus lodged therein exert influence over a hinterland. Because of technological supremacy or any other form of superior power, nearly all aspects of the peripheral region eventually come under the domination of decisions made by agencies that do not directly participate in the life of the provinces. To put it another way, the metropolis is the mother of the satellite, mediating the satellite's activities on the basis of determinations that reflect its own vested interests.

In discussing the colonial situation in the abstract, Hechter (1975) points to the way in which the metropolitan culture is superimposed over existing systems of differentiation, furthering the strain toward duality. To the extent that local people adopt this culture they will be rewarded, as with, for example, entry into higher status occupations; resistance, on the other hand, means being relegated to the bottom of the stratification ladder. In every instance, however, leadership positions tend to be reserved for those from the center itself. Because of the hegemony present throughout, the economics, commerce, administrative structures, and, ultimately, even the social programming of the periphery develop in complement to the core. Consequently, the values and the ideology of the periphery come to represent a kind of jingoism of the mind.

As a conceptual model, internal colonialism initially concentrated on geographic relationships and was replete with arguments about agricultural shifts, exploitation of natural resources, labor mobilization, and so on — all seen as developed primarily to be beneficial to the core. A second use of the internal colonialism replaces the spatial definitions of core and periphery with a figurative, symbolic relationship. In this case people of the hinterlands are marked not by territory but by social and psychological distance from the centers of power. Those on either side of the resultant power relationship become a distinctive status group, isolated from their counterparts by stereotype and myth. Borrowing a phrase from Gamson (1968), Hechter (1975) argues that once initiated, the politics of "stable unrepresentation" ensures the perpetuation of inequalities. With the addition of the realities of residential or occupational segregation, or with any other visible sign of separateness, the disadvantages will multiply. The disjuncture between this emblematic core and the periphery is no less acute, and may even be more real. Roles open to individuals and their access to the decision-making process, as well as their very consciousness, are de facto consequences of their position vis-à-vis control of socially meaningful resources. Internal colonialism has not been overtly applied to the study of the elderly in the United States.

**Dual Economy Models.** A dual economy model has begun to appear in the gerontological literature because of concern with unequal development in economic organization. It starts from the premise that contemporary market economies can no longer be depicted as encompassing a single competitive enterprise; over the last century, radical changes in the organization of the economy have left a significant share of productive capacity in the hands of a relatively small monopoly. The result is a bifurcation within capitalism, with center or core industries dominating the economic scene, while peripheral industries comprise firms struggling within a still competitive environment.

As characterized by Bluestone et al. (1973):

> The core economy includes those industries that comprise the muscle of American economic and political power. . . . Entrenched in durable manufacturing, the construction trades and to a lesser extent, the extraction industries, the firms in the core economy are noted for high productivity, high profits, intensive utilization of capital, and a high degree of unionization. What follows normally from such characteristics are high wages. The automobile, steel, rubber, aluminum, aerospace, and petroleum industries are ranking members of this part of the economy. Workers who are able to secure employment in these industries are, in most cases, assured of relatively high wages and better than average working conditions and fringe benefits. . . .

Beyond the fringes of the core economy lies a set of industries that lack almost all of the advantages normally found in center firms. Concentrated in agriculture, nondurable manufacturing, retail trade, and subprofessional services, the peripheral industries are noted for their small size, labor intensity, low profits, low productivity, intensive product market competition, lack of unionization, and low wages. Unlike core sector industries, the periphery lacks the assets, size, and political power to take advantage of economies of scale or to spend large sums on research and development.

Firms located within these industries reflect these characteristics, and the experiences of workers in them are circumscribed by this structure. For example, core firms tend to be capital intensive and use the latest technology; since workers must be trained to use this technology, they are an investment to their employers. As a result, they can command higher wages, job stability, pensions, and other benefits. The structure of the periphery, on the other hand, does not give employees the same source of power; as a result, these workers tend to be disadvantaged vis-à-vis their core counterparts. Thus, merely comparing occupational titles of employees cannot explain the wide-ranging disparities in income often found (Gordon, 1972); ultimately, such measures remain at the level of individual attributes because they ignore the structural location of jobs.

A more detailed description of research in this area will appear in the chapter on retirement. Yet it is apparent here that sectoral differences point to structural inequalities that arguably carry over into old age. Research has found that core and peripheral enterprises stratify workers on the basis of sex and race, with white men predominating in the more advantageous core sector (Tolbert et al., 1980; Hendricks and McAllister, 1983; Calasanti, 1985); such differential placement helps explain why women, for example, are more likely to be poor in old age (O'Rand and Henretta, 1982). Essentially the lack of control over resources earlier in one's life extends into the retirement years; it cannot be simply accounted for on the basis of personal characteristics. Even such indicators as "years in the labor force" can be misleading, because the structure of the periphery mandates intermittent work histories. Given the lack of career mobility between sectors (Tolbert, 1982), it becomes obvious that an individual's access to opportunity can be greatly constrained or enhanced by sectoral placement. Of course, it should be noted that while the organization of modern free market economics exerts considerable influence over individual experience, this does not mean that no vertical stratification exists within sectors or that human attributes do not make a difference. However, the "difference" that personal characteristics do make are further delimited by structural location, when greater education, for example, may increase the ability to command higher wages in the core while the same incremental change may not lead to remunerative enhancements for peripheral employees. In any case the point here is that the monopolistic pattern empirically identifiable in modern industrial systems circumscribes access to a wide range of opportunities for the elderly. It can affect not only the resources available to individuals but also their very outlook on life, including happiness in the latter stages of the life cycle (Dowd, 1980).

Beginning with the life course in general, it is apparent that the experiences of the elderly are affected by and affect structural arrangements in their access to opportunities. More specifically, the availability of medical care and the quality of nutrition, on the one hand, and differential patterns of retirement, on the other, are each intimately tied to structural level socioeconomic patterns. These in turn have crucial influences on the lives of older people. More sophisticated medical technology is available to members of the core; nutrition among poorer (peripheral) elderly is often marginal, putting them at a double disadvantage given their inability to acquire adequate medical care. One advocate of the political economy approach to medical care has aptly demonstrated that structure plays a significant role in the physical quality of life. A series of national studies reveals that both morbidity and mortality rates differ significantly among lower and upper level occupations, reflecting in many instances a differential exposure to health hazards and adequate care that are conditioned by structural location (Navarro, 1976a, 1976b, 1982).

Similarly, patterns of retirement reflect core and peripheral membership, whether that designation is at the intranational or international level. The elderly located in peripheral countries without institutionalized retirement plans are often forced to continue work when they are no longer capable, to be dependent on family and others, or to be left without resources altogether. Former peripheral employees in nations such as the United States that have a dual economic system do not reap the same benefits from nationally institutionalized retirement schemes as their core counterparts. Advantaged workers can accumulate assets for their past work years as well as count on much higher pensions, better medical care, and so on.

Beyond these basic issues, structural factors also have a profound effect on the everyday life of the elderly: their degree of participation in the life of the society, the range of their contacts, and the richness and variety of their lives. Those who continue to work may have more chance of being actively engaged in society than those who retire. Retired professionals and executives are often at the center of things, remaining active in community life, while those from the periphery who experience attrition of their social roles feel removed and isolated. Money, or the lack of it, drastically affects one's social life space. Those on severely limited incomes cannot afford to participate in many activities. In our highly mobile society, if they live at some distance from other members of their family, they will have less frequent contact. Education also tends to maintain the lifeworld of the elderly, by increasing inner resources for dealing with the vicissitudes of aging, knowing how to draw on what resources and support systems available, and having something to offer to the young.

Finally, extrapolation from these perspectives suggests that even the definition and evaluation of the self is closely tied to structural considerations (Estes et al., 1982). For example, in western industrial societies where personal worth is measured by income, an abrupt reduction in income at retirement may lead to a loss of self-esteem. Add in the potential for psychological distress resulting from inadequate nutrition, lack of access to medical care, and generally reduced circumstances, and the prospects can become even more bleak. A lack of access to political power may also increase feelings of inadequacy. This means that those who manage to retain both income and influence will tend to feel differently about themselves in old age than those who do not. Indeed, a major tenet of political economic approaches is that we cannot simply speak of the aged as a homogeneous group; while structural factors may cause the majority of elderly in one country to be devalued, in societies such as the United States where the state is involved in a struggle for both fiscal and social solvency, certain segments of older persons fare rather well while others reinforce the dependent stereotype. Of course, this is not to say that personal factors are unimportant; rather, individual characteristics are always a part of a context that may shape, reflect, respect, or devalue such attributes.

## Summary

Social gerontology has not escaped the common plight confronting most disciplines that attempt to integrate the theoretical with the applied. Solutions nearly always appear couched in the language used to formulate the problems. To date the theoretical frameworks are neither all that they should be nor could be, but the growth of explanatory models witnessed in the last decade or so definitely has laid the groundwork for significant advances in the near future. Along the way one of the primary lessons learned has been that "facts" can vary, depending on the point being made.

One of the original theoretical attempts, disengagement theory, with its assertion that aging is a process of quietly receding from view or at least of withdrawing from active participation, quickly met with criticism from all sides. Especially vocal were those activity theorists who contended older people do not change their minds about the importance of being involved even when they can no longer keep pace with the world around them. In an effort to account for differential adjustment among those who withdraw, as well as those who remain active, Rose (1965) suggested the possibility of an aged subculture, very much the counterpart of the widely recognized youth movement associated with the late 1960s. By becoming their own reference group and by recognizing their common predicament, older people will develop a new basis for adaptation, claims Rose, even to the point of evolving into a social movement with a political voice. Not content with any of these descriptions of why older people experience and react with the feelings they do, social-psychologically oriented gerontologists expressed reservations, asserting instead that it all depends on a person's psychological makeup and habitual methods of coping. It is true, they noted, that roles themselves may be discontinuous, but people are not; the repertoire of responses developed throughout a lifetime is not suddenly abandoned on the threshold of old age.

In the next wave of theoretical development the focus shifted to macro-level structural factors and the impact they have on the process of aging. Age stratification theory is an attempt to formulate a whole life conception of aging. A complicated model to say the least, age stratification views old age as a process of becoming socialized to new or revised role definitions, reflecting a fluid relationship among people, their social contexts, and their opportunities. How much change must be accommodated by individual actors is difficult to predict; it is dependent on an intertwined series of feedback loops revolving around the size of the aging population, the roles available, and the differences in the timing of individual and social needs.

Modernization theory has also focused attention on societal change and individuals' aging. Used primarily in cross-cultural and historical surveys, the model contends that structural factors undergoing alteration as societies develop mean important shifts in the roles accorded to people. Those whose skills most aptly fit an earlier era are thought to be particularly hard hit.

Exchange and social environmental perspectives depict aging as a negotiated sequence depending on resources held by the trading partners. Somewhat more situational than either of the two structural points of view that preceded them, the exchange and socioenvironmental theories posit a reciprocal process wherein actor and context shape one another.

Finally, the newest theories in social gerontology adopt a broad political economy approach. Once again the starting point is in the tradition of the older disciplines of sociology and economics. Application to questions of aging, however, has highlighted the point that context, actor, and theoretical model share a common root. Furthermore, the factors shaping all three reflect political and market ideologies. Implicit is the contention that all so-called statements of fact are also ideological.

# Discussion Questions

**Need for Theories**

1. In the discussion question about changes in the situation of older people in Chapter 1 you were asked to suggest some solutions. Now try to formulate a theory about the problem, your solution, and the links between the two.

**Making Sense of Aging**

2. How might your major or chosen profession, your economic and social situations and those of your parents, the historical circumstances in which you were born and grew up, and what you think is important in life influence what you think about the aging process?

**Evaluating Theories**

See questions on specific theoretical orientations.

**Focus of Social Gerontology**

3. How might the realization that retirement age is a socially constructed norm benefit both individuals and society?

**Explaining the Aging Experience**

4. What are the advantages and disadvantages of developing distinct theories about aging as a separate social process?

**Disengagement and Activity Theories**

5. a. What is disengagement theory trying to explain? Can you think of any physical or biological reasons why disengagement might take place?
   b. Are there phenomena or levels of analysis ignored by disengagement theory? If so, how does this affect the adequacy of disengagement theory?
   c. What perspective do you think disengagement theory starts from?

6. a. What is activity theory trying to explain? How well does it do this?
   b. Are there phenomena or levels of analysis ignored by activity theory? If so, how does this affect the adequacy of activity theory?

7. Do you think disengagement or an uncritical adherence to societally dominant value systems are the only alternatives open to the elderly? What other alternatives might there be?

8. The findings of Longino and Kart (1982) indicate well-being is enhanced by meaningful interaction with others. How would you characterize meaningful interaction? How do meaningful interaction, going through the motions, and disengagement differ from each other?

**Subcultural Theory**

9. a. What is subcultural theory trying to explain? How well does it do this?
   b. Are there phenomena or levels of analysis ignored by subcultural theory? If so, how does this affect the adequacy of subcultural theory?
   c. What perspective do you think subcultural theory starts from?

10. What might be the advantages and disadvantages of associating only with members of one's own subculture?

**Continuity Theory**

11. a. What is continuity theory trying to explain? How well does it do this?
    b. Are there phenomena or levels of analysis ignored by continuity theory? If so, how does this affect the adequacy of continuity theory?
    c. From whose or what perspective do you think continuity theory was developed?

12. What are the relative advantages and disadvantages of an internal focus (stable character norms) as opposed to an external focus (orientation to cultural and external norms) in adapting to changing social circumstances during the aging process?

13. Do you think people's characters change as they grow older? If so, how and why?

**Second Generation Theories**

14. Are there phenomena or levels of analysis that are taken into account by (a) age stratification theory and (b) modernization theory that were *not* addressed by early theoretical developments?

15. Are there any phenomena or levels of analysis that are ignored by (a) age stratification theory and (b) modernization theory? If so, how does this affect their adequacy as theories?

**Modernization Theory**

16. How have changes that have taken place during the lifetimes of people who are old today affected what they are now experiencing?

**Emergent Theories**

17. Are there any aspects of social life taken into account by (a) social environmental theory and (b) political economy that were ignored by earlier theories? How do the approaches

of social environmental theories and political economy differ from each other?

**18.** How do dependency theory, internal colonization, and dual economy models differ from each other?

**19.** Compare and contrast social environmental theories and the focus of political economy. To what extent do these theories deal with different questions and levels of analysis, and to what extent are they mutually exclusive?

# Pertinent Readings

Allen, V. L., and E. van de Vliert. *Role Transformations: Exploration and Explanations.* New York: Plenum Publishing Corporation, 1984.

Atchley, R. C. "Disengagement Among Professors." *Journal of Gerontology* 26, 4 (1971): 476–80.

Back, K. W. "Personal Characteristics and Social Behavior: Theory and Method." In *Handbook of Aging and the Social Sciences*, eds. R. H. Binstock and E. Shanas, pp. 403–31. New York: Van Nostrand Reinhold Company, 1976.

Bengtson, V. L., and J. J. Dowd. "Sociological Functionalism, Exchange Theory and Life Cycle Analysis." *International Journal of Aging and Human Development* 12, 1 (1980): 55–73.

Blau, Z. S. *Old Age in a Changing Society.* New York: New Viewpoints, a Division of Franklin Watts, Inc., 1973.

Bluestone, B., W. M. Murphy, and M. Stevenson. *Low Wages and the Working Poor.* Ann Arbor: The Institute of Labor and Industrial Relations, 1973.

Breytspraak, L. M. *The Development of Self in Later Life.* Boston: Little, Brown & Company, 1984.

Brim, O. G., Jr. "Foreword," In *Aging and Society*, vol. 3: *A Sociology of Age Stratification*, by M. W. Riley, M. Johnson, and A. Foner, pp. ix–xii. New York: Russell Sage Foundation, 1972.

Bronfenbrenner, U. *The Ecology of Human Development.* Cambridge, Mass.: Howard University Press, 1979.

Cain, L. D., Jr. "Life Course and Social Structure." In *Handbook of Modern Sociology*, ed. R. E. L. Faris, pp. 272–309. Chicago: Rand McNally & Company, 1964.

———. "Age Stratification Versus Age Status: Implications for Practice." Paper presented to World Congress of Sociology, Mexico City, 1982.

Calasanti, T. "Participation in a Dual Economy and Adjustment to Retirement." *The International Journal of Aging and Human Development* 21 (1985).

Covey, H. C. "A Reconceptualization of Continuity Theory: Some Preliminary Thoughts." *The Gerontologist* 21, 6 (1981): 628–33.

Cowgill, D. O. "Aging and Modernization: A Revision of the Theory." In *Dimensions of Aging*, eds. J. Hendricks and C. D. Hendricks, pp. 54–67. Cambridge, Mass.: Winthrop Publishers, Inc., 1979.

———, and L. D. Holmes. *Aging and Modernization.* New York: Appleton-Century-Crofts, 1972.

Cumming, E. "Further Thoughts on the Theory of Disengagement." *International Social Science Journal* 15, 3 (1963): 377–93.

———. "Engagement with an Old Theory." *Aging and Human Development* 6, 3 (1975): 187–91.

———, L. R. Dean, D. S. Newell, and I. McCaffrey. "Disengagement — A Tentative Theory of Aging." *Sociometry* 23, 1 (1960): 23.

———, and W. E. Henry. *Growing Old: The Process of Disengagement.* New York: Basic Books, Inc., 1961.

Dowd, J. J. "Aging as Exchange: A Preface to Theory." *Journal of Gerontology* 30, 5 (1975): 584–94.

———. *Stratification Among the Aged.* Monterey, Calif.: Brooks/Cole Publishing Company, 1980.

Eisenstadt, S. N. "Studies of Modernization and Sociological Theory." *History and Theory* 13, 2 (1974): 225–52.

Emerson, R. M. "Exchange Theory, Parts I & II." In *Sociological Theories in Progress,* vol. II, eds. J. Berger, M. Zelditch, and B. Anderson, pp. 38–87. Boston: Houghton Mifflin, 1972.

Estes, C., J. H. Swan, and L. E. Gerard. "Dominant and Competing Paradigms in Gerontology: Towards a Political Economy of Aging." *Aging and Society* 2, 2 (1982): 151–64.

Foner, A. "Age in Society: Structure and Change." *American Behavioral Scientist* 22, 2 (1975): 144–65.

———, and D. Kertzer. "Intrinsic and Extrinsic Sources of Change in Life-Course Transitions." In *Aging from Birth to Death,* ed. M. W. Riley, pp. 121–36. Boulder, Colo.: Westview Press, 1979.

Foner, N. "Some Consequences of Age Inequality in Non-Industrial Societies." In *Aging from Birth to Death,* vol. 2: *Sociotemporal Perspectives,* eds. M. W. Riley, R. P. Ables, and M. S. Teltelbaum, pp. 71–86. Boulder, Colo.: Westview Press, 1982.

Fox, J. H. "Perspectives on the Continuity Perspective." *International Journal of Aging and Human Development* 14, 2 (1981–1982): 97–115.

Gamson, W. A. "Stable Unrepresentation in American Society." *American Behavioral Scientist* 12 (1968): 15–21.

George, L. K. *Role Transitions in Later Life.* Monterey, Calif.: Brooks/Cole Publishing Company, 1980.

Gordon, D. M. "From Steam Whistles to Coffee Breaks." *Dissent* (Winter 1972): 197–210.

Gubrium, J. F. *The Myth of the Golden Years: A Socio-Environmental Theory of Aging.* Springfield, Ill.: Charles C Thomas, Publisher, 1973.

———. "Toward a Socio-Environmental Theory of Aging." *The Gerontologist* 12, 3, Pt. 1 (1974): 281–84.

Havighurst, R. J. "A Social-Psychological Perspective on Aging." *The Gerontologist* 8, 2 (1968): 67–71.

———, and R. Albrecht. *Older People.* New York: Longmans, Green, 1953.

———, J. M. A. Munnichs, B. Neugarten, and H. Thomae. *Adjustment to Retirement.* Assen, The Netherlands: Van Gorcum & Comp. N. V., 1969.

———, B. Neugarten, and S. S. Tobin. "Disengagement and Patterns of Aging." In *Middle Age and Aging,* ed. B. L. Neugarten, pp. 161–72. Chicago: University of Chicago Press, 1968.

Hechter, M. *Internal Colonialism: The Celtic Fringe in British National Development, 1536–1966.* Berkeley: University of California Press, 1975.

Hendricks, J. "The Elderly in Society: Beyond Modernization." *Social Science History* 6, 3 (1982): 321–45.

———, and T. M. Calasanti. "Social Policy on Ageing in North America." In *Ageing and Social Policy: A Critical Assessment*, eds. C. Phillipson and A. Walker. London: Heinemann Educational Books, 1986.

———, and C. E. McAllister. "An Alternative Perspective on Retirement: A Dual Economic Approach." *Ageing and Society* 3, 3 (1983): 279–99.

Henry, W. E. "Engagement and Disengagement: Toward a Theory of Adult Development." In *Contributions to the Psychobiology of Aging*, ed. R. Kastenbaum, pp. 19–35. New York: Springer Publishing Company Inc., 1965.

Hochschild, A. R. *The Unexpected Community*. Englewood Cliffs, N.J.: Prentice-Hall, Inc., 1973.

———. "Disengagement Theory: A Critique and Proposal." *American Sociological Review* 40, 5 (1975): 553–69.

Hoogvelt, A. M. M. *The Sociology of Developing Societies*. Atlantic Heights, N.J.: Humanities Press, 1977.

Huyck, M. H. "Psychological Perspectives on Adaptation in Later Life." In *Recent Advances in Gerontology*, eds. H. Orimo, K. Shimada, M. Iriki, and D. Maeda, pp. 643–48. Amsterdam: Excerpta Medica, 1979.

Kerckhoff, A. C. "The Status Attainment Process: Socialization or Allocation?" *Social Forces* 55, 2 (1976): 368–81.

Kuypers, J. A., and V. L. Bengtson, "Social Breakdown and Competence: A Model of Normal Aging." *Human Development* 26, 3 (1973): 181–201.

Langholm, S. "On the Concepts of Center and Periphery." *Journal of Peace Research* 8, 3 (1971): 273–78.

Laslett, P. "Societal Development and Aging." In *Handbook of Aging and Social Sciences*, eds. R. H. Binstock and E. Shanas, pp. 3–34. New York: Van Nostrand Reinhold Company, 1976.

Lawton, M. P. "Environment and Other Determinants of Well-Being in Older People." *The Gerontologist* 23, 4 (1983): 349–57.

Lemon, B. W., V. L. Bengtson, and J. A. Petersen. "An Exploration of the Activity Theory of Aging: Activity Types and Life Expectation among Inmovers to a Retirement Community." *Journal of Gerontology* 27, 4 (1972): 511–23.

Liang, J., L. Dvorkin, E. Kahana, and F. Mazian. "Social Integration and Morale: A Reexamination." *Journal of Gerontology* 35 (1980): 746–57.

Longino, C. F., and C. S. Kart. "Explicating Activity Theory: A Formal Replication." *Journal of Gerontology* 37, 6 (1982): 713–22.

Maddox, G. L. "Disengagement Theory: A Critical Evaluation." *The Gerontologist* 4, 2 (1964): 80–82.

———. "Themes and Issues in Sociological Theories of Human Aging." *Human Development* 13, 1 (1970): 17–27.

———, and J. Wiley. "Scope, Concepts and Methods in the Study of Aging." In *Handbook of Aging and the Social Sciences*, eds. R. H. Binstock and E. Shanas, pp. 3–34. New York: Van Nostrand Reinhold Company, 1976.

Marshall, V. W. "No Exit: A Symbolic Interactionist Perspective on Aging." In *Being and Becoming Old*, ed. J. Hendricks, pp. 20–32. Farmingdale, N.Y.: Baywood Publishing Company, Inc., 1980.

———, and J. A. Tindale. "Notes for a Radical Gerontology." *International Journal of Aging and Human Development* 9, 2 (1978–1979): 163–75.

Maxwell, R. J. "The Changing Status of Elders in Polynesian Society." In *In the Country of the Old*, ed. J. Hendricks, pp. 57–66. Farmingdale, N.Y.: Baywood Publishing Company, 1980.

————, and P. Silverman. "Information and Esteem: Cultural Considerations in the Treatment of the Aged." In *In the Country of the Old*, ed. J. Hendricks, pp. 3–34. Farmingdale, New York: Baywood Publishing Company, 1980.

McClelland, K. A. "Self-Conception and Life Satisfaction: Integrating Aged Subculture and Activity Theory." *Journal of Gerontology* 37, 6 (1982): 723–32.

McCrae, R. R., and P. T. Costa, Jr. *Emerging Lives, Enduring Dispositions*. Boston: Little, Brown & Company, 1984.

Miller, S. J. "The Social Dilemma of the Aging Leisure Participant." In *Older People and Their Social World*, eds. A. M. Rose and W. A. Peterson, pp. 77–92. Philadelphia: F. A. Davis Company, 1965.

Myles, J. "The Aged, the State and the Structure of Inequality." In *Structured Social Inequality*, eds. J. Harp and J. Hofley, pp. 317–42. Toronto: Prentice-Hall, 1980.

Navarro, V. *Medicine under Capitalism*. New York: Predist, 1976a.

————. "The Political and Economic Determinants of Health and Health Care in Rural America." *Inquiry* 13, 2 (1976b): 111–21.

————. *Imperialism, Health and Medicine*. Farmingdale, N.Y.: Baywood Publishing Company, 1982.

Neugarten, B. L., R. J. Havighurst, and S. S. Tobin. "Personality and Patterns of Aging." In *Middle Age and Aging*, ed. B. L. Neugarten, pp. 173–77. Chicago: University of Chicago Press, 1968.

Neysmith, S., and J. Edwardh. "Economic Dependency in the 1980s: Its Impact on Third World Elderly." *Ageing and Society* 4, 1 (1984): 21–44.

O'Rand, A., and J. Henretta. "Midlife Work History and Retirement Income." In *Women's Retirement: Policy Implications of Recent Research*, ed. M. E. Szinovacz, pp. 25–44. Beverly Hills, CA.: Russell Sage Publications, Inc., 1982.

Palmore, E., ed. *Normal Aging*. Durham, N.C.: Duke University Press, 1970.

————, and K. Manton. "Modernization and Status of the Aged: International Correlations." *Journal of Gerontology* 29 (1974): 205–10.

Parsons, T. "Evolutionary Universals." *American Sociological Review* 29, (1964): 339–57.

Phillips, B. S. "A Role Theory Approach to Adjustment in Old Age." *American Sociological Review* 22, 2 (1957): 212–27.

Portes, A. "On the Sociology of National Development: Theories and Issues." *American Journal of Sociology* 82, 1 (1976): 55–85.

Press, I., and M. McKool. "Social Structure and Status of the Aged: Toward Some Valid Cross-Cultural Generalizations." In *In the Country of the Old*, ed. J. Hendricks, pp. 47–56. Farmingdale, N.Y.: Baywood Publishing Company, 1980.

Ragan, P. K., and J. B. Wales. "Age Stratification and the Life Course." In *Handbook of Mental Health and Aging*, eds. J. E. Birren and R. B. Sloane, pp. 377–99. Englewood Cliffs, N.J.: Prentice-Hall, Inc., 1980.

————. "Aging and Social Change." In *Aging from Birth to Death*, vol. 2: *Sociotemporal Perspectives*, eds. M. W. Riley, R. P. Ables, and M. S. Teltelbaum, pp. 11–26. Boulder, Colo.: Westview Press, 1982.

————, R. P. Ables, and M. S. Teltelbaum. *Aging from Birth to Death*, vol. 2: *Sociotemporal Perspectives*. Boulder, Colo.: Westview Press, 1982.

Riley, M. W., and R. T. Campbell. "From Theory Generation to Theory Testing: Age Cohort Models." In *Recent Advances in Gerontology*, eds. H. Orimo, K. Shimada, M. Iriki, and D. Maeda, pp. 297–98. Amsterdam: Excerpta Medica, 1979.

————, M. Johnson, and A. Foner. *Aging and Society*, vol. 3: *A Sociology of Age Stratification*. New York: Russell Sage Foundation, 1972.

Rose, A. M. "The Subculture of the Aging: A Framework in Social Gerontology." In *Older People and Their Social World*, eds. A. M. Rose and W. A. Peterson, pp. 3–16. Philadelphia: F. A. Davis Company, 1965.

Rosenmayr, L. "Age, Lifespan and Bibliography." *Ageing and Society* 1, 1 (1981): 29–49.

Rosow, I. *Social Integration of the Aged*. New York: The Free Press, 1967.

————. *Socialization to Old Age*. Berkeley: University of California Press, 1974.

Schwartz, A. N. "A Transactional View of the Aging Process." In *Professional Obligations and Approaches to the Aged*, eds. A. N. Schwartz and I. M. Mensh, pp. 5–29. Springfield, Ill.: Charles C Thomas, Publisher, 1974.

Shanas, E. "Some Observations on Cross-National Surveys of Aging." *The Gerontologist* 3, 1 (1963): 7–9.

Sherman, S. R., R. A. Ward, and M. LaGory. "Socialization and Aging Group Consciousness: The Effect of Neighborhood Age Concentration." *Journal of Gerontology* 46, 1 (1985): 102–9.

Simmons, L. *The Role of the Aged in Primitive Society*. New Haven: Yale University Press, 1945.

————. "Aging in Preindustrial Societies." In *Handbook of Social Gerontology*, ed. C. Tibbitts, pp. 62–91. Chicago: University of Chicago Press, 1960.

Streib, G. F. "Are the Aged a Minority Group?" In *Applied Sociology*, eds. A. W. Gouldner and S. M. Miller, pp. 311–28. New York: The Free Press, 1965.

————. "Social Stratification and Aging." In *Handbook of Aging and the Social Sciences*, eds. R. H. Binstock and E. Shanas, pp. 160–85. New York: Van Nostrand Reinhold Company, 1976.

————, and C. J. Schneider. *Retirement in American Society*. Ithaca, N.Y.: Cornell University Press, 1971.

Tigges, L., and D. Cowgill. "Aging From a World Systems Perspective: An Alternative to Modernization Theory." Paper presented to The Gerontological Society of America, 1981.

Tindale, J. A., and V. W. Marshall. "A Generational Conflict Perspective for Gerontology." In *Aging in Canada: Social Perspectives*, ed. V. W. Marshall, pp. 43–50. Don Mills, Ontario: Fitzhenry & Whiteside, 1980.

Tolbert, C. M., III. "Industrial Segmentation and Men's Career Mobility." *American Sociological Review* 47, 4 (1982): 457–77.

————, P. M. Horan, and C. M. Beck. "The Structure of Economic Segmentation: A Dual Economic Approach." *American Journal of Sociology* 85 (1980): 1095–116.

Townsend, P. "The Structured Dependency of the Elderly." *Ageing and Society* 1, 1 (1981): 5–28.

Wallerstein, I. "The Rise and Future Demise of the World Capitalist System: Concepts for Comparative Analyses." *Comparative Studies in Society and History* 16 (1974): 387–415.

Williams, R. H., and C. G. Wirths. *Lives Through the Years*. New York: Atherton Press, 1965.

Zusman, J. "Some Explanations of the Changing Appearance of Psychotic Patients: Antecedents of the Social Breakdown Syndrome Concept." *The Millbank Memorial Fund Quarterly* 64, 1 (1966).

# PART TWO

# THE LIFEWORLD OF THE AGING PERSON

# 4

# THE PHYSIOLOGY
# OF AGING

**THE RELEVANCE OF
PHYSIOLOGY TO SOCIAL
GERONTOLOGY**

The Impact of Early Physiological
Theories
The Effect of Sociological Factors on
Physiology
Physiology as Part of the Social Context

**EARLY BIOLOGICAL THEORIES**

The Rate of Living Theory
The Stress Theory

**RECENT BIOLOGICAL THEORIES**

Cellular Theories
Molecular Theories
Somatic Mutation
Error Theory
Program Theory
Immunological Theory
Neuroendocrine Theory
Free Radical and Waste Product
Theories
Cross-Linkage Theory
Implications of Physiological Theories
of Aging

**FUNCTIONAL CAPACITY AND
AGE**

Functional Variability Within Age
Categories
The Picture of Function
Life-Style Factors and Functional
Variability

**SUMMARY**

**DISCUSSION QUESTIONS**

**PERTINENT READINGS**

# The Relevance of Physiology to Social Gerontology

Why include a chapter on physiology in a book on social gerontology? As we pointed out in Chapter 1, the physiological, psychological, sociocultural, and economic levels of life interact with each other and influence the experience of aging. A sociology of aging that totally ignored the physiological aspects of aging would be inadequate, and vice versa. Is aging in our cells, in our minds, or is it something that happens between people?

Social gerontology and the physiology of aging are interrelated in three major ways: (1) through popularizations of some of the earlier theories on the cultural traditions from which social gerontology arose, (2) through the impact of sociocultural and economic factors on physiology, and (3) because physiological processes are part of the context of cultural life. Physiological processes are often the rationale for discrimination in jobs, services, and in many other areas of life. Here we will briefly examine these facets of this interrelationship and survey some of the earlier theories. We will then look at the recent major theories on the physiology of aging and their implications for social gerontology.

## THE IMPACT OF EARLY PHYSIOLOGICAL THEORIES

As we shall see, earlier theories about aging were based on the idea of **entropy:** that the human organism is like a mechanism that runs down as it consumes energy in the process of living. The whole notion of entropy, based on the second law of thermodynamics, is intuitively appealing because it takes considerable energy to maintain a system state. Although entropic theories have fallen into disfavor, they have had considerable influence in shaping cultural stereotypes of aging, and, indeed, in the development of social gerontological theory. Gerontologists are no different from other people; if a biological model is presented as fact, there is a tendency to look for echoes of it in the social realm. A prime example of this is the predisposition to see old people as disappearing from view for physiological reasons (Cumming and Henry, 1961), which is the logic underlying the development of disengagement theory.

## THE EFFECT OF SOCIOLOGICAL FACTORS ON PHYSIOLOGY

Strehler (1977) proposes four criteria that must be met for a process to be considered characteristic of normal biological aging:

- Age-associated changes must be universal, occurring in all members of a species.
- The changes must be *intrinsic* to the organism rather than resulting from external factors.
- Physiological aging will be both gradual and progressive.
- Physiological aging is a process of declining functional capacity that makes death more probable.

These criteria may be more analytically than practically useful because they assume there is something in the way the organism itself is constituted that is an important factor in aging, and that it is important to distinguish the internally driven changes of aging from the externally stimulated ones. Hickey (1980) makes a similar point in developing his explanatory model of aging using the nature/nurture framework. He distinguishes between the concepts of *primary aging*, derived from nature, biology, and genetics, and *secondary aging*, which is the effect of the environment on development and health in old age. Walford (1983) goes even further in limiting biological theories. The point, however, is that the intrinsic and extrinsic facets of aging processes may be so closely aligned that biological research requires an explicit criteria to differentiate the two.

The real life application of any criterion is, however, restricted when we try to identify factors truly intrinsic to the organism. The question of universality, for example, is troublesome; when we say a physiological change is universal, do we mean all members of the species without exception will undergo it, or do we mean that all members of the species have the potential for undergoing it given the appropriate circumstances? We must also consider the enormous variability between members of a species even in the most generally distributed characteristics. Anyone who has had experience with anatomy and physiology or with the results of clinical laboratory tests will know drawings in anatomy and physiology textbooks and "normal" laboratory test results represent statistical estimates of the most general ranges rather than any kind of universal standard. Furthermore, because we can never observe an organism in isolation from its environment, how can we say that processes are completely intrinsic rather than extrinsic?

Although we can never be sure that a change is exclusively physiological, we can demonstrate that some changes and developments that are often thought to form part of the physiological aging process are associated with sociocultural factors and can be modified. For many years scientists thought that **atherosclerosis** (hardening of the arteries) was a condition common to all older people. Now, however, external factors such as nutrition, stress, and socioeconomic status are considered to account for most cases of atherosclerosis. One hundred years ago tuberculosis was the leading cause of death. Today there are few cases of tuberculosis in the United States. Not until streptomycin became available in the late 1940s was there a drug available to cure tuberculosis, but by then the death rates had dropped by roughly 75 percent within a few decades. Why did the death rate decline and why are the few cases we see today drawn from high-density, low-income urban or rural poverty areas? Overcrowding, poor nutrition, the isolation of infected individuals, and lack of pasteurized and sanitary milk and meats are responsible for the fact tuberculosis is virtually limited to the disadvantaged (Fries and Crapo, 1981). Similarly, a lack of exercise has also been identified as an important factor in accelerating osteoporosis in postmenopausal women. In Chapter 11 we will explore in more detail the socioenvironmental and life-style factors that influence the health and functional status of the elderly. Hickey and others distinguish two dimensions of the environment that affect physiological status in old age: (1) food, toxicity, chemicals, and stress and (2) life-style and behavior patterns (Hickey, 1980; Butler and Newacheck, 1981; Somers and Fabian, 1981). To these, others may add causal links with such macro-level concerns as economic policy, structure of the labor force, and the impact of commodity production (Estes et al., 1984; Doyal, 1979).

## PHYSIOLOGY AS PART OF THE SOCIAL CONTEXT

Although it is difficult to be absolutely sure which changes are intrinsic to an organism, physiological constraints and potentials form part of the context within which we live our lives. Figure 3.4 suggested physiological capabilities were part of one dimension of successful adaptation. Many of the physiological changes generally associated with aging may be modified by changes in life-style and social organization; others may not. One focus of the study of the physiology of aging that most captures the imagination is the search for factors that may be biologically manipulated to delay or retard the aging process. Perhaps an equally important contribution can be the knowledge of the physiological constraints within which most of the elderly live their lives.

The impact of this latter contribution has two facets. If we have some idea of what the physiological constraints and potentialities are, we can, if we wish, work toward ordering our social contexts in ways that will maximize functioning within the limits of the possible. If we have some realization of the variations in the levels of physiological functioning among the elderly, we will avoid stereotyping them on the basis of studies that look at those who are least functional. If the level of physical abilities is so predictable, how does one explain the existence of long-lived, creative, and active elderly people such as Dr. Spock, Justice Douglas, Picasso, or Claude Pepper?

The search for an elixir to ward off the maladies of old age is as old as civilization. Many have followed Ponce de Leon in seeking magic — whether it be healing waters, proverbial tiger testicle compounds, sexual encounters with adolescents, or rejuvenation from inhaling adolescent exhalations. To use such measures was believed to revitalize aging bodies, and all manner of claims were made on their behalf. Today scientists are convinced that changes in the inner mechanisms of our bodies, beginning at the molecular or cellular level, hold greater promise of revealing ways to intervene in aging.

Numerous journal articles report studies of changes in hormonal function and cellular and tissue composition that are associated with senescence. While everyone acknowledges the importance of basic research at this level as a prerequisite to understanding the physiology of aging — a higher level theory based on inaccurate assumptions about biochemical and cellular function would be worthless — many believe that the key to understanding the physiology of aging lies at a more systemic level. Society's ability to prolong life well beyond the reproductive years has brought about the existence of the *senescent* years during which the organism becomes ever harder pressed to recover from displacing stimuli; in many respects we have created the old age we now seek to unravel.

## Early Biological Theories

The list of the physical symptoms of aging — gray hair, poor eyesight, dental problems, wrinkled, sagging skin, hearing loss — goes on and on. The search for a cure continues, but a magic elixir has yet to be found. Nor is one likely to be discovered in the foreseeable future, except in science fiction. Injections, creams, and mystical prescriptions may temporarily make people feel younger, look younger, or engage in youthful pursuits, but no one really knows how to inhibit the process.

Although people have speculated about why we age at least since Ancient Greece, it was not until the later decades of the nineteenth century that scientific models began to appear. An interesting footnote to the history of gerontology is that precious little cumulative development took place until after World War II. There are, however, two main themes that emerge from the early biology of aging. One attributes aging to particular physiological systems or conditions. Foremost among these was the belief that *autointoxication* was a prime cause of aging. Elie Metchnikoff's 1904 claim that intestinal bacteria resulted from putrefaction in the digestive tract is illustrative of this research theme. The second tradition dates from the thirteenth-century work of Roger Bacon. It emphasized the wear and tear of living as a cause of aging. In the 1880s August Weismann updated the idea of tissue fatigue and the loss of regenerative ability and gave it an evolutionary twist.

The idea of tissue fatigue may come under the wider concept of entropy, an idea that also dates back to the Ancient Greeks but was further developed in the nineteenth century when attempts to understand the apparent order of the universe became formalized in two laws of thermodynamics. The first of these held that energy can neither be created nor destroyed and the amount of energy in the universe is finite. The second law contends that this energy becomes increasingly less available to do work or to maintain order. Though we shall not discuss it in great detail, it is the second law that is important for our purposes because the concept of entropy arose as one of its corollaries. Briefly, unless a system is already in equilibrium, it takes a greater amount of energy to maintain a stable state through time than would be necessary if its component elements became disorganized. An important variable controlling the speed with which a system loses its ability to do work, including maintaining its integrity, is the amount of energy originally involved. The degradation of the system once begun is irreversible, continuing until no further energy is available for its use. The system can then be said to have achieved equilibrium. This tendency for disorganization caused by energy loss as a function of time is referred to as entropy. Increasing entropy has been thought to be a common characteristic of all systems, whether mechanical, cybernetic, or human. Therefore it is easy to understand how a person might find the notion of entropy attractive in explaining aging and the ultimate disorganization of life's processes that we call death. Hippocrates (460–377 B.C.) himself, the progenitor of modern medicine and one of the first to discuss diseases of the elderly, referred to aging as a natural event involving a loss of body heat. Among contemporary physiological theories, entropy was initially attractive — prompting researchers to formulate their models in terms of a finite store of energy that when dissipated causes the disruption of the body's equilibrium.

What is sometimes called "living systems theory" was posed as an alternative to the idea of system depletion through entropy. It is based on the notion that all living systems obtain and use energy from their environments. Aging then may result from an impaired ability to assimilate ambient energy sources (Bertalanffy, 1968). Many contemporary biological theories can be construed as attempts to specify the mechanics by which the body ceases to assimilate what it needs to maintain itself.

## THE RATE OF LIVING THEORY

The rate of living theory (Pearl, 1928) used to be very popular, but is currently regarded with disfavor. On the surface, such a theory seems plausible. Many organisms appear to have a certain amount of energy stored within them, and once it is exhausted they die, much the way a fire dies after the wood is burned. If the theory were accurate for all activity, we would anticipate higher mortality rates among those organisms or individuals who engaged in the most exercise throughout their lives. The opposite is true, however. Regular exercise or work seems to maintain the body rather than hasten its demise.

The premise of the model is that some sort of "program" exists within the organism; the quicker the program is run through, the sooner death ensues. Metabolic rates considerably higher than those of humans are found primarily in animals with lower life expectancies; thus there might appear to be a reasonable basis for a rate of living hypothesis. But in fact life expectancies are not linked to finite energy reserves, and this research has fallen into disrepute in recent years (Comfort, 1979).

Since the survival of any species is predicated on living through the reproductive years, there is no intrinsic reason for the life program to last any longer than it takes to bear and rear offspring. Sophisticated variations of the program theory have surfaced in recent years as knowledge of information storage in the body increased. However, the idea of wear and tear on a system, no matter how attractive the analogy, has few if any adherents today.

## THE STRESS THEORY

Another general proposition related to the foregoing hypothesis is offered by a more contemporary view called stress theory (Selye and Prioreschi, 1960). It is unique because stress theory perceives no difference between the consequences of normal aging and those of pathological conditions. However, the theory does not encompass any kind of sociopsychological strain but refers instead to physical wear and tear from sudden and unexpected stressors over which we have no control. Rapid temperature changes, chemicals or other irritants, exhaustion, and so on are typical stressors on our bodies. Experiments conducted on both tissue samples and intact animals reveal a three-stage reaction pattern that the theory contends resembles aging. The only difference is one of time; the stress syndrome identified in the laboratory is assumed to be a telescoped version of what happens over the lifetime of an individual. The three-stage process of alarm, resistance, and exhaustion presumably leaves us indelibly scarred with fibrotic tissue that accrues with successive stressful events. Old age is then that period in which we are no longer capable of fighting off various insults as a result of the accumulation of wear and tear. Like the concept of fixed energy, the stress hypothesis is not now a widely accepted causal explanation of the aging process.

As previously noted, it has been demonstrated that exercise inhibits the decline of physical and mental functions (Jokl, 1983), but this seems to run contrary to the stress theory of aging. Selye himself saw successful activity, no matter how intense, as leaving one with comparatively few scars and providing the exhilarating feeling of youthful strength, even at a very advanced age. He cites the numerous examples of hard-working people, such as G. B. Shaw, Bertrand Russell, Voltaire, Michelangelo, Pablo Picasso, and Artur Rubenstein, who were active well into their seventies, eighties, or even late nineties (Selye, 1974).

# Recent Biological Theories

Recent efforts to unravel the mysteries of biogerontology have proceeded apace but without any particular cohesion. While social science is often thought of as the stepchild of the harder sciences because of its lack of specificity, a close look at recent biological theories of aging suggests the sister disciplines are not any more specific. Diverse theories of how and why we age abound. This is because changes over time appear in every aspect of our bodies from the molecular to the systematic levels. The specialty of the researcher seems to have as much relation to the explanatory framework he or she employs as do the actual facts of the aging process (Hayflick, 1985). Nearly all the theoretical models discussed have been criticized for their failure to consider even more fundamental changes. They have also been taken to task for their continual search for deficits, declines, and deterioration.

A new direction is needed. Unless there is a functional reason for senescence, in terms of the reproductive success of the species, evolutionary change is more likely to enhance stability than cause deleterious age changes. Hayflick (1985) notes in passing that a search for "longevity assurance genes" is one plausible new approach.

Where then does that leave the search for biological explanations of the aging process? They are still largely concentrating on single cause models, yet the **etiology** of aging is among the more complicated and interactive of physical processes. Multiple causation or a lack of systemic integration has not yet become a credible research focus. Similarly, little attention has yet been focused on **pleiotropic** processes, those that perform a positive function during the early phases of life but become maladaptive after the reproductive years. To date most attention has been paid to molecular processes, cellular change, immunological alterations, neuroendocrine system decline, organ changes stemming in part from cross-linkages between macromolecules, the accumulation of waste products, or free radical transformations. Other pet theories are also put forth periodically, gaining favor for a time before giving way to others.

Our discussion of the more plausible biological theories will necessarily be a topical review. The task of detailed analysis is best left to specialized biological and physiological courses or textbooks. The differences among the following theories are often more apparent than real; there is considerable overlap and complementarity among them. Despite their multiplicity, or because new models are still being formulated, none can be dismissed out of hand at present. Neither can any model be said to be totally incorrect; each has something to offer as an explanation.

## CELLULAR THEORIES

A high-powered electron microscope reveals that our bodies are made up of a variety of cell types as well as a scaffolding material that holds the cells in place. Basically these can be classified into two types of cells: **mitotic** cells such as those found in our skin, which divide or copy themselves, and **post-fixed mitotic** cells, which are incapable of duplication. Both types have a structure similar to that shown in Figure 4.1. Once the maximum number of the nondividing cells is attained, as, for example, in the central nervous system, which is composed of post-fixed mitotic cells, we cannot replace any that may be destroyed and so face an ever-dwindling supply. Although scientists have been able to duplicate the chemical composition of the cell, they have not yet been able to produce one in the laboratory. Apparently there is something about the way the components are organized that presently eludes us. Functionally, the cell has been called a molecular factory, because it carries out the processes necessary for sustaining life. To do so the cell must first support and maintain itself. Only then can it contribute to maintaining the organism. However, for numerous reasons cells die. It was once believed that mitotic cells were capable of reproducing themselves for an indefinite period; therefore, by implication, as far as aging was concerned, only the death of nondividing cells was important. Scientists now know that both types of cells have a maximum life span not appreciably longer than that of the whole organism.

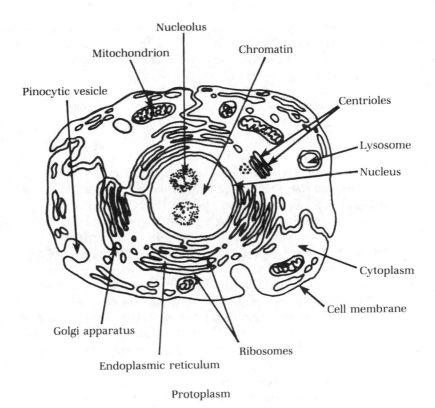

**FIGURE 4.1**
Diagram of a typical cell.

They also know that cells produced late in life show *morphological* differences from similar cells produced by a younger organism.

Since nondividing cells cannot be replaced, scientists have sought a life maintenance level for post-fixed mitotic cells below which the probability of the immediate death of the organism increases drastically. Cellular deterioration or **cell necrosis** could be the consequence of normal changes over time in catalytic chemical components of the cell or of rearrangements of the genetic material in the nucleus or the result of pathological conditions. In practice it is extremely difficult to distinguish among them. Once a certain degree of loss has occurred, the chances of death begin to increase. Though we know spinal *ganglia*, certain cells along nerve tracts, and brain cells decline in very old age to 60 to 80 percent of their number in younger organisms, these reductions do not appear to initiate aging. Nonetheless, cellular modifications are particularly important for aging. To meet its two principal tasks a cell must first produce the energy required by its internal components to sustain life, maintain its own and the organism's chemical stability, and, in the case of mitotic cells, accurately reproduce itself. If for any reason the coordination of these subtasks is interrupted, then cellular deterioration is likely to follow. We will examine some of the factors thought to bring about a disruption in normal cell functioning.

A key issue in cellular research is whether dividing cell lines have a finite life span beyond which they cease to divide and replicate. If not, then aging must occur on another level. For many years biologists thought dividing cells had the potential to continue, if not forever, at least for a very long time. Nourished by a correct medium, their life span was certainly longer than that of the host organism. The original research was surrounded by such acclaim, including a Nobel Prize, that subsequent challenges were attributed to faulty procedures and dismissed. But until the late 1950s, no such studies were carried out using human tissue; all research findings were based on animal samples, especially chick embryos, and the results were generalized to humans. As a chance adjunct to cancer research, it was discovered that human cells grown in culture doubled just as had been foreseen; yet after a number of doublings the rate of division began to decline, eventually coming to a halt, and the cells died.

Furthermore, cells *explanted* from older donors and grown **in vitro** divide proportionately fewer times than those taken from younger donors, and in either case the number of doublings remaining is directly related to the mean maximum life span of the species. Subsequent research in vitro suggests in-place cells reveal a similar tendency toward diminished function with the age of the host (Hayflick, 1979; Schneider et al., 1979).

In a series of carefully controlled experiments the youngest cells were observed to attain an average of fifty doublings before death, while older cells doubled proportionately less, depending on the age of the host. This in itself was enough to alter much of the thinking about physiological aging. Interrupting cellular division by freezing cells in liquid nitrogen at temperatures as low as −190°C or by other means and then returning them to the normal range does not alter the remaining number of doublings, suggesting there is indeed a built-in limit of life (Cristofalo and Stanulis, 1978). Interestingly, not only were dividing cell lines found to have a finite life span, but prior to ceasing their replicative capacity a number of physiological and biochemical decrements were observed.

These decrements are called the *Phase III* phenomenon, or alternatively, the *Hayflick limit*. This type of cellular research has spurred biogerontologists to search for the mechanisms whereby cells cease to function normally. Since the life expectancy of normal cells is beyond that of the host organism, cell necrosis in itself does not cause aging. But well before the cells die their functioning undergoes change. It does not matter that certain malignant cells appear to be immortal. In normally dividing cells, during the first two phases of nurturance and vigorous cell division, all changes are adaptive. Not until Phase III does division slow, intracellular changes appear, and metabolic byproducts begin to accumulate. Phase III does not appear to result from any external agent causing a malfunction; rather the change is intrinsic, perhaps due to a built-in time clock.

Various hypotheses have been advanced and rejected to explain how such a clock might work. Some have even challenged the validity of the observations from which Hayflick drew his conclusions, claiming that his findings fail to address the causes of aging. Others have sought resolution at the genetic level, looking for cumulative copying errors, cross-linking between information-carrying molecules, the functional role of **oncogenes** (especially the *MYC* gene), and general errors in genetic programs (Hayflick, 1985; Schneider, 1984; Fries and Crapo, 1981).

## MOLECULAR THEORIES

Because cell deterioration seems to be caused by more fundamental alterations, many biogerontologists have pointed to the molecule as the "epicenter" of age changes (Viidik, 1982). Years ago a research team noticed the life spans of pairs of identical twins were more similar than those of fraternal twins. What do the identical twins have in common that fraternal twins do not? Also, why do mammalian females live longer than males? In the case of identical twins the answer lies in their identical genetic material. As to the longer life span for females, some think it may relate to the presence of the second X chromosome that males lack. Even before the landmark discoveries of DNA, on the basis of chromosomal differences, biogerontology began to look for **genome**-based explanations.

In Figure 4.1 we see something labeled "chromatin" on the nucleus of the cell. Present in all cells, these are loosely coiled strands that split lengthwise as the cell divides. Human beings have forty-six chromosomes in every body cell which are composed of thousands of tiny genes that ultimately determine the character and function of the cell. The clock that regulates the functioning of the genes seems to slow down in the course of time, giving rise to the Phase III phenomenon.

**Somatic Mutation.** One explanation for why cells themselves undergo senescence centers about somatic mutation. First popular about twenty-five to thirty years ago, the somatic mutation theory evolved out of technological advances in radiobiology. Simply put, the proliferation of useless or harmful cell parts may cause what we call aging. In the process of division random inferior cells may be replicated. Cellular aberrations may also come about from external mutagenic agents present in the environment. Radiation and ultraviolet rays from the sun are ready examples. Another process that may cause mutations is a cross-linkage between molecules. And chromosomes from older donors are thought to have more abnormalities than younger donors (Curtis, 1971; Schofield and Davis, 1978).

With the discovery of DNA in the early 1950s, scientists also found that certain conditions brought about an alteration in the extremely precise arrangement of the chemical components of DNA. Basically, DNA is a spiral, ropelike ladder consisting of four compounds paired together much like tongue and groove flooring. The order the components take constitutes what we call the genetic code. These components, however, can be damaged by events in such a way that the message they provide will be incorrect. Older donors have more frequent abnormal arrangements than younger ones. Many knowledgeable experts were critical of the research on which somatic muta- tion theory was formulated, so it has not received a great deal of attention in recent years. But in light of the enormous advances in the methods of molecu- lar biology, especially recombinant DNA technology, the theory may be worth closer scrutiny. For reasons as yet unknown, recent experiments on senescent human lung fibroblasts have disclosed something quite remarkable: what are termed "amplified genes" have been found in extrachromosomal locations (Hayflick, 1985; Schneider, 1984; Shmookler-Reis, et al., 1983).

**Error Theory.** In addition to molecular mutations, mitotic cells may become inoperative because of *copying errors* in repeated divisions. For a message to be transmitted to the cell or to larger parts of the organism, DNA depends on the RNA stored in the nucleolus portion of the nucleus. The synthesizing or manufacture of protein enzymes is the chief task of the nucleolus, with a du- plicate copy of the mechanism being transferred during cell division. Since changes in the structure of RNA have been observed in samples from older donors, some have hypothesized that these may be a result of slight but pro- gressive modifications in copying. Such "error catastrophies" (Orgel, 1970) may so alter the protein produced by newer cells that they are incapable of recognizing essential components of themselves; this forces the body's immu- nologic system to work against itself. Cancer is the best known example of aberrant cells produced within our own bodies.

Error theory is in many respects tied to both the somatic mutation theory and to the notion of a biological clock. In one early formulation (Orgel, 1970) the error model was suggested as an explanation for the origin of harmful genes that interfere with crucial processes or for a random occurrence of in- active chromosomes. There is no agreement yet whether the changes rupture nonrepeated DNA sequences or cause inaccurate protein synthesis. Con- sensus does exist, however, that the functional link between these errors and aging lies in the multiplication of the mistakes that lead to cellular deteriora- tion (Hayflick, 1985).

**Program Theory.** Still another explanation of the increasing instability of crucial information contained on DNA is referred to as program theory. The underlying logic is that age changes cannot be simply random — stochas- tic — events. Instead the system that feeds information to the body simply runs out or turns off over time. Whether the genetic code is ultimately con- sumed, causing cells to fail, or whether some unidentified evolutionary mechanism causes it to stop to ensure the survival of new generations is un- known (Rockstein and Sussman, 1979). It is unlikely, however, that sex-linked genes play a role, because advocates of the model attribute gender differences in longevity to secondary characteristics or to social factors. Age declines may be caused by what Hayflick (1985) refers to as a "free-wheeling, non–genome-dependent continuation of the inertia developed from previously determined developmental events." In other words, the same forces promoting maturation may cause decline. What seems certain is that at the systemic level genetic "pacemakers" may alter thresholds in the hypothalamus, endocrine system, or hormone receptors on cell membranes (Moment, 1978).

## IMMUNOLOGICAL THEORY

One concrete finding accepted by biogerontologists is that in normal functioning, the immunological system undergoes involutionary changes after puberty. This affects aging in two ways. First, the body's production of antibodies necessary to fight off infections declines. Second, as normal immune patterns change in one direction, autoimmune responses change in the opposite direction. This is important because the body's ability to differentiate between itself and foreign organisms falters. As previously noted in the discussion of error theory, cancer is the most recognizable result. Others are rheumatoid arthritis and mature onset diabetes. In certain respects the kind of tissue rejection characteristic in transplants has symptoms that parallel aging: vascular and kidney impairment, hair loss, and a generalized failure to thrive (Walford, 1983).

Since immunologic functioning is controlled by the thymus, aging may stem from thymic atrophy. By old age immune capabilities are 5 to 10 percent of what they were at puberty. Both thymic mass and function deteriorate in the course of life, leading some investigators to look at T-cell production as a trigger for immunologic aging (Hayflick, 1985). Once again the mechanisms whereby immune systems decline are not clearly understood and no single explanation of the reasons for this decline is accepted by immune researchers. Just because a correlation has been noticed does not establish a causative link.

## NEUROENDOCRINE THEORY

As another systemic explanation of aging, neuroendocrine research focuses on the maintenance of **homeostasis.** Here attention is concentrated on the regulatory role of neurons and hormones for the whole body. Changes in the hypothalamus cause changes in pituitary glands, and many endocrine functions are affected. As Hayflick (1985) points out, steroid changes at menopause show up in the clinical diagnosis of osteoporosis in certain women.

Similarly, brain oxidative metabolism brings changes in **neurotransmission receptors.** Perhaps these alterations account for the senile plaques and neurofibrillary tangles characteristic of Alzheimer's disease and other organic dementias. Slow viruses — *prions* — have also been found to be associated with dementia. They too are thought to be related to neuroendocrine declines. Some have even suggested the existence of a "death hormone" (DECO) with wide-ranging ill-effects (Hayflick, 1985).

## FREE RADICAL AND WASTE PRODUCT THEORIES

For our purposes free radicals can be defined as unpaired electrons in atoms or molecules seeking a mate. If they pair with an otherwise stable unit, another radical is created and the process continues. In all respiring cells (cells that move oxygen and other materials in and out) free radicals are normally generated. They are also present in the environment, in all forms of metabolism, and in foods and tobacco. Regardless of their source, bonding with unsaturated fats brings about a byproduct, aldehyde, which is a cross-linking agent that damages membranes and even chromosomes. According to Harman (1981), aging itself may be the sum of free radical reactions continuing throughout life. Since free radicals are self-perpetuating and are not biodegradable, they may contribute to the development of **lipofuscin**, which is familiar to most of us as the liver spots we see on the skin of older people.

As a normal metabolic waste product, lipofuscin accumulates in every cell in our bodies. In the past few decades intensive study of the changing chemical morphology associated with aging has shown lipofuscin granules to be composed of a number of chemical elements normally present in the body combining to form lipofuscin as a consequence of chemical reactions necessary for metabolizing nutrients. We know it is found universally, first in the cytoplasm of nondividing cell lines, and that it is a reliable indicator of age; as yet, however, there is no conclusive information about its causal relationship with aging. We also do not know if it is the consequence of a copying error or some other phenomenon. It appears that lipofuscin begins to mass together early in life in active organ systems such as cardiac muscle and brain tissue, and gradually spreads, ultimately showing up on the skin. It is not, however, found in all tissue, nor is it deposited at a constant rate in the same tissue; rather it is related to the functional specialization of a tissue's cells. For example, as illustrated in Figure 4.2, after the age of ten, lipofuscin is deposited at a constant rate in both healthy and diseased heart muscles. If we lived to be ninety years old it would occupy approximately 6 to 7 percent of the intracellular volume in our *myocardium* (Strehler, 1977). Microscopic examination of the accumulation of age pigment in brain and nerve cells has shown similar progressive patterns. As further evidence of its relationship with aging, lipofuscin deposits are found extensively in cases of *progeria*, a rare form of premature aging among children (Timiras, 1972).

The collection site of lipofuscin in the cytoplasm of the cell is particularly important, since it is presumably involved in the inactivation of the Golgi apparatus, which are responsible for exporting substances from the cell. It may possibly have the same effect on the mitochondria, the transducers that furnish the enzymes and the energy for other essential processes. Finally, lipofuscin may also be associated with the lysosomes; the two have similar chemical components. Lysosomes produce the enzyme necessary for digesting nutrients and dissolving worn out cell parts. The enzyme they contain is so powerful that lysosomes have been called "suicide sacks," for if the enzyme were to be released accidently, the entire cell would be destroyed. If the appearance of age pigment

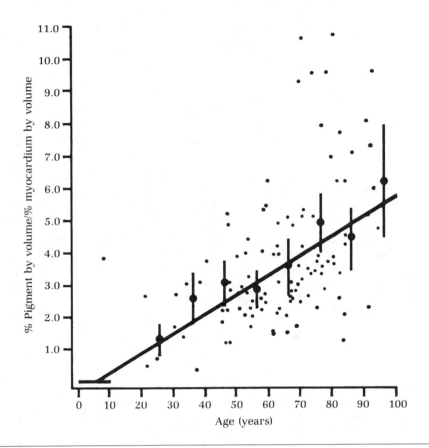

**FIGURE 4.2**

Relationship between age and pigment content of human myocardium. (*Source:* Strehler, B. L., et al. "Rate and Magnitude of Age Pigment Accumulation in the Human Myocardium." *Journal of Gerontology* 14, 4 [1959]: 433.)

interferes with the respiratory and energy-releasing functions of the cell, its implication for aging is most important (Strehler and Mildvan, 1962). Clearly, lipofuscin occupies a significant proportion of cell volume, reaching nearly 75 percent of certain central nerve cells by ninety (Strehler, 1977).

While we shall discuss nutrition in greater detail later, we should be aware that both disease and dietary habits are among the external factors contributing to the formation of age pigment. Lipofuscin has been associated with a deficiency of vitamin E and an oversupply of fatty acids. Further, the majority of us tend to eat too much for our own good — close to 1100 excess calories daily. Coupled with this, the manner in which we ingest our food makes a difference. Eating small amounts spread over several meals leads to a relatively innocuous oxidative process with few intermediate byproducts. However, if we gorge ourselves with our usual intake of 3300 calories in one sitting, an accumulation occurs that leads to a buildup of harmful byproducts (Bjorksten, 1969).

## CROSS-LINKAGE THEORY

Caloric intake may also be one of the causes of the biochemical vulcanization of certain cells and tissue that biologists call cross-linking (Bakerman, 1969). The basic principle is straightforward; macromolecules are linked *covalently* or by a hydrogen bond, thereby changing the structure and function of the molecules involved. Over time the molecules either become inert or they malfunction, leading to damage and eventually death. In the meantime solubility, permeability, and elasticity decline. Simultaneously, crowding within the cell and in the extracellular compartment occurs and the respiratory transport suffers (Hayflick, 1985). Since this cross-linking is observed most frequently in the extracellular protein found in collagenous fibers, its analysis has come to be known as *collagen theory*. Collagen, one of the most abundant forms of protein in our bodies, is present in all connective tissue such as ligaments, tendons, or muscles, in the walls of arteries, and in the ground substance holding our cells in place. Normal epidermal scar tissue is a good example of collagen fiber; it was known decades before the isolation of collagen that scars show age-related transformations. The formation of scars over the wounds of older individuals is slower, and the resultant tissue has a structure different from that found in younger people. Collagen composes 30 to 40 percent of body protein; it is found in the viscous gelatinlike ground substance surrounding the cells, in the walls of the arteries, and in connective tissue. Together with elastic and reticular fibers, collagen provides the support that holds the cells in place; it serves as a shock absorber to protect vital organs and it allows for the expansion and contraction of tissues. However, like a rubber band, collagen undergoes modification of its elastic properties over time.

The characteristic changes in skin provide some indication of what is happening to the collagen throughout our bodies. As collagen becomes denser and replaces other components in the ground substance, cells have greater difficulty acquiring nutrients and expelling wastes because the ground substance has lost much of its permeability. A lack of elasticity in the walls of the circulatory system spells the probable onset of atherosclerosis, higher blood pressure, and many related problems. Muscular effectiveness declines with age, most noticeably after fifty, partly as a consequence of the degenerative alteration in collagen fibers. Bones also become more brittle because of changes in the marrow collagen. While it is improbable that an alteration in collagen is the sole harbinger of aging, the pattern of cross-linking and its role in impairing functional capacities justify its inclusion among primary physiological explanations of the aging process (Bjorksten, 1969; Kohn, 1977).

## IMPLICATIONS OF PHYSIOLOGICAL THEORIES OF AGING

The variety of explanatory models in biogerontology help clarify the difference between the primary and secondary characteristics of the aging process.

Illness is in no way an intrinsic component of age. Primary or normal aging is universal, inevitable, and irreversible. All the theories presented in this chapter have been concerned with primary aging. Secondary aging — all those diseases, maladies, and chronic complaints that form the basis for the stereotypic portrait of an older person — is very plastic. Some people have more wrinkled skin or harder arteries than others. Thoughtful inquiry will probably reveal that some have spent more time in the sun and that others have eaten a diet that causes the secondary characteristics. While 80 percent of all old people have some chronic disease, the others have no symptoms of disease. Moreover, patterns of life for those who have chronic diseases probably contain good reasons why their health in the later years is not what they had hoped.

Primary theories of aging have to meet the criteria listed earlier in the chapter. To be valid they must incorporate anatomic, biochemical, behavioral, and physiological parameters, as well as changes in the ability to engage the environment (Wallace, 1977). They must also explain the Phase III phenomena, immunologic changes, and repair and metabolic correlations with the life span of the species (Walford, 1983). The search continues. If primary aging could be controlled, what would happen biologically, socially, economically, or in terms of health? The ramifications are staggering. If the rectangularization of the survival curve discussed earlier is attained, is society ready or even willing to deal with it? So far biological theories of aging have remained part of pure science; what will it mean if they become applied science?

# Functional Capacity and Age

The significance of the foregoing theories lies in their ability to explain the progressive loss of biological integrity over life. They provide us with a perspective on the underlying mechanisms of more widespread physiological changes. Alone they are hardly sufficient to tell us why one person dies at forty-five and another lives to be over 100. Longevity is a consequence of the reciprocal influences of normal physiological aging and a wide range of social and environmental factors. Generally speaking, our bodies are at their most vigorous when we are young, but at any time fitness depends on the dynamic interplay between intrinsic and extrinsic resources. We tend to forget that chronological age is a convenient indicator of functional capacity, not an absolute measure.

## FUNCTIONAL VARIABILITY WITHIN AGE CATEGORIES

An amazing degree of variability is as significant a hallmark of aging as is any other possible marker. It is not at all unusual in clinical examinations of the elderly to find a man of seventy with the eyesight of someone twenty years his junior, yet with the kidney function of one considerably older. An example of one such profile of a number of diverse physical parameters is shown in Figure 4.3. In this instance the individual is a noninstitutionalized male, and

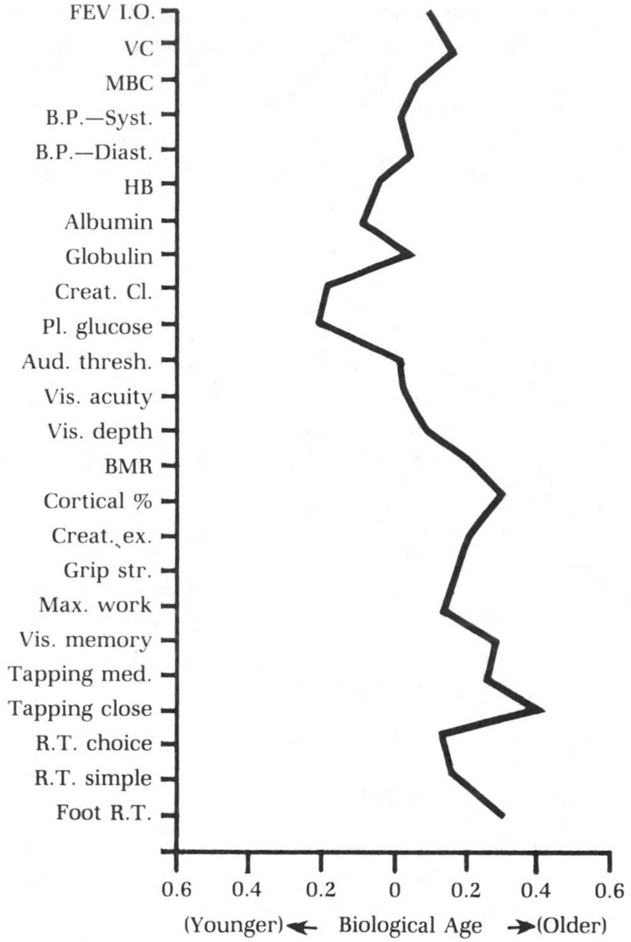

**FIGURE 4.3**

Biological age profile of a single individual. (*Source:* Borkan, G. A., and A. H. Norris. "Assessment of Biological Age Using a Profile of Physical Parameters." *Journal of Gerontology* 35, 2 [1980]: 180.)

clearly chronological age would provide only a rough approximation of his biological functioning (Borkan and Norris, 1980).

A number of questions are raised by the example shown: "Just how old are you?" "How do we measure age?" "Is it your muscles or your lungs?" Without definitive answers, the argument against arbitrary ages for events such as retirement is not as strong as it might sound. While technological advances and urbanization have alleviated many tensions our ancestors encountered in harsher environments, stress remains a relative concept. Physical capacities depend on use; if we are not called on to perform, it is hardly possible to develop our resources fully. Many social and economic factors impose differential pressures on functional capacity. Overall our ability to survive stressful episodes encountered from time to time in the normal course of events depends on the relative severity of the challenges, as well as on our reserve capacities. While measures of functional level show a linear decline with age, most of these reflect decrements under resting conditions. Similar observations of other groups or tests run during brief periods of maximum effort might show different patterns. Under stress situations we would expect to see a more precipitous decline, a greater displacement of normal levels, and extended recovery periods (Shock, 1977). Much remains to be uncovered about the physiological characteristics of the aged.

Regardless of the extent to which modern society mitigates the hard reality of physiological decline, one cannot avoid the gradual inevitable loss of life processes. Alterations at one level trigger changes at another; ultimately body composition and the functioning capacity of organ systems undergo debilitating transformations. Some of the major changes in body composition are set forth in Table 4.1 and Figure 4.3. It must be kept in mind the figures represent statistical averages and should not be taken as indicative of what is necessarily in store for a given individual. Some changes begin to occur relatively early in adult life while others may be postponed until quite late. As Timiras (1978) points out in her review, changes such as these should not be construed as a series of frames unfolding with a precise regularity. To do so would be to disregard the interplay of internal, social, and environmental factors.

Often the tendency to use functional age as a metaphor is overlooked. To have a heart like one forty years one's junior is not to have a heart forty years younger than the rest of one's body. Costa and McCrae (1985) remind us that just as there is no single theory or rate of aging, neither does the functional capability of the heart indicate how well any other organs work. They point out that aging may have many independent causes; hence the functional variability. If this is true, the idea of one overall functional index of age may be no more informative than chronological age. The implications of their contentions are profound and deserve serious reflection. If correct, it is possible biologists have been

**TABLE 4.1**

Comparison of a Tentative "Reference Person" Seventy with One Twenty-Five

|  | Age 25[a] | Age 70[b] |
| --- | --- | --- |
| Fat (%) | 14 | 30 |
| Water (%) | 61 | 53 |
| Cell solids (%) | 19 | 12 |
| Bone mineral (%) | 6 | 5 |
| Specific gravity | 1.068 | 1.035 |

[a]Brozek, J., Washington, D.C., Department of the Army, Office of the Quartermaster General, 1954.
[b]Fryer, J. H. In *Biological Aspects of Aging*, ed. N. W. Shock, p. 59. New York: Columbia University Press, 1962.
*Source:* Bakerman, S., *Aging Life Processes*, p. 8. Springfield, Ill.: Charles C Thomas, Publisher, 1969.

focusing their research on the wrong problems. If the causes of aging are due to a variety of factors, the search will have to be redirected.

A new level of sophistication may be called for, one that takes into consideration the complex interplay among biological processes, individual health, the capabilities one is born with, stress, and potent social forces (Costa and McCrae, 1985). The kind of profile shown in Figure 4.3 may not look especially innovative. It is, however, and close scrutiny reveals how useful such an idea may be. Variation around a given normative value for any particular age group suggests more precise intervention strategies. Medical care could be carefully tailored on the basis of individual age profiles such as those shown, and social policies and services could be targeted for precise problems.

## THE PICTURE OF FUNCTION

Coordination of organ systems is the key to most whole body functioning. Integrative processes and control mechanisms are crucial for maintaining homeostasis and may be more important than cellular alterations. Another key is the uniformity of internal environments through neural or endocrine regulatory capacities. After thirty a wide range of physiological functions show a linear decline of close to 1 percent each year; hence a number of integrative dependent properties must be undergoing a similar shift. Lest this seems too negative, it should also be noted that an equally large number of functions remain fairly stable under resting conditions until well past the seventh decade. As shown in Figure 4.4, there appears to be little change in the acidity, osmolarity, or sugar levels of our blood unless strong displacing stimuli occur (Shock, 1977). The reasons for this are related to alternative control mechanisms that are not found for other functions. Yet people rarely die of "old age"; that is, they do not actually wear out. More often they succumb to specific demands that surpass their remaining reserve capacity. The differences among people, and among organs within an individual, are a constant source of medical and interpersonal strain for the older person. Of major significance is that those functions dependent on the coordination of various organs show a greater deterioration with age than those of single organs. One example would be maximum vital capacity; though lessened, we seldom become aware of it unless exertion prompts a need for a rapid oxygen exchange. Only then do we discover that the muscles necessary for rapid breathing have also undergone decay, making it considerably more difficult to catch our breath than we remembered.

## LIFE-STYLE FACTORS AND FUNCTIONAL VARIABILITY

While the picture of functioning shown in Figure 4.3 describes averages, the range of variation among the general population actually increases with age. This means we age at different rates over time. Chronological age becomes a less reliable indicator of individual function for it conceals diverse capabilities. As Fries and Crapo (1981) ask, what is the reason behind the differences? To say plasticity is part of the human condition is not very informative.

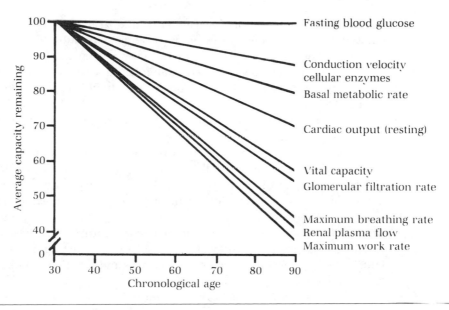

**FIGURE 4.4**

Simplified linear decline of physiological capacities with age; value at age 30 = 100 percent. (*Source:* Adapted from Shock, N. W. "Energy Metabolism, Calorie Intake and Physical Activity of the Aging." In *Nutrition and Old Age,* ed. L. A. Carlson. Uppsala: Almquist & Wiksell, 1972.)

Different people, different genetic endowments, and different biographies account for these variations. Not everyone follows the same pathway physically, psychologically, or socially. Perhaps part of the disparity can be explained by more people having chronic conditions in the later years. But the thoughtful gerontologist wants to know why specific medical conditions are present. What is the relation between life-style factors, the limits imposed by our social circumstances, and health and physical well-being?

In a ten-year follow-up of nearly 300 older individuals, Palmore et al. (1985) sought to predict functioning among their old-old study population in North Carolina. What they found was that declines were not accurate characterizations of all very old persons. The more socially advantaged elderly had no change in social or economic functioning and only a slight deterioration in global measures of physical and mental functioning. Though women and blacks showed rather marked deterioration, the authors attribute this to sexism and racism. Other sociological factors were also predictors of basic physiological, social, and psychological functions. The implications drawn by these experts is that social policy considerations are crucial for the physical and mental well-being of their sample population. If the advantaged in our society, by virtue of being able to acquire medical attention, sound nutrition, shelter, and other personal resources, live longer and better, then the ameliorative steps necessary for the less advantaged should be evident.

Although nothing lasts forever, Fries and Crapo (1981) offer a concrete suggestion for ensuring maximum physical viability until the very end of life. Figure 4.5 and Table 4.2 illustrate what they are saying. In their view, for a "vigor curve" to approximate the rectangular survival curve for a number of commonly used age markers, certain steps should be taken. Personal and societal choices are going to have to be made quickly. Personal decisions can enhance life, but social constraints are the background against which personal choices are made.

Of course, gerontology cannot provide a panacea against aging: even the most self-centered biologist will acknowledge all contexts are not equal. Even if they were equal, skin, arterial walls, kidney reserves, and so on would still show the effects of aging at different rates. It would be ideal but naive to say everyone makes a choice, so everyone has to live with the outcome. An undeniable body of evidence in the social science literature demonstrates that personal options reflect social location. To return to the Palmore et al. finding (1985) — to cite just one example: social status and functional status seem to go hand in hand.

In subsequent sections of this book it will become increasingly clear that socioeconomic considerations influence nearly all aspects of the aging process. They do not alter molecular structure, but they certainly provide the basis on which life is lived and circumscribe the opportunities to maximize our

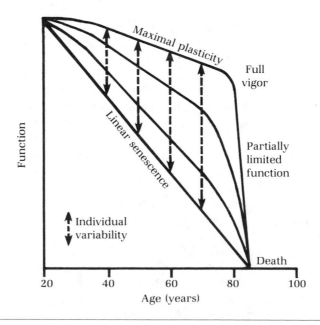

**FIGURE 4.5**

Individual rectangular curves for vigor representing a lifetime of vigor followed by terminal collapse.

options. Which causes the other is largely a question of which end of the telescope one looks through. They are, however, inextricably interwoven.

## Summary

It is unlikely that many of us will simply wear out and actually die of actual old age; the cause of death will probably be some specific disease that our bodies will no longer be able to fight. The process of senescence with its increasing vulnerability, is what is called normal aging. The theories introduced in this chapter are all attempts to explain why and how normal aging occurs. To date, however, no single theory of physiological aging has been broadly accepted. Furthermore, there is a considerable degree of overlap among them, and they all have something to contribute to our understanding.

One of the primary difficulties facing biogerontologists is distinguishing between primary and secondary aging patterns. It is no easy matter to determine what is intrinsic and what extrinsic. As we saw, a number of criteria have been suggested in an effort to delimit the field of inquiry, but as our knowledge increases, the boundary lines tend to shift. As a living system the human body interacts with both the physical and social environments. Each of these influences fundamental aging processes diversely according to the circumstances in which a given person lives out his or her life. Available nutrition, medical care, support, stress, and so on all interact with the aging organism.

Early biological models concentrated on the effects of metabolic rates and

**TABLE 4.2**

Modifiable Aspects of Aging

| Aging Marker | Personal Decision(s) Required |
| --- | --- |
| Cardiac reserve | Exercise, nonsmoking |
| Dental decay | Prophylaxis, diet |
| Glucose tolerance | Weight control, exercise, diet |
| Intelligence tests | Training, practice |
| Memory | Training, practice |
| Osteoporosis | Weight-bearing exercise, diet |
| Physical endurance | Exercise, weight control |
| Physical strength | Exercise |
| Pulmonary reserve | Exercise, nonsmoking |
| Reaction time | Training, practice |
| Serum cholesterol | Diet, weight control, exercise |
| Social ability | Practice |
| Skin aging | Sun avoidance |
| Systolic blood pressure | Salt limitation, weight control, exercise |

*Source:* Fries, J. F., and L. M. Crapo. *Vitality and Aging: Implications of the Rectangular Curve*, p. 125. San Francisco: W. H. Freeman & Company, 1981.

stress on the living organism. Both models contained implicit presumptions based on entropy as a factor in system depletion. Later efforts to explain intrinsic aging paid much greater attention to the mechanism by which essential processes deteriorate over time. From the molecular to the cellular to the systemic levels, each theory is faced with the task of accounting for more fundamental processes. Free radical, waste product, and cross-linkage models face similar obstacles but focus on the entire organism and the effect of the environment on the living system. The evidence that dividing cell lines have a finite life span is incontrovertible, but impairment of cellular functioning and duplication errors are likely implicated in aging to a greater extent than actual cell necrosis.

As a consequence of numerous societal and pathological circumstances, wide discrepancies between chronological and physiological age are common. Chronological age, therefore, is deceptive; it cannot be relied on as an accurate indicator of functional capabilities. A single index of functional age may also pose significant problems because it is a summary measure masking a great deal of variability. While there is evidence that some processes diminish gradually but steadily, others begin to undergo involution quite late, and still others show little change at all. As a consequence, it is difficult to say for sure which events herald old age, for they are many and varied; even within the same individual there is wide diversity.

Some researchers use the variations within a single individual to suggest aging may be caused by a range of processes. If so, the search for a single cause of all processes may be misleading. We need to redirect our energies if the mysteries of age in the whole organism are to be revealed. Interestingly, the range of functional variation increases as age increases. This suggests that life-style factors and social circumstances may be more significant than biogerontologists customarily acknowledge.

The reason behind the variation is the plasticity of the human condition. Part of the difference is the result of different genetic endowments, but an equal part has to be attributed to the different biographies of different people. Figure 4.5 illustrates the gap between a straight, linear pattern of senescence and the rectangularization of the survival curve that comes with plasticity. The implications of rectangular life curves were mentioned in Chapter 2 and will again be discussed in the following chapter. As Figure 5.1 shows, advances to date have come about from changes on the societal level. It is within the bounds of those alterations that individual factors influence an individual's life expectancy.

# Discussion Questions

**Relevance of Physiology to Social Gerontology**

1. Think of some problems in functioning that old people you know have. To what extent do you think these result from the normal physiology of aging? From illness? From life-

style? From the social circumstances in which these people find themselves?

2. What do you think could be done to alleviate these problems (a) medically, (b) by the elderly themselves, or (c) by changes in the environment in which they live?

3. What problems might arise from attributing physiological problems that are socially or environmentally caused to the normal aging process?

4. What would be the problem with a social theory of aging that ignored physiology?

**Early Biological Theories**

5. How has entropy shaped the development of a theoretical model for the physiology of aging?

6. What negative effects might the uncritical adoption of theories based on entropy have (a) for social policy or (b) for the way in which questions are formed in developing social theories of aging?

**Recent Biological Theories**

7. Discuss the potential contribution to understanding the physiology of aging of (a) theories at the molecular level, (b) theories at the cellular level, (c) theories at the systemic level, and (d) clinical studies of physiological functioning and organ systems in old people (such as exercise tolerance and other studies of the cardiovascular system).

**Functional Capacity and Age**

8. Compare the functional levels of some old people of similar ages. How do these people differ in terms of the material resources that have been and are available to them? Of their social support systems? Of their past and present lifestyles? Of their position in society? In what way do you think that differences in physiological functioning are related to the other differences between them?

9. Looking again at Figure 4.3, think about how your own profile might appear on any given day. What factors might cause it to change?

**Life-Style Factors and Functional Variability**

10. What social policy or service implications might be drawn from everyone having a functional profile available when they seek professional assistance?

# Pertinent Readings

Bakerman, S., ed. *Aging Life Processes.* Springfield, Ill.: Charles C Thomas, Publisher, 1969.

Bertalanffy, L. van. *General Systems Theory.* New York: George Braziller, Inc., 1968.

Bjorksten, J. "Theories." In *Aging Life Processes*, ed. S. Bakerman, pp. 147–79. Springfield, Ill.: Charles C Thomas, Publisher, 1969.

Borkan, G. A., and A. H. Norris. "Assessment of Biological Age Using a Profile of Physical Parameters." *Journal of Gerontology* 35, 2 (1980): 177–84.

Butler, L. H., and R. W. Newacheck. "Health and Social Factors Affecting Long-Term Care Policy." In *Policy Options in Long-Term Care*, eds. F. Meltzer, F. Farrow, and H. Richman. Chicago: University of Chicago Press, 1981.

Comfort, A. *The Biology of Senescence.* New York: Elsevier, 1979.

Costa, Jr., P. T., and R. R. McCrae. "Concepts of Functional or Biological Age: A Critical View." In *Principles of Geriatric Medicine*, eds. R. Andres, E. L. Bierman, and W. R. Hazzard, pp. 30–37. New York: McGraw-Hill Book Company, 1985.

Cristofalo, V. J., and B. M. Stanulis. "Cell Aging: A Model System Approach." In *The Biology of Aging*, eds. J. A. Behnke, C. E. Finch, and G. B. Moment, pp. 19–31. New York: Plenum Press, 1978.

Cumming, E., and W. E. Henry. *Growing Old: The Process of Disengagement.* New York: Basic Books, Inc., 1961.

Curtis, H. J. "Genetic Factors in Aging." *Advances in Genetics* 16 (1971): 305–24.

Doyal, L. *The Political Economy of Health.* Boston: South End Press, 1979.

Estes, C. L., et al. *Political Economy, Health and Aging.* Boston: Little, Brown & Company, 1984.

Fries, J. F., and L. M. Crapo. *Vitality and Aging: Implications of the Rectangular Curve.* San Francisco: W. H. Freeman & Company, 1981.

Harman, D. "The Aging Process." *Proceedings of the National Academy of Science* 78, 11 (1981): 7124–28.

Hayflick, L. "The Strategy of Senescence." *The Gerontologist* 14, 1 (1974): 37–45.

———. "Advances in Cytogerontology." In *Recent Advances in Gerontology*, eds. H. Orimo, K. Shimada, M. Iriki, and D. Maeda, pp. 104–105. Amsterdam: Excerpta Medica, 1979.

———. "Theories of Biological Aging." In *Principles of Geriatric Medicine*, eds. R. Andres, E. L. Bierman, and W. R. Hazzard, pp. 9–21. New York: McGraw-Hill Book Company, 1985.

Hickey, T. *Health and Aging.* Monterey, Calif.: Brooks/Cole Publishing Company, 1980.

Jokl, E. "Physical Activity and Aging." *Annals of Sports Medicine* 2 (1983): 43–48.

Kohn, R. R. "Heart and Cardiovascular System." In *Handbook of the Biology of Aging*, eds. C. E. Finch and L. Hayflick, pp. 281–317. New York: Van Nostrand Reinhold Company, 1977.

Moment, G. B. "The Ponce de Leon Trail Today." In *The Biology of Aging*, eds. J. A. Behnke, C. E. Finch, and G. B. Moment, pp. 1–17. New York: Plenum Press, 1978.

Morgan, M. "My Life with Dr. Spock." *Parade Magazine* (October 14, 1984): pp. 4–6.

Orgel, L. F. "The Maintenance of the Accuracy of Protein Synthesis and Its Relevance to Aging." *Proceedings of the National Academy of Science* 67 (1970): 1476.

Palmore, E. B., J. B. Nowlin, and H. S. Wang. "Predictors of Function Among the Old-Old: A 10-Year Follow-Up." *Journal of Gerontology* 40, 2 (1985): 244–50.

Pearl, R. *The Rate of Living.* New York: Alfred Knopf, 1928.

Rockstein, M., and M. Sussman. *Biology of Aging.* Monterey, Calif.: Brooks/Cole Publishing Company, 1979.

Sacher, G. A. "Evolutionary Theory in Gerontology." *Perspectives in Biology and Medicine* 25, 3 (1982): 339–53.

Schmookler-Reis, R. J., et al. "Extrachromosomal Circular Copies of an 'inter-alu' Unstable Sequence in Human DNA Are Amplified During In Vitro and In Vivo Aging." *Nature* 301 (1983): 394–98.

Schneider, E. "Biomedical Aging Research in 1983: Some Highlights." *Journal of the American Geriatrics Society* 32, 4 (1984): 293–95.

Schneider, E., et al. "The Effect of Aging on Cellular Replication in Vitro and in Vivo." In *Recent Advances in Gerontology,* eds. H. Orimo, K. Shimada, M. Iriki, and D. Maeda, pp. 106–07, Amsterdam: Excerpta Medica, 1979.

Schofield, J. D., and I. Davis. "Theories of Aging." In *Textbook of Geriatric Medicine and Gerontology,* ed. J. Brocklehurst, pp. 37–70. Edinburgh: Churchill Livingstone, 1978.

Selye, H. *Stress Without Distress.* New York: J. B. Lippincott Co., 1974.

Selye, H., and P. Prioreschi. "Stress Theory of Aging." In *Aging: Some Social and Biological Aspects,* ed. N. W. Shock, pp. 261–72. Washington, D.C.: American Association for the Advancement of Science, 1960.

Shock, N. W. "System Integration." In *Handbook of the Biology of Aging,* eds. C. E. Finch and L. Hayflick, pp. 634–65. New York: Van Nostrand Reinhold Company, 1977.

Somers, A. R., and D. R. Fabian. *The Geriatric Imperative.* New York: Appleton-Century-Crofts, 1981.

Steen, B., B. Isaksson, and A. Svanborg. "Body Composition at 70 and 75 Years of Age: A Longitudinal Population Study." *Journal of Clinical Experimental Gerontology* 1, 2 (1979): 185–200.

Strehler, B. L. *Time, Cells, and Aging,* 2nd ed. New York: Academic Press, Inc., 1977.

———, and A. S. Mildvan. "Studies of the Chemical Properties of Lipofuscin Age Pigment." In *Biological Aspects of Aging,* ed. N. W. Shock. New York: Columbia University Press, 1962.

Timiras, P. S., ed. *Developmental Physiology and Aging.* New York: Macmillan, Inc., 1972.

———. "Biological Perspectives on Aging." *American Scientist* 66 (Pt. 5) (1978): 605–13.

Viidik, A. "Biological Aging: Searching for the Mechanisms of Aging." In *New Perspectives on Old Age,* eds. H. Thomae and G. L. Maddox, pp. 53–73. New York: Springer Publishing Company, 1982.

Walford, R. C. *Maximum Life Span.* New York: W. W. Norton & Co., 1983.

Wallace, D. J. "The Biology of Aging." *Journal of the American Geriatrics Society* 25, 3 (1977): 104–111.

# 5

# HEALTH STATUS IN THE LATER YEARS

**DIMENSIONS OF HEALTH**

Definitions of Health
  *Perspectives on Health and Disease*
  *The Conceptualization of Health and Disease*
The Meaning of Health for the Elderly
  *Levels of Analysis*
  *Sociocultural Conceptualizations of Health in Old Age*
  *The Medicalization of the Social*
  *Functional and Experiential Definitions of Health*
  *Toward a Meaningful Definition of Health in Old Age*

**HEALTH PROBLEMS OF THE LATER YEARS**

Health and the Rectangularization of the Life Curve
Patterns of Mortality and Morbidity among the Elderly

**THE DISEASES OF LATER LIFE**

Cardiovascular Diseases
  *Atherosclerosis*
  *Heart Disease*
  *Cerebrovascular Accidents*
  *Hypertension*
Cancer
Arthritis and Rheumatism
Diabetes Mellitus
Oral and Dental Problems

**LIFE-STYLE AND HEALTH IN THE LATER YEARS**

The Sociocultural Context and Health
Control and Longevity
  *Improving Life Expectancy*
Life-Style Factors Affecting Health and Longevity
  *Tobacco Abuse*
  *Alcohol Abuse*
  *Environmental Factors and Health*
  *Nutrition and Diet*
  *Exercise*
  *Life Satisfaction and Health*

**HEALTH CARE SERVICES FOR THE ELDERLY**

Cost Effectiveness in Health Services for the Elderly
  *The Problem of Rising Costs*
  *Cost Effectiveness in Health Care for the Elderly*
Cost Containment and Health Expenditures
  *Diagnosis Related Groups*
  *Potential Problems with DRGs*
Appropriate Levels of Care for the Elderly
  *Alternatives to the Medicare Cost Control System*

**SUMMARY**

**DISCUSSION QUESTIONS**

**PERTINENT READINGS**

# Dimensions of Health

The normal physiological changes of aging result from a complex interaction of the human body with its physical and social environment. The concept of health is a multilevel phenomenon as well. Biological, psychological, cultural, and social structural factors determine its very definition. In this chapter we will examine some conceptualization's of health that focus on various levels and analyze their implications for health status in aging. We will also indicate the ways in which health and social policy issues intertwine. A more pointed discussion of social issues and legislation related to health will be reserved for Chapter 8.

## DEFINITIONS OF HEALTH

**Perspectives on Health and Disease.** Historically, paradigms of health and disease have focused on different analytic levels. While recognizing that discussions of the nature of health go back at least to the work of Galen, Kelman (1975) identifies the first scientific paradigm of health as the *bioindividual school*. From the era of the Enlightenment a machine model of the human body has been popular, and health has been considered the perfect working order of the human organism. The diagnosis and treatment of diseases were conducted on an individual biochemicosurgical basis, and ill-health was seen as existing within the individual organism. The germ theory of disease is one example of this point of view. While it may seem naive to more recent theorists who emphasize the part played by the sensitivity of the individual organism and by socioenvironmental factors in the etiology of disease, the germ theory made it possible to identify the etiologic agents of infectious diseases and to formulate effective treatments for these with antibiotics — a development that has led to a dramatic increase in average life expectancies in countries where antibiotics are readily available.

The second major paradigm in the discussion of health is the **social epidemiology** or *environmental approach*. As its name implies, it examines the effect of environmental factors on health and illness: impure water, diet, smoking, hazards in the workplace, and other life-style factors. Social epidemiology still suffers from the implicit assumption that health is biologically, not socially determined, however, and as such is an organically defined state. This approach tends to focus on screening for and treating environmentally induced disease rather than on identifying and modifying the social causes from which such conditions arise (Kelman, 1975).

The third approach identified by Kelman is somewhat akin to what Estes et al. (1984) call the *political economy of health*. This perspective analyzes the ways in which the structure of social relations and particular interests define health and illness, contribute to medical problems, and influence the organization of health care (Kelman, 1975; Estes et al., 1984). An example of a political economic point of view might be an analysis of how financial and marketing interests of manufacturers and hospitals shape the ways in which medical technology is developed and distributed.

**The Conceptualization of Health and Disease.** Perhaps the best known definition of health is that offered by the World Health Organization: "Health is a state of complete physical, mental and social well-being, and not merely the absence of disease or infirmity" (1946). This definition has since been criticized on a number of grounds. Its vagueness makes it difficult to operationalize, since not everyone would agree on what is meant by well-being. Others have criticized the WHO definition because it has paradoxically led to undesirable sociopolitical consequences that limit the freedom of the individual through the *medicalization of the social* (Zola, 1975; Conrad and Schneider, 1980). The WHO definition was doubtless meant to illustrate the ways in which the structure of social relations may limit or enhance the well-being of the individual and to encourage a rethinking of sociopolitical structures with this in mind. If mental and social well-being are seen as conforming to socially defined standards, discontent and dissent are judged illnesses to be medically treated rather than as points of view to be listened to and acted upon on their own merits. One of the major targets of critics in this school is the use of psychoactive drugs to handle psychosocial problems. Critics contend that this method represents a failure to deal with social problems at a societal level. For instance, Lennard quotes an advertisement that advocates the use of Librium, a tranquilizer, in managing intellectual curiosity that leads to increased sensitivity and apprehensiveness about unstable national and world conditions (Lennard et al., 1971).

Another line of concern is the practical usefulness of the WHO definition. Can we offer complete well-being to everyone, even supposing we agree on what it is? How much can we afford or are willing to spend on health? As will be seen in Chapter 6, by 2030 the potential expenditures on Alzheimer's disease will be enough to swamp the health care system. How do we set priorities for various health-related expenditures? Attempts to furnish more clearly delimited and practically useful definitions of health have focused on its functional aspects. For example, Parsons defined health as "the state of optimum capacity of an individual for the effective performance of the roles and tasks for which he has been socialized" (Parsons, 1972). Dubos' conceptualization combines functional and experiential elements and defines health as "a *modus vivendi* enabling imperfect men to achieve a rewarding and not too painful existence while they cope with an imperfect world" (Dubos, 1968). Clearly a complicated question is involved here: functional criteria imply quite different consequences than experiential ones. Functional perspectives stress an inability to perform one's roles regardless of how one feels: experiential criteria look at the actual feelings of people (Estes et al., 1984).

The bioindividual and epidemiological approaches have led to the development of alternative conceptual frameworks for thinking about health and disease. The first was developed by medical anthropologists and contrasted *biomedical* and *ethnomedical conceptions* of disease and illness. The biomedical approach concentrates on the physical substrates of disease, including such things as genes, diet, enzymes, physiological systems, organisms, microorganisms, climate, and stress. The ethnomedical approach focuses on how the illness is construed and handled by the people themselves (Fabrega, 1984). A crucial distinction between disease and illness particularly relevant in discussions of older persons may be traced back to the work of Mechanic (1962) and has been fully elaborated by Fabrega (1979, 1984) and by Kleinman and his colleagues (Kleinman et al., 1978; Kleinman and Mendelsohn, 1978). Disease is defined as the biological component of sickness, comprised of abnormalities in the structure and function of body organ systems and identified with neurophysiological and neurochemical factors. Illness, on the other hand, refers to the symbolic psychosocial aspects of sickness. Kleinman describes illness as "the human experience of disvalued changes in states of being and in social function" (Kleinman et al., 1978). Fabrega goes on, "From a general anthropological point of view, medical problems or illness may be defined as a disvalued change in the adaptation and functioning of an individual which gives rise to a need for corrective action" (Fabrega, 1984). It may include body symptom changes and an impairment in the ability to carry out expected tasks. The cultural experience of illness is influenced both by the physical properties of the disease from which the illness has been constructed and by the nature of the culture's theory of illness. It exploits universal human potentials and responds to universal limits in a culturally unique fashion. Although culturally constructed, illness tends to be based on physical symptoms, it need not necessarily have a corresponding disease. Of course, the converse is also true: someone may have a disease without being considered to be ill by his or her own culture.

Fabrega (1972) further distinguishes between two broad frameworks within which disease and illness are conceptualized: the *organismic perspective* and the *systems perspective*. The organismic view focuses on the person having the disease as a unit of analysis. It sees disease as a qualitative state that represents a disruption of normal function and has negative connotations. It may be seen as biological discontinuity, behavioral discontinuity, or phenomenological discontinuity (a change in states of being). The unified or systems perspective views disease and illness as a process. Health and disease are seen as phases of the multilevel phenomena that constitute the human condition (Engel, 1960).

## THE MEANING OF HEALTH FOR THE ELDERLY

**Levels of Analysis.** Each of the approaches just discussed may be useful in considering the health issues related to aging. Certain aspects of some problems are best handled using a biomedical approach. The changes in the lens of the eye that lead to cataracts are, as far as we now know, a result of normal physiological aging processes. They cannot thus be retarded by modifying environmental factors or social relations but are best handled by medical modalities such as surgery or implanted lenses. We need, however, to remember the psychosocial implications of cataract surgery for those who undergo it and the political economic implications of funding and decisions as to where and by whom it will be performed. Furthermore, an approach drawn from social epidemiology may be useful in evaluating the impact of environmental and life-style factors on the health of the elderly. For example, occupational diseases that are carried into retirement and the effects of tobacco, alcohol, and lack of exercise all call for a social epidemiological analysis.

Political economy and an analysis of the implications of the structure of social relations for the health of the elderly is important in a number of ways. As well as being a matter of personal life-style, the health hazards resulting from tobacco and alcohol also derive from the ways in which these products are marketed by the tobacco and alcohol industries. Similarly, we must examine the structure of social relations that both builds up stress and then makes tobacco, alcohol, and drug use a culturally acceptable way of coping with stress. To a significant degree, occupational diseases result from the organization of social groups and the distribution of power in the workplace. Finally, political economy is important in determining the share of the national budget spent on health care for the elderly, as well as the types of care made available to them. There are many reasons why most forms of medical insurance, including Medicare, are better suited for catastrophic conditions rather than the long-term chronic conditions of older persons. A political economy approach helps to illuminate those reasons.

**Sociocultural Conceptualizations of Health in Old Age.** The ethnomedical approach reminds us that our views of health status in old age, like illness, are socially constructed notions that may not correspond to the physical substrate. Old age has tended to be conceptualized as illness in our culture. On the one hand, this leads to a form of ageism that sees the old as infirm even when they are not: an illness without a disease. On the other hand, we may have diseases without being ill: physical changes that are caused by a disease may be perceived as part of the normal aging process and left unattended when effective treatment is available. As we will see in Chapter 6, a problem of this type that has recently received considerable attention is **dementia.** Many have been tempted to consider it a matter of "senility," while dementia is in fact always the outcome of a disease process. When both a disease and an illness are present, an understanding of the socially constructed reality of illness, as well as of the disease, can contribute to more effective management.

**The Medicalization of the Social.** Like the rest of us, the elderly may to some degree fall prey to the medicalization of the social. That is, difficulties rooted in societal problems are seen as caused by failing physical capacities that are the purview of the medical community. Overmedication is considered a major problem among the elderly, and questions are being raised as to whether some of the problems managed with psychoactive drugs might not be more appropriately handled by changing the social conditions from which they arise (Estes et al., 1984; Lee and Lipton, 1982). More effort seems to be given to finding cures for socioenvironmentally spawned diseases such as cardiovascular disease and lung cancer than to modifying the social causes that contribute to their prevalence. Furthermore, as Estes et al. (1984) and Townsend (1981) point out, the attribution of physical decline and incompetence to the aging process "depoliticizes" the ways in which dependence is created among the elderly.

**Functional and Experiential Definitions of Health.** Estes et al. (1984) and Kelman (1975) also contend that in a free market economy, the primary goal of which is maximizing profit, the emphasis tends to be on a functional definition of health in the sense of the ability to be economically productive. It does not matter if you feel ill as long as you are not sick in the sense that you can continue to produce. Clearly this has prejudicial effects for the elderly in two major ways. First, it casts doubt on their health and competency, because they are marginally productive in the work force by virtue of our social policies. Second, it has at least the potential for encouraging withdrawal of health care resources from members of society who are judged to be unproductive, a tendency reflected in the widespread attention given to the recent series of cost-cutting measures as we move toward the end of the 1980s.

**Toward a Meaningful Definition of Health in Old Age.** What criteria are we to use for assessing health in old age? As we have seen, an overemphasis on functional criteria for health at any age may lead to an insensitivity toward a person's sense of well-being and a reluctance to provide care to those who — for one reason or another — are unable or unwilling to produce according to society's terms. Experiential health, as a sense of complete physical, mental, and social well-being, however, is hardly a realistic goal in later life, particularly for the old-old. Perhaps the key lies in Dubos' definition: achieving a rewarding and not too painful existence while coping with an imperfect world (Dubos, 1968). Efforts toward maximizing the health of the elderly could be seen as creating social conditions and medical services that allow them to use whatever powers they have, to recover from treatable diseases, to live with the diseases that are not treatable, and perhaps to allow the elderly to contribute to the lives of others. As well as providing supportive services for today's elderly, such efforts might include a variety of preventive measures designed to help future generations avoid some of today's disabilities and illnesses.

# Health Problems of the Later Years

## HEALTH AND THE RECTANGULARIZATION OF THE LIFE CURVE

Over the past hundred years medicine has done more to improve the quality of life than in all previous centuries combined. Yet from the life tables presented in Chapter 2 it is clear that the most significant breakthroughs have been observed for those illnesses likely to affect people in their earliest years. The control of infectious diseases brought dramatic declines in infant mortality. With improved sanitary conditions and public health information, maternal mortality quickly subsided as a major contributor to the death toll during the childbearing years. Intestinal disorders, a major cause of death in the last century, have all but disappeared as a consequence of new food-handling techniques and other hygienic measures. Unfortunately, these problems have been replaced by diseases unique to industrial societies, primarily disorders of the upper respiratory system. Changes in the causes of mortality and the course of the illnesses themselves also reflect wide-ranging alterations in the kind of society we live in and the work we do. Within these parameters is some latitude for individual variation, but the limits are set by societal factors. Figure 5.1 illustrates the way in which various factors have contributed to the rectangularization of the life curve.

When younger people fall ill, it is most often a consequence of exogenous factors and frequently of infectious disease. The course such illnesses follow is traumatic, with a definite onset, crisis point, and self-limiting aftermath. In other words, they are **acute** conditions. Later in life the causes of illness change, becoming essentially endogenous and nonspecific. They are **chronic**, developing slowly, without a marked crisis point, and lingering for extended periods. In contrast to acute conditions, chronic illnesses usually involve a number of body functions and cannot be attributed to a single cause, thereby confronting both the patient and the physician with a more obstinate problem. Another difference is that unlike youthful illnesses the pathological conditions of later years seem to be progressive, leading to increased vulnerability rather than protective resistance. Besides combating those diseases likely to strike prior to biological maturity, medicine has scored its biggest victories over those conditions that have a specific **etiology** — that is, result from a single identifiable cause. Ironically, the illnesses that appear most often to accompany aging are not of this type and therefore have not benefited from medical research as rapidly. Yet contrary to popular stereotypes, the later years need not be a time of continual ill health, however much the two seem to be inevitably linked in our thinking. Not very long ago "old age" itself was frequently listed as the cause of death for people who died after sixty, because

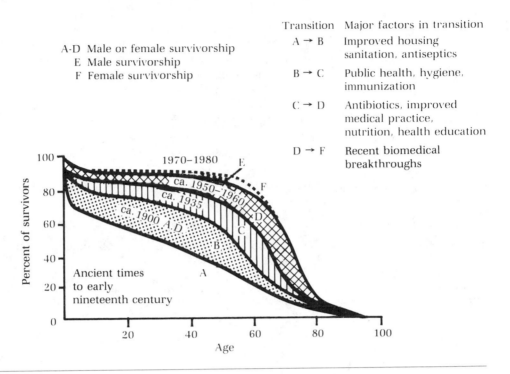

A-D  Male or female survivorship
  E  Male survivorship
  F  Female survivorship

| Transition | Major factors in transition |
| --- | --- |
| A → B | Improved housing sanitation, antiseptics |
| B → C | Public health, hygiene, immunization |
| C → D | Antibiotics, improved medical practice, nutrition, health education |
| D → F | Recent biomedical breakthroughs |

**FIGURE 5.1**

Human survivorship trends from ancient times to the present. These idealized curves illustrate the rapid approach to the limiting rectangular curve that has occurred during the last 150 years. The inset on the upper right lists major factors responsible for these transitions. Note that life expectancy for males has not changed since 1950 in the 50+ age group but that female survivorship has improved during this period, partially, at least, because of better treatment of reproductive system malignancies. (*Source:* Strehler, B. L. "Implications of Aging Research for Society." *Federation Proceedings* 34, 1 [1975]: 6.)

people believed that aging itself was a form of disease. A few countries still continue to refer to age as cause of death; in West Germany, for example, between 8 and 10 percent of the deaths of older people are officially attributed to "old age." Generally speaking, medical science no longer views illness and age as indistinguishable phenomena. Nonetheless, health is often used as a barometer of aging in many people's minds and chronic diseases are seen as unavoidable (Hickey, 1980; Kane et al., 1984).

Some recent investigators have suggested that advances in medicine may one day leave future generations of older people free from many of the degenerative diseases so extensive today. On the other hand, other scientists continue to view pathological disease as the fate of the aged regardless of future medical developments, apparently envisioning that once present conditions respond to treatment, a new set of impairments will take their place.

Whether this proves to be the case, the health status of older persons clearly represents the dynamic interplay of phenomena continually subject to change. One means of achieving a better understanding of health status among the elderly is to look at the ways in which the causes of death for various groups have been modified since the turn of the century.

## PATTERNS OF MORTALITY AND MORBIDITY AMONG THE ELDERLY

It is usually assumed that the illnesses from which human beings suffer have been fairly constant throughout history. No doubt those illnesses with which we are currently familiar have afflicted people for centuries, yet many of the diseases prevalent in the past no longer demand attention today. One example

**TABLE 5.1**

Primary Causes of Death in the United States, 1900–1981, and in Selected Countries[a]

| United States (1900) | Rank | United States (1981) | Canada (1982) | Japan (1982) | France (1981) | England and Wales (1982) |
|---|---|---|---|---|---|---|
| Influenza/ pneumonia | 1 | Diseases of heart | 1 | 3 | 2 | 1 |
| Tuberculosis | 2 | Malignant neoplasms | 2 | 1 | 1 | 2 |
| Gastroenteritis (includes diarrhea) | 3 | Cerebrovascular diseases | 3 | 2 | 3 | 3 |
| Diseases of heart | 4 | All accidents | 4 | 5 | 4 | 7 |
| Cerebrovascular diseases | 5 | Respiratory diseases[b] | 5 | 8 | 5 | 5 |
| Chronic nephritis | 6 | Influenza/ pneumonia | 6 | 4 | 14 | 4 |
| All accidents | 7 | Diabetes mellitus | 10 | 14 | 15 | 14 |
| Malignant neoplasms (all cancers) | 8 | Cirrhosis of the liver | 11 | 9 | 7 | 19 |
| Early infancy diseases | 9 | Atherosclerosis | 9 | 17 | 22 | 9 |
| Diphtheria | 10 | Suicide | 7 | 7 | 11 | 15 |
| | 11 | Homicide and legal intervention | 18 | 21 | 24 | 21 |
| | 12 | Early infancy diseases | — | — | — | — |

[a]Latest year available.
[b]Refers to bronchitis, emphysema, asthma, and other chronic respiratory diseases.
*Sources:* National Center for Health Statistics. *Monthly Vital Statistics Report,* 29, 2. Washington, D.C.: U.S. Government Printing Office, 1980; U.S. Bureau of the Census. *Statistical Abstract of the United States, 1985.* Washington, D.C.: U.S. Government Printing Office, 1985; and World Health Organization, *World Health Statistics Annual,* Geneva: World Health Organization, 1984 (adapted).

is rickets, once so commonplace it was considered a normal fate in England 200 years ago. The severity of still other diseases has been reduced over the years, although the conditions themselves are still observable. Measles, for instance, is rarely a source of alarm to any but the pregnant, despite the fact that during the last century measles was frequently fatal (and still is in some Third World countries), causing blindness and near epidemic numbers of deaths on occasion. By 1915 measles had given way to diphtheria, influenza, and other infectious diseases as primary causes of death. Historically, respiratory diseases, tuberculosis and bronchitis among them, have been closely associated with populations during rapid periods of industrialization, often appearing as a fatal condition among the older males in these populations. Medical anthropologists have long stressed the ecological relationship among diseases, culture, and the environment in which people live. Now, as much of the world gains access to modern medicine, the nature of ill-health will undoubtedly reflect those changes (Bourliere, 1978).

Since the early 1900s there has been a substantial decrease in those infectious diseases that had been so intractable in previous years. In the industrialized nations of the world, where improved sanitary and health conditions have been reflected by an increase in the average age of populations, a concomitant change has occurred in degenerative diseases, usually characteristic of older populations as primary causes of death. As shown in Table 5.1, retrogressive chronic diseases have replaced infectious viruses and tubercular diseases in the United States as the most commonly identified fatal illnesses. A comparison of current American patterns with mortality in four other countries is presented in Table 5.1 as well. While the rank order in the more industrialized countries parallels that in North America, current patterns among developing or Third World countries as exemplified by Table 5.2 differ, in part

**TABLE 5.2**
Primary Causes of Death in a Third World Country: El Salvador, 1981

| Rank | Causes of Death | Rank | Causes of Death |
|------|-----------------|------|-----------------|
| 1 | Homicide and other forms of violence | 7 | Respiratory diseases[a] |
| | | 8 | Senility without mention of psychosis |
| 2 | Signs, symptoms, and other ill-defined conditions | 9 | Malignant neoplasms |
| 3 | Early infancy diseases | 10 | Diseases of the digestive system[b] |
| 4 | Infectious and parasitic diseases | 11 | Cerebrovascular disease |
| 5 | All accidents | 12 | Influenza/pneumonia |
| 6 | Heart diseases | | |

[a]Includes chronic and unspecified bronchitis, emphysema, asthma, and other diseases of the respiratory system, excluding pneumonia and acute infections.
[b]Includes diseases of the digestive system other than peptic ulcers, appendicitis, hernias, cirrhosis, and malignant neoplasms.
*Source:* World Health Organization. *World Health Statistics Annual.* Geneva: World Health Organization, 1984 (adapted).

because of their lesser degree of industrialization and the limited availability of medical care.

A representation of age-specific mortality found in later adulthood can be seen in Table 5.3. Close inspection of the table reveals a subtle variation in the major causes of death in the second half of life. For both middle-aged and older people, heart diseases, cancer, and cerebrovascular lesions, predominantly strokes, appear as the most frequent causes of death, accounting for approximately 73 percent of the deaths among those over forty-five. Fully 46 percent of the fatalities can be directly attributed to heart diseases alone and a further 16 percent to malignant neoplasms. Moving beyond the first three causes of death, fatal conditions sort themselves into distinct groups by age. Among the middle-aged, violent deaths from accidents or suicides take a heavy toll. For older people these are surpassed by fatalities that result when physiological defenses have been vitiated by age. As is evident, however, from the right side, men and women sixty-five or over do not succumb uniformly to the same diseases.

While mortality data provide much information about the illnesses that most often result in death, they cannot reveal the extent to which the lives of the living are affected by these same or other conditions. It is necessary to look at the evidence gathered by health surveys to ascertain the incidence of those illnesses currently afflicting various segments of a country's population. Depending on whether the statistics are based on individuals who actually seek medical attention or are derived from a sample of all members of a designated group, the causes of **morbidity**, or a departure from full health, will vary somewhat. In either case, though, the diagnostic categories used have some impact on the results; that is, symptoms will be perceived and listed in a fairly well-defined range of expected conditions. Still, incidence surveys pro-

**TABLE 5.3**
Selected Causes of Death by Age and Sex in the United States, 1981

| Causes of Death (45–64) | Rank | Causes of Death (Over 65) | 65+ Male to Female Ratio |
|---|---|---|---|
| Diseases of heart | 1 | Diseases of heart | 1.344 |
| Malignant neoplasms | 2 | Malignant neoplasms | 1.886 |
| Cerebrovascular diseases | 3 | Cerebrovascular diseases | 1.008 |
| Accidents | 4 | Pneumonia | 1.565 |
| Cirrhosis of liver | 5 | Atherosclerosis | 1.065 |
| Diabetes mellitus | 6 | Accidents | 1.676 |
| Suicide | 7 | Diabetes mellitus | .965 |
| Pneumonia | 8 | Cirrhosis of liver | 2.188 |
| Atherosclerosis | 9 | Suicide | 7.595 |

Source: *Statistical Abstract of the United States, 1985.* Washington, D.C.: U.S. Government Printing Office, 1985 (adapted).

vide the most complete picture of the quality of health experienced by a majority of people.

In a very general way age itself can serve as a reliable indicator of the prevalence of both acute and chronic conditions. As a general rule, it may be said that older people are more likely to suffer chronic conditions and are less likely to be afflicted by acute illnesses at any given time. Of the more than twenty-five million people over sixty-five in the United States today, almost 28 percent are suffering from chronic heart conditions, 38 percent from hypertension, 8 percent from diabetes, 46 percent from chronic bronchitis, and 13 percent from deformities or orthopedic impairments. These figures may actually underrepresent impairment levels, since older persons often see them as normal aspects of the aging process to be expected rather than treated. Some conditions are also socially stigmatizing and are likely to be unreported. Urinary incontinence is an obvious example. Some estimates of incontinence range from 5 to 20 percent of the elderly in the community and as much as 75 percent among residents of long-term care institutions. Contrary to popular opinion, many forms of incontinence can be treated. As we can see from Table 5.4, the incidence of many disorders is relatively low in young people under seventeen and rises in middle and old age (Rowe, 1985; U.S. Census, 1985).

While older people continue to suffer at least one acute episode of illness every year, this represents a drastic decline from the actual number encountered at earlier ages. One significant change is that older people who have an acute condition are disabled longer. A similar pattern emerges for accidents; they happen less often for older people but result in longer periods of recuperation. Thus, nearly 29 percent of the young adult population fell victim to accidental injury in 1980, while only 20 percent of the group between forty-five and sixty-four were injured through accidents. Although fatal accidents continue to decline among the elderly, the overall percentage of accidents creeps up slightly, to 21.3 percent. Unlike the younger groups, who are usually involved in traffic accidents, two-thirds of the injuries of older people are a result of accidents around the house, an important factor to keep in mind

**TABLE 5.4**
Percent Incidence of Selected Chronic Conditions by Age, United States, 1981

|  | Under 17 | 17–44 | 45–64 | 65 and Over |
|---|---|---|---|---|
| Heart conditions | 2.04 | 3.79 | 12.27 | 27.7 |
| Hypertension | 0.14a | 5.42 | 24.37 | 37.86 |
| Chronic bronchitis | 3.84 | 2.81 | 4.09 | 4.61 |
| Arthritis | 0.28a | 4.77 | 24.65 | 46.47 |
| Diabetes mellitus | 0.14a | 0.86 | 5.69 | 8.34 |

aFigure does not meet standards of reliability or precision.
*Source:* Adapted from U.S. Bureau of the Census. *Statistical Abstract of the United States, 1985.* Washington, D.C.: U.S. Government Printing Office, 1985.

when planning living accommodations for older people. Among older women, accidents cause about four days of disability yearly, compared to about one day from accidents for men. As a consequence of their various health problems, both acute and chronic illness as well as accidental injury, older people have their activities restricted for nearly five weeks every year, up from the three and a half weeks for people in the forty-five to sixty-four age range (National Center for Health Statistics, 1983).

Many elderly find the aftermath of ill-health more threatening than thoughts of even their own death. From the middle years onward a large proportion of people live with at least one chronic health problem and the likelihood of more cropping up in successive years. The various respiratory ailments become the most frequent acute illnesses among older adults, accounting for seventy-two out of every 100 episodes of acute distress by forty-five, dropping to forty-six after sixty-five. Accidental injuries are second, representing slightly more than twenty-one and sixteen of every 100 episodes in the middle-aged and older categories, respectively. Diseases of the digestive tract are the third most common acute condition among older people; however, for the middle-aged they are preceded by infectious and parasitic diseases. Despite the many unanswerable questions, so far as researchers have been able to tell the treatments indicated for the acute illnesses observed in older persons are identical to those indicated for other age groups. The primary difference among the age groups is the presence of chronic conditions that may complicate the course followed by acute illnesses.

Far more significant than acute conditions are the chronic illnesses reported by the elderly and the limitations they impose. Looking first at the limitations on daily living, it is not difficult to appreciate why older people face the possibility of becoming socially isolated. During the middle years there is a noticeable increase in the number of people who relate the incidence of constraint in their daily routine, although interestingly enough, half the people sixty-five or over go about their business seemingly undeterred by any limitations. The percentage of adults who feel constrained in day-to-day activities by chronic conditions is illustrated in Figure 5.2.

As revealed by the figure, the proportion of severely limited individuals increases dramatically with age—nearly fourfold just among the ages specified. Not shown is the fact that after individuals reach their midseventies, they are even more inhibited by the effects of chronic illnesses, thereby facing still greater barriers to social interaction.

In the forty-five to sixty-five age group 78 percent of people consider their own health to be excellent or good, whereas 22 percent consider it to be fair or poor. Of people sixty-five and over, only 69 percent consider their health to be excellent or good, while 31 percent consider it to be fair or poor (National Center for Health Statistics, 1984a).

Given the potentially extensive health problems and diminished financial resources of older people, it is small wonder that many of them express a great deal of anxiety over possible dependency. This is not to say that all older

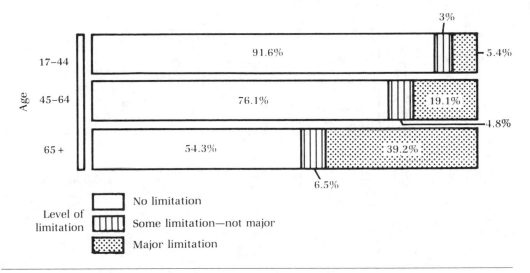

**FIGURE 5.2**
Percentage of adults with various degrees of activity limitation caused by chronic conditions.
(*Source: Current Estimates from the Health Interview Survey, 1981.* Vital and Health Statistics,
Series 10, No. 141. Washington, D.C.: U.S. Government Printing Office, 1981 [adapted].)

people experience the same health-related problems or that those they do cannot possibly be mitigated. Figure 5.3 provides a closer look at the information
presented in the previous figure. Obviously such factors as sex, race, and income are important components of the overall health picture. With few exceptions, women, nonwhites, and poor people suffer more from ill-health in the
process of becoming older. An understandable concern repeatedly voiced by
inquiring older citizens is why optimal medical attention is not available to all
as part of their retirement benefits. This is liable to become an even greater
concern given the recent cuts in Medicare funding.

## The Diseases of Later Life

The most frequently occurring chronic conditions afflicting older people are
the various forms of heart disease, hypertension or high blood pressure, and
the several forms of arthritis. In addition, a great many other illnesses and impairments cause varying degrees of distress. Foremost among these are
cancer, diabetes, cerebral hemorrhages, and circulatory problems, as well as
the impairments in hearing and vision discussed in Chapter 6. In Chapter 4 aging was emphasized as an intrinsic process distinct from the numerous pathol-
ogies so often associated with it, yet at the present time medical researchers
have difficulty in separating the manifestations of either. Multiple pathological
conditions compound the problems of accurate diagnosis, effective treatment,
and sensitive care. Once older people decide a visit to a physician is in order, it
is highly probable they will have a complex set of symptoms. Unlike acute ill-

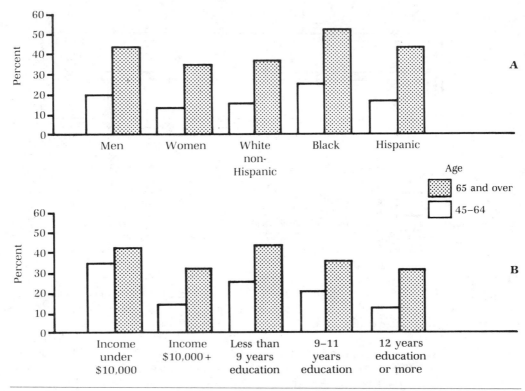

**FIGURE 5.3**

Percent of specified categories of persons suffering major activity limitation because of chronic conditions: United States, 1978–1980. *A*, By age, sex, and race. *B*, By income of family head and age and by education of family head and age. (*Source:* Adapted from National Center for Health Statistics. *Health Indicators for Hispanic, Black and White Americans.* Vital and Health Statistics, Series 10, No. 148; Table 14, pp. 52–53. Washington, D.C.: U.S. Government Printing Office, 1984.)

nesses, many chronic conditions appear in unison. This is of serious concern, and many of the textbook descriptions of disease the physician uses in evaluating patients will be misleading when applied to geriatric cases because the readily observable signs are altered among the elderly. Specially designed training is therefore necessary to detect root causes (Butler, 1979; Andres et al., 1985). It is all the more crucial then to gain some knowledge of the diseases and disabilities of the elderly if the wide range of problems they engender is to be dealt with in terms of the whole person. Most scientists agree people do not really die of old age per se; they succumb to one or more specific diseases.

## CARDIOVASCULAR DISEASES

**Atherosclerosis.** Estimates are that 55 percent of all deaths in the United States each year are caused either by coronary or by cerebral ischemia or infarction attributable to atherosclerosis. Closely aligned with all forms of heart disease is a particular set of vascular difficulties generally grouped under the label of *arteriosclerosis* (hardening of the arteries). The form most common in later years is called atherosclerosis, a thickening of the *intima* or interior walls of major vessels throughout the body. By the 1960s a report on the worldwide distribution of heart diseases by the World Health Organization noted that atherosclerosis is a nearly universal health problem that singularly stands in the way of any appreciable prolongation of life. The same report also predicted in those countries where the incidence of atherosclerosis is not yet a widespread cause of death, rapidly changing social and technological conditions portend future increases ("The World Health Situation," 1967). Evidence indicates this was clearly the case historically both in industrialized countries and in those currently undergoing rapid industrialization. The disease cannot be considered an exclusively modern malady, as it was described in explicit detail in ancient Greek medical literature. Examination of mummies also suggests it was known in Egypt and probably throughout the ancient world (Timiras, 1972).

Bierman (1985) reports that it is currently hypothesized that atherosclerosis is caused by the superimposition of both intrinsic aging processes and environmental factors (such as diet) on unknown genetic factors. That atherosclerosis is not simply the result of unmodified intrinsic biological aging processes is demonstrated by the fact that most mammalian species age without spontaneously developing atherosclerosis. Subpopulations in the world also age to the life span appropriate to the human species without developing the disease. Thus the considerable differences in the prevalence rates in various parts of the world are probably related to factors other than age per se, and preventive measures such as life-style changes in the young and middle-aged are some of the most promising avenues for managing atherosclerosis in future generations (Bierman, 1985).

For some years now age-specific death rates for diseases of the heart have been in slow decline. Still, the extent to which heart diseases including atherosclerosis claim lives is overwhelming. In the period between 1950 and 1980 deaths resulting from heart diseases among men in the sixty-five to seventy-four age bracket declined by roughly 20 percent. In the next ten-year age bracket the shift was even more dramatic. Among women no such downward shift has been noted (National Center for Health Statistics, 1984b).

Despite the recent slight decline, middle-aged American men stand about one chance in five of developing clinically significant cardiovascular problems before they reach retirement age; aside from Finnish men, Americans have the highest cardiac mortality rates in the world. Like so many other generic cardiovascular diseases, atherosclerotic conditions discriminate on the basis of sex; they occur among American males at a rate three times the incidence among similarly aged females. And like other chronic illnesses, atherosclerosis need not prove fatal or disrupt normal routines; its prevalence approaches 100 percent among the very old in certain populations, seriously impairing their way of life.

Only among sufferers of diabetes or other high-risk illnesses does atherosclerosis make much of an impact before late in the fourth decade, although its inception usually dates from early adolescence. Autopsies from casualties of war in Korea and Vietnam demonstrated a high prevalence of atherosclerotic changes in the arteries of American males as early as the second and third decades of life (Bierman, 1985). Individuals with a family history of heart disease seem particularly prone to cardiovascular disorders, although the mechanism by which susceptibility is transmitted is still a puzzle to medical science. The most important factors that have been linked to increased probabilities of arterial diseases are diets high in saturated fats, sedentary activities, obesity, cigarette smoking, and psychological stress.

Over the past century numerous theories have been formulated to explain the pathogenesis of atherosclerotic conditions, although to date none have gained universal acceptance. The 1980 public split and accompanying fervor, a rare event in medical circles, resulting from the controversial report of a blue-ribbon panel named by the National Academy of Sciences to study the issue is testimony of the controversy surrounding the importance of diet. The appearance of fatty streaks in the inner walls of the arteries has prompted many investigators to conclude that the blood deposits fatty substances that are absorbed through the **endothelial lining** separating the actual blood flow from the intima of the artery. These in turn are trapped inside the artery wall rather than passing through with the nutritive substances. Ultimately a roughening and swelling occur that promote the formation of fibrous plaques in the **lumen**, or artery channel. Once the irregularity has taken shape, further buildup follows, constricting the space through which blood may flow. The actual buildup is called a **thrombosis** and may eventually bring about a complete **occlusion**, or closing of the artery. Under stress, thromboses may break loose, floating through the artery until becoming lodged in one of the smaller branches. Since the artery is a living form of connective tissue, damage begins immediately after any individual cell dies, no matter what the cause. With tissue death comes calcification, loss of elasticity, and lowered permeability. Which factors actually initiate the damage is a hotly debated topic among physiologists.

Two basic mechanisms by which atherosclerosis causes serious — and in some cases life-threatening — clinical problems are clots and narrowing of the blood vessels, both of which lead to *ischemia* or inadequate blood supply. A clot, or *thrombus*, that breaks loose is called an *embolism*. It may lodge in an artery, cutting off circulation to a segment of the brain or the heart and thus cause tissue death or **infarction** of that segment; when this happens, it causes a cerebral or myocardial infarction. It may become caught in the lungs as a *pulmonary embolism*. In all cases these are potentially life-threatening conditions. In other instances a clot may block circulation to a leg, resulting in gangrene and possible amputation. *Stenosis*, or narrowing of an artery, may be so advanced that any contraction of the blood vessels will result in the circulation being temporarily cut off, a phenomenon known as a *transient* *ischemic attack. Angina,* or cardiac chest pain, results from the circulation in the coronary arteries being compromised. Stenosis of the *carotid arteries* in the neck that feed the head leads to transient ischemic attacks of the brain accompanied by transient episodes of confusion or loss of neurological function. Impairment of the circulation to the legs leads to cramps or *claudication* during exercise, a common condition among the elderly.

Various surgical techniques have been developed to deal with problems resulting from the stenosis of particular arteries when the rest of the circulatory system is in sufficiently good shape for a return of function if the blockage is circumvented. Arterial bypass involves replacing the blocked segment with grafts from other blood vessels or with prosthetic implants. When a surgeon performs an *endarterectomy,* he or she scrapes out the lumen of the blocked artery. This procedure is sometimes used to clear out thromboses from the **carotid arteries** when the patient is considered to be at risk for stroke and sometimes in an attempt to salvage a leg when a major blood vessel feeding it has thrombosed. A new noninvasive procedure known as *angioplasty* has been developed in the 1980s. It involves threading a narrow catheter through the blood vessels to the point at which the artery is stenosed. A balloon on the end of the catheter is blown up and used to dilate the artery gradually. Used initially to treat coronary artery disease, it is now being extended to treat stenosis of the arteries feeding the legs. While these techniques are important in that they promise prolonged function for those who are already affected by atherosclerosis, the real hope for future generations of the elderly lies in primary prevention.

**Heart Disease.** The chances of disability or fatality from various forms of heart disease increase with every decade of life. So pervasive is heart disease among people in their forties or older that until recently it was thought to be synonymous with aging itself. Hence it is particularly surprising that death rates for heart attacks declined markedly as the 1970s drew to a close. Epidemiologists had noted slight declines since the mid-1950s, but it was not until several years had passed that attention was focused on one of the most striking public health developments of our time. The rate of decline accelerated in the mid-1970s, so much so that the percentage change in little more than seven years surpassed the previous twenty years. Recent statistics indicate there has been a continuing dramatic decline in cardiac deaths in men for 1981, whereas cardiac death rates in women have remained relatively constant since 1960. As yet the reasons for the decline are not clear, and there is considerable debate over the relative roles of the many factors involved; the availability of advanced cardiac life support systems and coronary care units to get people through the crucial first forty-eight hours has been suggested as a major factor (National Center for Health Statistics, 1984b; U.S. Census, 1985).

Through the 1980s heart diseases continue to account for over half of all fatalities in the United States and Canada — claiming a victim roughly every minute. In many other industrial countries in the Western world the rates are very similar. The Scandinavian countries and the United Kingdom have a high incidence of coronary failure. Even when it does not result in death, nearly one in five of all adult disabilities are the result of heart-related problems. Though younger males are susceptible targets, it is among older men that rates begin to escalate. Apparently, premenopausal women have a hormonal protection that when lost exposes women to a greater likelihood of heart attack.

Despite the reductions in some age groups, death rates in the United States per 100,000 population in 1981 among males ranged from 278 in the forty-five to fifty-four age group to 4579 for those sixty-five and older. In women the rates were 84 in the forty-five to fifty-four age group and 3407 in those sixty-five and older. The National Center for Health Statistics estimates indicate that if heart disease alone could be eliminated, about a five-year gain in life expectancy might ensue (U.S. Census, 1985; Kannel and Brand, 1985).

For every group and for men and women alike the first twenty-four to forty-eight hours following an *infarction* are the riskiest. Once a heart attack has taken place, approximately one-third of all victims die before they receive medical attention. Yet immediate care is essential, as another 20 to 30 percent are likely to die in the twenty-four hours following infarction. Continued survival beyond this point and eventual rehabilitation depend not only on the severity of the attack but also on the patient's ability to come to terms with the fear and anxiety heart attacks inevitably engender. The nature of relationships with significant others and personal security seem to play crucial roles in successful recoveries. Thoughtful communication among the victim, his or her spouse, and the attending physician should alleviate many uncertainties about vital questions such as probable longevity or sexual performance, thus speeding recovery and preventing recurrences (Gentry and Williams, 1979).

For men, however, mortality doubles every decade or so, while it triples for women. In some Scandinavian countries the rate among women rises more precipitously, approaching a fourfold increase per decade. Among those over seventy-five, the differences between men and women are nearly eliminated. In addition to atherosclerosis and thromboembolic disease discussed above, Lindenfeld and Groves (1982) note that increased wall thickness and reduced elasticity of the aorta, resulting in **systolic hypertension** and an increased work load for the heart, are primary effects of senescence on the cardiovascular system.

The Framingham Heart Disease Epidemiology Study, started in 1949, investigated the risk factors associated with an increased susceptibility to heart disease by following a general population sample of 5209 men and women who were thirty to sixty-two at entry. On the basis of the longitudinal inquiry, Kannel and Brand (1985) identify the following risk factors as associated with increased risks of death from heart disease: high blood pressure, obesity, cigarette smoking, diabetes mellitus, and elevated levels of triglycerides in the blood. They suggest that the risk factors most amenable to intervention are hypertension and cigarette smoking. Control of lipids, weight control, and more exercise may also be helpful, and diabetes management may be effective if the other risk factors are dealt with along with control of blood sugar levels (Kannel and Brand, 1985).

**Cerebrovascular Accidents.** Cerebrovascular accidents, or strokes, rank as the third most common fatal affliction in the second half of life. Although there has been a significant decrease in the number of deaths from stroke since 1970 (when it was over 207,000), in 1981 strokes still claimed over 163,000 lives in the United States and left many times that number impaired. Table 5.1 shows that cerebrovascular disease was the third most frequent overall cause of death in the United States, Canada, France, and England and the second most frequent cause of death in Japan in the early 1980s. Death rates from cerebrovascular disease in the United States rise dramatically with age: in 1981 the rate was 62.9 per 100,000 in the fifty-five to sixty-four age group, 206.3 in those sixty-five to seventy-four, 715.6 among those seventy-five to eighty-four, and 2126.8 in those eighty-five and older (U.S. Census, 1985).

Although many traumatic events may cause brain damage, most of them stem from other circulatory difficulties. In referring to strokes, most practitioners mean cerebral hemorrhages caused either by *embolisms* that have traveled to the brain and occluded one of the cerebral arteries or by a thrombosis that develops in the brain's own *ventricular* system. In either event the result is oxygen-rich blood supplies are cut off to some part of the brain, with a subsequent degeneration of the affected sections. Other causes include hemorrhage, either within the brain itself (intracerebral hemorrhage) or within the meninges or membranes surrounding it (subarachnoid or subdural hemorrhage).

Strokes vary in severity according to the area of the brain in which they occur plus the intensity and extent of the damage sustained. The results of a stroke may range from mild difficulty in the use of the extremities to complete paralysis or death. Some of the deficits resulting from a stroke may fade away after a month or two, particularly with proper rehabilitative efforts. Some of them may also be permanent. Part of the insidious aftermath of a stroke is loss of memory, speech aphasia, emotional problems, partial paralysis, loss of bowel control, and so on. Epidemiological studies of stroke suggest they occur more frequently in industrialized countries than in the so-called underdeveloped nations and are more likely to strike nonwhites than whites, with both sexes equally susceptible under comparable occupational conditions and activity levels. Nearly all research agrees that cigarette smokers are at higher risk for developing cerebrovascular disease than nonsmokers. While immediate medical attention may alleviate many complications and rehabilitation can help stroke patients overcome still others, the neural injury can never be undone.

Various degenerative diseases of the brain are other pathological conditions affecting the elderly. Cerebral atrophy, senile plaques, Parkinson's disease, and numerous other disorders are generally lumped together under the term "organic brain damage" because of their diffuse character. As illustrated in Chapter 6, organic brain damage is difficult to diagnose, and often symptoms of functional disorders are incorrectly labeled as organic. Many of the related cerebral conditions are long-standing and only manifest themselves during stressful episodes in later life or when cardiovascular accidents trigger their appearance.

**Hypertension.** Hypertension, what most of us simply call high blood pressure, affects roughly the same percentage of older people as heart disease and, like other coronary problems, is much more prevalent among blacks. Part of the difficulty with diagnosing hypertension in older people is the general tendency for blood pressure to elevate throughout most of life, especially among women. Also, the issue of appropriate levels for a given individual poses problematic questions not easily resolved. In addition, blood pressure is affected by the presence of other illnesses, fever, obesity, and even air temperature. In turn hypertension may cause other body homeostatic functions to become unbalanced, contributing indirectly to death. Cerebral hemorrhage and cardiac failure appear to be the most frequent terminal conditions associated with high blood pressure, although *renal insufficiency* and *bronchopneumonia* are not unusual. Among the clinically significant symptoms are fluctuations in *systolic* and *diastolic* pressure, changes in the structure of certain parts of the eye, and mental confusion, especially late in the day. High blood pressure and its opposite, *hypotension*, or low blood pressure, are often silent — that is, their symptoms are not readily apparent. With hypertension, the narrowing of the lumen means the heart must work harder to move the same volume of blood while less blood reaches the vital organs. Being under greater pressure brings greater likelihood of organ damage.

## CANCER

Cancer is one of the major killers in industrialized countries. Table 5.1 shows that cancer ranks second only to diseases of the heart in the United States, Canada, and England and is first in France and Japan. Although cancer can occur throughout life, and death from cancer is seen as particularly tragic among the young, both incidence rates and death rates from cancer rise steadily with age, peaking after eighty-five. In the middle years, from thirty to approximately forty-four, mortality rates from cancer are somewhat higher among women than among men. In those under thirty death rates from cancer are slightly higher for men. After fifty in the case of death and after sixty in the case of incidence, men are at increasingly greater risk from cancer than are women. During the period 1978–1981 death rates from cancer in those eighty-five and older were 1557.5 per 100,000 population overall, 2314.2 for men and only 1224.8 for women. Overall cancer incidence rates from the same age group were 2361.7 per 100,000 population, with a rate of 3613 for men and only 1818 for women. From sixty on overall cancer incidence rates exceed 1000 per 100,000 population. A few primary sites — colorectal cancer, lung cancer, breast cancer in women, and prostate cancer in men — account for the majority of cancers in the older age groups, although there is also a significant incidence of cancer of the stomach, pancreas, bladder, non-Hodgkin's lymphomas and leukemias, and a few others (U.S. Department of Health and Human Services, 1984). An unfortunate but interesting change in patterns of cancer incidence over recent years has been the rapid rise in lung cancer among women, believed to result from the social acceptability of cigarette smoking. Among women in the sixty-five to seventy-four age bracket, lung cancer death rates climbed 13 percent in the 1979–1980 period alone. Halfway through the 1980s it appears lung cancer will overtake breast cancer and become the number one cancer killer of American women of all ages (American Cancer Society, 1985; Centers for Disease Control, 1982).

Cancer is an abnormal and uncontrollable growth of certain cells that invade and destroy other organs and deprive the body of nutrition. Its cause is uncertain, although recent work has concentrated on the breakdown of *immunological* defense mechanisms in the host and on genetic factors. Cancer seems to result from a combination of vulnerability on the part of the organism and precipitating factors such as carcinogens in the environment. More than 80 percent of all cases of lung cancer among men have been attributed to smoking (Centers for Disease Control, 1982), and rates of cancer of the bladder are known to be significantly higher among smokers than among the general population. Alcohol and tobacco abuse are associated with a significant increase in cancer of the mouth and upper digestive tract. Certain industrial carcinogens such as aniline dye, polyvinyl chloride (PVC), and asbestos have also been identified. Prolonged exposure to radiation is known to be definitely carcinogenic. Continuing research on diet suggests high fat and low fiber diets may be associated with higher incidence rates of breast and colon cancer, respectively. The consumption of cruciferous vegetables (cabbage, cauliflower, broccoli, and brussel sprouts) is believed to have a protective effect against cancer. Viruses, as in the case of Burkitt's lymphoma and carcinoma of the cervix, are also thought to be etiologic agents in the development of cancer.

While significant medical advances have been made against some cancers, particularly the childhood leukemias, and there have been a number of recent developments in managing cancer of the breast, overall mortality rates from breast and colorectal cancer — two of the most frequent types affecting older people — have not changed appreciably since 1949. There has been an overall slight increase in death rates from prostate cancer and a dramatic rise in death rates from lung cancer — representing a 224 percent increase in men and a 331 percent increase in women — over the same period (American Cancer Society, 1985). To some extent the declines may have resulted from targeting certain forms of cancer for intensive research. In any case, however, the best hope lies in preventive measures and in early detection. Breast examination and the use of screening techniques such as *mammography* are particularly important in elderly women, since there are excellent chances of cure for small lesions discovered early. Recent data from the National Cancer Institute indicate five-year survival rates of 85 percent for women with a localized disease, as opposed to 56 percent for women with a regional disease and only 10 percent for those in whom the disease had spread to a distant site (National Cancer Institute, 1984).

## ARTHRITIS AND RHEUMATISM

Arthritis and rheumatism are seldom identified as causes of death. Nonetheless, they are important conditions interfering with normal life for the elderly, appearing in about half the middle-aged and in up to four-fifths of people in their seventies. Arthritis and rheumatoid ailments are second only to heart disease as the most common reason for disabilities after midlife, accounting for over one-fifth of the causes for the infringement of normal activities. Again, these rates seem to be sexually related, climbing even higher for women in extreme old age. Among nonwhite Americans, especially blacks, arthritis is much less frequent than for whites.

Arthritic conditions are of two general types: *osteoarthritis* and *rheumatoid arthritis*. The demarcation between the natural involution of bone material and osteoarthritis as a pathological state is blurred, since a gradual demineralization of bones is usually thought to be a normal aspect of aging. The most serious ailments are a result of the breakdown of the bone structure in the lower back and in joints where the harder outer surface of bone cartilage wears away most rapidly. Dietary insufficiencies, alterations in bone metabolism, wear and tear, and even cold environments have been identified as probable causes of most arthritic conditions. Changes in collagen structure and ground substances are also assumed to be possible factors in the onset of arthritis, since this alteration allows bones to rub together, causing noticeable pain.

Rheumatoid arthritis is somewhat less frequently found among the elderly and strictly speaking cannot be termed a disease of old age, occurring as it does any time after infancy. The majority of cases develop in early adulthood, but because of the disease's chronic nature they only become clinically significant later in life. Rheumatoid conditions are found primarily in smaller joints, where the membranes lining the joint cavity wear thin, allowing the ends of the bones to scrape against one another. In its active phase bone marrow may also become involved, resulting in marked atrophy and muscular wasting. The role of the body's immunological mechanisms as a factor in the breakdown of connective tissue and the development of rheumatoid arthritis has been under investigation for many years. Currently the most widely held theory of its pathogenesis is that it is initiated by an antigen-antibody reaction resulting in autoimmunity (Berner, 1983).

## DIABETES MELLITUS

Diabetes mellitus is another pervasive ailment found among the elderly. It is characterized by an increase in blood sugar caused by relative or absolute insulin deficiency. Insulin is the body's major storage hormone, and when adequate levels of insulin are not available for use, the body cannot convert ingested foodstuffs into storage fuels; rather their byproducts remain in the bloodstream, causing elevated blood sugar levels, or *hyperglycemia*. The inadequate metabolism of fat and protein in diabetics can lead to *diabetic ketoacidosis*, a serious complication of diabetes that if not properly managed can lead to diabetic coma and death.

There are two major types of diabetes: insulin-dependent diabetes (formerly known as juvenile onset), and insulin-independent diabetes (formerly known as adult onset). The primary mechanism in insulin-dependent diabetes, which appears to be associated with genetically predisposing factors, is a failure to form and secrete insulin. In insulin-independent diabetes, which accounts for 85 to 90 percent of diabetes, the primary mechanism appears to be insulin resistance in the liver and in the peripheral tissues, particularly muscle. Insulin resistance is intensified by obesity, which is present in 80 percent of diabetics (Berner, 1983).

Diabetes mellitus was the seventh most frequent overall cause of death in the United States in 1981. Death rates for both sexes in the older age groups were 61.9 per 100,000 population in the sixty-five to seventy-four age group, 127.7 for those seventy-five to eighty-four, and 217.2 for those eighty-five or older. In all three categories women appear slightly more susceptible than men. At all ages, nonwhites have diabetes more often than whites. Even when death does not immediately result, the incidence rate of diabetes mellitus in persons over sixty-five interferes with normal functioning. Current estimates are that over 8.3 percent of all older persons in the United States suffer from diabetes (U.S. Census, 1985).

The relative impact of diabetes goes beyond simply having the condition. It is also associated with a number of other disabilities in the elderly. Diabetics are more likely than nondiabetics to develop atherosclerosis, heart attacks, strokes, or gangrene of the lower extremities. Poorly controlled diabetes can lead to *diabetic retinopathy*, changes in the blood vessels of the retina of the eye resulting in vision loss; cataracts also occur more frequently in diabetics, making diabetes the leading cause of blindness in this country today. Diabetes may also lead to severe renal disease and to damage to peripheral nerves, resulting, for example, in a lack of sensation in the soles of the feet. Diabetics are also more susceptible to infection than the general population. In some cases diabetes may be controlled by diet alone; others may be difficult to control even with oral agents or with insulin injections.

## ORAL AND DENTAL PROBLEMS

Oral and dental problems, decay, loss of teeth, and periodontal diseases have not received the attention they deserve given their role in the elderly's sense of well-being. Recent upgrading of dental care, patient awareness, and fluoridation should lessen premature loss of teeth (endentulousness) in the future, but among the middle-aged and elderly today, one-fourth to one-half of those in each age group have lost all their teeth. Of this number, roughly three-fourths of the middle-aged and over half of the elderly who have lost their own teeth have been fitted with dentures. Judging from the best nationwide data available, a look into the mouth of anyone over forty-five who still has his or her own teeth would reveal an average of twenty teeth either filled, missing, or decayed. In the forty-five to sixty-four age group slightly less than half the permanent teeth are still in place, while in the group aged sixty-five to seventy-nine an average of twenty-five teeth are missing. Periodontal inflammation affecting the gums and other tissues is the other major oral disease of the elderly, the consequences of which may be even more serious than caries. Regional variations exist, but according to the National Center for Health Statistics (1983), nine out of ten people over sixty-five have some clinically significant form of periodontal disease. The percentage is nearly as high for the middle-aged, with 85 percent of the men and 76 percent of the women afflicted with painful gum diseases. For a variety of reasons the old and the poor seem hesitant to visit their dentists; in contrast to physician checkups, the number of dental visits declines with age. Of course, the latter are not covered by most private or federal health insurance programs. If present patterns continue, up to three-quarters of the older and half of all middle-aged people will not have seen a dentist for two years. Socioeconomic differences are important, since nearly twice as many people with incomes considered to be adequate go to the dentist compared to their financially poorer counterparts.

# Life-Style and Health in the Later Years

### THE SOCIOCULTURAL CONTEXT AND HEALTH

It is true, as we claimed in Chapter 4, that all organisms age in species-specific patterns. Still, the environment in which life transpires will have a profound impact on the unfolding of not only intrinsic factors but also pathological conditions. Comparing information from diverse cultures to gain a better understanding of health is a risky business — too many variables enter into what we take to be the facts. Nevertheless, even partial comparisons can shed a great deal of light on the health problems characteristic of the elderly in different places. From Figure 5.1 it is evident that living conditions can drastically alter what appears to be the normal life course.

Accordingly, this brief overview is to enable the reader to reach a better understanding of the dynamic character of health conditions without offering an in-depth look at the countries surveyed. It is immediately apparent from a comparison of industrial and nonindustrial societies that the age structure of the latter differs in predictable ways from the former, where technological change long ago altered people's relationship with nature and each other. As noted in previous chapters, nonindustrial societies are characterized by high mortality rates throughout life, but particularly during infancy. An inescapable consequence of living at near subsistence levels is long-term nutritional deficits that preclude large segments of the population from living long enough to collect retirement benefits they would be entitled to as residents of most industrial societies. Ironically, the opposite problem, too much food, shortens life expectancy in many technologically advanced societies. While the same chronic deleterious conditions can be found around the world, as is evident in Tables 5.1 and 5.2, their rank ordering differs according to a complex of environmental and genetic factors.

Epidemiologists studying either type of society attempt to identify the role played by three diverse sets of facts. *Biotic* factors refer to the living organisms in a given **ecosystem**. This living environment includes such things as food supply, its utilization and potential, naturally occurring pathogens, and parasites. *Abiotic* factors refer to all physical and chemical elements of the ecosystem, whether natural or the result of civilization. Climate, altitude, soil conditions, pollutants, and so on are examples of abiotic variables. An illustration of their importance is the twofold increase in fatal bronchitis in urban areas. *Socioeconomic* factors constitute the third category that differentiates life expectancy and health profiles. Working conditions, stress, access to medical care, and ethnic or cultural advantages or disadvantages are included here (Bourliere, 1978).

Japan is an interesting example of a recently industrialized country that is undergoing many diverse changes, including health and mortality patterns. In some respects Japan resembles older industrialized giants, though it presents a different pattern in terms of the illnesses and the normal physiological parameters of age. Improved nutritional programs have recently given younger generations of Japanese a larger stature than their parents, but, like their parents, they do not normally experience a weight gain between ages twenty-five and forty-five, which is characteristic of people of European origins. Among Japanese who have moved to Hawaii and the mainland United States, rates of coronary heart disease increase. Mainland residents who have become acculturated develop cardiovascular problems approximating the same rates as Americans of European heritage; however, the rate for those who live in Hawaii or maintain close cultural proximity to traditional life-styles is appreciably lower (Marmot et al., 1979). Traditionally, nearly all Asians have consumed a heavily vegetarian diet supplemented by fish; as a consequence, their blood cholesterol levels have been lower than those found in people whose diets include a large amount of animal fats. On the other hand, higher salt intake in fish-consuming groups, as in Japan, results in elevated blood pressure. Vegetarians around the world show similarly low cholesterol levels. In such diverse groups as the bushmen of the Kalahari and the Ituri pigmies whose diets are extremely low in animal fats, blood cholesterol levels are reportedly near zero, with both arteriosclerosis and heart attacks being rare (Bourliere, 1978).

Throughout most of Africa, coronary heart diseases are seldom ranked among the primary causes of death, although people suffer from other illnesses closely tied to their way of life. For example, Yoruba tribesmen who have left the country to live in urban areas develop high blood pressure and atherosclerotic patterns much more comparable to their black counterparts in North America than those of the tribes who remain in the country. Bantu or Kurumba tribesmen who continue their traditional way of life show a much lower incidence of atherosclerosis than is observed for black Americans in the

United States. South Africans also exhibit many urban-rural differences related to life-style, such as a higher incidence of both cancer and diabetes in the cities, where dietary consumption is influenced by the predominantly westernized patterns. Although peptic ulcers are uncommon ailments across Africa, other nutritional disorders are familiar, especially those closely related to protein deficiency. Among the Masai, intestinal infections and liver diseases are frequent conditions, while arteriosclerosis and heart diseases are nearly unknown. While oral hygiene is a concept little known in most African societies, both tooth decay and periodontal diseases are relatively rare (Dubos, 1959). In northern India in the provinces near New Delhi, medical research has provided additional insight into the relationship between diet and coronary diseases. As in Africa, the lower social categories in India traditionally have diets that are low in animal fat; their more affluent neighbors on the other hand have adopted many Western ways of living, especially dietary habits, and have consequently shown a marked increase in calcification of the arteries and related vascular problems (Bourliere, 1978).

## CONTROL AND LONGEVITY

As the proportion of older people in the population continues to grow, questions regarding the control of illness and the prolongation of life will become ever more pressing. Ask a group of biologists or medical scientists if they have any prospects for lengthening life and you will hear a collective yes. Ask by what factor and by how many years, and likely as not a collective shrug of the shoulders and an "it all depends" answer will be forthcoming. Some search for ways to slow the pacemakers of life. The goal is not so much to lengthen the life span as it is to prolong the vigorous years — to effect perhaps a five-year "marking of time" at any given chronological age, after which bonus life would continue as before. Such a gain would stall biological aging for individual and societal benefit, thereby decreasing the relative dependent years. Others seek to control the pathological conditions that rob people of their vitality. As has been discussed, the years of rapid extensions in life expectancy are behind us. Medical science is entering a new era. Having conquered, for all intents and purposes, infectious diseases, attention must turn to relieving chronic degenerative conditions.

The change of the character of the life tables shown in Chapter 2 reflects the breakthroughs of yesterday. As long as variations in length of life occur, researchers are convinced that both the length of life and the quality of old age experienced by most people can be improved. The real short-term hope for achieving a rectangular survival curve lies in evening out inequalities among social groups. This applies not only to the dramatic differences between the quality of life and the life expectancies in the industrialized nations as opposed to Third World countries, but also to differences between groups in the United States.

For example, sixty-five-year-old white women in America may look forward, on the average, to another 18.4 years of life, while white men have no more than about fourteen years left. Older nonwhite men and women both have even fewer years remaining to them than their white counterparts. The differences are largely the result of socioeconomic characteristics such as occupation, income, education, marital status, and knowledge of and access to medical care rather than inexorable or intrinsic factors. For these same reasons we may expect the quality of life, in terms of health, to be sufficiently optimized to allow the vast majority to have as few illnesses and impairments as those in the most advantaged social categories.

To be sure, the high prevalence of chronic conditions in advanced industrial societies is in part caused by an increased life expectancy resulting from advances in combating acute infectious diseases and the other factors illustrated in Figure 5.1. For instance, those who once would have died of tuberculosis today live long enough to die of cancer or atherosclerotic heart disease. The greater number of elderly diabetics around today is partly related to improvements in the management of diabetes that allow those who suffer from it to live longer. The chronic degenerative diseases are also, however, partly the result of life-style, cultural, and environmental factors. Control of the latter would result in considerable improvements in life expectancy and quality of life for many of the elderly. But what roads can be taken to achieve this end?

**Improving Life Expectancy.** Preventive medicine can go a long way toward improving the quality of life among older people. For epidemiologists studying the distributions of disease, prevention is discussed in terms of primary and secondary strategies. *Primary prevention* entails attempts to avert the onset of disease. It combines public health measures to lessen the occurrence of illnesses with the lowering of specific risk factors by modifying the diet, activity level, personal habits, customs, health examinations, and so on.

While there is often a tendency to focus on primary prevention at the individual level, a more comprehensive approach to preventive medicine would require attending to social structural factors that are detrimental to health. The structure of work puts some groups in positions of higher risk because of their employment. Societal factors, as previously noted, often create stress and then encourage tobacco and alcohol abuse as a means of coping with it. Socioeconomic differences most clearly evident in sex, race, and education disparities in mortality are obvious indicators of the direction ameloriative efforts might well take.

*Secondary prevention* is intended to fend off the more severe states of existing maladies or their complications through the use of therapeutic drugs, palliative measures, and counseling. A crucial component of secondary prevention of the disabilities likely to affect the elderly lies in an extensive reshaping of the negative attitudes held both toward the elderly and by older people themselves, described earlier.

## LIFE-STYLE FACTORS AFFECTING HEALTH AND LONGEVITY

**Tobacco Abuse.** Many heavy smokers die young. The elderly who smoke also tend to be in poorer health than those who do not. Social epidemiologists consider widespread smoking cessation as the single most effective action possible in controlling chronic diseases. As mentioned earlier, smoking is associated with greatly increased risks of heart disease and stroke. It has also been estimated that approximately 30 percent of cancer deaths are caused by smoking. Not only cigarette smokers, but also pipe smokers, cigar smokers, and tobacco chewers are at increased risk for cancer of the mouth, larynx, and esophagus. Cigarette smoking is also a known causative agent in chronic bronchitis and *emphysema*. As we saw in Table 5.1, chronic respiratory diseases were the fifth most frequent cause of death in the United States in 1980. Smoking has also been found to be associated with increased risks of osteoporosis, hip fracture, and postmenopausal tooth loss. In a five-year controlled study of seventy-year-old men, smokers were found to have higher losses in body weight; impaired functional capability because of lower bone mineral density, pulmonary function, and muscle strength; and a significantly higher incidence of cancer, chronic bronchitis, peptic ulcers, and intermittent claudication than a comparable group of nonsmokers (Mellstrom et al., 1982).

**Alcohol Abuse.** Alcohol has been implicated as an important causative factor for many chronic diseases. Clearly differences exist between use and abuse. The effects of abuse can be devastating, causing a person to spend his or her last years as a chronic invalid. One of the most significant effects of alcohol abuse is liver damage, which impairs other organ systems. Liver damage may take the form of fatty replacement of the liver cells, alcoholic hepatitis, or cirrhosis, a chronic inflammatory disease of the liver in which functional cells are replaced by scar tissue. In the mid-1980s cirrhosis has become the eighth most frequent cause of death in the United States. Liver damage influences diseases that to the uninitiated appear quite remote. For example, people with advanced cirrhosis may develop varicose veins in their esophagus, which, when damaged by the passage of food, causes them to bleed to death. Other digestive system complications of alcohol abuse include alcohol gastritis, gastric and duodenal ulcer disease, and malabsorption of nutrients. Alcohol is related to an increased risk of cancer of the tongue, mouth, pharynx, and liver.

Alcohol also affects the cardiovascular system. One of its more serious effects is alcoholic cardiomyopathy, in which alcohol-related damage to the muscles of the heart results in low output and depressed contractibility. It may lead to significant increases in blood pressure and to damage to muscles other than those of the heart. Each of these obviously has potentially fatal consequences.

A variety of central nervous system problems can result from a heavy alcohol intake. Detoxified alcoholics have been shown to have significant evidence of organic brain syndrome, including deficits in sensorimotor performance, perceptual capacities, conceptual shifting, visual-spatial abstracting abilities, and memory function. Alcohol withdrawal may be complicated by *delirium tremens*, an acute psychotic state characterized by profound confusion, hallucinations, overactivity, insomnia, elevated temperature, an increased pulse rate, and tremors. Mortality rates from delirium tremens have been as high as 20 percent, although they have declined because of better medical management. Nonetheless, delirium tremens still presents a serious management problem in heavy drinkers who are abruptly withdrawn from alcohol because of unexpected hospitalization. One of the most devastating aftermaths of chronic alcohol abuse is Wernicke-Korsakoff's syndrome. During the early phase, called Wernicke's encephalopathy, neurological deficits become apparent. The patient suffering from Korsakoff's psychosis suffers from severe amnesia, a tendency to invent to cover memory deficits, and remarkable personality alterations characterized by passivity, indifference, and lack of affect. Many of these patients are institutionalized for the remainder of their lives.

Finally, alcohol is an important contributory factor in malnutrition; it has been suggested as the most common cause of vitamin and trace nutrient deficiency in the United States. Thiamine deficiency alone is a major cause of *Wernicke's encephalopathy*. Alcohol-derived nutritional deficiencies result in general poor health and contribute to such health problems as anemia, convulsions, small bowel dysfunction, ataxia, motor palsies, and nystagmus. Alcohol also interacts with prescription, over-the-counter, and illicit drugs and has been reported to be the most frequent cause of drug-related crises in the United States (Eckardt et al., 1981).

Some alcoholics live to be old; others take up drinking in their later years. In either case the impact of alcohol on the elderly can be particularly severe. Because of reduced liver and other organ functions, increased sensitivity of the aging brain to the effects of alcohol, a tendency to have higher alcohol blood levels with the same intake as younger people, and taking a variety of drugs with which alcohol may interact, older drinkers face greater risks. Alcohol may disturb the sleep and sexual performance of these people and significantly impair their cognitive functions. It may result in accidents, falls, and serious injury (Hartford and Samorajski, 1982). Prevention of alcohol abuse would thus be a second important step toward improving the health and well-being of the elderly. While secondary concern is an immediate necessity for the alcoholic, primary intervention will do more in the long run to stop what many consider to be a modern-day epidemic.

**Environmental Factors and Health.** Many aspects of the lives of older persons reflect the specific environments in which they reside. The wrinkled faces of life-long dwellers of the desert Southwest will be quite distinct from those who have grown old in the humid Northwest. As pointed out in Chapter 3, Lawton (1977; Nahemow and Lawton, 1976) and others spoke of the environmental press — the demands the environment places on people — to describe the dialectical interaction between people and the world around them. Such pressures are thought to range along a continuum from hospitable to very demanding. In terms of health the environment exerts a steady and continuing influence over the life course. Epidemiologists have adopted a holistic, multifactorial perspective on the environment that includes its organic, inorganic, and cultural constituents (Armelagos et al., 1978).

Over the past 100 years we have greatly altered the physical environment. We have also introduced new health hazards. Organic changes as the by-products of industrialization, agriculture, transportation, and energy consumption have been immense. From such everyday occurrences as starting our cars to wearing out tires, we are faced with air pollutants of carbon monoxide, nitrogen oxides, sulfur dioxide, photo-oxidants, asbestos, and so on. In the process of "improving" our lives through chemistry used in farming and manufacturing, we have also introduced many thousands of new synthetic chemicals — close to 1000 every year — into our lives. Inorganic changes have been no less dramatic: the multiple kinds of radiation, temperature, noise, vibration, and innumerable other stressors are constants in many of our lives. Cultural changes have also added to the environmental press — they are no less real than organic or inorganic alterations. Where and how we live, what we do to earn a living, what we eat, the things we invent and do to comfort, amuse, and distract ourselves, and stressful life events that come with the way we organize our lives are all part of the same environment — each is capable of affecting our health (Public Health Service, 1979).

Consider just one or two examples: the risk of cancer is greater for people who live in the industrial Northeast. People who work in the dye or rubber industries have increased risks of bladder cancer; workers in any form of manufacturing involving the use of polyvinyl chloride are at high risk for liver cancer. Exposure to asbestos can lead twenty years later to cancer of the membranes lining the chest cavity (malignant mesotheliona). For those who were exposed to Agent Orange during the Vietnam War, leukemia and other related health hazards seem to be one of the consequences (American Cancer Society, 1985). Epidemiologists can point to the pattern of many forms of cancer and other diseases; while they cannot always explain the configuration, it does not seem to be the result of mere chance.

There are other hazards than cancer that result from earning a living. For example, one review of a number of national studies suggests at least four million workers contract work-related diseases every year, with perhaps as many as 100,000 deaths. The rates vary according to occupation, clustering around occupations at the lower end of the socioeconomic scale partly as a result of serious health hazards on the job (Navarro, 1976; Wilson, 1970). In the United States this is nowhere more evident than in the coal mining industry. Black lung affects one in five underground miners (Navarro, 1976). In the cotton industry the sister malady, brown lung, resulting from inhaling cotton fiber, is an occupational hazard with an incidence rate close to that for black lung. For those who work in and around silos in the Midwest, breathing grain dust creates a version of the same condition. Occupational safety and health hazards are such that nine out of ten workers in the United States are not protected from exposure to at least one of the 163 most common hazardous industrial chemicals, according to the Surgeon General. The full consequences are unknown and may take many years before they are clinically significant. The Occupational Safety and Health Administration has already identified intervention procedures; it is up to industry, however, to implement these. By modifying the work environment, many risks could be controlled, but such concerns have not yet become a priority. Until they are the health of older persons will continue to be at risk as a consequence of their occupations (Public Health Service, 1979).

Underlying the question of implementing protective measures is the question of priorities: how far are we willing to compromise the future health of today's workers? Who will bear the cost of their disabilities in old age? Might not funds be better concentrated on measures designed to eliminate hazards in the workplace? Approaches to controlling environmental hazards in the workplace would have to be multifaceted if they are to work. They would need to include identifying financially feasible but effective control measures, enforcement procedures, and possibly aids to implementation for industry, safeguards to ensure that workers cannot be penalized by management for abiding by safety standards, and worker education, since it has been frequently found in safety studies that workers themselves ignore protective measures. The result in either case is that during retirement conditions contracted perhaps years earlier on the job become clinically evident.

**Nutrition and Diet.** Concern with the role of nutrition in affecting the aging process has grown significantly in the last decade. Despite controversies over whether lowering cholesterol and saturated fat levels, increasing fibrous foods, and lowering salt intake have any effect on health and mortality, the consensus is that dietary intervention forestalls many of the negative consequences of aging. Like so many other areas in gerontology, nutrition is a multifaceted phenomenon with physiological, psychological, and sociological aspects. Eating consists of far more than biological sustenance. Diet makes a difference, but what is good for the body may not reflect what is important for the soul, the self-concept, or the social status one is accorded by what he or she eats (Calasanti and Hendricks, 1986).

With one-third to one-half of the health problems of the elderly stemming directly from nutrition, modifying the habits of a lifetime is clearly one of the principal life-style considerations conducive to prolonging life. Despite the limitation imposed on nutritional adequacy for 20 percent of all older people in the United States, overabundance appears to play a major role in vitiating life for the remainder. If by some stroke of fate medical science discovered a way to prevent obesity, an average of over four years might be added to life expectancy at birth, just about double the extension that might be realized from eliminating various forms of cancer (Freeman, 1965).

How much to eat is a complicated question, depending on everything from activity levels to body surface area and lean body mass. Daily food consumption in the United States is around 3300 calories, far in excess of the amount advisable. According to the best estimates, few men require more than 2900 calories daily and few women need over 2100. With normal declines in metabolic rates averaging 3.5 percent every decade after maturity, caloric requirements in later years are reduced even further. At most, middle-aged men and women should maintain an intake of between 2400 and 1700 calories. Curtailments of between 8 and 10 percent per decade are recommended thereafter, for a total caloric reduction of over one-third between twenty-five and seventy. In sections of Kashmir and the Caucasus, or in the Ecuadorian village of Vilcabamba, where extreme longevity is commonplace and many people remain active for over 100 years, average daily food consumption comes to only 1200 to 1900 calories (Busse, 1978).

In addition to the number of calories, there is the question of what we eat. An adequate balance of protein and carbohydrates combined with essential vitamins and minerals is crucial. Dietary surveys in Europe and North America found the required 50 to 65 grams of protein daily are surpassed by nearly 40 percent of the younger people, while the elderly more often fall short of optimum amounts. Dramatic improvements in health would be observed if the average cholesterol intake of nearly 600 milligrams was reduced by half. The elimination of egg yolks, probably the highest cholesterol food most people eat on a regular basis, would go a long way toward lowering blood cholesterol levels. Unfortunately, in most other cases foods high in cholesterol are also sources of essential protein, which must be retained for optimum diets. The elderly also find themselves with too little calcium, too few vitamins, and an overabundance of fats and carbohydrates in their diets. The calcium is important to offset other declines that lead to the possibility of *osteoporosis*, while vitamins aid in maintaining the secretion of enzymes that normally diminish with age. Iron and $B_{12}$, for example, are beneficial supplements to the stomach's natural juices, aiding the absorption of nutrients and assisting in the production of amino acids used for energy and as the body's building blocks. One of the liabilities associated with vegetarian diets is the inadequate supply of high-quality proteins and the increased incidence of liver diseases. On the other hand, too large an ingestion of saturated fats from animal sources adds to the lipids in the bloodstream, exacerbating the risk of atherosclerosis and other coronary diseases. Further problems arise when the caloric intake at any one meal is too high, resulting in harmful metabolic byproducts that add to the buildup of atherosclerotic plaques, even if total daily allowances are not exceeded. Currently, the recommended pattern is four or five light meals a day rather than one or two large ones. Preliminary evidence suggests that to some extent, earlier dietary improprieties may be partially reversed by replacing saturated fats with polyunsaturated fats, with the possible result of a limited regression of atherosclerotic plaques (Stamler, 1975).

Food should not be thought of simply as a source of nutrition or a means of avoiding hunger. It is also imbued with wide-ranging symbolic connotations inextricably interwoven with the rest of our lives. One of the reasons lifelong patterns are so resistant to change and why even programs such as meals-on-wheels, which provide healthful meals, cannot ensure adequate nutrition, is the all too frequently neglected social significance of eating. Meals are social events, a time for socializing. Isolated people who are often lonely are less likely to secure proper nourishment regardless of the availability of appropriate food merely because eating alone is emotionally distasteful (Hendricks and Calasanti, 1986). Similarly, the habits of a lifetime are quite difficult to break. Changing them entails major emotional adjustments that few of us, particularly the elderly, are prepared or able to make. Among the other contributions to inadequate nutrition are ill-fitted dentures, trouble with swallowing, diminished sense of taste and smell, and the inability to shop or prepare food, all predisposing factors that seem to characterize the lives of many older people (Natlow and Heslin, 1980).

Among the more important issues affecting the nutritional status of older persons, the role of socioeconomic status cannot be overlooked. Its implications go well beyond questions of whether the disadvantaged do not have enough or the right foods to eat or whether the upper classes overindulge. Socioeconomic factors also influence what are viewed as prestige foods such as butter and bakery and convenience products. Among today's generation of older people, dietary intake reflects financial constraints, as well as compensation for foods that were in scarce supply at some point during their lives. Red meats, rare and expensive during the Depression and the war years of the 1940s, constitute a staple in the diets of those who are now old. Nutrition is generally poorer among older persons who live alone than for those who live with a spouse or some other family member. The emotional factors stemming from role loss, depression, and loneliness all interact with the symbolism of food and are associated with eating disorders found among older persons (Candy-Gibbs and Turner, 1986). A myriad of normative social and psychological components of aging affect diet; each must be taken into consideration if nutritional intervention is to improve the lives of older people.

**Exercise.** Sedentary life-styles are part of modern life for many people. Many diseases can be combated by increasing the level of physical activity; for example, recent declines in heart disease are attributed to the growing popularity of various moderate exercise regimes. Improvements in the cardiovascular system, the respiratory system, musculature, body composition, and a general sense of well-being are the general result. Exercise helps alleviate osteoporosis in postmenopausal women, and for all older people it aids in the consumption of lipids and in preserving functional capacity in many organ systems. The Framingham longitudinal study mentioned earlier clearly points to a correlation between increased health risks and decreased physical activity. Blood pressure, blood sugar, glucose tolerance, and blood lipids all respond positively to exercise. Psychological changes have also been noted, especially in such psychomotor responses as reaction time, attention, and memory. Beyond these improvements, self-concept, body image, and mood states, also affecting many other health conditions, show marked enhancement among older persons who take up or continue moderate levels of physical activity (Jokl, 1983; Fries and Crapo, 1981).

**Life Satisfaction and Health.** At a basic level, Henry (1982) asserts, emotions can override neuroendocrine feedback controls that maintain homeostasis. This leads to pathophysiological changes and disease states. The symmetrical relationship between health and life satisfaction has fascinated gerontologists for a number of years. While it is true poor health undermines morale, it is also true that those who are more satisfied also rate their own health more positively. The relationship is not as simple as it appears, however. Some of us seem to be preoccupied with our body functions and are unable to think beyond our physical selves. Others tend to transcend their bodies, to rise above their physical being to exert more control over their lives (Peck, 1956). To unravel this relationship not only must investigators have adequate psychological assessments, but they must be able to distinguish between self-rated health and actual clinical evaluations. The central focus is not really on whether a person's feeling can replace a physician's clinical observations (they seem to be rather closely related anyway) but instead on the consequences of positive or negative self-perceptions. Though the complexities continue to elude resolution, researchers have discovered that self-rated health may be more important than objective health status as far as future longevity is concerned (Maddox and Douglass, 1974; Palmore, 1981; Botwinick, 1984).

When evaluating their personal health, the parameters the elderly take into account are their individual health histories; that is, are they as healthy as previously? How are they doing compared to others their age or to those who live in similar situations? If for any reason they conclude that they are at a disadvantage, observed clinical health begins to deteriorate regardless of how good it was. Apparently, objectively verifiable factors only enter into the elderly's sense of life satisfaction when they become subjectively meaningful in terms of self-evaluated health (Tissue, 1972). Among a complex range of social conditions that seem to provide a stable health picture are intact marriages, adequate financial resources, stress-free lives, and a cohesive psychological profile (Pfeiffer, 1974). While health status tends to decline following major crises, as with the death of a loved one, we must exercise caution before making any generalizations. According to popular conceptions, retirement often results in more illnesses. Mortality rates for males reach a peak in the years immediately after they retire. Is it not also the case that a large percentage of older men claim ill-health as a reason for not seeking additional employment in the postretirement years? Both statements are doubtlessly true, yet the best indications are that retirement has little direct effect on health. Whatever changes seem to occur among retirants also happen among those who have been able to continue working. It may also be that claims of impaired health are really rationalizations for not seeking new jobs, functioning partially as a face-saving device to offset the displaced status accompanying retirement. As has often been pointed out, the sick role may actually be a replacement for the loss of primary roles that cannot be resumed. Intense social involvements providing a purpose and a sense of confidence through furnishing alternative roles would go a long way toward upgrading self-reported health status among many elderly (Palmore and Luikart, 1974).

# Health Care Services for the Elderly

The number and kinds of health care services that should be provided for the elderly is a complex issue involving not only medical questions but also social policy matters and decisions about the allocation of resources within society. In this section we begin by looking at the issue of rising costs and the potential impact of the most recent attempt to control these through diagnosis related groups (DRGs) as mandated by the Tax Equity and Fiscal Responsibility Act of 1982 on the health of the elderly. We then outline some considerations that should be considered in planning appropriate health care services for the elderly. In Chapter 11 we will turn our attention to health policy in the more general context of social policy and examine both the legislative history of health care for the elderly in the United States and how it compares with similar legislation in other countries.

## COST EFFECTIVENESS IN HEALTH SERVICES FOR THE ELDERLY

**The Problem of Rising Costs.** In the early 1980s the problem of rising costs surfaced, and health care costs have been a topic for major national concern ever since. The first Medicare bill was passed by Congress in July 1965 and became effective with the next fiscal calendar year. Part A, providing basic hospitalization insurance, is automatic for all those who qualify for Social Security or railroad pensions and includes their dependents under stipulated conditions. Part B, after an annual deductible, covers certain aspects of outpatient care and is open for voluntary enrollment at a supplemental fee that is withheld from Social Security payments. At the time of its inception the annual cost of the Medicare program was $3 billion. By 1985 it had risen to over $50 billion. In 1950 total national health expenditures amounted to $12.7 billion, or 4.4 percent of the gross national product. By 1982 they had risen to $322 billion, or 10.5 percent of the gross national product, of which 42 percent was spent on hospital care (Fifer, 1984). In 1983 it was estimated that Medicare would spend $39 billion, or 68 percent of its budget, on hospital services alone and that the costs of these services were rising at a rate of 19 percent a year (Hunt, 1983). Iglehart (1983) reported that the annual increase in Medicare expenditures was nearly as large as the total budget of the National Institutes of Health. Medicare outlays had increased at an average annual rate of 17 percent since 1970, and, according to recent projections by the Congressional Budget Office, the Hospital Insurance trust fund would be depleted before the end of the decade and would run increasing deficits in the years afterward. By 1995, if trends current in 1983 continue, Medicare's hospital trust fund would be $300 billion below its expenditures.

Clearly, something needed to be done to alleviate the impending fiscal crisis, and it was in this climate that the Tax Equity and Fiscal Responsibility Act of 1982 mandating the development of a prospective payment system for Medicare hospital costs was signed into law. Before discussing this act and its potential implications for the health care of the elderly, it is important to consider the issues involved in the concept of cost effectiveness in health care.

**Cost Effectiveness in Health Care for the Elderly.** Two basic issues are customarily discussed in cost effectiveness in health care: the need for cost control by means of *efficiency* in managing available resources and the need for *effectiveness* in terms of producing the right results. In the case of health services this translates into saving lives and getting people well. Some are tempted when evaluating the cost of health care to focus on cost efficiency — keeping the outlay for care down — because this is easier to measure. As we shall see one of the major criticisms of DRGs is that they do precisely this. Cost effectiveness in health care is often considered in functional terms: does providing a treatment mean that this patient will again become socioeconomically productive? Are outlays for a particular health program likely to increase national productivity? While it is important to use resources wisely, we also suggest that other issues need to be considered in evaluating the cost effectiveness of care for the elderly. Does a particular way of financing and organizing health care lead to the best possible quality of life for the elderly under these circumstances? To what extent are rising health care costs for the elderly a result of increasing numbers of elderly in the population as opposed to the inefficient use of resources? In view of the past contributions of the elderly to the economy, to what extent should federal budget cuts be directed toward health care for the elderly? How far are we willing to risk compromising the quality of care to save money? In sum, providing cost-effective health services involves balancing two considerations: not wasting available resources while providing an appropriate quality of care (Lang, 1984).

## COST CONTAINMENT AND HEALTH EXPENDITURES

**Diagnosis Related Groups.** Prior to the development of the prospective payment system, Medicare reimbursement was for reasonable costs on the basis of services rendered. This practice, it was argued, encouraged health care providers to expend more resources in the care of Medicare patients — the more services used and the higher their cost, the greater the reimbursement received for patient care. Critics maintained the system had no incentive for cost consciousness. Furthermore, unpredictable and rising costs made it difficult to budget accurately for financial requirements for hospital care. Legislators and planners therefore looked for a system of controlling costs by setting reimbursement limits in advance.

In September 1982 President Reagan signed the Tax Equity and Fiscal Responsibility Act into law. This act contained two broad measures directed toward controlling the costs of Medicare. An interim program of tighter Medicare controls on hospitals was put into place that insiders estimated would cut reimbursements by $5 billion in a three-year period. The act also issued a directive to develop a prospective payment system that when implemented would impose an effective ceiling on Medicare payments. This was a response not only to the rising cost of health care but also to the political proclamation of the need to impose budget reductions on health as part of the overall curtailments contained in the president's tax reduction plan.

In April 1983 the revisions to the Social Security Act, including the Medicare Prospective Payment Plan, became law with a three-year transition period. The overriding importance of the regulations thus put into effect was the development of DRGs involving payment of a flat fee to hospitals for treatment. Payment schedules are nonnegotiable and are to be considered as full payment. If hospital costs amount to less than the DRG reimbursement, the hospital pockets the difference. If hospital costs amount to more than the DRG reimbursement, the hospital must absorb the cost. The theory is that more costly cases should offset less costly cases, allowing the hospital at least to break even if not make a profit. Thus hospitals will be rewarded for careful management of resources while enabling them to keep costs down. In setting DRG payment rates the country was divided into nine regions, each with separate urban and rural rates. Initially, fee schedules were regionalized, though payments based on national averages are to be implemented by 1987; a sliding ratio was to be in effect during the transition. Direct costs of medical education for teaching institutions are excluded from the prospective payment system and are to be passed through. Capital costs were originally excluded from the prospective payment system, but as of 1986 are to be incorporated as well.

DRGs made their first appearance in 1975 when researchers at Yale University defined expected lengths of patient stay to identify atypical patients in reviews of hospital utilization patterns. They were next implemented for third-party reimbursement purposes in twenty-six hospitals in New Jersey and a lesser number in Maryland. In the course of national implementation the original Yale classification has been modified somewhat. It is now comprised of a refined listing of 467 DRGs based on ICD-9-CM codes grouped into 23 major diagnostic categories on the basis of body organ system affected. In addition, three residual categories for exceptional cases require automatic review by Medicare representatives. The DRGs are classified as medical or surgical, according to procedures performed, with five variables used in determining payment:

- Specific operative procedure (cost assigned on the basis of the most resource-intensive procedure)
- Principal diagnosis (reason for admission to the hospital)
- Age of the patient (higher rates for patients seventy or older)
- Significant complications arising while the patient is hospitalized
- Co-morbidities (significant secondary problems present at the time of admission)

The Health Care Financing Administration estimates that approximately 5.1% of all patient admissions will not fit normal patterns. In those cases, called outliers, when the patient's conditions confound classification procedures, the hospital is reimbursed for additional costs at 60 percent of the difference between the hospital's adjusted cost for the DRG and the cost outlier threshold or 60 percent of the per diem rate for the category. Slightly higher reimbursement adjustments are available for teaching hospitals to cover the indirect costs of medical education; for rural referral hospitals, which are eligible for urban rates; for sole community hospitals; and for cancer hospitals, recognizing that the types of patients treated in these institutions are liable to incur more costs than those treated elsewhere. The national standard prices for DRGs are set and updated by the Secretary of the Department of Health and Human Services based on recommendations from a fifteen-member advisory commission. There have, however, been questions raised regarding whether the committee's advice is actually being heeded. Beginning in 1986 fee schedules will be subject to review every four years to compensate for inflation, new technologies, and related factors affecting hospitalization expenses. In addition, hospitals are required to contract with an independent peer review organization for review of the appropriateness of a sampling of admissions, of all outliers, and of a random sampling of discharges each quarter (Lang, 1984; Iglehart, 1982a, 1982b, 1983).

**Potential Problems with DRGs.** Criticisms of the DRG prospective payment system have centered on three major issues: quality of care, access to care, and how effective the system actually is in containing costs as opposed merely to shifting them. Four underlying problems with DRGs have been identified as contributing to deficiencies in these areas. First, the data base used to construct DRGs is inadequate in that charges on which categories are based do not necessarily reflect costs. Furthermore, some studies have estimated error rates in diagnosis and procedure coding as high as 35 percent. Second, DRGs are focused on controlling costs for single admissions for a particular diagnosis and not the overall costs of treatment for the disease or of total patient care expense. Third, there is a lack of sophistication in estimating the intensity of care requirements, with no provisions for estimating the relative severity of an illness within a DRG. Third, a number of studies have indicated that the importance of particular DRGs vary from one area of the country to another; that is, conditions having the same DRG classifications are not identical across the United States. Fourth, some critics have expressed a fear that in spite of quality assurance requirements, DRGs provide a built-in incentive for hospitals to place more priority on keeping costs down than on quality of care (Lang, 1984; Horn, 1983; Horn and Schumacher, 1982).

Another overriding concern expressed by many authors is that the prospective payment system may promote the commercialization of medicine and a "bottom-line mentality" in hospital administrators that will sacrifice the principle of providing access to quality care in favor of the financial well-being of the institution. Adverse effects on the quality of care may include the provision of less costly, but also less effective services, a curtailment of the amount of service given, and early discharge before the patient is fully recovered. The House Select Committee on Aging has affirmed some of these fears. In a report released in early 1985 the committee indicates that patients leaving hospitals operating under DRG prospective payment systems are sicker and require more posthospital care than before the enactment of DRG legislation. Rural patients discharged from hospitals were found to be even sicker, while the facilities from which they came were themselves having financial difficulty (Select Committee on Aging, 1985). Another problem has also surfaced. Some DRGS seem to contain incentives to giving certain forms of treatment that may not necessarily be the most desirable. For instance, the surgical DRGs for peptic ulcers and various forms of cardiovascular disease reimburse more than the medical DRGS for these diagnoses. The prospect then may be a temptation to resort to surgical treatment of those conditions rather than using nonintrusive treatments. The concern is not, however, limited to critics outside of the health care system. Physicians fear that patterns of medical practice may also be subtly influenced by medical staff credentialing procedures that emphasize the cost effectiveness of the physician as opposed to clinical competence alone (Omenn and Conrad, 1984; Lang, 1984).

Still further trepidation has been voiced over the question of access to care. As previously noted, DRGs do not take into account the varying degrees of severity that may exist within a disease covered by a single DRG classification. Therefore tremendous variation in the costs of caring for a particular type of illness without significantly affecting the length of stay is possible. A study of cerebrovascular cases falling within the same DRG at Johns Hopkins Hospital revealed costs ranging from $450 to $58,000, the result primarily of variations in severity.

Cost variability within diagnostic categories may lead hospitals to deny access to patients who are more severely ill or who consume more resources, as well as to patients who are likely to have long stays because of their socioeconomic status and lack of alternative support systems. The failure of DRGs to provide payment for standby services, medically necessary for managing potential complications in high-risk patients, is still another disincentive to the treatment of the severely ill. What this may mean is that certain institutions, such as public and county hospitals, may become choices of last resort for the severely ill. In the absence of special considerations for hospitals treating a high proportion of the very ill, such facilities may find it difficult to survive. Hospitals may also be tempted to drop services that lose money to concentrate on those that are more profitable. While specialization among facilities could lead to improvements in quality, this practice can also lead to limitations in access: some unprofitable services may be dropped by all hospitals in the community. Finally, there is also a concern that DRGs will limit the development and adoption of new technology, since categorization is based on traditional medical practices (Hunt, 1983; Iglehart, 1982b, 1983; Lang, 1984; Omenn and Conrad, 1984).

Questions have also been raised about the extent DRGs really cut costs as opposed to shifting them. Since the DRG system only looks at payment for individual admissions, physicians could potentially discharge and then readmit a patient rather than having one long, financially unprofitable stay. Strategies for circumventing regulations became commonplace so quickly that something known as DRG "creep" developed. Another way of outwitting the system is to manipulate a patient's principal diagnosis to get a higher payment. To cite one example, the outlier rate in New Jersey was approximately 30 percent in 1984 as opposed to the 5 to 6 percent rate for Medicare outliers predicted by the Health Care Financing Administration. Of course, this may well reflect problems with the whole DRG plan and not an attempt to "play" the system. Shifting of costs also affects other third-party payers who may have to offset losses from DRGs. As a result, prospective payment schemes are currently being considered by a number of insurance carriers. Finally, while Medicare hospital expenditures may fall, the cost of outpatient and nursing home care may rise as a result of shifting care needs. Careful attention will have to be paid to improved discharge planning and to developing cost-effective step-down care for those released from hospitals (Lang, 1984; Iglehart, 1982b; Pettingill and Westell, 1984).

## APPROPRIATE LEVELS OF CARE FOR THE ELDERLY

**Alternatives to the Medicare Cost Control System.** The critiques of the DRG system pose two major challenges to the Medicare cost control system: (1) the need to take into account severity levels within illness categories so payments may be adjusted in order not to penalize those who take care of the severely ill and (2) the need to evaluate cost effectiveness in terms of total patient care rather than seeking cost efficiency only on hospital expenditures. One alternative some have suggested is a system similar to that of the health maintenance organizations (HMOs). Under such a plan an agency would be paid a basic rate for each participant to provide total health care, including inpatient, outpatient, short-term, and long-term care. Such an approach it is argued would provide an incentive to reduce admission rates and lengths of stay, to perform surgery on an outpatient basis, and to use long-term care and home health services as alternatives to hospitalization (Fifer, 1984). In short, rather than reimburse for procedures, Medicare payments could focus on outcomes.

A number of policy questions underlie decisions regarding the financing and delivery of health care for the elderly. It is important to be aware of these rather than to muddle along on an ad hoc basis. One question is how much the nation is willing to commit to health care expenditures for the elderly on the basis of their needs given other demands on available funds. This issue will be more fully explored in Chapter 11. Here we merely take note of one suggestion: it is perhaps more fruitful to pose the question in terms of how much and what kind of health care each person would consider appropriate at different times in his or her life given the availability of resources, rather than formulate the debate in terms of a battle for resources between young and old. Once having decided on the investment we are willing to make, we then have to decide the type or types of care to provide. Should we, for instance, concentrate on preventive or curative measures? Preventive measures would be particularly important for today's younger cohorts so that when they are tomorrow's elderly they will not have the same range of disabilities with which to contend. At the same time, curative medicine must be available to those who already have to deal with illness and disability. Allocation, when resources are short, should be on the basis of immediate medical need (Clark, 1985).

## Summary

No period of life is free from illness or disability, though the types of health problems we face change. In youth and in the middle years acute conditions are the most prevalent, only to be replaced in the later years by chronic ailments. Too frequently overlooked is that an older person's ills have been a long time coming. The mild stiffness that robs the young of their jaunty step gives bad backs or trick knees to the middle-aged and finally settles in to debilitate the elderly. Through the course of life a host of social and economic factors influences one's health, shaping not only the significance attached to various conditions but the probable outcomes. In industrialized cultures people no longer fear the infectious epidemics that formerly killed large numbers before they could reach what we now consider middle age. Instead, respiratory ailments and degenerative diseases take their toll, often remaining constant companions in life for decades. What permits the health problems of the second half of life to be so resistant to medical science is their multiple etiologies, stemming from diffuse and gradual alterations. As causes of death some diseases, cardiovascular impairments and malignant neoplasms among them, are more common than others, occurring among men and women, nonwhites and whites at differential rates. On the other hand, many nonfatal, or at least not necessarily fatal, illnesses may be found in nearly all of the elderly living in modern industrial societies; atherosclerosis is far and away the outstanding example. Provided some segment of the population is exempt from the health problems faced by the rest of the population, there is room to improve the quality of life experienced by the vast majority.

As we have seen, even the task of deciding what constitutes illness and disease is not as simple as it might at first appear. Beyond the mere physical properties of ill health lie a myriad of social and cultural factors. As we grow older, the problems of differentiating one state from another are multiplied many times. Before we can offer definitive conclusions about the health conditions older people encounter, we must also look at the organization of the medical profession and the values of our society.

With increased survival rates, what is now being found is that older persons suffer a fairly predictable range of health problems. Foremost among these are cardiovascular diseases and cancer. In the past decade the pattern of heart diseases is changing to reflect evidence of increased health awareness. Rates for men are declining but the incidence among women is not. What is striking about this short-term shift is the evidence of how rapidly intervention can make a difference. Life-style and social factors, in combination with advances in patterns of medical care, have altered what for years seemed a normative pattern. Cancer, unfortunately, has not responded as readily. In part because of the multiple causes of the process — perhaps because cancer is more a group of diseases than a unified disease process — the development of cancerous conditions has continued to confound the medical community. Immunological breakdown and environmental influences interact to frustrate attempts to identify causative linkages to date.

Short of life-threatening maladies, a number of other problems are common among the elderly and delimit the quality of their lives. Again the range is broad, running from arthritis to diabetes to dental problems. To some extent these too depend on the societal level, personal habits, and life-styles. The obvious impact of social structure is apparent in cross-cultural comparisons made by social epidemiologists. Within the framework of industrialization and the free market economies of Western nations, choices have been made regarding the priorities of primary and secondary intervention. It is a mistake, however, to assume that such choices are irrevocable. During times of economic distress, cutbacks in secondary treatment for certain groups within the society are often proposed. What is not so apparent is that the same economic factors implicated in the shortfalls are intertwined with the manifestation of health problems. Other solutions are feasible, but they are political rather than medical. We will return to an explorations of such questions in Chapter 11.

The "buzz-word" of the current political season is "cost effectiveness." It has spawned the emergence of prospective payments systems whereby health care systems are reimbursed by hospital admission rather than for outcomes and according to fixed payment schedules rather than for costs of care. Two results have become apparent in the relatively short time the program has been in effect. First, many costs are being shifted rather than contained. Second, the political agenda provides no guarantee that past service will ensure adequate care now.

Advocates of prospective payments systems argue that retrospective reimbursement on the basis of cost leads to excessive spending by hospitals and unnecessary procedures. Critics, however, point out that fixed, prospective payments — whether to hospitals or to health maintenance organizations — may have the opposite effect, leading to withholding potentially beneficial procedures because of cost considerations and resulting in less than optimal care. In choosing between systems of health care — whether on the social, political, or clinical level — we must answer two challenges: to keep the level of expenditures within the limits of available resources (always remembering that these limits are themselves socially constructed) and to choose those avenues that are most likely to enhance the lives of the elderly. The ultimate goal of a health care system should be to add life to the years of the elderly (Clark, 1985), not merely to add years of dependency and suffering to their lives.

# Discussion Questions

**Dimensions of
Health**

1. Choose a specific illness that affects old people. Discuss the causes, treatment, and prevention of this illness (a) from the biomedical point of view, (b) from the point of view of social epidemiology, (c) from the point of view of the political economy of health, (d) as a socially constructed illness reality, and (e) from the systems perspective.

2. Give some examples of the medicalization of social problems of the elderly. What other specific approaches could be used to explain these problems?

3. Discuss the advantages and disadvantages for the elderly of conceptualizing health (a) in functional terms and (b) in experiential terms.

4. Describe some instances of disease without illness and illness without disease in the elderly.

5. Write your own definition of health for the elderly. In doing so, think about what you would like your own old age to be like.

**Health Problems
of the Later Years**

6. Propose a research project designed to identify the most effective way of improving longevity over the next fifty years.

**The Diseases of
Later Life**

7. Choose one of the diseases discussed in this section. Develop a comprehensive plan for managing this disease in the elderly, including primary prevention, secondary prevention, treatment, and psychosocial support. How would you organize treatment? How would you decide on appropriate levels of treatment? Should older persons receive chemotherapy?

**Life-Style and
Health in the Later
Years**

8. You are a consultant to a state government. Design a comprehensive public health program for promoting physical health in the elderly. Incorporate (a) public education regarding risk factors, (b) measures that could be taken in the workplace to ensure that people will be healthier at the time they retire, and (c) support services and health promotion programs for the elderly.

9. How far do you think the life-style factors that affect health are a matter of personal responsibility? How far do you

think they result from the culture or social structure? What would you do about them to improve the health of the elderly?

**Health Care Services for the Elderly**

**10.** What do you think cost-effective health care for the elderly means? What would be the major goals of a cost-effective health care system?

**11.** What are the advantages and problems of DRGs?

**12.** You are a member of a congressional committee concerned with health planning. The ideas discussed in question 8 are sent to your committee to put into a comprehensive plan. How would you finance this system and make it cost effective?

## Pertinent Readings

American Cancer Society. *1985 Cancer Facts and Figures.* New York: American Cancer Society, 1985.

Andres, R., E. L. Bierman, and W. R. Hazzard, eds. *Principles of Geriatric Medicine.* New York: McGraw-Hill Book Company, 1985.

Armelagos, G. J., A. Goodman, and K. H. Jacobs. "The Ecological Perspective in Disease." In *Health and the Human Condition,* eds. M. H. Logan and E. E. Hunt, Jr., pp. 71–84. Belmont, Calif.: Wadsworth Publishing Company, 1978.

Berner, J. J. *Effects of Diseases on Laboratory Tests.* New York: J. B. Lippincott Company, 1983.

Bierman, E. L. "Aging and Atherosclerosis." In *Principles of Geriatric Medicine,* eds. R. Andres, E. L. Bierman, and W. R. Hazzard, pp. 42–50. New York: McGraw-Hill Book Company, 1985.

Botwinick, J. *Aging and Behavior.* New York: Springer Publishing Company, 1984.

Bourliere, F. "Ecology of Human Senescence." In *Textbook of Geriatric Medicine and Gerontology,* ed. J. C. Brocklehurst, pp. 71–85. Edinburgh: Churchill Livingstone, 1978.

Busse, E. W. "How Mind, Body and Environment Influence Nutrition in the Elderly." *Postgraduate Medicine* 63, 3 (1978): 118–25.

Butler, R. N. "Medicine and Aging: An Assessment of Opportunities and Neglect." National Institutes of Health, Department of Health, Education and Welfare, NIH Publication No. 79-1699. Washington, D.C.: U.S. Government Printing Office, 1979.

Calasanti, T., and J. Hendricks. "A Sociological Perspective on Nutrition Research Among the Elderly: A Call for Theory." *The Gerontologist* 25 (1985).

Candy-Gibbs, S. C., and H. B. Turner. "Psychological Dimensions of Nutrition." In *Nutritional Aspects of Aging,* ed. L. Chen. Boca Raton: CRC Press Inc., 1986.

Centers for Disease Control. "Smoking and Cancer." *Mortality and Morbidity Weekly Report* 31 (1982): 77–80.

Clark, P. G. "The Social Allocation of Health Care Resources: Ethical Dilemmas in Age-Group Competition." *The Gerontologist* 25, 2 (1985): 119–25.

Conrad, P., and J. W. Schneider. "Looking at Levels of Medicalization: A Comment on Strong's Critique of the Thesis of Medical Imperialism." *Social Science and Medicine* 14A (1980): 75–79.

Dubos, R. *Mirage of Health.* Garden City, N.Y.: Anchor Books, 1959.

———. *Man Adapting.* New Haven: Yale University Press, 1965.

———. *Man, Medicine and Environment.* New York: Praeger Publishers, 1968.

Eckhart, M. J., et al. "Health Hazards Associated with Alcohol Consumption." *Journal of the American Medical Association* 246, 6 (1981): 648–66.

Engel, G. I. "A Unified Concept of Health and Disease." *Perspectives in Biology and Medicine* 3 (1960): 459–85.

Estes, C. L., et al. *Political Economy, Health and Aging.* Boston: Little, Brown & Company, 1984.

Fabrega, H. "Concepts of Disease: Logical Features and Social Implications." *Perspectives in Biology and Medicine* 15 (1972): 583–616.

———. "The Scientific Usefulness of the Idea of Illness." *Perspectives in Biology and Medicine* 22, 4 (1979): 554–58.

———. "Culture and Psychiatric Illness: Biomedical and Ethnomedical Aspects." In *Cultural Conceptions of Mental Health and Therapy,* eds. A. J. Marsella and G. M. White, pp. 39–68. Boston: D. Reidel Publishing Co., Inc., 1984.

Fifer, W. R. "Prospective Payment Strategy — Is It Working?" *Pennsylvania Medicine* 87, 12 (December 1984): 38–42.

Frankenberg, R. "Functionalism and After? Theory and Developments in Social Science Applied to the Health Field." In *Health and Medical Care in the U.S.: A Critical Analysis,* ed. V. Navarro, pp. 21–37. Farmingdale, N.Y.: Baywood Publishing Company, 1975.

Freeman, J. T. *Clinical Features of the Older Patient.* Springfield, Ill.: Charles C Thomas, Publisher, 1965.

Fries, J. F., and L. M. Crapo. *Vitality and Aging: Implications of the Rectangular Curve.* San Francisco: W. H. Freeman & Company, 1981.

Gentry, W. D., and R. B. Williams, Jr., eds. *Psychological Aspects of Myocardial Infarction and Coronary Care.* St. Louis: The C.V. Mosby Company, 1979.

Gerstenblith, G. M., L. Weisfeldt, and E. G. Lakatta. "Disorders of the Heart." In *Principles of Geriatric Medicine,* eds. R. Andres, E. L. Bierman, and W. R. Hazzard, pp. 525–26. New York: McGraw-Hill Book Company, 1985.

Hartford, J. T., and T. Samorajski. "Alcoholism in the Geriatric Population." *Journal of the American Geriatrics Society* 30 (1982): 18–24.

Hendricks, J., and T. Calasanti. "Social Dimensions of Nutrition." In *Nutritional Aspects of Aging,* ed. L. Chen. Boca Raton: CRC Press, Inc., 1986.

Henry, J. P. "The Relation of Social To Biological Process of Disease." *Social Science Medicine* 16, 3 (1982): 369–80.

Hickey, T. *Health and Aging.* Monterey, Calif.: Brooks/Cole Publishing Company, 1980.

Horn, S. "Does Severity of Illness Make a Difference in Prospective Payment?" *Healthcare Financial Management* 37, 5 (May, 1983): 49–53.

———, and D. N. Schumacher. "Comparing Classification Methods: Measurement of Variations in Change, Length of Stay, and Mortality." *Medical Care* 22, 5 (1982): 489–500.

Hunt, K. "DRG — What It Is, How It Works and Why It Will Hurt." *Medical Economics* 60, 18 (September 5, 1983): 262–70.

Iglehart, J. K. "The New Era of Prospective Payment for Hospitals." *New England Journal of Medicine* 307, 20 (November 11, 1982a): 1288–92.

——. "New Jersey's Experiment with DRG Based Hospital Reimbursement." *New England Journal of Medicine* 307, 26 (December 23, 1982b): 1655–60.

——. "Medicare Begins Prospective Payment." *New England Journal of Medicine* 308, 23 (June 9, 1983): 1428–32.

Jokl, E. "Physical Activity and Aging." *Annals of Sports Medicine* 1, 2 (1983): 43–48.

Kane, R. L., J. G. Ouslander, and I. B. Abrass. *Essentials of Clinical Geriatrics.* New York: McGraw-Hill Book Company, 1984.

Kannel, W. B., and F. N. Brand. "Cardiovascular Risk Factors in the Elderly." In *Principles of Geriatric Medicine*, eds. R. Andres, E. L. Bierman, and W. R. Hazzard, pp. 104–19. New York: McGraw-Hill Book Company, 1985.

Kelman, S. "The Social Nature of the Definition of Health." In *Health and Medical Care in the U.S.: A Critical Analysis*, ed. V. Navarro, pp. 3–20. Farmingdale, N.Y.: Baywood Publishing Company, 1975.

Kleinman, A., and E. Mendelsohn. "Systems of Medical Knowledge: A Comparative Approach." *Journal of Medicine and Philosophy* 31 (1978): 314–30.

——, L. Eisenberg, and B. Good. "Culture, Illness and Care: Clinical Lessons from Anthropologic and Cross-Cultural Research." *Annals of Internal Medicine* 88 (1978): 251–58.

Lang, H. L. "A Physician Looks at DRGs." *The Western Journal of Medicine* 141, 2 (1984): 248–55.

LaRue, A., L. Bank, L. Jarvik, and M. Hetland. "Health in Old Age: How Do Physicians' Rating and Self-Rating Compare?" *Journal of Gerontology* 34, 5 (1979): 687–91.

Lawton, M. P. "Impact of the Environment on Aging and Behavior." In *Handbook of the Psychology of Aging*, eds. J. E. Birren and K. W. Schaie, pp. 276–301. New York: Van Nostrand Reinhold Company, 1977.

Lee, P. R., and H. L. Lipton. *Drugs and the Elderly: A Background Paper.* Policy Paper No. 3. San Francisco: Aging Health Policy Center and Institute for Health Policy Studies, University of California, 1982.

Lennard, H. L., et al. *Mystification and Drug Misuse: Hazards in Using Psychoactive Drugs.* San Francisco: Jossey-Bass, Inc., Publishers, 1971.

Lindenfeld, J., and B. M. Groves. "Cardiovascular Function and Disease in the Aged." In *Clinical Internal Medicine in the Aged*, ed. R. W. Schrier, pp. 87–123. Philadelphia: W. B. Saunders Company, 1982.

Maddox, G., and E. B. Douglass. "Self-Assessment of Health." In *Normal Aging II*, ed. E. Palmore, pp. 55–62. Durham, N.C.: Duke University Press, 1974.

Marmot, M. G., et al. "Japanese Culture and Coronary Heart Disease." In *Recent Advances in Gerontology*, eds. H. Orimo, K. Shimada, M. Iriki, and D. Maeda, pp. 476–79. Amsterdam: Excerpta Medica, 1979.

Mechanic, D. "The Concept of Illness Behavior." *Journal of Chronic Disease* 15, 1 (1962): 189–94.

Mellstrom, D., et al. "Tobacco Smoking, Ageing and Health Among the Elderly. A Longitudinal Study of 70 Year Old Men and an Age Cohort Comparison." *Age and Ageing* 11 (1982): 45–68.

Nahemow, L., and M. P. Lawton. "Toward an Ecological Theory of Adaptation and Aging." In *Environmental Psychology: People and Their Physical Settings*, eds. H. M. Proshansky, W. H. Ihelson, and L. G. Riven, pp. 315–21. New York: Holt, Rinehart & Winston, 1976.

National Cancer Institute. *The Breast Cancer Digest.* NIH84-1691. Bethesda: National Institutes of Health, 1984.

National Center for Disease Statistics, Department of Health, Education and Human Services. *Health in the United States: Chartbook.* Washington, D.C.: U.S. Government Printing Office, 1980.

———, B. Bloom. *Current Estimates from the National Health Interview Survey, United States, 1981.* Vital and Health Statistics, Series 10, No. 141 (PHS No. 83-1569), Public Health Service. Washington, D.C.: U.S. Government Printing Office, 1982.

———, C. S. Willder: *Disability Days: United States, 1980.* Vital and Health Statistics, Series 10, No. 143 (PHS No. 83-1571), Public Health Service. Washington, D.C.: U.S. Government Printing Office, 1983.

———, F. M. Trevino, and A. J. Moss: *Health Indicators for Hispanic, Black and White Americans.* Vital and Health Statistics, Series 10, No. 148 (PHS No. 84-1576), Public Health Service. Washington, D.C.: U.S. Government Printing Office, 1984.

———, L. Fingerhut: *Changes in Mortality among the Elderly, United States, 1940–1978,* Supplement to 1980. Vital and Health Statistics, Series 3, No. 22a (PHS No. 84-1406a), Public Health Service. Washington, D.C.: U.S. Government Printing Office, 1984b.

Natlow, A. B., and J. Heslin. *Geriatric Nutrition.* Boston: CBI Publishing Company, Inc., 1980.

Navarro, V. *Medicine Under Capitalism.* New York: Prodist, 1976.

Omenn, G. S., and D. A. Conrad. "Implications of DRGs for Clinicians." *New England Journal of Medicine* 311, 20 (November 15, 1984): 1314–17.

Palmore, E. *Social Patterns in Normal Aging: Findings from the Duke Longitudinal Study.* Durham, N.C.: Duke University Press, 1981.

———, and C. Luikart. "Health and Social Factors Related to Life Satisfaction." In *Normal Aging II,* ed. E. Palmore, pp. 185–200. Durham, N.C.: Duke University Press, 1974.

Parsons, T. "Definitions of Health and Illness in the Light of American Values and Social Structure." In *Patients, Physicians and Illness,* ed. E. G. Jaco, pp. 107–27. New York: The Free Press, 1972.

Peck, R. "Psychological Development in the Second Half of Life." In *Psychological Aspects of Aging,* ed. J. E. Anderson. Washington, D.C.: American Psychological Association, 1956.

Pettingill, B. F., and H. C. Westell. "Unanswered Questions Facing DRGs." *Hospital Topics* 62, 4 (July/August, 1984): 3–5.

Pfeiffer, E. "Survival in Old Age." In *Normal Aging II,* ed. E. Palmore, pp. 269–80. Durham, N.C.: Duke University Press, 1974.

Public Health Service. *Healthy People: The Surgeon General's Report on Health Promotion and Disease Prevention.* PHS No. 79-55071A. Washington, D.C.: U.S. Government Printing Office, 1979.

Rowe, J. W. "Health Care of the Elderly." *The New England Journal of Medicine* 312, 13 (March 28, 1985): 827–35.

Select Committee on Aging, U.S. House of Representatives, 1985.

Sheldon, A., F. Baker, and C. P. McLaughlin, eds. *Systems and Medical Care.* Cambridge, Mass.: The M.I.T. Press, 1970.

Stamler, J. "Diet Related Risk Factors for Human Atherosclerosis: Hyperlipidema, Hypertension, Hyperglycemia, Current Status." *Advances in Experimental Medicine and Biology* 60, 1 (1975): 125–58.

"The World Health Situation." In *World Health Chronicle*, No. 21. Geneva: World Health Organization, 1967.

Timiras, P. S., ed. *Developmental Physiology and Aging*. New York: Macmillan, Inc., 1972.

Tissue, T. "Another Look at Self-Rated Health among the Elderly." *Journal of Gerontology* 27, 1 (1972): 91–94.

Townsend, P. "Structured Dependency of the Elderly: Creation of Social Policy in the Twentieth Century." *Ageing and Society* 1, 1 (1981): 5–28.

U.S. Bureau of the Census. *Statistical Abstract of the United States, 1985*. Washington, D.C.: U.S. Government Printing Office, 1985.

———. *Cancer Incidence and Mortality in the United States, 1973–1981*. NIH 85-1837. Bethesda: National Cancer Institute, 1984.

Wilson, R. N. *The Sociology of Health*. New York: Random House, 1970.

Zola, I. "Medicine as an Institution of Social Control." *Sociological Review* 20 (1972): 487–504.

———. "In the Name of Health and Illness: Some Sociopolitical Consequences of Medical Influence." *Social Science and Medicine* 9 (1975): 83–87.

# 6

# PSYCHOLOGICAL FACTORS IN ADULT LIFE

**MULTIPLE FACETS OF THE PSYCHOLOGY OF AGING**

**SENSORY AND COGNITIVE FUNCTIONING**
Sensory Modalities
 *Kinesthetic Sensitivity*
 *Audition*
 *Visual Acuity*
Reaction Time and Psychomotor
 Response
Learning, Remembering, and
 Forgetting
 *Metamemory*
 *Sensory Memory*
Intelligence and Creativity
 *Multidimensionality of Intelligence*
 *Age-Related Artifacts in Testing*
 *Cognitive Ability and Impending Death*
 *Creativity*

**STABILITY AND CHANGE OVER THE LIFE CYCLE**
Stage Theories of Development in
 Adulthood
Alternatives to Developmental Models
Sex Roles and Adult Life

**PSYCHOLOGICAL DISORDERS IN THE LATER YEARS**
Mental Health and Mental Disorders
Mental Health in Later Life
 *What It Feels Like to be Old*
 *Intrinsic and Situational Factors*
 *Sex Differences*

**MENTAL DISORDERS AMONG THE ELDERLY**
Psychogenic Disorders
 *Affective Disorders*
 *Neurotic Disorders*
 *Psychotic Disorders*
 *Other Self-Destructive Behaviors*
Organic Brain Syndromes
 *Alzheimer's Disease*
 *Multi-Infarct Dementia*
 *Other Disorders*
Treatment and Intervention
 *Medication*
 *Psychotherapy*

**SUMMARY**

**DISCUSSION QUESTIONS**

**PERTINENT READINGS**

# Multiple Facets of the Psychology of Aging

As psychologists are fond of saying, no one ever encounters the problems of old age unprepared. Each person brings a lifetime of hard-won coping techniques designed to alleviate stress and to bolster self-concept. Life at any given moment is a reflection of biological capabilities, social inputs from the environment, and a sense of one's own skills, goals, and alternatives. To evaluate how well a person is doing emotionally it is necessary to understand how these three realms interact and merge. In this, as well as the preceding chapter on health, we review some of the many conditions that might affect the elderly — we shall see that often the observed problem is not the only problem; it is also the attitude one has. We are all subject to many of the same events, but as the result of a life of continuous growth and development, we impose our own unique twist on what might otherwise be termed objective circumstances.

In a society that extols the virtues of youth and denigrates its elderly, it is little wonder that psychological risks might be thought to run high along with age. Nevertheless, among the elderly, as in every other age group, only a relatively small percentage can be considered to be suffering from serious psychological problems. Why then do older people constitute a disproportionate number of both admissions to psychiatric facilities and suicides committed each year? Perhaps the source lies with the existence of increased or unexpected tensions in their lives. Why are they but a small percentage of private or outpatient psychiatric clients? Maybe it is because stereotypes die hard and the biases of health care personnel are not so different from the rest of the population. Charting a course of successful aging is synonymous with maintaining a balance between personal and social resources on the one hand and perceived demands and obligations on the other. Without a feeling of permanence or consistency, the risk of emotional trauma is exacerbated. To clarify some of the misconceptions about psychological factors in later life, this chapter will summarize what is known about alterations in psychomotor capacities, developmental adaptation, and what is commonly labeled psychopathology.

Over the course of the life span, sensory and perceptual modalities are in a constant state of flux, and as changes occur, cognitive and intellectual adjustments and compensations are increasingly required. One of the central themes emerging from life span analyses of adult development and aging is the continuity of the adaptive responses in the face of losses accruing with each successive life stage. In addition, acceptance of the limitations imposed on physical abilities over time involves learning new skills and reorienting personal desires or expectations. Recognizing that youthful capacities generally fade to be replaced by other attributes is a crucial developmental task that must be accomplished if a person is to feel competent or satisfied in his or her later years.

Just as positive accommodations are cumulative, so too are responses that eventually become maladaptive, even though they might originally have been functional. Psychological disorders that appear in later life usually have their origin in an earlier period. Nor do they stem solely from an individual's psychological makeup; rather, they reflect stresses to which one is exposed and the availability of appropriate resolutions. The psychological problems of older people resemble those of the rest of society, except that older people are more vulnerable to organic disorders than are younger people. To fully understand these as well as the more normal aspects of the psychological dimensions of the aging process, it is important to appreciate the ways in which the various components change over the life cycle.

# Sensory and Cognitive Functioning

## SENSORY MODALITIES

Sensory processes have received considerable attention in the investigation of the effects of age on mental capacities. Of the five basic senses psychologists customarily study, taste and smell will not be addressed here beyond noting they show age-related decrements that frequently result in an inability among the very old to distinguish among various foods or odors. In the case of taste the tongue loses *papillae* with age, there are fewer taste buds on the remaining number, and hormonal changes reduce their functioning. The best evidence indicates that until age sixty the ability to perceive sweet, sour, bitter, and salt — the four basic tastes — changes not at all. During the sixties some gradual erosion is noticed, most particularly with salty flavors, but even these are minor. If food in the diet of an older person does not taste as he or she thinks it should, the cause is usually not a problem of the taste receptors. The inability to distinguish various tastes or flavors that is sometimes noted is often caused by other things; among these, smell appears to play a large role. Taste is also thought to represent a number of psychological factors.

Anyone who has had a cold knows food may taste bland. The experience of food is seemingly based on a combination of taste and olfactory stimulation. Research on the sense of smell is contradictory, but most investigators contend there is some minor deterioration over time. Throughout life odor recognition varies greatly among individuals. Some older people never had much of a sense of smell, some experience a decline in the later years, while others do not seem to perceive a change. When a decline occurs, the root cause may be an atrophy of olfactory bulbs in the nose.

The remaining three senses — sight, hearing, and kinesthesis — are more pertinent here because they are apt to be directly related to psychological well-being. An individual's potential for interaction with the environment is grounded in his or her receipt of and response to sensory inputs. Fortunately, most people have sensory acuities far in excess of what is normally required for simple awareness. In addition to ample surpluses, initial losses are often minimized by compensatory mechanisms called into operation when a given modality no longer provides essential information. After a certain point, however, any further depreciation of sensory processes is likely to manifest itself in behavioral or psychological aberrations.

For stimuli to be consciously recognized a two-step process, more distinct in analysis than in fact, must operate. First, the stimulus must be of sufficient magnitude to activate receptor organs and associated nerve tracts. If the stimulus is below the organ's *threshold*, or if the receptors are not working properly, no stimulation message is received by the brain. Once a message reaches the brain, it must be catalogued according to preexisting experiences before recognition takes place and a response is formulated. Innumerable factors, ranging from the type of stimulus or disorders in higher order cerebral functioning to socially ingrained habits, may intervene between stimulus and response. That a response to a given stimulus may be perfectly appropriate under certain conditions and inappropriate under others renders the search for invariable explanations a difficult, and at times impossible task. Generally, threshold levels increase with advancing age; the more specialized the sense, the greater the increment of change over time. Of equal importance is the complexity of the response or the degree of stimulus discrimination required, so that those responses calling for the greatest articulation between systems usually show the largest decrements. On the other hand, habitual response patterns are less likely to deteriorate provided no sudden changes interrupt customary response patterns.

**Kinesthetic Sensitivity.** Why do older people seem to fall often, or why do they sometimes appear to be clumsy as though their bodies are not quite coordinated? The answers are at least in part linked to changes in somatic (or kinesthetic) sensitivity. Over time the unthinking integration of somatic sensation mediated by vestibular cues for maintaining balance seems to deteriorate.

Perhaps the most expedient way to explain kinesthetic sensitivity, without going into great detail, is by a series of examples. Few young people have any difficulty in recognizing when they are sitting upright or partially prone. Nor do they often err when called on to locate their feet relative to their knees, such as when climbing on uneven terrain. Usually they are able to make generalized postural adjustments when getting to their feet, compensating for slight misalignments without giving the matter any thought. Many elderly, on the other hand, do not have the luxury of unconsciously controlling body position or movement, since the loss of their kinesthetic senses leaves them vulnerable to accidental falls and postural instability. For each of us the sense of movement, touch, and position depends in part on receptors located in muscles, joints, and the skin. Further, the **proprioceptive** system, as kinesthesis is called by physiologists, relies on visual cues and on vestibular controls. Obviously all are important, yet few of us experience postural confusion in the dark, primarily because our limbs and muscles send their own messages to the brain, advising of their location relative to other parts of the body. Fluid balances in the semicircular canals of the inner ear also help maintain spatial orientation, acting much like the gyroscope or artificial horizon in an airplane that shows the craft's altitude relative to the earth's surface. Each of the three semicircular canals extends in a different plane and each contains a liquid that activates tiny hair receptors that transmit a message to the cerebral cortex and the thalamus when the equilibrium is disturbed (Barrett, 1972). For various reasons, some of which can be traced to sensory impairments and some to a breakdown of the brain's integrative capacities, the dizziness or vertigo reported by many elderly is attributed to dysfunctions in these two areas. The specific causes of kinesthetic malfunctions are yet to be discerned. Motion sickness and a rare disease known as Meniere's syndrome are thought to be extreme examples of the nausea and locomotion difficulties encountered among older people.

**Audition.** The ability to hear is one of the most valuable of our senses; when it becomes impaired, it places people at a disadvantage of which they are only too painfully aware. Current estimates suggest approximately 7 percent of all middle-aged Americans suffer hearing losses of a magnitude that hinders social interaction. By sixty-five or so the percentage has jumped to over half of all men and 30 percent of all women (National Center for Health Statistics, 1982). Normally young adults can hear pure tones in frequencies up to 15,000 vibrations per second. Beginning around twenty-five, *presbycusis*, an age-related loss of the ganglion cells necessary for conduction, causes erosion of the upper threshold, and after sixty-five or seventy sounds above 4000 vibrations per second may be inaudible. Conversely, low-range tones (below 1000 cycles) do not appear to be appreciably affected by age. Volume, or loudness measured in decibels, is a more common measure of hearing. Humans can hear sounds between 0 decibels, well below the level of a whisper, which averages about 8 decibels, to those in excess of 130 decibels, though pain and nausea are associated with the latter. Since the range of normal conversation is around 60 decibels, severe hearing impairments are said to occur when an individual's threshold exceeds 35 decibels.

Age-related declines in the hearing of high-frequency sounds may be traced to a deterioration of receptor hair cells, neurons, and vascular changes in the inner ear or membranes within the inner ear. Depending on which decline is most prominent, the ability to hear different types of sound will be affected.

The best evidence at this time appears to support the contention that the association between age and hearing loss of all types is strong. Wax buildup and a constant ringing called tinnitus resulting from a variety of pathological conditions will also reduce auditory acuity. In addition, any sustained noise above 70 decibels will eventually cause hearing loss. Thus, increased noise pollution has also been indicated as a source of decreased auditory ability. Hearing loss has also been shown to be related to lower levels of education, posing even greater risks for those who work in noisy environments. Listening to loud music also compromises the ability to hear well, so future generations of old people may show even greater deficits.

Testing for hearing loss is usually carried out under controlled laboratory conditions using constant and variable pure tones, as well as speech uttered at different volumes. From all indications the declining acuity exhibited by the aged in laboratory tests suffers still greater aggravation in the less favorable circumstances of daily routines. While many of the changes are a consequence of retrogressive alterations, or diseases of the inner ear, vascular difficulties, environmental assaults, and other variables such as sex or intelligence are also implicated. Across the age span, women, and those people who by virtue of their training pay close attention to speech patterns, experience the least hearing loss as they become older. Men and blacks experience greater real declines, especially at higher frequencies. One of the most obvious results of severely impaired hearing is a sense of isolation and loneliness, quite possibly coupled with emotional distress. Butler and Lewis (1982) note that the emotional upsets associated with reduced reality testing and decreased auditory perception may lead to reactive depressions and paranoid ideational states if impairments are sufficiently severe and continue for any lengthy period of time. There is no evidence, however, that hearing deficits in any way reduce intelligence when procedures on verbal testing are controlled (Thomas et al., 1983).

**Visual Acuity.** By the late 1980s approximately 11.5 million people in the United States will suffer visual impairments. Like so many other chronic conditions affecting us, the prevalence rates climb with age. In fact, age is the single best predictor of visual limitations or blindness; if we live long enough nearly all of us will have vision problems. Over half of the nearly half a million legally blind persons in the United States are over sixty-five, and by the year 2000 their number will climb to between 272,000 and 367,000. Using a broader definition of visual impairment — an inability to read newsprint without corrective lenses — about 1,760,000 older people will have trouble seeing. These figures represent a 78 percent increase over what was the case at the beginning of the decade. Most of them will be among the old-old and will probably be women. They will also be on the lower levels of the socioeconomic scale, be more disadvantaged according to most standard indicators, suffer multiple chronic conditions, be limited in their normal routines for up to one month out of every year, and be disproportionately minority members of our society (Lowman and Kircher, 1979; Hendricks, 1986).

Such a claim grows out of existing patterns and information reported over the last decade. Like so many other physical conditions affecting the elderly, visual impairment is likely to be influenced by a disadvantaged position in the social structure. Prevalence rates seem to be linked with relative social disadvantage; the pattern holds for income, education, gender, and race (National Center for Health Statistics, 1981). The peripheral position the disadvantaged elderly experience may also be reinforced by their vision problems. Whether the visually impaired are disengaged is a difficult issue: some say there is a centripetal tendency, whereas others disagree. Knowledge in this area is sparse at best. What is certain is that age-related deficits in visual capability or any other sensory change means a loss of wholeness — if only for symbolic reasons (Bader, in press; Sekuler et al., 1983; Monbeck, 1973). What experts in vision impairment call a "blind attitude" — a pattern of discrimination based on the inability to see — seems to affect not only those who only occasionally interact with the nonsighted but those who experience the condition as well.

Visual acuity is the measure most often used when speaking of vision. It is a summary index of efficiency most often reported in the ability to discriminate test objects at a distance of twenty feet. If an individual has 20/20 vision, that means he or she can read an eye chart as well as normal people at that distance, with smaller ratios indicating progressively poorer eyesight. For example, vision rated as 20/70 means objects distinguishable at twenty feet with impaired eyesight can be discriminated at seventy feet by the normally sighted. Resulting from morphological changes in the eye, most declines become noticeable by late in the fourth decade, appearing slightly earlier for nonwhites than whites. Hence seven out of eight people over forty-five find it necessary to wear glasses, compared to three out of ten younger than forty-five. Fewer than 20 percent of those over sixty-five cannot obtain a corrected vision of at least 20/40, more than adequate for normal activities (Butler and Lewis, 1982).

A variety of ocular problems afflict older eyes, the most frequent being cataracts, glaucoma, and macular diseases. Over the past five years or so the increasing availability of new surgical techniques for managing visual impairment has brought at least some relief to many of the visually impaired elderly. A major cause of visual decline and eventual blindness has been cataract formation: with age, the lens of the eye, which should be crystal clear, becomes cloudy and white, no longer allowing light to pass. Providing there is no other disease of the eye, sight may be restored by removing the lens (or cataract) from the eye. This was once a serious operation requiring prolonged hospitalization, but the operating microscope and other improvements in surgical technique have made cataract extraction a relatively low risk procedure that can be performed on an outpatient basis if the person is otherwise healthy. Implantable lenses and contacts for cataract patients have replaced the need for heavy cataract glasses. Other developments include the increasing frequency of corneal transplants and the use of **scleral buckle procedures** and the laser to retinal detachment and hemorrhage.

The old person squinting at a newspaper held out at arm's length has been a source of humor for many years. But **presbyopia,** or the inability to change the eye's focal length, is so common during the last half of life that most people over forty have experienced it. A similar decline in the eyes' ability to adapt to darkness tends to inhibit reading and driving at night among the aged. Nonetheless, carefully controlled illumination can minimize a large share of the problems that might otherwise interfere with a person's daily routine (Keeney and Keeney, 1980).

Regardless of ability to read a newspaper, changes in vision also affect sensitivity to glare and depth perception. Bright illumination is hard for old eyes to adapt to. Declines in acuity and hypersensitivity to glare also lead to decrements in an older person's sense of depth and relationship. Some deterioration in breadth of field has also been observed. Finally, recent research has indicated an apparent slowing in the speed with which visual information is processed because of a longer refractory period following neural stimulation (Botwinick, 1984). Consequently, perceptual flexibility in visual sensation undergoes a gradual involution with age. Clearly, if thresholds are altered in any of the senses, contact with the immediate environment may be threatened. As indicated in Chapter 3, the ability to engage components of the context in which behavior is acted out is a critical personal resource. Without that ability an eddying effect is likely to sweep through many facets of cognitive and social well-being.

## REACTION TIME AND PSYCHOMOTOR RESPONSE

Declining sensory acuity and the often concurrent slowing of behaviors involving the central nervous system are seen most clearly in evaluations of psychomotor performance of older populations. The relationship is by no means simple or direct. As noted in Chapter 4, diminished conduction velocities, the speed at which impulses travel neural pathways, account for only a small fraction of the delay in reaction times that accompanies advanced age. Traditionally, reaction time has been defined as the lag between stimulation and the initiation of a response. Any assessment of reaction time is complicated by such factors as the nature of the signal, the complexity and type of response required, motor skills, testing artifacts involving experiences, practice or the amount of irrelevant information, plus a wide range of sociopsychological variables including attention or motivation. In contrast to many younger test recruits, older respondents appear willing to sacrifice speed in favor of accuracy, thereby exhibiting slower overall profiles but more precise responses (Botwinick, 1984).

It is most important to remember that laboratory test results are quite difficult to translate into equivalent performances in daily life, since daily activities are generally influenced by unexpected and extraneous environmental inputs and are seldom limited to the narrow range of choices characteristic of test situations. Nonetheless, age decrements in performance tests of reaction time have substantial practical implications. The rapidity with which decisions based on coordination of cognitive and motor capacities may be implemented seems to depend almost entirely on the functioning of the cerebral cortex, where signal-to-noise ratios show a steady age-related deterioration. Some researchers have suggested poorer performances are a consequence of heightened ambient arousal states in the cortex of older persons that exceed the limits of efficient functioning. This necessitates a longer time to discriminate between random impulses and those to which a response is required. Without the pressure of time, evidence indicates that older people are as capable of acting effectively as their younger counterparts. Whether they do reflects as much personality and educational variables or emotional states as psychological motor skills per se (Welford, 1969). It is known that reaction time lengthens with lethargic or depressed moods, although continued activity may stimulate possible improvements within certain limits (Botwinick, 1984).

Circulatory deterioration, depressed cerebral metabolism, or suppressed brain rhythms also tend to correlate with slower reaction times and lessened mental functioning. Apparently the propensity toward cardiovascular problems may also retard simple reaction sequences that the elderly cannot overcome regardless of their exercise levels (Botwinick and Storandt, 1974).

Our response to a stimulus perceived is comprised of three interrelated phases: transmission, interpretation, and execution. The interpretation phase, or the central processing, involves a series of subroutines whereby decisions are reached. Because very little if any decline in response speed for simple tasks has been reported, most investigators point to higher order cerebral processing as responsible for delays in more complicated tasks. As Schaie and Geiwitz (1982) point out, even these differences may be the result of technique; younger persons use cues better to anticipate the required response. When split-second preparation is precluded, many of the age differences also disappear (Gottsdanker, 1982).

## LEARNING, REMEMBERING, AND FORGETTING

As with a computer, when we learn we process information from a variety of sources. It is perceived, classified, stored, interpreted, and finally retrieved. Our memories are similar to computer disks on which bits of data are stored; if we can prove we filed it, we are thought to have learned something. But also like the computer there can be bugs in the process. Unlike the machine, however, we do not get an error message specifying the nature of the default. Consequently, finding where the process went wrong is not easy. Even distinguishing learning from memory is a dilemma. How can one be demonstrated without the other?

Learning studies have tended to focus on *verbal learning;* that is, they involve testing language skills to demonstrate the assimilation of a body of material. In so doing they may mask true capabilities with the artifacts of testing.

Memory assessment is also tricky. In an effort to sort out components within this complex process, recent efforts have distinguished between metamemory, sensory, as well as short-term and long-term memories. These categories are used to guide our discussion to attain a clearer picture of the effects of age on the various aspects of memory.

While few longitudinal studies of learning, memory, and forgetting have been undertaken (Robertson-Tchabo and Arenberg, 1985) and methodological problems are quite complex, what do we know about how either of these two facets of cognitive processing change with age? At the outset it cannot be stressed too strongly that older people can and do learn. Studies seeking to ascertain learning capacities and memory in older people in the past have reinforced the popular notion that in both cases the elderly are at a disadvantage. Many of the earlier investigations stumbled over conceptual and procedural obstacles, confusing learning with the demonstration of knowledge and making broad generalizations extremely hazardous. It has been widely accepted that the older the respondent, the less likely he or she is to fare well on performance tests designed for learning or memory skills, provided intelligence levels are not disparate. Disagreements arise when it comes to the question of whether such tests are indeed measuring capacity factors or are referring instead to artifacts of the test situation (Horn and Engstrom, 1980). As illustrated in Figure 6.1, in tests requiring rapid responses there does appear to be an ordinary slowing of reaction time and arousal of the central nervous system. Again, however, results must be considered cautiously, for evidence suggests that verbal fluency or numerical skills do not suffer during timed performance tests (Horn, 1975). Under conditions allowing for self-pacing, the magnitude of the age decrements in timed tests is lessened considerably.

The best evidence indicates that when all factors are taken into consideration some decay occurs after sixty-five. It may be because older people are too anxious or too cautious during testing. They may not be motivated to do well in laboratory situations for the sake of some young psychologist or in the types of tests learning assessment requires. Perhaps they also lack an appropriate strategy for learning new material or taking tests. We do know that with practice everyone, including older people, improves his or her performance. Under the right circumstances all of these problems might be corrected, so in many respects the question still remains whether older people learn as easily as younger people. Until the methods for assessing improve, little in the way of definitive statements can be made (Perlmutter and Hall, 1985; Botwinick, 1984).

The distinction between learning and memory is confusingly vague, since the demonstration of learning necessarily involves retrieving data from the brain's memory bank. Precisely where learning leaves off and the memory begins is yet unclear. In a seminal discussion of the issues, Botwinick (1984) points out that, though the exact division may be arbitrary and is frequently blurred, the two processes represent independent phenomena. In attempting to answer the question, psychologists have created a multistage model of the

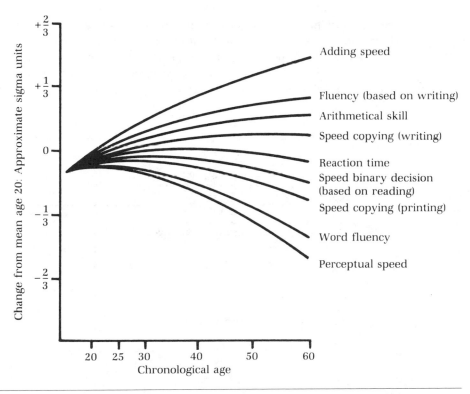

**FIGURE 6.1**

Age differences and age changes in timed aspects of intelligence: summary data. (*Source:* Horn, J. L. "Psychometric Studies of Aging and Intelligence." In *Genesis and Treatment of Psychological Disorders of the Elderly*, eds. S. Gershon and A. Raskin, p. 33. New York: Raven Press, 1975.)

three interrelated aspects that must also be borne in mind: encoding, storage, and retrieval. While it may be more analytically distinct than real, it is a good guide for sorting out dimensions of memory. The two axes of memory are shown in Figure 6.2.

**Metamemory.** Metamemory refers to encoding and retrieval strategies, that is, the ways of organizing information for efficient storage and ultimately recall. Although this may relate to the fact they are not in situations that require memorization or other factors, older people do not seem to develop spontaneous techniques for committing information to memory. Under conditions where natural learning as opposed to laboratory testing is measured, Perlmutter and Hall (1985) found that metamemory strategies seems to be retained. Indeed, older people may actually do better than younger persons.

**Sensory Memory.** Sensory memory may be viewed as a short-term holding tank; information is either sorted for further processing or used and discarded. The time lapse of sensory memories is just fractions of a second. If information is retained, it is in the form of *short-term memory*. As shown in Figure 6.2, it is a type of deeper storage that uses explicit cognitive sorting. An example might be the retention of a telephone number from when it was looked up to dialing the phone. Once used, or if the sequence is interrupted, it

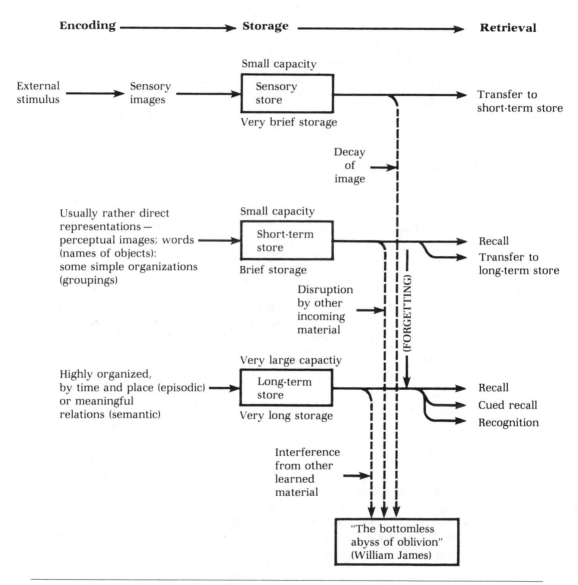

**FIGURE 6.2**

Visual representation of memory system. Two dimensions are shown: (1) three phases of encoding, storage, and retrieval and (2) three storage levels. (*Source:* Schaie, K. W., and J. Geiwitz. *Adult Development and Aging,* p. 309. Boston: Little Brown & Company, 1983.)

is forgotten unless sent to *long-term memory*. Here is a seemingly limitless store of long past experiences, information, frequently dialed phone numbers, and general knowledge about the world. Long-term storage is much like a junk drawer of the mind. We are not ever sure what is in there until we have occasion to go looking for something. When asked to retrieve information, it is brought back to short-term storage, then recited or used in some other way.

How does age enter into this complicated arrangement? Age-related memory deficiencies have been widely reported in the psychological literature. While short-term recall seems to decay with age, perhaps as a consequence of poorer sorting strategies, long-term memories of remote events do not show similar changes. However, the character of long-term memories needs to be carefully examined before any definitive conclusions can be drawn. It may well be that only practical long-term memories, those frequently recalled, can be readily remembered. Do unrehearsed memories also resist dissolution? The answer certainly has practical significance for all levels of mental functioning. In nearly every instance, well-educated, mentally active people do not have the same decline as their age peers who do not have similar opportunities to flex their minds. Nevertheless, with few exceptions the time required for memory scanning is longer for both recent and remote recall among older people, probably more the result of social and health factors than any irreversible effects of age (Perlmutter and Hall, 1985; Botwinick, 1984). In one twenty-year analysis of mental functioning, women were found to retain an advantage over men as they moved further into old age. While the opposite might be expected to be the case, as men are customarily perceived as being more active, the researchers suggest the differences may stem in part from higher morbidity and earlier mortality among men (Blum et al., 1972).

## INTELLIGENCE AND CREATIVITY

If assessing learning and memory is difficult, the issue of intelligence is exponentially more problematic. By definition, intelligence testing was originally linked to scholastic performance in the educational system. A score of 100 was obtained by a statistical procedure and used to indicate the average intelligence quotient (IQ) for a given age group. In this way a first grader, a college senior, and a retired person may each have an IQ of 100, 120, or whatever. For many years the youth-oriented content of standardized questions militated against the older person, or anyone else not closely aligned with mainstream education, from scoring as well. For an equally long time intelligence was generally discussed as a single concept as shown by the score. Fortunately, intelligence testers have become more sophisticated. The old idea that intelligence waned with age has come under close scrutiny, and new conceptualizations of what an IQ is comprised of and sophisticated methodological analyses have changed the way we think of intelligence. No longer do psychometrists say intelligence is what intelligence tests measure. To anticipate the proverbial bottom line: IQ is a multifaceted phenomenon, with facets that change at different rates and are affected by a variety of contextual factors; further, declines that occur are not noticeable until quite late in life.

**Multidimensionality of Intelligence.** It is frequently forgotten that intelligence as we normally speak of it is a composite statistical measure of several distinct though interrelated capacities rather than of any single attribute. Intelligence is infinitely more than the score a person achieves on a test; rather, it is the ability to combine available information in pursuing a specifiable goal. Some psychologists have broadened the concept of intelligence to encompass effective utilization of all environmental factors. Performance, intelligence as estimated by psychological tests, is usually determined through a series of subtests that theoretically tap all dimensions of intellectual capacity. The Wechsler Adult Intelligence Scale (WAIS), for instance, groups eleven subtests under the verbal and performance scales. On the verbal series oral answers are required to test comprehension, information, vocabulary, similarities, arithmetic, and digital span. Thus, on the similarities test individuals must explain why a series of paired objects seem to belong together. In response to an information question about the origin of rubber, they must provide the simplest reasonable answer to receive a correct score. The performance tests, which include arranging and completing pictures, assembling objects, block design, or digital symbol tasks, require respondents actually to manipulate materials in accordance with instructions.

Depending on which type of test is used, performance by age may decline or increase. Customary laboratory studies using cross-sectional age comparisons nearly always contend older persons do less well. In some cases the decline is said to be at about thirty; in others scores start to drift downward after fifty (Botwinick, 1984). On the other hand, on tests intended to demonstrate the application of knowledge to the solution of real-life puzzles, middle-aged and older adults score much higher in practical performance (Kogan, 1982; Demming and Pressey, 1957). Finally, use of the Army Alpha intelligence test to measure change led to the conclusion that verbal scores increase with age, while arithmetic scores decline (Perlmutter and Hall, 1985). What then is the correlation of IQ with age?

**Age-Related Artifacts in Testing.** In a longitudinal investigation of IQ spanning three decades Schaie and his colleagues provide what is surely one of the most penetrating looks at intellectual functioning over the course of adult life. In 1956 the study team administered a battery of instruments from the Primary Mental Abilities Test (PMA) to 500 adults ranging in age from twenty-two to seventy. In 1963 and again in 1970, 1977, and 1983 Schaie and his colleagues returned to retest as many of the original participants as could be located.

On each occasion a series of cognitive profiles was obtained for individuals and then aggregated for each five- or seven-year age cohort. In an effort to discover what changes, if any, appeared as individuals became older, Schaie and his coworkers distilled thirteen separate measures of intellectual functioning into four dimensions. Intellectual skills acquired by means of either formal or informal education were labeled *crystallized intelligence*. As on most

IQ tests, Schaie assumes conceptual, verbal, and arithmetic skills as well as logical thinking are reflected in this particular dimension. In practical terms, crystallized intelligence is thought to enable people to assimilate new knowledge or to learn quickly. *Cognitive flexibility* represents the ability to shift between accustomed modes of thinking or to accommodate changes in stimulus situations or a new set of instructions. *Visuomotor flexibility* is thought to express competence in adjusting to unfamiliar routines or tasks involving both cognitive and motor capabilities. Finally, *general visualization* indicates an aptitude for working with visual materials, as evidenced by the ability to find a figure concealed against a similar background or to identify objects only partially displayed. Of the four dimensions, the last has been acknowledged by Schaie and colleagues as less defensible than the others (Baltes and Schaie, 1974; Schaie, 1979; Schaie and Hertzog, 1985).

Age-related patterns of intellectual performance over time are shown graphically in Figure 6.3. As can be seen, the original data, shown by the heavier dark line, appear to affirm a gradual deterioration in intellectual performance with age. Likewise, focusing only on the follow-up data collected seven years later might lead one to assert a definite age-related decline in intelligence. On all four dimensions older adults seem to be at an increasing disadvantage when compared to successively younger respondents. Yet when each cohort is compared to its own earlier performance, shown by dashed lines, later scores turn out to be higher on two of the dimensions. Definite improvements in both crystallized intelligence and visualization aptitude are manifested across the age span. Cognitive flexibility is not strongly related to age. Among younger adults there was a slight decline in the ability to transfer between familiar modes of thinking, while older people exhibited some improvements over their own previous scores. Only the dimension tapping visuomotor skills reveals a marked age-related deficit. According to Schaie and his colleagues, the majority of downward trends found in cross-sectional analyses reflect the impact of generational differences, not of age itself. In other words, an age bias built into intelligence tests by the types of information or skills required is at the heart of much of the presumed decrements exhibited by older people. In short, intellectual abilities of older people do not decline, though they do become obsolete. To begin with older people are usually further removed from their formal educational experiences; in most cases they left educational institutions earlier than today's generation, thereby missing out on certain important influences. Extraneous factors unrelated to intellectual talents are also more likely to affect older test takers; foremost among these is probably fatigue. Perhaps most significantly the socially stultifying or impoverished circumstances in which the elderly sometimes find themselves may be an intellectual handicap, interfering with optimal behavior (Schaie, 1974, 1979, 1985; Hertzog, 1985). As the situational constraints are removed and the educational levels of future generations are upgraded, the relative intellectual declines historically thought to characterize older people will be moderated considerably.

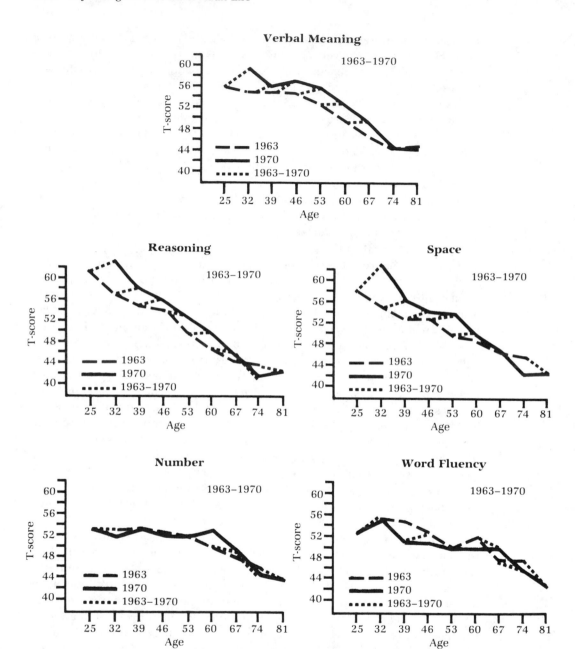

**FIGURE 6.3**

Comparison of longitudinal and cross-cultural patterns of intellectual performance. (*Source:* Schaie, K. W., and G. Labouvie-Vief. "Generational Versus Ontogenetic Components of Change in Adult Cognitive Behavior: A Fourteen-Year Cross-Sequential Study." *Developmental Psychology* 10 [1974]: 305–20. Copyright 1974 by the American Psychological Association. Reprinted by permission.)

Why the difference in IQ between cross-sectional and longitudinal studies? As Schaie (1985) points out and as noted in Chapter 1, cross-sectional studies assess people born at very distinct points in time. Thus, their test scores may reflect cohort or generational differences. More simply, people who went to school in the 1930s, for example, were taught a different way and learned different things than people who went to school in the 1970s and 1980s. Today more people go to school, attend school longer, and study subjects that intelligence tests ask questions about. Consider an alternative case. Since the early 1960s younger cohorts have been scoring lower than their counterparts did in previous years. Cross-sectional studies conducted in the 1990s might suggest that people actually get smarter over time. Clearly that too would be a result of the time of testing (Schaie and Geiwitz, 1983). Longitudinal studies are obviously required (better yet, the type of cross-sequential design Schaie and his research team used and as is shown in Figure 6.3) if any sense is to be made of intelligence testing. Only in this way can the many influences affecting IQ be explicitly taken into consideration. Specifically, those age-graded, historically variant, and nonnormative critical life events that influence how an individual interacts with his or her environment will affect performance on psychological tests (Willis and Baltes, 1980).

**Cognitive Ability and Impending Death.** One factor thought by some to influence performance on psychological assessments is the proximity of death — an example of an age-graded mediator. Looking again at data provided by the Schaie team (see Figure 6.4), it is possible to see a downturn in test scores for the oldest age groups. Can a genuine decline in intelligence be inferred from the test scores or are the changes indicative of a breaking down of cognitive processes — a coming unglued as it were — in advance of death? If this is indeed a possibility, a *terminal decline* or *drop* occurring among those who have relatively little time left to live suggests changes in test performance might be used to predict survival. To illustrate, a person is tested once, again, and perhaps a third time; then he or she dies. If on the later trials there was a poorer performance, it might well signal the beginning of the end.

The first report of a **terminal drop** in diverse cognitive abilities in advance of death prompted others to return for a retrospective look at the test performance of deceased sample members, comparing their scores to those of the survivors. The results of a longitudinal investigation of twins in which surviving members scored better on intelligence tests than nonsurvivors (Jarvik and Falek, 1963) spurred further interest in the possibility of a decline in cognitive functioning prior to death. Not only were deteriorating health and impending death reflected in the measures of intellectual capacity, but projective and reproductive tests requiring the interpretation of a fairly unstructured stimulus were also modified by the nearness of death. Two American psychologists studying elderly Germans found not only that the deceased had performed less well up to five years before their deaths, but, remarkably, that those respondents who were unwilling to become involved in the first retest

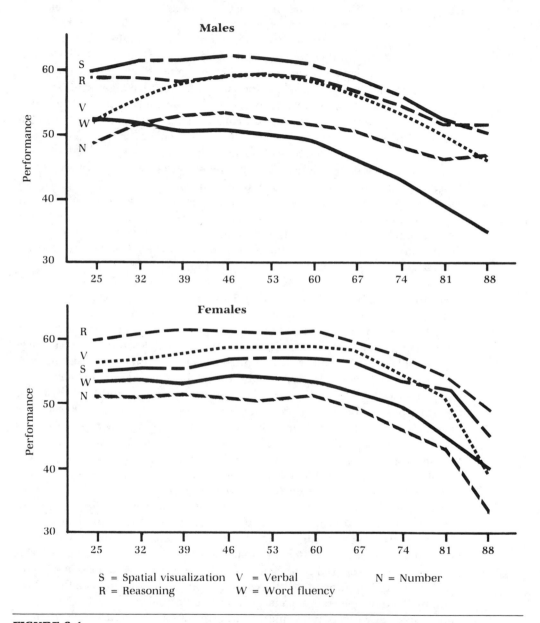

**FIGURE 6.4**

The effect of age on five mental abilities in longitudinal research. (*Source:* Schaie, K. W. The Seattle Longitudinal Study: A Twenty-One-Year Exploration of Psychometric Intelligence in Adulthood. In *Longitudinal Studies of Adult Psychological Development,* ed. K. W. Schaie. New York: The Guilford Press, 1982.)

also died at a rate in excess of those who had cooperated — perhaps intimating a cognizance of their own decline (Riegel and Riegel, 1972).

Lending additional credibility to the notion of a terminal drop, reports issuing from the eleven-year study of healthy older men carried out on behalf of the National Institute of Mental Health have confirmed the tendency for survivors to manifest markedly stable intellectual functioning. Combined with this is a social dimension in which survivors experience a near absence of emotional problems and a high degree of continuity in their personal lives. On almost all measures of IQ, morale, and activity, the participants who died had scored lower and showed less consistency in their overall performances when compared to the group still alive after eleven years. Not surprisingly, a large number of the survivors coped with their circumstances through an instrumental orientation to life, though they exhibited few tendencies toward disengagement or withdrawal (Granick and Patterson, 1971). Data analyzed by Palmore (1982) and by Siegler et al. (1982) on longitudinal data from the Dule studies also confirm the interaction of cognitive abilities and the nearness of death.

Though questions remain, and many studies have been unable to discover any decline in intellectual functioning, the implications are fascinating. It might just be possible that changes in the cognitive realm herald health changes not yet apparent to an examining physician. Subtle cerebrovascular changes, high blood pressure, and other physiological alterations may first become evident through performance scores for intellectual functioning. Botwinick et al. (1978) identified a complex set of abilities in which changes are apparently precursors for health changes among approximately two-thirds of their sample who either died or survived. Some of their measures had more to do with self-assessment than other psychological measures; however, they found that respondents' information was more predictive of survival than physicians' diagnoses.

**Creativity.** Creativity is another aspect of intelligence. The stereotype has it that older people are rigid, unwilling to consider new ways of doing things or alternatives to their habitual patterns. Psychologists call the converse of rigidity *divergent thinking*, the ability to seize any viable mechanism, no matter how novel it may be, to function effectively in the environment or at a job. Those of us who are always looking for new ways of putting things together — be it in art, music, or our own daily lives — are called *autodidactic* (Butler, 1974). Autodidacts seldom accept reality as it is presented; they willingly try innovative approaches. While creativity of this type is usually associated with highly acclaimed and gifted persons, ordinary people can also be creative in this way, continually reworking the scripts of their lives.

Despite innumerable anecdotal accounts of famous artists who literally ward off death until the completion of their last great creative effort or who begin very late in life, such as Grandma Moses, we know precious little about the effects of age on creativity. From Chapter 2 it is evident that a negative conception of the creative abilities of older people has broad historical roots. As early as the Civil War period, American scientists expressed doubts as to the productive usefulness, creativity, and abilities of older people, although it was not until Lehman's work (1953) that systematic inquiries began in earnest. Unfortunately, no one listened to Lehman's caveats about not drawing any causal inferences from his studies. Using a technique involving the frequency with which a contributor was cited by others in his or her profession, Lehman charted periods of maximum productivity both quantitatively and qualitatively for living and deceased persons. Exact ages varied by the field of endeavor, but generally the decade of the thirties was found to be a high point, succeeded by a long and gradual diminution of creative effort. Responding to Lehman's work, Dennis (1966) attempted to introduce the effects of life expectancy in evaluating creative production. Obviously, there are more creative people alive at thirty than at sixty according to Dennis; hence it is natural that the largest number of respected contributors would be produced at a relatively early age. If the analysis focuses only on long-lived creators, Dennis agrees that creative productivity reaches a plateau at approximately the age Lehman claimed, or perhaps a few years later, which is maintained until very late in life. However, combining long- and short-lived contributors tends to exaggerate the decline.

As many gerontologists are quick to point out, Lehman and Dennis might be comparing apples and oranges — quality and quantity — because the number of contributions may not provide a valid or reliable index of the magnitude of the effort. Regardless of this important issue, an equally relevant consideration is the context in which a contribution is made or recognized. A creative effort too far out of step with current thinking may be dismissed as foolhardy, just as a comparably adventurous breakthrough, coming after a highly acclaimed but more glamorous achievement may also go without recognition. In spite of these findings such investigations do not shed much light on the creative possibilities encountered by the vast majority of people living their lives outside of the professional limelight.

To identify creative thinking in individuals who do not live out their lives in the public eye, Taylor (1974) sought to enumerate what kind of people are creative. According to his argument, creative people shape their environment, organizing it in response to specific quests. However, Taylor notes they transform the problem at hand through metaphors or analogy into one capable of a fruitful solution. Implicit in Taylor's analysis is the need for people of all ages, not simply the aged, to receive stimulation and rewards for their efforts lest they cease and fall back into routinized patterns. In American society, which has thus far paid scant attention to the lives or potential contributions of its elderly citizens, few creative outlets currently exist to provide an opportunity for older people to live to their utmost potential. Whatever declines occur in divergent thinking over the life course can seemingly be offset by increased opportunities to explore new approaches. If we are able to judge by the life-long patterns of creative women who have demonstrated divergent thinking and who remain actively creative throughout their lives, no significant decline is likely to take place (Crosson and Robertson-Tchabo, 1983).

# Stability and Change Over the Life Cycle

Studies of personality and coping styles over the life course have expanded considerably over the past decade. Research on life span development is now divided into two fairly clear-cut disciplines, but both represent a departure from the older **ontogenetic view.** In the original formulation one of psychology's most recognized and debated contributions to a process-centered approach to life contended that we all passed through a sequence of developmental stages that were determined from within. Following in the footsteps of Charlotte Buhler, Eric Erikson became one of the more vocal and certainly the most visible advocate of such a view. Erikson and the Swiss psychologist Piaget set the stage for looking at development as shifting patterns of intellectual functioning, personality traits, and resolving stage-generated tasks (Erikson, 1982; Piaget, 1983). For the most part their approach to development focused on fixed ontogenetic stages that unfold irrespective of contextual variation. Unfortunately, the educated public seized on the idea of staged development, much like it embraced astrology and tea-leaf reading (Brim, 1976). While the academic community searched for an alternative model, the racks of popular bookstores were filled to overflowing with titles promising to unravel the crises of life wrought by developmental stages.

In the ensuing section we will review Erikson's popular model of ontogenetic change. This will be followed by a review of some of the alternative formulations that maintain adult life may be more aptly characterized as an aleatory interaction of psychological, social, and historical forces, quite contrary to a closed chronological sequencing. We will also suggest ways in which each paradigm influences research findings and shapes the way gerontologists look at the life course.

## STAGE THEORIES OF DEVELOPMENT IN ADULTHOOD

Regardless of disagreements about the number of stages or the rate of change, most developmental theorists assert that for individuals to remain reasonably satisfied over the years, they must undergo slight modifications in the ways they think of themselves and their environments. Erikson, for example, maintains there are eight distinct periods in our lives, each marked by a crisis or task that must be overcome or resolved if we are to move successfully to the next period. Failure to progress is thought to result in a gradual but inevitable accumulation of stress. Not surprisingly, since Erikson's special interest was in the childhood years, five of the eight stages are concluded prior to biological maturity. Moving from adolescence to young adulthood people pass through a sixth stage during which the choices range between *intimacy*, establishing close interpersonal relationships, or *isolation*, being self-absorbed and having little concern for others. Though he does not specify exact chronological ages,

Erikson describes two other phases that cover the bulk of our adult years. The seventh period is one in which our attention is directed either toward *genera-tivity*, an attempt to contribute lastingly to others, or *stagnation*, feeling bored and being preoccupied with our own body changes. The last stage is one of consummation, a time of *integrity* versus *despair*. Healthy resolution results in an acceptance of life for what it is, without any deep-felt sense of having lost anything along the way. The alternative, for those who have not reached suc-cessful resolutions along the way, is a sense of despair over what might have been and foreboding about prospects for tomorrow (Erikson, 1963).

Erikson's well-crafted theory seems to reflect the changing pattern of in-tellectual functioning, personality evaluation, and reactions to stress. Perhaps because of its seeming applicability to many of life's problems it encouraged an organismic perspective on personality change with a resultant career-like conception of the various interlocking periods. Viewing Erikson's last two stages as insufficiently detailed, first Kolberg (1964) and later Peck (1968) sub-divided the latter half of life into an additional number of phases. In Kolberg's case the search centered on stages of moral development he assumed were universal. For Peck the issue revolved around developmental tasks and the achievement of a perspective in which intellectual pursuits, sociability without sexual connotations, and emotional flexibility were desirable attributes. Like Erikson, Peck viewed retirement as a time when new sources of gratification must be elaborated along with an ability to transcend physical states if a per-son is to maximize personal adjustment.

Two more recent developmental models have been formulated by Gould and Levinson. Beginning with a clinical study augmented by a sample of over 500 adults, whose ages ranged between sixteen and sixty, Gould has intro-duced the most explicit age intervals for a life course trajectory. As might be expected, people in the youngest categories continue to align themselves as members of the parental family unit. But in the next phase, between eighteen and twenty-one, some changes have taken place, so that by the third phase in-dependent adult attitudes have become stabilized. The fourth phase, lasting from twenty-nine until thirty-six, marks the beginning of self-reflection and deeper feelings, while the next phase, up to forty-three, is characterized by some personal and marital unrest, although financial worries are no longer as overriding as they were previously. Life becomes stable once more in the sixth period, with friendships and emotional ties increasing in importance. By Gould's seventh phase, time has become the central issue, with typical concerns con-verging on the allocation of temporal resources and health. The particular man-ner in which these general tendencies are expressed quite naturally varies; how-ever, there is a progressive building between the stages. It is unfortunate that Gould did not include later age phases in his research, since the stages he dis-cusses provide empirical validation of Erikson's heuristic suggestion (Gould, 1975, 1978).

Levinson's model (1978), also enjoying some popularity now, is based on a series of intensive interviews with a group of forty men between thirty-five and forty-five. Without attempting to control for other social characteristics, he gathered information through biographical interviews from his sample of hourly workers, executives, academic biologists, and novelists. In depicting the anatomy of life cycles Levinson identifies three major eras, each lasting approximately twenty years, which can be subdivided into a series of shorter periods. He hypothesizes that the eras and periods found exist throughout humankind, since they are grounded in presumably intrinsic properties of our biological, psychological, and social complexions.

The notion of staged development has been used to make sense of changes in intelligence scores, stress and depression symptoms, personality changes, cognitive style, time perspective, and other psychological variables (Botwinick, 1984). Regardless of the verifiability of the actual stages, the paradigm has been a useful heuristic device for organizing the myriad research findings of gerontological research. At the same time, critics have charged that the paradigm masks important sex role differences and the impact of normative social involvements, simplifies personality, and is a middle-class orientation more reflective of academic career aspirations than the lives of real people (Gubrium and Buckhold, 1977; McCrae and Costa, 1984; Guillemard, 1982; Gergen, 1980).

In refinements of the earlier frameworks, and in the work of those who openly challenge the idea that "life inherently cycles" in some progressive fashion (Gubrium and Buckhold, 1977), a variety of contextual factors have been posited as needing to be integrated with an emphasis on the evolution of social and psychological attributes. A number of investigators maintain that at the very least the three factors of race, sex, and social class, and related subcultural variables, exert an inexorable influence over life and may blunt or even alter the way in which developmental stages occur. According to those who place greater stress on contextual or environmental factors, how an individual meets the world at any period of life cannot be anticipated without attention to the social, cultural, and historical factors defining appropriate alternatives. In his review of developmental and life course perspectives, Elder (1975) places special stress on the necessity of considering the impact of socially determined experiences on the dynamics of developmental stages.

## ALTERNATIVES TO DEVELOPMENTAL MODELS

Having established that relativity is the controlling idea and that age boundaries shift over time and place, the issue becomes: How should we employ our appreciation of these facts in our theoretical frameworks and intervention strategies? Here again new ground is being broken. What Bronfenbrenner (1979) termed the "ecology of human development" is a provocative approach and one that is likely to enrich the conceptual apparatus of developmental studies. Psychological attributes are cast as dynamic qualities whose manifestations are influenced by context. Foremost among the new conceptualizations of the life course is an emerging theory that sees age as a stratum variable that intersects life trajectories.

Another school of thought maintains that personality tracts do not undergo marked developmental change but rather are fairly constant. Such a view maintains that common personality traits — assertiveness, sociability, emotionality, stability, and so on — may ebb and flow but are not predictable on the basis of age (McCrae and Costa, 1985). In short the personality dispositions of a young person will be those of an old person thirty or forty years hence. While opportunities to learn and contexts of interaction deflect the way in which basic traits are played out, basic styles of personality are thought to persist. Two advocates of the stability model, McCrae and Costa (1984), assert that eighteen basic facets of personality inhabit three global domains. Referring to it as the Neuroticism, Extraversion, and Openness (NEO) model, they present a credible argument that fluctuations in the relative prominence of the constituent elements accounts for what they call developmental unfolding. When marked changes in personality appear, they may indicate pathological conditions.

## SEX ROLES AND ADULT LIFE

To generalize anything about the course of adult life to members of the opposite sex is risky business. The recognition of the transactional quality of life's unfolding spurred a number of investigators to see what, if any, gender-based differences might exist between women and men in the way they deal with the trials and tribulations of their later years (Rossi, 1985). Lowenthal (1975) and Lowenthal et al. (1975), in their cross-cultural and longitudinal studies, found that in many instances gender-linked variables were better explanations of the patterning of adult life than those discovered by means of developmental stages. Although they identified a sequence of career-like stages of life based on a transitional flux of social roles, they found a number of attitudes, perspectives, and behaviors to be less indicative of stages than they had expected.

Both Neugarten (1968) and Lowenthal et al. (1974) found that the dominant goals and problems faced by women and men during the later phases of life may actually be quite different. Women do not yet appear to suffer the same occupational or health-related stresses as do men, though as we saw in Chapter 5 the incidence of certain conditions previously thought to be more characteristic of men is increasing among middle-aged and older women. Whereas women have traditionally been more preoccupied with expressive and familial crises, there is a growing debate, however, as to who faces the most threatening hurdles, who is most likely to develop new coping strategies, and how such strategies will be devised and differ.

Role transitions in later life require that one strike an ever new balance between available resources and expectations. There is growing evidence to suggest that men have greater difficulties than women if only because they have not learned to be as flexible. In his cross-cultural analyses of men in their middle years, Guttman (1976, 1977) points to the influence culturally determined sex role identities have as mediators of adjustment. While he suggests some masculine traits are more or less impervious to cultural disparities, sex role prescriptions do vary. In those societies in which power and dominance are preeminent values, middle-aged and older men will continue to struggle against the passivity and receptivity that life's unfolding currents hold for them. Guttman asserts that as a consequence psychosomatic illness, alcoholism, and other symptoms of emotional strife are likely to remain part of men's passage through the life course. In contrast, when traditional sex roles are more loosely defined, the lives of the elderly have the potential to be vastly enriched.

For a long time people maintained there was a double standard of aging — that women reached what could be considered their declining years earlier than men. One of the more pernicious aspects of such a belief is that women were forced into lying about their ages and were not likely to consider as eligible companions men who were younger or even the same age. Fortunately, women are being recognized as having more resilience than they have been traditionally accorded. Another facet of the old double standard held that the so-called *empty nest* years were harder for women to accept. Once again recent studies are recognizing this too is a misconception—children leaving home is not particularly stressful for either women or men. Instead, being relieved of responsibilities for one's children may have a positive impact on self-esteem (George, 1980). Women may begin to assert themselves and take a more active role in mastering their own situations.

Changing age role and sex role identities for both women and men are crucial aspects of developmental growth. All too frequently there is a pervasive tendency to assume the roles appropriate to a woman's developmental needs are found largely within the context of her family. Yet from early youth to the grave, impermanence is the norm for most women, with instability a constant component of adaptive strategy. As Sinnot (1977, 1982) and others have pointed out, perhaps a lesson can be learned from the kind of fluid adjustments characteristic of a woman's experience. The declining specificity of gender roles in itself poses its own development risks to successful adjustment. The blurring of traditional definitions of what is appropriate for one sex or the other, *androgyny*, is one viable way to reduce sexual and age inequalities while at the same time maximizing personal fulfillment (McGee and Wells, 1982).

# Psychological Disorders in the Later Years

## MENTAL HEALTH AND MENTAL DISORDERS

Whether to label someone as mentally ill or healthy depends a great deal on who is doing the diagnosing. No concrete boundary line exists between or within global categories of mental disorders. Obviously there are extremes, but there is also a large gray area. Since most clinical diagnoses are based on psychological or behavioral syndromes or patterns, many things must be taken into account when evaluating behavior. The mental health professional is challenged to categorize the symptoms of any particular person. In doing so, however, it is always a question of what seems to be most descriptive without worrying whether the defining features are exclusive to any given category. Further, people who come to the attention of mental health professionals may manifest more than one condition, which compounds the difficulties of diagnosis and treatment. Questions of quality and quantity of care must also be dealt with by those who want to help the individual manage distress. Finally, the range of clinical options is broad, reflecting a variety of conceptual orientations. Similar to the situation pointed out in our discussion of health, psychiatry and clinical psychology work with diverse models — the medical, psychological, behavioral, and social are the most common. Which is adopted determines what treatment will be used.

For all intents and purposes the American Psychiatric Association's Diagnostic and Statistical Manual of Mental Disorders (DSM) is the bible of mental health professionals. Presently in its third edition (DSM-III), it is updated and changed periodically to reflect changes in the treatment of disorders. Each revision prompts a great deal of interest and debate as it goes through successive drafts. The reasons for the impassioned concern range from new views on the state of the art to debate over the causes of mental disorders and theoretical and political decisions and disagreements. A prime example is the absence of the broad category of homosexuality in the DSM-III as a mental disorder. In the earlier volumes it was listed as a psychosexual malfunction that needed curing; now only homosexuality that is unacceptable to the individual is included. By implication it appears that by and large homosexuality is no longer thought of as a type of sexual dysfunction.

Just as there is room for a difference of opinion on what constitutes a mentally healthy sexual orientation, there is room for diverse opinions on many other types of psychological conditions. It is not only that some conditions pass out of fashion; the values and norms of society also evolve over time, altering perceptions and the evaluation of behaviors. What is maladaptive under certain circumstances need not be so under other conditions. In the discussion to follow we will concentrate on generally agreed upon categories; these are not, however, absolute. It may well be that the next edition of the DSM will delete certain categories as maladapative, modify others, and perhaps include conditions not now thought to constitute a disorder.

Despite the caveats commonly attached to descriptions of mental disorders as general typologies, not everyone with a specific diagnosis will be identical. Having the defining features of a condition does not mean people will not differ in important respects. Furthermore, the discussion is of mental disorders, their classification and description; it is not a description of people per se. How a person interacts with his or her environment, friends, family, and formal support systems influence how a disorder is manifested. Multiply that by a lifetime of experiences and the problem of drawing a concise picture of mental health and mental disorder among the elderly becomes far more problematic than for the rest of the population. Old people show remarkable variability, but that is what makes them normal. Why should it be otherwise?

## MENTAL HEALTH IN LATER LIFE

**What it Feels Like to be Old.** Imagine you find yourself in a situation where the rules are changing, where your familiar props — those things you use to affirm your sense of self — may be eroding, where other people's stereotypes of you are strong enough that you have to work hard to convince them you are not what they think you are. How do you think you might react? Alternatively, place yourself in a context where you find yourself a member of a minority subgroup, where the rules, vague as they may be, are made by a powerful majority, where the things you are most familiar with are not valued, where change seems to happen so quickly that the routine you knew does not work much of the time. Project yourself fifty, sixty, or seventy years into the future, to a time where the changes since the Wright brothers, the invention of television, computers, mass transportation, and so on have doubled or even doubled again. How do you think you would do?

Remarkably, you would probably adapt. You would change and fit in, perhaps not without stress, but to a considerable degree you would think of yourself as still being part of the mainstream. At the risk of oversimplification, that is what older people have to deal with and how they think of themselves. For some, adaptation causes stress, for others it is no problem. As a group, older persons may encounter a higher risk than any other age category, but then no time of life is free from emotional distress. Whenever the national economy is uncertain or volatile, many individuals show greater stress reactions. Not surprisingly then, any threats to the financial well-being of the elderly are likely to heighten the kinds of insecurities that harm emotional well-being. Thus, feeling threatened does not automatically make someone mentally ill; it may represent a realistic reaction to an external problem.

**Intrinsic and Situational Factors.** Two issues contribute to the incidence of defined psychological problems found in later life. To begin with, so-called mental illness knows no time dimension. Developmental stresses, unresolved conflicts, and even organic disruptions are cumulative, often taking years before they become clinically observable. The problems of later life represent the summation of all that has gone before. A second dimension has to do with the increasing interdependence between people and their everyday life contexts. If the feedback received does not reinforce self-concepts, then difficulties are certain to follow. On reaching what is normatively defined as old, an entire cohort is systematically exposed for the first time to a range of risks previously affecting only certain individuals. Deprive a person of familiar and supportive social contacts and the newly imposed burdens will exacerbate whatever problems may already exist — if weaknesses were present, even if unnoticed, they will present themselves unmistakably (Fozard and Thomas, 1975).

How people react to the stresses they encounter will depend on their personal skills and on their supportive networks; for some it is conceivable that the challenges of becoming old may even generate new-found strengths. For the majority, however, weaknesses carried over from earlier life will be magnified in old age. The factors contributing to what is commonly thought of as mental illness are not well understood. In fact, the whole phenomenon of psychiatric deviance is as elusive as any in the argot of social science. Of necessity, then, our discussion will confine itself to a general overview of the psychological facets of the aging process.

While a concise outline of the stresses that possibly foster the undermining of people's mental health would doubtlessly omit certain crucial issues, in his effort to bring some order to the classification of stress-induced factors, Rosow (1973) has succeeded in presenting a usable summary. In addition to the cohort liability just pointed out, he contends the loss of roles experienced by the elderly often excludes them from absorbing memberships and devalues their potential impact on society. What makes the exclusion even more devastating to many is that their socialization has not prepared them for such a fate, nor are their new lives infused with clear structural guidelines that would allow an easy transition. The ill-defined circumstances in which most elderly find themselves naturally generate considerable strain, often leading ultimately to a profound sense of anxiety and malaise. Under similarly stressful and anxiety-provoking conditions, the majority of us would probably react analogously. The difference would be of course in the supportive networks to which we could turn for the reaffirmation of our self-concepts. For a number of elderly, successive role losses have left them bereft of compensatory feedback so that they must rely solely on their own personal resources to shore up their mental health. When physiological deprivations and poor health are compounded with the social adversities incurred by the elderly and the lack of understanding of their plight, it is no wonder they are susceptible to emotional upsets.

Like the physical conditions discussed in the previous chapter, mental conditions often have an age bias. As we will see later, the diagnosis reflects in part the expectations of those doing the evaluation. Still, it is possible to assert that the incidence of mental disorder increases, but not until the decade of the seventies. Prior to that time the pattern for the frequency of psychological dysfunction is relatively flat across the majority of adult life. Contrary to popular opinion, no acute midlife crisis nor any empty nest neuroses are unique to certain periods of life. Nor is retirement so traumatic that depression automatically occurs. Depression of course does result from losses (Butler and Lewis, 1982), and the losses of later life are poignant because not all are voluntary. Who would not feel depressed if much that was supportive was gone? Organic brain disease also becomes more common in the latter years, but only in a small minority of the elderly.

**Sex Differences.** There is also a pattern of sex differences, but it is difficult to explain. Such variations appear in diagnosis, treatment, prescription of psychotherapeutic drugs, reactions to stress, and so on. According to most experts, men have a higher risk in the years after sixty-five, yet women are seen more frequently by mental health professionals and receive the majority of prescription medication. A significant part of the reason women are medicated more frequently has to do with the biases of the medical profession and not any actual condition the women may have. Though women are relatively more powerless throughout their lives, at least traditionally, this may lead to an ability to adapt to environmental stress; therefore they are not caught off-guard by whatever old age brings. Men, on the other hand, are used to imposing their will on the world around them. Even so, men are often reluctant to seek assistance; furthermore, when they do they are not as likely as women to receive prescription medication or long-term care. A key factor in an older person's mental stability is physical health. Those who experience somatic distress more frequently suffer from emotional disorders than those who have no particular complaints about their physical health. Of course, those with emotional problems also tend to have physical distress, and it is difficult to say which is the cause.

# Mental Disorders Among the Elderly

It is a mistake to think of old people as senile. To begin with there is no such diagnosis in the DSM-III. Furthermore, when the term is used in popular psychology it is an indistinct category generally taken to mean old people do strange things. Everyone does strange things at some points in time, and the elderly are like everyone else.

Regardless of the legitimacy of the term, it is often mistakenly thought that old people are mentally incompetent. The best estimate is that somewhere between 10 and 15 percent of the older population have emotional problems of sufficient magnitude to require mental health attention. Some investigators claim that even this estimate is overly conservative when the number of elderly facing high-risk situations is considered. Add in the million or so persons already residing in various kinds of institutions, the seven million who face severe stresses from living below the poverty line, and the two million who have chronic diseases, and the proportion of the population disposed to emotional disorders increases rapidly (Butler and Lewis, 1982). When all of the forms of psychopathology experienced by the elderly both inside and outside institutions are tallied, the proportion of elderly who may be suffering serious mental distress could easily range from 25 to 60 percent.

What does this mean? Epidemiologists who study the pattern and distribution of mental illness in late life use figures such as these to remind us that the largest majority, from 50 to 80 percent of all old people, do not have psychiatric impairment (Blazer, 1983). In other words, older persons are only at slightly greater risk than the rest of the population. Depending on whether the figures are derived from elderly persons living independently in their communities, from those receiving treatment as outpatients, or from those living in long-term care institutions, rates will vary. For those elderly living in the community approximately 10 to 20 percent have some degree of mental impairment. It is difficult to state this with certainty, since such information is gleaned from self-reports and personal evaluations. Patients who seek outpatient treatment are also self-selecting; they think they need help or they would not be there, so once again caution must be exercised in making generalizations. There is little doubt, however, that among those admitted to long-term care facilities the rates increase. Almost half the population of institutions have significant impairment, while another 40 percent have mild to moderate psychiatric difficulties (Blazer, 1983). These findings are not too surprising because these are after all mental care facilities. But what about those elderly persons living on their own in their communities? Are older persons more disturbed than middle-aged or younger persons?

Probably not, although some research suggests that the proportion of people who are not yet old and who may experience mental health problems in old age will be greater than among today's generation of elderly (Gatz et al., 1980). The difference will probably be the result of a cohort effect. Because of more perceived stress, a lifetime of access to a network of supportive services, or perhaps a growing ideology of self-help, they will be more willing to admit to suffering distress.

Is the rate of impaired mental functioning in the elderly in the United States higher or lower than that found in other industrialized countries? Interestingly, it is just about the same. In Japan, for instance, the 10 to 20 percent prevalence is considered reliable, with an additional 4 to 6 percent suffering from severe mental problems. Unlike the Western pattern, however, the peak risk years are thought to be somewhat earlier, between fifty and fifty-four. As further testimony of the higher risks incurred by the elderly and of the likelihood of an age bias operating in the delivery of mental health services, we have only to note that in the United States older people comprise nearly 30 percent of institutionalized mental patients. A comparable percentage of institutionalized elderly in Japan ranges around 15 percent; in West Germany it is 22 percent, while in England it is nearly identical to that found in the United States (Redick et al., 1973; Shinfuku, 1978). Unfortunately, both in the United States and abroad there is a long history of "therapeutic nihilism" that may contribute to the relatively large number of institutionalized elderly residing in mental hospitals and the relatively small number (somewhere around only 3 percent) who are seen as outpatients (Rosenfeld, 1978).

## PSYCHOGENIC DISORDERS

Despite the impossibility of drawing a hard and fast line between psychogenic and organic disorders, the typology is a useful framework for classification and treatment. By far the majority of psychogenic problems, sometimes called functional disorders, found among the elderly are of long duration, resulting from earlier maladjustments that may go unnoticed until the later years. Doubtlessly some people first manifest symptoms of psychological distress relatively late in life, but these probably are a small minority and are subsumed under a particular diagnostic label. Most practitioners agree that the reaction patterns developed over the course of a lifetime are fairly resilient, regardless of whether they are helpful, adaptive responses or dysfunctionally negative. Again, we find widely diverse estimates of the incidence of psychogenic disorders among older people. Some suggest up to half of all psychological disruptions are attributable to functional causes (Butler and Lewis, 1982; Blazer, 1983). At present, however, these figures must be viewed as rough approximations, since the whole question of psychological disorders in later life is being rephrased as we acquire new insights into the problem.

**Affective Disorders.** The most common psychogenic illnesses found after the middle years are termed affective disorders. Generally speaking, affective disorders can be described as alterations in personality or normal mood states, marked by a growing lack of self-respect and unresolved turmoil. Many affective disorders are diverse forms of depressive reactions, though elation and bodily preoccupation may also occur. Depression, whether based on mild reactive responses to identifiable situational factors or on serious psychogenic states that have no apparent link with external events, is the single most frequent functional disorder. The symptoms of depression usually involve a mood of despair in which individuals withdraw from active participation in most interactions, concentrating their attention instead on depreciating their own self-worth and potential, though they remain capable of angry outbursts against real or imagined wrongs.

A wide gamut of psychosomatic symptoms usually accompany affective disorders. Such irregularities as loss of appetite, sleeping difficulties, constipation, and fatigue may all indicate emotional upset. No doubt at least a portion of the anecdotal accounts reported in newspapers about older people repaying income taxes or debts outstanding for twenty years can be attributed to the feelings of guilt and retribution that are also part of many depressive syndromes. Those relatively rare depressive reactions that crop up late in life seemingly without prior history are customarily diagnosed as a form of *involutional melancholia*. The label was used originally to refer to postmenopausal women who found themselves unable to muster normal emotional responses. It is now used for many affective disorders that appear for the first time during later life. Sensory deprivations such as deafness may often have a psychogenic component, manifested in psychological distress as the sufferer becomes increasingly isolated. Hyperemotional reactions, including those classified as manic behavior, are a less common affective disorder, though they occur frequently enough to be identified as similar to the depressive mood states characteristic of younger people. Manic-depressive disorders seem to afflict wom-

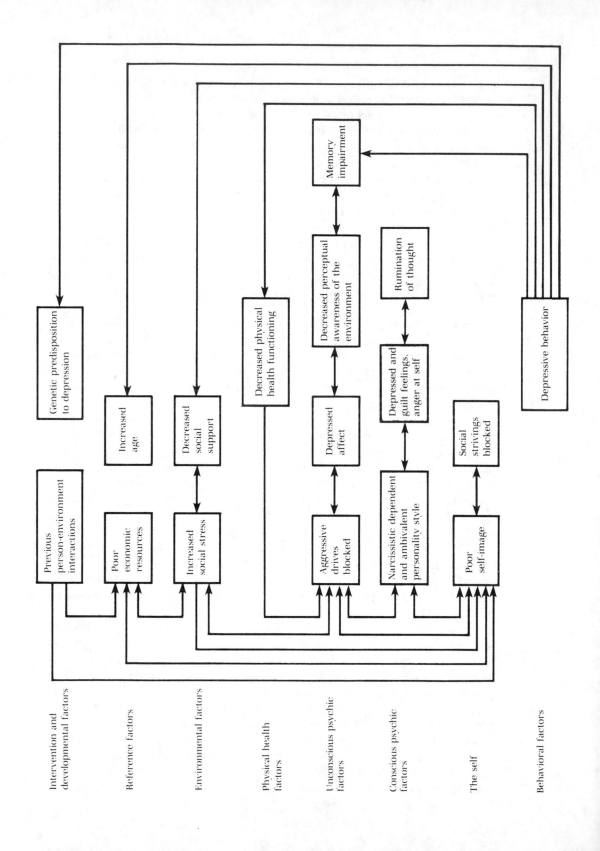

en and professional people more often than men or blue collar workers, but whether this remains the case among older populations is by no means certain.

Despite the difficulties of distinguishing between what mental health professionals label reactive versus endogenous states, there can be little doubt that depression among the elderly reflects their physical health and social situation. It is of course a complicated relationship, so it is erroneous to assume that the incidence of depression increases as a direct consequence of age. In fact, among older persons who are healthy and socially advantaged, depression is no more common than it ever was. The increase comes among those who suffer from chronic health impairments or attempt to cope with late life deprivations. In general, depression is characteristic of only 10 to 18 percent of the elderly (Murrell et al., 1983).

The causes (Blazer, 1983) of depressive reactions among older sufferers are highly treatable. At the risk of oversimplification, Figure 6.5 illustrates how the causes of depression might be conceptualized. Looking first at this figure, then at Figure 6.6, possible approaches to alleviate one of the more pervasive affective disorders of the later years should be apparent. Taken together these two graphs highlight the interaction of three facets of aging — physical, social, and psychological — and how they come together to affect individual adaptation.

**Neurotic Disorders.** Neurotic disorders likely to be encountered among the elderly also follow the patterns for the rest of the population. With the possible exception of obsessive-compulsive traits, it is safe to say the neurotic disorders experienced by the elderly have evolved over a number of years. Usually the symptoms of an obsessive-compulsive reaction involve an inability to shake off disquieting thoughts and a need to engage in ritualized behavior. Not infrequently, the compulsive behavior acquires meaning as a purifying or protective act guarding against some dreaded consequence. Most often, neurotic reactions are marked by considerable anxiety and may be interpreted as the patient's futile attempt to grapple with unfavorable external circumstances beyond his or her control. *Dissociative* and *conversion neuroses* represent the serious breakdown of cognitive functioning and entail psychosomatic complaints of considerable magnitude. Some gerontologists are convinced that threatened displacements or depreciations of identity bring about neurotic reactions as a kind of defense against overwhelming psychological disjunctures. Hypochondriasis is another form of functional disorder exhibited by the depressed, although one difference is that the depressed patient may be unable or unwilling to seek professional treatment, while the hypochondriac cannot

**FIGURE 6.5 (opposite)**
Etiology of depression in later life. (*Source:* Blazer, D. "The Epidemiology of Mental Illness in Later Life." In *Handbook of Geriatric Psychiatry*, eds. E. W. Busse and D. G. Blazer, p. 209. New York: Van Nostrand Reinhold Company, 1980.)

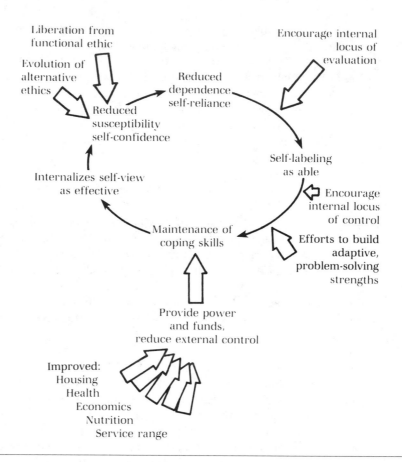

**FIGURE 6.6**
Reducing the likelihood of psychological distress among the elderly. (*Source:* Kuypers, J. A., and V. L. Bengtson. "Social Breakdown and Competence: A Model of Normal Aging." *Human Development* 16, 3 [1973]: 197.)

gain enough attention. Somatic complaints reflect a preoccupation with body functioning and an exaggerated concern with normal aches and pains. According to Pfeiffer and Busse (1973), after middle age, women are more disposed to hypochondriasis than men, perhaps partially as a compensatory strategy against other role losses or threats of personal failure.

Whether we have in mind functional disorders in general or hypochondriasis in particular, the research literature suggests a clear connection between neurotic symptoms and social interaction. Lack of power, control, and attention all seem to be pivotal in the manifestation of neurotic complaints. If, as Butler (1975) suggests in his Pulitzer Prize winning book on old age, the later years are a time of greater externally imposed stress, whether physical or social, the consequence is often an internalization (analogous to blaming the victim) that manifests itself in various forms of neurotic behavior (Busse and Blazer, 1980).

**Psychotic Disorders.** The various types of psychotic disorders comprise a more serious category of impairment, since they reflect a break with normative definitions of reality and a disintegration of logical processes. Hallucinations and delusions of grandeur are the most stereotypical examples of psychoses, but cases in which there is a complete personality alteration, as in the legendary psychotic who believes himself to be Napoleon, are no longer given as much credibility as previously. *Paranoid* states are characterized by feelings of persecution for some presumed wrongdoing. Unlike other psychotics, paranoids do not necessarily manifest disrupted intellectual capacities; once their initial assumptions are accepted, a logical development follows. Paranoid reactions occur more often among already institutionalized elderly or among those who are suddenly thrust into adverse situations. Sensory impairment, as in the loss of vision or hearing, or social isolation may also bring on paranoid fears. Fortunately, most paranoid reactions are fairly short, and often they do not even fall too far outside what is considered the normal range of suspiciousness. For this reason they are frequently difficult to detect, merging into ordinary experiences in such a way that while seeming a bit strange, their behavior may not be so strange as to attract attention. The diagnosis of *schizophrenia* covers nearly half of all patients admitted to mental hospitals in the United States. In Europe, when hallucinations, cognitive breakdown, abandonment of social facades, and so on occur in later life, the disorder is labeled *paraphrenia*. Apart from the reference being applicable to elderly schizophrenics, other distinctions are probably nebulous. Schizophrenia, as one of the more intractable forms of psychotic disorders, has a poor prognosis. It is a formidable task to attempt to communicate with patients who are at best only occasionally lucid and capable of responding to normal therapeutic contact. Few schizophrenics become so only at an advanced age; more often this disorder is chronic, dating as far back as late adolescence, though it might remain secondary until declining physical health or some other crisis brings it to the surface.

The difficulties of diagnosing psychotic disorders late in life stem in part from a lack of precision in diagnostic protocols for older persons and from their behavioral similarity to organic brain dysfunction. Few reliable statistics are available, but best estimates suggest about 10 percent of all mental disorders among older persons are the result of psychotic disorders (Eisdorfer, 1980).

**Other Self-Destructive Behaviors.** A number of other types of self-destructive behaviors have traditionally been considered forms of emotional disorders requiring societal intervention in many Western cultures. The outstanding example of self-destructive behavior is of course suicide. Each year a disproportionate number of suicides are committed by people over sixty-five.

**TABLE 6.1**

Suicide Rates in the United States, 1970–1981

| Age | Male | | | | | | | |
| --- | White | | | | Black | | | |
| | 1970 | 1975 | 1980 | 1981 | 1970 | 1975 | 1980 | 1981 |
| All ages[a] | 18.0 | 19.9 | 19.9 | 20.0 | 8.0 | 9.9 | 10.3 | 10.2 |
| 5–14 years | 0.5 | 0.8 | 0.7 | 0.8 | 0.1 | 0.3 | 0.3 | 0.2 |
| 15–24 years | 13.9 | 19.3 | 21.4 | 21.1 | 10.5 | 12.7 | 12.3 | 11.1 |
| 25–34 years | 19.9 | 24.0 | 25.6 | 26.2 | 19.2 | 23.4 | 21.8 | 21.8 |
| 35–44 years | 23.3 | 24.4 | 23.5 | 24.3 | 12.6 | 16.0 | 15.6 | 15.5 |
| 45–54 years | 29.5 | 29.7 | 24.2 | 23.9 | 13.8 | 12.4 | 12.0 | 12.3 |
| 55–64 years | 35.0 | 31.9 | 25.8 | 26.3 | 10.6 | 10.7 | 11.7 | 12.5 |
| 65 and over | 41.1 | 39.0 | 37.5 | 35.7 | 8.7 | 11.2 | 11.4 | 12.2 |

[a]Includes other age groups not shown separately. Rate per 100,000 in specified age group.
*Source:* U.S. Bureau of the Census. *Statistical Abstract of the United States, 1985*, p. 79. Washington, D.C.:
U.S. Government Printing Office, 1985.

The elderly number over one-quarter of all recognized self-inflicted deaths per year in the United States. An additional number go unreported (perhaps as many as 40 percent more) since, contrary to the myth, most suicides do not leave notes. As can be seen in Table 6.1, overall the rate of suicide has risen somewhat over the past several years. Because the figures lag some four or more years behind, it is difficult to say what if any impact current economic constraints are having, but historically suicide rates are in inverse proportion to the country's economic well-being. Among men, whites are more likely with every decade of life to commit suicide; the rate for black men peaks in the decade after twenty-five. For women of both races the peak comes during the decade of the forties. Abroad the rates are higher. While all people react to a given predicament in individual ways, divorced, widowed, or single people are more likely to end their own lives. The same holds true for people who have recently experienced an unresolved crisis. Among the most culpable precipitating factors is the absence of supportive networks to assist with coping (Miller, 1979).

Alcoholism, as was seen in the last chapter, is very self-destructive. With approximately nineteen million people in the United States being heavy drinkers (four or more drinks a day), it is not too surprising that roughly 10 percent of the elderly fall into that category. The figure would probably be higher were it not for the shorter life expectancy of those who drink immoderately. Of course alcoholism, as with any other type of substance abuse, is symptomatic of a desire to alter one's moods. Do older persons depend on such substances as a coping mechanism to deal with the stresses they feel, the loneliness, boredom, depression, grief, and pain? Butler and Lewis (1982) say that is exactly the reason.

| Age | Female | | | | | | | |
|---|---|---|---|---|---|---|---|---|
| | White | | | | Black | | | |
| | **1970** | **1975** | **1980** | **1981** | **1970** | **1975** | **1980** | **1981** |
| All ages[a] | 7.1 | 7.3 | 5.9 | 6.2 | 2.6 | 2.7 | 2.2 | 2.4 |
| 5–14 years | 0.1 | 0.2 | 0.2 | 0.3 | 0.2 | 0.1 | 0.1 | 0.1 |
| 15–24 years | 4.2 | 4.9 | 4.6 | 4.9 | 3.8 | 3.2 | 2.3 | 2.4 |
| 25–34 years | 9.0 | 8.8 | 7.5 | 7.7 | 5.7 | 5.4 | 4.1 | 4.6 |
| 35–44 years | 13.0 | 12.6 | 9.1 | 9.5 | 3.7 | 4.0 | 4.6 | 4.2 |
| 45–54 years | 13.5 | 13.8 | 10.2 | 11.1 | 3.7 | 4.0 | 2.8 | 2.5 |
| 55–64 years | 12.3 | 11.5 | 9.1 | 9.4 | 2.0 | 3.4 | 2.3 | 2.9 |
| 65 and over | 8.5 | 8.4 | 6.5 | 6.3 | 2.6 | 2.2 | 1.4 | 2.3 |

Whether functional psychological disorders are the cause or the consequence of chronic physical illness is still open to question, although it is known that among older people the two usually occur close together. Thus far the discussion has focused on functional disorders, but a significant portion of elderly hospitalized mental patients are victims of organic brain disorders rather than psychogenic responses to the stresses of age. In neither case, however, do the two types usually appear in pure form. People who develop organic impairments may later show neurotic or psychotic symptoms as their social world becomes even more intolerant and unresponsive. Psychological disruptions may also operate in the opposite direction, and functional disorders may be joined by organic complications, with the symptoms of each becoming intermingled. From either source it is fruitless to address one without treating the other at the same time. Diagnostic problems are manifold, since clinical evaluations depend as much on cognitive functioning as they do on neurological signs. In both types of disorder patients may fall well within the normal range of performance for people their age while experiencing organic or psychogenic damage to their well-being.

## ORGANIC BRAIN SYNDROMES

Any cerebral impairment that interferes with normal mental functioning may be diagnosed as one or another form of organic brain syndrome. *Dementia* — physiological pathology of the brain — has become a priority area of investigation in the neurosciences under the aegis of the National Institute on Aging and other sponsoring agencies. Between 1976 and 1984 federal funds for Alzheimer's disease research increased tenfold, to $37.1 billion. Until fairly recently the kinds of conditions associated with organic brain disease were sometimes thought to be accelerated presentations of normal involutional changes. In Europe, especially, this was the prevailing opinion, but today dementia is widely accepted as a pathological condition (Cohen and Eisdorfer, 1985).

Because of the recent emphasis on understanding dementia, major gains have been made since the early 1980s. The DSM-III presents a major reclassification of various organic brain disorders. Seven major subtypes with a constellation of behavioral or psychological symptoms are described without reference to etiology (American Psychiatric Association, 1980). For our purposes the discussion will be confined to two broad subtypes: Alzheimer's disease and multi-infarct dementia.

Generally speaking, all organic brain syndromes have the following behavioral features (Butler and Lewis, 1982):

- Impaired memory (difficulties may occur in registration, retention, or recall)
- Impaired intellect (problems with comprehension, organization, calculation, and information)
- Impaired judgment (disability in the formulation of opinions, selection, and appropriate actions)
- Impaired orientation (disorientation as to time, place, and person)
- Lability of affect (either excessive or shallow emotional response or inappropriate affect)

Clearly each of these is subjective, based on personal history and circumstances. Furthermore, diagnosis is more difficult in the presence of compounding conditions.

How widespread are organic brain syndromes? Recent epidemiological work suggests they are the most common cause of psychiatric disorder in later life, affecting about 4 to 6 percent of the young-old and over 20 percent of those over eighty-five. Depending on the type of categorization, they are either the fourth or fifth cause of nonaccidental death in the United States. Of those who die from an organic brain disorder, over half have Alzheimer's disease (Rasool and Selkoe, 1985; Cohen and Eisdorfer, 1985; Raskind and Storrie, 1980). In view of the growing proportion of the population in their eighties and older it is likely dementia will become ever more common in the near future.

Organic brain disorders, especially Alzheimer's disease, are insidious. By the time they become apparent both the sufferer and those who suffer alongside them may be fully cognizant that something has gone terribly wrong. During what has been called the prediagnosis stage, cognitive declines will have occurred, language and memory lapses will be haunting, and aberrant emotions may have put heavy stress on affection and friendship. To then be told things will only get worse strains whatever emotional resources left to an even greater extent. Behavioral manifestations vary widely; some people retain motor skills but have speech problems, while in others the reverse is true. Some have impaired executive processing, while others do not. To a fair degree social amenities remain intact through the early phases, but glaring gaps are also present. No wonder Alzheimer's disease is called the "death of the mind" (Blass, 1984).

In attempting to provide a guide for the clinical management of patients who suffer from Alzheimer's disease and other irreversible disorders, Cohen et al. (1984) provide a sequential model for dealing with the ravages wrought by a disease for which there is no effective means of preventing, reversing, or arresting. From the prediagnosis stage with its silent onset, their model progresses through concerns over reactions to the diagnosis, to anger, guilt, sadness, coping strategies, maturation, and finally a separation from self when the disease has progressed quite far. At that point only a shell of the mind remains. Not only are families pressed to the limit, but community support services are being challenged to meet a growing need. The financial strain alone is enormous. Eisdorfer estimates that the total nursing home bill came to about $30 billion in 1984 — at least 40 percent was destined for dementia patients. Of this amount, roughly 40 percent was paid by the patients, with the remainder coming largely from Medicaid funds (Medical News, 1985).

**Alzheimer's Disease.** Referred to as senile dementia before recent refinements, Alzheimer's disease is by far the most common primary degenerative dementia. In addition to those symptoms just listed, personality changes are startling: aggressiveness, sexual preoccupation, and paranoia are common. The rates of prevalence mentioned earlier are indicative of most industrialized countries, not merely the United States (Kay and Gergman, 1980). Since autopsy is the only definite way to identify Alzheimer's disease, at present most epidemiological estimates are inferred from behavioral protocols and by ruling out other possible problems. Therefore such figures are subject to some degree of error. However, observing an Alzheimer's disease patient, especially when the disease has progressed to some extent, leaves little doubt about the diagnosis. Fortunately, the statistics provide some reassurance: among the young-old, 95 percent *will not* experience dementia; after eight-five the figure drops to 70 to 80 percent. Among families with a history of Alzheimer's disease the odds are a little less favorable, however (Henig, 1981; Zarit et al., 1985).

Little is yet known of the cause of Alzheimer's disease. Neurofibrillary tangles and senile plaques — macropathological structural damage — have been identified for some time. It is not known what causes these gross distortions, however. Tangles occur within the brain cell while plaques are outside, primarily in the cerebral cortex. The tangles are of abnormal protein fibers wrapped in helical filaments, leading researchers to look for altered protein metabolism. Hyperactive and defective cells are thought to be responsible in the misspecification of protein synthesis. Plaque material is also comprised of protein and is found in normal as well as demented older persons. The difference seems to be one of density, with greater amounts of plaque correlated with intellectual deterioration. The question is whether these structural changes are a byproduct of more basic neurochemical alterations. Attention has lately been focused on an enzyme called choline acetyltransferase (CAT) necessary for neural transmission; immunological changes are another possibility. Still other factors are also being explored; foremost among these are the presence of a slow virus or the possibility of metal deposits. While much research is being conducted, obviously considerable work remains (Rasool and Selkoe, 1985; Cohen and Eisdorfer, 1985).

**Multi-Infarct Dementia.** Occurring in roughly 12 to 17 percent of all cases of organic brain disease, multi-infarct dementia stems from a severing of blood supplies to areas of the brain. Those with a history of high blood pressure are more likely to have multi-infarcts. Since the condition is caused by a cutting off of blood, the appearance of this disorder is much more sudden than is the case for Alzheimer's disease. The diagnosis is usually based on the person's ability to carry on his or her routines and hence may be affected by social variables and may be offset by intensive types of therapy. Short of a marked crisis other symptoms to watch for are dizziness, headaches, decreased vigor — both mental and physical — and vague somatic complaints. Complete neurological workups are necessary in all cases where brain damage is suspected.

In many instances it is impossible to distinguish clinically between particular organic disorders. Careful observation over time and sophisticated CT scanning are necessary (Bucht et al., 1984). The course of multi-infarct dementia is uneven, erratic, but downward; it is not, however, as obviously linear as Alzheimer's disease. The intermittent cycle of improvement followed by decline is relative of course; there are periods of lucidity followed by further deterioration of memory and other cognitive impairments. Psychomotor incapacity may be present and speech dysarthria noticeable (Butler and Lewis, 1982). In severe cases we refer to it as a stroke, but more frequently the brain damage is more diffuse. In either instance psychomotor impairment may be obvious, either transient or permanent.

**Other Disorders.** Other brain disorders may also strike older persons and mimic Alzheimer's disease or multi-infarct dementia. In many cases these other disorders may be reversible. Stemming in part from such causes as head trauma, alcohol, malnutrition, and drugs, such reversible dementias will respond well to proper treatment and will pass. Environmental cues that are clear and distinct are quite therapeutic and will likely lead to the short-term amelioration of the disorder. Many depressive reactions also mimic dementia, however, so caution must be exercised in doing diagnostic workups.

As already noted, organic disorders falling under the general heading of "dementia" are expensive and take a major toll on both the patient and the support system. Today over $12 billion is annually spent providing long-term care for older persons with dementia. By 1990 the figure may more than triple — reaching some $43 billion a year. By the year 2030 some say the total costs for dementia could rise to $750 billion, overwhelming the health care system. One or another form of dementia may be the most common reason why old people are placed in long-term care institutions, as organic brain disorders are found in over half of all nursing home residents (Medical News, 1985; Rowe, 1985).

## TREATMENT AND INTERVENTION

There is little doubt that much of the suffering endured by older people afflicted with psychogenic or organic disorders could be alleviated by early rehabilitative treatment. However, preventive measures designed to avert the occurrence of psychological difficulties would be far more effective. In most cases the emotional upheaval that interferes with normal functioning does not take place in isolation, without societal involvement. By changing or redesigning normative perspectives regarding the status of the aged, entire generations might escape some of the high risks that challenge the ability of today's elderly to withstand stress. Primary prevention would entail large-scale efforts at reeducating people about what it means to age in terms of developmental goals. A concerted program aimed at offsetting traditionally negative images about aging would go a long way toward restoring a sense of competence to the lives of older people. Further, ensuring adequate levels of income, providing responsive medical attention, and encouraging active participation in the decisions affecting their lives, while emphasizing personal worth developed from much more than productive contributions or youthful capacities, would surely mediate those factors that presently increase the likelihood of emotional breakdowns. In practical applications, various elements of preserving or restoring optimal functioning appear in Figure 6.6.

Recalling the previous chapter about the social construction of illnesses, it is possible to see how few areas of the lives of the elderly provide a better example than their cognitive and mental well-being. The widespread stereotype of their having impaired sensory capabilities and being senile creates illnesses where there might not be any. How normal psychomotor changes are construed is surely a crucial element in anyone's emotional stability.

Unfortunately, mental health professionals are not much different than the rest of the population. Too frequently they have personal or professional biases that prompt them to look for cognitive and emotional disorders. They then diagnose them and treat the conditions they have defined. A person seeking a particular treatment is likely to be seen as being in need of exactly that. Few health professionals intentionally manufacture an impairment, but we all find what we are trained to see.

Yet some real disorders require real treatment. Many families, friends, and patients with organic brain syndromes, depressive reactions, and so on are at a loss at what to do. The geriatric specialist is pressed for answers; diatribes about society's insensitivity are quite beside the point. Attention is needed now. A number of treatments are available to the geriatrician, and within each a continuum of care exists. Which options are exercised depends on personal preferences, resources, reimbursement, appropriateness, and cost effectiveness. An additional problem is that a very small percentage of mental health professionals have been trained in geriatric therapy or other specialties. Today neither the professions nor the mental health system in the United States is geared to the particular needs of older persons (Gatz et al., 1980).

**Medication.** As pointed out earlier, diagnosis and effective treatment reflect an implicit or explicit choice in conceptual models. Geriatrics has increasingly had a role in the "tranquilizer revolution" (Butler and Lewis, 1977). Older persons are prescribed a disproportionate number of drugs each year. Some estimate that over one-quarter of all prescribed medications and a large percentage of over-the-counter products are given to the elderly (Butler and Lewis, 1982). Partially this is a result of physicians prescribing blanket medications in lieu of more targeted forms of intervention for the elderly. Drugs are a big business. By the end of the decade the drug industry is expecting a 60 percent growth in the number of antianxiety and antipsychotic drugs sold in 1985 — a $2 billion market in this category alone (*USA Today*, 1985).

These factors indicate a heavy use of medications among the elderly. First, there is a steady increase in drug use throughout the adult years. Averages after sixty-five amount to almost eleven prescription drugs for the noninstitutionalized elderly and nearly fifteen among those in institutions. Among those persons taking prescription drugs, women received more prescriptions and for a greater number of drugs. Second, the *pharmacokinetic* factors — how the body reacts — for older persons may be quite different, and since older persons are seldom included in clinical trials the effects are largely unknown. Third, Medicare does not cover medications taken on an outpatient basis (Simonson, 1984; Storandt, 1983).

What constitutes a judicious use of drugs is a question likely to prompt considerable debate. Too frequently psychotropic drugs are intended as much for management as for therapy. Tranquilizers, antidepressants, hypnotics, and sedatives not only control older patients' anxieties but also those of the care providers (Butler and Lewis, 1982). To use drugs to resolve problems of living is to avoid the problem. Drugs will pacify depressed elderly people, but much of the time they will do nothing to resolve problems. In the case of organic brain syndromes, however, medications to augment CAT neurotransmitters and vasodilators are believed to be of therapeutic value and their use is indicated (Botwinick, 1984). Generally, mental functioning will respond as the cerebral damage is controlled. In the case of organic brain disorder, however, medication without supportive attention to situational, psychological, and social interaction factors will not be as effective as it could be.

Until the causal factors involved in organic disorders are better understood, specific therapy cannot be achieved. Vascular disorders outside the brain are thought to be involved in the onset of dementias whose control seems to result in the remission of organic symptoms or at least in a lessening of behavioral disruptions. While the physical causes of organic brain syndromes do not now respond to treatment, attention to psychological well-being has been helpful. Although much patience and perseverance is required, efforts to maintain the older patient's contact with reality through traditional therapy, including occupational therapy or behavioral modification, do ameliorate the extent of the patient's disorientation.

**Psychotherapy.** Historically, psychodynamic models have reflected their freudian biases against effective therapy for anyone over forty. Older patients therefore have not often received therapy. However, some progress has been made in recent years, and for the older person dealing with one or more functional disorders, a variety of therapeutic techniques are available. In her review of counseling modes Storandt (1983) outlines the effective use of the psychodynamic theories of Freud, Jung, Adler, and others, as well as behavioral techniques, cognitive, family, and group strategies. Most apparent from her extensive review of the more prominent forms of therapy is that those tailored for the needs of older clients have been slow to develop.

Despite this, private psychiatric care has been very potent in treating the kinds of problems frequently found among older patients. Many private psychiatric facilities have been more successful than public hospitals in reversing certain psychiatric conditions, which suggests there may be a relation between the ability to pay and treatability. Why are so few older patients found among practitioners' lists of clients? Such issues as therapists' concerns about their own aging, their parents, their effectiveness, lack of training, and cultural bias complicating physical illnesses among patients are answers most commonly cited (Bridge and Wyatt, 1980; Butler and Lewis, 1982). The elderly themselves may also be hesitant about submitting to therapy because of personal prejudices and fears. Accordingly, the large majority who need mental health services are not receiving attention until their disorders have advanced to severe stages or until no other alternatives are available. Once an older person is institutionalized, his or her prognosis does not greatly improve. Some research actually indicates it may exacerbate dependency.

Secondary prevention aimed at lessening the extent of psychological impairments must necessarily be determined by the nature of the disorder. Most older patients with affective disorders will respond to either individual or group psychotherapy. Of course, the therapist must take into consideration the practical, defensive role many psychogenic disorders play. The question then becomes: If a defense is working, if a patient's ego is being protected, should we by therapy attempt to right the disorder? Since many anxious or depressed patients have a difficult time perceiving or verbalizing the cause of their complaints, it may be more efficient to wait for the spontaneous remissions that often occur.

In all psychogenic cases, however, the principal goal is to restore positive self-esteem in terms of the patient's available resources. In doing so, the situation of the older patient often demands a more active involvement by the therapist than is usual for younger patients. Supportive interaction may be far more beneficial than rational analyses, partially because the dependencies that originally brought about the crisis are usually part of an inescapable reality. Similarly, therapy that enables patients to continue normal routines is very important; allowing the patient to remain at home or with the family is not only reassuring but also provides an opportunity for reality testing not available in most institutions. What the patient may need most of all is a facilitator who will furnish an opportunity for a review of previous experiences, with the goal of bringing about a progressive realignment of disparate self-images (Butler and Lewis, 1982).

# Summary

The psychological facets of aging are multiple, diffuse, and complex. They include normal, primary aging and secondary or pathological changes. The maintenance of a sense of personal well-being requires active participation with the social life space and an ability to adapt to changing psychomotor and cognitive functioning. Since we do not exist as distinct psychological entities in isolation from the rest of the world, having the personal resources necessary for engaging the environment is crucial. The interaction of social structural factors and individual competencies is nowhere more apparent than in a discussion of the psychology of aging.

Current evidence suggests that sensory decay over time is modest at worst; most older people will not experience significant enough declines to threaten their interaction patterns. Changes do of course occur, but until these alter threshold levels, few if any will be perceived as significant. Vision and hearing undergo the greatest deterioration, but a number of ameliorative measures are available to offset many difficulties. Regardless of real change, the stigma of assumed handicaps prompts some degree of withdrawal. Since much of this pattern is a socially constructed attitude, it too can be altered. Even the lengthening of reaction times is usually not sufficient to impair abilities to do most of the tasks of everyday life. By the time they reach their sixth decade, most people have had a lifetime of adaptation and adjustment experience that they utilize in grappling with the limitations and disabilities they encounter.

The myth of age-related declines in intelligence has only recently been challenged by new evidence. Schaie, as the leader of a research team, has shown that intelligence and sensory declines do not go necessarily hand in hand. What had previously been identified as an age-related decline is now thought to be caused by conceptual inadequacies or biases built into most psychological tests. While certain cognitive capacities involving motor skills are lost with age, these, too, have been grossly overestimated. When evaluation is made by cohort-appropriate means, the debilities simply do not appear. Of course there are individual exceptions; capacities may be modified by ill-health, by unfavorable social circumstances, and, ultimately, by the nearness of death. In practical terms we must restructure the nature of formal educational opportunities to allow for and encourage later participation if we value optimal well-being for our elderly.

In attempting to make sense of life, psychologists have developed many developmental models. Beginning with an ontogenetic perspective on the life course, it was originally assumed that sequential development was universal, inevitable, and predictable. Later models shifted their attention to give greater credence to the normative structuring of life's stages. In this alternative formulation, plasticity and social involvements mold the timing, shape, and sequence of developmental stages. A culture that stresses progress and change is likely to foster a developmental psychology that sees these as basic human attributes when they are actually imposed by socialization and interaction. In a still later refinement, models stressing gender differences in coping and adjusting during the adult years have expanded the notion of normative development to suggest the two sexes may have distinct life trajectories. Yet another view sees personalities as multiplex entities comprised of many distinct attributes. The shifting pattern of those subfacets are responsible for the patterning of personality types and reaction modes. While much remains to be done, the debates surrounding these latest theoretical models are promising in that they have opened up new avenues both for research and for individual variation in coping.

The prime example of secondary aging faced by psychologists revolves around the question of mental illness and mental health. Even identifying the cause and consequence of psychological disorders is a difficult task. Most of the functional disorders — neurotic, psychotic, and affective — found among the elderly do not suddenly arise in later life. Rather, they only become apparent once the social backdrop of interaction begins to change. Depressive reactions are the most frequently observed nonorganic condition in the later years. Depending on a number of factors, the model for treatment and intervention to improve the lives of those with psychological disorders will vary widely. The general practitioner or psychiatric professional, however, relies on medication to control symptoms. This tendency toward the medicalization of social problems has been observed in a number of distinct dimensions of our lives.

Organic brain disorders are another issue. Here the basic categories are reversible and nonreversible. It is this nonreversible group, primarily Alzheimer's disease and multi-infarct dementia, that is so pernicious. The silent onset and progressive deterioration of these disorders are very taxing for the sufferer and support networks. With multi-infarct conditions the disruption is more abrupt and more suited to therapeutic intervention but at the same time they will likely lead to ever greater difficulties over time. Several forms of therapy are available and have been effective with clients in their later years.

Both diagnosis and treatment are socially prescribed; they reflect conditions created by the vocabulary of the profession. Social factors envelop all aspects of everyone's life at all times. Accordingly, there is complicity in an older person's psychological disorder that points to factors often beyond their control. This is not to say they are lumps of clay to be molded; rather, the social backdrop constitutes the stage on which they act out their roles. As negative perspectives on the cognitive and emotional dimensions of the elderly are replaced by enlightened opinion, future generations of old people will ideally receive the kind of treatment and support they need.

# Discussion Questions

**Multiple Facets of the Psychology of Aging**

1. Think of an old person you know well. How would you rate his or her psychological well-being? To what extent do you think this person's state of mental health is the result of (a) past experience, (b) factors in his or her present situation, or (c) character traits or attitudes toward what happens?

**Sensory Modalities**

2. What functional and psychological problems are likely to be related to decreases in (a) kinesthetic sensitivity, (b) hearing, or (c) visual acuity? If you had to suffer partial or complete loss of one sense, which would you choose to lose?

3. List as many ways as possible of compensating for the various sensory deficits that may affect old people and of encouraging maximum function.

**Reaction Time and Psychomotor Response**

4. In real life situations what are the advantages of choosing (a) speed over accuracy or (b) accuracy over speed? What criterion might one use to balance the two? What factors might lead older people to prefer accuracy over speed whereas the young prefer speed over accuracy?

**Learning, Remembering, Forgetting**

5. How would you explain differences between the performance of old and young people in laboratory testing?

6. What memory or learning deficits are found in old people? What measures would you suggest for preventing or remedying these?

**Intelligence and Creativity**

7. What do intelligence tests test? How well do you think they serve? Suggest some alternative ways of assessing intelligence and ability.

8. What do you think it means to say that someone is more intelligent than someone else? Do you think the older people you know are more or less intelligent than younger people? List some reasons for apparent differences in intelligence between older and younger people.

**9.** Do you think that a decline in cognitive ability is caused by being close to death or contributes to the terminal process? Why?

**Creativity**

**10.** Do you think that how often someone's work is cited is an adequate measure of creativity? What factors might lead to frequent citation? What other measures might be used to assess creativity, particularly in the case of people outside the academic world?

**Stage Theories of Development**

**11.** What are the strengths and weaknesses of stage theories of development (a) as models for describing the actual way people age or (b) as suggesting developmental goals?

**Alternative Approaches**

**12.** In what ways do you think NEO-type models of continuity are likely to contribute to or break down ageism?

**Sex Roles and Adult Life**

**13.** How does the aging process of women differ from that of men? How did it differ thirty years ago? What useful lessons might we learn by comparing sex role differences in aging?

**Mental Health and Mental Disorders**

**14.** What factors affect the way in which mental health is defined? How would you define it? Do you think that what it means to be mentally healthy for old people is different from what it means for young people? If so, how?

**15.** What factors affect the mental health of the elderly? How do these operate in (a) the psychogenic or functional disorders and (b) the organic brain syndromes?

**16.** You are a consultant to a state government. Prepare an outline of a proposal for a comprehensive mental health program for the elderly. Be sure to discuss the following: (a) public education and other measures aimed at preventing mental disorder and maximizing mental health in the elderly; (b) ways of rehabilitating and ensuring maximum functioning for those who have functional or organic mental disorders; (c) the role of community-based outpatient services in institutionalization; (d) guidelines for institutions designed to maximize the well-being of the institutionalized elderly; (e) guidelines for using various modes of intervention, measures designed to solve problems in living, psychotherapy, and using medications; and (f) the role of various types of professionals in promoting mental health for the elderly.

# Pertinent Readings

American Psychiatric Association. *Diagnostic and Statistical Manual of Mental Disorders.* Washington, D.C.: American Psychiatric Association, Inc., 1980.

Bader, J. E. "Socio-Economic Aspects of Aging." In *Vision and Aging,* eds. A. A. Rosenbloom and M. Morgan. Chicago: Professional Press (in press).

Baltes, P., and K. W. Schaie. "The Myth of the Twilight Years." *Psychology Today* 10, 7 (March 1974): 35–40.

Barrett, J. H. *Gerontological Psychology.* Springfield, Ill.: Charles C Thomas, Publishers, 1972.

Blass, J. P. "Stages of Alzheimer's Disease." *Journal of the American Geriatrics Society* 32, 1 (1984): 4.

Blazer, D. B. "The Epidemiology of Depression in Later Life." In *Depression and Aging: Causes, Care and Consequences,* eds. L. D. Breslav and M. R. Haug, pp. 30–50. New York: Springer Publishing Company, 1983.

Blum, J. E., J. L. Fosshage, and L. F. Jarvik. "Intellectual Changes and Sex Differences in Octogenarians: A Twenty-Year Longitudinal Study of Aging." *Developmental Psychology* 7, 2 (1972): 178–87.

Botwinick, J. "Intellectual Abilities." In *Handbook of the Psychology of Aging,* eds. J. E. Birren and K. W. Schaie, pp. 580–605. New York: Van Nostrand Reinhold Company, 1977.

———. *Aging and Behavior.* New York: Springer Publishing Company, 1984.

———, and M. Storandt. "Cardiovascular Status, Depressive Affect, and Other Factors in Reaction Time." *Journal of Gerontology* 29, 5 (1974): 543–48.

———, J. R. West, and M. Storandt. "Predicting Death from Behavior Test Performance." *Journal of Gerontology* 33, 5 (1978): 755–62.

Bridge, T. P., and R. J. Wyatt. "Paraphrenia: Paranoid States of Later Life. I. European Research" and "II. American Research." *Journal of the American Geriatrics Society* 28, 5 (1980): 193–205.

Brim, O. G. "Theories of Male Mid-Life Crisis." *Counseling Psychologist* 6, 1 (1976): 2–9.

Bronfenbrenner, U. *The Ecology of Human Development.* Cambridge, Mass.: Howard University Press, 1979.

Bucht, G., R. Adolfsson, and B. Winblad. "Diagnosis of Alzheimer Type and Multi-Infarct Dementia: A Clinical Description and Diagnostic Problems." *Journal of the American Geriatrics Society* 32, 7 (1984): 491–98.

Busse, E. W., and D. Blazer. "Disorders Related to Biological Functioning." In *Handbook of Geriatric Psychiatry,* eds. E. W. Busse and D. G. Blazer, pp. 390–414. New York: Van Nostrand Reinhold Company, 1980.

Butler, R. N. "The Creative Life and Old Age." In *Successful Aging,* ed. E. Pfeiffer, pp. 97–108. Durham, N.C.: Center for the Study of Aging and Human Development, Duke University, 1974.

———. *Why Survive?: Being Old in America.* New York: Harper and Row Publishers, 1975.

———, and M. I. Lewis. *Aging and Mental Health: Positive Psychological Approaches.* St. Louis: The C. V. Mosby Company, 1977, 1982.

Cohen, D., and C. Eisdorfer. "Major Psychiatric and Behavioral Disorders in the Aging." In *Principles of Geriatric Medicine,* eds. R. Andres, E. L. Bierman, and W. R. Hazzard, pp. 867–908. New York: McGraw-Hill Book Company, 1985.

———, G. Kennedy, and C. Eisdorfer. "Phases of Change in the Patient with Alzheimer's Dementia." *Journal of the American Geriatrics Society* 32, 1 (1984): 11–15.

Crossen, C. W., and E. A. Robertson-Tchabo. "Age and Preference for Complexity Among Manifestly Creative Women." *Human Development* 26, 1 (1983): 149–55.

Demming, J. A., and S. L. Pressey. "Tests 'Indigenous' to the Adult and Older Years." *Journal of Counseling Psychology* 4 (1957): 144–48.

Dennis, W. "Creative Productivity Between the Ages of 20 and 80 Years." *Journal of Gerontology* 21, 1 (1966): 1–8.

Eisdorfer, C. "Paranoia and Schizophrenic Disorders in Later Life." In *Handbook of Geriatric Psychiatry*, eds. E. W. Busse and D. G. Blazer, pp. 329–37. New York: Van Nostrand Reinhold Company, 1980.

Elder, G. H., Jr. "Age Differentiation and the Life Course." In *Annual Review of Sociology*, eds. A. Inkeles, J. Coleman, and N. Smelser, pp. 165–90. Palo Alto, Calif.: Annual Reviews, Inc., 1975.

Erikson, E. H. *Childhood and Society*, 2nd ed. New York: W. W. Norton & Co., 1963.

———. *The Life Cycle Completed.* New York: W. W. Norton & Co., 1982.

Fozard, J., and J. C. Thomas. "Psychology of Aging." In *Modern Perspectives in the Psychiatry of Old Age*, ed. J. G. Howells, pp. 107–69. Larchmont, N.Y.: Brunner/Mazel, Publishers, 1975.

Gatz, M., M. A. Smyer, and M. P. Lawton. "The Mental Health System and the Older Adult." In *Aging in the 1980s: Psychological Issues*, ed. L. W. Poon, pp. 5–18. Washington, D.C.: American Psychological Association, Inc., 1980.

George, L. K. *Role Transitions in Later Life.* Monterey, Calif.: Brooks/Cole Publishing Company, 1980.

Gergen, K. J. "The Emerging Crisis in Life-Span Developmental Theory." In *Life-Span Development and Behavior*, vol. 3, eds. P. B. Baltes and O. G. Brim, pp. 31–63. New York: Academic Press, Inc., 1980.

Gottsdanker, R. "Age and Simple Reaction Time." *Journal of Gerontology* 37, 3 (1982): 342–48.

Gould, R. "Adult Life Stages: Growth Toward Self-Tolerance." *Psychology Today* 8, 9 (1975): 74–78.

———. *Transformations.* New York: Simon & Schuster, 1978.

Granick, S., and R. D. Patterson, eds. *Human Aging II: An Eleven-Year Followup Biomedical and Behavioral Study.* DHEW Publication No. (HSM) 71-9037. Washington, D.C.: U.S. Government Printing Office, 1971.

Gubrium, J., and D. Buckhold. *Toward Maturity.* San Francisco: Jossey-Bass, Inc., Publishers, 1977.

Guillemard, A. M. "Old Age Retirement and the Social Class Structure: Toward an Analysis of the Structural Dynamics of the Later Stage of Life." In *Aging and Lifecourse Transitions: An Interdisciplinary Perspective*, eds. T. K. Hareven and K. J. Adams, pp. 221–44. London: Tavistock Publications, 1982.

Guttman, D. "Individual Adaptation in the Middle Years: Developmental Issues in the Masculine Mid-Life Crisis." *Journal of Genetic Psychiatry* 9, 1 (1976): 41–59.

———. "The Cross-Cultural Perspective: Notes Toward a Comparative Psychology of Aging." In *Handbook of the Psychology of Aging*, eds. J. E. Birren and K. W. Schaie, pp. 302–26. New York: Van Nostrand Reinhold Company, 1977.

Hendricks, J. "Societal Aspects of Aging and Visual Impairment." In *Handbook of Aging and Vision*, eds. S. Timmermann and R. Kaarlela. New York: American Foundation for the Blind, 1986.

Henig, R. M. *The Myth of Senility.* Garden City, N.Y.: Anchor/Doubleday, 1981.

Horn, J. L. "Psychometric Studies of Aging and Intelligence." In *Genesis and Treatment of Psychological Disorders in the Elderly*, eds. S. Gershon and A. Raskin, pp. 19–43. New York: Raven Press, 1975.

———, and G. Donaldson. "Faith Is Not Enough: A Response to the Baltes-Schaie Claim that Intelligence Does not Wane." *American Psychologist* 32, 3 (1977): 369–73.

———, and R. Engstrom. "Apprehension, Memory, and Fluid Intelligence Decline Through the 'Vital Years' of Adulthood." Paper presented to Association for Gerontology in Higher Education, Denver, Colo., 1980.

Jarvik, L. F., and A. Falek. "Intellectual Stability and Survival in the Aged." *Journal of Gerontology* 18, 2 (1963): 173–76.

Kay, D., and K. Gergman. "Epidemiology of Mental Disorders Among the Aged in the Community." In *Handbook of Mental Health and Aging*, eds. J. E. Birren and R. B. Sloane, pp. 34–56. Englewood Cliffs, N.J.: Prentice-Hall, Inc. 1980.

Keeney, A. H., and V. T. Keeney. "A Guide to Examining the Aging Eye." *Geriatrics* 35, 2 (1980): 81–91.

Kogan, N. "Cognitive Styles in Older Adults." In *Review of Human Development*, eds. T. M. Field et al., pp. 586–601. New York: Wiley-Interscience, 1982.

Kolberg, L. "Development of Moral Character and Moral Ideology." In *Review of Child Development Research*, vol. 1, eds. M. Hoffman and L. Hoffman. New York: Russell Sage Foundation, 1964.

Lehman, H. C. *Age and Achievement*. Princeton, N.J.: The Princeton University Press, 1953.

Levinson, D. J. *The Seasons of a Man's Life*. New York: Alfred A. Knopf, Inc., 1978.

Lowman, C., and C. Kirchner. "Elderly Blind and Visually Impaired Persons: Projected Numbers in the Year 2000." *Journal of Visual Impairment and Blindness* 73 (1979): 69–73.

Lowenthal, M. F. "Psychosocial Variations Across the Adult Life Course: Frontiers for Research and Policy." *The Gerontologist* 15, 1 (1975): 6–12.

———, et al. *Four Stages of Life*. San Francisco: Jossey-Bass, Inc. Publishers, 1975.

McCrae, R. J., and P. T. Costa, Jr. *Emerging Lives, Enduring Dispositions: Personality in Adulthood*. Boston: Little, Brown & Company, 1984.

———. "Personality, Stress, and Coping Processes in Aging Men and Women." In *Principles of Geriatric Medicine*, eds. R. Andres, E. L. Bierman, and W. R. Hazzard, pp. 141–44. New York: McGraw-Hill Book Company, 1985.

McGee, J., and K. Wells. "Gender Typing and Androgyny in Late Life: New Directions for Theory and Research." *Human Development*, 25, 1 (1982): 116–39.

Medical News. "Research on Aging Burgeons as More Americans Grow Older." *Journal of the American Medical Association* 253, 10 (March 8, 1985): 1369–85.

Miller, M. *Suicide After Sixty*. New York: Springer Publishing Company, 1979.

Monbeck, M. E. *The Meaning of Blindness*. Bloomington: Indiana University Press, 1973.

Murrell, S. A., S. Himmelfarb, and K. Wright. "Prevalence of Depression and Its Correlates in Older Adults." *American Journal of Epidemiology* 117, 2 (1983): 173–85.

National Center for Health Statistics. *Prevalence of Selected Impairments*. Health and Vital Statistics, Series 10, No. 134. Washington, D.C.: U.S. Government Printing Office, 1981.

———. *Hearing Ability of Persons by Sociodemographic and Health Characteristics: United States*. Health and Vital Statistics, Series 10, No. 140. Hyattsville, Md.: Public Health Service, 1982.

Neugarten, B. L. "The Awareness of Middle Age." In *Middle Age and Aging*, ed. B. L. Neugarten, pp. 93–98. Chicago: The University of Chicago Press, 1968.

Palmore, E. B. "Predictors of the Longevity Difference: A 25-Year Follow-Up." *The Gerontologist* 225 (1982): 513–18.

Peck, R. C. "Psychological Developments in the Second Half of Life." In *Middle Age and Aging*, ed. B. L. Neugarten, pp. 88–92. Chicago: University of Chicago Press, 1968.

Perlmutter, M., and E. Hall. *Adult Development and Aging*. New York: John Wiley & Sons, Inc., 1985.

Pfeiffer, E., and E. W. Busse. "Mental Disorders in Later Life — Affective Disorders: Paranoid, Neurotic and Situational Reactions." In *Mental Illness in Later Life*, eds. E. W. Busse and F. Pfeiffer, pp. 89–106. Washington, D.C.: American Psychiatric Association, Inc., 1973.

Piaget, J. "Piaget's Theory." In *Handbook of Child Psychology*, ed. P. H. Mussen, pp. 103–28. New York: John Wiley & Sons, Inc., 1983.

Raskind, M. A., and M. C. Storrie. "The Organic Mental Disorders." In *Handbook of Geriatric Psychiatry*, eds. E. W. Busse and D. Blazer, pp. 305–28. New York: Van Nostrand Reinhold Company, 1980.

Rasool, C. G., and D. J. Selkoe. "Sharing of Specific Antigens by Degenerating Neurons in Pick's Disease and Alzheimer's Disease." *New England Journal of Medicine* 312, 11 (March 14, 1985): 700–05.

Redick, R. W., M. Kromer, and C. A. Taube. "Epidemiology of Mental Illness and Utilization of Psychiatric Facilities among Older Persons." In *Mental Illness in Later Life*, eds. E. W. Busse and E. Pfeiffer, pp. 199–231. Washington, D.C.: American Psychiatric Association, Inc., 1973.

Riegel, K. F. and R. M. Riegel. "Development, Drop and Death." *Developmental Psychology* 6, 2 (1972): 306–19.

Robertson-Tchabo, E. A., and D. Arenberg. "Mental Functioning and Aging." In *Principles of Geriatric Medicine*, eds. R. Andres, E. L. Bierman, and W. R. Hazzard, pp. 129–40. New York: McGraw-Hill Book Company, 1985.

Rosenfeld, A.H. *New Views on Older Lives*. Washington, D.C.: National Institute of Mental Health, Department of Health, Education and Welfare, 1978.

Rosow, I. "The Social Context of the Aging Self." *The Gerontologist* 13, 1 (1973): 82–87.

Rossi, A., ed. *Gender and the Life Course*. New York: Aldine Publishing Company, 1985.

Rowe, J. W. "Health Care of the Elderly." *New England Journal of Medicine* 312, 13 (March 28, 1985): 827–35.

Schaie, K. W. "The Primary Mental Abilities in Adulthood: An Exploration in the Development of Psychometric Intelligence." In *Life Span Development and Behavior*, eds. P. B. Baltes and O. G. Brim, Jr. New York: Academic Press, Inc., 1979.

————, and J. Geiwitz. *Adult Development and Aging*. Boston: Little, Brown & Company, 1981.

————. and C. Herzog. "Measurement in the Psychology of Adulthood and Aging." In *Handbook of the Psychology of Aging*, eds. J. E. Birren and K. W. Schaie, pp. 61–92. New York: Van Nostrand Reinhold Company, 1985.

Sekuler, R., D. Kline, K. Dismukes and A. J. Adams. "Some Research Needs in Aging and Visual Perception." *Vision Research* 23, 3 (1983): 213–16.

Shinfuku, N. "Current Status and Scope of Gerontopsychiatry." In *Aging in Japan*, ed. S. Nasu, pp. 45–47. Tokyo: Japan Institute for Gerontological Research and Development, 1978.

Siegler, I. C., S. M. McCarty, and P. E. Logue. "Wechsler Memory Scale Scores, Selective Attribution and Distance from Death." *Journal of Gerontology* 37, 2 (1982): 176–81.

Simonson, W. *Medications and the Elderly.* Rockville, Md: Aspen Systems Corporation, 1984.

Sinnot, J. D. "Sex-Role Inconstancy, Biology, and Successful Aging." *The Gerontologist* 17, 5 (1977): 459–63.

———. "Correlates of Sex Roles of Older Adults." *Journal of Gerontology* 37, 5 (1982): 587–94.

Storandt, M. *Counseling and Therapy with Older Adults.* Boston: Little, Brown & Company, 1983.

Taylor, I. A. "Patterns of Creativity and Aging." In *Successful Aging,* ed. E. Pfeiffer, pp. 113–17. Durham, N.C.: Center for the Study of Aging and Human Development, Duke University, 1974.

Thomas, P.D., W. C. Hunt, P. J. Garry, R. B. Hood, J. M. Goodwin, and J. S. Goodwin. "Hearing Acuity in a Healthy Elderly Population: Effects on Emotional, Cognitive and Social Status." *Journal of Gerontology* 38, 3 (1983): 321–25.

USA Today. "Today's Tip-off — Sales of Psychotherapeutic. . . ." *USA Today,* April 24, 1985, p. C-1.

Welford, A. T. "Age and Skill: Motor, Intellectual and Social." In *Decision Making and Age,* ed. A. T. Welford, pp. 1–22. Basel, Switzerland: S. Karger, 1969.

Willis, S. L., and P. B. Baltes. "Intelligence in Adulthood and Aging: Contemporary Issues." In *Aging in the 1980s: Psychological Issues,* ed. L. W. Poon, pp. 260–22. Washington, D.C.: American Psychological Association, Inc., 1980.

Zarit, S. H., N. K. Orr, and J. M. Zarit. *Caring for the Patients with Alzheimer's Disease: Families Under Stress.* New York: New York University Press, 1985.

# 7

# EVERYDAY WORLD OF THE ELDERLY

**KEY QUESTIONS**
**FAMILY RELATIONS IN LATER LIFE**
The Nature of Family Ties
  *Family Patterns*
  *Family Interaction*
  *Elderly Families*
  *Separation and Widowhood*
Structural Factors and Family Relations
  *Modernization and the Elderly*
  *Family Interaction*
Abuse and Conflict in Families
The Meaning of Sexuality
  *Sexual Functioning*
  *Incidence and Interest*
  *Sexual Response Cycles*

**LIVING ARRANGEMENTS**
The Elderly in the Community
  *Where the Elderly Live*
  *The Meaning of Place*
  *The Trauma of Relocation*
Congregate Living Facilities
  *Retirement Communities*
  *Nursing Homes*
  *Institutional Environments*
  *Institutional Alternatives*

**ISSUES OF DAILY LIFE**
Leisure, Diversions, and Time
  *Leisure Pursuits*
  *Education*
  *Friendships*
  *Voluntary Participation*

**ISSUES FOR THOUGHT**
Concerns About Crime
The Role of Religion
Anticipating Death
Temporal Orientation

**SUMMARY**

**DISCUSSION QUESTIONS**

**PERTINENT READINGS**

# Key Questions

What is life like after age sixty-five? From national surveys we know older people are concerned about their incomes, health, dependency, and a variety of other frailties of everyday life (NCOA, 1981). In most ways older people are not much different than younger people in their worries. Aside from puzzling over the meaning of the world, the nature of retirement, or financial matters, what are older people concerned with as they go about their normal routines? Like everyone else they generally worry about day-to-day occurrences. Idle moments are occupied in reflection — wondering about oneself, friends, marital relations, what to do tonight or tomorrow, even the nearness of death and the purpose of religion. Even though we all speculate occasionally whether anyone thinks the way we do or handles life in the same manner, we generally believe ourselves to be somehow exceptional — not necessarily better but unique. It is difficult to fathom that others might have quite similar thoughts and concerns.

This chapter focuses on topics that affect the quality of everyday life for the elderly. The quality of life experienced by the elderly is directly related to their growing numbers, improving health status, and changing societal values. Here we will concentrate on daily occurrences. While statistics cannot provide a truly sensitive portrayal of daily life, they can help give an overall picture and indicate reference points for evaluating specific instances. We will discuss family life, intergenerational relations, and community and institutional living arrangements. We will also discuss self-perceptions and what roles and activities occupy the elderly during the retirement years. Finally, we discuss sexual identity and some of the most prominent fears, especially the concern with crime.

# Family Relations in Later Life

### THE NATURE OF FAMILY TIES

The family life of older people is a key resource in maintaining a sense of well-being. As we saw earlier, the notion of **filial responsibility** has a checkered history — often being more idealistic than realistic. Still, the emotional bonds

254

between older people and their families may be a stronghold against any adversity. Accordingly, one purpose of this chapter is to examine the family life and living arrangements of the elderly. We will also look at family composition, relationships, and independent and institutional residential possibilities. In addition, we will provide a realistic picture of the role of the family — good and bad — in determining how older people face the daily hurdles of life. As will be evident, not everything about the living patterns of old people is what we might expect (Nydegger, 1983).

Living arrangements are one of the more critical factors in fostering a sense of security throughout life. Although no hard and fast connections can be drawn between housing patterns, family relationships, and satisfaction in later life, some relatively clear indications exist to show they are often associated. For instance, gerontologists are convinced people who live in isolation and without family ties generally encounter more serious problems in their later years. They are also in a disadvantaged position financially, more often live in substandard housing, have more serious health problems, and are more likely to experience a sense of loneliness and despair than their peers, who are part of a family. Traditionally, research has focused on social isolates, although significant attention is now being paid to the means by which nearly all elderly, whether living alone, or with others, might be able to remain independent members of the community instead of becoming institutional residents. Currently, roughly one in twenty people lives in one or another kind of institution. Many observers assert even this represents too large a proportion compared to the aged actually requiring those services obtainable only in institutions.

**Family Patterns.** For decades the impact of family life on the present circumstances and future adjustments of all individuals regardless of age has been readily acknowledged. Almost without exception, societies around the world have a fairly rigid, clear-cut kinship structure, although provisions for alternate family systems have generally existed alongside the normative pattern. The most pervasive unit is the **nuclear family** — the immediate family consisting of parents and children. **Extended families**, including the nuclear family and various relatives spread over more than two generations, are also found in many parts of the world. Extended families are customarily prevalent where the nuclear unit is not able to supply sufficient economic and emotional support.

It is frequently, though perhaps erroneously, asserted that extended families were common in Europe and North America in the nineteenth century. Recent evidence has called into question assumptions regarding the prevalence of three-generation families living under one roof, suggesting that such arrangements were temporary and seldom widespread or, in the case of the United States, more often nonexistent. Figures vary, however, but the norm during the past century appears to have been that older parents continued to maintain independent households, with less than one in ten older women and one in twenty older men residing with children and grandchildren (Laslett, 1985, 1984; Quadagno, 1982).

In the twentieth century many alterations in family structure have derived in part from greater life expectancy, tendencies toward earlier marriage, and fewer children. In its own way each of these contributes to the likelihood that more people than ever before will have at least one living grandparent during their early adulthood. Now, as we move through the 1980s, still further changes will have an effect on structural arrangements. The rate of change in family life is likely to slow down. Factors such as lower birth rates have declined about as far as they are likely to. At the same time the educational level, which had steadily increased since World War II, seems to have reached a plateau. Similarly, though over half of all women are in the labor force, the rate of increase will probably also slacken. The proportion of men working or seeking work has been on the decline for about two decades, but now, with the changes in retirement policies and the ease with which young women and men enter the labor force, a stabilization will occur. According to most experts, all of these trends will retard any future change in family life (Glick, 1979).

Other changes in the family life cycle that will have an impact on the elderly of tomorrow include the longer dyad period when couples live alone following the departure of their last child — now nearly fifteen years, or one-third of their total married life. How extensive this will become is difficult to say given divorce statistics and a trend that became apparent in the late 1970s toward later first marriages. Finally, unmarried couples of opposite sexes are a rapidly increasing phenomenon — though still relatively small in number, accounting for approximately two million households in recent years (U.S. Census, 1984). Though this number is a scant 2 percent of the couple households in the United States, comparable information for countries such as Sweden shows a rate of about 12 percent and it is rising. What this will mean for long-term family relationships or late-life living arrangements cannot yet be said. However, unmarried couples, while primarily young, exist among all age groups, with those over sixty-five making up over 6 percent of the unmarried couples. Clearly, alternative family life-styles will become very real possibilities in the years ahead. For the past decade and a half the number of unmarried couples has been growing by roughly 100,000 households a year; about 82 percent are in the twenty-five to forty-five age bracket, and soon this group will be counted among the ranks of the young-old.

Among the elderly, alternative family arrangements are becoming increasingly visible. While the number of intact couples has increased by nearly one-quarter, among blacks the increase is still greater; it is still true that most older men are married and living with their spouses but most older women are not. Of course, variations are broad, and sharp contrasts exist between the young-old and the old-old. Given that the current differential in life expectancy is approximately eight years, and that women customarily marry men three to five years older than themselves, it should come as no surprise that with each passing year fewer women live as part of a couple or family unit. With each successively older cohort, sex ratios are even less advantageous for older women. By the year 2000 for every 100 men over eighty-five there will be an excess of twenty-five women. Unless women begin marrying men nearly eight years younger than themselves, they will face a continuing necessity to redefine the nature of their family lives during their later years. It is unlikely, however, that remarriages will play much of a role in such adjustments since only 2 percent of all grooms and 1 percent of all brides are over sixty-five. Even when companionship is sought, there are few incentives to marry in the later years. Both social and economic factors militate against such unions (Glick, 1979; Aisenberg and Treas, 1985).

Figure 7.1 shows that the risk of widowhood is not distributed equally between the sexes or between blacks and whites. In the United States, for example, approximately five-sixths of older men are married, while less than one sixth are widowed. For women only slightly more than one-third are still living in a marital household and over one-half are widowed. Remarriage is higher for men both because of the favorable sex ratios and because societal values enable them to find younger partners more easily than women can. Remarriage rates among older men are about seven times higher than among older women (U.S. Census, 1983).

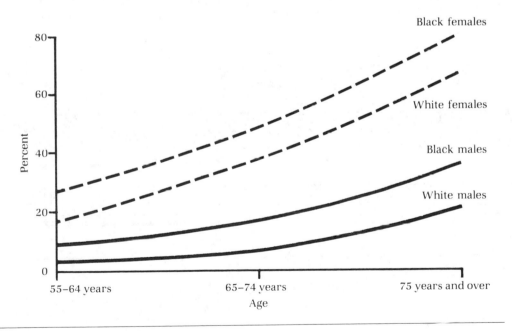

**FIGURE 7.1**

Widowhood of persons fifty-five and over, by race and sex, 1982. (*Source:* U.S. Bureau of the Census. *America in Transition: An Aging Society*, p. 21. Current Population Reports, Series P-23, No. 128. Washington, D.C.: U.S. Government Printing Office, 1983.)

The information in Figure 7.1 does not reveal the whole story of the loneliness and isolation that face some older citizens. From fifty onward, death begins to take its toll on married couples. In the United States today a majority of the women over sixty-five are widows, with 40 percent of them living alone. In 1982 over seven million elderly persons lived alone, the majority of whom were women. The figures on marital status among the elderly have changed little over the last decade for men but quite a bit for women. The proportion of women living in families declined by 10 percent between 1965 and 1981, so that only 10 percent of the older women and 5 percent of the older men are living with either their children or other relatives. As shown in Figure 7.2, a far larger percentage of women now live out their later years by themselves (or with nonrelatives). Today just over half of all older women live as part of families, in contrast to approximately 80 percent of older men still living in a family situation. Those older persons referred to as primary individuals (those who live alone or with nonrelatives) face a far different life situation than do those in a family context.

It is not unusual to find the elderly themselves quite militant in defending their independence; a large majority say they view too much help from their adult children as a form of charity they would rather do without. The cultural emphasis on individualism and self-help most definitely carries over into the later years. For the recently retired or for the affluent elderly, living alone may not cause many problems, but for the vast majority independence is like a

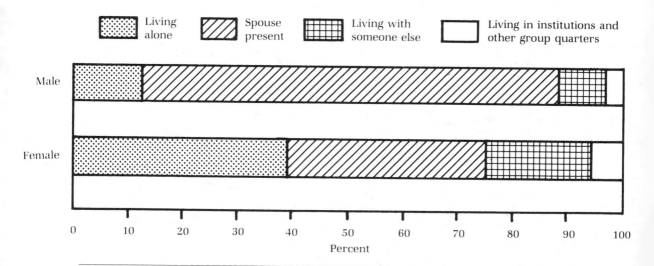

**FIGURE 7.2**
Distribution of the male and female populations sixty-five years old and over by living arrangements, 1981. (*Source:* U.S. Bureau of the Census. *Demographic and Socioeconomic Aspects of Aging in the United States*, p. 87. Current Population Reports, Series P-23, No. 138. Washington, D.C.: U.S. Government Printing Office, 1984.)

commodity that becomes ever scarcer and more expensive the older they get. Given that generally neither adult children nor parents relish the prospect of living together, it is surprising so few elderly actually live in institutions.

This is not to say relationships between older parents and children have deteriorated. No evidence exists to support the myth that older parents have been more respected in the past. Family relations in preindustrial societies may have been colder and more distant than in Western societies today. When respect was granted it was in part because valuable resources, especially land, were passed from parents to children. A real component of meaningful inter-action between the generations is a sense of mutual independence and re-ciprocal assistance. Today a variety of interaction and support patterns can be found, each of which reflects negotiated relations. It will be interesting over the rest of the decade to see how the new federalism, with its tendency to shift economic and care responsibilities even more onto family networks, affects the expressive quality of intergenerational solidarity (National Institute on Aging, 1981; Mutran and Reitzes, 1984; Sussman, 1985).

**Family Interaction.** Ideally, the debate over whether industrialized societies have corrupted the extended family, thus creating isolated nuclear family units out of either economic or practical necessity, has been settled. All the evidence in the gerontological literature indicates that extended families in the past were largely a myth (Hareven, 1978). Actually a modified form of the extended family is more likely today than in the past, since only in the twentieth century have life expectancies been high enough for multiple generations of a single family to be together. By the year 2000 the typical family is likely to have four generations alive at the same time, in contrast to two generations in the early 1900s. This does not mean the total family support system will grow accordingly. The reduced fertility rate of the last few decades means older persons after the year 2000 will probably have fewer lineal descendants. Another significant change will be in the distribution of the generations themselves. For the first time in history we are seeing a parent-children relationship among those over sixty-five. The ratio of parents in their eighties to children in their sixties has shifted from twenty-nine in the older age category to 100 in the young-old category in 1950 to fifty-three to 100 as we entered the 1980s. By the year 2000 there will be ninety-six persons alive over eighty for every 100 in the sixty to sixty-four age range. What this means is that the extremely elderly surviving parent will rely on children who are themselves reaching retirement age. They in turn will have middle-aged children and adult grandchildren. The implications of this trend for possible financial and emotional responsibilities are tremendous (U.S. Census, 1984).

Although few households, less than one in ten, are actually composed of three generations, the vast majority of older people, almost 80 percent, live within an hour's distance of their children and manage to see them at least weekly. There are, however, a few differences by social class (Sussman, 1985; Lacy and Hendricks, 1980). Adult children of middle-class backgrounds are likely to live somewhat farther away from their parents than their working-class counterparts, yet patterns of mutual aid and contact are equally viable in both cases. The primary reasons that middle-class children are not as physically close to their parents are more a reflection of their occupational statuses than of any desire to disassociate themselves; they are simply willing to live apart to pursue careers. Greater distances of course result in fewer visits; nonetheless, when made, the visits last longer than those experienced by working-class families. Judging from the best data available, some compensation for the absence of one's children may be provided by the pride elderly parents take in the accomplishments of their children. Most families can and do share with one another, though it is the emotional bond that is most important — affection between middle-aged children and their aged parents runs high (Rosenfeld, 1978; Shanas, 1979).

The modified extended family in modern mass societies can be described in terms of the type and extent of interaction, the residential propinquity, and the exchange of values and services among its members. The latter category encompasses both material and intangible forms of mutual aid. One unfortunate consequence of the myth of dependence among the elderly is that assistance can and does go both ways, but this is often ignored. For example, recent widows derive the most essential forms of support from their aged parents (Bankoff, 1983). Similarly middle-aged children going through divorces frequently return to their parental home for varying durations. Because of their greater mobility, middle-class children tend to concentrate on tangible forms of reciprocity, whereas working-class generations residing in closer proximity exchange household chores, child care, and so on. Of course, available income is important, and recent research suggests that increased earnings encourage interhousehold transfers (Moon, 1983). Preliminary findings suggest that the greater amount of giving and receiving help found among black families is closely related to socioeconomic factors. Among black families, intergenerational respect seems to be a significant factor in giving and receiving family support (Mutran, 1985). Further, cross-cultural research reveals that regardless of social class, 80 to 90 percent of all old people with serious health problems are able to rely on assistance from family members (Shanas et al., 1968; Shanas, 1979). It must not be assumed, however, that intergenerational assistance is limited to crises. In fact, integrating the oldest living generation into the day-to-day interaction in families seems to be on the increase (Bengtson et al., 1985). Gender seems to be a significant factor in the type and extent of this interaction: thus, while both sons and daughters are equally likely to maintain contact, daughters are more likely to participate in helping activities and sharing resources than are sons (Kivett, 1985). Daughters are also likely to feel considerable pressure on occasion from their responsibilities to both older and younger family members. Women often feel as if they are caught between two generations looking to them for assistance. With household concerns and family cares compounded with participation in the labor force, it would be surprising if some degree of strain did not appear.

In general, it still appears that the intergenerational conflict implicit in the notion of a generation gap is not as pernicious as many have believed. Intergenerational interaction does not always run smoothly of course, but neither is it necessarily hostile. Rather, it is dynamic, subject to negotiation and change and reflects structural factors, self-concepts, and the actors' constructions regarding the type of interaction (Mutran and Reitzes, 1984). While successive generations may have their own interests and conflicts may erupt, unrelated individuals within the same cohort may display even greater value disparity (Bengtson et al., 1985; Bengtson and Treas, 1980). That less than a third of the elderly live with their children is probably more closely related to their desire to retain independence (Rosenmayr, 1977) than to the breakdown of the family. Indeed, even constant contact with children among independent elderly parents may be perceived as an unwanted intrusion into their sense of autonomy and privacy (Cohler, 1983). Certainly research has shown that the elderly do not feel a need for constant social interaction, nor is this lack a negative aspect of their lives (Larson et al., 1985).

**Elderly Families.** During the 1970s the number of older families increased until today they account for over one-fifth of the American household units. With the demographic projections for the years ahead, it seems reasonably certain that both their number and proportion will continue to increase. Still, many older people are spending their last years alone, or out of necessity living with combinations of unrelated individuals. Of all the people in the United States who live by themselves, 40 percent are sixty-five or over and, among these, four-fifths are women. Many of these women have been widowed and feel as long as they are able they want to retain their independent life-styles. There has also been an increase, about 13 percent, in the number of elderly families in which the woman is considered the head of the household. Among whites, roughly 8 percent of the older families are headed by women. Among blacks, the percentage of older women who are the head of the household is nearly twice as high. For those of Spanish origin, who may be of any race, women consider themselves as the head of the household 3 to 4 percent more often than do white women. In a great many of these cases the wife has assumed the provider role because her husband may have disabilities — putting an additional strain on their marriage (U.S. Census, 1984; Fengler and Goodrich, 1979).

The marital status of older Americans, as shown in Table 7.1, illustrates patterns found in most Western countries. Perhaps the most noteworthy changes in the two age categories are the shifts in couples and those affected by death. Among the young–old men, nearly eight out of ten are still married, a figure that declines to slightly more than two-thirds among the old-old. As already noted, women are far more likely to have been faced with the death of their spouses; less than half the younger group and one-fifth of the older women still live as part of a couple. What the table does not show are racial differences. Among the elderly black and those of Spanish origin, the statistics

**TABLE 7.1**

Percent Distribution of the Population Sixty-five and Over by Family Status, by Sex, 1965–1981

(Total resident population excluding members of the Armed Forces in military barracks. Figures are for March of year indicated.)

| Family Status | Both Sexes | | | |
| --- | --- | --- | --- | --- |
| | 1981 | 1975 | 1970 | 1965 |
| Total | 100.0 | 100.0 | 100.0 | 100.0 |
| In families | 64.1 | 65.8 | 67.1 | 70.4 |
| Householder | 35.3 | 36.2 | 36.3 | 37.2 |
| Married, spouse present | 29.4 | 30.0 | 28.9 | 29.2 |
| Other family householder | 5.9 | 6.2 | 7.3 | 8.0 |
| Spouse of householder | 21.2 | 20.7 | 19.3 | 18.7 |
| Other relative | 7.6 | 9.0 | 11.5 | 14.5 |
| Not in families | 35.9 | 34.2 | 32.9 | 29.6 |
| Nonfamily householder | 29.7 | 28.0 | 26.6 | 23.3 |
| Secondary individuals | 1.0 | 1.2 | 2.1 | 2.3 |
| Inmates of institutions | 5.2 | 4.9 | 4.1 | 4.0 |

NA = not applicable.

*Source:* U.S. Bureau of the Census. *Demographic and Socioeconomic Aspects of Aging in the United States.* Current Population Reports, Series P-23, No. 138. Washington, D.C.: U.S. Government Printing Office, 1984.

vary to some degree but the same trends are observed. One significant departure is the much greater tendency for minority group elderly to have responsibility for a youngster — either their own or someone else's — in approximately 20 percent of the older minority families. Apart from these differences, older family life-styles are fairly similar in most industrial countries.

Another facet of the life-styles of older families revolves around what has been termed the **family life cycle** or the timing of certain benchmark events. While the events shown in Figure 7.3 are not intended as an exhaustive list of critical stages, they indicate the continuous evolution experienced by all families. Much like the developmental paradigms discussed in Chapter 6, many researchers assume families also go through sequential stages during which readjustments occur in the way family roles are carried out. Fluctuations in the timing of certain key events are readily apparent; they reflect not only changing economic and social climates but also characteristics of the marital couple. For example, the extension of what are often called the *empty nest* years, when couples once again live alone, means dramatic life-style changes as women reenter the labor force, reestablish identities not based on caring for dependent children, and generally attempt to accommodate themselves to the new parameters of their marriage. At present most couples can plan on spending over fifteen years together after their children leave home. Yet with the gains women are experiencing in life expectancy, they still face almost two decades of late-life widowhood (Glick, 1977).

| | Male | | | | Female | | |
|---|---|---|---|---|---|---|---|
| 1981 | 1975 | 1970 | 1965 | 1981 | 1975 | 1970 | 1965 |
| 100.0 | 100.0 | 100.0 | 100.0 | 100.0 | 100.0 | 100.0 | 100.0 |
| 80.3 | 79.8 | 79.1 | 80.2 | 53.2 | 56.1 | 58.5 | 62.9 |
| 73.2 | 76.0 | 72.9 | 71.2 | 9.6 | 8.4 | 9.8 | 10.7 |
| 70.3 | 73.1 | 69.0 | 66.8 | 1.6 | (NA) | (NA) | (NA) |
| 2.8 | 2.9 | 3.9 | 4.4 | 8.0 | 8.4 | 9.8 | 10.7 |
| 3.0 | (NA) | (NA) | (NA) | 33.5 | 35.0 | 33.3 | 33.3 |
| 4.0 | 3.7 | 6.3 | 9.0 | 10.1 | 12.7 | 15.4 | 18.8 |
| 19.7 | 20.2 | 20.9 | 19.8 | 46.8 | 43.9 | 41.5 | 37.1 |
| 14.7 | 14.8 | 14.9 | 13.9 | 39.8 | 37.3 | 35.2 | 30.6 |
| 1.3 | 1.2 | 2.4 | 2.4 | 0.9 | 1.3 | 1.9 | 2.3 |
| 3.8 | 4.2 | 3.6 | 3.5 | 6.2 | 5.3 | 4.4 | 4.3 |

**Separation and Widowhood.** The emotional turmoil caused by the death of a spouse is an experience that is not easy to communicate to others. For most couples a mutual dependency develops over the years, so that suddenly being alone naturally evokes feelings ranging from grief, loneliness, and confusion to guilt, anger, and a sense of abandonment. With the current attention being focused on myriad behavioral facets of death and dying, many new insights are coming to light about a subject most of us consider not only private but unique. First-hand accounts supplemented by the findings of social scientists have recently provided a poignant new look at what life is like for the surviving partner (Lopata, 1979; Matthews, 1978; O'Laughlin, 1983).

While prior marital relations will affect the emotional reaction to a spouse's death, the suddenness with which this event occurs will exert an enormous influence. The ability to anticipate a death, coupled with financial security, helps the surviving partner adjust, as does extensive involvement in roles and interests that went beyond the marital bond. Thus, for example, the social isolation of some widows can be a reflection not only of psychological factors but also of a dependence on the husband's social contacts as a basis for her own friendships. That increasing numbers of married women in their late forties and early fifties are currently employed — about 48 percent — is a positive sign not only because it furnishes an additional income but perhaps more importantly because it provides for a potentially supportive network in the event of a husband's death (U.S. Census, 1983).

**FIGURE 7.3**
Median age of mothers at the beginning of selected stages of the family life cycle, 1900–1970. (*Source:* U.S. Bureau of the Census. *The Future of the American Family.* Current Population Reports, Series P-23, No. 104. Washington, D.C.: U.S. Government Printing Office, 1980.)

The greater likelihood of outside social contacts enables widowers to re-tain their levels of social participation more often than widows. Women, however, may do better overall in resuming the routines of life. Although re-search findings are inconsistent (Kalish, 1985), widowers tend to remarry within a relatively short time. Relating to gender differences in patterns of adjustment, professionals and retired professionals adapt more readily than blue-collar workers (Atchley, 1975). That women are less likely to hold such white-collar positions may mean that those who are employed still face greater obstacles in bereavement than men. In other words, gender differences may be partially attributable to structural rather than psychological constraints.

Adjustment modes are affected by many factors, including ethnicity, per-sonality, husband's occupation and income, and marital relations or family ties. In all cases, however, coping with bereavement is made easier when there is a support network. Grief in its most profound sense represents a real loss in the personal security that had come from intimate relationships. The most effective forms of family support usually come from close kin; contradictory to popular belief, however, the presence of children in the home neither lessens the shock nor hastens the recovery process (Bankoff, 1983; Lopata, 1979; Glick et al., 1974). In addition, in old age the surviving partner who has adjusted to retirement, departure of children, and other changes unique to the late phases of family life with the spouse present is often the hardest hit by death of a mate. Naturally the surviving partner will often experience a reactive depression with all the symptoms described in Chapter 6. Of course, not everyone is bereaved by the death of a family member — relationships do vary and *conflicted grief* is common — but when it is felt, the sense of futility and pointlessness is very nearly enveloping for a time. The sense of loneliness and despair prompts some people to withdraw, to lose their ability to concentrate, and to redefine what had previously seemed to be important events and activities. For the elderly the death of a loved one also fosters a new sensitivity to their own health. All of this is normal, and like the mythical phoenix rising from the ashes, life is eventually renewed.

Finally, while widowhood is a very personal experience, the process of recovery seems to include some fairly typical situations. Of course, ethnicity, cultural heritage, and social class background affect how grief and recovery are expressed, but seemingly a set of ritualized activities occur within all subcultures. While years spent with a spouse leave an indelible mark, only a very small minority are totally unable to cope, and for most people acute grief dissipates within less than a year. During this period some are dependent on children, but most widowed persons are quite self-sufficient; indeed, three-quarters live alone (U.S. Census, 1984). In the case of widows the death of a spouse might even lead to a freedom that challenges them to expand and use dormant skills (Kalish, 1985; Lopata, 1979; Seltzer, 1979).

In our culture death has been isolated to such an extent that it mostly takes place out of sight. We also view death as appropriate for the very old but premature otherwise. With death relegated to the old, does this mean aged persons are particularly sensitive to the prospect of their own death? Certainly it prompts a recognition that time is not infinite. The realization that the time left for living is finite prompts what Butler (1975) has termed the "life review process," when people attempt to integrate their lives through reflective review. Ideally, the outcome is a sense of insight and resolution rather than anxiety or dread. Undergoing a meaningful life review is not a magical process that helps stave off any subsequent problems; it is more a way of buttressing self-concept through a reiteration of the steps that have led to the present. Seemingly the life review also alters the symbolic meaning of death for persons at various phases of the life cycle. At present the dominant opinion is that older persons face the specter of their own death better than do younger people. Indeed, the prospect of death among older persons is less disconcerting than incompetence, dependency, discomfort, or loss of dignity (Marshall, 1980a).

## STRUCTURAL FACTORS AND FAMILY RELATIONS

**Modernization and the Elderly.** That in many contemporary industrial societies age-graded roles for older family members are not imbued with any particular prestige or authority is taken by some older people to imply that industrialization is inherently detrimental to their status. As pointed out in Chapter 3, however, this notion that modernization necessarily leads to an erosion of the position of the elderly neglects two important caveats: (1) that the elderly were not always accorded positions of respect in preindustrial societies (Laslett, 1985) and (2) that industrialization need not follow one single pattern nor have dire consequences for older persons in a society. While the term "industrialization" implies a particular means of production, this does not encompass the potentially varied ways in which production is socially organized. For example, while United States and the Soviet Union are both industrialized nations, they have very divergent forms of productive organizations. Social relations, including those within the context of the family, are endemic to these different economic forms and will have the greatest impact on family forms and interactions; hence the position of the elderly within these societies.

A comparison of the status of the elderly in other countries may shed some light on this issue. However, the following focuses only on social relations as they are shaped by the process of production. Historical and cultural considerations are also important, but we will not address them here. In Great Britain Walker (1983) has highlighted the relationship between the needs of capitalism, the state, the elderly, and the family structure. Retirement, for example, as implemented by the state, systematically excludes the elderly from the work force to promote efficiency in production. Old age policies, he contends, have not only increased age stratification and dependence but have also been formulated on assumptions that reflect both exclusion from the productive process and the sexual division of labor within the family. Policies thus presuppose that women are care givers and are able to devote themselves to this effort. Those programs that do exist provide substitutes for rather than support to family care providers. The result is decreased social status not only for the elderly but for the wives or daughters who give care and forego income and career opportunities to provide support. Similarly, in Italy the social organization of production is integral to the dependent status of the elderly within both the economic world and the family. Giori (1983) points to the marginalization of the elderly — their removal from the labor force to aid the process of mechanization — maintaining that this has also created an image of the elderly as weak and useless, thus justifying their dependence and exclusion. Such labels carry over into family relations wherein care of the elderly, short of internment, is confined to the private sphere. The nuclear family is increasingly asked to adapt to the structural limitations imposed by the social organization of production; within this framework, older persons can be tapped for either domestic service within the homes of their children or as a cheap temporary labor pool, thus enhancing accumulation. Further, given the uneven economic development of Italy, the dependent situation of the elderly is exacerbated in the southern region, where business expansion has been kept to a minimum to aid capital accumulation in the industrialized North (Bonanno and Calasanti, 1985).

The elderly in the Soviet Union, on the other hand, have a somewhat different relationship to the productive process and hence family relations. While there are retirement policies and state pensions, the state has continued to emphasize the value of work and hence still uses large numbers of the aged in the labor force. Approximately 60 percent of the retired elderly are still involved in the official economy, although they often hold low status jobs and are paid accordingly. In addition, many older persons participate in the second economy that provides goods and services not met by the official economy. More important, they contribute to a family's financial well-being by taking care of grandchildren, thus freeing adult children to expand their role in social production (Porket, 1983). While such grandparenting contributions are not unique (they are also found in other countries), the Russian grandparent is accorded more respect partially as a result of continued participation in the economy, which contradicts a dependency stereotype. Hence, while the aged in the Soviet Union have access to pensions, in the organization of production they still are an integral part of the productive activity, more so than in Great Britain or Italy.

The relationship between the economic sphere and family relations becomes more apparent when we shift the focus to Third World countries. While many of these are capitalist nations, their rate of industrialization is underdeveloped partly because of their relationship to already modernized countries such as the United States. Traditionally, it has been assumed that these nations do not need social policies to help care for the elderly because they are supported by strong family networks not yet eroded by industrialization. However, as Third World governments increasingly strive to partake in capitalist ventures, the ability of families to care for their older members will be severely constrained. The majority are subject to a variety of conditions that simultaneously increase profits for enterprises and lead to individual poverty, such as low wages and poor working conditions. Combined with the need to migrate to secure employment, the capability of families to support older persons becomes tenuous. As in other countries, the elderly contribute to the family's survival by performing household tasks that free parents to work for the maintenance of the group, a necessity when wages are low. When they are unable to continue these tasks and need care, however, they are a drain on the entire unit (Neysmith and Edwardh, 1984).

**Family Interaction.** In the United States the view of older persons, especially grandparents, also entails some structurally induced ageism. The distinction between paid and unpaid activities is in part responsible, but so too are the frequent political debates that undermine the legitimacy of older people's claims to a share of the wealth. The situation created by these debates, however well-intended they may be, has created attitudes in which the attributes of the elderly are held in low esteem. The polarities turning up in families are therefore not entirely of their own making. The media presentation of sweet, well-adjusted, but passive older persons resembling more things than independent individuals denies them authority and respect.

Still another characteristic of family relations that fosters a picture of the elderly as unessential is their relegation in many cases to a largely affective role of grandparent. Working-class and minority families with low mobility and financial resources may be exceptions, but generally speaking, conceptions of grandparenthood are quite trivial (Troll et al., 1979). While middle-class families retain important emotional ties with their elders, in all likelihood the elderly play no significant financial role in the family. Clearly, different styles of grandparenting are possible, and a fivefold complex has been described by Neugarten and Weinstein (1964):

- Formal, tradition-oriented
- Fun seeker, younger, more indulgent
- Parental surrogate, daily interaction
- Reservoirs of family wisdom, patriarchal types
- Distant figures, appear on ritualistic occasions

None of the types, with the possible exception of the surrogate role, reflects an active involvement in production, an important cultural value in a capitalist society such as the United States. While the expressive nature of grandparenting is both important and worthwhile, social status in the United States is generally predicated on the basis of material possessions or contributions. In most cases grandparenting is nonremunerative and does not play such a contributory role in the financial security of families and therefore does not command the same respect as in the Soviet Union. This is coupled with the individualist and self-reliant thrust of social policy, which will be detailed in Chapter 11. The result is that neither cultural roles nor social programs that are intrinsic to the political economic structure of the United States enhance the position of the elderly in the family. At best they are doting grandparents; at worst a burden to be borne by the children.

As this review implies, the relative position of older family members or the importance accorded the roles they fulfill, as well as the experience of the elderly engaged in these activities is intimately bound to social structural constraints. This does not deny individual variation but points to the role of structural factors in delimiting the possible ranges of experience. Just as child-rearing role of women in the United States is honored and yet undervalued because it is nonremunerative, so fulfilling affective roles or helping with household tasks does not necessarily mean the elderly will be accorded a high status. The culturally defined orientation toward older family members reflects the values implicit in the organization of the working world. As Rosenmayr (1985) cogently notes, age norms, values, and societal structure are merely facets of the mode of production. The former all derive from and interact with the latter. In modern mass societies it makes little sense to speak of the status of older people within the family without taking into consideration the generative quality of the mode of production (Streib, 1985).

## ABUSE AND CONFLICT IN FAMILIES

One of the more unsavory aspects of the structured inequalities in family relations is abuse of the elderly, most often dependent parents. Media attention in recent years has tended to portray mistreatment as a recent and burgeoning epidemic. Without in any way minimizing the incidence of abuse, neither assumption is correct. As we shall see, accurate statistics are difficult to come by; the best estimates, however, put the figure for physical abuse at over a million per year — roughly 4 percent of all older people. Why do we see this tendency for family brutality? Why are we seeing the elderly, mostly women over the age of seventy-five who are in a dependent position vis-à-vis their families, being battered or otherwise abused?

The brutalization of the elderly, the most common type of abuse, is not new. Historical and cross-cultural inquiries have found evidence that maltreatment is neither novel nor limited. Family violence toward older members can be documented in court proceedings of the seventeenth and eighteenth centuries, is evident in a wide varieties of cultures, East and West, modern and premodern, and cuts across all socioeconomic categories. Comforting as it might be for the rest of us to believe those who resort to violence are mentally ill, the prevalent pattern of reported abuse points to a number of culpable factors. Cultures that condone violence as a way of resolving conflicts will manifest cycles of family violence (Steinmetz, 1978; Foner, 1984; Pedrick-Cornell and Gelles, 1982).

Regardless of cultural explanations, the prevalence of abuse became more visible in the early part of the 1980s, partly because of the size of the aged population. As the population age structure shifts and the proportion of the old-old increases, there will be more elderly to abuse. Second, as the number of frail elderly grows, so too does maltreatment. Third, financial pressures appear to contribute to the incidence of violence. Economic hardships within the family often accompany mistreatment. Can we hypothesize, therefore, that further financial burdens on the elderly and their families will bring more brutality to the surface? Some researchers think so. They say inflation and inadequate support networks will likely exacerbate the problem in the next few years (Kosberg, 1983; Steinmetz and Amsden, 1983).

The acceptability of aggressive behavior certainly contributes to the abuse problem. Physical confrontation is a very common response in our society. The individual psychopathology of the abuser cannot be dismissed, nor can a history of intrafamily violence. Enforced shared housing and the burden of caring for those who cared for us are thought to be crucial factors (Lau and Kosberg, 1979; Block and Sinnott, 1979).

The focus so far has been on physical violence, but that is only the most shocking. Neglect, emotional traumatization, or financial exploitation also fall into the same category, but they are even more difficult to document. Administering medication as a way to manage disruptive behavior, shouting at a vulnerable family member, confining family members, or not providing sanitary conditions are forms of assault. Some fall clearly on the side of abuse; no one is likely to challenge sexual assaults as abuse; for others most of us would say it is contingent on certain conditions. Is there a pattern, is it meant to intimidate, does it violate human rights? Each of these issues has to be addressed if we are to gain a complete understanding of what abuse is. Generally speaking, we must think in terms of physical treatment, psychological negligence, and the exploitative dimensions of interaction; when these are all considered, the incidence of maltreatment most probably approaches 10 percent (King, 1984; Select Committee on Aging, 1979).

Who are the main perpetrators of elderly abuse? Potentially almost any family member is capable of violence. Though the abused are often reluctant to complain, offenders of record include daughters, sons, grandchildren, spouses, and other family members or care givers. In light of the responsibilities placed on the caregiver and the difficulties of dealing with growing dependency, it should not be too surprising that middle-aged daughters have been singled out by some as particularly prone to give abuse (Pedrick-Cornell and Gelles, 1982). Before making any sweeping generalizations, however, much more research needs to be done. The amount of publicity has pointed out the problem, but any conclusions now are premature. Sons also batter their parents. Cases of grandchildren as abusers, with and without parental complicity, have come to light. Offenders in abuse cases are of both high and low social standing, so the search must go beyond any given subculture (Straus et al., 1980).

## THE MEANING OF SEXUALITY

Sexuality involves much more than its physical aspects, and certainly much more than intercourse alone. Sexuality is a complex interweaving of physical, psychological, and social — including social structural — aspects; thus while it has some of its roots in physiological functions, it is, in the same sense as aging, a social construction. In Western societies the physical aspects of sexuality have not been considered appropriate topics for public discussion. There has, however, been an increasing openness about the physical aspects of sexuality in the past twenty years. Still we must not fall prey to a tendency to concentrate on the physical at the expense of social and psychological factors. Many claim the use of sexuality by the advertising industry is part of this trend. By using sex to sell commodities, advertising tends to foster a view of sex itself as a commodity. Sexual satisfaction may have become a mark of prestige that one can buy because one is a success. Advertising also tends to ignore the sexuality of the elderly: possibly because, with their fixed incomes, they are not a market for many of the products being sold. Weekly expenditures for personal care products are highest between thirty-five and fifty-four; they are lower for those over sixty-five than for any other group except for those under twenty-five (Department of Labor, 1983). While the focus on educating people in sexual techniques is laudable, it can also lead to a view of sexuality as a competitive performance, leaving people feeling inadequate and humiliated if they do not reach certain preconceived norms.

In our discussion we explore the physical aspects of the sexuality of the elderly. We emphasize, however, that the sexuality of the elderly, like that of all of us, is a complex phenomenon that involves all components of the personality and is shaped by cultural and structural circumstances. Certainly it is an aspect of interpersonal and family relations that must be discussed openly.

A generation ago sexuality did not create problems of the same magnitude for older people, for life expectancy seldom exceeded the reproductive years by much. With advances in longevity came the emergence of certain sex-related enigmas. The sensual grandparent is outside the thinking of many people — aging is often equated with neutering, so that with time genital arousal and orgasmic release are unthinkable (Huych, 1977). Not only is this the view of the younger generation, judging by their amusement and expressions of surprise on hearing of it, it is also the feeling of the grandparents.

**Sexual Functioning.** Without doubt, physiological changes alter sexual capacities in later life, yet their influence is vastly exaggerated. Psychological elements are probably far more consequential in determining the character of older people's sex lives. The myths proliferate, affecting women and men alike. Common opinion has it that middle-aged men fare somewhat better than women as far as sexual opportunity is concerned; they are allowed to seek out companions considerably younger than themselves — a prerogative not granted women. This is certainly true, but as long as they are presumed to be sexually active, older men are burdened with the onus of performance standards better suited to men thirty years their junior. Paradoxically, another ingredient of the myth of male sexuality is the widely held belief that the loss of a man's erective capacity is a natural concomitant of aging. While men do indeed experience some delayed reactions in their sexual response cycles, the changes are functionally minimal compared to other physiological involutions. Most important, men do not naturally lose their capacity for erection as a result of these changes.

An equally inappropriate stereotypic notion is that sex loses its appeal to women by the end of their procreative years. Menopause is viewed as the great divide, and women on the other side of it are not supposed to be interested in sex. Again, the facts are quite the contrary. Among current generations of older women, concern with sex never seems to have been as prominent as with men, though neither does it stop with their menses. Like men, older women find themselves surrounded by sexual fallacies so strong they are hesitant to admit to anything other than socially prescribed norms. Physically, women retain their capacity to enjoy sex far more satisfactorily than men, and with mild hormone therapy there is no reason why postmenopausal women cannot remain active as long as they desire (Comfort, 1980). As one well-known authority phrased it when remarking on society's tendency for "hocusing" older people out of their sexuality in the same way they have been hocused out of other valuable activities:

> . . . old folks stop having sex for the same reasons they stop riding a bicycle — general infirmity, thinking it looks ridiculous, no bicycle — and of these reasons the greatest is the social image of the dirty old man and the asexual, undesirable older woman (Comfort, 1974).

**Incidence and Interest.** Only with the clinical investigations carried out by Masters and Johnson and the data gathered as part of the Duke longitudinal studies of aging has sexual activity among the elderly been given significant attention. Subsequent research has begun to augment these initial reports, although for basic information the earlier studies remain the most reliable and complete. Despite older people being enormously underrepresented among Kinsey's (1953) respondents, he reports an increasing incidence of male impotence over the years, coupled with declining activity levels. Notwithstanding, the oldest men do not relinquish their activity levels with any greater speed than younger men. Sexual intercourse occurs less frequently among older women than their younger sisters; however, Kinsey suggests this is more a reflection of male than female partners. The Masters and Johnson and the Duke research studies illuminate what Kinsey barely implied. Together they provide a fairly broad overview of the effects of age on sexual interest and responsiveness. The following discussion is based largely on the information made available from these studies.

Sexual interest and involvement are clearly related to a host of variables, yet the best predictors of whether older people will maintain their sexual activities are continuity and past behavior. Among both men and women, those who have enjoyed a long and recurrent sex life without lengthy interruption are most likely to remain active far longer than their age mates who have not had a similar history. Despite declines in the late sixties and seventies, there is no decade this side of 100 in which sexual activity is completely absent. As a rule men are more active than women at every age. At sixty few men have ceased to engage in sex; by age sixty-eight somewhat less than three-quarters continue to have sexual intercourse, although some portion of those who abstain are still interested — talking and speculating even when they are prevented from actual participation. By the time they reach their late seventies only 25 percent of the men are still active and will continue to engage in some form of sex for the rest of their lives. In fact, there is even a moderate increase in the proportion of eighty- and ninety-year-olds who acknowledge sexual activity. Marital status apparently does not have much impact on men's activity levels; unmarried men are nearly as active and certainly as attracted as men who live with their spouses (Pfeiffer, 1979).

For women the situation is somewhat different. As with men, sexual interest is greater than actual incidence, even though sex is less often a topic of contemplation. Marital status is the crucial factor in continued involvement; women who do not have a spouse have far fewer sexual outlets than their married counterparts. On the other hand, the number of outlets they have established persists far longer than for married women. Previous enjoyment more than simple frequency of sexual relationships is of particular importance for women in determining how they currently feel about sex — while for men both factors are equally relevant. A woman who has enjoyed her sexual experiences in earlier years, regardless of their regularity, will generally persist in those activities in her later years. Above all else, the presence of a sexually capable, socially sanctioned partner is particularly reflected in a woman's level of sexual involvement. In middle age, the years around fifty, seven-eighths of all married women regularly engage in coitus. Ten years later, participation has declined to about 70 percent, and by sixty-five only about half still engage in intercourse. Both members of the older couples in the Duke studies tend to attribute the cessation of intercourse to the husband, because of illness, lack of interest, or impotence. Reports issuing from the Duke investigations suggest masturbation is an alternative practiced by approximately one-quarter of the women responding to the sexual questions (Christenson and Gagnon, 1965; Pfeiffer et al., 1970).

Among that portion of the older population who are sexually involved in their later years, the frequency of intercourse gradually diminishes. The patterns shown in Table 7.2 were exhibited some years ago, yet they do not differ substantially from data reported elsewhere. What such overall trends generally mask is that married people, those from lower socioeconomic statuses, and blacks are many times more active than are singles, those from the upper classes, and whites (Newman and Nichols, 1970). Judging from these data, there appears to be a slight increase in the occurrence of intercourse for the cohorts listed over what the Kinsey team reported about thirty years ago. One possible interpretation of this upward shift entails the presumed changes in sexual morality, implying that present generations of elderly are less conservative about sex than previous generations. It also implies that if contemporary trends toward more openly sensual relationships are durable, future cohorts of older people should be even more sexually active (Starr and Weiner, 1981).

**Sexual Response Cycles.** Physiologically, Masters and Johnson (1970) indicate men experience more of an age-related deficit than women, though in neither case are the changes serious enough to interrupt the sex lives of the elderly. Clinically, the four stages of the sexual response cycle begin to change sometime during middle age. The *excitation stage*, marked in men by an erection and in women by vaginal lubrication, gradually requires more time than in previous years. The erection that used to be achieved in seconds takes minutes in later life, and even then it is neither as full or as demanding as that of a young man. Because of hormonal changes and the involution of the vaginal lining, postmenopausal women do not lubricate as thoroughly, which sometimes results in painful intromission. The *plateau* stage in older men is lengthened, preejaculatory emissions are reduced, and apparently there is less

**TABLE 7.2**

Frequency of Sexual Intercourse in Later Life[a]

|  | Group | Number | None | Once a Month | Once a Week | 2–3 Times a Week | More Than 3 Times a Week |
|---|---|---|---|---|---|---|---|
| **Men** | | | | | | | |
|  | 46–50 | 43 | 0 | 5 | 62 | 26 | 7 |
|  | 51–55 | 41 | 5 | 29 | 49 | 17 | 0 |
|  | 56–60 | 61 | 7 | 38 | 44 | 11 | 0 |
|  | 61–65 | 54 | 20 | 43 | 30 | 7 | 0 |
|  | 66–71 | 62 | 24 | 48 | 26 | 2 | 0 |
|  | Total | 261 | 12 | 34 | 41 | 12 | 1 |
| **Women** | | | | | | | |
|  | 46–50 | 43 | 14 | 26 | 39 | 21 | 0 |
|  | 51–55 | 41 | 20 | 41 | 32 | 5 | 2 |
|  | 56–60 | 48 | 42 | 27 | 25 | 4 | 2 |
|  | 61–65 | 44 | 61 | 29 | 5 | 5 | 0 |
|  | 66–71 | 55 | 73 | 16 | 11 | 0 | 0 |
|  | Total | 231 | 44 | 27 | 22 | 6 | 1 |

[a]Percentages.

*Source:* Pfeiffer, E., A. Verwoerdt, and G. C. Davis. "Sexual Behavior in Middle Life." *American Journal of Psychiatry* 128, 10 (1972): 1264.

urgency to reach orgasm. Women seemingly experience fewer age-related changes in the plateau phase. In spite of a modest reduction in the size of the clitoris with age, there is not any apparent loss of sensitivity. The *orgasmic* phase is roughly analogous in both men and women. The normal pattern among younger men is a series of contractions that are relatively steady through actual emission. In men over fifty, however, the expulsive contractions may change rhythm earlier or be less severe, while seminal emissions are reduced. Middle-aged or older women may experience a shorter orgasmic phase compared to that of younger women, though hormonal treatments often inhibit significant alterations. As with men, women experience several contractions during orgasm, but among the aged these are shorter or may even take the form of spasms accompanied by some abdominal pain.

Finally, the *resolution* phase is again characteristic of both male and female cycles. For men over forty the refractory period may be considerably extended. In young men the resolution phase transpires in a few minutes and a limited erection may be maintained throughout, while for the middle-aged or older man erections disappear more swiftly and hours may pass before intercourse is again possible. At any age the refractory period for women is far less than for men. Among middle-aged and postmenopausal women, the return to a physiological equilibrium is fairly rapid and in many respects parallels that of the older man. For the man, reduced ejaculatory demand may translate into little need to ejaculate at all, thereby prolonging both immediate and long-term sexual functioning and shortening the resolution phase (Solnick and Corby, 1983).

Unfortunately, most people know little about their own body processes and any alterations in sexual functioning signal the beginnings of distress. Impotence is the most common sexual disorder among men over forty-five, sometimes precipitating serious emotional turmoil accompanied by health or mental problems (Kent, 1975). There is some evidence that men in their later fifties or sixties experience a kind of *climacteric* that is somewhat equivalent to menopause; as yet, however, little solid information is available with even less to indicate such a change might interfere with sexual activity. More likely, psychological predisposition plays a far greater role in declining sexual interest. Based on their extensive analyses, Masters and Johnson (1966) have isolated several integral components of male sexual inadequacies. Lack of prowess is often related to disenchantment and marital monotony, preoccupation with extraneous pursuits such as a career, emotional or physical fatigue, overindulgence in either food or drink, mental or physical infirmities, and, finally, fears regarding sexual performance. All can effectively preclude any kind of sexual response. Another commonly expressed fear arises in the aftermath of heart attacks. Like many other ideas, this misconception has little medical support and ought to be abandoned. Actually, sex requires no more exertion than taking a brisk walk or climbing a flight of stairs. Along with the cultural views of older people's sexuality, the lessening need and frequency of ejaculation contribute an additional personal strain insofar as a woman may inadvertently feel threatened by a partner who does not ejaculate. Both partners should understand changing sexual functionings, learning to take more time to be emotionally demonstrative if they are to avoid confounding their relationship with unrealistic expectations (Comfort, 1980; Masters and Johnson, 1970).

Of all the aspects of human sexuality, the female menopause is a leading candidate for the most maligned. Why the termination of the menses is such a clouded issue is a complex question, yet overriding all other considerations is cultural conditioning. Behaviorally, the changes attributed to menopause are in many cases merely an accentuation of already existing tendencies previously held in check. Even the clinical features of the so-called menopausal syndrome are far from uniform. In the Western world hot flashes, emotional turmoil, chronic fatigue, occipital headaches, neckaches, plus myriad other subjective factors are common complaints. Because of hormonal changes in the reproductive system, additional changes include an introversion of the vaginal walls and a loss of lubricating secretions that may occasionally result in painful intercourse. Lest the many fallacies surrounding menopause be reinforced, it cannot be stressed too strongly that psychological factors are equally, if not more important as hormonal factors in influencing subsequent sexual interests and functioning. A woman's subjective perception of herself is most often what damages her sexual outlook; if she believes herself to be unattractive or too old, sex will in all probability become a thing of the past.

One last point needs to be made. Intercourse is not the only means of expressing emotions; it is a serious mistake to think of its termination as the end of sensuality. At all ages coitus is but a single element in the communication of love. It is not unusual for it to be of less importance than other manifestations of the sexual bond. For older couples, being physically or spiritually close or showing tenderness or respect may be valued even more.

# Living Arrangements

At the outset of this chapter a few introductory comments were made regarding the complex interrelationships between living arrangements and the daily adjustment of the elderly. Having spent some time examining the social location of older people within the family structure, we will now look at the physical environment. In most respects the physical ecology of aging is certainly as multifaceted as the social. It is often subtle, almost always powerful, and as fascinating as it is frustrating to those who might wish to alter its appearance or impact. A statistical picture of where older people live is not sufficient in itself; a graphic description must also entail close attention to the way individual personalities and ecological factors interact with one another. It is, however, a beginning from which general implications may be drawn and applied to localized settings.

## THE ELDERLY IN THE COMMUNITY

**Where the Elderly Live.** There is considerable variation in where the elderly live. Not only are they not spread equally across geographical regions, but within cities and in rural areas predictable patterns of older persons' residence can be observed. The place, locale, and accessibility of people's homes determine a great deal about their behavior. To understand how these factors affect older people, it is important to remember the concept of social life space introduced earlier and to remember that local traditions may not be transferable if a move becomes necessary. While the urbanization of the United States dates back to the 1920s, the suburbanization of our cities did not accelerate until the 1950s. By this time most of those who are now thought of as old had settled into a family home. Unless forced to move, it is quite likely they are still living there. The migration of younger workers under thirty-five first to the cities and then to suburban developments left behind pockets of elderly in rural and central city locations.

As of the early 1980s over two-thirds of the elderly population lived in the nation's metropolitan areas. Of these, over half lived outside the central cities — a shift since the 1970 census when most older people resided in these areas. Today only about one-third of all older people live in what we would think of as inner-city neighborhoods. The exception is the minority elderly: over 55 percent of older blacks live in the heart of the central city with another 12 percent in other metropolitan areas. Some central cities still have elderly enclaves, but they are not nearly as widespread as concentrations of racial or ethnic enclaves. Once again a distinction between the young-old and the old-old must be made. The old-old cluster in some inner-city neighbor-hoods; after all, that is where they moved forty years ago. Accordingly, they reside in older and now substandard housing units that consume 30 to 38 per-cent of their incomes to maintain. This range is some two to three times great-er than for younger people. Even then deferred maintenance is often the norm (Lawton, 1985).

Actually, the suburban population is aging more rapidly than any other, since nearly 40 percent of the elderly now live in suburban rings just outside of central city areas. By the end of the century we can expect to find a gray belt around the cities. While some older persons have moved out to the suburbs, others have grown old in place; they moved into more comfortable quarters in midlife, raised their families, and remained there after their children had grown up and left. Changes in family status, suitability of the dwelling, or quality of life are not enough to get many of us to move; more than 40 percent of older persons have been in the same residence for over twenty years. Only declining health or financial hardship are enough to get people to move (Fitzpatrick and Logan, 1985; Golant, 1984).

Nearly one in four older persons live in rural areas, mostly in small towns. Generally, the smaller the rural community the greater the concentration of the elderly, although this is not true of actual farms. In the decade leading up to the latest census the number of elderly living on farms declined from 4.5 to 3 percent. To a large extent the high concentration of the elderly in America's hamlets is a result of the out-migration of younger persons and low fertility rates over the past several decades. In the western North Central part of the United States, including Kansas, Missouri, Nebraska, and Iowa, the farm belt in general has witnessed a growth in the proportion of old people. Florida also has a high percentage of the population over sixty-five but for different reasons. In recent years its attractiveness as a retirement site has grown, and large numbers of older migrants have moved in. Arizona and Texas are simi-larly becoming places for retirement. There are states with larger absolute numbers of elderly, such as New York, Pennsylvania, Ohio, and California, but the actual percentage of the population over sixty-five is lower there because the overall size of the population is so much greater (Flynn et al., 1985; Clif-ford et al., 1985).

**The Meaning of Place.** What does it matter where older people call home? For one thing accessibility to essential services — such as shopping centers or medical care — is crucial. Designing service programs, delivering those ser-vices, providing alternatives, and transporting older people to health and social care providers is becoming increasingly problematic. In rural areas, for example, difficulties in providing assistance to older people are distinct from those encountered in suburban and inner city locales. The psychological sig-nificance of place and physical surroundings must also be taken into account. The landmark work by Lawton (1977, 1980) stressed the transactional and synergistic nature of person-environment integration and made researchers aware of the impact of space, place, and territory on the sense of well-being among the elderly. Place is a symbolic anchor for being in the world, an arena where mastery over things outside the self originates. Adaptability, coping, and **environmental press** are crucial facets of the point Lawton has been making for years in reference to the well-being of the elderly. A familiar place or definite social life space spawns an active, as opposed to a passive or inappropriate, stance in coping with what needs to be dealt with. Home and place are buffers, mediating how the world is perceived. Without these safe havens the elderly would likely suffer considerably more stress (Scheidt and Windley, 1985; Rowles and Ohta, 1985; Kahana, 1982).

As is clear from Figure 7.4, older people sometimes relocate. Though they are a relatively small percentage, elderly movers go from one house or apartment to another, to congregate living facilities, and to other states. In some instances the moves represent changing family life-styles, economic or health needs, or other necessities. Much has been made of retirement migration to the sunbelt states during the 1970s, but the pattern is by no means simple. Migration to retirement communities has been increasing; today over half of those older people who migrate move to sunbelt states. Those elderly who travel to the southern crescent of the United States are no longer just the very wealthy. Some are affluent, but they have also been joined by middle-class retirees with incomes double or better the current poverty level. Many go to Florida, Arizona, and similar states because of the weather. Some older migrants have special needs in their new locales and increase the demand for service provisions; in California especially this seems to be the case (Longino, 1984; Bigger et al., 1984).

**The Trauma of Relocation.** Why is it that some older people are disinclined to move even when it might improve their living accommodations? First, there is the issue of money, or rather the lack of it, to use in securing newer or at least less dilapidated housing. The irony, however, is that the elderly with the least money move most frequently, not because they want to but often as a consequence of condemnation proceedings or urban renewal, which forces them out of the deteriorated sections of town where they can afford the rent. Second, not everyone welcomes change even if it is for the better. Simply because a person is dissatisfied with the present situation does not necessarily inspire a desire to move that will actually be carried through. Despite the nuisances, ineffable social conditions, or perceived lack of safety, all of which undeniably affect morale, the thought of moving to new and unknown places may cause even greater consternation. Relocation is a traumatic event; it means leaving behind neighborhood ties and friendships built on long years of living in the same place. Familiar surroundings furnish a sense of security or stability, and even those elderly who might really have wanted to move and who enjoy their new environment may end up grieving for their lost home. The losses mourned are physical, social, and psychological, since the move is a separation from the person's heritage and the cues that bolster old memories (Lawton, 1980; Kasl and Rosonfield, 1980).

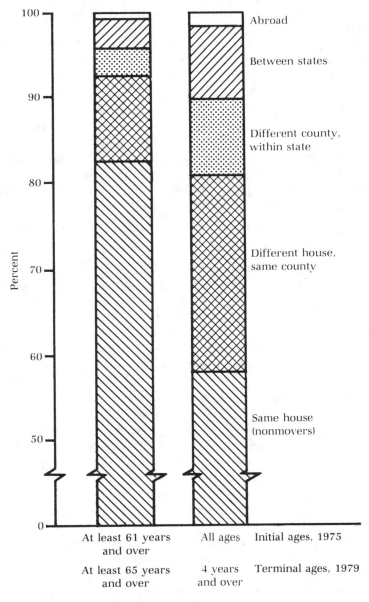

**FIGURE 7.4**
Mobility and migration status of the population sixty-five and over and four and over in 1979,
1975–1979. (*Source:* U.S. Bureau of the Census. *Demographic and Socioeconomic Aspects of Aging
in the United States*, p. 33. Current Population Reports, Series P-23, No. 138. Washington, D.C.:
U.S. Government Printing Office, 1984.)

The prospect of a move does not affect all of the elderly in the same way; therefore, the question becomes one of accounting for the differences. To date there are few longitudinal studies that attempt to discern the true impact of housing changes on morale, but what little evidence is available offers some important practical suggestions. As one would expect, personality and friendship patterns are important in determining whether a move is viewed with foreboding and dread or as a welcome relief. Anticipation, knowing far enough in advance to prepare for the move, and, if possible, making preliminary visits to the new apartment or house also facilitate adjustment. The expectations an older person has regarding the new location and the nature of the situation being left behind inevitably contribute to the effects of the move. Unsurprisingly, physical health is also a major factor. Given sufficient preparation and sensitive handling of the change, new housing often has a positive impact on morale and life satisfaction. Nonetheless, some findings suggest that when older people move, whether willingly or involuntarily, some deterioration of their health will result (Lawton, 1985; Ferraro, 1983).

## CONGREGATE LIVING FACILITIES

Among the possible destinations for older movers are one or another form of congregate living facilities. Retirement communities or homes in the sunbelt states are one attractive alternative. Another type of residential change, but one often laden with many negative connotations, is the move into institutions, be they personal care facilities, nursing homes, or graduated care compounds. In the following section we will discuss each of these briefly and then review some of the alternatives to institutionalization.

**Retirement Communities.** Retirement communities probably conjure up an image of Sun City or some similar place that looks like a country club, with deck chairs and golf clubs. Actually, gerontologists use the label to refer to any age-segregated living arrangement for the independent elderly who relocate there after retiring at least once. Within the general category two subtypes exist: planned and unplanned. The first comes closest to the country club image, though it may also be an urban high-rise, housing project or apartment conversion in a northern city. The second may be just one of those places that act as a magnet for older persons, drawing them in such numbers that others also consider it de facto a retirement place. Such retirement communities may or may not be subsidized by governmental agencies to make units more affordable to low- and moderate-income persons (Kart, 1985).

Aside from having age eligibility requirements, planned retirement communities have other features in common. They range in size from a few dozen to 7,000 dwelling units, provide structured activities and services, and include a purchase price and monthly maintenance fee. In some instances the purchase price is for life only, and the units revert to the community's organizers on the death of the purchasers. In other cases the unit can be inherited and then used or sold depending on the situation of the heirs. Obviously, the private planned communities are primarily designed for the affluent middle classes and are not generally within the reach of the disadvantaged elderly. There are some exceptions, however, in the urban areas of the country where subsidies underwrite construction or maintenance costs, thereby lowering the necessary income threshold of residents.

Increasingly we are seeing life-care plans in which residents are assured of occupancy for the remainder of their lives regardless of the extent of dependency. As a rule such facilities are built on a cluster plan that incorporates self-care units, meals-only options, and skilled nursing capabilities. While these and other retirement communities promote close ties with age peers and seem to foster a high degree of life satisfaction, they do not sever family ties or cut people off from the outside world. True, self-perceived age boundaries are more apparent, but as many researchers have pointed out, and as the subcultural model discussed in Chapter 3 suggests, the equality of interaction thus established can be beneficial for older residents (Longino et al., 1980; Keith, 1982; Streib, 1985).

Retirement communities act as status buffers in the face of the structured inequalities endemic in free market economies. As such, they provide what Streib (1985) refers to as protective shields in the wake of the downward mobility and superannuation characteristic of the movement into old age. For their residents there is often an obliviousness to outside status ranking that buttresses their morale. If they also engender an age-group consciousness, the spread of such communities could become a political force to be reckoned with in the future. But this now seems to be only a potential, not a reality. One thing has become sure, however, for those who are able and chose to move to retirement complexes: the outlook on life is better in the long run than among those who remain in age-integrated communities.

**Nursing Homes.** Another type of congregate living most elderly (as well as the majority of the public) view with trepidation is the nursing home. The majority of the elderly enjoy independent lives. But what are older people to do if there comes a time when, even though they are not seriously ill, they can no longer fend for themselves in what may be an unaccommodating environment? For those who have families or financial reserves there are a number of alternatives, but for those who have neither family ties nor adequate resources entering an institution may be the only way of getting the help they need. In Europe the availability of domiciliary homes for the elderly goes back to sixteenth-century alms houses for the indigent old. During the Middle Ages care of the elderly was sporadic and generally perceived of as a moral obligation of the church. In England the Poor Law of 1601 settled the responsibility of caring for the poor and infirm in each community. Based on a localized system of taxation, the law was intended to equalize the burdens of supportive services by requiring each community to contribute only its proportionate share of money and assistance. This was one of the earliest nationally sanctioned measures of relief. Ironically, 375 years later many of the difficulties inherent in such a program are still being addressed by societies. It is only in the present century that similar facilities have been provided in the United States, and many of these came about as a consequence of social legislation during the Depression.

The prospective payment plan for Medicare-Medicaid portends an increase in the importance of nursing homes. According to findings by the Senate Special Committee on Aging (1985), acute care hospitals are discharging older patients "quicker and sicker." Some fall between categories, ending up in a no-care zone without medical recourse; others are placed in long-term care nursing homes where admissions screenings have confirmed a marked decline in over-all health status among new patients since the advent of DRGs. Provisions under Medicare for institutionalization will be discussed in Chapter 11; suffice it to say that the expense for nursing home care is staggering, averaging $18,000 a year. Medicare covers only a fraction of these costs and to obtain Medicaid coverage means "spending-down" assets to qualify. Across the board about 60 percent of the total nursing home bill is paid from public funds. By 1990 it is projected that the cost will total over $75 billion a year.

Who goes to nursing homes? Demographically, seven out of ten residents are widows. As they age, this likelihood increases, so that by eighty-five over four of five persons in long-term care facilities are women. Among other note-worthy characteristics of nursing home residents are that 92 percent are white, only 12 percent are married, and the prospect of admission is greater among those who are without family or other support networks (Kart, 1985). In general, the further one moves into old age the more likely the risk of insti-tutionalization becomes. Between sixty-five and seventy-four an estimated 1.5 percent are in nursing facilities; in the next ten-year bracket that figure in-creases to around 6 percent, and by eighty-five nearly one-quarter of the el-derly are in institutions. Overall, the total comes to about 1.4 million elderly or about 5 percent of all older persons in the United States. In Soviet and eastern block countries where communal care policies receive greater emphasis, rates of institutionalization are considerably lower (Lesnoff-Caravaglia, 1984). In Canada, Britain, and on the European continent, the proportions of the elderly found in institutions at any given time are comparable to those in the United States. Of course, these figures reveal nothing of those who may have been in an institution in the past or may find themselves in one in the future. Kasten-baum and Candy (1973) pointed out the fallacies implicit in using the smaller figure in making generalizations.

With the old-old growing at the rate they are, it is certain that questions about institutionalization are going to proliferate. Who are the elderly most likely to find themselves residents of nursing homes? How much does it cost? What role can the family play? Are there alternatives? The questions continue, but the answers are slow in coming. Heretofore, a clean environment was con-sidered adequate; now we have come to realize how important the qualitative dimensions of the environment are in shaping behavior.

The institutions in which older people are confined vary from old age homes that provide little more than custodial care or general supervision to state mental hospitals and skilled nursing facilities. Unfortunately, a latent function of the federal legislation aimed at strengthening health care services has been the increased reliance on institutionalization to solve relatively minor problems of aging. At the same time it has promoted the propagation of proprietary nursing homes whose profit motives may be at variance with the best interests of their residents. Standards maintained in the different types of institutions have been established by federal legislation resulting in a labyrinth of regulations imposed by successive laws governing their operation. Homes for the aged, sometimes called **domiciliary care** homes, provide protective living accommodations to residents who require minimal supervision in a sheltered environment and who are otherwise able to take care of their own needs. In the event serious illnesses necessitate medical attention, residents are transferred to more appropriate facilities, either **personal care** homes with nursing services or, for those who can medicate themselves, personal care homes without nursing facilities. Most retirement communities and elderly residential hotels or apartments fall into these categories, which comprise nearly one-fourth of the institutional alternatives. **Skilled nursing** facilities may offer complete or intermediate levels of care. In either case they must furnish around-the-clock nursing service based on personal need and provide medical and dietary supervision. Such institutions may be **extended care** facilities serving as convalescent units for general hospitals or they may admit residents without prior hospitalization. As outlined in Chapter 11, Medicare requires at least a three-day stay in a hospital and certified medical need if financial assistance is to be supplied by the federal government.

Today, of the over 25,000 nursing homes in the United States, close to 80 percent are commercial operations where sizable profits are occasionally made. Housing two-thirds of all institutionalized elderly, the business potential of such homes is indeed enticing. Unfortunately, unscrupulous owners have found ways to curtail services to enhance the return on their money (Butler and Lewis, 1982; Townsend, 1971). Despite the establishment of an Office of Nursing Home Affairs to oversee the enforcement of governmental regulations, the task is formidable. During much of 1980 the government grappled with revising regulations and requirements for facilities accepting Medicare and Medicaid payments. One of the first tasks was to draft a patients' bill of rights. Naturally, there is a price tag attached, and implementing the proposals for adequate intake evaluations, timetable planning for patients, and new staff requirements are projected to cost roughly 15 cents per patient day at the outset according to officials of the Department of Health and Human Services.

**Institutional Environments.** While there is no denying that many older people could benefit from a sheltered environment, the extent to which the various forms of institutionalization satisfy the emotional needs of the elderly is another question. Too many institutions deprive residents of their sense of integrity by depersonalizing the environment for the convenience of staff members. Almost all personal property is taken from residents, and the milieu is much like a strict hospital. Despite the need for a portion of the setting to be oriented to adequate, sometimes efficient, and extensive medical service, there is no reason why it cannot be more flexible. An awareness of psychological needs and residents' rights should be just as strong an element in the architectural design, especially in domiciliary age homes, as the technical aspects of health care. In actuality, it would easily be possible to achieve a warmer feeling in all geriatric institutions; most gerontologists agree there is no justification for elevating institutional expediency over the provision of something approximating the residents' own unique life space. Both physical layout and functioning could easily incorporate more resident input, thereby gratifying a desire to continue to exercise some element of control over their living arrangements (Brody, 1977; Koff, 1982; Eustis et al., 1984).

As a consequence of what is sometimes referred to as *psychological railroading* within highly routinized environments, some older residents are prone to a kind of **institutional neurosis**. Chief among its symptoms is a gradual erosion of the uniqueness of one's personality traits so that residents become increasingly dependent on staff direction for even the most mundane needs. Visitors often complain about the sense of distance between themselves and the resident or the resident's seeming lack of interest in events outside the institution. It is not necessarily that personnel in the institution are insensitive to the older person's plight; rather, the operational procedures themselves breed a kind of docility leading in turn to a leveling of character attributes. In attempting to counter the hospital constraints insofar as practical and to set up the institution as an extension of the community, some investigators point out that many of the negative connotations of institutionalization could be minimized. With the number of older people over seventy-five expanding far more rapidly than the older segment of the population in general, the need for some kind of supportive environments will continue to expand in the near future. If indeed part of our value framework is the humane treatment of the elderly, ways must be found to restructure institutions to emulate the normal rhythms and needs of the residents. Building in opportunities for the elderly to have a sense of active participation in their own affairs is the first step.

Although preserving a sense of well-being inside old age institutions is difficult, in responsive facilities many remotivation aids have been tried and found to have a positive influence on morale. With only a little effort, nursing home and long-term care patients can be helped to stave off negative labels, self-concepts, or deleterious mental languor. Activities as simple as in-house newspapers, participation in planning routines, excursions, and so on all improve self-concepts and attitudes (Brody, 1977). Of course, adequate intake procedures aimed at socializing the incoming patient can prevent many problems before they occur. Even the proper design, the absence of architectural barriers, and the physical features of the care setting have been recognized as having a mediating effect on patients' activity levels, well-being, interaction, and mortality. Such things as a well-defined personal space, carpeting, and personal belongings have been shown to be supportive (Lawton, 1977; Moos and Lemke, 1980; Stein et al., 1985).

With the importance of congruence between treatment environment and client needs well recognized by long-term care planners, individualized and coordinated management plans are the idealized goal. Under prodding for reform, standardized patient records have been endorsed by the National Center on Health Statistics. Together with two interlocking systems called Patient Appraisal Care Planning (PACE) and Patient Care Management Systems (PCMS), the potential exists for focused and individualized intervention procedures (Butler and Lewis, 1982). Then why do we keep reading exposés? Why do nursing homes not change? Obviously, the media concentrate on the bad homes, not the ones that are run properly for maximum patient benefit. No one knows how many homes provide inadequate services; we evaluate only the physical plants and certain certification levels for staff. Most likely the bad ones constitute a very small percentage and are greatly outnumbered by homes that do the best job they can. Furthermore, operating a nursing home is a complicated process. As Figure 7.5 suggests, many diverse levels are involved in the decision-making process. To have any marked impact on the quality of care all components must cooperate. But what is the incentive? Three-quarters of all nursing homes fall into the proprietary category, and as long as they comply with minimum standards, they are doing well as far as the overseeing agencies are concerned. Even those homes that are not run for profit are not immune from staff insensitivity or they may be unaware of the alternatives. Ombudsmen help, and many communities have instituted voluntary programs of this type to point the way, cajole, and if necessary, threaten. Until the law is changed, however, nursing homes permit ombudsmen in at their own discretion. The law could be altered, but to date powerful lobbying groups have precluded serious consideration of any type of monitoring. Regular visits also increases the prospect of accountability. Reform is a question of priorities (Ward, 1984; Spilerman and Litwak, 1982).

**Institutional Alternatives.** Because no one wants to live in an institution and in many cases placement is made because no other remedies are readily apparent, there is an obvious need to maximize alternative arrangements. It is estimated that roughly 15 to 40 percent of those people already living in institutions could easily be maintained in the community if adequate supplemental home care could be obtained. Similarly, in her survey of five industrial countries Shanas suggests at least one-fifth to one-third of the noninstitutional aged in various countries could benefit from these same services so that institutionalization might be avoided (Shanas, 1971). As others have pointed out, the idea of alternatives to institutions has been with us for some time. "Alternative" may not be the best term, as the proposed programs are basically designed to encourage and facilitate community living and to relegate institutions to the supplemental role they were initially intended to fill. The point is not simply to keep people at home because it seems like a better thing to do, but to ameliorate those conditions pressing them into institutions in the first place. Presently there are approximately 3000 organizations qualified under Medicare regula-

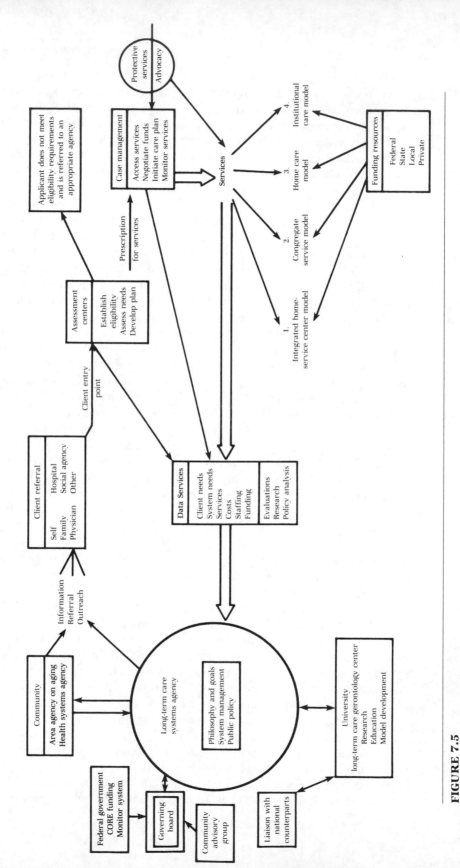

**FIGURE 7.5**
Multiple components in long-term care. (*Source:* Koff, T. H. *Long-Term Care: An Approach to Serving the Frail Elderly*, p. 93. Boston: Little Brown & Company, 1982.)

tions to offer home health care, and since proprietary agencies are allowed to offer therapeutic services to the noninstitutionalized elderly, this number is likely to increase rapidly. The problem will be in making sure that the target population of needy elderly are fully aware of the choices they have available.

The trend away from institutionalization, mandated by the Older Americans Act, reflects not only a humanitarianism but an effort to hold down expenditures. An increase in the rate of use of nursing homes, especially by the old–old, has come about in part because past legislation created situations in which maximum benefits were paid only when beneficiaries were institutionalized, not when domiciliary care by families was attempted. Changes in family structure are adding to this trend, but proposed incentives for personal care, such as tax credits, are now being considered as first steps toward reversing the direction and providing alternatives. California, for example, is the one state with a long tradition of "family-based attendant care" (Callahan et al., 1980). By providing families with $400 to $600 monthly, depending on the level of impairment, the relatives of the elderly are able to purchase services from professionals or even other family members. Naturally, there is a potential for abuse, as there always is, but at the same time the benefits are numerous. It remains to be seen how this program and others in Texas, Oklahoma, Michigan, Wisconsin, and New York respond to charges of gouging, virtual imprisonment of the elderly by their needy families, and related criticisms.

Day hospitals where older people can go to get medical and social services have existed in Britain for two decades, while in America the idea of daycare centers for the elderly has attracted attention only in the past few years. Generally, day care centers focus on providing social services; however, they are beginning to offer a complete range of facilities paralleling those furnished by institutions themselves. Among the more important elements of alternative services are health maintenance, physical therapy, housekeeping and shopping services, transportation help, meals, and financial and general counseling. Not only are these options financially feasible compared to institutionalization, they are practical in terms of personnel requirements. The biggest obstacle appears to be the bureaucratic red tape in the federal agencies and the bias in favor of institutional services. Rather than viewing institutions and their alternatives as either-or propositions, the two could be made to work in conjunction, so that the elderly might exercise some freedom of choice in deciding which is the more desirable.

One intermediate arrangement containing elements of both institutional and home maintenance is the retirement community or residence organized on a graduated or concentric basis. Normally these programs are designed to provide a minimally sheltered environment for those who are no longer satisfied living in the community but who do not yet require any extensive assistance. Residents either purchase or rent living accommodations and make use of other facilities as they desire. There is an element of risk under the purchase plan, with the result that longevity, treatment, and profits may be indirectly related. As one observer characterizes the plans, the administrators count on a stable death rate — hence sufficient turnover — to meet their mortgage commitments. On the other hand, the residents wish to maximize their investment by living long enough to get a good return on the high entrance fee without running out of money to meet monthly payments (Marshall, 1980b). Usually there are programs for the elderly who prefer to live elsewhere but wish to come to the center during the day for meals or other services. In addition, a team visits the aged person to provide homemaker assistance or to deliver hot meals. For those in need of more help than is practical under independent living arrangements, a second level of care exists where more complete personal attention is given in an intermediate nursing facility, though there is still a full measure of independence. Finally, there is a unit for nonambulatory older people requiring close nursing supervision. The support systems of these facilities are intended to bridge the continuum from guarded independence to long-term care for the frail elderly.

Ideally, the multipurpose daycare centers, outreach programs, congregate or independent living accommodations, and the long-term nursing facilities can offer a total service program in which elderly individuals select only the assistance they desire, feeling as though the choice is indeed theirs to make. Part of the problem with the present state of community services springs from the lack of integration among agencies and the underrepresentation of elderly clients. Community mental health programs, for instance, are less involved with their potential elderly clients than would be indicated in terms of their needs, though it may well be that services enabling the older community resident to remain active at home make up for some of the deficiencies left unaddressed by mental health agencies. Such programs as free transportation, contact with health care facilities, and mediation between the elderly resident and social welfare agencies, landlords, and local governmental bureaucracies have been deemed crucial by community planners. Organizations that facilitate resident involvement in the community also serve the important function of sensitizing other community members to the needs and desires of the elderly who often are an invisible and fragmented sector of the population (Bennett, 1980; Butler et al., 1979–1980).

## Issues of Daily Life

What do the independent elderly do with their days? Do they spend all their time watching television or playing bingo at the local drop-in center? Do they no longer seek out new experiences or the opportunity to learn? Just what is important to someone over the age of sixty-five? When asked what they think about every day, older people say they think about their families, current events, the meaning of their lives — generally what people of all ages think about. One of their other important concerns is crime and the possibility they may be victimized. As they near the end of their lives, do older people think more about religion; are they afraid of dying? The stereotype is that people become more religious as they get older. Is this true, and if so, is it a function of age or historical factors? Actually, like everyone else, the things older people do and think about are those issues closest to their daily lives — age does not bring many changes in that regard.

## LEISURE, DIVERSIONS, AND TIME

Assuming that retirement brings much free time, what do people actually do with this time? Retirement is not simply an event marked by a ceremony, perhaps a token of appreciation, then a trip or some other long-sought respite. At some point retirement implies that a new mosaic of roles comes into being, but most of us have only a vague idea of what this entails. To capture the ambiguities gerontologists have referred to retirement as a *roleless role* (Shanas, 1972; Burgess, 1960). But that implies the shift is discontinuous — that retirement is an either-or proposition — and that work had previously been the central life interest.

Whether working was a primary source of identity, retirement eventually results in unstructured time, time that must be filled one way or another to maintain a social identity. While it may well be a middle-class bias that all time has to be spent in pursuit of something meaningful, most of us do need diversions. The fact that so many elderly in national surveys report they would like to continue working, regardless of financial necessity (*Public Opinion*, 1985), is ample evidence of the need for the structure of the workaday world. What then occupies the elderly after they retire?

**Leisure Pursuits.** Some 80 percent of the older persons in the country spend much time watching television. They are also the most frequent subscribers to daily newspapers, and seem to try to be informed about current events. Reflecting the stage of their family lives, they spend considerable time visiting with friends, which is the leading preference among things to do for a large majority. Television, reading, and visiting all take up about six hours daily. More than half of the elderly take at least one so-called vacation every year. Crafts and hobbies are also important; at least 42 percent of the elderly have such activities that occupy them on a regular basis. Diversions cut across the general spectrum of activities that the entire population engages in, but age groups do not usually participate in the company of one another. For the most part there is a fairly rigid segregation in leisure pursuits because of generational preferences or because of what has been labeled the *portent of embarrassment*; that is, older people avoid situations, as do many of us, when the prospect of less than acceptable performance is likely (Miller, 1965). Perhaps that is why less than 10 percent have been involved in active sports and why the rate of participation declines steadily with age (Bammel and Bammel, 1985). This trend does, however, seems to be reversing as the elderly enroll in fitness programs in greater numbers along with the rest of the population.

**Education.** Another leisure activity for the elderly that has shown remarkable growth over the last decade is education. Over half a million older people are taking classes of some kind. In the years ahead this trend is expected to continue; indeed many educational institutions are counting on it as the lower birth rate lessens the number of younger learners (Hendricks, 1983). As the trend pointed to in Figure 7.6 illustrates, we are all spending an increasing proportion of our time outside of work. While women are not shown in the graph, because of the interrupted character of their work histories in the past, they too face the same expansion of leisure time in their later years. With the general rise in the educational level, future generations of the elderly will be returning to school in ever greater numbers. Since little in the educational background of most workers prepares them for living outside their work roles, the return to education will help enhance the quality of life among the elderly, teach them new or renewed skills, and help them be more active socially (Sterns and Sanders, 1980). The spread of Elderhostel programs in which older learners meet for concentrated short-term courses in specialized areas means that the elderly across the United States, Canada, and abroad are given opportunities to learn. Enrollments have been increasing annually by 20 percent with three-quarters of those who come returning; the mailing list responding to inquiries is currently over 350,000. Two out of three attendees are women; their average age is sixty-eight, and 80 percent have some experience in higher education. In 1983 some 100,000 older people were expected to be students in Elderhostels (Elderhostel, 1985). Many other local opportunities

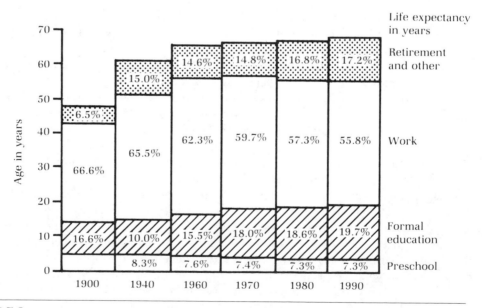

**FIGURE 7.6**
Lifetime distribution of education, work, and leisure for American men, 1900, projected through 1990. (*Source:* Best, F. "The Future of Retirement and Lifetime Distribution of Work." *Aging and Work* 2, 3 [1979]: 174.)

for taking courses exist, from the YMCAs and YWCAs to city-wide recreation departments and extension programs. The expects say the demand and the need are insatiable.

**Friendships.** What becomes readily apparent in looking at recreation and leisure is that ties to other people are common. What people do in their spare time they generally do with others. The opportunity to form these associations can aid in maintaining an optimistic attitude (Ward, 1985).

Intimate friends are a great source of strength, since they provide reference points from which adaptive reformulations of one's self-concept can be forged. By having several friends or a single close friend with whom they can share their thoughts, fears, interests, or objective problems, older people are protected from many of the negative definitions imposed by the larger society and from some of the liabilities growing out of the attrition of their social roles. Peer groups as socializing agents form the basis for the subcultural perspective discussed in Chapter 3; as such, they are influential and highly salutory for all people, the elderly being no exception. For this reason the value of friends is apt to redouble during adult life; at the same time the nature of friendships also changes. As indicated in the previous section, older people's reluctance to move to improved housing stems partly from neighborhood ties based on long-term residency and friendship bonds that are often very deeply rooted. Given the opportunity to relocate, many elderly prefer to stay put because that is where their friends are.

As a personal resource, friends are less significant as long as there are children to raise, jobs to perform, and places to go. Relieved of many full-time family obligations, middle-aged people discover that their friends become a major source of satisfaction. Since friends are usually at a similar point in the family life cycle and have many of the same concerns and interests, there are ample grounds for solid, intimate relationships to take root. With the narrowing of the social life space beginning in late middle age, ties are strengthened; consequently, those most often cited by older people as trusted friends have usually been involved in long-standing relationships carried over from the middle years. Interaction or visiting back and forth is regular, weekly at least, and is apparently unassociated with the frequency of contact among parents and children except among the most disadvantaged. For this latter group, Rosow (1970) reports he and others have found what amounts to an inverse relationship between contact with friends and neighbors on the one hand and children on the other. For those not severely affected by the hardships of age or by the absence of children in the immediate vicinity, however, the two sets of relationships are thought to be largely independent. There is no doubt about the salience of familial bonds; they continue to be the single most important factor in the lives of most elderly. But by themselves family members have a difficult time sustaining morale. Friends also boost morale, and their presence or absence may be an overriding consideration among interpersonal factors contributing to a sense of well-being. Interestingly, the aged almost never turn to their friends for financial assistance; they look only to the family for monetary help, though in the case of illness friends and neighbors are viable substitutes for the family (Rosow, 1970; Blau, 1973).

While friendships are important in sustaining psychological adjustment, it should not be inferred that isolated individuals *necessarily* fare less well. In some cases people who have been isolated all of their lives have been reported as having average or even higher morale and are no more disposed to psychological distress requiring hospitalization. It is mostly those who have tried and failed to make friends or else have lost their intimate ties who are particularly vulnerable to emotional upset. The majority of the elderly have fewer contacts with their friends as they enter the further reaches of old age for reasons not solely attributable to death rates. Some evidence reveals that social networks based on work or marital status are the most susceptible to dissolution, although the middle-class elderly have a greater chance of retaining friends compared to their working-class peers. Not only do they have a larger number of friends, but unlike their less advantaged age mates, they augment older friends with those only recently met. Localized friendships also reflect class patterns; here the working-class elderly are more prone to having a preponderance of friends who are also neighbors. Perhaps as a consequence of their greater sociability, married people more often have intimate friends than nonmarried people, while women feel they have a greater number of friends than do men. In all cases friends resemble one another fairly closely; thus married people's friends are usually married and of the same social class, age, and sex (Babchuck, 1978–1979; Kandel and Heider, 1979; Roberto and Scott, 1984–1985).

So important do these friends become, so vital are they to a sense of well-being, that many residents and age peers often leave legacies to one another, their clubs, and their organizations in their wills (Rosenfeld, 1979). The strength of primary bonds makes for a true sense of community. In her study of Les Floralies, a retirement residence in France, Keith noted that the true emotions of friendship — positive and negative alike — imparted a sense of belonging, of interdependence, and of sociality. In later comparisons with similar settings in the United States she found remarkable parallels in the emergence of personal ties (Keith, 1982).

**Voluntary Participation.** Another mechanism for maintaining personal ties and promoting a sense of worth is through volunteer work. Well over 100 years ago, de Tocqueville graphically described Americans as a nation of joiners. From an analysis of participation rates in six Western democracies, Curtis (1971), however, deems the assumed uniqueness of the American propensity for joining voluntary associations to be overrated. According to his research, approximately half of the American population belongs to various nonunion associations, yet the extent of affiliation in the United States is second to Canada's. In Great Britain and West Germany the number who participate in at least one voluntary organization is roughly 33 percent, followed by Italy at 25 percent and Mexico at 15. Including union membership does not alter the ordering even though the percentages are somewhat higher. The proportion who belong to a multiple number of associations is less of course: 33 percent in both Canada and the United States, 11 percent in Britain, and less than 9 percent in the other countries. Hardly surprising, such factors as sex, social class, marital status, and age are important variables in every instance. Except for the United States and Canada, where men are only slightly more likely than women to join various kinds of nonunion organizations, the rate of membership for men is two to three times that of women. People of higher social class backgrounds and married people claim involvement in voluntary organizations more often. Affiliations according to age approximate a normal curve, reaching a peak in the middle years between thirty-six and fifty, remaining at a plateau until the sixties, and slowly declining thereafter. Recent studies have shown that contrary to expectations older women are remaining active in the later years and both men and women may remain affiliated until their eighties (Babchuck, 1978–1979).

It is difficult to say what proportion of our older population is actually involved in voluntary associations, since most of the studies focusing on this question have been cross-sectional analyses unlikely to include the truly isolated elderly. In addition, most people are cognizant of societal norms endorsing participation in voluntary groups, and in all probability they exaggerate their reported activity. Estimates of participation rates for those in their sixties and beyond vary, ranging from a low of about one-fifth to a high of 70 percent. Although the evidence is scanty, for every three memberships retained, older people apparently cancel two, generally those most closely linked with earlier stages of the life cycle (Smith, 1966). However, among the elderly as among the general citizenry, membership is closely tied to socioeconomic background; hence the more advantaged are represented in disproportionate numbers. Since most organizations are comprised of a small nucleus of the dedicated surrounded by a few regular meeting-goers and a large number of nominal dues-paying members whose commitment is more ideological than concrete, who is active and who is not is a debatable issue.

One of the many paradoxes of voluntary membership is that, socioeconomic and contingent roles notwithstanding, blacks are involved far more extensively than whites or members of any other ethnic group. In their study of voluntary affiliations in Texas, Williams et al. (1973) found that structural variables explained the lower participation of Chicanos and the middle level rates among whites but did little to clarify why blacks are so active. Cuellar (1978) contends, however, that the establishment of the Asociación Nacional Pro Personas Mayores is likely to increase the activity levels of older Chicanos. Basing his conclusions on observations in Los Angeles barrios, Cuellar notes the growing political orientation of both men and women who are active in voluntary associations. In a study of lower income black and white elderly in Philadelphia, church affiliations were found to predominate among the activities of black respondents — followed by social and recreational memberships — but this was not sufficient to explain why so many more elderly blacks remain highly engaged (Hirsch et al., 1972; Clemente et al., 1975). Ad hoc explanations tend to emphasize the compensatory function served by active membership, offsetting those needs unmet by the larger society, but these are seldom generalizable to the elderly of other minority groups.

Regardless of ethnic or racial background, for those who choose to retain active memberships in voluntary associations, the rewards are most beneficial. In many respects there is either an explicit or implicit age grading in the majority of organizations; therefore, older people are brought into close contact with others their age. Out of their interaction, friendships blossom and there is a mutual exchange of information and opinion. As might be expected, those expressing the greatest involvement also derive the highest degree of satisfaction. Voluntary groups furnish one situation that older people can avail themselves of to talk over aspects of their lives not easily discussed with their adult children. They raise consciousness, permitting the elderly to realize they are not alone in their problems nor personally to blame for all their hardships. What will be the picture for voluntary membership in the future? Rising educational levels and socioeconomic improvements may be the foundation for increased activity, while the publicity focused on new roles for the elderly might provide the motivation. For many older people who have an inclination for becoming involved, this is all to the good. It must not be overlooked, however, that it is undesirable to force all elderly into accepting an activity model. Furthermore, the potential for exploiting their willingness to contribute voluntarily to essential social services cannot be ignored.

# Issues for Thought

Older people muse and contemplate as do the rest of us, but are they concerned about the same topics? Yes and no. Some of what they think about results from the particulars of their situation at the end of the life course. Some investigators contend that we become more reflective with age and therefore turn to more philosophical topics. This may be true for some, but actually older people tend to focus on immediate and often pragmatic issues.

## CONCERNS ABOUT CRIME

A great deal of media attention has been directed to the fear of crime and victimization among the elderly. While the statistics do not bear out the presumption that old people are hounded at every corner or in their homes by criminals, the fear persists. As long as older people feel they must alter their daily routines to avoid being victims, the fear is very real. But what do the statistics say? Basically the data indicate there is a decreasing rate of crime among progressively older ages. As is obvious from the general trend shown in Figure 7.7, the elderly are the least likely age category to be victimized. Despite this fact, some 25 percent of the elderly claim crime as an issue of personal concern (see Table 2.1). A closer look at the figures in Table 7.3 reveals some interesting things. First, assuming these figures are correct, while the elderly are

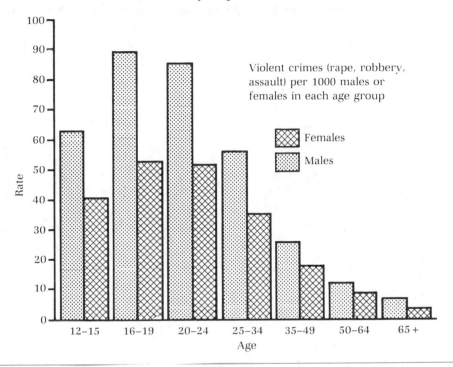

**A National Crime Survey Report**

Violent crimes (rape, robbery, assault) per 1000 males or females in each age group

Females
Males

FIGURE 7.7

Criminal victimization by age. (*Source:* Department of Justice, Bureau of Justice Statistics. *Criminal Victimization in the United States, 1982.* Washington, D.C.: U.S. Government Printing Office, 1984.)

less likely to fall prey to crime, some older persons run higher risks than others because of such factors as sex and race. Informed opinion also suggests place of residence is important. Inner-city elderly are targets as often as the rest of the population in the same locale. Of course, part of the contradiction between the fear of crime and actual victimization might be explained by the fact that some of the elderly are so paralyzed by apprehension they do not venture out as much as they would like. If their concerns curtail involvement in any activity — shopping, transportation, or socialization — it is serious regardless of what the actual rates of victimization might show (Johnson and Williamson, 1980; Lee, 1983; Department of Justice, 1984).

Added to the perceived dangers outside, there is a whole scheme of frauds that plague people in their homes. These frauds are especially pernicious because of the tremendous economic burden facing the victims and their desire to get a hedge against further inflation. Paradoxically, here too the fear is greater than the rate of victimization. The elderly are no more likely to be duped than others; it is just that they have fewer resources upon which they can fall back (Criminal Justice and the Elderly, 1979).

**TABLE 7.3**

Types of Criminal Victimization by Age, Race, and Sex (rate per 1000 population in each age group)

| Race, Sex, and Age | Crimes of Violence | Crimes of Theft |
|---|---|---|
| *White* | | |
| Male | | |
| 12–15 (6,149,000) | 61.1 | 140.1 |
| 16–19 (6,576,000) | 89.3 | 136.0 |
| 20–24 (8,856,000) | 85.9 | 149.4 |
| 25–34 (16,735,000) | 56.0 | 106.8 |
| 35–49 (16,874,000) | 24.3 | 74.0 |
| 50–64 (14,053,000) | 12.1 | 46.3 |
| 65 and over (9,468,000) | 6.9 | 25.3 |
| Female | | |
| 12–15 (5,875,000) | 41.5 | 122.8 |
| 16–19 (6,493,000) | 51.8 | 126.9 |
| 20–24 (9,018,000) | 50.9 | 124.7 |
| 25–34 (16,752,000) | 35.5 | 86.1 |
| 35–49 (17,348,000) | 17.4 | 76.8 |
| 50–64 (15,581,000) | 7.9 | 47.6 |
| 65 and over (13,710,000) | 4.0 | 21.9 |
| | | |
| *Black* | | |
| Male | | |
| 12–15 (1,068,000) | 80.8 | 125.3 |
| 16–19 (1,100,000) | 90.5 | 114.7 |
| 20–24 (1,276,000) | 85.4 | 141.1 |
| 25–34 (2,062,000) | 66.4 | 122.3 |
| 35–49 (1,832,000) | 36.6 | 71.3 |
| 50–64 (1,336,000) | 21.8 | 54.8 |
| 65 and over (849,000) | 14.2[a] | 19.1 |
| Female | | |
| 12–15 (1,065,000) | 37.9 | 105.5 |
| 16–19 (1,153,000) | 62.9 | 99.0 |
| 20–24 (1,485,000) | 61.4 | 68.7 |
| 25–34 (2,487,000) | 39.4 | 105.0 |
| 35–49 (2,266,000) | 18.8 | 58.4 |
| 50–64 (1,699,000) | 11.0 | 56.4 |
| 65 and over (1,285,000) | 9.1[a] | 26.9 |

NOTE: Numbers in parentheses refer to population in the group.
[a]Estimate, based on ten or fewer sample cases, is statistically unreliable.
*Source:* Department of Justice, Bureau of Justice Statistics. *Criminal Victimization in the United States, 1982*, p. 27. Washington, D.C.: U.S. Government Printing Office, 1984.

If the statistics are accurate, why are the elderly so apprehensive? Why is the fear of crime persistently reported as the number one problem confronting those over sixty-five? General displaced anxiety, awareness of physical decline, a sense of vulnerability, and other cohort factors have been cited. In an insightful analysis of fear on the street, Cutler (1979–1980) posits a combination of stress, cohort awareness, and their differential impact in a period when crime in general is more visible. He also notes that as long as fear impedes mobility, the elderly are paying a relatively higher price and therefore deserve special attention.

## THE ROLE OF RELIGION

The main form of voluntary participation is through religious activities. But aside from providing a place to go or a range of volunteer roles, is religion itself a major factor in the lives of the elderly? First, we have to recognize that going to church and being religious are not necessarily the same thing. Next we have to bear in mind the differences between age and cohort effects. The first would suggest that people do become more concerned with spiritual matters over time. The second implies that if people are religious when they are young, they will probably be religious when they become old. If it seems that older persons are more religious than other groups, it may be because during the formative years of their lives, many decades ago, religion was more central in our culture.

Like age grading, religion is a cultural universal. Questions of a true deity aside, all societies associate valued traditions with religious qualities, thereby making them more sacrosanct. In addition, two themes relevant to the spiritual nature of later life are visible in all Judeo-Christian religions. Essential to all creeds is a belief in the existence of an afterlife where humans will be delivered from the trials and tribulations of life on earth. To maximize the potential benefits of that afterlife, people must closely adhere to the teachings of the church. A second universal is a portrayal of the most pious and the most virtuous as gray-haired servants of the word — no matter if they are spiritual entities or earthly elders. In its own way each of these themes has added to the aura of the *religiosity* of old people. In fact, patterns of belief, religious orientation, activity, and the importance of religion remain fairly stable over time (Blazer and Palmore, 1976). Old people who are religious were once young religious people; few dramatic conversions one way or the other take place. This is in contrast to the folklore of aging that has the elderly turning to religion as a solace in dealing with troubles or misfortune.

The results of a nationwide Harris poll (1975) show that more than 70 percent of those over sixty-five, compared to just about half of the younger adults assess religion as "very important" in their lives. While only 3 percent of the elderly claim they have no religious preferences, gerontologists are divided on whether religious interest or activities increase with age and whether religion is beneficial in promoting life satisfaction. Although many studies have shown both increases and better adjustment in the later years, others have found little association between religious involvement and daily functioning. In his review of the literature on both sides of the issue, Moberg (1975) concludes there apparently is a positive connection between adjustment, religious interest, and activities, though it may in turn reflect the presence of other factors. As a result, he is unwilling to draw any causal inferences. In general there does not seem to be any widespread tendency toward greater religiosity with age. Patterns found among today's elderly have either persisted from youth or else indicate broad social currents.

In summarizing the research on religious practices, Moberg (1970) finds that while church-related activities outside the home diminish in the later years, the elderly compensate by reading the Bible more, listening to broadcasts of religious programs, or praying in their own homes. Obviously, practical considerations such as ill-health or lack of transportation cannot be dismissed. Nor can the feelings expressed by some older people that churches are guilty of neglecting them be glossed over. Religious organizations have addressed themselves to the plight of the old for centuries, but few modern clergy have received pastoral training appropriate for dealing with elderly parishioners. One small study in the midwestern United States revealed that less than 30 percent of the ministers had been given specific advice on meeting the needs of older people and that still fewer felt their training was adequate — this in spite of the fact that one-third to one-half of their work is directly tied to older people (Moberg, 1975). Attendance among elderly Jews does not decline, lending additional support for this view, since their religion has traditionally done more for its elderly than most Catholic or Protestant denominations.

Church attendance and religion among older blacks is higher than among whites. Perhaps black churches are more responsive to the needs of their aged members. Cohort differences may also be responsible for the black elderly's feelings of attachment and participation in their religions. Since the black church is also a locus of many social programs beneficial to older people, attendance does not decline until it is impeded by health or transportation difficulties (Heisel and Faulkner, 1982; Guy, 1982; Hirsch et al., 1972). For blacks and for whites most of the evidence is in favor of a correlation between religion and a more abundant sense of life satisfaction. Aside from the spiritual benefits religion has to offer, it seems to lend a sense of emotional security, perhaps through providing an immediately accessible reference group — often lacking for those not closely affiliated with a church. In the face of death, religion seems to infuse its adherents with more positive attitudes as long as they are confident of their own redemption. Yet as Moberg (1975) and others have repeatedly cautioned, adjustment may be the result of other factors, and it is impossible to say if the adjusted simply belong to churches or if belonging to a church promotes adjustment. Either way, an affiliation with an organized religious body is a reliable sign of greater rates of participation in other realms of life.

## ANTICIPATING DEATH

Sooner or later life inevitably terminates. Maybe that is why most of us think it is natural when an old person dies but that death is premature for everyone else. In most hospitals, for example, when the call lights of old and young patients are illuminated, priority is usually given to the young; on the wards and in the emergency room, heroics are first exhibited when the more youthful are in jeopardy (Sudnow, 1967). In the same vein a conspiracy of silence greets the elderly when questions of finality are raised in the company of those younger than themselves, the assumption being that the older one is the more fearful of death he or she becomes. This is another of the myths about age. The conclusion of a large number of studies is the opposite — old people seldom express serious fears about their own demise. In most instances their views are more realistic, accepting the inexorable more easily than those who still see their own natural deaths as far in the future. Despite the tenacity of the assumption that those closest to death are the most fearful, little evidence indicates older people are particularly apprehensive (Sands and Parker, 1979–1980; Kalish, 1985).

It is an enlightening experience to talk with older people about death. In many cases it is a welcome opportunity for them to discuss their feelings and to look back on things in the past to reach a new understanding of themselves. Unfortunately, they are reluctant to raise the issue with younger people, whom the elderly assume are uncomfortable in such a conversation. Before middle age, few people have reason to reflect on their own finality; after all none of life's challenges has yet been insurmountable. Horizons have always receded to reveal ever broader vistas and health has rarely presented much of a problem. With the onset of those physical and social changes that characterize middle age, the mode of *bodily transcendence* that had previously predominated gradually dissipates and, as Erikson points out, people quietly begin reckoning how much time they have left. Parental deaths, which today may be postponed until children are in their forties or even older, bring mortality into personalized relief that becomes increasingly more distinct. Throughout the remainder of life the possibility of death is often a matter of reflection, though not necessarily consternation. As pointed out earlier, after middle age it is less a cause of anxiety than are thoughts of illness and dependency.

There are older people, just as there are people at every age, who seem to worry a great deal about dying; yet age itself is a poor indicator of who is most likely to experience marked death anxiety. As is the case with other psychological adjustments, attitudes toward death will reflect reaction patterns long integral to one's personality. Religious beliefs, higher educational levels, longstanding social relationships, and an overall sense of security also exert an ameliorative influence over whatever anxiety death may potentially induce. The impact of religion must be qualified to a certain extent; to be beneficial, religion must be accompanied by a certainty of salvation, for those who are not free of fears of retribution may not experience any greater calm (Jeffers and Verwoerdt, 1969). Generally, only a small minority of the elderly openly verbalize a heightened sense of fear. Among the factors seemingly characteristic of the most fearful are physical and social isolation, minimal educational levels, or chronic depressive states.

Contrary to popular assumptions, seriously impaired health does not in itself portend feelings of dread or fright. Actually, those who are sick or have long-term ailments may be more accepting — death may be perceived as a welcome relief. What is interpreted as fearfulness perhaps results from the situations in which most people die. Hospitals, where every task is originally intended to preserve life, have become the place where most everyone goes to die. Few people die at home anymore; the vast majority are banished to demoralizing, impersonal wards where their questions are met with silence. As death draws near, the terminal patient is literally avoided, for the priorities lie with those who will live. Physicians visit less frequently and for shorter periods. No wonder the dying are afraid, though it is not death they fear but abandonment, pain, and confusion. What many desire most is someone to talk with, to tell them their life has not been meaningless (Sudnow, 1967; Kubler-Ross, 1969). A general discussion of terminal care would lead too far afield; however, there is much insightful research that carefully addresses this issue. The crucial point here is simply that death is not the cause of many of the fears attributed to it. Innovative terminal care facilities are just beginning to emerge in the United States. Modeled after the long-established St. Christopher's Hospice in London, St. Luke's Hospital in New York and the New Haven Hospice in Connecticut were the first American efforts oriented specifically toward terminal care. Each maintains patients outside the hospital for as long as is practical, and then arranges a transfer to a supportive medical setting where an interdisciplinary team supplies counseling to patients and families along with appropriate medical attention. Early indications are that dying becomes much easier and fears are of little more than passing concern (Kalish, 1985; Kastenbaum, 1985).

## TEMPORAL ORIENTATION

Retirement is a time to think and wonder, to reflect on passages, futures, and how much is left. In many ways temporality is part of the conscious worldview of the elderly. Usually little dissonance is evoked by the prospect of a limited number of tomorrows, but time is fundamental to the self-concepts of the elderly. Locating the self in time is basic to maintaining adjustment across the life course.

In Chapter 4 the idea of entropy was introduced as one way of conceptualizing the physical process of aging. Time is also a basic constituent of the theoretical frameworks proposed by social gerontologists to interpret progressive changes over the life cycle (Fry, 1983). Cumming and Henry's disengagement model is predicated on personal and societal recognition of a foreshortening of the future as the impetus for withdrawal. Empirical forays into subjective perceptions of temporal duration have generally found that the aged are indeed sensitive to the fleeting character of time and how little of it appears to remain. As people age they sense time is somehow speeding up: the past recedes ever more swiftly and the future becomes now all too soon. Yet a paradox exists, for on a personal level *futurity* is foreshortened as individuals age. For some this is a cause for anxiety as they realize all their tomorrows are quickly becoming history; others are content with just being — living one day at a time, with little regard for temporal horizons. This is not to imply, however, that the future cannot be an abstract concept insightfully used as a means of categorizing experience. Within these two dimensions the question becomes: How do older people view time and tomorrow?

A fundamental component of temporal experience is an awareness of a sense of motion. Children probably become cognizant of time as they come to recognize before and after relationships. Gradually they are able to distinguish memory from now and to differentiate anticipations of what is yet to come; by early adolescence most have attained a mature sense of time and are able to conceive of themselves in the future. Futurity for them is a circumscribed reference; they know they are in the process of *becoming*, of moving away from and toward something else, but their future is very near. In a sense it is as if they recollect the future; what is going to happen to them is no more than what has happened, and consequently, their thoughts about the second half of life are nearly barren. Adolescents also seem to "blank out" the past unless asked, giving little thought to what is behind them. The emphasis on future extensions continues to grow until middle age, when most people admit to themselves that they have become whatever it is they are going to be and begin to concentrate on reinforcing their positions. The future is still out there, as the time between now and death, but the "real me" already is (Kastenbaum and Aisenberg, 1972).

Whether from an awareness of the scarcity of time left, the cumulative impact of experiences and memory, or something else, the rate of temporal passage is perceived as if it is speeding up. Experimental studies of time estimation with few exceptions report that successively older respondents consistently underestimate measured time intervals. It should be emphasized, however, that intelligence, socioeconomic status, education, activity levels, and morale have also been found to exercise discrete influences over subjective temporal estimates. Some of these factors themselves may be closely related to advancing age. Aside from various possible physiological explanations, a recurrent theme rests on the value ascribed to time by those doing the judging. As long as older people place greater importance on time than do other respondents, their judgments will tend to reflect a quickened tempo (Kastenbaum, 1983; Wallach and Green, 1968; Cottle and Howard, 1972).

Many people learn early in life to defer gratification, to think of the future. Through at least middle age people can think of the promise of the future as being better than the present, which is in turn an improvement over the past. It encompasses events, goals, and aspirations set and planned for. Although this may not entail an explicitly chronological schedule, having a broad conception of what is to come is helpful, often promoting emotional and practical adjustment. Some researchers have suggested a natural decline in futurity is concomitant with the aging process, and this is the reason so many elderly seem to dwell on the past. To support such a view observers point to the amount of time older people spend reminiscing — perpetuating the past because it is very much brighter than their future prospects or as a way of bringing about a reintegration of their self-concepts and of achieving a degree of self-validation (Merriam, 1980). Besides, the elderly say, what is there to talk about in the future? If it exists at all in a personal sense, it is the counterpart of the adolescent's view — not extending much beyond the near tomorrow and focused primarily on mundane considerations. Actually, close attention to how people respond to temporal considerations should reveal efforts to face what comes next. Restructuring the past may be a necessary preliminary step before turning to face tomorrow. Only those who have settled past experiences and have found the appropriate pigeonholes in which to categorize their memories forget the past and focus more on living out their years. On the practical level of daily life, assisting people to work out and accept their personal time frames is crucial if they are to maintain their social adjustment and personal autonomy (Kastenbaum, 1983).

Time course and time perspective in the lives of the elderly reflect a merging of past and future — organized around topics of immediate concern. The lived time of old age is influenced by the inescapable components of health, well-being, financial status, sociability, and control of resources, all factors that create life rhythms. The underlying theme is a concern with maintaining a continuity of self. Of course, internal physiological processes impose a biological cadence, but temporal cognizance is tinged by intentional concerns, whether these be anxiety-laden or optimistic. As part of the life space of old age, the meaning of time reflects the same composite of factors that affects life satisfaction, morale, and personal evaluations of control (Hendricks, in press).

## Summary

One of the more pervasive myths about old age is that the elderly are abandoned by their families to face life's challenges solely through their own devices. In our look at the social and physical situations of older people in the United States and a few selected countries abroad, little evidence was found to support such a view. On the contrary, a network of extended families appears to be alive and well, if somewhat modified. At least half of all older people appear to be incorporated into three-generational families who live in close proximity. If the staging of family life cycles continues to advance to even earlier ages, there is reason to believe that four-generation networks will become more common as middle-aged people become grandparents. The place of grandparents in family life is invariably tied to cultural traditions, but these too seem to exhibit certain patterns that cut across national boundaries. While fewer older Americans share the same physical living space with their children, like their counterparts abroad, the majority participate in kinship networks providing emotional and material supports to one another. Over 80 percent of the elderly in the United States and in other industrial countries see their children weekly, if not daily, generally living within easy commuting distance of each other.

Older families change their complexion as they move into the later phases of the family life cycle. Living as couples again for the first time in several decades appears to cause some stress, as the divorce rate among middle-aged and older couples has been on the increase in recent years. With widowhood come still further readjustments. Given the differences in life expectancy, the average woman is likely to be widowed for an extensive period. Under the circumstances, it is reasonable to assume that alternative life-styles for the elderly will evolve. What shape these will take cannot yet be forecast with any certainty, but several possibilities, including old age communes, are already gaining attention. As a highly individualized event, the death of a spouse might not appear to result in any predictable consequences. Once again, researchers are finding the avenues to recovery are not nearly as unique as those involved usually believe. Traditions against remarriage for women are gradually lessening, though widowed men have long shown a greater tendency to take another spouse. *But more prospective mates for men.* Without intending to paint too bleak a picture, older women are more likely to become socially isolated, and therefore more dependent on their children, than are men. For the widowed and the elderly in general, families are important in promoting adjustment and satisfaction during the later years.

The picture is not entirely rosy, however. One of the more reprehensible aspects of family relations in later life shows up in the statistics on abuse. Definitional and reporting problems preclude any definitive statements about the abuse of older family members, but dependency and financial burdens appear to exacerbate the strains.

Another dimension of the daily concerns of the elderly often is subsumed under the euphemism of marital relations — or sexuality. One of the stereotypes is that sexual relations cease before the Social Security checks arrive. The facts do not support such a view. There is no decade this side of 100 in which some people do not enjoy sex. On a biological level men undergo more changes than women; yet these are hardly sufficient to interfere with their ability to engage in sex. Probably the greatest constraint for the present generation of elderly women is the lack of socially sanctioned partners, since physiologically menopause has little to do with continued sexuality. With age, both men and women have somewhat slower response cycles, though this is complemented by the appreciation of more varied and thoughtful sexual interaction. While hormone therapy may occasionally be required, without counseling it cannot by itself reestablish satisfactory sexual relations. The lack of privacy encouraged by institutional design is just one indication of the common assumption that older people are entirely sexless.

The housing characteristics of older people in the countries surveyed show some variation in single-family homes as contrasted to congregate living arrangements, with the former predominating in America. In most respects, however, very similar patterns emerge. In all cases the elderly tend to live in older, less desirable accommodations that often present serious maintenance problems. Despite the inconveniences involved, relatively few elderly are willing to move away from neighborhoods they have considered home for an average of twenty-five years. For those who do move, there is often a period of mourning for the lost residence and for all it symbolizes. If the relocation was voluntary, morale usually is better. Confronted by the supposedly cleansing forces of urban renewal, or simply out of a desire to lighten the burdens carried by some of the elderly, upgrading existing housing is an important opportunity for intervention, where real and immediate benefits may be realized if it is handled sensitively.

Almost everyone finds the thought of residing in an institution chilling. Like so many other facets of aging, the probability of institutionalization is little understood. At any given time nearly one and a half million elderly are living in institutions. For those between sixty-five and seventy-five, the probability is less than for those over seventy-five, when the chances increase with each additional year. Even though over 5 percent of the aged are institutionalized on any given day, many move in, some move out, and others die; the population of nursing homes turns over regularly. Life in some homes is neither what it could be nor should be. Federal legislation or local licensing procedures should not be seen as a panacea, for what is really needed is more viable options. At present, efforts are just beginning to be made in this direction, with the establishment of stepwise centers that facilitate a sense of independence, allowing clients to select only those services and assistance they feel they require. In many respects the United States lags behind European countries in offering a full spectrum of social services for the elderly. The American emphasis on self-sufficiency in an age in which no single individual can control all aspects of life has resulted in an underdeveloped and nonintegrated service delivery system stressing remedial measures for problems that might be fairly easily prevented.

Part of the focus in the daily lives of the elderly is on leisure and diversion. Until recently, fewer elderly engaged in very physical leisure pursuits. Though only a minority of older people are involved in education, those who are benefit by friendships, associations, and mental acuity that helps offset the stereotype that older people do not learn easily.

The elderly's extensive concern over victimization stems in part from a fear of physical injury and a loss of self-esteem. While religion is also important, the evidence is mixed about how important it is for people in their later years. There does not appear to be any particular sensitivity to the prospect of their own demise; old people may actually be the most realistic of any of us. Reminiscing is another daily preoccupation the importance of which should not be underestimated as it is invaluable in adjusting temporal orientation and a sense of self.

# Discussion Questions

**Key Questions**

1. What effect do living conditions have on the morale of older people?

**Family Relations in Later Life**

2. Using your knowledge of older members of your own family, what effect might living alone have? Do you consider these older relatives members of your immediate family?

3. What effect did historical conditions or personal factors have on the timing of key events in the family lives of your parents and grandparents?

4. In what ways do you think life review might help people in coming to terms with the inevitability of death and in making better use of the time that is left to them?

5. Design a labor market policy and a retirement policy that would strengthen the position of the elderly within the family.

6. What factors do you see as most crucial in leading to the abuse of the elderly? (Consider possible social structural, economic, cultural, and psychological explanations.) Do you think that psychological or societal factors play the greatest role?

7. What criteria would you use to define abuse of the elderly? (Be sure to consider psychological as well as physical abuse.)

**The Meaning of Sexuality**

8. In what ways do you think sexuality could be a source of anxiety or enhance the lives of the elderly? How central do you think sexuality is or should be throughout life?

**Living Arrangements**

9. Are there any areas in which the elderly are concentrated in your city or state? If so, what has led to this concentration? Would they benefit by moving to a retirement community?

10. How do you think service needs, patterns of service delivery, and the difficulty involved in these would differ in rural and urban areas?

**Congregate Living Facilities**

11. What do you think could be done to improve the quality of life of elderly people who live in nursing homes? Consider

both programs that could be implemented within the existing structure and possible innovations in the structure of nursing home organization. What supplementary or alternative services would you offer? How would these be integrated with nursing home services?

**Issues of Daily Life**

12. Why do you think embarrassment is a factor in the leisure pursuits of the elderly?

**Issues for Thought**

13. Have you ever thought about being in school when you are sixty-five or seventy? How do you feel about it? What factors must change in the educational system for older people to return more often?

14. Doing things with other people provides a real sense of satisfaction. What other reinforcements derive from close friendships and associations?

15. Crime is an issue for everyone: why do old people view it differently?

16. What is meant by age and cohort effects on religion? What will religious involvement in old age look like for your generation? Why?

17. What reasons might underlie different meanings of death at various phases of life? How do your views of death differ from those of your parents or grandparents?

# Pertinent Readings

Aisenberg, R., and J. Treas. "The Family in Late Life: Psychosocial and Demographic Considerations." In *Handbook of the Psychology of Aging,* eds. J. E. Birren and K. W. Schaie, pp. 169–89. New York: Van Nostrand Reinhold Company, 1985.

Atchley, R. C. "Dimensions of Widowhood in Later Life." *The Gerontologist* 15, 2 (1975): 176–78.

Babchuck, N. "Aging and Primary Relations." *International Journal of Aging and Human Development* 9, 2 (1978–1979): 137–51.

Bammel, L. L. B., and G. Bammel. "Leisure and Recreation." In *Handbook of the Psychology of Aging,* eds. J. E. Birren and K. W. Schaie, pp. 848–63. New York: Van Nostrand Reinhold Company, 1985.

Bankoff, E. "Aged Parents and Their Widowed Daughters: A Support Relationship." *Journal of Gerontology* 38, 2 (1983): 226–30.

Bengtson, V. L., and J. Treas. "The Changing Family Context of Mental Health and Aging." In *Handbook of Mental Health and Aging,* eds. J. E. Birren and R. B. Sloane, pp. 400–28. Englewood Cliffs, N.J.: Prentice-Hall, Inc., 1980.

————, N.E. Cutler, D. J. Mangen, and V. W. Marshall. "Aging Generations and Relations Between Age Groups." In *Handbook of Aging and the Social Sciences*, eds. R. Binstock and E. Shanas, pp. 304–38. New York: Van Nostrand Reinhold Company, 1985.

Bennett, R. "Living Conditions and Everyday Needs of the Elderly with Particular Reference to Social Isolation." In *Institutionalization and Alternative Futures*, ed. J. Hendricks, pp. 10–29. Farmingdale, N.Y.: Baywood Publishing Company, 1980.

Bigger, J. C., C. B. Flynn, C. F. Longino, and R. F. Wiseman. "Sunbelt Update: The Migration of the Elderly in 1980." *American Demographics* 6, 12 (December 1984): 22–25, 37.

Blau, Z. S. *Old Age in a Changing Society*. New York: New Viewpoints, a Division of Franklin Watts, Inc., 1973.

Blazer, D., and E. Palmore. "Religion and Aging in a Longitudinal Panel." *The Gerontologist* 16, 1, Pt. 1 (1976): 82–85.

Block, M. R., and J. R. Sinnott. *The Battered Elderly Syndrome: An Exploratory Study*. College Park, Md.: Center on Aging, University of Maryland, 1979.

Bonanno, A., and T. M. Calasanti. "The Political Economy of the Rural Elderly." Paper presented to Midwest Sociological Society, April 1985.

Brody, E. M. *Long-Term Care of Older People*. New York: Human Sciences Press, 1977.

Burgess, E. W. *Aging in Western Societies*. Chicago: University of Chicago Press, 1960.

Butler, R. N. *Why Survive? Being Old in America*. New York: Harper & Row, Publishers, 1975.

————, and M. I. Lewis. *Aging and Mental Health*. St. Louis: The C.V. Mosby Company, 1982.

————, et al. "Self-Care, Self-Help, and the Elderly." *International Journal of Aging and Human Development* 10, 1 (1979–1980): 95–117.

Callahan, J. J., Jr., et al. "Responsibility of Families for their Severely Disabled Elders." *Health Care Financing Review* 1, 3 (1980): 29–48.

Christenson, C. V., and J. H. Gagnon. "Sexual Behavior in a Group of Older Women." *Journal of Gerontology* 20, 3 (1965): 351–56.

Clemente, F., P. A. Rexford, and C. Hirsch. "The Participation of the Black Aged in Voluntary Associations." *Journal of Gerontology* 30, 4 (1975): 469–72.

Clifford, W. B., et al. "The Rural Elderly in Demographic Perspective." In *The Elderly in Rural Society*, eds. R. T. Coward and G. R. Lee, pp. 25–55. New York: Springer Publishing Company, 1985.

Cohler, B. J. "Autonomy and Interdependence in the Family of Adulthood: A Psychological Perspective." *The Gerontologist* 23, 1 (1983): 33–39.

Comfort, A. "Sexuality in Old Age." *Journal of the American Geriatrics Society* 22, 10 (1974): 440–42.

————. "Sexuality in Later Life." In *A Handbook of Mental Health and Aging*, eds. J. E. Birren and R. B. Sloane, pp. 885–92. Englewood Cliffs, N.J.: Prentice-Hall, Inc., 1980.

Cottle, T. J., and P. Howard. "Temporal Differentiation and Undifferentiation." *Journal of Genetic Psychology* 121, 2 (1972): 215–33.

Criminal Justice and the Elderly. "Elderly Duped No More Often, But Harmed More, by Consumer Fraud." *Criminal Justice and the Elderly Newsletter* (Summer 1979): 3.

Cuellar, J. "El Senior Citizens Club." In *Life's Career — Aging*, eds. B. G. Myerhoff and A. Simic, pp. 207–29. Beverly Hills, Calif.: Sage Publications, Inc., 1978.

Curtis, J. "Voluntary Association Joining: A Cross-National Comparative Note." *American Sociological Review* 36, 5 (1971): 872–80.

Cutler, S. J. "Safety on the Streets: Cohort Changes in Fear." *International Journal of Aging and Human Development* 10, 4 (1979–1980): 373–84.

Department of Justice, Bureau of Justice Statistics. *Criminal Victimization in the United States, 1982.* Washington, D.C.: U.S. Government Printing Office, 1984.

Department of Labor, Bureau of Labor Statistics. *Consumer Expenditure Survey: Diary Survey, 1980–81.* No. 2173. Washington, D.C.: U.S. Government Printing Office, 1983.

Dumazedier, J. *Sociology of Leisure.* Amsterdam: Elsevier, 1974.

Elderhostel. *Annual Report, 1984.* Boston: Elderhostel, 1985.

Eustis, N., J. Greenberg, and S. Patton. *Long-Term Care for Older Persons: A Policy Perspective.* Monterey, Calif.: Brooks/Cole Publishing Company, 1984.

Fengler, A. P., and N. Goodrich. "Wives of Elderly Disabled Men: The Hidden Patients." *The Gerontologist* 19, 2 (1979): 175–83.

Ferraro, K. F. "The Health Consequences of Relocation Among Aged in the Community." *Journal of Gerontology* 38, 1 (1983): 90–96.

Fitzpatrick, K. M., and J. R. Logan. "The Aging of the Suburbs 1960–1980." *American Sociological Review* 50, 1 (1985): 106–17.

Flynn, C. B., et al. "The Redistribution of America's Older Population." *The Gerontologist* 25, 3 (1985): 292–296.

Foner, N. *Ages in Conflict.* New York: Academic Press, Inc., 1984.

Fry, C. L. "Temporal and Status Dimensions of Life Cycles." *International Journal of Aging and Human Development* 17, 4 (1983): 281–300.

Giori, D. "Old People, Public Expenditure and the System of Social Services: The Italian Case." In *Old Age and the Welfare State,* ed. A. Guillemard, pp. 187–211. Beverly Hills, Calif.: Sage Publications, Inc. 1983.

Glick, I. O. "Updating the Family Life Cycle." *Journal of Marriage and the Family* 39, 1 (1977): 5–13.

———. "The Future Marital Status and Living Arrangements of the Elderly." *The Gerontologist* 19, 3 (1979): 301–09.

———, R. S. Weiss, and C. M. Parkes. *The First Year of Bereavement.* New York: John Wiley & Sons, Inc., 1974.

Golant, S. M. *A Place to Grow Old: The Meaning of Environment in Old Age.* New York: Columbia University Press, 1984.

Guy, R. F. "Religion, Physical Disabilities, and Life Satisfaction in Older Cohorts." *International Journal of Aging and Human Development* 15, 3 (1982): 225–32.

Hareven, T. *Transitions: The Family and the Life Course in Historical Perspective.* New York: Academic Press, Inc., 1978.

Harris, L., et al. *The Myth and Reality of Aging in America.* Washington, D.C.: The National Council on the Aging, Inc., 1975.

Heisel, M. A., and A. O. Faulkner. "Religiosity in an Older Black Population." *The Gerontologist* 22, 4 (1982): 354–58.

Hendricks, J. "Higher Education's Pursuit of the Lifelong Learner." *Gerontology and Geriatric Education* 3, 4 (1983): 253–58.

———. "Time: Biological, Personal, Social and Historical." In *The Encyclopedia of Aging.* New York: Springer Publishing Company (in press).

Hirsch, C., D. P. Kent, and S. L. Silverman. "Homogeneity and Heterogeneity among Low-Income Negro and White Aged." In *Research Planning and Action for the Elderly: The Power and Potential of Social Science,* eds. D. P. Kent, R. Kastenbaum, and S. Sherwood, pp. 484–500. New York: Behavioral Publications, Inc., 1972.

Huych, M. H. "Sex and the Older Woman." In *Looking Ahead: A Woman's Guide to the*

*Problems and Joys of Growing Older,* eds. L. E. Troll, J. Israel, and K. Israel, pp. 43–58. Englewood Cliffs, N.J.: Prentice-Hall, Inc., 1977.

Jeffers, F. C., and A. Verwoerdt. "How the Old Face Death." In *Behavior and Adaptation in Late Life,* eds. E. W. Busse and E. Pfeiffer, pp. 163–81. Boston: Little, Brown & Company, 1969.

Johnson, E. S., and J. B. Williamson. *The Social Problems of Aging.* New York: Holt, Rinehart and Winston, 1980.

Kahana, E. "A Congruence Model of Person-Environment Interaction." In *Aging and the Environment: Theoretical Approaches,* eds. M. P. Lawton, P. G. Windley, and T. O. Byerts, pp. 97–121. New York: Springer Publishing Company, 1982.

Kalish, R. A. "The Social Context of Death and Dying." In *Handbook of Aging and the Social Sciences,* eds. R. Binstock and E. Shanas, pp. 149–70. New York: Van Nostrand Reinhold Company, 1985.

Kandel, R. F., and M. Heider. "Friendship and Factionalism in a Triethnic Housing Complex for the Elderly in North Miami." *Anthropological Quarterly* 52, 1 (1979): 49–59.

Kart, C. S. *The Realities of Aging.* Boston: Allyn & Bacon, Inc., 1985.

Kasl, S. V., and S. Rosonfield. "The Residential Environment and Its Impact on the Mental Health of the Aged." In *Handbook of Mental Health and Aging,* eds. J. E. Birren and R. B. Sloane, pp. 468–95. Englewood Cliffs, N.J.: Prentice-Hall, Inc., 1980.

Kastenbaum, R. "Time Course and Time Perspective in Later Life." In *Annual Review of Gerontology and Geriatrics,* ed. C. Eisdorfer pp. 80–102. New York: Springer Publishing Company, 1983.

————. "Death and Dying: A Life-Span Approach." In *Handbook of the Psychology of Aging,* eds. J. E. Birren and K. W. Schaie, pp. 619–43. New York: Van Nostrand Reinhold Company, 1985.

————, and R. Aisenberg. *The Psychology of Death.* New York: Springer Publishing Company, Inc., 1972.

————, and S. E. Candy. "The 4% Fallacy: A Methodological and Empirical Critique of Extended Care Facility Population Statistics." *Aging and Human Development* 4, 1 (1973): 15–21.

Kent, S. "Impotence: The Facts Versus the Fallacies." *Geriatrics* 30, 4 (1975): 164–69.

Keith, J. *Old People as People: Social and Cultural Influences on Aging and Old Age.* Boston: Little, Brown & Company, 1982.

King, N. R. "Exploitation and Abuse of Older Family Members: An Overview of the Problem." In *Abuse of the Elderly,* ed. J. J. Costa, pp. 3–12. Lexington, Mass.: Lexington Books, 1984.

Kinsey, A. C., et al. *Sexual Behavior in the Human Female.* Philadelphia: W. B. Saunders Company, 1953.

Kivett, V. R. "Consanguinity and Kin Level: Their Relative Importance to the Helping Network of Older Adults." *Journal of Gerontology* 40, 2 (1985): 228–34.

Koff, T. H. *Long-Term Care: An Approach to Serving the Frail Elderly.* Boston: Little, Brown & Company, 1982.

Kosberg, J. ed. *Abuse and Maltreatment of the Elderly.* Boston: Wright PSG, 1983.

Kubler-Ross, E., *On Death and Dying.* New York: Macmillan, Inc., 1969.

Lacy, W. B., and J. Hendricks. "Developmental Models of Adult Life: Myth or Reality." *International Journal of Aging and Human Development* 11, 2 (1980): 89–110.

Larson, R., J. Zuzanek, and R. Mannell. "Being Alone Versus Being With People: Disengagement in the Daily Experience of Older Adults." *Journal of Gerontology* 40, 3 (1985): 375–81.

Laslett, P. *The World We Have Lost Further Explored.* New York: Charles Scribner's Sons, 1984.

————. "Societal Development and Aging." In *Handbook of Aging and the Social Sciences,* eds. R. Binstock and E. Shanas, pp. 199–230. New York: Van Nostrand Reinhold Company, 1985.

Lau, E. E., and J. I. Kosberg. "Abuse of the Elderly by Informal Care Providers." *Aging* 299–300 (1979): 10–15.

Lawton, M. P. "The Impact of Environment on Aging and Behavior." In *Handbook of the Psychology of Aging,* eds. J. E. Birren and K. W. Schaie, pp. 276–301. New York: Van Nostrand Reinhold Company, 1977.

————. *Environment and Aging.* Monterey, Calif.: Brooks/Cole Publishing Company, 1980.

————. "Housing and Living Environments of Older People." In *Handbook of Aging and the Social Sciences,* eds. R. Binstock and E. Shanas, pp. 450–78. New York: Van Nostrand Reinhold Company, 1985.

Lee, G. R. "Social Integration and Fear of Crime Among Older Persons." *Journal of Gerontology* 38, 6 (1983): 745–50.

Lesnoff-Caravaglia, G. "Service Provision in the Soviet Bloc: Bulgaria and the USSR Contrasted." *Ageing International* 10, 4 (1984): 17–18.

Longino, C. F., Jr., "Migration Winners and Losers." *American Demographics* 6, 12 (December 1984): 27–29, 45.

————, K. McClelland, and W. Peterson. "The Aged Subculture Hypothesis: Social Integration, Gerontophilia and Self-Conception." *Journal of Gerontology* 35, 5 (1980): 758–67.

Lopata, H. Z. *Women as Widows: Support Systems.* New York: Elsevier, 1979.

Marshall, V. W. "Socialization for Impending Death in a Retirement Village." *American Journal of Sociology* 80, 5 (1975): 1124–44.

————. *Last Chapters: A Sociology of Death and Dying.* Monterey, Calif.: Brooks/Cole Publishing Company, 1980a.

————. "Game-Analyzable Dilemmas in a Retirement Village: A Case Study." In *Institutionalization and Alternative Futures,* ed. J. Hendricks, pp. 146–52. Farmingdale, N.Y.: Baywood Publishing Company, 1980b.

Masters, W. H., and V. E. Johnson. *Human Sexual Response.* Boston: Little, Brown & Company, 1966.

————. *Human Sexual Inadequacy.* Boston: Little, Brown & Company, 1970.

Matthews, S. H. *The Social World of Older Women: Management of Self-Identity.* Beverly Hills, Calif.: Sage Publications, Inc., 1978.

Merriam, S. "The Concept and Function of Reminiscence: A Review of the Research." *The Gerontologist* 20, 5 (1980): 604–09.

Miller, S. J. "The Social Dilemma of the Aging Leisure Participant." In *Older People and Their Social World,* eds. A. Rose and W. Peterson, pp. 77–92. Philadelphia: F. A. Davis Company, 1965.

Moberg, D. "Religion in the Later Years." In *The Daily Needs and Interests of Older People,* ed. A. M. Hoffman, pp. 175–91. Springfield, Ill.: Charles C Thomas, Publisher, 1970.

————. "Needs Felt by the Clergy for Ministries to the Aging." *The Gerontologist* 15, 2 (1975): 170–75.

Moon, M. "The Role of the Family in the Economic Well-Being of the Elderly." *The Gerontologist* 23, 1 (1983): 45–50.

Moos, R. H., and S. Lemke. "Assessing the Physical and Architectural Features of Sheltered Care Settings." *Journal of Gerontology* 35, 4 (1980): 571–83.

Mutran, E. "Integenerational Family Support Among Blacks and Whites: Response to Culture or to Socioeconomic Differences." *Journal of Gerontology* 40, 3 (1985): 382–89.

———, and D. C. Reitzes. "Intergenerational Support Activities and Well-Being Among the Elderly: A Convergence of Exchange and Symbolic Interaction Perspectives." *American Sociological Review* 49, 1 (1984): 117–30.

National Council on Aging. *America in the 80s: America in Transition.* Washington, D.C.: Louis Harris and Association, Inc., National Council on Aging, 1981.

National Institute on Aging. *Aging and the Family.* Washington, D.C.: U.S. Government Printing Office, 1981.

Neugarten, B., and K. Weinstein. "The Changing American Grandparent." *Journal of Marriage and the Family* 26 (1964): 199–204.

Newman, G., and C. R. Nichols. "Sexual Activities and Attitudes in Older Persons." In *Normal Aging,* ed. E. Palmore, pp. 277–81. Durham, N.C.: Duke University Press, 1970.

Neysmith, S. M., and J. Edwardh. "Dependency and Third World Elderly." *Ageing and Society* 4, 1 (1984): 21–44.

Nydegger, C. N. "Family Ties of the Aged in Cross-Cultural Perspective." *The Gerontologist* 23, 1 (1983): 26–32.

O'Laughlin, K. "The Final Challenge: Facing Death." In *Older Women,* ed. E. W. Markson, pp. 275–96. Lexington, Mass.: Lexington Books, 1983.

Pedrick-Cornell, C., and R. J. Gelles. "Elder Abuse: The Status of Current Knowledge." *Family Relations* 31, 4 (1982): 457–65.

Pfeiffer, E. "Sexuality and Aging." In *Clinical Geriatrics,* ed. I. Rossman, pp. 568–75. Philadelphia: J. B. Lippincott Company, 1979.

———, A. Verwoerdt, and H. S. Wang. "Sexual Behavior in Aged Men and Women." In *Normal Aging,* ed. E. Palmore, pp. 299–303. Durham, N.C.: Duke University Press, 1970.

Porket, J. L. "Income Maintenance for the Soviet Aged." *Ageing and Society* 3, 3 (1983): 301–23.

Public Opinion. "Opinion Roundup — America Through the Ages: Studying the Elderly." *Public Opinion* 8, 1 (1985): 30–35.

Quadagno, J. S. *Aging in Early Industrial Society.* New York: Academic Press, Inc., 1982.

Roberto, K. A., and J. P. Scott. "Friendship Patterns Among Older Women." *International Journal of Aging and Human Development* 19, 1 (1984–1985): 1–10.

Rosenfeld, A. H. *New Views on Older Lives.* Washington, D.C.: U.S. Government Printing Office, 1978.

Rosenfeld, J. P. "Bequests from Resident to Resident: Inheritance in a Retirement Community." *The Gerontologist* 19, 6 (1979): 594–600.

Rosenmayr, L. "Changing Values and Positions of Aging in Western Culture." In *Handbook of the Psychology of Aging,* eds. J. E. Birren and K. W. Schaie, pp. 190–215. New York: Van Nostrand Reinhold Company, 1985.

———. "The Family-A Source of Hope for the Elderly of the Future." In *Older People, Family and Bureaucracy,* eds. E. Shanas and M. B. Sussman, pp. 132–57. Durham: N.C.: Duke University Press, 1977.

Rosow, I. "Old People: Their Friends and Neighbors." In *Aging in Contemporary Society,* ed. E. Shanas, pp. 57–67. Beverly Hills, Calif.: Sage Publications, Inc., 1970.

Rowles, G., and R. J. Ohta, eds. *Aging and Mileau: Environmental Perspectives on Growing Old.* New York: Academic Press, Inc., 1985.

Sands, J. D., and J. Parker. "A Cross-Sectional Study of the Perceived Stressfulness of Several Life Events." *International Journal of Aging and Human Development* 10, 4 (1979–1980): 335–41.

Scheidt, R. J., and P. G. Windley. "The Ecology of Aging." In *Handbook of the Psychology of Aging,* eds. J. E. Birren and K. W. Schaie, pp. 245–58. New York: Van Nostrand Reinhold Company, 1985.

Select Committee on Aging, U.S. House of Representatives. *Elder Abuse.* Washington, D.C.: U.S. Government Printing Office, 1979.

Smith, J. "The Narrowing of Social Life Space." In *Social Aspects of Aging,* eds. I. H. Simpson and J. C. McKinney, pp. 226–42. Durham, N.C.: Duke University Press, 1966.

Seltzer, M. M. "The Older Woman: Facts, Fantasies and Fiction." *Research on Aging* 1, 2 (1979): 139–54.

Shanas, E. "Measuring the Home Health Needs of the Aged in Five Countries." *Journal of Gerontology* 26, 1 (1971): 37–40.

———. "Adjustment to Retirement: Substitution or Accommodation." In *Retirement,* ed. F. Carp, pp. 219–44. New York: Behavioral Publications, 1972.

———. "The Family as a Social Support System in Old Age." *The Gerontologist* 19, 2 (1979): 169–74.

———, et al. *Old People in Three Industrial Societies.* New York: Atherton Press, 1968.

Solnick, R. L., and N. Corby. "Human Sexuality and Aging." In *Aging: Scientific Perspective and Social Issues,* eds. D. S. Woodruff and J. E. Birren, pp. 202–24. Monterey, Calif.: Brooks/Cole Publishing Company, 1983.

Special Committee on Aging, U.S. Senate. "Heinz Says First DRG Study Flags Potential Hazards for Older Americans." *News* (February 25, 1985).

Spilerman, S., and E. Litwak. "Reward Structures and Organizational Design: An Analysis of Institutions for the Elderly." *Research on Aging* 4, 1 (1982): 43–70.

Starr, B. D., and M. B. Weiner. *The Starr-Weiner Report on Sex and Sexuality in the Mature Years.* New York: Stein & Day Publishers, 1981.

Sterns, H. L., and R. E. Sanders. "Training and Education of the Elderly." In *Life-Span Developmental Psychology: Intervention,* eds. R. R. Turner and H. W. Reese, pp. 307–30. New York: Academic Press, Inc., 1980.

Stein, S., M. W. Linn, and E. M. Stein. "Patients' Anticipation of Stress in Nursing Home Care." *The Gerontologist* 25, 1 (1985): 88–94.

Steinmetz, S. K. "Battered Parents." *Society* 15, 15 (1978): 54–55.

———, and G. Amsden. "Dependent Elderly, Family Stress and Abuse." In *Family Relations in Later Life,* ed. T. Brubaker, pp. 173–92. Beverly Hills, Calif.: Sage Publications, Inc., 1983.

Straus, M. A., R. J. Gelles, and S. K. Steinmetz. *Behind Closed Doors: Violence in the American Family.* New York: Anchor Books, 1980.

Streib, G. F. "Social Stratification and Aging." In *Handbook of Aging and the Social Sciences,* eds. R. Binstock and E. Shanas, pp. 339–68. New York: Van Nostrand Reinhold Company, 1985.

Sudnow, D. *Passing On.* Englewood Cliffs, N.J.: Prentice-Hall, Inc., 1967.

Sussman, M. B. "The Family Life of Old People." In *Handbook of Aging and the Social Sciences,* eds. R. Binstock and E. Shanas, pp. 415–49. New York: Van Nostrand Reinhold Company, 1985.

Townsend, C. *Old Age: The Last Segregation.* New York: Bantam Books, 1971.

Troll, L., S. Miller, and R. Atchley. *Families in Later Life*. Belmont, Calif.: Wadsworth Publishing Company, 1979.

U.S. Bureau of the Census. *America in Transition: An Aging Society*. Current Population Reports, Series P-23, No. 128. Washington, D.C.: U.S. Government Printing Office, 1983.

————. *Demographic and Socioeconomic Aspects of Aging in the United States*. Current Population Reports, Series P-23, No. 138. Washington, D.C.: U.S. Government Printing Office, 1984.

Walker, A. "Social Policy and Elderly People in Great Britain: The Construction of Dependent Social and Economic Status in Old Age." In *Old Age and the Welfare State*, ed. A. Guillemard, pp. 143–67. Beverly Hills, Calif.: Sage Publications, Inc., 1983.

Wallach, M. A., and L. R. Green. "On Age and the Subjective Speed of Time." In *Middle Age and Aging*, ed. B. Neugarten, pp. 481–85. Chicago: The University of Chicago Press, 1968.

Ward, R. A. *The Aging Experience*. New York: Harper & Row, Publishers, 1984.

————. "Informal Networks and Well-Being in Later Life: A Research Agenda." *The Gerontologist* 25, 1 (1985): 55–61.

Williams, J. A., N. Babchuck, and D. R. Johnson. "Voluntary Associations and Minority Status: A Comparative Analysis of Anglo, Black and Mexican Americans." *American Sociological Review* 38, 5 (1973): 637–46.

# PART THREE

# AGING IN SOCIAL CONTEXT: SOCIAL POLICY, STRUCTURAL FACTORS, AND THE AGING

# 8

# WORK, FINANCES, AND THE GOLDEN YEARS

**WORK AND AGING IN MASS SOCIETY**
Changes in the Economy, Labor
    Patterns, and Retirement
Two Perspectives on Work and
    Retirement
    *Individual Approach*
    *Structural Approach*

**WORK PATTERNS AND THE LIFE CYCLE**
Social Construction of Careers
Models of Career Development
    *Sociologically Oriented Models*
    *Psychologically Oriented Models*
    *Social Meaning of Careers*

**THE MEANING OF WORK**
Worker Stereotypes
Status Displacement
Age Discrimination
Work and Self-Image
Anticipating Retirement
    *Individual-Level Explanations*
    *Structural Explanations*

**WORKING AROUND THE WORLD**
Trends in Western Countries
Countries in Transition:
    Japan and the Soviet Union
Working Women
Minorities and the Labor Market

**FINANCES IN THE LATER YEARS**
Income during the Golden Years
    *Indicators of Income*
    *Income Patterns during the Golden
        Years*
    *Income Satisfaction*
Expenditures during the Golden Years
    *Minority Finances in the Golden Years*

**SUMMARY**

**DISCUSSION QUESTIONS**

**PERTINENT READINGS**

In the midst of the debate over national deficits, budgets, domestic programs, and national defense many have suggested that government transfer programs for the elderly be reduced. As will be seen in Chapter 11, social policies reflect political decisions as much as ameliorative concerns. While some say the elderly themselves or their families should take greater responsibility for financial support, others claim such a view amounts to little more than blaming the victim for the problems encountered after a lifetime of work. To understand the issue it is necessary to have a grasp of how the elderly got to be in the position that characterizes retirement today.

This chapter examines patterns of work and their financial implications for aging. Particular attention will be paid to the meaning of the individual's position vis-à-vis social structures for patterns of work and retirement. Thus, we will consider work and retirement in different countries, in different segments of the economy, and how women's work experiences differ from that of men. We shall also explore the implications of attitudes toward older workers and retirement in advanced industrial societies. In many respects the normative properties of life events stemming from the social organization of the work world provide the pattern by which the sequence of roles and associated activities unfold. If we are to make sense of adult development and aging, we must examine all sides of the issue. Work and careers are what occupy most people throughout their lives and must therefore be included (Abeles et al., 1980; Kohli et al., 1983).

# Work and Aging in Mass Society

## CHANGES IN THE ECONOMY, LABOR PATTERNS, AND RETIREMENT

Today all segments of the work force have become aware of the instability of national economies, inflation, and the precarious interdependence of world powers. Particularly relevant to older workers nearing retirement is the necessity of extending savings, pensions, and Social Security benefits during times of financial insecurity, confronted as they are by lengthening life expectancies and increasingly higher costs of living. Many economic problems once considered peculiarly the province of the aged are now recognized as facets of the everyday world of middle-aged and younger workers. Labor market fluctuations have become crucial for younger workers, as well as for those nearing retirement. It is not simply those who lack any or specific skills who are affected by economic ills. Coupled with the traditional exclusion of workers with outdated skills or knowledge is the increasing focus on professional and white-collar bureaucratization of the labor force. This change in the occupational structure of the United States is occurring throughout the Western industrialized world. The occupational histories of workers nearing retirement today do not mirror the structural changes being identified. However, workers in their middle years show marked differences in their occupational histories from the older workers. Such differences will have a discernible impact on the nature of work and retirement among those who will be elderly at the turn of the century.

Compulsory retirement programs not only encompass the majority of all workers but they also have had a notable impact on the shifting structure of the labor force. Most people assume retirement to be the special concern of those over sixty and, as a result, many find they have labored under mistaken or clouded perceptions of the hard realities. Almost without exception, everyone subscribes to and works for financial security that will furnish today's essentials as well as tomorrow's cushion. The question of course is how many ever realize this dream? What are the changing criteria for its achievement? Yet we must also consider the importance work has for those presently middle-aged; only recently has there been the possibility that endeavors other than work may become the central focus in our lives. Accordingly, this chapter addresses itself to work-related events as they affect the lives of middle-aged and older workers and the potential for the dynamic interplay among participants in the labor force.

The impact of technology on industrialized societies may be seen clearly in the character of work and leisure within society. In the early 1970s economists forecast the lowering of compulsory retirement age, the decline in number of days worked per week or weeks per year with full and constant growth in productivity (Kreps, 1976). Although fluctuations in the economic and labor spheres have made observers cautious about making predictions, some have been made and countered. The U.S. Department of Labor classifies full-time workers as those persons employed thirty-five hours or more each week. There has been an increase in demands during the past decade among labor unions and other employee advocate groups for shorter workweeks and longer vacation times, several of which are turned down because the expectations of society run high; think, for example, of the postal workers' and management sponsorship of the elimination of Saturday mail delivery. Most workers can plan on spending approximately 240 days a year on the job. Though the work rate among older citizens is declining, the average workweek remains at forty-one hours, not appreciably different from 1940 (Schulz, 1980). Estimates that the workweek would decline by several hours may have been off because younger workers are aware that retirement will enforce leisure time and provide economic disincentives to continued labor force participation. Workers postpone leisure time and pursuits and substitute work at younger ages (Burk-hauser and Tolley, 1978). Nonetheless, if workers spend twelve hours a day eating and resting, only 42 percent of their time is devoted to work. The re-mainder is available for other pursuits (Clague, 1971). On the surface, most people might seem to be well prepared for the enforced leisure of their retire-ment years. That this is a more complex issue than might first be thought will become clear.

## TWO PERSPECTIVES ON WORK AND RETIREMENT

In attempting to provide an explanatory framework for making sense of an in-dividual's work and retirement patterns, gerontologists use two alternative frameworks. To date, the dominant paradigm in social gerontology has been one that sees individuals and their personal attributes as the appropriate unit of analysis in nearly all aging research. In recent years there have been in-creasing calls for an alternative model that concentrates instead on normative structural arrangements. The status attainment model, as the older of the two perspectives is called, looks primarily at **human capital** variables, those in-dividual characteristics that people accumulate over their lives.

**Individual Approach.** A close look at retirement satisfaction and adjust-ment research from the individualist approach shows it to be marked by three distinct yet interrelated foci. First, considerable attention has been directed to evaluating the relative psychological and social status of retirees. The corpus of research relating retirement to such issues as life satisfaction, morale, alien-ation, and psychological functioning is indeed large and often adopts some type of a generalized social stratification model as an explanatory framework (Henretta and Campbell, 1976; Streib and Schneider, 1971). The second pri-mary focus deals more explicitly with the nature of financial status in the pre- and postretirement years. Here, too, a similar inventory of topical areas, plus such things as health, interpersonal relationships, attitudes, and so on, are all related directly to financial adequacy (Barfield and Morgan, 1978; Herzog, 1978). Finally, in recent years there has been a growing concern with inter-vention strategies. In this regard there have been calls to extend pension cov-erage and preretirement planning programs and to change Social Security programs to promote a better foundation on which to base adjustment in later life (Kreps, 1979; Viscusi, 1979). On both sides of the Atlantic, social scientists have centered the principal thrust of their research efforts on these topics (Atchley, 1976).

In studies of psychological well-being, life satisfaction, morale, and so on, dilemmas of the retired in general are linked to problems of individual re-sources. In nearly all instances the relative decline in financial resources, abetted by personal attitudes toward retirement, is the foundation on which the research is based (Beck, 1982). Implicitly, one consequence of these re-search endeavors has been an overemphasis on a functional conception of social roles and statuses. Such a statement is not meant to imply a conscious desire on the part of either scholars or government officials to maintain prevailing social conditions. Rather, it means that gerontologists take existing structural factors as givens rather than as socially created and therefore malleable. By relying on status attainment variables only we define not only the nature of the *problem* but also circumscribe acceptable solutions.

As long as research strategies continue to look only at the personal attributes of the individual worker or retiree, explaining differential rewards and opportunity structures for similar investments will remain problematic. The existence of an invisible hand shuffling the labor force according to abilities can no longer be assumed, much as Adam Smith might have wished it. Widespread incongruities imply other factors may also be influencing the "return" on given individual characteristics.

**Structural Approach.** Of late a number of studies have challenged the traditional explanatory model. Among these challenges is one characterized variously under such terms as "structuralism," the "new structuralism," or "dual economy" perspectives. While there are a number of important differences between them, generally these models stress that human capital variables, including education, skill, or age, operate within the context of a segmentalized industrial order that demarcates the lives of individual workers or retirees independently of personal attributes. For example, despite striking similarities in a number of human capital dimensions — general education, vocational training, tenure with current employer, attachment to the labor force, and so on — male and female workers reveal marked disparities in reward structures (Bibb and Form, 1977). Black women earn substantially less than white women even when all possible human capital variables are controlled (Treiman and Terell, 1975). A differential may be observed among various sectors of the economy based on a worker's place in the productive sectors and the competition and command of core resources within each market. Thus, workers in primary markets will receive relatively more of the fruits of production than workers in peripheral markets. Seemingly, comparable investments in human capital attributes will not, in and of themselves, level differentials in returns on those investments (Beck et al., 1978).

An uncritical acceptance of later life problems as a result of retirement per se or as the consequence of differences in human capital would be misleading (Phillipson, 1982; Friedman and Orbach, 1974). As Walker (1980) reminds us, an analysis of the social and economic situation of the elderly must be set in the larger "context of the prevailing social and economic structure and values." In other words, the economic situation of older people, as well as its correlates, is not solely the result of personal investments in human capital, individual choice, or initiative. Rather, retirement benefits and experiences may also be a consequence of structural impositions resulting from the location in one or the other principal economic sectors. Occupational history, location of employment, and mobility each shape social relations before and after retirement. To understand more fully how personal adjustment ensues we must look at all relevant factors and explore possible connections that create the need for and the ability to adjust.

Neither the individualist nor the structural approach is sufficient in itself to explain the diverse phenomena of work and retirement; each must complement the other. In the following descriptions of factors evolving out of the world of work it is important to remember how interpretative models are used in data collection and analysis.

# Work Patterns and the Life Cycle

## SOCIAL CONSTRUCTION OF CAREERS

To consider fully the lives of older workers we must examine career patterns. Much previous research has been focused on the features of occupational careers, from both psychological and sociological perspectives. In either case several factors repeatedly surface in the literature dealing with work and occupations. The classic definition of *career* was offered by Wilensky (1961): an orderly succession of related jobs arranged in a hierarchy of prestige through which individuals move in more or less patterned sequences. Careers are embedded in an institutional framework, so that the organization of the workplace and the differential system of rewards for productivity and mobility are particularly important. Mobility may be either vertical (upward or downward in social rank) or horizontal (involving a change in function without a change in reward, such as a delivery person becoming a salesperson or a clerk becoming a receptionist).

The meaning attached by workers to their occupations, their attitudes, and their commitment appears to contribute to the shape of career patterns. Factors influencing careers are both individual and situational; neither can be understood in isolation. It is true, however, that the segmented labor markets in highly industrialized countries produce distinct differences in workers' abilities to command and garner resources and to participate in health and retirement benefits (Dowd, 1980). While a worker's expectations are important in defining activity and future direction, his or her place in the labor market is critical in determining the range to which such expectations and efforts will be confined.

Depending on where a worker is employed, both in terms of the sector of the economy and the type of industry or occupation, career trajectories will differ significantly. The orderly progression of job assignments implicit in the definition of a career assumes occupational structures remain fairly stable and that cohort factors are not relevant. In reality the pace of social change causes occupational skills to become quickly outmoded. The nature of work is changing rapidly partly because of the accelerating pace of technological innovation and shifting age pyramids. Each has an impact on opportunities for advancement and job shifts. Careers have been the mechanism by which socially structured transitions are given meaning by individuals and studied by the social sciences. The meaning structure used to interpret life, even the notions of the progression toward retirement and life scripts, entails implicit career trajectories.

## MODELS OF CAREER DEVELOPMENT

**Sociologically Oriented Models.** One of the earliest developmental models in the study of careers was the "trait-factor" theory, which assumed a matching process took place between an individual's specific abilities and certain vocational opportunities. Many variations of this approach have been articulated, the basic assumption of all the models being that occupational choice reflects personality traits. Partly in response to this trend a sociological paradigm was offered that posited occupational selection as beyond the immediate control of an individual (Osipow, 1968). One of the early studies of occupations in the United States found that the majority of workers sampled showed little upward mobility; among lower status occupations a significant proportion of children had followed in their fathers' footsteps, while the reverse was observed for those of higher status. For both groups, jobs held during the time when the worker was finishing his or her education and working a variety of odd jobs were seemingly prophetic of subsequent career developments (Davidson and Anderson, 1937). A decade later another study of work histories led to the description of several typical career patterns, each of which was based on a succession of five work stages: the preparatory, initial, trial, stable, and retirement stages. The preparatory stage consists of all behaviors leading up to selecting the first job. During the initial stage workers are pursuing their education and hold a series of temporary jobs. For three years or so after completing their education many workers continue to look around for other jobs, but during this trial stage they move toward their ultimate choice. The stable stage is the selection of a long-term occupation, although workers do not necessarily stick with one job, as is illustrated by people in the professional and white-collar jobs who change jobs but not occupations. The final stage is retirement, that period after individuals leave their usual full-time occupations (Miller and Form, 1951).

Gusfield (1961) has promoted a similar developmental model of career stages. In his scheme three phases of career growth are linked to two distinctive career shapes. The phases, paralleling those of Miller and Form, are the trial, stable and established career phases. From these Gusfield develops the directed and undirected career shapes. The directed career is stable and focused, established either immediately or through gradual development. This pattern is represented most commonly by professional and white-collar workers. Blue-collar workers, on the other hand, more often demonstrate the undirected career, which is characterized by lack of commitment, frequent change, and impermanence. These career shapes may reflect the differential placement of workers in the labor markets. Within the larger category of blue-collar jobs we find both employees who participate in highly organized and competitive industries and those who work in peripheral industries that are neither organized nor highly paid. The development of workers' careers is certainly influenced by the positions their jobs occupy in the productive spheres.

**Psychologically Oriented Models.** A model that places more emphasis on psychological factors was proposed by Super (1957). Super contends that basically an occupation is selected because of its potential for self-expression. While factors external to the individual determine the exact manner of expression, particular vocational behaviors reflect the individual's stage of life development, with self-concept becoming more stable as vocational activities also become stabilized. Four career patterns are assumed. These include the stable pattern (where an occupation is entered early and permanently), the conventional pattern (where several jobs are tried, one of which leads to a stable job), the unstable pattern (where a person holds a series of trial jobs that may lead to temporary stability followed by disruption), and a multiple trial pattern (where an individual pursues several relatively stable jobs). The shape of a worker's career is determined by "vocational maturity," defined by Super as the worker acquiring appropriate attitudes and displaying suitable behavior for his or her life stage.

In the stable model, Super (1957) outlined successive stages of *crystallization, specification, implementation, stabilization,* and *consolidation.* Phase one and two normally take place during the search for possibilities and suitability of the teenage years. Phase three is thought to occupy people in their early twenties, while phase four begins by the mid-twenties. By the mid-thirties the consolidation period has begun and will characterize the remainder of working life. Having moved through such an orderly sequence, people are thought to arrive at the threshold of retirement after a long, gradual movement upward in their chosen profession or occupation.

**Social Meaning of Careers.** These models are important to bear in mind during the following discussion of work and preparation for retirement. We might anticipate that attitudes toward and the eventual adjustment to retirement or demand for continued work will be conditioned by occupational background and by individual adaptation to the sequential development described in Chapter 6. For example, in light of Super's model, those professionals who have had stable careers may be less willing to accept retirement than certain blue-collar workers with unstable patterns. The professionals have developed a higher degree of commitment to and identification with their occupations, creating possible resistance to retirement careers that do not incorporate a degree of continued involvement with the profession. If occupational choice reflects personality traits, factors related to adjustment in retirement ought to differ among workers. Retirement counselors might then use the probable attitudes associated with each occupation, career pattern, and personality type. At the present time, however, little resembling a well-ordered approach to counseling predominates among preretirement programs. The stability and security pointed out by Miller and Form and by Gusfield also have an impact on later work life and on the transition to retirement. Retirement may be viewed by workers as a welcome phase in their occupational careers, either because it is another logical step or because it puts an end to a succession of tangentially related jobs and an unstable career pattern. Or it may be dreaded as a time of impending role loss or of relative poverty because of a reduction in income.

The interaction of life-span development and careers in work are well integrated into the American consciousness. Most people have some conception of whether they are on or off schedule and use that notion to evaluate their lives. Socially recognized turning points throughout much of adulthood are rooted in two primary spheres, the family and work. It is crucial to realize that the expectations and mindsets thus created are subject to change and variability; they are *not* absolute (Hagestad and Neugarten, 1985).

This point is emphasized because the typical idea of a career, however applicable it may have been in the past, needs reexamining. Regardless of structural changes in the nature of the work experience, a number of factors intervene in the unfolding of careers. First, variability at the age of entry will alter the sequencing and the timing of events. Second, interrupted trajectories may result in repeated entry-level positions without any upward mobility. Third, the traditional career model may not be applicable to both sexes. Women's transition points and progression sometimes reflect family formation decisions; thus their careers and the occupational attainment they achieve are affected. Heretofore some women have shown more disjointed career patterns and therefore different earnings, benefits, and retirement anticipation. Even among those whose careers have been mirror images of the pattern of men, retirement benefits, mobility, and earnings have still shown a constricted return (Marini, 1980, 1984; Rosenfeld, 1980, 1983; Rosenfeld and Sorensen, 1979; Trieman, 1985; O'Rand and Henretta, 1982).

Structural factors also operate in the working world. The social organization of free market economies in segments or sectors affects individual income, status attainment, and the shape of careers. In their overview of these macro-level impositions on individual patterns, Beck et al. (1978) note demonstrable differences between sectors — in their case core and periphery, "which cannot be explained by the racial, sexual, human capital, or occupational characteristics of their respective labor forces." In other words, organizational barriers in the labor market affect the return on human capital. These structural factors have profound ramifications for the careers of women and men who find themselves occupying positions in different spheres of the market. Baron and Bielby (1985) note this structural differentiation is "pervasive, almost omnipresent, sustained by diverse organizational structures and processes." In their analysis, which focused in this instance on women's career opportunities, they concluded that major obstacles limit mobility and benefits. In sum, the women in their study were concentrated in secondary labor markets devoid of advancement opportunities, which accorded them fewer benefits for the positions they attained.

The social consequences of structural placement and the organization of production has been hypothesized to extend to the impact of technology on the organization of work. The key characteristics of core industries, primary labor markets, and career mobility involve a complex of similar factors. They each involve stable employment, increasing autonomy and responsibility, increasingly higher wages, better working conditions, benefits, and an internal mobility ladder. As production moves along the continuum from labor to capital to technologically intensive processes, an increasingly large pool of workers may find themselves in a position analogous to being employed in secondary labor markets or in peripheral industries. They will have less ability to exercise control in performing their jobs, they will have greater instability in their careers, they will have restricted wages and mobility, and they will have fewer fringe benefits such as pension planning, insurance programs, and so on — those job-related factors that promote optimum adjustment in the later years. With the diffusion of what is now the fifth generation of automated equipment, large portions of future generations may not encounter the kind of careers they anticipate. Obviously, some new positions will be created by technology that will require well-developed skills and permit maximum autonomy but the bulk of workers may find a dampening of their career opportunities (Hendricks, 1984).

# The Meaning of Work

## WORKER STEREOTYPES

What is the relationship among a worker's age, job performance, satisfaction, and self-esteem? In turn, how are these conditioned by the beliefs others hold about aging workers? As has become apparent, older people are not easily or neatly categorized. Chronological age is only one facet of a complex whole. Furthermore, as was made clear in Chapter 4, even the idea of functional age is misleading, since a person's different capacities vary widely.

It is often fallacious and perhaps foolhardy to adhere to or even make generalizations about the performance of older workers. Nevertheless, one hears about the cycle of anxiety and frustration created where older, unskilled, women or nonwhite workers somehow experience feelings of failure as an unavoidable concomitant of participation in the labor force. Although scant research can be found to support assumptions about emotional, cognitive, or temperamental declines in the capacities relevant to occupational performance, many pervasive societal stereotypes reflect negative appraisals, which undermine confidence and self-esteem among older workers. In addition, such stereotypes tend to create implicit resistance and prejudice among those responsible for hiring workers, with the result that older workers often find themselves rejected for employment or advancement on the basis of an age criterion alone.

Myths concerning older workers abound. While some changes in specific performance levels occur over a person's work life, general performance rarely declines. Several factors are likely to account for the slight differences observed. As noted in Chapter 6, older persons who participate in experiments do less well on those tasks involving speed or time pressures than younger workers, partially because of their unfamiliarity with laboratory test procedures and partially because of their desire to perform well. Also, when productivity is the unit of measure, the type of job may have an effect on a worker's output. In some retail positions age is perhaps a less acceptable quality; thus, customers may not approach older clerks because of their own age biases. Differential productivity occurs less often among office or clerical personnel. Research conducted by the Bureau of Labor Statistics has repeatedly challenged the belief that older workers are less accurate or consistent than their younger colleagues or that their rates of absenteeism are higher. Not only are older workers more likely to remain on the job, they are also less likely to incur job-related injuries. Despite the realities, people in charge of hiring or promotion often have accepted the myths and negative stereotypes and attempt to avoid the pitfalls alleged to accompany hiring workers over forty. As we have seen from the discussion of theoretical models in gerontology, it may be reasonable to characterize the work environment with its potential for negative labeling as contributing to perceived or actual decrements in performance, rewards, and competence. The stereotypes condition not only the reactions of employers but also may establish and reinforce negative self-assessments among older workers (Jacobson, 1979; Stagner, 1985).

Even if we assume older workers lack newer, more technical skills desired in the primary labor markets, other characteristics, whether actual performance, dependability, loyalty, experience, or a desire to maximize growth and development, are valuable in work (Clark and Spengler, 1980). One of the fundamental considerations in employment possibilities has been said to be job satisfaction and meaning in a worker's life. This is a sharp, double-edged sword. The notion of job retraining implies a poor fit between worker and job. The issues of midcareer redirection, transfer of skills among diverse occupations, and flexible hours are gaining popularity among those whose goal is promoting the adaptation of older workers to changes in the character of industrial work. It was generally assumed that the loss of a job or occupational role, age discrimination in reemployment, and impending retirement signaled the onset of a diminution in one's feelings of self-worth and respect. This was believed to be true for men but not for women; women were thought to escape such stresses for the most part, because their primary identity arose from their family relationships and their role as familial lifegivers and care providers. These assumptions are under scrutiny and increasingly have been qualified as research and critical attention have been focused on them (George and Maddox, 1977). Clearly, the composition of the labor force is undergoing significant change. So, too, will the range of individual adaptations and reactions to demands and stereotypes in the worker's world alter.

However, many workers forced out by mandatory retirement programs often cannot help but view their separation from work as a personal failure or rejection. People who voluntarily retire may do so unconsciously under social pressure; they may feel they are saving face or that they are affirming their active participation in the decision-making process. The psychological price exacted from those workers who have thoroughly internalized the positive cultural attitudes toward work and production must indeed be high. Required to withdraw at an arbitrary age, they relinquish not only their central roles in the productive schema but also possibly the foundation of their identities. With industrialization has come a particularly heavy emphasis on productive accomplishments, so much so that even nonwork activities are managed within the framework of a worklike orientation; often we fill our spare time with worklike pursuits or with activities that more closely resemble work than leisure.

While these reactions may indeed be true for some workers, they are not universal. Associated with the increasing degree of industrialization and technological sophistication is a complex division of labor. In many instances, although it consumes a large portion of life, work does not contribute the most significant reinforcements or rewards in an individual's life. Many jobs are simply not inherently stimulating or satisfying to the people who must perform them. Rather, work has meaning in life because it facilitates interpersonal contacts or provides economic independence enabling the worker to engage in more meaningful pursuits. Despite that a worker might not miss the duties of his or her work per se, anticipating retirement carries with it the reality of a multitude of changes. Work gives or imposes a formal structure on an individual's life, with free time usually defined as time left over from work. The fusion of work and leisure roles and the concept of leisure as a new social role are becoming alternatives to the notion of work as the inescapable central role of each individual's life (Gordon et al., 1976; Kaplan, 1979). Work provides a ready means by which people may categorize one another, thus creating and demanding specific responses. Certainly, the nature of one's work, leisure, and prospective retirement brings both common and unique experiences to be shared, rendering broad generalizations about older workers difficult at best. In a cross-national analysis of older workers in Britain, Denmark, and the United States, Shanas et al. (1968) found demographic factors were the most outstanding common characteristics among those who were able to continue working beyond the customary retirement age. Most of these older workers were married men who were healthy and slightly younger than the majority of the retired population. An interesting difference between the United States and Britain is that most of those who work past retirement age in America are white-collar workers while in Britain they are generally blue-collar workers.

## STATUS DISPLACEMENT

It is common for older workers who are having some occupational difficulties to experience what is called **status displacement.** Regardless of their skills, older workers who lose their jobs as a result of negative stereotypes, economic fluctuations, or automation face a number of hurdles in attempting to locate new employment. Because they are middle-aged, they are usually tied down and have less geographical mobility than their younger counterparts who have not yet established residential stability. Unemployment tends to be lengthy, and personnel directors hesitate before offering job opportunities to older workers, often because of the negative stereotypes mentioned earlier (Jaffe, 1978). Providing the prejudicial attitudes manifested by personnel officers are overcome and a job found, the older worker frequently experiences a change in occupation, slipping a rung or two in status, with a corresponding reduction in salary. Seemingly, newly acquired jobs are also most often with smaller businesses providing either services or retail trade (Schulz, 1985; Sheppard, 1976).

## AGE DISCRIMINATION

The other common type of occupational displacement comes about because of age discrimination. The basis for age discrimination in employment is apparent from even a brief examination of cultural values evident in industrialized societies. Using the United States as an example, it is possible to see that during the developmental period of the nineteenth and twentieth centuries, emphasis was placed primarily on youthfulness, productivity, the work ethic, achievement motivation, and self-sufficiency. The American cultural motif shuns references to decay, decline, or debility. Partially because of the manner in which most people are channeled into a single occupation or profession, age discrimination becomes much more common because employers need only look to the pool of younger workers to quickly replace workers approaching retirement. In an effort to counteract the tendency reported by the Secretary of Labor in 1964 that unemployment among workers over forty-five costs the American economy over one million man years of productive time each year, Congress enacted the Age Discrimination in Employment Act (ADEA) in 1967.

The original legislation and amendments enacted in 1974 and 1978 are designed to prevent and provide redress for discrimination prior to age seventy in hiring, compensating, promoting, discharging, and retiring individuals in any part of the labor market in firms that employ twenty or more people. For federal employees there is no upper limit. There are exceptions based on critical performance criteria and for executives with large salaries, but by and large the ADEA covers the majority of all workers. While the ADEA will be discussed more fully in Chapter 11, let us merely say here that though the ideal was strongly supported in Congress and by labor unions, the effects are mixed at best (Casey, 1984; Wanner and McDonald, 1983).

What is the employment experience of older workers like since the inauguration of federal policies in the United States? Has the situation improved? Age discrimination in individual cases is difficult to document, but the general trend suggests ageism in the labor market is still with us. In the past three decades there have been sharp declines in the numbers of older men who are still working. After about forty-five, job instability becomes increasingly common. As is shown in Table 8.1, the pattern for men in the United States is more dramatic than for women. Men are not as active in labor markets as they once were. Among women, labor force participation rates in the middle-aged categories have increased appreciably, whereas participation rates for those over sixty-five have remained relatively low. Comparing the United States labor participation rates over time provides an interesting commentary on the effect of the ADEA for categories of workers approaching sixty-five. As is apparent, despite federal legislation barring age discrimination, fewer workers remain active in exactly those age categories the act was designed to protect. Clearly, one must consider the occupations in which workers of these ages have been employed as well as the general trend of business cycles.

To make sense of the wide-ranging changes that mean displacement and dislocation for older workers, we must take business cycles, product market characteristics, occupational patterns, and attitudes toward older workers into consideration. Technology, too, has a major impact, and according to Samuel Ehrenhalt, Commissioner of Labor Statistics for the New York Federal Region, there is already evidence to suggest its impact is being disproportionately set-

**TABLE 8.1**
Labor Force Participation Rates by Age and Sex in Five Industrialized Countries

| Age | USA | | | | | Japan | | |
|-----|------|------|------|-------|-------|--------|------|------|
| | 1950 | 1979 | 1982 | 1990[c] | 2000[c] | 1950[b] | 1975 | 1982 |
| **Men** | | | | | | | | |
| 20–24 | 81.9 | 87.6 | 85.9 | | | 96.3 | 79.1 | 70.2 |
| 25–44 | 92.3 | 95.0 | 94.5 | | | 97.0 | 98.2 | 97.4 |
| 45–54 | 91.9 | 92.3 | 90.8 | 91.3 | 91.0 | | 97.8 | 96.4 |
| 55–59 | 86.7 | 82.2 | 81.3 | 78.7 | 77.0 | 92.4 | 94.7 | 91.1 |
| 60–64 | 79.4 | 61.8 | 56.4 | 55.9 | 52.8 | 65.2 | 85.4 | 76.0 |
| 65–69 | 39.0[a] | 20.0[a] | 26.5 | 23.2 | 19.9 | | 49.7[a] | 57.4 |
| 70+ | | | 12.1 | 11.3 | 9.8 | | | 28.4 |
| **Women** | | | | | | | | |
| 20–24 | 43.2 | 69.3 | 70.0 | | | 49.2 | 66.8 | 71.1 |
| 25–44 | 33.1 | 62.1 | 67.9 | | | 53.2 | 47.6 | 56.4 |
| 45–54 | 32.8 | 60.3 | 61.5 | 67.1 | 69.6 | | 60.3 | 62.7 |
| 55–59 | 25.9 | 48.7 | 49.4 | 49.7 | 50.2 | 48.2 | 50.9 | 50.3 |
| 60–64 | 20.5 | 33.9 | 33.1 | 33.8 | 33.7 | 27.2 | 39.2 | 38.6 |
| 65–69 | 7.3[a] | 8.3[a] | 14.7 | 14.1 | 13.6 | | 15.8 | 26.6 |
| 70+ | | | 4.7 | 4.0 | 3.6 | | | 10.6 |

[a]65+.
[b]Age categories for 1950 are 25–39, 40–49, 50–59, and 60+.
[c]Projected.
[d]Younger age categories grouped together.

tled on workers, especially men, over forty-five (*USA Today*, 1983). Few, if any, labor economists doubt there will be a continuing decline in labor force participation among middle-aged and older workers (Morrison, 1982). According to recent government statistics, unemployment rates for those over fifty-five are increasing more rapidly than for any other age group. In 1982, the most recent year for which figures are available, unemployment increased 24 percent for workers in the fifty-five to sixty-four age bracket, compared to a 16 percent increase for the rest of the working population. Once unemployed this group is also three times more likely to get discouraged and give up their search for another job (Select Committee on Aging, 1982). In short, they experience an involuntary early retirement as their niche in the labor market disappears. In the so-called smokestack industries, 86 percent of laid-off workers over forty-five do not find reemployment. Though one in six workers is a man over forty-five, only one in twenty-three jobs created in the first half of 1983 was filled by men in that age group (Hendricks, 1984; *USA Today*, 1983).

Other than unemployment, three other aspects of the job experiences of older workers suggest some degree of age discrimination. First, when reemployment takes place, it is often in positions lower than the previous job. Sec-

| Age | France | | | West Germany | | | Sweden | | |
|---|---|---|---|---|---|---|---|---|---|
| | 1946 | 1975 | 1982 | 1950 | 1978 | 1982 | 1950 | 1975 | 1982 |
| Men | | | | | | | | | |
| 20–24 | 91.2 | 81.5 | 79.0 | 93.4 | 80.9 | 80.9 | 90.0 | 73.4 | 83.9 |
| 25–44 | 96.4 | 96.0 | 96.2 | 95.7 | 94.3 | 95.2 | 97.2 | 91.2 | 95.1 |
| 45–54 | 94.7 | 93.8 | 92.8 | 95.1 | 94.9 | 94.9 | 96.3 | 91.1 | 94.1 |
| 55–59 | 85.4 | 81.8 | 74.8 | 87.4 | 83.8 | 82.3 | 92.5 | 85.5 | 87.2 |
| 60–64 | 76.3 | 54.3 | 39.7 | 73.0 | 43.0 | 43.6 | 79.7 | 68.5 | 68.3 |
| 65–69 | 51.6[a] | 10.6[a] | 8.5 | 26.8[a] | 8.4[a] | 9.7 | 40.1[a] | 11.0[a] | 15.7 |
| 70+ | | | 2.4 | | | 4.9 | | | 10.5 |
| Women | | | | | | | | | |
| 20–24 | 59.9 | 66.0 | 67.6 | 70.4 | 69.9 | 71.3 | 57.3 | 65.5 | 81.7 |
| 25–44 | 49.4 | 57.1 | 63.9 | 43.8 | 56.8 | 59.7 | 32.3 | 67.1 | 86.0 |
| 45–54 | 50.8 | 49.0 | 55.3 | 34.9 | 48.4 | 51.8 | 30.3 | 71.8 | 85.6 |
| 55–59 | 46.1 | 41.9 | 44.3 | 29.4 | 39.0 | 39.9 | 26.3 | 57.7 | 71.9 |
| 60–64 | 40.2 | 27.8 | 21.0 | 21.2 | 12.2 | 13.3 | 18.9 | 35.1 | 46.2 |
| 65–69 | 22.0[a] | 5.0[a] | 3.5 | 9.7[a] | 3.4[a] | 4.5 | 8.6[a] | 3.5[a] | 6.1 |
| 70+ | | | 1.9 | | | 2.0 | | | 1.8 |

Sources: *U.N. Demographic Yearbook, 1956*, pp. 319–38. New York: United Nations, 1956; *Yearbook of Labour Statistics, 1979*, pp. 24–29. Geneva: International Labour Office, 1979; *Yearbook of Labour Statistics, 1983*, pp. 13–37. Geneva: International Labour Office, 1983; and U.S. Bureau of the Census. *Demographic and Socioeconomic Aspects of Aging in the United States*, p. 116. Current Population Reports, P-23, No. 138. Washington, D.C.: U.S. Government Printing Office, 1984 (adapted).

ond, upward job mobility slows and then stops for older workers. By fifty to fifty-nine career progression settles with much less overall mobility. Third, earnings profiles, even when all relevant intervening variables are taken into consideration, are lower for older workers. Age-related declines in earnings are remarkable but not distributed equally between salaried and hourly workers nor for union and nonunion employees. Clearly, we need to look at occupational obsolescence and industrial sectors to understand completely why older workers suffer financially (Tolbert, 1982; Wanner and McDonald, 1983; Hendricks and McAllister, 1983).

## WORK AND SELF-IMAGE

What possible reactions might a person have as he or she faces either retirement or early job displacement? The combinations are numerous, certainly including such feelings as failure, guilt, fear because no regular pattern of activity exists anymore, or even a general denial of aging. While some are able to adjust fairly well to the initial transition, others may immediately search for new work, some may retreat into themselves, and others may internalize society's view of them as too old to be a viable and valuable part of the productive process. A crucial aspect of any of these reaction patterns is the change one's self-concept undergoes. No matter how one rationalizes discrimination it is personally experienced as somehow reflective of one's own faults or weaknesses. Even if this is natural, the results can be exceedingly destructive. An individual may intellectually apprehend the processes of compulsory retirement policies and yet be emotionally unable to accept them as beyond control. If the older worker incorporates the negative societal stereotypes, a gradual shift in self-image will occur, one that is difficult to overcome in the retirement years. When the negative appraisal summarized in "We see you as a bumbling old fool" becomes internalized to "I am a bumbling old fool," a downward spiral is set in motion that is difficult to break.

Social cues and reinforcements are both subtle and overt. As the need for exchange and input varies, the quest for information regarding job performance and standards, ability to manipulate the work situation, and the general desirability of one's presence may become more salient. Attitudes toward work also vary; individuals who derive less of their identity from their work roles may find diminution or loss of that role less threatening or oppressive than previously assumed (Cohn, 1979; Johnson and Williamson, 1980).

To prevent the vicious cycle of anxiety and poor self-evaluation among older workers, programs aimed at sensitizing personnel managers and occupational counselors are necessary. More individualized attention could easily be given to workers who appear to be developing anxieties about their performance and their futures. By constructing individual job profiles and offering personalized encouragement in counseling sessions, feelings of inadequacy might be eliminated long before they reached the point of being harmful. It would no doubt help some merely to know that many older workers possess skills on which management places a premium. Adequate adjustment to the

**TABLE 8.2**

Ratio of Population Actively Involved in the Labor Force in Third World and Eastern Bloc Countries

| Age | Ethiopia 1980 | Honduras 1982 | Pakistan 1983 | Peru 1981 | Czechoslovakia 1980 |
|---|---|---|---|---|---|
| Men |  |  |  |  |  |
| 6– 9 |  |  |  | 1.2 | 72.4[d] |
| 10–14 | 50.4 | 27.0 | 30.9 | 4.7 |  |
| 15–19 | 76.1 | 72.0 | 67.7 | 35.4 | 29.0 |
| 20–24 | 89.5 | 88.8 | 88.2 | 75.5 | 86.5 |
| 25–44 | 97.0 | 95.3 | 96.9 | 96.4 | 98.2 |
| 45–54 | 96.5 | 94.3 | 95.7 | 97.6 | 94.4 |
| 55–59 | 93.5 | 91.3 | 91.8 | 94.5 | 84.2 |
| 60–64 | 88.5 | 85.7 | 82.3 | 87.7 | 46.3 |
| 65–69 | 64.3[a] | 79.1 | 56.9[a] | 63.1[a] | 30.3 |
| 70+ | ____ | 55.4 | ____ | ____ | 12.1 |
| Total | 54.6 | 49.2 | 52.3 | 56.5 | 56.2 |
| Women |  |  |  |  |  |
| 6– 9 |  |  |  |  | 53.4[d] |
| 10–14 | 33.2 | 2.7 | 6.3 | 3.5 |  |
| 15–19 | 58.5 | 15.7 | 12.1 | 18.3 | 29.8 |
| 20–24 | 61.5 | 23.0 | 12.7 | 29.2 | 83.4 |
| 25–44 | 63.8 | 19.7 | 14.4 | 29.9 | 91.8 |
| 45–54 | 53.8 | 14.8 | 12.5 | 26.3 | 84.9 |
| 55–59 | 41.6 | 13.0 | 12.3 | 23.4 | 40.8 |
| 60–64 | 34.2 | 10.8 | 7.4 | 22.9 | 21.5 |
| 65–69 | 11.7[a] | 8.3 | 5.4[a] | 12.5[a] | 12.2 |
| 70+ | ____ | 5.2 | ____ | ____ | 4.0 |
| Total | 35.3 | 9.7 | 7.9 | 19.0 | 46.7 |

Note: For legends and sources, see Table 8.1.

retirement role would also be facilitated by preretirement programs sponsored by business or social service agencies. The planning aspects of such programs alert workers to potential problems they will encounter in retirement. Seminars or discussion groups with others approaching retirement not only help prepare the workers for the new role, but counseling programs may also enable them to retain or transfer jobs. Formal preretirement programs have their greatest value as a mechanism for **anticipatory socialization.** The present exercises conducted by unions and employers usually deal only with specific issues, including pension and medical benefits, tax advice, insurance, wills, and so on. Only a few are more comprehensive, covering attitudes toward work and retirement, meaningfulness in life, and potential activities and roles of interest to the retiring worker (Siegel and Rives, 1978; Schulz, 1985).

Some gerontologists have proposed that social service agencies might adopt preretirement counseling as an important function, since an agency approach would certainly bring a broader range of alternatives than those provided by unions or companies (Beattie, 1976; Monk, 1972).

Another possibility might be to use retired people in community service programs, which will give them a vital sense of belonging. They have valuable skills to offer and can provide services that might otherwise be unavailable in times of fiscal shortfalls. Examples of such programs include voluntary consulting services for those establishing a small business, to use retired persons to counsel school-age children, advise new employees, and so on. The variety of retired senior volunteer (RSVP) type programs is immense. They are also an invaluable means of using the skills and buttressing the self-concepts of older persons.

In Western societies occupational prestige has traditionally been associated with the masculine role. It is interpreted as a negative reflection of a man if he loses his job, becomes ill for an extended period, or even retires. As previously suggested, feelings of inadequacy, marginality, and possible rolelessness may contribute to ill-health to an extent not yet understood. Additionally, the traditional correlates of occupational roles, whether prestige or stress, should be observed among women who work in increasing numbers in spheres previously closed. Requiring individuals to remove themselves from active participation in the labor force when they may view their participation as the sole or at least the primary legitimation of their existence is bound to create psychological, physical, and social problems that might fruitfully be addressed either by changing or flexible retirement policies or by insightful social programming. Flexible retirement programs based on ability and desire have several arguments in their favor. First, they would eliminate the age discrimination inherent in compulsory programs. Flexible policies also offer a better opportunity to use the experience and abilities of older members of the work force. There is a possibility that further work would raise the amount of income among retired workers, thereby relieving some of the burden from Social Security and pension programs and reducing the number of elderly living at or below poverty levels. Finally, flexible retirement policies would increase morale and satisfaction among those people who want to remain active in the labor force (Butler, 1978; Drucker, 1978; Morrison, 1978).

To meet the needs of those who want to remain active in their occupations a range of alternative work options are also available. Among them are phased retirement, job sharing, job redesign, transfer and retraining programs, labor pools, and individualized positions for older workers. Whether these options have been developed to appeal to older consumers, to deal with labor shortages, or to respond to federal legislation, the result is the provision of employment opportunities for the elderly who benefit from working less than 1000 hours a year (ERISA regulations set part-time work at 1000 or fewer hours per year). The expectation is that these programs will expand as long as they are cost effective for employers. Unfortunately, most options are designed to serve white-collar, professional, and some service workers but not blue-collar workers. Given economic exigencies, their continued existence is rather tenuous. Finally, part-time work does not pay very well and may therefore be demeaning for older workers who may chose not to do it (Andrisani and Sandell, 1984; Jondrow et al., 1983).

## ANTICIPATING RETIREMENT

**Individual-Level Explanations.** The critera used by researchers to ascertain work satisfaction or life adjustment are a mixture of culturally prescribed values reflecting a dominant emphasis on happiness and high morale at the expense of other equally plausible dimensions. In assessing the degree of adjustment among any group of people, particularly among the elderly, one must carefully distinguish between contentment and that behavior the elderly themselves have been socialized to emulate. Industrialized societies differ significantly from other societal forms in which low productivity is accompanied by a high degree of mutual dependence among members. In such a societal transition many elderly lose control of property as well as their monopoly on *strategic knowledge* (Dowd, 1980). Increasingly, automation helps reduce the number of low- to mid-range jobs, so that older workers often either face an early but unplanned retirement or an extended period of unemployment prior to reaching pensionable age, since they are seldom seen as possessing skills or training that are readily transferable to new jobs. By contrast, higher status workers may find it easier to apply their general skills in replacement jobs. It has also been suggested that workers in higher status occupations routinely deal with abstract concepts; thus, anticipating the future in retirement may come more easily to them (Simpson et al., 1966).

Attitudes toward retirement are influenced by a variety of factors. Commitment to work, the nature of one's occupation, sex, anticipated financial situation during retirement, health status, preretirement counseling, the friendship network, and general life satisfaction are all believed to be associated with an individual's perceptions of impending retirement (Atchley, 1976; Palmore et al., 1982; McConnell, 1983). Workers in those societies with similar industrial and capital modes of organization have been presumed to experience the same concerns with and expectations of their retirement. A study of urban French male managers found that a favorable preretirement attitude toward retirement was related to health status, a high degree of life satisfaction, and a full exploration of leisure pursuits. Contrary to what is often hypothesized, no inverse relationship between commitment to work and the attitude toward retirement was found (Poitrenaud et al., 1979). Another recent study of preretirement attitudes and life-styles of urban Canadian men between fifty-five and sixty-four revealed that few actually made formal plans for their retirement, although those in higher socioeconomic categories more frequently made definite plans. Voluntary associations may be vital in establishing and socializing aging members' attitudes toward retirement. Perceived health status and general life satisfaction also influenced the decision to plan for retirement as well as the anticipation of it (Robinson et al., 1985).

A few studies have found that the positive preretirement attitudes toward impending retirement shift toward more negative feelings later. Hindsight is always 20-20; thus, a significant number of individuals are able to appreciate their own unpreparedness for retirement only after the fact. Of course, these results differ by employment status as well as by the nature of the research design. Monk (1972) found in his analysis of professional men in their fifties that their attitudes toward planning for retirement indicated a low valuation of preretirement programs; the participants felt planning was nearly worthless. Their rationales for not taking advantage of counseling programs included beliefs that they would not live long enough to have to worry about it, that rampant inflation effectively negated any possible savings for a comfortable retirement, or that retirement was contrary to their personal objectives of remaining actively involved in life until death. As would be expected, however, the weight of the evidence does not bolster their rather naive perspectives. In the large-scale Cornell study of workers approaching retirement the investigators consistently observed that expectations before retirement were more negative than the subsequent evaluations of retirement (Streib and Schneider, 1971). Further support is lent by the three-nation study carried out by Shanas et al. (1968). Among American white-collar and blue-collar workers, only three of every ten retired workers said they found little or nothing to enjoy about retirement. Ironically, among retired agricultural workers, traditionally seen in an idealized light, this figure increased to approximately five out of ten.

Accompanying greater life expectancies, increasing educational attainment, and changes in labor force participation, planning for retirement is a reality incumbent on both individual and employer. The piecemeal, narrowly focused programs currently offered must be expanded to address the social and psychological changes faced by aging workers. Financial advising is critical for all who envision the reduction of income; however, such programs would be of even greater value if offered earlier in the work-life career (Foner and Schwab, 1981).

Adjusting to retirement may be influenced by positive self-esteem or it may be linked with the relation of retirement activities to preretirement occupation. For some individuals, adjusting to retirement is eased by a continuation of activities using preretirement occupational skills. For others, focusing on similar skills and activities may rob the retirement years of their intrinsic reward. It is becoming apparent, however, that as life expectancy has increased, and since the technological revolution seems unlikely to slow its pace, one career throughout life, selected at about twenty-two or so, is an unreasonable expectation for many individuals. It seems at least as efficient and productive to integrate school and work throughout a person's lifetime, enabling midlife career changes and revamped expectations of productivity among older workers. This does not mean that all or even a majority of workers would change jobs or occupations, only that the potential would exist for those who wished to take advantage of it. Of equal importance would be continuing education programs to enable workers to renew their skills periodically and to keep up with ongoing developments in their fields.

Similarly, to facilitate adjustment to retirement variations of the five-day, fifty-week work year have been proposed. In addition to four-day work weeks and longer vacation periods, a work *sabbatical* has been designed for United States Steel workers. With every five years of service the worker is entitled to a three-month vacation intended to provide time for rest and relaxation. Such a program not only implicitly advocates retraining and relaxation but also anticipates the unstructured free time that comes with retirement (Robinson et al., 1985).

**Structural Explanations.** Attitudes toward retirement and the decision to retire are ready examples of the individualist focus of much gerontological research. The use of structural perspectives is still in its infancy but does suggest that other factors also affect how individual workers approach retirement. Dowd (1980) phrased the issue succinctly when he noted:

> Hidden among all of the statistics and accounts of the problems faced by old people in modern American society is the simple fact that some old people live fairly well while others face certain impoverishment. This fact has nothing to do with individual skills, abilities, personality attributes or other personal qualities; rather it has to do with social structure. By *social structure*, I mean the division of the American economy into sectors: one sector is highly organized and characterized by high wages and pension systems, and the other is marked by low wages and few, if any, fringe benefits (p. 77).

The differences between economic segments extends to pension plans, health benefits, and so on, so that individual workers are affected by sectoral placement even after retirement (Dowd, 1980).

A single illustration will help highlight the impact of locale as discussed in Chapter 3. It is a given among gerontologists that two important predicates mitigating all subsequent adjustment are financial status and health. Financial well-being in retirement derives from a combination of public, private, and personal sources; health is dependent on adequate insurance coverage enabling those who are ill to obtain medical attention. If anything disrupts the optimum levels of either monetary or physical well-being, most other social psychological attributes suffer accordingly. Table 8.3 shows the extent of private pension plans and collective health coverage by core and peripheral sectors of the economy. A cursory look at the figures is enough to suggest the salience of sectoral factors in affecting retirement. Other structurally generated differences have also been identified (O'Rand and Henretta, 1982; Beck, 1982; Guillemard, 1982; Baron and Bielby, 1985).

**TABLE 8.3**

Structural Differences in Private Pension Coverage and Health Insurance Plans in the United States, 1981

### Percentage of Employees with Present Pension Coverage by Industry[a]

| Core | | Periphery | |
|---|---|---|---|
| Mining | 57.0 | Agriculture, forestry, | |
| Construction | 36.1 | fisheries | 10.4 |
| Manufacturing[b] | 58.9 | Wholesale trade[b] | 42.7 |
| Transportation, public | | Retail trade | 19.3 |
| utilities[b] | 65.1 | Business services | 27.0 |
| Finance, real estate, | | Personal services | 9.6 |
| insurance[b] | 47.7 | Entertainment and recreation | 16.5 |
| Professional and related[b] | 50.8 | | |
| Public administration | 76.4 | | |
| Total | 57.15 | Total | 25.59 |

Total employees with pension: 44.3

### Percentage of Employees with Group Health Plans by Industry

| Core | | Periphery | |
|---|---|---|---|
| Mining | 84.1 | Agriculture, forestry, | |
| Construction | 58.9 | fisheries | 24.1 |
| Manufacturing[b] | 82.0 | Wholesale trade[b] | 71.4 |
| Transportation, public | | Retail trade | 38.9 |
| utilities[b] | 81.0 | Business services | 52.2 |
| Finance, real estate, | | Personal services | 20.4 |
| insurance[b] | 70.0 | Entertainment and recreation | 31.8 |
| Professional and related[b] | 61.5 | | |
| Public administration | 76.8 | | |
| Total | 73.51 | Total | 46.29 |

Total employees with group health: 62.0

[a]Based on a scheme developed by Tolbert et al. (1980).
[b]Since many industries are lumped together in this classification scheme, it was necessary to designate sectoral location on the basis of best fit. Therefore, these industrial groups are predominantly core or predominantly peripheral.
*Source:* Hendricks, J. and T. M. Calasanti. "Social Policy and Aging in North America." In *Ageing and Social Policy*, eds. A. Walker and C. Phillipson, London: Heineman (in press).

# Working Around the World

## TRENDS IN WESTERN COUNTRIES

Western industrialized countries tend to show a trend toward declining labor force participation among late middle-aged and older men and increasing labor force participation among women, particularly in their middle years. Third World countries, however, tend to show relatively high labor force participation rates for men throughout life and relatively low rates for women. The trends in the industrialized countries may result in part from economic problems affecting many of the sectors in which men are traditionally employed, changing social mores that make it more acceptable for women to work, a shift from manufacturing toward service industries, and the development of government-sponsored pension programs in response to political and economic pressures.

Tables 8.1 and 8.2 contrast five countries with free market economies, underdeveloped countries, and one eastern bloc nation. As can be seen in Table 8.1, peak labor force activity among men in industrialized countries comes early and begins to decline after forty-five. Between forty-five and fifty-four the percentage begins to decline, and from fifty-five on the proportion of men still working or seeking employment declines drastically, to well below 30 percent in every country except Japan. Interestingly, patterns in the eastern bloc country of Czechoslovakia, shown in Table 8.2, are similar to those in the United States. Other Third World countries are included to provide a further comparison. They exhibit a diffused pattern throughout life with well over 50 percent of those sixty-five and over still economically active; in addition, economic activity may begin as early as six. No similar childhood figures are available in Western countries because labor force participation is thought not to begin until fifteen or sixteen.

Women are most active between twenty and twenty-four, before taking on the obligations of parenthood. In Sweden the peak years come in the next age bracket because women delay starting families. As is also indicated, increasing numbers of women in all capitalist countries are working during their middle years; generally over half are economically active up to sixty. Between sixty and sixty-five the number declines, so that only one in three women work, and after sixty-five the number drops still further, to less than one in ten. Again, Japan is an exception: older Japanese women have a labor force participation rate nearly twice that of women in Western industrialized countries or even in Czechoslovakia.

Table 8.1 also provides figures that give some insight into the changing character of labor force participation. As is evident from an examination of the rates for working men in the countries selected, the proportion actively involved in the labor force has steadily declined over the past three decades for those over sixty. Although the official retirement age was sixty-five throughout the earlier decades, the first five years after formal retirement were still the most common working years, with participation rates decreasing thereafter.

Somewhat less than six of every ten American men are working between sixty and sixty-four. This represents a decline of two of every ten workers in this age range since 1950. During the same period the number of men over sixty-five in the American labor force has also declined. It has actually been cut in half, to less than one in five (17.1 percent). The projected figures for 1990 and 2000 show still further evidence of a downward shift in labor market participation rates for the older age categories. A recent study of age at retirement in successive cohorts revealed the same tendency; almost 55 percent of the 1916 cohort of men were retired at sixty-three and sixty-four, as opposed to only slightly over 30 percent of the 1904 cohort at the same age. Furthermore, over 30 percent of the 1922 cohort was retired by sixty-one (Rones, 1985).

Japanese men and women over sixty-five are far more likely to be employed than older citizens in any of the other selected countries. Over one-half of Japanese men and one-fifth of Japanese women sixty-five to sixty-nine are active in the labor force; of those seventy and over, one in three Japanese men and one in ten women are still in the labor force. The higher incidence of labor force participation is probably related to distinctive pension programs and benefit levels characteristic of the booming economy in Japan. While participation rates have declined since 1950, levels remain quite high and, despite forecasts of reduced productivity, are expected to exceed those in other industrialized nations for the remainder of this century (Kii, 1979; Maeda and Asano, 1979).

The situation for Swedish men is analogous to the American pattern, with very similar rates of decline. In Britain there have been decreases in labor force participation rates in almost all age groups because of the current economic situation. The greatest drop, however, has been among men fifty-five to sixty-five; the 91.3 percent participation rate in 1970 dropped to only 76.8 percent in 1983. Among the sixty-five and over group, the numbers were 20.2 percent and 8.1 percent in 1970 and 1983, respectively (U.S. Census, 1985a). The figures for France are somewhat misleading, since the earlier census taken in 1946 reflects the effects of a country still mobilized for a war economy. This accounts for some measure of the apparently large decline in the participation of older French workers, but much of the remainder is a result of rapid industrialization and the simultaneous phasing out of older workers. Although male labor force participation rates since 1950 have remained relatively stable up to sixty, there has been a significant expansion of the proportion of women actively working during middle age over the past two decades. The most noteworthy changes have occurred in the United States, Sweden, and Britain for middle-aged women between forty and sixty.

In the United States in 1983 more than sixty percent of women in the forty-five to fifty-four age group were active in the labor force. In Sweden in 1982 approximately eight of ten middle-aged women were working: there had been a 50 percent increase in the proportion of women between twenty-five and fifty-four participating in the labor force since 1950, while for those between fifty-five and fifty-nine the increase was about forty percent. In Britain between 1970 and 1983 there were significant increases in the numbers of women twenty to twenty-four and twenty-five to fifty-four in the labor force, while labor force participation rates for all other groups in Britain either fell or remained approximately the same. As is apparent, in most countries there has been an expansion in the number of women in the oldest category active in the labor force (U.S. Census, 1985a).

As just noted, one essential component of any comparison of working patterns involves unemployment. Both in the United States and in the European Common Market countries periodic unemployment may be more frequent

among the younger age groups, but long-term unemployment is more characteristic of older workers. During nearly every kind of crisis the first to suffer
are the youngest and the oldest workers, with the middle-aged workers remaining relatively insulated. Long-term unemployment among the elderly is
particularly acute in France, where in 1984 approximately 44 percent of those
who had been unemployed for two years or more were at least fifty-five. In
Britain the percentage of long-term unemployed in the fifty-five and older
group fell in 1983 and 1984 as compared to previous years, possibly the result
of instituting programs of early retirement to alleviate the employment crisis
(U.S. Department of Labor, 1984a, 1984b; Eurostat, 1984a).

A further cross-national comparison will help reveal the impact of industrialization on labor force participation in various countries. As will become
clear, the results of demographic aging, technology, and the social organization of production are not uniform.

## COUNTRIES IN TRANSITION: JAPAN AND THE SOVIET UNION

Japan is an interesting case of a non-Western country that has undergone
rapid industrialization over a very few years. While the technologically sophisticated, highly productive realm of the Japanese economy is continually expanding, as compared to the United States, a significantly larger proportion of
workers are still employed in agriculture, fishing, forestry, and unpaid family
work. Following World War II, labor surpluses helped establish strict rules
governing entry into industrial jobs. Combined with more recent pressures
created by growing affluence, including a gradual erosion of the traditional
status accorded the society's elders, many older Japanese are presently confronted by strains not previously experienced. With retirement coming between fifty-five and sixty, plus meager pension benefits, it is no wonder many
older Japanese are encountering considerable stress during the last twenty
years of their lives. Elderly Japanese find there is often a seemingly abundant
supply of jobs for younger workers, while their own opportunities are largely
restricted.

Paradoxically, in recent years Japan has experienced something of a labor
shortage arising in part from the burgeoning labor demands of a booming
economy. The shortage has facilitated some movement of middle-aged people
into industry, as well as the postponement of retirement in a small range of industries, but whether this trend will continue is highly questionable. Although
large industrial companies set retirement at fifty-five to sixty, the Japanese
government has attempted to promote employment of the elderly by offering
temporary and continuous subsidies to employers who hire or retain older
workers. Elderly Japanese are subject to the present inadequate coverage of
the country's immature pension programs; currently only three-fifths of the
older population receive pension benefits. Despite that over one-third of the
older population works, the same proportion of families and individuals receiving public assistance is comprised of the elderly. As will be seen in our discussion of American women later in this chapter, Japanese women move in

and out of the labor market; however, they constitute even greater proportions of the active work force. Interrupted work histories contribute to lower, if any, pension benefits allowable to retiring women, despite their earlier age of qualification. Although retirement benefits doubled in 1973, observers agree that Japan's pension programs are still in their infancy (Kii, 1979; Maeda and Asano, 1979; Stewart, 1974). At least one observer has stated the propensity of older Japanese workers to participate actively in the labor force may be attributed to societal expectations that they continue working. Though finances may be inadequate, four out of five elderly live with their children. The long-noted sense of filial duty also extends to the economic support of aging parents. Older workers cite duty and the fact that it is normal to work as long as possible rather than to retire as reasons for maintaining employment (Palmore, 1975).

Similar to Western countries, the Soviet Union has recently experienced innumerable growing pains as the pace of industrialization gained momentum following World War II. For one thing the number of people reaching retirement age has expanded considerably since 1940, up from a scant 6.8 percent to nearly 12 percent in 1970. In addition, Soviet workers are now eligible for retirement at earlier ages than allowed in Western countries, women at fifty-five and men at sixty, but these ages are flexible according to occupation, with the more strenuous jobs permitting earlier retirement (Social Security Administration, 1984). At present, just over one-third of the Soviet labor force is forty to fifty-nine, despite the possibility of early retirement. Because of severe labor shortages, the use of retired workers who have valuable skills and experience is widely endorsed; hence many people continue to work beyond the age at which they could retire. While women number half of the overall labor force, they represent a majority in some occupations. In public health, for example, over 85 percent of all workers are women. Women comprise 70 percent of the medical doctors, about the same percentage as for school teachers.

The impact of a growth-oriented economy is clearly reflected in Soviet programs over the past twenty years. In 1956 benefits of old age pensions were bolstered to such an extent that the percentage of older workers declined from 50 percent in 1956 to below 10 percent in 1962. In the decade since, however, the need for a larger labor force has prompted governmental programs aimed at encouraging older workers to remain on the job. If they continue to work, older workers may obtain full pension benefits in addition to any wages that they might earn. This has fostered an upswing of the number of men over sixty in the labor force since 1963 to 53 percent. About 17 percent of the Soviet women continue working past retirement age, but a large proportion assume the role of unpaid family workers so their children can work without worrying about caring for their own homes or offspring. Additionally, as was pointed out in Chapter 7, many older people participate in a second economy. Thus, in the Soviet Union the majority of those past retirement age continue to contribute to the productive sphere by working in either the regular or second economic sphere or else by assuming household duties and thereby freeing others to join the labor force.

## WORKING WOMEN

Just as Table 8.1 reflects the dramatic decline in labor force participation among older men for the past thirty years, so too it reflects the steady increase of women active in the labor forces of the Western countries. More women work now than ever before, and more middle-aged women are returning to employment than at any previous time. Only one-third of the women in the United States were in the labor force in 1950 compared to over one-half in 1983. In 1950 men were two and a half times as likely as women to be in the labor force, but in 1982 only one and a half times. By 1985 women constituted slightly over half of civilian workers in the United States, whereas they had constituted only 38 percent in 1970. In fact, women have accounted for the major share of labor force growth since the 1960s and are projected to account for seven out of ten additions to the labor force in the 1980s.

Between 1950 and 1977 the number of years an average twenty-year-old woman could expect to spend in the labor force nearly doubled, from 14.5 to 26 years. In 1950 only 11.9 percent of women with children under six, and 28.3 of those with children six to seventeen worked; in 1983 fully 49.9 percent of women with children under six and 63.8 percent of women with children six to seventeen were employed. At the same time the number of families maintained by women almost doubled between 1970 and 1983, so that one of every six families was headed by a woman; approximately 60 percent of these women were in the labor force. As shown in Figure 8.1, labor force participation rates among women fifty-five to fifty-nine have risen significantly since the 1950s, whereas those for women sixty to sixty-four have remained relatively constant despite a slight rise in the early 1970s (U.S. Department of Labor, 1984a; U.S. Census, 1983a; Waldman, 1983). In the European Common Market countries women's participation also increased, though there were significant variations in the rates between countries. In 1982 the range was from a low of a little over 21 percent in Ireland to a high of over 46 percent in Denmark. Here again, as we see from Table 8.1, participation rates tend to be fairly high among middle-aged women (Eurostat, 1984a, 1984b).

Since 1947, unemployment rates among women have tended to be higher than those for men. As shown in Figure 8.2, however, a reversal began in 1982 (U.S. Department of Labor, 1983a). DeBoer and Seeborg (1984) attribute this transition to the fact that female-dominated service occupations in peripheral industries are growing faster than male-dominated manufacturing industries. For a number of reasons, including self-concept, training, and so on, unemployed men who had previously worked in manufacturing tend not to seek jobs in service industries.

Despite that unemployment rates for women have fallen below those for men, it should also be noted from Figure 8.2 that these figures have tended to rise since the 1960s for both sexes. In 1982 the unemployment rate in the United States was significantly higher than in any of the other industrialized nations, with the exception of Great Britain and Canada. Unemployment is not, however, evenly distributed among industries, occupations, races, or the sexes. Among women, for example, unemployment is higher among blacks

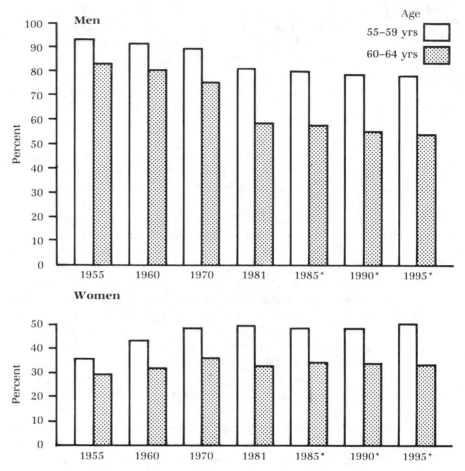

*Projected figure. NOTE: Figures are monthly averages. Total noninstitutional population. Projections are based on current labor force participation ratios through 1979 and current population estimates through 1976.

**FIGURE 8.1**

Labor force participation rates among workers fifty-five to sixty-four by sex. (*Source:* U.S. Bureau of the Census. *Demographic and Socioeconomic Aspects of Aging in the United States,* p. 116. Current Population Reports, Series P-23, No. 138. Washington, D.C.: U.S. Government Printing Office, 1984 [converted from numeric data].)

and Hispanics than among whites; it is higher among those with less education, particularly high school dropouts; and it is higher among younger women, particularly those sixteen to nineteen. Economically, women who maintain families seem to do poorly overall. Their unemployment rates are higher; over 10 percent in 1981 as opposed to approximately 6 percent for wives. Further,

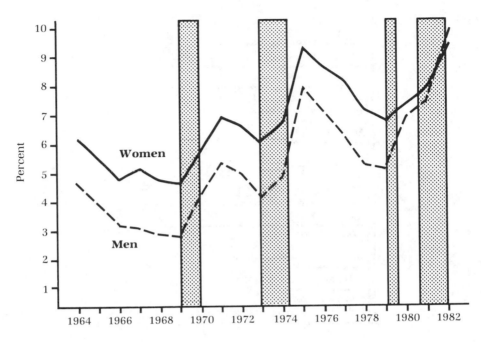

NOTE: Shaded areas denote recessions.

**FIGURE 8.2**

Male and female unemployment rates, 1964–1982. (*Source:* DeBoer, L., and M. Seeborg. "The Female-Male Unemployment Differential: Effects of Changes in Industry Employment." *Monthly Labor Review* 107, 12 [1984]: 8–15.)

women who are heads of households have average family incomes less than half of that for husband and wife families in 1981. Well over 30 percent of families maintained by women were in poverty, compared to well under 10 percent of husband and wife families (Johnson et al., 1983; U.S. Department of Labor, 1983b).

As can be seen from Figure 8.3, women as a group tend to earn less than men; generally women are paid at a rate of 60 to 65 percent of men's overall earnings, with this ratio remaining constant at least since the 1960s. A major factor contributing to lower rates of pay for women is their distribution within the labor market. In short, job segregation exists. Women tend to be concentrated in the lower paying clerical and service occupations. When women work in the manufacturing industries, they tend to be concentrated in the lower paying peripheral industries and are underrepresented in the higher paying ones. Although women are actually more likely than men to work in the professional and technical groups, they are less likely to hold higher prestige positions (Mellor, 1984). Though they obtain positions, they remain in entry-level jobs while men move up. Lower educational levels among women

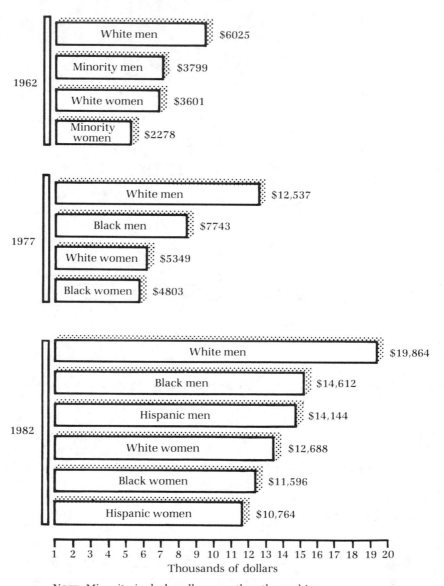

NOTE: Minority includes all races other than white.

**FIGURE 8.3**

Average earnings of American workers by sex and race, 1962, 1977, and 1982. (*Sources:* U.S. Department of Labor, Bureau of Labor Statistics. *Employment and Unemployment During 1979.* Washington, D.C.: U.S. Government Printing Office, 1980; U.S. Department of Labor, Women's Bureau. *Women Workers Today.* Washington, D.C.: U.S. Government Printing Office, 1974; and Mellor, E. F. "Investigating the Differences in Weekly Earnings of Women and Men." *Monthly Labor Review* 107, 6 [1984]: 17–28 [adapted].)

have been thought to contribute to these patterns in the past; data from a 1981 study showed that women tended to make only 59 to 66 percent as much as men even when they had comparable levels of education (U.S. Department of Labor, 1983c). While the proportion of women obtaining a higher education has been increasing, with 50.3 percent of bachelor's degrees, 50.8 percent of master's degrees, and 32 percent of doctorates being earned by women in 1982, women are still underrepresented in the professions and in managerial and executive positions (Sieling, 1984; Shack-Marquez, 1984; Scientific Manpower Commission, 1985). Similarly, discontinuous work patterns do not explain either occupational segregation or lower levels of pay because women with continuous work histories do not demonstrate a greater likelihood of being employed in higher paying jobs (England, 1982).

Despite the equal employment opportunity laws prohibiting employment discrimination on the basis of sex, occupational distribution in the marketplace has not been altered dramatically since 1963. On the federal level, women may use the provisions of the 1963 Equal Pay Act, Title VII of the Civil Rights Act of 1964, Title IX of the Education Amendments of 1972, and Executive Order 11246, which prohibit employment discrimination by federal contractors, to enforce their rights to equal employment opportunities (Wallace, 1976). The challenge is one not easily met, nor one on which all members of society agree. As long as women and minorities fill secondary positions in the labor markets, no matter their gains in education and income, they will continue to command fewer resources and have available correspondingly fewer chances for control over the financial and physical issues raised during the later years than do those who occupy positions in the primary labor markets. The ability to command resources based on education, training, and occupation does not necessarily overcome the effects of discrimination based on sex or race (Quinn, 1979). The generalization to be made is not that older women are certain to be poverty stricken, in ill-health, and lonely but that they are at a much higher risk of having such experiences. Indeed, at the United Nations Conference on Women held in Africa in 1985, the same theme was articulated by a variety of speakers: the economic crises of the world are borne most often by women whose relative positions have worsened since 1975.

## MINORITIES AND THE LABOR MARKET

Like women, minorities also tend to be disadvantaged with regard to the labor market. This not only bodes ill for their later years but also puts black and Hispanic women in double jeopardy. Since minority aging will be discussed more completely in Chapter 9, the focus here will be on a global work-related discussion. Notwithstanding federal programs, there is a marked differential between white and minority incomes in the United States. Furthermore, there are noticeable disparities between minorities. Asian Americans do quite well, with average incomes only slightly below that of the majority population. Cubans do better financially than other Hispanic people, while Puerto Ricans earn the least. Cubans are somewhat of a paradox; the wave of immigrants who moved to the United States around 1960 have done very well, while later arrivals are among the least well paid of anyone working in the United States. Blacks, too, have income averages that cluster near the lower end of the scale. The incomes shown in Figure 8.3 indicate part of the story; what they do not convey is the per capita income in families or how the income is disbursed. Given differences in family size and the proportion of incomes spent on shelter and other necessities, the quality of family life is sharply lower among minorities.

The figures also do not show how minorities are more affected by the vagaries of the ebb and flow of business cycles. Over the past twenty years black incomes, for example, moved from being about 55 percent that of whites to a high of 61 percent, only to return to approximately their initial level during the recession of the early 1980s. Hispanic incomes, while higher than among blacks, have been similarly affected by the state of the economy. Unemployment rates are also far higher among blacks and Hispanics than among whites. In 1982 and 1983 blacks were twice as likely to be unemployed as whites; Hispanics were one and a half times as likely as whites, though unemployment rates for Puerto Ricans approached the black rate. In 1982 the unemployment rate for non-Hispanics was 9.5 percent, as compared to an overall rate of 13.4 percent for Hispanics and 17.3 percent for Puerto Ricans. Blacks represented 20.1 percent of the unemployed yet comprised only 10.3 percent of all workers. Similarly, Hispanics represented 7.7 percent of unemployed workers and only 5.4 percent of all workers. Of those who were employed, whites were more likely than Hispanics and blacks to have worked fifty-two weeks of the year, with blacks being likely to have worked for shorter periods than Hispanics. Among women, minority group unemployment rates in 1982 were similar to the overall rates, with black women being twice as likely as white women to be without a job and Hispanic women rather more than one and a half times as likely as white women to be jobless (U.S. Census, 1985b; U.S. Department of Labor, 1983b, 1983d, 1984a).

All the data show that blacks and Hispanics have lower income levels than whites and are more likely to fall below the poverty level. This is not the place to engage in a general review of the politics of poverty, but official government statistics do point to devastating poverty among minorities and show that in the two decades since the Civil Rights Act of 1965 poverty levels for minorities have actually increased. In 1983 the overall percentage of persons below the poverty level nationwide was 15.2 percent. The percentage among whites was only 12 percent, as compared to 36 percent for blacks. In 1982 over 25 percent of Hispanics were below the poverty level; among Puerto Ricans, 43 percent fell into this category. Of married couple families, 6.9 percent of white families were in poverty, as opposed to 15.6 percent of black families and 19.3 percent of Hispanic families. Of families maintained by men, 12.6 percent of white families were below the poverty level, as compared to 25.0 and 18.4 percent of black and Hispanic families, respectively. In contrast, among families maintained by women, the situation was particularly acute:

fully 28.9 percent of white families, 56.1 percent of black families, and 55.5 percent of Hispanic families were below the poverty line. Both median family income and the distribution of family income brackets favored whites against blacks and Hispanics, with Puerto Ricans faring worst among the Hispanics. In part this is attributable to the large number of Puerto Rican households maintained by women. In 1981 the median family income for blacks was only 60 percent of that for whites. Among women head of households, white median family income in 1982 was $13,145, far higher than that for black ($7489) and Hispanic ($7611) families. Nationwide, the overall percentages of families with incomes under $5000 in 1982 were 4.6 percent for whites, 17.0 percent for blacks, and 10.1 percent for Hispanics. In the highest income bracket ($50,000 and over) we find 11.9 percent of whites but only 2.6 percent of blacks and 3.9 percent of Hispanics (U.S. Census, 1985a, 1985e, 1983a; Johnson et al., 1983).

Other indicators predictive of financial hardship are equally potent. Lower levels of education as well as labor market locale and concentration in peripheral sectors of the productive sphere are also characteristic of minorities. Certainly, years of schooling explain a large share of the earnings differential, but even when minority education is comparable to whites, salaries are still considerably less. All things being equal, education helps; however, additional years of school help white males far more than anyone else. A black man with a college degree earns approximately the same as a white high school graduate. A study cited in the Employment and Training Report of the President for 1982 found that even when controlling for sex, age, race, education, and other observable characteristics, the return on human capital was inequitable: education helps, but it helps whites more. Puerto Rican and Central and South American men experience the worst employment discrimination; as already noted, blacks are similarly clustered in low-paying, low status jobs.

We can conclude that a pervasive pattern of job discrimination is found in the United States. When minorities obtain jobs, they are primarily in service and what are called operative occupations. They experience little upward mobility, receive less return on human capital investments than whites, and are most affected by economic recession. The best news relatively speaking is found among Asian Americans who are consistently better off and experience less overt discrimination. It is a myth, however, to think no discrimination exists. The evidence is there when refined indicators are used. Income levels are higher than among other minority groups but more family members work to bring family incomes to the levels they reach. Of course, not all Asian Americans come from the same country of origin or ethnic background, and their experiences in the United States are as heterogeneous as Hispanics. Among Asian Americans, poverty rates are half again higher than for whites, while financial returns for comparable educations are lower — both are evidence of labor market discrimination. When the Commission on Civil Rights (1980) controlled for all possible intervening factors, both Japanese and Chinese Americans were found to be highly disadvantaged relative to whites (U.S. Census,

1985a; Scientific Manpower Commission, 1985; Commission on Civil Rights, 1980).

A final word must be included on an often ignored group, the Native Americans. With the lowest per capita income and education levels, as well as the highest poverty and unemployment rates, this group probably has the poorest quality of life of any other living in the United States. With age come even greater inequalities and hardships with virtually no recourse for amelioration. For all minorities and the disadvantaged the struggle to stay above the poverty level during their working years leaves little opportunity to prepare for retirement. Few, if any, have access to private pensions and few acquire assets they could liquidate if necessary. Futhermore, years of struggling with poverty, inadequate nutrition, less than optimal medical care, and so on makes the prospect of an old age that the white elderly aspire to extremely unlikely. Indeed, the probability of even reaching what the general population thinks of as old age is significantly lower.

# Finances in the Later Years

Almost without exception, financial status in old age reflects relative standings throughout the working life. As will be seen in Chapter 11, the distribution of public pension policies is predicated on lifetime earnings profiles. Since the majority of all people over sixty-five receive the largest share of their monies from government transfer programs, little redistribution or realignment takes place. Those who were well paid before retirement will be relatively better off than those whose previous incomes were low. One might argue that other consumption entitlements, such as health and social services, redress some of the inequalities. Nonetheless, the social dynamic of old age is rooted in the structure of participation in the labor market. In other words, the array of benefits, resources, power, and the very legitimacy of older people's claims are influenced by the same factors that guide the economy and politics in general. The wages of retirement and all they portend stem from the wages of work (Myles, 1984; Estes et al., 1984).

However much financial status in retirement is said to be the result of individual activities, the fact remains that public pension entitlements channeled through governmental agencies are linked to "market criteria" (Myles, 1984). They reflect political choices that once become operative are often reified and seen as irrevocable. Just how golden, then, are the golden years? Are the same people who are disadvantaged by wage-based inequalities before retirement still at the bottom of the system after they retire?

## INCOME DURING THE GOLDEN YEARS

Analyzing the financial situation of the elderly in comparison to that of younger cohorts is not a simple task. As pointed out in Chapter 1, when looking at statistics, the answers identified depend very much on the questions asked. Some questions and concepts make the financial situation of the elderly look rather positive; others make it look decidedly negative. In either case, however, the patterns derive from the distributive qualities of the labor market. To get a complete picture of the finances of the elderly we need to ask a range of questions and be aware of controversies and limitations surrounding the indicators used in reporting and comparing income levels. In deciding whether retirement income is adequate, as was pointed out with regard to health, it is not a case of looking at economics as a competition between generations, or as deferred wages, or as priorities in the national budget, but in terms of a balancing of resources throughout life. Do citizens have a right not to be faced with economic insecurity at the end of their lives (Myles, 1984)?

**Indicators of Income.** One issue in comparing the incomes of those sixty-five and over with the rest of the population is whether to use figures for families or individuals. In 1980 the median income of families with householders sixty-five and over was 58 percent of that of all families. However, the per capita income of families with householders sixty-five and over was 81 percent of the per capita income for all families. Analysts think per capita family income gives an overly negative view of the financial situation of the elderly, since the families of the older persons tend to be smaller than those of the young and middle-aged, and thus the income per person is higher than the figures for families would lead one to believe. On the other hand, a comparison of per capita income may make the situation of the elderly seem more favorable than it really is, because of economies of scale in younger families and because of the differing needs of the elderly, including, for instance, increased expenses for medical care (U.S. Census, 1984).

Another major question is that of non-monetary benefits, which generally are not included in income estimates. Public non-monetary benefits available to the elderly in the United States include Medicare, Medicaid, food stamps, and publicly owned or subsidized housing. In other free market economies of the West a similar range of non-monetary entitlements exist for older persons, and in all cases they account for a larger share of the national budget than they do in the United States (Myles, 1984). It has been estimated that public non-monetary benefits add about 10 percent to the income of the elderly in the United States. In addition to these programs, a variety of related benefits are offered to older people, including discounts on transportation and other services provided by businesses. Then, too, there is the assistance provided by friends and family. How should that be counted? Except for Medicare, participation in public non-monetary benefit programs among the elderly is relatively low. In addition, there is the problem of how to quantify the value of non-monetary benefits for those who receive them. To use the market value may be misleading, because an excess of one type of support (for example, housing or food) does not compensate for a deficiency in another kind of support (for example, medical care). Finally, if we are looking at comparisons between the financial status of the elderly and the rest of the population, we need to remember that the young and those in the middle years may also receive a variety of noncash benefits, including such things as public education. Chen proposes using a variety of measures for estimating the value of different types of non-monetary subsidies and suggests that including non-monetary benefits in estimates of income for the elderly would reduce the poverty rate by between 4 and 10 percent depending on the measures used (U.S. Census, 1984: Chen, 1985).

The poverty index, originated by the Social Security Administration in 1964, and updated each year since, has also come under fire. Because it is based on the income necessary to maintain subsistence level diets, some have contended that the "near poverty" benchmarks (income at 125 percent of poverty level) would be a more appropriate indicator of economic hardship, given the increased expenditures for health care that comes with age (Chen, 1985). As may be seen from Figures 8.4A and 8.4C, which indicator is selected radically affects the appearance of poverty rates among the elderly. Based on actual poverty levels, the rate among the elderly for 1983 is 14.1 percent. If, however, 125 percent of the poverty level is taken, rates jump to 22.4 percent. The first is slightly lower than that found among the general population, while the second is some two points above (U.S. Census, 1985e).

As has been pointed out, the use of summary indicators may obscure variability within groups. A relatively high mean income may result if a small group of high income individuals are averaged along with a relatively large group of the poor. While median income is a better indicator, it still obscures

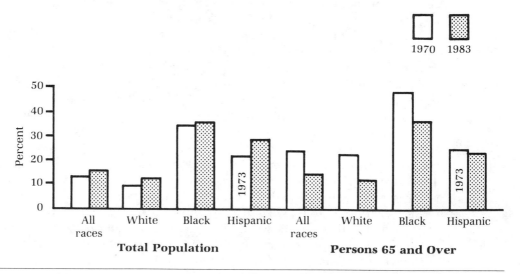

**FIGURE 8.4A**

Trends in percentages of population below the poverty level, 1970–1983: persons sixty-five and over compared to total population by race. (*Source:* U.S. Bureau of the Census. *Characteristics of the Population Below the Poverty Level: 1983.* Current Population Reports, Series P-60, No. 147. Washington, D.C.: U.S. Government Printing Office, 1985 [converted].)

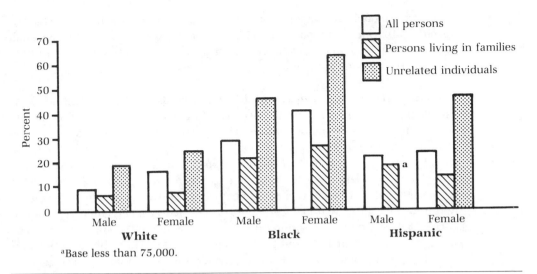

a Base less than 75,000.

**FIGURE 8.4B**
Percent of persons sixty-five and over below the poverty level by family status, sex, and race.
(*Source:* U.S. Bureau of the Census. *Characteristics of the Population Below the Poverty Level: 1983.*
Current Population Reports, Series P-60, No. 147. Washington, D.C.: U.S. Government Printing
Office, 1985 [converted].)

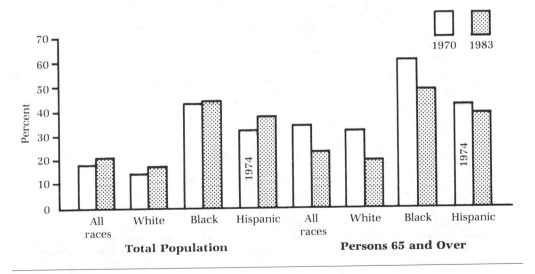

**FIGURE 8.4C**
Trends in percentages of population below 125 percent of poverty level, 1970–1983: persons
sixty-five and over compared to total population by race. (*Source:* U.S. Bureau of the Census.
*Characteristics of the Population Below the Poverty Level: 1983.* Current Population Reports, Series
P-60, No. 147. Washington, D.C.: U.S. Government Printing Office, 1985 [converted].)

variation, particularly that all those in low-income categories may come from a specific subgroup of the population. As shown in Figure 8.4B, and as we shall see later in this chapter, relatively moderate overall poverty rates may hide soaring rates among some minority populations.

**Income Patterns during the Golden Years.** Is the financial situation of the elderly good or bad? On the positive side there has been a noticeable decrease in poverty rates among the elderly over the last few decades, both overall and as compared to the general population. In 1959 poverty rates for those sixty-five and over was 35.2 percent as opposed to a rate of 22.4 percent for the general population; by 1983 it was slightly under the general rate of 15.2 percent. Based on the 125 percent indicator, in 1969 35.2 percent of the elderly found themselves within 25 percent of the poverty level, while in 1983 the percentage was only 22.4; among the general population, comparable figures were 17.4 percent in 1969 and 20.3 percent in 1983. There has also been an improvement in median income among the elderly as compared to the general

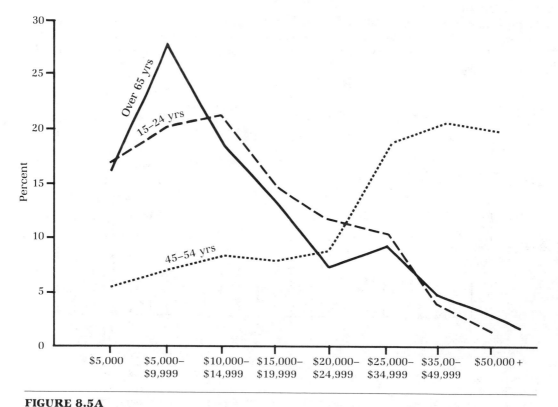

**FIGURE 8.5A**

Money income of households: percent distribution by money income level by age, 1983. (*Source:* U.S. Bureau of the Census. *Statistical Abstract of the United States, 1985*, 105th ed. Washington, D.C.: U.S. Government Printing Office, 1985 [converted].)

population. Between 1972 and 1982, because of the increase in Social Security, median incomes of the elderly grew at about twice the rate of those of the general population. Between 1951 and 1981, in terms of constant dollars, the median income of the elderly more than doubled (U.S. Census, 1983b, 1985e).

While these indicators represent some very real improvements in the financial situation of the elderly, there is no room for complacency. The recent political climate threatens to halve the cost of living increases for the retired. Furthermore, these positive indicators should not obscure the negative side of the financial situation of the elderly. As shown in Figure 8.5, median money income for householders sixty-five and over was less than that for any other group in 1983. Those over sixty-five (like the young) tend to be disproportionately represented in the lower income groups when their pattern of income distribution is compared to those in middle life. It is clear that substantial numbers of the elderly live in real poverty and some groups are at very high risk. In addition to sex and race, factors affecting income levels among old people include health and the survival of a spouse, a person's health and ability to continue to work at acceptable levels, and living arrangements. As shown in Figure 8.4B, all groups, elderly unrelated individuals living alone or with nonfamily members, are at greater risk for poverty. There are also telling differences among those who continue to work, as compared to those who are retired. In 1980 the median income of a family maintained by an elderly per-

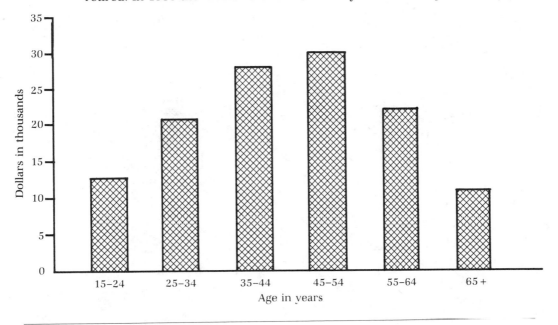

**FIGURE 8.5B**
Median income of households by age, 1983. (*Source:* U.S. Bureau of the Census. *Statistical Abstract of the United States, 1985,* 105th ed. Washington, D.C.: U.S. Government Printing Office, 1985 [converted].)

son who did not work was only $11,550, as compared to $24,280 among those who worked full-time, twenty-seven to fifty-two weeks a year. After sixty-five, income also declines dramatically with increasing age. In 1983 the poverty rate for those sixty-five to seventy-one was 10.8 percent; for those seventy-two and over, a period when medical expenses begin to climb precipitiously, it was 16.9 percent (U.S. Census, 1984a).

As illustrated in Figure 8.6, major sources of income for the elderly include Social Security benefits, earnings, property income, and private and

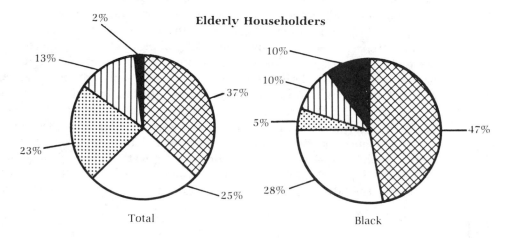

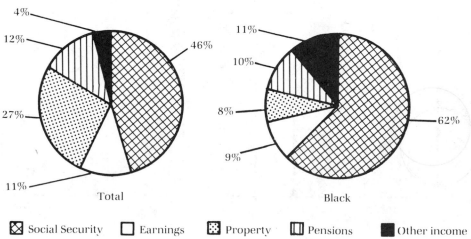

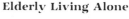

**FIGURE 8.6**
Source of money income in 1981, by race, for elderly householders and persons living alone.
(*Source:* U.S. Bureau of the Census. *America in Transition: An Aging Society.* Current Population Reports, Series P-23, No. 128. Washington, D.C.: U.S. Government Printing Office, 1984.)

public pensions. As might be expected from the discussion of labor force participation patterns, since the 1960s there has been a decline in the importance of earnings and increased reliance on retirement income from Social Security, public and private pensions, and assets. There is also greater dependence on Social Security with increasing age. Elderly unrelated individuals, who tend to constitute the lowest income group among the elderly, are also likely to rely almost wholly on monies other than earned income. The decision about whether to continue working after people are eligible for retirement seems to be related to whether they are liable to have a significantly higher income if they continue to work (U.S. Census, 1984; Chen, 1985).

**Income Satisfaction.** Public opinion polls have shown elderly people as a whole to be reasonably satisfied with their financial situation. Surveys conducted by the National Opinion Research Center from 1982 through 1984 showed only 15 percent of older people to be not at all satisfied with their financial situation; 42 percent were more or less satisfied, and 43 percent were fairly well satisfied. Among younger age cohorts, 25 percent of those fifty-five to sixty-four were not satisfied at all, while fully 37 percent of those between twenty-five and thirty-nine were not at all satisfied. Among those sixty-five or over, 66 percent thought their income was average or above average, while 28 percent thought it was below average and 6 percent thought it far below average. It should be noted, however, that 17 percent of the elderly thought not having enough money to live on to be a very serious problem and 24 percent found it a problem, while 58 percent considered it to be no problem. Furthermore, the relatively high overall levels of satisfaction again obscure serious problems among ethnic minorities: 42 percent of black respondents saw impending poverty as a problem and 52 percent of Hispanics felt likewise. A lifetime of living in near poverty certainly teaches coping skills necessary for dealing with reduced resources in the retirement years. Among those who retire, financial considerations seem to weigh heavily in the decision about whether to retire early. Indeed, a majority of persons felt they would like to continue some type of paid part-time work after retirement (*Public Opinion*, 1985; NCOA, 1981).

Advocacy among American labor unions of early retirement programs continues, not only to provide older workers with a chance for a relaxed life of leisure but also to maximize job opportunities for younger union members (Claque et al., 1971; Stagner, 1978). Older workers may feel pressure to retire from younger workers, management, and their unions. What impact are these trends having? To date no precise answers have emerged; however, the evidence indicates that adequate income and health status are related to the decision to retire early. Health factors range from perceived health problems to the actual incidence of time lost from work. Whatever the reason, there is a continuing decline in the age at which unionized workers are retiring (Barfield and Morgan, 1974, 1978; Holtzman et al., 1980).

To assess the need for flexible careers it is necessary to distinguish between jobs and careers. Jobs are specific work positions with related duties, responsibilities, and income. An individual may keep the same job throughout his or her work life, yet change employers repeatedly; for instance, a mechanic, teacher, or engineer who retains the same duties despite working for different employers. Conversely, an individual might work for the same employer for many years and change jobs as he or she ascends the hierarchy of the particular company. Added to the idea of job change is the notion of a career; to the examples given earlier might be added an individual changing from the role of lawyer to banker, teacher to social worker, or athlete to small business entrepreneur to illustrate the concept of a career. These considerations, plus internal or external pressures and the availability of job and career opportunities, must enter into any examination of career changes among workers (Murray et al., 1971).

The idea of career and retirement flexibility has grown in importance over the past few years because of the character of industrialized employment. Lower status jobs are continually being abolished by automation, while many clerical positions have expanded. Modern technology enables a country to use less human energy in the process of creating more economic surplus, and, in turn, the larger the surplus, the greater the potential for supporting sizable numbers of nonproductive people. In addition, the health and medical improvements during this century have contributed to longer lives, so that the period of retirement is now averaging as long as ten to fifteen years. It is entirely possible, however, that the advantages of mandatory retirement as far as the industrial sector is concerned may be outweighed by the disadvantages incurred in the personal and social spheres of life. The same critics who loudly decry economic waste often seem blissfully ignorant of the ramifications of psychic waste. Tired of seeing older workers dissatisfied and their collective experience underutilized, the idea of flexible retirement has become a rallying point for all those who choose to emphasize human potential and life alternatives as crucial as economic growth. Caution must be exercised, since the amount of psychological cost levied against those who could no longer explain their retirement as the result of an inflexible system has yet to be determined.

It is entirely feasible that workers in most industrialized countries could retire as early as age fifty or fifty-five during the 1980s without sacrificing productivity (Kreps, 1976). The unemployment rate over the next few years will probably have more significance than overall productivity, however. As unemployment increases, so does the number of applicants for existing jobs; consequently, more pressure is exerted on the extremes of the age continuum to delay their entry or to hasten their exit from the labor market. National Social Security regulations have a way of responding to economic pressures, as represented by the three-year reduction in the earliest pensionable age for men in the United States in 1961. This change occurred after a period of recession during which unemployment rates averaged 6 percent, up from the 3 percent observed in the early years of the 1950s. Economic growth in America after the middle 1960s saw unemployment again drop to between 3 and 4 percent, but the cycle has come full circle and the boom has been succeeded by economic crises and unparalleled unemployment rate. One possible outcome may be to place renewed emphasis on expanding flexible and early retirement programs; some even suggest the economic incentives for early retirement present in both private pension and the Social Security program in the United States may have to be addressed in future legislation (Schulz, 1985).

## EXPENDITURES DURING THE GOLDEN YEARS

One of the difficulties in comparing the income of the elderly with that of the young is that because of their differing situations and varying needs, some of the expenditures of the elderly are higher than those of the young. Two particular items are housing and health care costs. For elderly families, the four largest items of the budget are (in order) housing, food, transportation, and health care. For younger families, they are housing, food, transportation, and recreation (U.S. Census, 1984). Even when dollar amounts are roughly comparable, the proportion of total income spent on these and other necessities is considerably greater among the elderly. Remember, too, as noted in Chapter 7, the elderly tend to live in older homes for which repair and maintenance costs are high. Also the average out-of-pocket per capita expenditures for medical care for those over sixty-five in 1984 was $1059; 5.6 percent went for hospital costs, 21.4 percent to physicians, 41.6 percent for nursing home care, and 31.3 percent for other care. This figure has almost doubled from the 1977 figure of $522 (Waldo and Lazenby, 1984). Older people also spend more on food than younger people, possibly because of consumption patterns that focus on restaurant meals and convenience foods bought in small quantities. These expenditures represent approximately 23.5 percent of income before taxes for the elderly as opposed to only 16 percent in the under twenty-five group (U.S. Department of Labor, 1983e). Both health and housing expenditures tend to increase even more the further one moves into old age, whereas, as noted earlier, income tends to decrease.

In spite of these problems, there has been some improvement in the number of retired persons able to cope because of federally established lower, intermediate, and higher budgets for urban retired couples. In 1970 the income of 49 percent of couples was below the intermediate budget and 51 percent above it, while in 1980 the numbers were 35 percent and 65 percent, respectively. Although similar advances were made in the lower budget, 1.2 million couples still fell below the lower limit, which means that many people are going without necessities (Chen, 1985).

**Minority Finances in the Golden Years.** The distribution of financial hardship and poverty is not equal during retirement. Looking again at Figure 8.4B, blacks and Hispanics tend to do worse than whites, and women worse than men, on all counts. They have higher poverty levels, lower median incomes, and tend to rely more on Social Security than on other sources of income such as earnings that as we saw earlier, means increased poverty. This is a reflection of a variety of structural factors; as we saw in the sections on working women and minorities, these groups tend to have higher unemployment rates and are concentrated in lower paying jobs with fewer retirement benefits. This in turn leads to an impaired opportunity to save for retirement, less likelihood of a pension, and an increased propensity to retire relatively early for health reasons. In retirement, as during their working life, blacks are at a greater disadvantage than even Hispanics, and black and Hispanic women are at double risk. Among women who never married, the risks are far greater than for most other categories. In 1983 63.4 percent of elderly black women living alone were below the poverty level (O'Rand and Henretta, 1982; U.S. Census, 1985e).

# Summary

The experiences of older members of the work forces of industrialized societies are influenced by many factors, ranging from position in primary or secondary labor sectors, career patterns, occupational status, and, to some degree, individual choice. Workers who are women or members of minority groups, who fill lower status jobs, who exhibit unstable career patterns, or, in many instances, who age at the wrong time and place are confronted with tremendous challenges in their attempts to command resources, ensure security, or reenter the labor market once they have left. Myths proliferate regarding the declining capacities and inefficiency of aging employees, coupled with the costliness of occupational transfer programs. These myths, however, are not supported by research data. The older person actually has many valuable skills and traits that could easily be recognized and used by personnel managers and employers.

Adjusting to retirement is associated with occupational background, willingness to retire, and financial security. Many people keenly feel the loss of their work role, yet many others view retirement with favor or equanimity. Financial considerations are among the most important resources shaping the exigencies of the retirement years. All too frequently middle-aged workers see retirement as an event rather than as a period of life and a process in its own right. Accordingly, too little preparation for retirement characterizes the majority. For some, however, structural factors make preparation difficult, if not impossible.

Two alternative models can be used in attempting to observe how people adjust to and how satisfied they are with their retirement. The human capital approach is the more individualistic of the two. It looks primarily at those individual resources in which people invest themselves over the course of their lives to explain what they encounter after leaving the labor force. The dimensions of financial well-being are cast as the outcome of personal attributes such as education, occupation, health, marital status, and so on. The structural perspective may examine these same factors but they are treated as consequences of macro-level processes beyond the control of individual workers. In this view occupation, health, finances, and so on are thought to reflect locale vis-à-vis the social organization of production. In reality the two models are complementary, viewing the retirement experience as a complex interplay of structural, cultural, and individual factors.

The concept of a career is crucial in the ways many people think about their own lives and in the analytic template gerontologists use to make sense of changes during adult life. Most of us think of the future as a passage through a sequence of positions, each of which builds on the one preceding. Even when we do not experience such a progression ourselves, it is the usual standard by which success is measured. The nature of the economy and the changing growth patterns in production have a major impact on how individual career trajectories take shape. As we enter an era where demographic and technological changes are altering the way work is performed, we need to re-examine how we think of careers. The vast bulk of the labor force is now employed in service occupations in which the opportunities for advancement are far different than in the manufacturing sector. Likely as not there will be widespread dampening of upward mobility once entry-level positions are obtained. Furthermore, technological innovations may create the need for changes of occupation in midlife. It may well be, therefore, that the career patterns of our parents and grandparents may not be replicated by future generations of the elderly.

Labor force participation rates and returns depend on a combination of factors. Worker stereotypes maintain that older workers are neither as productive nor as capable as their younger counterparts. The result is wide-scale dislocation and displacement of workers in their middle and later years in the labor force. As early as forty-five, differential labor market experiences discriminate against those who are that age or older. The results can be devastating both economically and psychologically.

A cross-cultural comparison of work experience suggests that not all mass societies have industrialized in the same way. Markedly different patterns are found not only among the free market economies of the West but between them and developing or still underdeveloped economies. Narrowing the focus to the United States also shows a range of experiences are the norm. White men do far better as a group than any other category of workers. Women and minorities in the labor market encounter significantly less return on their own investments and greater discrimination in unemployment and upward mobility.

These lifelong patterns continue to structure the lives of people long after they have left the labor force. Public pension programs are predicated on earnings in the productive sphere and help to legitimate its ramifications. Varying degrees of financial hardship characterize subpopulations of the elderly, but overall most of the elderly think their situation is acceptable. Depending on which indicators are used, the picture of relative standing will appear differently. One thing is clear: for those whose lives are constrained by living at or only slightly above the poverty level, itself a political definition, the prospects of a trouble-free old age are dimmer than for those whose finances place them in an advantaged position. For the most part, those advantages accrue to the white male portion of the labor force, with all other workers arrayed behind, reflecting structural factors that have influenced their work experience. Women and racial and ethnic minorities may invest in human capital, but to date the returns during their retirement years have tended to leave them at comparatively greater risk. Black and American Indian minority workers may have suffered the greatest inequities of all.

# Discussion Questions

**Work and Aging in Mass Society**

**1.** What are the possible implications for retirement of economic upheavals experienced earlier in working life?

**2.** What might the advantage be of working shorter hours throughout the life cycle and never really retiring? Answer in terms of the workers themselves, the employers, the workers' families, the economy, and those who purchase goods and services.

**3.** How would the plight of the elderly poor be explained by (a) the individualist approach, and (b) the structural approach? What are the strengths and weaknesses of each? How might they be synthesized?

**Work Patterns and the Life Cycle**

**4.** To what extent do you think career patterns are determined by (a) social factors or (b) psychological factors? How do these operate? How are changes in the economy and in technology likely to affect the concept of career development?

**5.** How might we deal with problems that technological and economic change pose? Propose a model of working life that might be more appropriate to current conditions than the career development model.

**The Meaning of Work**

**6.** What are the advantages and disadvantages of work having a central meaning in people's lives?

**7.** What factors underlie age discrimination in employment? How might these be overcome?

**8.** How could the negative impact of status displacement among older workers and retirees be minimized? Consider possible structural, cultural, and psychological interventions in your answer.

**9.** How would the issue of preparation for retirement be considered (a) within the individual model and (b) within the structural model?

**Working Around
the World**

**10.** How do you think the differences in labor force participation patterns between industrialized and Third World countries can be explained?

**11.** What are the causes of labor market segregation between men and women? What are the probable implications of this for women during their working lives and in retirement? Do you think there should be equal employment opportunity and pay for women?

**12.** How would you explain labor market segregation between whites and ethnic minorities? What are its potential implications for retirement?

**Finances in the
Later Years**

**13.** What are the key questions in assessing the financial situation of the elderly? What indicators would you use in answering these questions?

**14.** Design an income policy for the elderly taking into account the role of public and/or private pensions, the role of retirement, and opportunities for continued employment.

**15.** What are the positive and negative aspects of the current financial situation of the elderly? What are the problems in comparing the ability of the young and the elderly to meet necessary expenditures?

# Pertinent Readings

Abeles, R. P., L. Steel, and L. L. Wise. "Patterns and Implications of Life-Course Organization: Studies From Project TALENT." In *Life-Span Development and Behavior*, vol. 3, eds. P. B. Baltes and O. G. Brim, pp. 308–37. New York: Academic Press, Inc., 1980.

Andrisani, P. J., and S. H. Sandell. "Technological Change and Its Labor Market Situation of Older Workers." In *Aging and Technological Advances*, eds. P. K. Robinson, J. Livingston, and J. E. Birren, pp. 99–111. New York: Plenum Press–NATO Scientific Affairs Division, 1984.

Atchley, R. C. *The Sociology of Retirement*. New York: Halsted/Wiley, 1976.

Barfield, R. E., and J. Morgan. *Early Retirement: The Decision and the Experience and a Second Look*. Ann Arbor: Institute for Social Research, 1974.

———. "Trends in Satisfaction with Retirement." *The Gerontologist* 18, 1 (1978): 19–23.

Baron, J. N., and W. T. Bielby. "Organizational Barriers to Gender Equality: Sex Segregation of Jobs and Opportunities." In *Gender and the Life Course*, ed. A. S. Rossi, pp. 233–51. New York: Aldine Publishing Company, 1985.

Beattie, W. M., Jr. "Aging and the Social Services." In *Handbook of Aging and the Social Sciences*, eds. R. H. Binstock and E. Shanas, pp. 619–42. New York: Van Nostrand Reinhold Company, 1976.

Beck, E. M., P. M. Horan, and C. M. Tolbert. "Stratification in a Dual Economy: A Sectoral Model of Earnings Determination." *American Sociological Review* 43, 6 (1978): 704–20.

Beck, S. N. "Adjustment to and Satisfaction with Retirement." *Journal of Gerontology* 37, 5 (1982): 616–24.

Bibb, R., and W. H. Form. "The Effects of Industrial Occupational and Sex Stratification on Wages in Blue-Collar Markets." *Social Forces* 55, 3 (1977): 974–96.

Burkhauser, R. V., and G. S. Tolley. "Older Americans and Market Work." *The Gerontologist* 18, 5 (1978): 449–53.

Butler, R. N. "Alternatives to Retirement." Testimony before the Subcommittee on Retirement Income and Employment. House Select Committee on Aging. July 25, 1977. DHEW Publication No. (NIH) 78–243. Washington, D.C.: U.S. Government Printing Office, 1978.

Casey, B. "Recent Trends in Retirement Policy and Practice in Europe and the USA: An Overview of Programmes Directed to the Exclusion of Older Workers and a Suggestion for an Alternative Strategy." In *Aging and Technological Advances*, eds. P. K. Robinson, J. Livingston, and J. E. Birren, pp. 125–37. New York: Plenum Press–NATO Scientific Affairs Division, 1984.

Chen, Y. P. "Economic Status of the Aging." In *Handbook of Aging and the Social Sciences*, eds. R. Binstock and S. Shanas, pp. 641–65. New York: Van Nostrand Reinhold Company, 1985.

Clague, E. "Work and Leisure for Older Workers." *The Gerontologist* 11, 1, Pt. II (1971): 9–20.

———, B. Palli, and L. Kramer. *The Aging Worker and the Union: Employment and Retirement of Middle Aged and Older Workers.* New York: Praeger Publishers, 1971.

Clark, R. L., and J. J. Spengler. *The Economics of Individual and Population Aging.* Cambridge, Mass.: Cambridge University Press, 1980.

Cohn, R. M. "Age and Satisfactions from Work." *Journal of Gerontology* 34, 2 (1979): 264–72.

Commission On Civil Rights. *Success of Asian-Americans: Fact or Fiction?* Washington, D.C.: U.S. Government Printing Office, 1980.

Davidson, P. E., and H. D. Anderson. *Occupational Mobility in an American Community.* Stanford, Calif.: Stanford University Press, 1937.

DeBoer, L., and M. Seeborg. "The Female-Male Unemployment Differential: Effects of Changes in Industry Employment." *Monthly Labor Review* 107, 12 (1984): 8–15.

Dowd, J. J. *Stratification Among the Aged.* Monterey, Calif.: Brooks/Cole Publishing Company, 1980.

Drucker, P. F. "Flexible-Age Retirement: Social Issue of the Decade." In *The Future of Business*, ed. M. Ways. New York: Pergamon Press, Inc., 1978.

England, P. "The Failure of Human Capital Theory to Explain Occupational Sex Segregation." *Journal of Human Resources* 17 (1982): 358–70.

Estes, C. L., L. E. Gerard, J. S. Zones, and J. H. Swan. *Political Economy, Health and Aging.* Boston: Little, Brown & Company, 1984.

Eurostat (Statistical Office of the European Communities). *Employment and Unemployment.* Luxembourg: Office for the Official Publications of the European Communities, 1984a.

———. *Employment and Unemployment, 1984* (Statistical Yearbook). Luxembourg: Office for the Official Publications of The European Communities, 1984b.

Foner, A., and K. Schwab. *Aging and Retirement.* Monterey, Calif.: Brooks/Cole Publishing Company, 1981.

Friedman, E. A., and H. L. Orbach. "Adjustment to Retirement." In *American Handbook of Psychiatry*, ed. S. Arieti, pp. 609–45. New York: Basic Books, 1974.

George L. K., and G. L. Maddox. "Subjective Adaptation to Loss of the Work Role: A Longitudinal Study." *Journal of Gerontology* 32, 4 (1977): 456–62.

Gordon, C., C. M. Gaitz, and J. Scott. "Leisure and Lives: Personal Expressivity across the Life Span." In *Handbook of Aging and the Social Sciences*, eds. R. H. Binstock and E. Shanas, pp. 310–41. New York: Van Nostrand Reinhold Company, 1976.

Guillemard, A. M. "Old Age, Retirement, and the Social Class Structure: Towards an Analysis of the Structural Dynamics of the Latter Stage of Life." In *Ageing and Life Course Transitions*, eds. T. K. Hareven and K. J. Adams, pp. 221–43. London: Tavistock Publications, 1982.

Gusfield, J. R. "Occupational Roles and Forms of Enterprise." *American Journal of Sociology* 66 (1961): 571–80.

Hagestad, G. O., and B. L. Neugarten. "Age and the Life Course." In *Handbook of Aging and the Social Sciences*, eds. R. Binstock and E. Shanas, pp. 35–61. New York: Van Nostrand Reinhold Company, 1985.

Hendricks, J. "Impact of Technological Change on Older Workers." In *Aging and Technological Advances*, eds. P. K. Robinson, J. Livingston, and J. E. Birren, pp. 113–24. New York: Plenum Press–NATO Scientific Affairs Division, 1984.

————, and C. McAllister. "An Alternative Perspective on Retirement: A Dual Economy Approach." *Ageing and Society* 3, 3 (1983): 279–99.

Henretta, J. C., and R. T. Campbell. "Status Attainment and Status Maintenance: A Study of Stratification in Old Age." *American Sociological Review* 41, 6 (1976): 981–92.

Herzog, B. R., ed. *Aging and Income: Programs and Prospects for the Elderly*. New York: Human Sciences Press, 1978.

Holtzman, J. M., J. Berman, and R. Ham. "Health and Early Retirement Decisions." *Journal of the American Geriatrics Society* 28, 1 (1980): 23–28.

International Labour Office. *Yearbook of Labour Statistics, 1983*. Geneva: International Labour Office, 1983.

Jacobson, D. "The Social Environment: A Neglected Dimension in the Study of Older Workers' Job Performance." In *Recent Advances in Gerontology*, eds. H. Orimo, K. Shimada, M. Iriki, and D. Maeda, pp. 377–78. Amsterdam: Excerpta Medica, 1979.

Jaffe, A. J. "Notes on the Recent Labor Force Experience of Older Workers." *Aging and Work* 1, 2 (1978): 135–38.

Johnson, B., L. Johnson, and E. Waldman. "Most Women Who Maintain Families Receive Poor Labor Market Returns." *Monthly Labor Review* 106, 12 (1983): 30–34.

Johnson, E. S., and J. B. Williamson. *Growing Old: The Social Problems of Aging*. New York: Holt, Rinehart & Winston, 1980.

Jondrow, J., F. Brechling, and A. Marcus. *Older Workers in the Market for Part-Time Employment*. Project on National Employment Policy and Older Americans. Washington, D.C.: National Commission for Employment Policy, 1983.

Kaplan, M. *Leisure: Lifestyle and Lifespan*. Philadelphia: W. B. Saunders Company, 1979.

Kii, T. "Recent Extension of Retirement Age in Japan." *The Gerontologist* 19, 5 (1979): 481–86.

Kohli, M., J. Rosenow, and J. Wolf. "The Social Construction of Ageing Through Work: Economic Structure and Life-World." *Ageing and Society* 3, 1 (1983): 23–42.

Kreps, J. M. *Women and the American Economy: A Look to the 1980s*. Englewood Cliffs, N.J.: Prentice-Hall, Inc., 1976.

————. "Aging and Social Policy." *The Gerontologist* 19, 4 (1979): 340–43.

Maeda, D., and H. Asano. "Public Policies for the Aged in Japan." *Aging* 301–302 (Nov.-Dec., 1979): 36–45.

Marini, M. M. "Sex Differences in the Process of Occupational Attainment: A Closer Look." *Social Science Research* 9, 2 (1980): 307–61.

———. "Age and Sequencing Norms in the Transition to Adulthood." *Social Forces* 63, 1 (1984): 229–44.

McConnell, S. R. "Retirement and Employment." In *Aging: Scientific Perspectives and Social Issues*, eds. D. S. Woodruff and J. E. Birren, pp. 333–50. Monterey, Calif.: Brooks/Cole Publishing Company, 1983.

Mellor, E. F. "Investigating the Differences in Weekly Earnings of Women and Men." *Monthly Labor Review* 107, 6 (1984): 17–28.

Miller, D. C., and W. H. Form. *Industrial Sociology*. New York: Harper & Row Publishers, Inc., 1951.

Monk, A. "Factors in the Preparation for Retirement by Middle-aged Adults." *The Gerontologist* 11, 4 (1971): 348–51.

———. "A Social Policy Framework for Pre-retirement Planning." *Industrial Gerontology* 15 (Fall 1972): 63–70.

Morrison, M. H. "Flexible Distribution of Work, Leisure, and Education: Potentials for the Aging." In *Aging and Income: Programs and Prospects for the Elderly*, ed. B. R. Herzog, pp. 95–127. New York: Human Sciences Press, 1978.

———. *Economics of Aging: Future of Retirement*. New York: Van Nostrand Reinhold Company, 1982.

Murray, J. R., E. A. Powers, and R. J. Havighurst. "Personal and Situational Factors Producing Flexible Careers." *The Gerontologist* 11, 4, Pt. 2 (1971): 4–12.

Myles, J. *Old Age in the Welfare State: The Political Economy of Public Pensions*. Boston: Little, Brown & Company, 1984.

National Council on Aging. *Aging in the Eighties: America in Transition*. Washington, D.C.: National Council on Aging, 1981.

O'Rand, A., and J. Henretta. "Midlife Work History and Retirement Income." In *Women's Retirement: Policy Implications of Recent Research*, ed. M. Szinovacz, pp. 25–44. Beverly Hills, Calif.: Sage Publications, Inc., 1982.

Osipow, S. H. *Theories of Career Development*. New York: Appleton-Century-Crofts, 1968.

Palmore, E. *The Honorable Elders: A Cross-Cultural Analysis of Aging in Japan*. Durham, N.C.: Duke University Press, 1975.

———, L. K. George, and G. Fillenbaum. "Predictors of Retirement." *Journal of Gerontology* 37, 6 (1982): 733–42.

Phillipson, C. *Capitalism and the Construction of Old Age*. London: Macmillan, Inc., 1982.

Public Opinion. "Opinion Roundup: America through the Ages: Studying the Elderly." *Public Opinion* 8, 1 (1985): 30–42.

Poitrenaud, J., et al. "Factors Related to Attitude Towards Retirement Among French Preretired Managers and Top Executives." *Journal of Gerontology* 34, 5 (1979): 723–27.

Quinn, J. F. "Wage Determination and Discrimination Among Older Workers." *Journal of Gerontology* 34, 5 (1979): 728–35.

Robinson, P. K., S. Coberly, and C. E. Paul. "Work and Retirement." In *Handbook of Aging and the Social Sciences*, eds. R. Binstock and E. Shanas, pp. 503–27. New York: Van Nostrand Reinhold Company, 1985.

Rones, P. L. "Using the CPS to Track Retirement Trends Among Older Men." *Monthly Labor Review* 108, 2 (1985): 46–50.

Rosenfeld, R. A. "Race and Sex Differences in Career Dynamics." *American Sociological Review* 45, 4 (1980): 583–609.

———. "Sex Segregation and Sectors." *American Sociological Review* 48, 5 (1983): 637–55.

———, and A. B. Sorensen. "Sex Differences in Patterns of Career Mobility." *Demography* 16, 1 (1979): 89–101.

Schulz, J. H. *The Economics of Aging*, 1st and 2nd eds. Belmont, Calif.: Wadsworth, Inc., 1980, 1985.

Scientific Manpower Commission. "Women and Minorities: Their Proportions Grow in the Professional Work Force." *Monthly Labor Review* 108, 12 (1985): 49–50.

Select Committee on Aging, U.S. House of Representatives. *Unemployment Crisis Facing Older Americans* (97–367). Washington, D.C.: U.S. Government Printing Office, 1982.

Shack-Marquez, J. "Earnings Differences Between Men and Women: An Introductory Note." *Monthly Labor Review* 107, 6 (1984): 15–16.

Shanas, E., et al. *Old People in Three Industrial Societies*. New York: Atherton Press, 1968.

Sheppard, H. L. "Work and Retirement." In *Handbook of Aging and the Social Sciences*, eds. R. H. Binstock and E. Shanas, pp. 286–309. New York: Van Nostrand Reinhold Company, 1976.

Siegel, S. R., and J. M. Rives. "Characteristics of Existing and Planned Preretirement Programs." *Aging and Work* 1, 2 (1978): 93–100.

Sieling, M. S. "Staffing Patterns Prominent in Female-Male Earnings Gap." *Monthly Labor Review* 107, 6 (1984): 29–33.

Simpson, I. H., K. W. Back, and J. C. McKinney. "Work and Retirement." In *Social Aspects of Aging*, eds. J. H. Simpson and J. C. McKinney, pp. 45–54. Durham, N.C., Duke University Press, 1966.

Social Security Administration. *Social Security Programs Throughout the World—1983*. Research Report No. 59. Washington, D.C.: U.S. Government Printing Office, 1984.

Stagner, R. "The Affluent Society Versus Early Retirement." *Aging and Work* 1, 1 (1978): 25–31.

———. "Aging in Industry." In *Handbook of the Psychology of Aging*, eds. J. E. Birren and K. W. Schaie, pp. 789–817. New York: Van Nostrand Reinhold Company, 1985.

Stewart, C. D. "The Older Worker in Japan: Realities and Possibilities." *Industrial Gerontology* 1, 1 (1974): 60–76.

Streib, G. F., and G. J. Schneider. *Retirement in American Society: Impact and Process*. Ithaca, N.Y.: Cornell University Press, 1971.

Super, D. E. *The Psychology of Careers*. New York: Harper & Row Publishers, Inc., 1957.

Tolbert III, C. M. "Industrial Segmentation and Men's Career Mobility." *American Sociological Review* 47, 4 (1982): 457–77.

Treiman, D. J. "The Work Histories of Women and Men: What We Know and What We Need to Find Out." In *Gender and the Life Course*, ed. A. S. Rossi, pp. 213–31. New York: Aldine Publishing Company, 1985.

———, and K. Terell. "Sex and the Process of Status Attainment: A Comparison of Working Women and Men." *American Sociological Review* 40, 1 (1975): 174–200.

*USA Today*. "Older Men Left in Job Squeeze," p. 1. November 28, 1983.

U.S. Bureau of the Census. *Population Profile of the United States: 1982*. Current Population Reports, P-23, No. 130. Washington, D.C.: U.S. Government Printing Office, 1983a.

————. *America in Transition: An Aging Society*. Current Population Reports, Series P-20, No. 128. Washington, D.C.: U.S. Government Printing Office, 1983b.

————. *Demographic and Socioeconomic Aspects of Aging in the United States*. Current Population Reports, Series P-23, No. 138. Washington, D.C.: U.S. Government Printing Office, 1984.

————. *Statistical Abstract of the United States, 1985*, 105th ed. Washington, D.C.: U.S. Government Printing Office, 1985a.

————. *Persons of Spanish Origin in the United States: March 1982*. Current Population Reports, Series P-20, No. 396. Washington, D.C.: U.S. Government Printing Office, 1985b.

————. *Economic Report of the President, 1985*. Washington, D.C.: U.S. Government Printing Office, 1985c.

————. *Characteristics of Households and Persons Receiving Selected Noncash Benefits: 1983*. Current Population Reports, Series P-60, No. 148. Washington, D.C.: U.S. Government Printing Office, 1985d.

————. *Characteristics of the Population Below the Poverty Level*. Current Population Reports, Series P-60, No. 147. Washington, D.C.: U.S. Government Printing Office, 1985e.

U.S. Department of Labor, Bureau of Labor Statistics. *Handbook of Labor Statistics*. Bulletin 2175. Washington, D.C.: U.S. Government Printing Office, 1983a.

————. *Women at Work: A Chartbook*. Bulletin 2168. Washington, D.C.: U.S. Government Printing Office, 1983b.

————. Women's Bureau. *Time of Change: 1983 Handbook on Women Workers*. Bulletin 298. Washington, D.C.: U.S. Government Printing Office, 1983c.

————. *Workers Without Jobs: A Chartbook on Unemployment*. Bulletin 2174. Washington, D.C.: U.S. Government Printing Office, 1983d.

————. *Consumer Expenditure Survey, 1980–1981*. Bulletin 2173. Washington, D.C.: U.S. Government Printing Office, 1983e.

————. *Our Changing Economy: A BLS Centennial Chartbook*. Bulletin 2211. Washington, D.C.: U.S. Government Printing Office, 1984a.

————. *Work Experience of the Population in 1981–1982*. Special Labor Force Report. Bulletin 2199. Washington, D.C.: U.S. Government Printing Office, 1984b.

Viscusi, W. K. *Welfare of the Elderly: An Economic Analysis and Policy Prescription*. New York: John Wiley & Sons, Inc., 1979.

Waldman, E. "Labor Force Statistics for a Family Perspective." *Monthly Labor Review* 106, 12 (1983): 16–30.

Waldo, D., and H. C. Lazenby. "Demographic Characteristics and Health Care Use and Expenditures by the Aged in the United States: 1977–1984." *Health Care Financing Review* 6, 1 (1984): 1–29.

Walker, A. "The Social Creation of Poverty and Dependency in Old Age." *Journal of Social Policy* 9, 1 (1980): 49–75.

Wallace, P. A. "Impact of Equal Employment Opportunity Laws." In *Women and the American Economy*, ed. J. M. Kreps, pp. 123–45. Englewood Cliffs, N.J.: Prentice-Hall, Inc., 1976.

Wanner, R. A., and L. McDonald. "Ageism in the Labor Market: Estimating Earnings Discrimination Against Older Workers." *Journal of Gerontology* 38, 6 (1983): 738–44.

Wilensky, H. L. "Orderly Careers and Social Participation." *American Sociological Review* 26, 4 (1961): 521–39.

# 9

# AGING AT THE MARGINS OF SOCIETY

**MINORITY AGING**
Aging at the Margins
The Minority Experience
The Logic of This Chapter

**AGING AND MINORITIES IN THE UNITED STATES**
Multiple Jeopardy: The Minority
    Experience
    *Health*
    *Economics*
    *Labor*
Aged Black Americans
    *Demographic Characteristics of Black*
        *Americans*
    *Aging and the Black Experience*
    *Health and Social Situations*
Aged Hispanic Americans
    *Profile of Hispanic Americans*
    *Aging and the Hispanic Experience*
Older Native Americans
    *Profile of Native Americans*
    *The Native American Experience*
    *Elderly Native Americans: The Issues*

Aged Asian Americans
    *Asian Americans: Model Minority or*
        *Marginal People?*
    *The History of Asian American*
        *Immigration*
    *Elderly Chinese Americans*
    *Elderly Japanese Americans*
    *Elderly Filipino Americans*
Ramifications of Ethnicity

**AGING IN THE THIRD WORLD**
    *Family Life*
    *Theoretical Perspectives*

**SUMMARY**

**DISCUSSION QUESTIONS**

**PERTINENT READINGS**

# Minority Aging

## AGING AT THE MARGINS

Throughout this book we have drawn attention to the ways in which the experience of aging for certain groups reflects the contexts of their lives. In the United States the process of growing old among blacks and Hispanics differs from the experience of aging among the middle class in advanced industrial society. Indeed, aging in Third World countries more closely approximates what we see among minorities than among the majority population in the United States. Minorities and people in the Third World to some degree share certain experiences pertaining to aging: shorter life expectancies, ill-health, inadequate financial resources, and many other structurally induced disadvantages. The term "marginality" is used here to describe those who are excluded because of personal or structural factors from many of the benefits enjoyed by those at the center of the social structure. In this chapter we will draw these elements together and focus on aging in minority groups.

What can be learned from looking at patterns of aging among diverse minority groups? First, it will help eliminate the notion that the United States is one large melting pot fostering cultural homogeneity. Second, we have seen already that minority group members have lower incomes, education, occupational levels, and so on — things that generally comprise social class standing. While not much is known about the effect of ethnicity per se (much of the information presented here will center on social class factors), comparing ethnic groups may help highlight some of the crucial impacts of these factors on aging. As noted in the last chapter, earlier texts on aging in mass societies have dealt predominantly with white aging. Ethnic minorities are an important segment of these societies, however, and their experiences have an essential place in any book on aging. Finally, an examination of aging at the margins according to the ways in which structural factors affect the lives of minorities and Third World peoples highlights the manner in which social policies and social structures influence the experience of us all. It may thus make us more aware of the consequences of the ways in which we organize our society and of the possibility of structural change.

## THE MINORITY EXPERIENCE

The extent to which ethnic minorities are different from the majority has long been a topic of debate in the social sciences. Some of those who focus on the differences work with individual-level models. These paradigms attribute differences between ethnic minorities and whites to something unique about the people who make up the minorities. Others are neostructuralists in that they see the differences between the experiences of whites and ethnic minorities as resulting in some ways from the social system.

The idea that disparities are the expression of some kind of biological difference between races has a long history and has been revived in recent years by scholars such as Jensen (1980) and Herrnstein (1973). Others have seen it as a matter of culture; for instance, the "culture of poverty" that prevents the advancement of Hispanics (Banfield, 1974) or a lack of motivation in Native Americans (McClelland, 1967). According to the bias of the theorist, this type of explanation of differences may lead to one of two attitudes: (1) minorities are inferior and therefore deserve what they get or (2) minorities are unable to look after themselves and therefore need special help and attention.

In reaction to the scorn or paternalism resulting from either of these attitudes, there has been a tendency to emphasize the similarities between whites and ethnic minorities; that is, we share a common humanity. The ethnic experience is different from that of whites because ethnic minorities are reacting to a complex of social structural factors that shape their experience. Others have pointed out the enormous variation among the cultures and life-styles of the ethnic minorities. There are striking differences between blacks, Hispanics, and Asian Americans, or even among members of one group; for example, Puerto Ricans differ greatly from Cubans or Mexicans.

Actually, two paradoxes are involved in assessing the minority experience. Focusing too heavily on the differences tends to lead to the conclusion that minorities and Third World peoples are somehow inferior, or second-class citizens. Concentrating on the similarities, on the other hand, may lead to overlooking very real problems that minorities face and the damage that has been done by years of discrimination in education and in the labor market. In short a pluralization of lifeworlds determines access to goods and services. Blaming all the problems on the structure closes off personal initiative; attributing difficulties exclusively to individual-level factors ignores very real structural constraints. We maintain that broad structural tethers generally circumscribe the lives of minorities and Third World peoples. There is, however, room for some latitude of response within these constraints, and an effort should be made to understand the differences among the cultures and the experiences of diverse peoples. More important, these limitations can be modified by social policy changes. Minorities in general, and the minority elderly in particular, should be involved in shaping social policy rather than being treated as its objects.

## THE LOGIC OF THIS CHAPTER

While we acknowledge the importance of the enormous cultural differences among the various ethnic minority groups in the United States and the heterogeneity of the Third World countries, because this book is sociological in its approach, the primary focus here will be on the ways in which structural factors circumscribe aging along the margins. Minorities are defined in part by their social and psychological distance from power. We will begin by surveying the impact of structural factors on the lives of the various ethnic minorities in general. We will then look at the implications of these for aging among black Americans, Hispanic Americans, Spanish Americans, Native Americans, and Asian Americans in particular. In the section on the Third World we will look briefly at the questions posed by the differences between aging in the Third World and in advanced industrial societies, and the implications of the relations between these societies for aging.

# Aging and Minorities in the United States

## MULTIPLE JEOPARDY: THE MINORITY EXPERIENCE

We have implied that entitlement structures and the allocation of resources among individuals are neither fortuitous nor a reflection of purely personal attributes. Both women and minorities, as we saw in Chapter 8, are groups whose economic life chances are largely circumscribed by differential access. The difficulties encountered by minorities are aggravated by age, in part because of the increasing structural limitations imposed on the majority of all older people in our society. Today's minority elderly also matured at a time when inequalities of opportunity were even more severe than they are today, with the result that their current problems are particularly acute. In the case of minority elderly the term "triple jeopardy" has been used to describe the risks imposed by being old, poor, and members of a racial or ethnic minority (Bengtson, 1979).

In 1983 white Americans accounted for 85.4 percent of the population, black Americans made up 11.9 percent, and Hispanics made up 5.7 percent. In 1980, the last year for which figures are readily available, Asians and Pacific Islanders comprised 1.7 percent of the population, and 0.07 percent were Native Americans, Eskimos, and Aleutians. Between 1980 and 1984 the black population grew at a much more rapid rate than the white population: 6.7 percent as compared to 3.2 percent. The growth rate for all other races combined was even more dramatic: 29.8 percent. However, high immigration rates for races other than black and white accounted for two-thirds of this growth. The remainder can be attributed to higher fertility rates. These higher rates to some degree also account for the relatively young population age structure of ethnic minorities illustrated in Figure 9.1. As is apparent, the proportion of persons over sixty-five in the white population is much higher than that for other races. Most significant, however, are shorter life expectancies among the ethnic minorities. In 1981 the life expectancy at birth for white men was 71.1 years, as opposed to only 64.4 years for black men, and 78.5 years for white women as opposed to 73 years for black women (U.S. Census, 1985a, 1985b). In the same year the life expectancy of Native Americans was approximately eight years less than that of the general population (National Indian Council on Aging Quarterly, 1981).

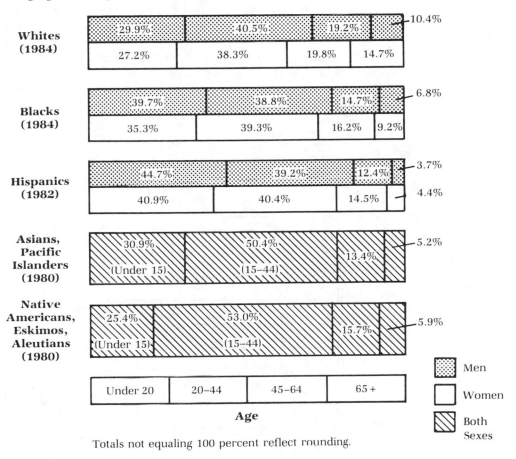

Totals not equaling 100 percent reflect rounding.

**FIGURE 9.1**

Age distribution by race. (*Sources:* U.S. Bureau of the Census. *Estimates of the Population of the United States, by Age, Sex, and Race: 1980 to 1984.* Current Population Reports, Series P-25, No. 965. Washington, D.C.: U.S. Government Printing Office, 1985; U.S. Bureau of the Census. *Persons of Spanish Origin in the United States: March, 1982.* Current Population Reports, Series P-20, No. 396. Washington, D.C.: U.S. Government Printing Office, 1985; and U.S. Bureau of the Census. *Statistical Abstract of the United States, 1985,* 105th ed. Washington, D.C.: U.S. Government Printing Office, 1985 [adapted from numerical data].)

**Health.** The general health situation of ethnic minorities is poorer than that of whites, both in health status and in access to care, which foreshadows shortened life expectancies and possibly greater degrees of disability in old age. Figure 9.2 shows that Hispanics, and particularly blacks in all age groups, are more likely to perceive their health as only fair or poor than are whites. Ethnic minorities, primarily Native Americans and Puerto Ricans, are also more susceptible to infectious conditions associated with poverty than is the general population. As noted in Chapter 5, Hispanics and blacks are also more likely to suffer from chronic activity limitations than are whites, but they are less likely to have seen a physician or dentist in the last year or to be covered by health insurance (U.S. Department of Health and Human Services, 1983a; National Center for Health Statistics, 1984).

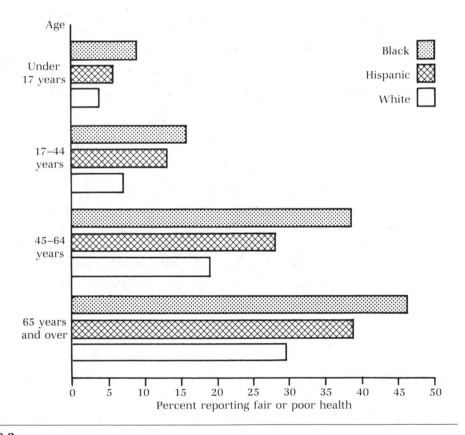

**FIGURE 9.2**

Self-reported fair or poor health among ethnic groups by age. (*Source:* U.S. Department of Health and Human Services. *Health Indicators for Hispanic, Black and White Americans*, p. 55. National Center for Health Statistics, Series 10, No. 48. Washington, D.C.: U.S. Government Printing Office, 1984 [adapted from numerical data].)

**Economics.** Economic disadvantage is associated with poor health and the lack of access to health care throughout life; the pattern carries over into old age. As we see in Figure 9.3, blacks, Native Americans, and Hispanics are much more likely to be below the poverty level than are whites. This is true of those who work full time and of those who are unemployed (U.S. Department of Labor, 1984a). The reasons stem in part from labor force segmentation, as was pointed out in Chapter 8. The poverty rate among Asian Americans and Pacific Islanders does not appear to be significantly higher than that among whites. In assessing the situation of the elderly, however, this is deceptive, since there are significant numbers of poor among the Asian American elderly.

As is illustrated in Figure 9.4, unemployment rates for blacks and Hispanics are double those for whites. While the figures for Native Americans are only slightly higher than those for whites, the proportion of Native Americans who do not participate in the labor force is much higher, reflecting a serious constriction of economic opportunity. Among Asian Americans and Pacific Islanders, including a high proportion of young professionals, unemployment rates are lower than for whites. Again, this should not obscure the fact that certain segments of the Asian American population have significant economic problems and suffer from labor force discrimination. In Figure 9.5 we see that the income distribution for both the white and Asian American populations peaks in the $25,000 to $49,999 range, with relatively low percentages having incomes below $5000 a year. The median income for both whites and Asian Americans is above the median income for the population as a whole; if one remembers that the data for Asian Americans and Pacific Islanders are from a slightly earlier period than that for whites, it becomes apparent that the median income for Asian Americans and Pacific Islanders tends to be slightly higher.

The statistics for blacks and Hispanics, however, are significantly below those for whites in 1982, the median income of blacks being approximately 55 percent that of whites. The comparable figure for Native Americans, Eskimos, and Aleutians was about 69 percent that of all other races in 1979. Significant numbers of Hispanics and even more Native Americans and blacks are at the lower end of the income scale, but they are underrepresented in the higher income brackets. Real median income for white households increased by 1.7 percent in 1982 and 1.4 percent in 1983, while median incomes for black and Hispanic families showed no increases over the same period (U.S. Census, 1984a, 1984b).

**Labor.** Undeniably, there is labor market segmentation even among those of equal educational levels. Although education is a key factor in advancement in the labor market, investments in education return more to whites than to members of minority groups; minority groups are more likely to be employed in the primary sector, where years of schooling enhance mobility and income levels. For those who lack basic skills and, in some cases, proficien-

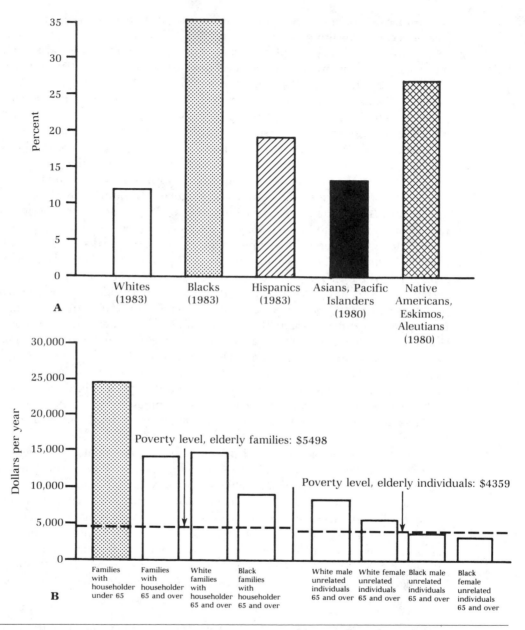

**FIGURE 9.3**

**A.** Percent of persons below the poverty level by race. (*Source:* U.S. Bureau of the Census. *Statistical Abstract of the United States, 1985,* 105th ed. Washington, D.C.: U.S. Government Printing Office, 1985 [adapted from numerical data].) **B.** Poverty level comparisons for families and elderly individuals, 1981. (*Source:* U.S. Bureau of the Census. *America in Transition: An Aging Society,* p. 9. Current Population Reports, Series P-23, No. 182. Washington, D.C.: U.S. Government Printing Office, 1983.)

cy in English, job opportunities are severely limited. As indicated in Figure 9.6, Hispanics are most disadvantaged with regard to education, with fully 39.8 percent of them having eight or fewer years of schooling. Whites, Asian Americans, and Pacific Islanders are most likely to have had at least some high school education; blacks, Native Americans, and Hispanics are much less likely to have had much high school education. Because of the influx of educated professionals, Asian Americans and Pacific Islanders are rather more likely than whites to have had a college education. Native Americans, blacks, and Hispanics fall far behind whites in having received a college degree.

In considering the situation of the minority elderly it is important to remember the disadvantages minorities usually suffer. The minority elderly are caught within this structure of disadvantage, and a lifetime of struggling with it is liable to have marked them in ways that carry over into old age. For example, as we saw in Chapter 8, labor force participation has important ramifica-

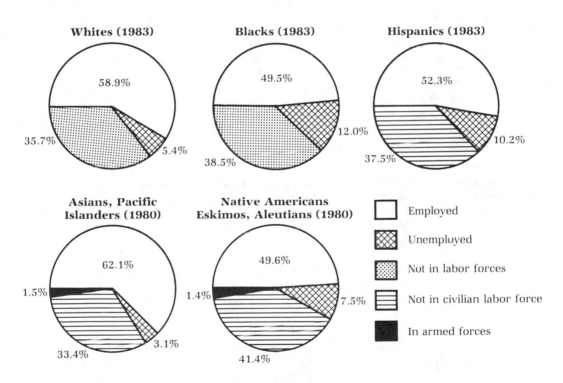

Note: Percentages for Whites and Blacks are based on the civilian labor force.

**FIGURE 9.4**
Labor force status by race. (*Source:* U.S. Bureau of the Census: *Statistical Abstract of the United States, 1985,* 105th ed. Washington, D.C.: U.S. Government Printing Office, 1985 [adapted from numerical data].)

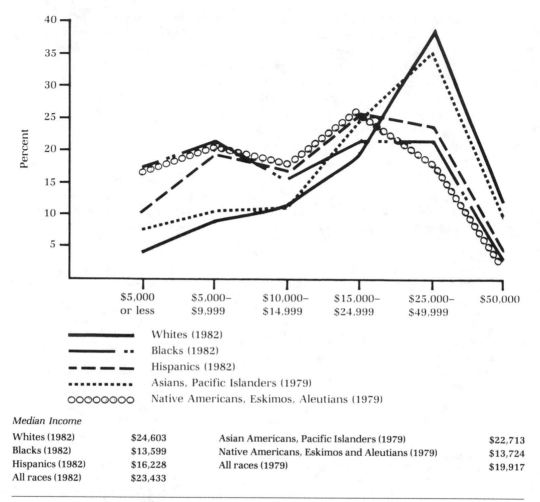

| Median Income | | | |
|---|---|---|---|
| Whites (1982) | $24,603 | Asian Americans, Pacific Islanders (1979) | $22,713 |
| Blacks (1982) | $13,599 | Native Americans, Eskimos and Aleutians (1979) | $13,724 |
| Hispanics (1982) | $16,228 | All races (1979) | $19,917 |
| All races (1982) | $23,433 | | |

**FIGURE 9.5**

Distribution of family income by race. (*Source:* U.S. Bureau of the Census. *Statistical Abstract of the United States, 1985,* 105th ed. Washington, D.C.: U.S. Government Printing Office, 1985.)

tions for financial security in old age. Access to medical care and the overall quality of life are also strongly influenced by previous employment history. As we have seen, the educational level of most minorities is below that of whites; however, even when we control for years of schooling, we find that minorities are disproportionately located in secondary markets and peripheral industries. Not only does such a structural location have important implications for later life finances but also workers within these industries are more likely to suffer from work-related illnesses and injuries that continue to plague them in old age (Beck et al., 1980).

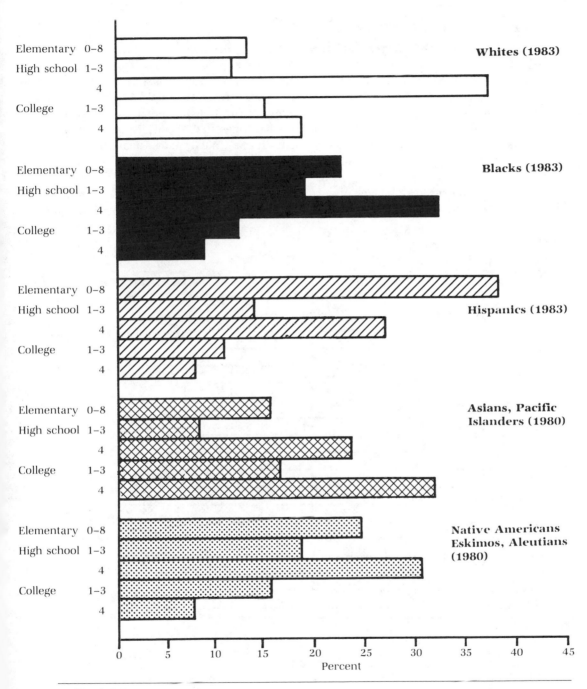

**FIGURE 9.6**
Years of education completed by race. (*Source:* U.S. Bureau of the Census. *Statistical Abstract of the United States, 1985*, 105th ed. Washington, D.C.: U.S. Government Printing Office, 1985 [adapted from numerical data].)

## AGED BLACK AMERICANS

**Demographic Characteristics of Black Americans.** As we have seen, by 1984 black Americans comprised 12.1 percent of the total population. As Figure 9.7 dramatically illustrates, the black population has a much younger population structure than the white population. In 1984 only 8.1 percent of blacks were sixty-five and over, compared to 12.6 percent for whites. Although both the white and black median ages have been rising for many years, echoing the general aging trend in the United States today, the black median age in 1984 was only 26.3, almost six years younger than the white median age of 32.2 (U.S. Census, 1985b).

Historically, the black population has been concentrated in the South; this is still true today. Approximately 53 percent of all blacks live in southern

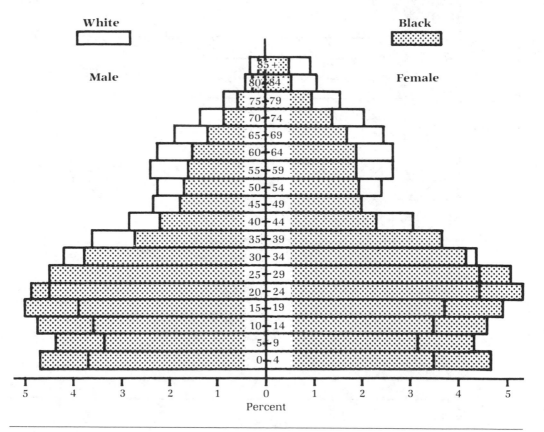

**FIGURE 9.7**

Percent distribution of the white and black populations by age and sex, July 1, 1984. (*Source:* U.S. Bureau of the Census. *Estimates of the Population of the United States, by Age, Sex and Race: 1980 to 1984.* Current Population Reports, Series P-25, No. 965. Washington, D.C.: U.S. Government Printing Office, 1985.)

states, where they comprise about one-fifth of the population. Another 20.2 percent live in the Midwest, while 18.3 percent live in the Northeast; only 8.5 percent live in the West.

Although general patterns of residential location have changed very little in the last few decades, a major shift is occurring within metropolitan areas. From the early 1960s until the present, the percentage of blacks in metropolitan regions grew, until recent estimates place over 53 percent of all blacks in urban environments, with the central cities housing six of every ten. At the same time, the number of whites in central cities has been continually declining so that just about 30 percent are now living in the inner core of any metropolis. Seventeen percent of the blacks live in the suburbs or at the fringes of urban areas, 24 percent less than the comparable proportion of whites. The exodus of whites, who command higher wages, from the more concentrated population centers leaves these areas without a sufficient tax base, an essential component for providing social services for all ages. While the white, black, and Hispanic elderly are all more likely to live in metropolitan than nonmetropolitan areas, the black and Hispanic elderly are more concentrated in the central areas while whites tend to live in the suburbs (U.S. Census, 1985a; 1983).

In light of the enactment of affirmative action legislation twenty years ago, it would be nice to say all inequities have been eliminated or were at least decreasing. Yet in income, occupational placement, and mobility, blacks continue to lag far behind whites. According to recent information, black Americans are only just beginning to occupy middle management positions and remain all but absent from executive positions (Kaufman, 1980). In 1983 black men were only half as likely as white men to hold executive, administrative, and managerial positions; black women were also only half as likely as white women to do so (U.S. Department of Labor, 1984b). During the 1980s income comparisons between black and white wage earners in the years before retirement continue to reveal wide disparities. The mean income for white families in the ten years preceding retirement was $28,358 in 1982. During this same period black families had a mean income of $16,635. Comparable income statistics for individuals show an even greater differential: the per capita income for blacks in the ten years before retirement ($5375) was less than one-half of that for whites ($11,807) (U.S. Census, 1985a). Four out of five elderly black women had incomes less than $5000 in 1981, as compared with about one-half of white women and black men and one-fifth of white men. Naturally, the inflationary spiral of the last few years will have changed the dollar amounts considerably, but if history is any indication, the gap will not have closed. In the period between 1969 and the mid-1970s no relative improvement occurred; it took two wage earners in most black families to bring in their lower incomes. During 1982 blacks with labor force experience were one-half again as likely as whites to be unemployed, and blacks who worked full time were almost twice as likely as whites to be below the poverty level (U.S. Department of Labor, 1984c).

**Aging and the Black Experience.** With relatively few exceptions, the stressful circumstances faced by the black minority are exacerbated with age. Actuarial calculations highlight differential life expectancies between blacks and whites, a partial explanation of why older people comprise little more than 8.1 percent of the black population. At birth today whites average six more years of life expectancy than blacks; by sixty-five the gap has narrowed and after seventy-five a crossover occurs, with black age-specific death rates being lower than whites. Why this occurs cannot be satisfactorily explained, but it probably has to do with a combination of genetic and socioenvironmental factors contributing to risk (Wing et al., 1985; Manton, 1982). Black women, like white women, outnumber men in later life. Accordingly, in the sixty-five to seventy-four age group only 33 percent of black women were married with their husbands still alive, while 50.2 percent were widowed and 6.2 percent were divorced; once past seventy-five, just under three-quarters were widowed, 3.3 percent were divorced, and only 17.6 percent were still married and living with their husbands (U.S. Census, 1983, 1984c, 1985b). One of the major controversies about black family life concerns whether it can be characterized as matriarchal. Little reliable evidence is available, yet given higher mortality rates for men, it is possible to appreciate the central role of black mothers and grandmothers in maintaining familial ties. This does not address the question of the alleged dispensability of black men; instead, it merely suggests that women are capable of carrying on the familial responsibilities of emotional and physical support after the men die (Jackson, 1980).

Regardless of racial characteristics, families are the ultimate source of aid for old people, though one difference many have noted is the seemingly greater prestige accorded the black elderly within the family. For example, if the value hierarchy of the black subculture emphasizes survival against all odds, older people, managing to live as long as they have, would naturally be accorded a measure of respect not granted to most whites. Then, too, there are the economic realities of black life in which older people do not experience as radical a decline as their white age peers in falling below the income standards of the rest of the population. Having less throughout life means that one has less to lose in retirement. Still, approximately 36 percent of the black elderly, compared to 12 percent of the white, live in poverty. Because of differential savings histories, aged blacks are far more dependent on current incomes, never having had much discretionary income in the first place. Seldom do they have more than very limited access to either personal savings or credit nor do they have income from other than Social Security. Prior to the Supplemental Security Income (SSI) Program in 1974, 80 percent of the blacks, compared to 90 percent of the whites, received cash payments. In the last decade coverage has increased significantly, however: over 154 percent for retired black workers. Nonetheless, there remains a differential in the amount of benefits received, and until blacks and whites have similar work careers, there will be a disparity in their respective retirement incomes. Among workers newly entitled to Social Security benefits, two-thirds of the black men and nearly 90 percent of the black women were concentrated in the lowest economic category characterized by low previous earnings on which benefit levels are based. The comparable rates for white men and women were one-third and two-thirds. When Social Security is supplemental, other sources such as private pensions are more often found among whites, while blacks rely on public assistance and Supplemental Security Income (Jackson, 1985; U.S. Census, 1983b). In one study looking across the two decades prior to retirement and one decade into retirement, incomes among blacks were found to decline an average of 55 percent. This decline is significantly more than the 36 percent drop among whites but less than the 62 percent observed for Mexican Americans. Hence, despite federal support programs, the sizable income gap among the three groups in their middle years grows even larger after sixty-five (Dowd and Bengtson, 1978).

Financial status during retirement hinges on race, sex, health, the survival of a spouse, and the ability to continue working. Educational attainment, lifetime earnings, and investments are also crucial. As is already clear, differentials between men and women and between whites and blacks are striking throughout life. In retirement the status quo is perpetuated. Older black men had an annual income of $4900 in 1981, roughly 57 percent that of older white men. At every age women's incomes are considerably less than men of the same race. In retirement black women received $3500 annually in 1981, with white women exactly equal to black men (U.S. Census, 1983). In an analysis of two large-scale national data sets, Fillenbaum et al. (1985) noted that among black men (data were unavailable for women) impaired economic circumstances attenuate retirement. Major concerns were economic and health issues, but among older white men a broader range of matters determined the shape of retirement. Without SSI and other income subsidies, the situation among black men would have been worse. As it was, preretirement incomes had been so low that relatively few economic changes occurred with retirement.

Whether elderly blacks will command high status in their subculture in the future is questionable. In her analysis of the black elderly, Jackson (1985) envisions a gradual erosion of the position of older people as they become less essential economically to their families and as the proportion of the black elderly increases. All things considered, it is probable elderly blacks are somewhat better integrated into their family groups than whites from equivalent socioeconomic backgrounds. Younger families often have only meager assets themselves and thus are unable to extend their resources to cover the needs of the elderly. In all other respects family ties are at least as viable as among whites. The issue of money aside, nearly half of elderly blacks who have children see them more often than once a week.

In 1983 black women seventy-five and over were more than 70 percent less likely than white women of the same age to live alone. Black women in the sixty-five to seventy-four age group, however, were slightly more likely to live alone than their white counterparts. Black men, on the other hand, were somewhat more likely than their white counterparts to live alone, particularly in the sixty-five to seventy-four age group. Evidence exists to suggest that the black elderly, like the white elderly, prefer their intimacy at a distance. Affective kinship relations appear to be structured on a matrilocal basis, with families living in the vicinity of the wife's mother, although not sharing the same house. Hence it is fair to say a modified extended family is the norm in urban areas (Cantor, 1979; Hirsch et al., 1972; Jackson, 1972a; U.S. Census, 1984c).

Since blacks are most often residents of an inner city, it is common occasionally to find large multigenerational households in the same neighborhood. In spite of what was noted earlier about urban renewal programs, older blacks do not move more often than whites and have much less tendency to change residences than the younger members of the black population. Also, despite that older blacks are less likely than older whites to own their own homes, significant numbers of those families headed by a person over sixty live in owner-occupied dwellings. Equity in a home is viewed by a majority of both older blacks and whites as a significant measure of security equaled for some only by close family ties or perhaps a sizable savings account. The symbolic importance of home ownership transcends all racial and ethnic categories, appearing to be a basic thread in the fabric of the American dream. After a lifetime of lower earnings, it should not be startling that the homes owned by older blacks are less costly than those owned by whites. On the average, their value is at least $5000 lower than for the homes owned by the majority of the elderly.

**Health and Social Situations.** With a lifetime of inequalities behind them and living closer to subsistence levels in general, would it not seem logical that health conditions of the black elderly will reflect a combination of these factors? On such fundamental physiological measures as stature, the evidence suggests aged blacks undergo greater losses than do their white counterparts (McPherson et al., 1978). To what extent these and other maladies are a consequence of racial vs socioeconomic background is a question to which no satisfactory answer exists. There is contradictory information on whether older black people are sicker than older whites. Some research says no, because older blacks are a surviving elite. Yet national survey data reveal an incidence of chronic disabilities among blacks almost twice as high as among whites. Hospitalization is also higher, and hospital stays are longer, and self-reported health is poorer among blacks than among whites (National Center for Health Statistics, 1984). Looking at Table 9.1 we can easily see that no consistent pattern of causes of death emerges clearly. Blacks and other nonwhites die more often from some causes but less often from others.

There is some indication that blacks feel older than whites of comparable ages — in light of differential life expectancies they may actually be older. In commenting on the difference, and to offset some of the biological or social inequities experienced by blacks, Jackson has called for a lowering of the retirement age at which blacks would qualify for Social Security. Her reasoning derives from the differential actuarial values for the two groups; since blacks die

**TABLE 9.1**

Ratios of Black and Other Races to White Death Rates for the Ten Leading Causes of Death for the Population Sixty-five and Over, by Age, 1978

| Cause of death by rank[a] | 65 and Over | 65 to 74 | 75 to 84 | 85 and Over |
|---|---|---|---|---|
| All causes | 0.972 | 1.223 | 1.057 | 0.603 |
| 1. Diseases of the heart | 0.862 | 1.100 | 0.954 | 0.547 |
| 2. Malignant neoplasms | 1.021 | 1.120 | 1.061 | 0.694 |
| 3. Cerebrovascular diseases | 1.096 | 1.836 | 1.193 | 0.599 |
| 4. Influenza and pneumonia | 0.842 | 1.413 | 0.977 | 0.490 |
| 5. Arteriosclerosis | 0.720 | 1.345 | 0.931 | 0.467 |
| 6. Diabetes mellitus | 1.528 | 1.993 | 1.572 | 0.783 |
| 7. Accidents | 1.050 | 1.423 | 1.092 | 0.555 |
| Motor vehicle | 1.083 | 1.160 | 1.133 | 0.685 |
| All other | 1.039 | 1.573 | 1.078 | 0.540 |
| 8. Bronchitis, emphysema, and asthma | 0.457 | 0.481 | 0.470 | 0.411 |
| 9. Cirrhosis of liver | 0.856 | 0.912 | 0.706 | 0.523 |
| 10. Nephritis and nephrosis | 2.522 | 3.234 | 2.737 | 1.442 |
| All other causes | 1.163 | 1.345 | 1.250 | 0.844 |

[a]Based on National Center for Health Statistics. *Eighth Revision International Classification of Diseases, Adapted for Use in the United States.* PHS Pub. No. 1693, Public Health Service. Washington, D.C.: U.S. Government Printing Office, 1967. The ten leading causes were defined on the basis of rates for the population sixty-five and over for all races combined.
*Source:* U.S. Bureau of the Census. *Demographic and Socioeconomic Aspects of Aging in the United States.* Current Population Reports, Series P-23, No. 138. Washington, D.C.: U.S. Government Printing Office, 1984.

earlier, they ought to be able to draw benefits sooner than whites to recoup some fair share of their investment (Jackson, 1980, 1972b). As we noted in Chapter 5, most people assess their own health as quite good. There are, however, ethnic diversities in self-reported poor health. General trends are shown in Figure 9.2. When careful attention is paid to holding socioeconomic factors steady, the pattern still persists, implying that discriminatory practices indeed take their toll (Dowd and Bengtson, 1978).

If older blacks tend to remain economically active for longer periods and are more engaged in family life, does this result in higher morale or better adjustment? Once again the evidence is contradictory; this time part of the confusion may be an offshoot of the "happy black" stereotype and the reluctance of older blacks to complain, especially to a white interviewer. It is highly unlikely that race in itself exerts a significant influence over morale; more probably other situational factors have to be taken into consideration before any valid generalizations could be made. With insufficient incomes, inhospitable physical surroundings, poor or at least impaired health, and an arduous life overall, it would be unusual not to find some degree of pessimism as a pervasive element in an individual's outlook. However, an exploratory study of majority and minority elderly in Rochester revealed that less than half of the old blacks and whites in that city had serious complaints and those who did expressed desires that are fairly conventional among older people irrespective of race. An interesting sidelight of the Rochester study is the finding that blacks are seemingly better able to accommodate themselves to a racially mixed situation without its having any visible impact on their own sense of well-being. In other studies of black and white adjustment patterns it has been found that over time differences tend to diminish (Wellin and Boyer, 1979; Dowd and Bengtson, 1978).

One dimension of morale some investigators feel might have a profound influence on adjustment is the quest for adequate social services. It is often inferred that because of their lack of formal education, misinformation, or whatever, older black people are not as aware of or do not utilize agency programs designed to serve them, suffering unnecessarily as a result. Judging from the Rochester data and from similar information derived from a parallel analysis of service provision in Houston, it would appear that, if anything, blacks may be up to twice as knowledgeable about local programs and more than willing to use them to advantage. This may arise partly because whites are more threatened by the need to request assistance, a reluctance that might be dispelled by an educational outreach project aimed particularly at correcting their misconceptions of the services offered. Of course, there are social class differences within each racial category, and inevitably, those most lacking are the least likely to avail themselves of agency supports to meet the demands of their later years. An often neglected facet of the use of services is the clients' perceptions of the responsiveness of agency personnel to their needs. Aged blacks rarely view local or state agencies as being willing to meet their personal needs, whether they be health, financial, or social services. Unfortunately, there may be some truth in their perceptions (Jackson, 1980; Sterne et al., 1974; McCaslin and Calvert, 1975).

## AGED HISPANIC AMERICANS

If there is an error in assuming the black elderly are homogeneous, the error is compounded among Hispanic Americans. Hispanic Americans may be of Mexican, Puerto Rican, Cuban, Central or South American, or of other origins. While there are many similarities that characterize them, there are also distinct differences. Next to blacks, people of Hispanic origin are the largest minority in the United States, yet appreciably less is known about their accession to old age. Two reasons account for the little systematic information that is available. Since they claim ancestry from at least one of five distinct nationalities, the very heterogeneity of their backgrounds is a major factor precluding ready categorization and generalization. Data gathered from Mexican Americans living in the Southwest are hardly applicable to Cubans in Florida or Puerto Ricans in New York. In addition, the Hispanic subpopulation is a very youthful group beset with so many far-reaching problems that the comparatively small number of old people has not been a special concern.

In the past half dozen or so years the Asociación Nacional Pro Personas

Mayores, like similar groups formed to represent other special interest groups, has increased the visibility of the Hispanic elderly so that many of the unknowns of the 1970s are beginning to come to light. In recent years publications of the U.S. Bureau of the Census, the Department of Labor, and the Department of Health and Human Services frequently provide statistics on persons of Hispanic origin, and, in some cases, give breakdowns by area of origin. Nonetheless, information is relatively sparse and tends not to focus on the Hispanic elderly per se.

**Profile of Hispanic Americans.** As shown in Figure 9.8, Mexican Americans predominate among the over 14 million persons of Hispanic origin, followed by Puerto Ricans, Central and South Americans, those who trace their family history from elsewhere, and Cubans. With so large a percentage

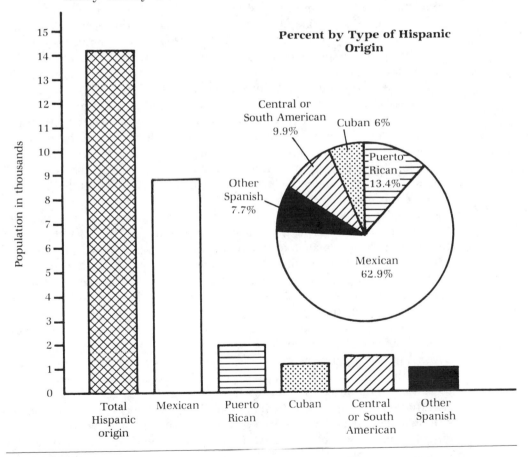

**FIGURE 9.8**
Composition of the Hispanic American population, March 1982. (*Source:* U.S. Bureau of the Census. *Persons of Spanish Origin in the United States: March, 1982.* Current Population Reports, Series P-20, No. 396. Washington, D.C.: U.S. Government Printing Office, 1985.)

originally coming from Mexico, it is reasonable to find the greatest concentrations of the Hispanic population in the West and the South. Overall, more than 42 percent of Hispanics reside in the West and approximately 31 percent live in the South. In the West they account for about one of every six residents. In the South they represent a somewhat lower proportion of the general population, approximately one in seventeen. Puerto Ricans and Dominicans are concentrated in the Northeast, particularly in New York, New York City, and New Jersey. Cubans, both in the earlier wave of the 1960s and those who arrived in the 1980s, settled largely in Miami and Dade county, though roughly one quarter live in the Northeast. Given their rural heritage and the stereotypical view of migrant farmers and laborers, it is somewhat surprising to find over 85 percent of Hispanics living in metropolitan areas, with almost one half of these living in central cities. Referring back to Figure 9.1, we see that the Hispanic population is a more youthful collection of people when compared to other groups in the figure. One of every nine Hispanic Americans is not yet five years old and the median age is only 23.7 years, almost seven years younger than the norm for the general United States population. On the other end of the continuum, only 4 percent are over sixty-five, a figure that has changed little over the last decade or so. Cubans are the sole exception, since their median age is 38.1, almost eight years older than the norm for the general population, and the proportion of persons sixty-five and over in the Cuban American population is 12.2 percent. Mexicans and Puerto Ricans have the youngest population structure, with a median age of approximately twenty-two years, while Central and South Americans and persons of other Spanish origin fall somewhere in the middle, with median ages of 26.8 and 27.9, respectively (U.S. Census, 1985a, 1985c).

Why the age structure of the Hispanic American minority is so skewed toward the earlier years is a multifaceted phenomenon. In their attempts to formulate some explanation for the distinctive age distribution of the Mexican segment, and by extrapolation all other people of Hispanic origin, researchers have offered four plausible and interrelated reasons. To begin with, Hispanic Americans, like other minority and poverty-bound peoples, die younger than the general population; from birth onward their life expectancy is less. Fertility patterns are a second important dimension; while the birth rate has been declining for much of the population, there has been little change among Hispanic Americans. Both the number of children born and the family size are greater than the national average, with large families, those containing six or more members, observed twice as frequently as in the general population. Non-Hispanic families were much more likely to have only two persons. Immigration and repatriation patterns are also important complicating factors. Traditionally, younger people are those most likely to pull up stakes and move to a new country, and this continues to be the case among recent Hispanic arrivals. Once again, Cubans are the exception because large numbers of professional and white-collar workers immigrated to the United States during the period of governmental reorganization under Fidel Castro.

While repatriation among Cubans has been negligible, the same is not true of Mexicans. Periodic massive deportations took place during the 1920s, in the Depression of the 1930s, and in the 1950s. Furthermore, there is a significant voluntary movement back to Mexico among middle-aged and older members of the population, especially as they near retirement. As future generations come to be increasingly native born, fewer people will return to Mexico, thereby contributing to a moderate expansion of the older population (Grebler et al., 1970; Moore, 1971; U.S. Census, 1979c).

Despite recent improvements in their incomes and occupational statuses, it is clear Hispanics continue to lag behind the rest of the country. In 1982 the unemployment rate of Hispanics was 13.4 percent, almost four percentage points higher than the rate for non-Hispanics, though again they show wide variations in unemployment rates. As noted in Chapter 8, Puerto Ricans are the most severely disadvantaged, with an unemployment rate of 17.3 percent, while the rate for Cubans was much lower (10.8 percent) although still above the rate for non-Hispanics. Hispanic women were more likely than men to be unemployed, and when they were employed, their median income was only about 62 percent of that of Hispanic men. Overall, median earnings of Hispanics average about 81 percent of those of non-Hispanics, but there was wide variation by country of origin. The median income for Puerto Rican families in 1982 was a mere $11,300, only a little over half the median income for all families ($22,400) and less than half the income for families not of Hispanic origin ($22,800). Cuban families had a somewhat higher median income ($18,000), although this was still well below the median income for the population at large. Median incomes for Mexican families and families of other Hispanic origin were $16,900 and $17,900, respectively. Fully 43.5 percent of Puerto Rican families had incomes below $10,000, as opposed to only 22.8 percent of Cuban families. At the other end of the scale, over twice as many Cuban families had incomes over $25,000 than did Puerto Rican families (U.S. Census, 1984b).

While the proportion of Hispanics holding professional or technical jobs is well below the national average, there are marked differences between subgroups. Mexicans and Puerto Ricans are much less likely to hold white-collar jobs than are Cubans. Barriers to success in the job market confronting Hispanic Americans include a lack of proficiency in English, low levels of formal schooling, and discrimination. Again, Mexicans and Puerto Ricans are, on the whole, much more poorly educated than are persons of other Spanish origin and Cubans. The low levels of education of Hispanics and possibly their sense of marginality are reflected in equally low levels of political participation: in the 1984 election a little over half as many Hispanics voted as did whites (U.S. Census, 1985c, 1985d; National Commission for Employment Policy, 1982).

Economic deprivation and the marginality of Hispanic Americans also affect their health status. Among Hispanics, Puerto Ricans have the greatest incidence of acute conditions, the highest proportion of persons who perceive their health as only fair or poor, and the greatest average number of days of restricted activity per year. Cuban Americans have the highest percentage of persons with activity limitation caused by chronic conditions. This is the result, however, of the older age structure of the Cuban American population, and after adjusting for the age differentials, the proportion of Cuban Americans with a major activity limitation more closely resembles the rate for whites (National Center for Health Statistics, 1984).

**Aging and the Hispanic Experience.** In most respects older Hispanic Americans are more disadvantaged than successively younger generations, which is common among older people everywhere. At least half the elderly have less than an elementary school education, and among the Mexican American elderly, a larger percentage lack even a rudimentary education. As we might anticipate, income follows a similar pattern since the two are often closely linked (U.S. Census, 1985c).

In most opinion surveys 52 percent of Hispanic Americans report that not having enough money to live on is a very serious problem for them, a larger proportion than among the elderly as a whole (*Public Opinion*, 1985). In 1983 the incidence of living at or below the poverty level among the Hispanic American elderly, though less than that of blacks, was almost twice that of the white elderly. In 1981 median income of men of Mexican and other Hispanic origin sixty-five and older was less than half the income earned by Mexican and Hispanic men in their middle years, whereas the income of elderly Mexicans and Hispanic women was only a little over half that of their younger counterparts. The percentage of black and Hispanic origin elderly who own their homes is nearly the same, although for both groups, fewer are likely to do so than the white elderly. In comparison to blacks, overcrowding is more of a problem among middle-aged and elderly Hispanic Americans, but this may be somewhat equalized because their residences are better equipped on the average (U.S. Census, 1985d).

The sex and marital characteristics of older Hispanic Americans are roughly parallel to other groups of elderly. Elderly Hispanic American women tend to live somewhat longer than men; they also outnumber men, though to a lesser degree than is seen for the general population. As is true in almost all other instances, they remain widowed after the death of their spouses. Perhaps as a reflection of their cultural heritage, older men in this group are more often married or remarried than in any other minority; about three-quarters of elderly Hispanic men were living with their spouses in 1982, though less than half of the older women did so.

One interesting ethnic difference is the number of Hispanic women who continue to have children into their late forties or early fifties; the middle-aged birth rate is twice as high as that recorded for Anglo women in the same age range. Paradoxically, Hispanic Americans perceive the onset of old age as beginning earlier than anyone else; however, job opportunities may play more of a role in this than ethnic status. Clustered as they are in low income tertiary or manual labor occupations, it is not surprising to find a dearth of workers who are old; hence the enforced unemployment of middle-aged and elderly Hispanic American men may make them feel of little value and therefore older (Crouch, 1972). In describing the aging experiences of Mexican American women, Moore (1971) suggests that fertility patterns may be a contributing factor to their particular modes of aging. The ethnographic studies of Mexican Americans carried out in San Francisco by Clark and Mendelson (1969) affirm this; they imply the matriarchal power of older Hispanic American women is strong enough to keep their adult children in a semidependent status until they are well into their own middle age. Spanish American families may be unusual in the amount of esteem they accord older members, but the evidence here is less than definitive.

The early literature on Hispanic Americans frequently contended that intergenerational help and assistance, particularly among Mexican Americans, was customary. The family cared for its own, including the elderly, who openly turn to the family for help. More recent findings have shown that there are, in fact, significant numbers of the Hispanic American elderly living alone, although this does not, as we saw in Chapter 7, necessarily lead to loneliness. In 1983 approximately a third of Hispanic American women sixty-five and over and about 13 percent of elderly Hispanic men lived alone; nearly three quarters of the men and one-sixth of the women were family householders, and another 10 percent of the men and about one-half of the women lived with their families (U.S. Census, 1985c). Lacayo et al. (1980) found that Puerto Ricans were most likely to live alone (about 38 percent), and Cubans were least likely to do so.

Whether the process of acculturation gradually erodes the traditional role of the Hispanic American aged or whether they continue to live their lives free of the discontinuities some feel to be characteristic of Anglo aged is debatable; however, at least among the present generation, there is still a place for the elderly person. While all older people continue to exert some authority over the family, a persistent dilemma involves the relative status of male and female roles. Some researchers have sharply criticized the common observation of male dominance; such a view may betray a certain naiveté, since in-depth analyses indicate that women of all ages have a profound influence in the family decision-making process. Norms of public decorum discourage an open display of this influence, however. With age, women may assume ever more important positions, guiding not only their immediate household but the lives of their offspring's families as well. The significance of these extended family networks cannot be overstated in providing a sense of usefulness among older people. The elderly provide intergenerational contact for the whole neighborhood and help with household and childcare responsibilities while being what may be the only link to past histories. Adaptation to the dominant cultural mode is extensive among the middle-aged, yet the growth of ethnic pride or *chicanismo* has infused both young and old with a new desire to preserve their cultural roots (Cuellar, 1978; Lacayo, 1978; Moore, 1971).

The heterogeneity of the Hispanic aged, with their wide cultural and economic variation, should not be underestimated. Not only is it one of the fastest growing segments of the population but portions of it are remarkably upwardly mobile. Because of the youthfulness of the age distribution, the rapid growth in the number of elderly has been masked. In light of their low educational backgrounds, less than five years on the average, most of the current generation of the elderly continue working to supplement their meager retirement or SSI benefits. As might be expected, immigrant status imposes additional hardships on those who came into the country illegally even though they may have worked here for thirty or forty years. For the same reason, plus cultural values, many Mexican American elderly hesitate to use available health care delivery systems. The legal barriers do not face Puerto Ricans, of course, nor do they seem to impede Cubans as significantly. Cubans also differ by virtue of their relatively old median age, 38.1 at last estimate, and high economic status — nearly equal to nationwide averages (Lacayo, 1978; Valle and Mendoza, 1978).

The future status of all Hispanic elderly hinges on a number of factors, including their own awareness of what they can expect. In the past it has often been said that the elderly in general and the minority elderly in particular lack a sense of political efficacy. However, rates of registration and voting among Hispanics in the forty-five to sixty-four and sixty-five and over age groups are much higher than among younger Hispanics (U.S. Census, 1985c). With the development of lobbying groups designed to heighten their visibility and awareness, there is some indication that minorities are leading the way to greater involvement in their own well-being. Among the Mexican American elderly living on the West Coast, the growth of age-based associations has restored a feeling of affiliation. Whether or not they are able to right all perceived wrongs, the clubs provide a vitality and an aura of personal worth to their members. Perhaps there is a lesson to be learned from Hispanics who are beginning to take an active hand in structuring their own social life space. As Mexican Americans assimilate values promoting a more flexible sex-role orientation, these efforts are likely to pay even greater dividends (Torres-Gil and Becerra, 1977; Cuellar, 1978; Markides and Vernon, 1984).

## OLDER NATIVE AMERICANS

**Profile of Native Americans.** Since World War II, Native Americans have become one of the fastest growing minorities in the United States. However, starting from such a small base, their growth has not altered their proportional representation all that much. By 1984 they still comprised less than 1 percent of the total population (U.S. House of Representatives, 1984).

The largest concentrations are found in the southwestern states of Oklahoma, Arizona, California, and New Mexico, followed by North Carolina, Washington, South Dakota, and New York. Quite unlike other minorities, a majority of Native Americans continue to live in rural areas, though the remaining 45 percent are urbanized. Other than for very general trends, less systematic data are available for Native Americans than for the other minority groups discussed so far. The two federal agencies responsible for collecting basic information, the Bureau of Indian Affairs and the Census Bureau, frequently disagree in their estimates. With high birth and death rates, Native Americans' life expectancy is approximately eight years less than that of the general population; in fact, the U.S. Department of Health, Education and Welfare (1978) contends that the age distribution of Native Americans in the 1970s closely resembled the 1880 profile of the United States population as a whole. In view of the diversity among Native American cultures and the scarcity of reliable data, we must hesitate before making too hasty a description of aged Native Americans. Undoubtedly, many commonalities exist, if only because of the governmental regulations under which Native Americans live out their lives.

**The Native American Experience.** The Native American minority stands apart from all other minority groups because of its special history and relationship with the federal bureaucracy. While most other minorities have attempted to accommodate themselves to the main currents of American life, Native Americans have been isolated on reservations, cultural islands apart from the rest of the population. In addition, Native Americans have long been considered wards of the government to the point that the Bureau of Indian Affairs has assumed the responsibility for deciding who may call themselves Native Americans and who may not. It should not be surprising that under these conditions Native Americans have become an extremely vulnerable group, filled with mistrust, yet realistically unable to reject the sinecures keeping them dependent on the government. The paternalistic regulations of the Bureau, though intended to ensure basic support, have come under serious criticism from Native Americans and the general population for their inflexibility and their denial of traditional cultural values. Two examples illustrate the main thrusts of these arguments. Under certain conditions, Native Americans who leave their reservations, for whatever reason, and remain absent for over a year lose their eligibility for many of the social services granted those on reservations. If a Native American seeks a job off the reservation and is away for the specified period, he or she is no longer entitled to medical care in the eyes of the Indian Health Service. Historically, land and grazing privileges have been extended to all tribal members for as long as they desired; today, elderly Native Americans must transfer their grazing rights to their heirs before they can qualify for sorely needed supplemental financial assistance. The extra income is of course a welcome addition, but nonetheless, the way the program operates deprives the old of their traditional position within the tribal structure (Levy, 1967; Jeffries, 1972).

Native Americans are also a young and economically depressed population, characteristics that are likely to remain for some years to come. As shown in Figure 9.1, over 5 percent of them are over sixty-five, though the median age is barely twenty. The median income for Native Americans is barely above the poverty level. In some areas as many as 75 percent of all Native Americans may be unemployed, while two-thirds have incomes below federal poverty levels. Paradoxically, the economic stagnation that has beset Native Americans in general has also preserved the status of old people whose incomes may account for as much as 60 percent of the family income (Williams, 1980; Murdock and Schwartz, 1978; U.S. Census, 1985a).

Of the minorities discussed here, Native Americans are the most economically disadvantaged. High poverty risk is a constant throughout life for nearly all Native Americans. By forty-five incomes have usually peaked for men and decline thereafter. Women seldom earn as much as one-half the income of men, putting them in the worst position of all minority members. It should be noted, though, that despite the importance of wages and other sources of income, there are alternatives to a strictly cash economy on the reservation. This is not to say that Native Americans are not living on the ragged financial edge, for they are certainly one of the poorest groups economically in the United States. However, barter and other modes of exchange work in the rural environments and these are not normally included in the assessments furnished by the government (U.S. Department of Health, Education and Welfare, 1978).

The health problems associated with poverty are particularly acute among Native Americans. As is apparent from Table 9.2, in 1980 death rates from tuberculosis were six times as high as those for the general population, while deaths from diabetes mellitus were twice as frequent (Table 9.3). On some reservations up to 40 percent of all adults were estimated to have diabetes. Other significant health problems include high rates of chronic and acute *otitis media* leading to hearing impairment in both adults and children, hypertension, and eye diseases, including refractive errors, cataracts, and glaucoma. As is evident from Table 9.2, alcoholism is a serious public health problem among Native Americans, and alcohol-related deaths were over five times higher than for the general population. Despite these significant health problems, per capita health care expenses for Native Americans have de-

**TABLE 9.2**

Age-Adjusted Mortality Rates in the Native American Population for Selected Causes Compared to Rates for the General Population, 1980

| Cause of Death | Rate per 100,000 in Native American Population | Ratio to Rate for United States, All Races |
|---|---|---|
| Alcoholism | 41.3 | 5.5 |
| Diabetes mellitus | 22.6 | 2.2 |
| Gastrointestinal diseases | 4.0 | 1.3 |
| Homicide | 18.1 | 1.7 |
| Suicide | 14.1 | 1.2 |
| Tuberculosis | 3.6 | 6.0 |
| Infant mortality | 14.6 | 1.1 |

Source: *Indian Health Care: An Overview of the Federal Government's Role.* A staff report for the use of the Subcommittee on Health and the Environment of the Committee on Energy and Commerce, U.S. House of Representatives, 1984.

creased in recent years, while per capita health care expenditures for the general population have been increasing. In 1984 the per capita health care costs for Native Americans was only $707.72, as opposed to $1177.23 for the general population (U.S. House of Representatives, 1984; Indian Health Service, 1982; *National Indian Council on Aging Quarterly*, 1981).

**Elderly Native Americans: The Issues.** A special session of the 1981 White House Conference on Aging was devoted to issues relating to Native Americans. The findings of this session were reported to the Select Committee on Indian Affairs of the United States Senate during the first session of the 97th Congress. Testimony on that occasion highlighted the marginality of Native Americans and their elderly in a number of respects and also called for both realizing the value of Native Americans as a resource and supporting their continued participation in community life.

While the Native American population is among the fastest growing groups in the nation, it is also one of the smallest. Despite that it is a young population, and becoming younger, there have been dramatic rises in the numbers of older persons over recent decades. Between 1970 and 1981 the number of the Native American elderly rose from 63,000 to 109,000, a 72 percent increase. For reasons that size alone should indicate, relatively little is known about the situation of this increasingly significant group (*National Indian Council on Aging Quarterly*, 1981).

As noted, the life expectancy of Native Americans is approximately eight years less than that of the general population. One of the most obvious reasons for this is that chronic serious health problems are rampant. Fewer Native Americans over fifty-five are able to carry on the activities of daily living without assistance than are the rest of the population who are sixty-five and over. Seventy-three percent of middle-aged and older Indians are impaired to some extent in their efforts to cope with the circumstances of daily

**TABLE 9.3**
Age-Specific Diabetes Mellitus Death Rates (Rates per 100,000 Population)

| Age | Rate in Native American Population | Ratio to Rate for United States, All Races |
|-----|-----|-----|
| 15–24 | 0.7 | 2.3 |
| 25–34 | 2.0 | 1.2 |
| 35–44 | 10.4 | 2.7 |
| 45–54 | 37.0 | 3.9 |
| 55–64 | 73.8 | 2.7 |
| 65–74 | 156.3 | 2.4 |
| 75–84 | 239.4 | 1.6 |
| 85+ | 236.6 | 1.1 |

*Source:* Indian Health Service. *FY 1984 Budget Appropriation. "Chart Series" Tables.* Rockville, Md.: Indian Health Service, 1983.

life. Although health care for elderly Native Americans is available through the Indian Health Service, Medicare, and Medicaid, three-quarters of aged Native Americans are not eligible for Medicaid coverage even though their incomes are truly inadequate. Barriers to health care among the Native American elderly on reservations include lack of transportation, a lack of information about health services, and an absence of cultural sensitivity by health care providers. The urban Native American elderly also suffer from the lack of facilities designed to provide care for those without health insurance and who have insufficient incomes to pay for health care. The White House Conference called for the development of home health care designed specifically for the older Native American population. It also called for research into mental health issues, as far greater degrees of depression and anxiety have been documented among Native Americans than among the general population (*National Indian Council on Aging Quarterly*, 1981).

The economic situation of aged Native Americans is more precarious than that of most of the nation. Nearly two-thirds of their elderly had incomes below the 1980 national poverty level. Needless to say, the average income of these minority elderly is insufficient to cover the costs of food, clothing, shelter, fuel, and medical care. Native Americans have suffered unduly as a consequence of federal regulations and across the board standards. On the whole, the elderly are unable to participate in retirement programs because of the shortened life expectancies that result from the greater health problems and harsher environments they face. The White House Conference Report goes to great lengths to point out the inequalities wrought by the structural constraints imposed on this particular group. It even suggests the need to develop different Social Security eligibility requirements for a population with lower life expectancies.

Housing is one area in which the living conditions of Native Americans as a whole, and their elderly in particular, fall below that of the general population. More than one-quarter of the houses on reservations are without plumbing. The houses of elderly Native Americans on reservations tend to be old, dilapidated, and lacking in amenities. For example, sleeping quarters are at a premium; more than one-quarter of aged Native Americans occupy bedrooms shared by three or more persons. In Alaska 44 percent are without heating during at least a portion of the winter (*National Indian Council on Aging Quarterly*, 1981).

Family ties are an important personal resource among Native Americans. Generally, the Native American elderly on reservations are well integrated into their families. The White House Conference report called for reinforcing these ties and systems of family support for the elderly. More than one-quarter of the aged Native Americans were caring for at least one grandchild, and 58 percent had two or more persons residing in their homes. Fully two-thirds lived within five miles of their relatives and called on them for assistance. In view of the high levels of limited activity among the Native American elderly and the relatively strong supportive family systems, the conference called for providing options for long-term care of the aged on the reservations, including home health care. Particular attention has been paid to the lack of nursing homes on reservations for those who can no longer be cared for by their families and the detrimental effect of removing the Native American elderly to nursing homes outside the reservation where they are cut off from their families and from their traditional culture (*National Indian Council on Aging Quarterly*, 1981; Select Committee on Indian Affairs, 1983c).

In rural areas elderly Native American women generally live in an extended family and take responsibility for managing the finances of the family. More than half of these women over sixty are widowed; they tend to live in abysmal financial circumstances. Nearly 60 percent of them are barely able to meet current monthly expenses, while two-thirds feel they do not have enough resources to meet future needs (*National Indian Council on Aging Quarterly*, 1981).

The White House Conference has called for recognizing the Native American elderly as a valuable national resource for their contributions to the maintenance of their cultural heritage and religious traditions, as well as to the health and well-being of Native American children, families, and society. It drew attention to the role of aged Native Americans in programs such as the Senior Employment program enacted by Title V of the Older Americans Act and the foster grandparents program. Contrary to the pervasive stereotype, 17.2 percent of the Native American elderly were working or seeking employment, as opposed to only 11.6 percent of the aged in the rest of the population. There is a real need for education and training in job skills among Native American adults, since more than one-quarter of them over sixty had less than a fifth grade education and only 18 percent of them had attended high school. Among Native Americans sixty or older, 65 percent described their life's occupation as semiskilled, unskilled, or farm laborer (*National Indian Council on Aging Quarterly*, 1981).

In an unusual step the conference report pointed to a need for policies going beyond solving problems to promotion of wellness among the Native American elderly in the sense of harmony, balance, and well-being throughout the physical, mental, spiritual, and social aspects of life. While this may seem a somewhat idealistic goal, something is to be learned from the Native American conception of old age as a time when people have a great deal to offer and their call for the integration of the elderly into the broader community.

## AGED ASIAN AMERICANS

**Asian Americans: Model Minority or Marginal People?** As is the case with Native Americans, Asian Americans are a fast-growing minority. In 1980 there were 3.7 million Asians and Pacific Islanders in the United States, comprising approximately 1.7 percent of the population, a 67 percent increase over the 1970 figure. Kim (1983) estimates that there were approximately half a million elderly Asian Americans in the United States in 1980–1981, about three-quarters of whom had grown old in the United States, with the remain-

der being late-life immigrants (U.S. Census, 1985a). These Asian Americans
come from a wide variety of backgrounds, and despite the tendency to lump
them together in official statistics, they form a rather heterogeneous group
comprised of eighteen ethnic groups.

Unfortunately, the U.S. Bureau of the Census, U.S. Commission on Civil
Rights, and Department of Justice do not seem to be able to reach a consensus;
each uses a different classification scheme. While the list is not exhaustive, the
nominal category of Asian Americans includes Japanese, Chinese, Filipinos,
Vietnamese, Burmese, East Indians, Koreans, Hawaiians, Micronesians, Samoans, and Taiwanese, among others. More than half of them live in the three
western states of California, Hawaii, and Washington. There is also a significant concentration of Asian Americans in New York City; overall, about 12
percent of Asian Americans live in either New York or in New Jersey. In the
following discussion we will give an overview of some of the myths and realities about Asian Americans and the Asian American elderly. We will then look
at historical trends in Asian American immigration and how the situation of
particular ethnic groups is shaped by their immigration to the United States.

Having said that, it is time for a disclaimer: there is a notable lack of data
about Asian Americans. They were not included in the decennial census as a
separate category until 1980, and even now, current population reports do
not give data regarding them. Although some data are available on the Asian
American elderly in this country, primarily through the efforts of the San
Diego State University Center on Aging, most studies, such as the 1977 U.S.
Commission on Civil Rights investigation of Asian Americans in New York City
or the field survey of Asian Americans in urban environments (U.S. Commission on Civil Rights, 1977; U.S. Department of Health, Education and Welfare,
1977), tend to have a regional focus. As a consequence, we know very little
about national trends.

From the data presented in the comparative figures at the beginning of
this chapter, Asian Americans appear to do rather well compared to other
ethnic groups, including whites. Overall poverty rates among Asian Americans are barely above those among whites; they have lower unemployment
rates than whites, a higher median income, and are more likely to have a college education. On the basis of statistics such as these, a recent article called
Asian Americans "a model minority" and "the promise of America" (Michaels,
1985). These summary statistics, however, obscure some harsh realities and
perpetuate the myths regarding Asian Americans that, in the past, have led to
an inattention to their needs. Cabezas (1980) identified three myths regarding
the socioeconomic success of Asian Americans and presented evidence to
challenge them. In contradiction to the myth that Asian and Pacific Americans
are not discriminated against in employment and are found in all sectors of industry, he presented evidence from studies by the United States Equal Employment Opportunity Commission and other groups demonstrating significant discrimination against Asian Americans in the labor market. To refute the
myth that Asian and Pacific Americans do well because they go to college and

therefore their income exceeds that of whites, he gave data demonstrating that Asian Americans receive comparatively poor returns of income for their educational levels, and that higher family incomes among Asian Americans are in part the result of more family members working. To counterbalance the myth that Asian and Pacific Americans are in business for themselves and are very successful, he pointed out that generally Asian firms are in retail trade and selective service with modest gross receipts, which can hardly be seen as representing business success (Cabezas, 1980). In recent years there has been a considerable effort in the literature on aging among Asian Americans to refute the myth that the elderly are integrated into their families, that Asian Americans can take care of their own, and that therefore there is no need for creating special service delivery systems (Kim, 1983; Lum, 1983; White House Conference on Aging, 1981).

Lum (1983) asserts that contrary to popular opinion, the Asian American elderly are indeed at multiple jeopardy: they are poor, elderly, members of a minority, and non-English speaking. The Asian American elderly are at significant risk for socioeconomic problems for a number of reasons despite the relatively favorable statistical profile of the Asian American population as a whole. As we noted earlier, Asian Americans are a heterogeneous mix, and some ethnic groups among them, such as Filipinos who tend to be primarily farm laborers, are particularly prone to poverty. Furthermore, as we shall see later, at the time when many Chinese and Filipino men immigrated to the United States, restrictive immigration policies prevented them from marrying, which means that they are now old alone, with all of the liabilities we have seen that can bring. They also tend to have scant formal education and training and poor English skills. A number of programs designed to improve English language skills of Asian Americans exist, but they are directed primarily at younger age groups (White House Conference on Aging, 1981).

The 1981 White House Conference on Aging identified a number of serious problems among elderly Asian Americans. They tend to have more debilitating and long-term health problems than the general population of the elderly. For example, the incidence rates for tuberculosis among Asian Americans and Pacific Islanders in 1980 were twelve times greater than those among whites (U.S. Department of Health and Human Services, 1983b). Nonetheless, they make less use of health care services, in part because they rely on traditional systems of folk medicine and in part because of a lack of Medicare coverage stemming from their position in the labor market. The Asian American elderly are also disadvantaged in terms of income. At the time of the 1981 White House Conference, more than one in five Asian American and Pacific Islander elderly had an income below the poverty level, a proportion 33 percent higher than the national average. The poverty rates were even worse among elderly women who were heads of households or unrelated women, about 31.1 to 40.4 percent higher. While 30 percent of the Asian American elderly participated in the labor force, because of language problems and low levels of education and training, they were primarily involved in service industries, farming, or were self-employed. Some groups, such as Filipino migrant farmers, were without Social Security coverage. Also as a function of their position in the labor market, most had no public or private pensions. Despite these difficulties, they tend to underuse social services, in part because of language and cultural barriers. A sensitive service delivery program has to be cognizant of the Asian concept of "filial piety" and that turning older family members over to external assistance is a normative violation censured by the cultural community. Similarly, they encounter special nutritional problems because of their reliance on ethnic foods and their difficulties in obtaining them. Many, for instance up to 67 percent of Chinese elderly women and 70 percent of Japanese women, live alone rather than admit a lack of family support, and those receiving minimal Social Security or SSI incomes had significant difficulty in financing their housing needs (Snyder, 1984; Kim, 1983; Lum, 1983; Gelfand, 1982).

**The History of Asian American Immigration.** While it is true that those who have come to the United States from the Orient derive from widely divergent cultures, with different religions and languages, their experiences in a country dominated by people from European backgrounds reflect a certain similarity. The first waves of male Chinese immigrants arrived in the 1850s to serve as unskilled laborers for the railroads and in the mines of the West. From the outset they faced prejudice and racial discrimination, and by the 1880s, with over 80,000 Chinese on the West Coast, there were widespread fears of eventual Oriental domination. Exclusionary laws prohibiting intermarriage, the immigration of women and families, or ownership of real property were passed in the following decades, with the result that the flow of Chinese to the United States had been stopped entirely by the time of the Depression in the early 1930s. The flood of Japanese immigration did not really begin until the 1890s, when large numbers of men arrived from Japan and Hawaii to work in the fields or as unskilled urban laborers. Until the mid-1920s Japanese immigrants were not so strictly regulated as the Chinese; consequently, more extensive familial settlements were established along the Pacific coast. With the passage of the Alien Exclusion Act in 1924, however, new arrivals dwindled. Despite a prior "gentlemen's agreement" between the two countries that curtailed the influx of the unskilled and women, skilled men were still allowed entry into the country in sizable numbers. Filipino migration to the United States was hardly noticeable until after World War I, although Hawaii had been the site of Filipino relocation for more than a decade previously. Like the Chinese, nine out of ten Filipinos traveling to America were men who came for economic reasons and found work in migratory agricultural jobs or in other low-paying, unskilled jobs. Before the late 1920s little attention was given to the new entrants; however, in 1929 violent demonstrations erupted in the West because of their high levels of employment at a time when field jobs were becoming scarce. During the same period, a bill was introduced in Congress to bar immigration by declaring Filipinos aliens, though they have been technically considered nationals since the islands were ceded to the United States in 1898. The enactment of the Philippine Independence Bill in 1934 granted commonwealth status to the islands, with independence following ten years later. In the process Filipinos were reclassified as aliens and immigration quotas were set at a meager fifty per year.

As a result of legislation in 1965 repealing immigration quotas, there has been a wave of Asian immigrants since the beginning of the 1970s. Though quotas were abolished, certain categorical qualifications exist based on professional and occupational groups, family reunification, and refugees. In addition, the 1968 Immigration Act exempts parents and spouses of United States citizens from any limitation the qualifications might otherwise have imposed. In contrast to their earlier counterparts, many of these — one in five since 1965 — are trained professionals who fulfill an important need in the United States. They also account in part for the relatively favorable overall picture of Asian immigrants. In 1979 the three major categories of Asian immigrants were Chinese-Taiwanese, Koreans, and Filipinos. During the early 1980s there has been a significant influx of Vietnamese refugees; in 1980 there were 166,727 refugee arrivals from Vietnam, Laos, and Kampuchea alone, though this figure had fallen to 36,167 by 1983 (Kim, 1983; U.S. Bureau of the Census, 1985a). Because of the support given by refugee resettlement programs — in contrast to the discrimination encountered by earlier Asian refugees — these refugees have better prospects than did Asian refugees arriving earlier in the century.

**Elderly Chinese Americans.** In traditional China the family was the basic associational unit, with all else, including the state, considered an appendage to it. An individual's identity was based totally on familial membership, and the bond between the two could never be broken. What was considered good for the family was naturally good for the individual, while personal achievements or failures were always seen as a reflection on the family. Although all older people were revered and worshiped by other members, the oldest man exerted absolute authority over business and even emotional matters. Throughout life children were obliged to obey and comfort their parents, to the point of valuing their parents' lives over those of their own children. Ideally, old age was a warmly anticipated, if not welcome, period of life in which people were gradually relieved of burdensome responsibilities without losing any of their security or veneration. Indeed, the position of the elderly in traditional China was so entrenched that the term **gerontocracy** was often used to describe the Chinese social order.

In the years since the Communist changeover other institutions have supplanted many of the family's roles, especially among the elderly. Although family units are still primarily responsible for teaching children to be good citizens, the state rather than the family is now emphasized as the unit most worthy of allegiance. In China, as in much of the Western world, the elderly are of another era and therefore are no longer viewed as a repository of wisdom. At the same time a redefinition of sexual roles has gradually taken place in which wives are not subordinate to their husbands and both may retain their family names or property after marriage. Divorces were possible in traditional China, though they were initiated almost entirely by the husband. Even if he should leave for the United States on what was to be a temporary absence but from which he never returned, the wife was duty-bound to passively await his homecoming (Welty, 1970). During the last century immigration obviously exerted a disruptive influence on family life, both at home and abroad. For one thing it was limited almost exclusively to men, resulting in a lack of men at home and a preponderance in the new country. In 1900 women comprised only 7 percent of the Chinese population in America and today men still continue to outnumber women among the older generations. Responsive to the ideology of material success inherent in the new country, Chinese traditions often have been abandoned in favor of small, economically feasible family units. Hence the value of filial piety has lost much of its former suzerainty in the lives of native-born children.

According to recent estimates, the Chinese population in the United States is approximately 891,000, clustered overwhelmingly in urban areas. The median age among Chinese Americans does not differ greatly from that of the general population, but the proportion of those over sixty-five is significantly lower.

Most of today's generation of the elderly were originally from Canton province. Departing for the United States to earn their fortunes as laborers, they had every intention of returning to their homelands once they had accumulated sufficient wealth. There is also a contingent of Mandarin-speaking elderly from the northern provinces who immigrated as political refugees after the establishment of the Communist government in 1948. Despite this later influx, the elderly still reflect the predominately male immigration of the early years. Along with the Filipino population, the Chinese display a unique sex ratio, since men outnumber women. Fully two-thirds of the aged men are presently married, compared to about 40 percent of the women, while only about one-fifth of the men, but one-half of the women, are widowed. Because of their lack of training, old world ways, and changing cultural conditions, many of these older Chinese find themselves with perilously few resources to draw on in their later years. Median incomes for the older segments of the Chinese American population differ by sex: men have an annual income just over one-third that of all other Chinese men, while older women earn about half as much as younger women. Part of the reason their financial situation is so bleak is because most Chinese Americans have spent a lifetime in low-paying jobs or in employment not covered by Social Security. With no source of income other than what is provided to the indigent elderly, the outlook is indeed grim (U.S. Census, 1984b; Wu, 1975).

With suicide rates three times as high among the Asian American elderly as among their white peers and with over one-third having never seen a physician or a dentist, there is every reason to believe that serious problems beset the aged. After years of discrimination and living under the fear of deportation, they are often reluctant to seek help from anyone in a bureaucracy. At the same time the older Chinese Americans are equally loathe to become burdens on their families, since this is not seen as legitimate within the context of their adopted culture. Cultural isolation is a very real problem in the lives of the elderly in any transplanted minority. Among the Chinese Americans it has resulted in an unusually high rate of drug use, particularly among older men without family or ideological ties to the larger community. The absence of bilingual service personnel or of programs geared to Chinese culture, dietary habits, and customs means that even those who are receiving services such as sheltered housing or income maintenance are less than satisfied. Some solutions are undoubtedly at hand, provided an element of flexibility becomes a basic, foundational principle in service delivery.

Unfortunately, no extensive effort has been made as yet to accommodate those elderly Chinese Americans who seek assistance. One of the first attempts to deal in a culturally specific way with the difficulties facing the Chinese elderly in the continental United States was launched in San Francisco's Chinatown several years ago. The organization Self-Help for the Elderly intends to gather all available resources under one system, making them easily accessible to older people living in the community. Ideally, this will facilitate the search for and provision of services without imposing the added disadvantage of dealing with outsiders who are perceived as threats. Other programs have since been inaugurated in other West Coast cities from Seattle to Los Angeles and in Hawaii. The projects range from providing sheltered housing, day-care centers, ethnic meals, and outreach treatment to liaisons with appropriate governmental agencies. All are intended to meet the distinctive needs of older Chinese Americans and the aged of other Asian ancestry (Kalish and Moriwaki, 1979; Cheng, 1978).

**Elderly Japanese Americans.** In marked contrast to the Chinese, the Japanese represent the ideal of the American success story. First-generation immigrants, the *issei*, left rural and lower-class backgrounds to travel to the United States in search of their fortunes. Instead, they found hard work, low wages, and overwhelming discrimination. Prohibited from owning land themselves, they acquired it in the name of friends and their American-born children. Once they had gained a foundation in their new land, injury was added to insult when 110,000 were placed in relocation camps during World War II. The end of the war brought peace and freedom, but it also brought new economic hardship when they returned to find their property and money had disappeared or been confiscated. Beginning again, the 600,000 plus Japanese Americans have by today managed to eke out incomes some $3000 or more above the national average. Educational levels among the second and third generations, the *nisei* and *sansei*, are higher than any other segment of the population and their occupational achievements are unsurpassed.

Women, being dutiful, usually deferred to men, and because of the system of inheritance, father-son relationships often took precedence over all others. Marriages were also family affairs arranged at the behest of the father through an agent who was responsible for maintaining family solidarity. If, for example, a family name was in danger of dying out because of a lack of sons, the agent might ask the groom to assume the wife's family name. With such traditions, the Japanese in America were understandably reluctant to marry outsiders, and many made the long trip home to find a wife or, if unable to return, selected their mates by mail through an agent in Japan. Customary family practices were adapted to a new way of life, but over the years and with a larger number being American born, customs slowly changed. Wives became companions, styles of clothing changed, and community ties resembled local norms, particularly after World War II. What will happen as the fourth generation, the *yonsei*, takes its place in society? Will the erosion of solidarity only hinted at among the nisei and sansei finally exact a price (Montero, 1980a, 1981)?

Old people account for little more than 8 percent of Japanese Americans, and six out of ten of the elderly are women. The median age is over thirty-four for women and nearly thirty for men. Over 80 percent of all Japanese Americans live in the western states, and they are predominantly an urban minority, with only 10 to 14 percent living outside of urban areas. Though they still occupy positions of prestige, they do not have as much status as in Japan. Still, most of the Japanese American elderly are firmly ensconced in a healthy and supportive network (Montero, 1980b; Kiefer, 1974). They do not, however, make friends readily outside of their own ethnic communities, but once friendships are formed, they are tightly knit. The effects of the World War II relocations and the stratagems used to hold property may have been deleterious to the vertical hierarchy of Japanese family life. Still, adjustments have been made and most of the issei are content with the respect they are accorded. Most of those studied by Montero (1981) report satisfaction with their achievements, financial status, and family relationships. Other activities also reflect mental and emotional contentment. Nine out of ten voted in the last election, most take at least a passive interest in politics, and at least 40 percent participated in religious or voluntary associations.

Living arrangements among the elderly reflect their *meiwako* values against being an imposition on others, especially on family members; a familial pattern in which they live an independent life insofar as possible seems typical. Although the responsibility of caring for aged parents does not rest solely on the eldest son as it did in the past, adult children still care for elderly family members, and apparently they experience serious emotional turmoil if they are incapable of fulfilling their own expectations. In traditional Japan families occupied the same position of importance they did in China. The extended family unit was the primary associational and supportive institution, and all members shared individual incomes with the rest of the family. The recent advent of convalescent facilities for the Asian elderly along the West Coast is further evidence of the gradual acculturation of both the older and middle-aged generations, though the older Japanese will likely continue their close family ties despite the inevitable strains of institutionalization (Osako, 1979; Kitano, 1969).

As pointed out in the discussion of health in Chapter 5, Japanese Americans have an incidence of cardiovascular diseases approximating that of the general population rather than their country of origin. Other dimensions of health tend to follow a similar pattern. Nevertheless, elderly Asian Americans in general are remarkably healthy, exhibiting fewer chronic disabilities than their majority group age mates. Symptoms of psychological distress are not surprising in view of the incongruities in an older person's values, expectations, and reality combined with the strong emphasis the Japanese place on saving face by not admitting to outsiders that serious problems exist. Though a problem for only a small percentage, older men appear to be the most vulnerable, and their hospitalization rates in Japan and the United States are very similar. The most frequent classification is schizophrenia and defensive withdrawal; however, cultural factors are important here, as they are in the diagnosis of emotional problems among all minority groups. The delineation of overt psychopathological conditions can only be carried out within a particular cultural context; what is learned as appropriate behavior under certain circumstances could easily be viewed as mental illness under other conditions. Hence the factors resulting in the disproportionate presence of Japanese Americans in California state mental hospitals may not have nearly the same significance in Hawaii or Tokyo. Nonetheless, that the patients are in California and not elsewhere indicates the existence of some disjunctures in their lives whether they originate from within the patients' own psyches or are a function of living in what remains an alien country. As the nisei and successive generations of native-born Japanese Americans move into old age, there is reason to predict they will manifest physical and psychological symptoms, both in etiology and behavior, closer to the general population than their older relatives have.

**Elderly Filipino Americans.** The aging experience of Filipino Americans required a distinct adaptive strategy. Following World War I young men from the low-land rice farming and fishing areas of the Philippines immigrated to the United States. Once in the United States, they worked primarily in agriculture, often encountering violent discrimination, as in the race riots of 1929. With the enactment of the Philippine Independence Bill in 1934, immigration was cut off, and those men already here gave up most hope for marrying women from their own cultural background. Living together in homogeneous camps of agricultural workers, the young men continued to speak their native language and preserve many of their cultural traditions. Now numbering slightly more than one-third of a million, Filipinos are the smallest of the three Asian minorities considered in this discussion. More than half of the population is male, a proportion that increases dramatically with age. Among the 6.2 percent who are over sixty-five, men outnumber women by more than four to one, higher even than among the Chinese. Under these circumstances, a smaller percentage of the women, about 40 percent, are widows. The median age is over twenty-six with a four-year spread between men and women. Income differentials between the young and old are similar to those in other minority groups.

Due to a highly mobile life-style, most Filipinos are employed as agricultural, domestic, or other traveling workers. Unlike the Japanese or Chinese, the Filipino community has yet to stabilize; as a consequence, older people more often face their later years without close ties to families or neighborhoods. Many of the elderly do not have strong bonds to other minority members, but for Filipinos this provokes special anxieties, because they were usually reared in a culture that emphasized the social nature of the self. Clinical evidence points to a weaker sense of self when deprived of close ties than is the case for most westerners. Like the Japanese or Chinese, Filipinos have a long tradition of subjugating individual needs in deference to familial demands; thus, without family ties they are at a loss (Marsella and Quijano, 1974). Another serious problem for the elderly is a language barrier they have never surmounted because of their lack of formal education. Paradoxically, cultural and linguistic traits stress personal status, and considerable maneuvering occurs between individuals as each ascertains the other's place before their interaction can continue. The older Filipino American, no matter how disadvantaged, is reluctant to seek any form of nonfamilial assistance. This tendency adds to their hardship, since relatively fewer of them have families on which they can call.

Unfortunately, little published research is available focusing on the plight of older Filipinos. With the exception of the Manilatown Information Service in San Francisco, very few service delivery systems have been set up to meet their special needs. In a San Diego area study only 10 percent of the Filipino respondents indicated they would seek assistance from local agencies as a first recourse. Part of the reason seems to be the Filipino value of reciprocity; without equivalent exchange they are hesitant to go outside of their informal networks for help. Because the oldest Filipinos are usually men, living alone or with other men, deteriorating health and financial resources result in serious difficulties (Kalish and Yuen, 1971; Peterson, 1978).

As is true of other Asian minorities, future generations of older Filipino Americans will present a far different picture. Intermarriage is becoming common among the younger generations, and nearly three-quarters of all those approaching middle age have a high school degree. Native-born people are a very small percentage of the current generation of older people, but they are in a majority in the younger age ranges. Taken together, education and birthplace are enough to predict that more adequate financial resources will be characteristic of the future aged because they will have been employed for higher pay in jobs covered by Social Security. Problematic as Social Security coverage may be in terms of adequacy when it is the sole or primary financial resource, it will still provide for relative improvement among aged Filipinos.

Whether family patterns will gradually reflect these changes cannot yet be forecast with any certainty, yet if the Filipino minority follows the trends of other Asian peoples who have settled in the United States, we may expect them to work out a middle position between their traditional cultures and the general American patterns. Absent the kind of large-scale physical communities characteristic of the Chinese or Japanese, Filipinos may move further away from traditional customs. With the lifting of the National Origins Quota in 1965, a new wave of immigration began and swelled the ranks of Filipino Americans to 30,000 annually throughout most of the 1970s. Though these newcomers are different in many respects, comprised of the highly educated and professionals, it remains to be seen how they will alter the prospects for aging among Filipinos.

## RAMIFICATIONS OF ETHNICITY

This discussion of ethnic factors in aging points to special issues that must be considered. Membership in one or another ethnic group means having certain ascribed characteristics simply by virtue of identification. To the extent that these circumscribe lifetime achievements they must be given their due when speaking of the process of aging. In addition, ethnic status portends a world-view and a culturally generated complex of values that are discernible from that of mainstream populations. These in turn mean additional adjustment problems in old age over and above what is implied by age itself. Furthermore, if culturally derived stereotypes or culturally normative values impede the acquisition of supportive services when they are needed, still greater hardships may be piled on various subpopulations of the elderly (Gelfand, 1982).

Assimilation may be one form of recourse, but it creates an equal number of problems. In a pluralistic society such as the United States there is no sound reason why social policies cannot be molded to take account of ethnicity. One set of values, for example, those that view seeking external formal assistance as shameful, should not be subjugated in favor of another set of values, for example, bureaucratic expediency. Involving ethnic leadership in formulating entitlement programs could be an effort that will prove beneficial to those not otherwise reached (Bechill, 1979). Even gathering useful statistics would be a step in the right direction. To date, Census enumerations have been seriously criticized for undercounting minorities or lumping diverse groups into residual categories that negate their individual identities. Finally, cultural roles accorded older persons within all ethnic groups vary by generation and social class, as well as by orientation to tradition (Gelfand and Kutzik, 1979).

# Aging in the Third World

Although our discussion has focused on aging in advanced industrial societies, and the study of aging in the Third World in all its diversity deserves its own volume, some attention to the issue of aging in the developing countries will be useful for comparison. At the international level the major concern in the past has been focused on the graying of the industrialized countries and the social problems this phenomenon presents. In the developing countries, as we saw in earlier chapters, with their relatively young population structures and shorter life expectancies, there has been a legitimate focus on high infant mortality rates and the economic, social, or health-related factors that lead to short and difficult lives for the majority of these people. The young population structure obscures a tremendous growth in absolute numbers of the elderly. As shown by Figure 9.9, the elderly in the developing countries will represent an increasingly high proportion of the world's elderly by the year 2025. Between 1950 and the end of the century, according to United Nations estimates, the world population of persons over sixty will have increased more

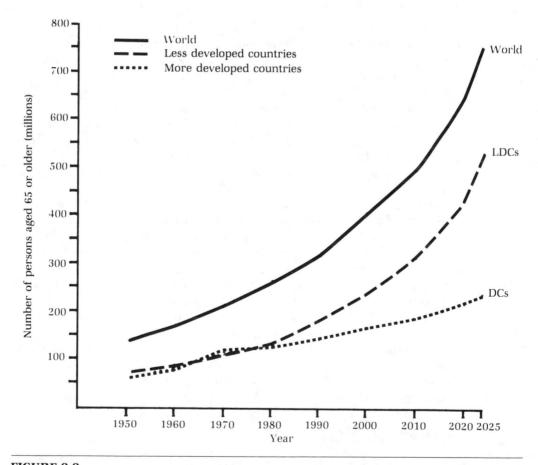

**FIGURE 9.9**

Aged population in underdeveloped and developed countries. (*Source:* United Nations, Department of International Economic and Social Affairs. *Demographic Indicators of Countries: Estimates and Projections as Assessed in 1980*, pp. 58–63. New York: United Nations, 1982 [adapted from numerical data].)

than threefold; 60 percent of these elderly people will be living in the less developed countries. By the year 2025 nearly three-quarters of the world's elderly will be living in the Third World; the elderly population of Africa alone is projected to rise from 16.6 million to 54.3 million by the end of the twentieth century. In both developed and Third World countries there will be an excess of women over men, and the elderly will be found in both urban and rural environments (Hampson, 1985; United Nations, 1983). Thus, the numbers and the plight of the Third World elderly is fast becoming a matter for international concern of which the student of gerontology should at least be aware. Furthermore, the issue of the elderly in the Third World is relevant to advanced industrial societies for two reasons: (1) the current situation of the elderly in the Third World is in part a function of the historically grounded structure of relations between advanced industrial societies and developing countries and (2) the dilemmas facing the Third World elderly may highlight some of the issues facing advanced industrial societies. In the course of this book, by way of international comparison, we have given illustrations of the characteristics of the situation of the elderly in many Third World countries. This section is designed to draw attention to some of the issues involved.

**Family Life.** As with certain ethnic minorities, considerable attention has been devoted in recent decades to dispelling the myth that families in Third World countries can take care of their own and that the situation of the elderly there is relatively favorable — at least until modernization has made its mark (Lewis, 1982). As noted in Chapter 2, many of those who would have been old in underdeveloped countries have died rather unpleasant deaths in their earlier years. Those who do live to old age, even in traditional societies, are apt to share with the rest of the population a life of chronic ill-health and poverty. While there may be more respect for the elderly — although even that is a matter of dispute — respect and authority are not interchangeable substitutes for good nutrition and health. Neither is social status a unified concept; rather it is composed of a number of dimensions, including biological, psychological, social, economic, and health status, among others, which vary somewhat independently (Goldstein and Beall, 1982).

**Theoretical Perspectives.** In Chapters 2 and 3 we touched on two theoretical perspectives that are sometimes used to explain the situation of the developing countries and consequently of their elderly: modernization theory and dependency theory. Modernization theory suggests that the failure to develop is somehow the result of impediments inherent in the traditional culture of Third World countries that must be removed by the developed countries. Dependency or world systems theory, however, holds that both the development of the industrialized countries and the underdevelopment of the Third World countries are sustained by the same force: the structure of relations between Third World and advanced industrial societies. Neysmith and

Edwardh (1984) maintain that the structure of this relationship is crucial for aging. It determines who grows old, the quality of their lives, the nature of state policy toward the elderly, and the forms of assistance developed nations offer to Third World countries to meet the needs of their elderly. Table 9.4 shows the ways in which the social policies — either implicit or explicit — fostered by this type of arrangement operate to the detriment of the elderly (Hendricks, 1982; Neysmith and Edwardh, 1984). In the relationship between

**TABLE 9.4**

Economic and Social Costs of the Politics of Aging in Developing Countries

| Policy Arena | De Facto Social Policies | Policy Outcomes | Impact on Old People |
|---|---|---|---|
| Labor | Lowest possible real wage | Wages and fringe benefits are 10–20 percent of those in industrial Western countries | |
| | | Increasing employment of women at wages 20–50 percent lower than men | |
| | | Increasing employment of minors and children under 14 at wages lower than those paid to women | |
| | | Planned high turnover rates of 50–100 percent per year so that labor never receives higher wages or benefits | Subsistence-level incomes |
| | | Workers are dismissed after they suffer disabling accidents, debilitating illness, or exhaustion | Destitution/pauperism Breakup of families Obsolescence, social and physical |
| | | High unemployment rates | |
| | | Forced mobility | Premature aging |
| | Increased work intensity | Extension of the working day, longer average working hours (45–58 hours) in underdeveloped countries than developed ones (40–44 hours) | Persecution Break with tradition Stress Abandonment of old people |
| | | Productivity is enhanced solely through extracting more from labor rather than through the introduction of labor-saving technology | Chronic disease |
| | Dangerous working conditions | Temperature, noise, light, crowding, clothing, and other protective measures are poor | |
| | | Disabling accidents | |
| | | High morbidity and mortality rates — heart, respiratory, cancer, and so on | |

*Source:* Neysmith, S. M., and J. Edwarth. "Economic Dependency in the 1980's: Its Impact on Third World Elderly." *Ageing and Society* 4, 1 (1984): 36–37.

**TABLE 9.4, cont'd**

Economic and Social Costs of the Politics of Aging in Developing Countries

| Policy Arena | *De Facto* Social Policies | Policy Outcomes | Impact on Old People |
|---|---|---|---|
| State authority | Programs to guarantee stability | Institutionalization of repression<br>Militarization<br>Labor laws prohibit the growth of trade unionism | |
| Income distribution | Highly stratified society | Widening gap between high and low income earners<br>Marginalization of subpopulations economically and socially through unemployment and poverty<br>Largest gains have occurred to the better organized upper middle class (managers and technocrats)<br>Privatization — little redistribution of income through state employment, welfare, and other social expenditures | Subsistence-level incomes<br>Destitution/pauperism<br>Breakup of families<br>Obsolescence, social and physical<br>Premature aging<br>Persecution<br>Break with tradition<br>Stress<br>Abandonment of old people<br>Chronic disease |
| Social welfare | Meeting need is defined as a private responsibility<br>Limited investment in physical infrastructure<br><br>No planned urban environment<br>Inadequate preventive health services<br>Inadequate educational services | Deplorable living conditions: housing; clean water; sanitation; transportation<br>Diseases of poverty — tuberculosis, malaria, tetanus, acute diarrhea, diphtheria, acute poliomyelitis<br>High infant mortality — malnutrition; mental illness<br>Illiteracy | |

free market economies and Third World countries, industrialized countries appropriate the surplus generated by Third World nations through capital drain — the structure of trade relations and unequal exchange — thus depriving the Third World countries of the resources necessary for their own development. Satellite nations are at their highest level of development when their relations with the core are weakest, since this arrangement provides less opportunity for draining resources from the satellite nation. The most underdeveloped regions are those that had the strongest relations with core countries in the past. These Third World countries are characterized by highly stratified societies comprised of small foreign and national elites, a small urban middle class, a stable working class, and an impoverished peasantry. Their large marginal underclass includes many of the elderly.

Third World countries have, on the whole, tended to replicate programs for the elderly, such as Social Security, developed by the advanced industrial societies. These programs, however, usually only cover government employees, those in core industries, or, at best, those in the formal labor market, amounting to coverage for approximately 10 percent of the economically active population (Hampson, 1985; Neysmith and Edwardh, 1984; U.S. Department of Health and Human Services, 1984). This leaves peasants, those who participate in informal labor (such as taking in laundry), and those who, for one reason or another, are not economically active uncovered, dependent for help on what family they have. At the same time the introduction of industry by core countries tends to break down traditional family structures by encouraging the outmigration of young people to the cities in search of jobs. As Neysmith and Edwardh (1984) suggest, insisting in these circumstances that the care of the elderly should fall on their families is converting a public issue into a private trouble.

Questions have been raised as to the appropriateness of Western-style systems of Social Security in developing countries. It has been pointed out that these systems tend to reinforce the stereotype of the elderly as dependent. Furthermore, although the extension of Social Security to the populations of Third World countries as a whole might be financially feasible at the outset because of a relatively young population structure, the increasing number of elderly in future years will place impossible strains on the system — a situation that is already to some extent being encountered by advanced industrial societies. Alternative forms of old age security are beginning to be explored, such as cooperative farms designed to be relatively self-sustaining, where the elderly would work as they are able and be provided for when they were not (Hampson, 1985; Neysmith and Edwardh, 1984). In future years it will perhaps become apparent in advanced industrial societies too that enforced retirement on a pension defines the elderly as dependent and their situation as a social problem.

## Summary

Any discussion of aging as a social process would be incomplete without considering the experiences of the minority elderly. Regardless of whether the heritage is black, Hispanic, Native American, or Asian, each of the subcultures described imposes its own distinctive normative structure on the aging individual. Obviously, certain dimensions of life, such as psychomotor processes, have little or nothing to do with ethnicity directly. The areas where ethnic status makes a difference are in that range of behaviors easily shaped by social or environmental factors. One of the more pressing issues involves not so much whether basic patterns are distinguishable by ethnic categories, but how the differences are interpreted by those involved. Suppose both Hispanic and Anglo Americans show some age-related alteration in sensory capacities: do both impute the same meaning to the change? Because of the worldview implicit in the dominant value structure, the shift in sensory capacities might be cause for all kinds of remedial measures designed to return the individual to an optimum level. The same event might be seen simply as part of one's fate, a natural concomitant of aging, to be accepted and endured, by the Hispanic American (Gelfand, 1979–1980).

In commenting on the uniqueness of the minority experience one must be mindful of the dilemma implicit in singling out minorities for special attention. In doing so they are set apart for good or ill. Are minorities different from any other group in the population because of some inherent characteristic or because of the way they are dealt with by the social system? Saying there are no differences negates the consequences of a lifetime of limited access. Some have characterized the results as multiple jeopardy that increases the hazards to which older minority group members are exposed. One need look only as far as life expectancy or health impairments to see the realities of the peril imposed.

Further evidence of a lifetime of disadvantage is provided by the statistics on unemployment and earnings. Blacks, for example, are far more likely to live below the poverty line than are whites. Even when education is held constant, members of minorities receive lower returns in such personal investments than do whites. Only among certain Asian Americans is the probability of education offsetting other hardships improved; when the number of wage earners contributing to family incomes is taken into consideration, however, the pattern of discrimination apparent among minorities in general is replicated. Ideally, the information in this discussion will put the old cliché about Asian Americans being a model minority to rest. Among aged Filipino Asian Americans, risk factors are higher than for other members of the Asian and Pacific minority. Here, too, the effects of immigration provisions and lifetimes of low earnings in occupations not always covered by Social Security result in a circumscribed quality of life for the elderly.

Perhaps no other group is as disadvantaged as are the Native Americans. Native Americans have lower life expectancies, more impaired health, and less adequate financial resources than any other group discussed in this chapter. The bureaucratization of the Native American experience has simultaneously blinded us to their past, present, and future potential contributions to society. It has also placed them in a restricted, often untenable, position.

One of the most interesting differences between whites and the minorities discussed is the role accorded the elderly minority group member. While there are clearly differences within the groups discussed, and in all cases status hierarchies add to the diffusion of traditional values, some real strengths emerge. In almost every instance the minority aged have closer ties to non-aged family members than the stereotype suggests. Part of the reason stems from cultural values that have not yet been diluted by assimilation into mainstream American culture.

The recent acknowledgment of the need for specially designed programs aimed at each segment of the American population is only the beginning. Without rapid and extensive expansion, services will be inadequate to rectify the inequities that exist. In addition to socioeconomic disadvantages, language barriers cannot be overemphasized. Programs that ignore cultural and linguistic backgrounds are not only inefficient but also unlikely to benefit the target groups. It should be evident that the elderly deserve better. As crucial as this initial glimpse of the general outlines of minority aging is, it does not provide sufficient grounds on which to formulate conclusive opinions — to do so would indeed be premature.

One conclusion warranted by the evidence, however, is that being located on the margins of social policy and political forces has a cumulative effect over the life course. As Third World countries move toward industrialization, many social policies are imported wholesale from the free market economies with which they trade. The future for those nations that adopt social and financial security programs modeled after those in the United States may encounter many of the same types of structurally induced patterns. By beginning with the differential access characteristic of subpopulations in the United States, they will have an opportunity to avoid perpetuating many of our shortcomings.

# Discussion Questions

**Minority Aging**

1. What is marginality? What are the consequences of marginality for people's lives and for their old age? To what extent do you think marginality is a consequence of (a) individual-level factors or (b) structural factors?

2. What can be learned from studying ethnic minorities? In your answer consider both aging at the individual level and in terms of social policy.

3. How are the elderly in ethnic minorities different from the elderly in the majority? Why?

**Aging and Minorities in the United States**

4. Choose a specific minority group or groups and answer the following questions: (a) In what way is the situation of the elderly better or worse in that minority group than among whites? Be sure to consider specific dimensions of the situation of the elderly, such as economic status, health, activity levels, integration into family and community, living arrangements, and psychological well-being. (b) How far do you think patterns of aging for members of that minority are shaped by historical and cultural factors, social-structural factors, and/or individual-level factors?

5. Do you think that the key to improving the situation of the minority elderly lies in integration into the mainstream of American culture, in a strengthening of the sense of cultural identity among the minorities, or in a combination of both? Why?

6. Do you think Social Security and other benefits should be determined differently for minorities with a significantly shorter life expectancy than the white majority?

7. Design a social policy plan targeted to address the problem of a particular ethnic minority discussed in this chapter. Begin by stating the particular problems and strengths of this minority. Next, state overall policy goals, outline policies to deal with particular problems, and describe how your policies would fit into the general picture of the social policy of aging.

**Aging in the Third World**

8. Do you agree economic and political relations between the industrialized nations and Third World countries affect the situation of the elderly in the Third World countries? What changes would be required in these relations to improve the situation of the elderly in Third World countries?

9. Imagine you are a government minister in a Third World country. Design a social policy to deal with the needs of the elderly in your country. Be sure to consider the needs of the elderly, the population structure and demographics of your country, and the availability of resources. What changes, if any, in relations between your country and other countries would be required to implement your policy? To what extent would the policy you have developed be applicable to an advanced industrial society such as the United States?

## Pertinent Readings

Banfield, E. C. *The Unheavenly City Revisited.* Boston: Little, Brown & Company, 1974.

Bastida, E. "Reconstructing the Social World at 60: Older Cubans in the United States." *The Gerontologist* 24, 5 (1984): 465–70.

Bechill, W. "Politics of Aging and Ethnicity." In *Ethnicity and Aging*, eds. D. E. Gelfand and A. J. Kutzik, pp. 137–48. New York: Springer Publishing Company, 1979.

Beck, E. M., P. M. Horan, and C. M. Tolbert. "Industrial Segmentation and Labor Market Discrimination." *Social Problems* 28, 2 (1980): 113–30.

Bengtson, V. L. "Ethnicity and Aging: Problems and Issues in Current Social Science Inquiry." In *Ethnicity and Aging*, eds. D. E. Gelfand and A. J. Kutzik, pp. 9–31. New York: Springer Publishing Company, 1979.

Cabezas, Amado. "Presentation on Employment Issues. U.S. Commission on Civil Rights." In *Civil Rights Issues of Asian and Pacific Americans: Myths and Realities*, pp. 389–93. Washington, D.C.: U.S. Government Printing Office, 1980.

Cantor, M. H. "Effect of Ethnicity on Life Styles of the Inner-City Elderly." In *Dimensions of Aging*, eds. J. Hendricks and C. D. Hendricks, pp. 278–93. Cambridge, Mass.: Winthrop Publishers, Inc., 1979.

Cheng, E. *The Elder Chinese.* San Diego: The Campanile Press, San Diego State University, 1978.

Clark, M., and M. Mendelson. "Mexican-American Aged in San Francisco: A Case Description." *The Gerontologist* 9, 2, Pt. I (1969): 90–95.

Cottle, T. J. *Hidden Survivors: Portraits of Poor Jews in America.* Englewood Cliffs, N.J.: Prentice-Hall, Inc., 1980.

Crouch, B. M. "Age and Institutional Support: Perceptions of Older Mexican Americans." *Journal of Gerontology* 27, 4 (1972): 524–29.

Cuellar, J. "El Senior Citizens Club: The Older Mexican-American in the Voluntary Association." In *Life's Career — Aging,* eds. B. G. Myerhoff and A. Simic, pp. 207–30. Beverly Hills: Sage Publications, Inc., 1978.

Dowd, J. J., and V. L. Bengtson. "Aging in Minority Populations: An Examination of the Double Jeopardy Hypothesis." *Journal of Gerontology* 33, 3 (1978): 427–36.

Fillenbaum, G. G., L. K. George, and E. B. Palmore. "Determinants and Consequences of Retirement Among Men of Different Races and Economic Levels." *Journal of Gerontology* 40, 1 (1985): 85–94.

Gelfand, D. "Ethnicity, Aging and Mental Health." *International Journal of Aging and Human Development* 10, 3 (1979–1980): 289–98.

———. *Aging: The Ethnic Factor.* Boston: Little, Brown & Company, 1982.

———, and A. J. Kutzik. "Conclusion: The Continuing Significance of Ethnicity." In *Ethnicity and Aging,* eds. D. E. Gelfand and A. J. Kutzik pp. 357–61. New York: Springer Publishing Company, 1979.

Goldstein, M. C., and C. Beall. "Indirect Modernization and the Status of the Elderly in a Rural Third World Setting." *Journal of Gerontology* 37, 6 (1982): 743–48.

Grebler, L., J. W. Moore, and R. C. Guzman. *The Mexican American People.* New York: The Free Press, 1970.

Hampson, J. "Elderly People and Social Welfare in Zimbabwe." *Ageing and Society* 5, 1 (1985): 39–67.

Hendricks, J. "The Elderly in Society: Beyond Modernization." *Social Science History* 6, 3 (1982): 321–45.

Herrnstein, R. J. *I.Q. in the Meritocracy.* Boston: Little, Brown & Company, 1973.

Hirsch, C., D. P. Kent, and S. L. Silverman. "Homogeneity and Heterogeneity Among Low-Income Negro and White Aged." In *Research Planning and Action for the Elderly: The Power and Potential of Social Science,* eds. D. P. Kent, R. Kastenbaum, and S. Sherwood, pp. 484–500. New York: Behavioral Publications, Inc., 1972.

Jackson, J. J. "Aged Negroes: Their Cultural Departures from Statistical Stereotypes and Rural-Urban Comparisons." In *Research Planning and Action for the Elderly: The Power and Potential of Social Science,* eds. D. P. Kent, R. Kastenbaum, and S. Sherwood, pp. 501–13. New York: Behavioral Publications, Inc., 1972a.

———. "Black Aged: In Quest of the Phoenix." In *Triple Jeopardy — Myth or Reality,* pp. 27–40. Washington, D.C.: National Council on Aging, 1972b.

———. *Minorities and Aging.* Belmont, Calif.: Wadsworth Publishing Company, 1980.

———. "Race, National Origin, Ethnicity and Aging." In *Handbook of Aging and the Social Sciences,* eds. R. Binstock and E. Shanas, pp. 264–303. New York: Van Nostrand Reinhold Company, 1985.

Jeffries, W. R. "Our Aged Indians." In *Triple Jeopardy — Myth or Reality,* pp. 7–10. Washington, D.C.: National Council on Aging, 1972.

Jensen, A. R. *Bias in Mental Testing.* New York: The Free Press, 1980.

Indian Health Service. *Indian Health Service Report. Fiscal Year 1981 Outpatient Summary of Leading Causes.* Rockville, Md.: Indian Health Service, 1982.

————. *FY 1985 Budget Appropriation. "Chart Series" Tables.* Rockville, Md.: Indian Health Service, 1983.

Kalish, R. A., and S. Moriwaki. "The World of the Elderly Asian American." In *Dimensions of Aging*, eds. J. Hendricks and C. D. Hendricks, pp. 264–77. Cambridge, Mass.: Winthrop Publishers, Inc., 1979.

Kalish, R. A., and S. Yuen. "Americans of East-Asian Ancestry: Aging and The Aged." *The Gerontologist* 11, 1, Pt. II (1971): 36–47.

Kaufman, J. "Black Executives Say Prejudice Still Impedes Their Path to the Top." *Wall Street Journal*, July 9, 1980, p. 1.

Kiefer, C. W. "Lessons for the Issei." In *Late Life: Communities and Environmental Policy*, ed. J. F. Gubrium, pp. 167–97. Springfield, Ill.: Charles C Thomas, Publisher, 1974.

Kim, P. K. H. "Demography of the Asian-Pacific Elderly." In *Aging in Minority Groups*, eds. R. L. McNeely and J. L. Cohen, pp. 29–41. Beverly Hills, Calif.: Sage Publications, Inc., 1983.

Kitano, H. H. L. *Japanese Americans: The Evolution of a Subculture.* Englewood Cliffs, N.J.: Prentice-Hall Inc., 1969.

Lacayo, C. G. "Preliminary Findings of the National Study to Assess Service Needs of the Hispanic Elderly." Paper presented to COSSHMO's National Hispanic Conference on Families, Houston, Texas, 1978.

————, et al. *A National Study to Assess the Service Needs of the Hispanic Elderly. Final Report.* Los Angeles, Calif.: Asociación Nacional Pro Personas Mayores, 1980.

Levy, J. E. "The Older American Indian." In *Older Rural Americans: A Sociological Perspective*, ed. E. G. Youmans, pp. 221–38. Lexington: University of Kentucky Press, 1967.

Lewis, M. "Aging in the People's Republic of China." *International Journal of Aging and Human Development* 15, 2 (1982): 79–105.

Lum, D. "Asian-Americans and Their Aged." In *Aging in Minority Groups*, eds. R. L. McNeely and J. L. Cohen, pp. 85–94. Beverly Hills, Calif.: Sage Publications, Inc., 1983.

Manton, K. G. "Differential Life Expectancy: Possible Explanations During the Later Ages." In *Minority Aging, Sociological and Social Psychological Issues*, ed. R. C. Manuel, pp. 63–68. Westport, Conn.: Greenwood Press, Inc., 1982.

Markides, K. S., and S. W. Vernon. "Aging, Sex-Role Orientation, and Adjustment: A Third-Generation Study of Mexican Americans." *Journal of Gerontology* 39, 5 (1984): 586–91.

Marsella, A. J., and W. y Quijano. "A Comparison of Vividness of Mental Imagery Across Different Sensory Modalities in Filipinos and Caucasian Americans." *Journal of Cross-Cultural Psychology* V, 4 (1974): 451–64.

McCaslin, R., and W. R. Calvert. "Social Indicators in Black and White: Some Ethnic Considerations in Delivery of Service to the Elderly." *Journal of Gerontology* 30, 1 (1975): 60–66.

McClelland, D. C. *The Achieving Society.* New York: The Free Press, 1967.

McPherson, J. R., D. R. Lancaster, and J. C. Carroll. "Stature Change with Aging in Black Americans." *Journal of Gerontology* 33, 1 (1978): 20–25.

Michaels, M. "Where the Family Comes First." *Parade Magazine*, June 2, 1985, p. 4.

Montero, D. *Japanese-Americans: Changing Patterns of Ethnic Affiliation Over Three Generations.* Boulder, Colo.: Westview Press, 1980a.

————. "The Elderly Japanese-Americans: Aging Among the First-Generation Immigrants." *Genetic Psychology Monographs* 101 (1980b): 99–118.

————. "The Japanese Americans." *American Sociological Review* 46, 4 (1981): 829–39.

Moore, J. W. "Mexican-Americans." *The Gerontologist* 11, 1, Pt. II (1971): 30–35.

Murdock, S. H., and D. F. Schwartz. "Family Structure and the Use of Agency Services: An Examination of Patterns Among Native Americans." *The Gerontologist* 18, 5 (1978): 475–81.

National Center for Health Statistics. *Health Indicators for Hispanic, Black and White Americans.* Vital and Health Statistics, Series 10, No. 148, PHS No. 84-1576, Public Health Service. Washington, D.C.: U.S. Government Printing Office, 1984.

National Commission for Employment Policy. *Hispanics and Jobs: The Barriers to Progress.* Report No. 14. Washington, D.C.: U.S. Government Printing Office, 1982.

*National Indian Council on Aging Quarterly.* Special Issue: White House Conference on Aging: The Indian Issues, 1, 4 (1981).

Neysmith, S. M., and J. Edwardh. "Economic Dependency in the 1980s: Its Impact on the Third World." *Ageing and Society* 4, 1 (1984): 21–44.

Osako, M. M. "Aging and Family Among Japanese-Americans: The Role of Ethnic Tradition in the Adjustment to Old Age." *The Gerontologist* 19, 5 (1979): 448–55.

Peterson, R. *The Elder Philipino.* San Diego, Calif.: The Campanile Press, 1978.

Public Opinion. "Opinion Roundup: America Through the Ages: Studying the Elderly." *Public Opinion* 8, 1 (1985): 30–42.

Select Committee on Indian Affairs, United States Senate. *Indian Health Issues, Anchorage, Alaska.* Washington, D.C.: U.S. Government Printing Office, 1983.

Snyder, P. "Health Service Implications of Folk Healing Among Older Asian Americans and Hawaiians in Honolulu." *The Gerontologist* 24, 5 (1984): 471–76.

Sterne, R. S., J. E. Phillips, and A. Rabushka. The *Urban Elderly Poor: Racial and Bureaucratic Conflict.* Lexington, Mass.: D.C. Heath & Co., 1974.

Torres-Gil, F., and R. M. Becerra. "The Political Behavior of the Mexican-American Elderly." *The Gerontologist* 17, 5 (1977): 392–99.

United Nations. *Vienna International Plan of Acting on Aging.* Vienna: United Nations, 1983.

U.S. Census. *Population Characteristics.* Current Population Reports, Series P-20, No. 336. Washington, D.C.: U.S. Government Printing Office, 1979.

———. *America in Transition: An Aging Society.* Current Population Reports, Series P-23, No. 182. Washington, D.C.: U.S. Government Printing Office, 1983.

———. *After-Tax Money Income Estimates of Households: 1982.* Current Population Reports, Series P-23, No. 137. Washington, D.C.: U.S. Government Printing Office, 1984a.

——— *Money Income and Poverty Status of Families and Persons in the United States: 1983* (advance data from the March 1984 Current Population Survey). Current Population Reports, Series P-60, No. 145. Washington, D.C.: U.S. Government Printing Office, 1984b.

———. *Marital Status and Living Arrangements: March, 1983.* Current Population Reports, Series P-20, No. 389. Washington, D.C.: U.S. Government Printing Office, 1984c.

———. *Demographic and Socioeconomic Aspects of Aging in the United States.* Current Population Reports, Series P-23, No. 138. Washington, D.C.: U.S. Government Printing Office, 1984d.

———. *Statistical Abstract of the United States, 1985,* 105th ed. Washington, D.C.: U.S. Government Printing Office, 1985a.

———. *Estimates of the Population of the United States, by Age, Sex and Race: 1980 to 1984.* Current Population Reports, Series P-25, No. 965. Washington, D.C.: U.S. Government Printing Office, 1985b.

————. *Persons of Spanish Origin in the United States: March, 1982.* Current Population Reports, Series P-20, No. 396. Washington, D.C.: U.S. Government Printing Office, 1985c.

————. *Voting and Registration in the Election of 1984.* Current Population Reports, Series P-20, No. 397. Washington, D.C.: U.S. Government Printing Office, 1985d.

————. *Characteristics of the Population Below the Poverty Level: 1983.* Washington, D.C.: U.S. Government Printing Office, 1985e.

U.S. Commission on Civil Rights. *The Forgotten Minority: Asian Americans in New York City.* Washington, D.C.: U.S. Government Printing Office, 1977.

U.S. Department of Health, Education and Welfare. *Social, Economic and Health Characteristics of Older American Indians, Part II.* Washington, D.C.: U.S. Government Printing Office, 1978.

————. *Health and Prevention Profile: United States, 1983.* Washington, D.C.: U.S. Government Printing Office, 1983a.

————. *1980. Tuberculosis in the United States.* Washington, D.C.: U.S. Government Printing Office, 1983b.

————. *Social Security Programs Throughout the World — 1983.* Research Report No. 59, Washington, D.C.: U.S. Government Printing Office, 1984.

U.S. Department of Health, Education and Welfare. *Asian American Field Survey: Summary of the Data.* Washington, D.C.: U.S. Government Printing Office, 1977.

U.S. Department of Labor. *Linking Employment Problems to Economic Status.* Bulletin 2201. Washington, D.C.: U.S. Government Printing Office, 1984a.

————. *Families at Work: The Jobs and the Pay.* Bulletin 2209. Washington, D.C.: U.S. Government Printing Office, 1984b.

————. *Work Experience of the Population in 1981–1982.* Bulletin 2199. Washington, D.C.: U.S. Government Printing Office, 1984c.

U.S. House of Representatives, Subcommittee on Health and the Environment. *Indian Health Care: An Overview of the Federal Government's Role.* Washington, D.C.: U.S. Government Printing Office, 1984.

Valle, R., and L. Mendoza. *The Elder Latino.* San Diego: The Campanile Press, San Diego State University, 1978.

Wellin, E., and E. Boyer. "Adjustments of Black and White Elderly to the Same Adaptive Niche." *Anthropological Quarterly* 52, 1 (1979): 39–48.

Welty, P. T. *The Asians: Their Heritage and Their Destiny.* Philadelphia: J. B. Lippincott Company, 1970.

White House Conference on Aging. *Special Concerns Sessions Reports: Asian American Elderly, Aging and Aged Blacks, the Elderly Indian, Spanish Speaking Elderly.* Washington, D.C.: U.S. Government Printing Office, 1971.

————. *Report of the Miniconference on Pacific/Asian Elderly: Pacific/Asians the Wisdom of Age.* Washington, D.C.: U.S. Government Printing Office, 1981.

Williams, G. C. "Warriors No More: A Study of the American Indian Elderly." In *Aging in Culture and Society,* ed. C. L. Fry, pp. 101–11. New York: J. E. Bergin Publishers, Inc., 1980.

Wing, S., K. G. Manton, E. Stallard, C. G. Hames, and H. A. Tyroler. "The Black/White Mortality Crossover: Investigation in a Community-Based Study." *Journal of Gerontology* 40, 1 (1985): 78–84.

Wu, F. Y. T. "Mandarin-speaking Aged Chinese in the Los Angeles Area." *The Gerontologist* 15, 3 (1975): 271–75.

# 10

# THE AGED AND
# THE POLITICAL ARENA

**THE NATURE AND STRUCTURE OF POLITICS**

The Nature of Politics
The Structure of Politics

**THE ELDERLY AS A SOCIAL MOVEMENT**

Age Groups in the Political Arena
The Advent of Age-Based Social Movements
The Second Coming: Developments Since the 1950s
Age Group Identification

**POLITICAL ATTITUDES AND OPINIONS**

Aging and Sociopolitical Attitudes
Party Affiliation
Taking a Stance on Social Issues

**POLITICAL PARTICIPATION**

Voting and Participation in the Political Process
Other Political Behavior

**THE POLITICAL FUTURE OF THE ELDERLY**

A Generational Alliance
Politics of Tomorrow

**SUMMARY**

**DISCUSSION QUESTIONS**

**PERTINENT READINGS**

# The Nature and Structure of Politics

## THE NATURE OF POLITICS

The politics of aging covers many topics. Two primary dimensions of political involvement, orientation and participation, are the subjects of this chapter. In the past these have often been the exclusive focus in discussions of politics and the elderly. There are, however, broader issues that must also be incorporated. Accordingly, in the next chapter the focus will be expanded to include questions of social policy and legal issues pertaining to the elderly. Political orientation is generally defined as social psychological components that underlie participation, namely, attitudes, consciousness, ideology, party affiliation, and so on. The latter in turn ranges from relatively passive forms, such as voting, to more active attempts to influence the political process. Generally, voting is thought to be part of a continuum of participation with involvement on one end running through campaigning and lobbying to actually holding office on the other end (Hudson and Strate, 1985). Accordingly, we will first look at factors influencing the political orientation of older person, including the development of an awareness of the legitimacy of older people's claims and the influence of age, period, and cohort effects on their political outlook. Next we will examine actual political involvement. Our attention in the last section will be devoted to voting behavior and selected examples of more active manifestations of participation.

## THE STRUCTURE OF POLITICS

The structure of American politics can be characterized in various ways. A few view the political arena as the domain of interested individuals taking the time and making the effort to have their voices heard. Others see it as dominated by wealthy corporate associations wherein the individual is subordinate. Still another scenario puts political power in the hands of organized interest groups that compete and cooperate among themselves to further their own vested interests. Thus groups, not individuals, forge public policy, and as was clearly demonstrated in the 1970s, these groups may escape strict accountability for the actions they authorize. The potential power of the elderly is established within this framework. The political stage is witness to the efforts of numerous interest groups to influence governmental processes. For any group the issue of power depends in part on whether it is able to adopt a uniform stance for a particular question. This is of pressing concern to groups dealing with or representing the elderly. Some have argued that special interest groups compete for limited resources, although the basic policies underlying the provision of funding may never be challenged (Estes, 1979). Indeed, the dominant structural values often are silent testimony to interest group activity that bargains for roles in carrying out programs for the aging. Age-based political movements have engendered some interest and some concern for potential political clout, yet at no time since the Depression has an effective age-based political movement sustained momentum for any length of time.

A number of common presumptions continue to appear in the discussions of politics and power now popular among social commentators and observers. The assumed conservatism of the elderly electorate, their increasing lack of opinions on contemporary social problems, the alleged reduction in their participation across the entire political spectrum, and their unwillingness to foster programs benefiting youth are often repeated. As will be seen, a number of the old assumptions have been largely discounted or at least challenged by new research. Nonetheless, stereotypes about the politically apathetic elderly have been popularized in the eyes of the public. Rather than fixing chronological age as a major factor significantly affecting political behavior, it may be more meaningful to consider the various circumstances under which age might or does make a difference in political activity. It would be deceptive simply to look at the results of a poll in which the opinions of the youth and the elderly are very different and to label one group as more conservative than the other. While this has often been the case in many public opinion surveys, we should be aware that numerous other variables are also important and must not be overlooked in any interpretation of the relationship between age and political views or activities. Attitudinal and behavioral variations reflect not only the historical epoch during which an individual was reared but also the peer influences of his or her own age cohort, in addition to those factors that can be attributed to the results of aging or maturation (Cutler and Bengtson, 1974; Hudson and Strate, 1985).

Social scientists have been hard pressed to account for activity in and differences within the political arena using age as a sole or even major criterion. The relationships between age and political activity and public policies with respect to aging are complex and do not lend themselves to ready, straightforward analysis.

## The Elderly as a Social Movement

Regardless of their actual impact, the emergence of age-based social movements has been a symbol to nurture an aging group consciousness. If they do nothing else, such groups garner increased visibility for the concerns of the elderly. Activism is widely hailed as a means to an end in the ideology of American politics; it creates real or perceived political power. The advent of old-age associations marked the beginning of a long and continuing process of legitimation. Interest groups of this type work to influence public policies affecting their constituencies. This requires a constituency that has coalesced around some set of issues; further, they have to create an image, communicated through the media, that they are responsible, concerned, and important. They must also be able to exert direct or indirect pressure on the legislative process, governmental agencies, and decision makers. To do so they must appear to have expertise, to be able to lobby effectively, and to raise money or votes on behalf of their supporters.

## AGE GROUPS IN THE POLITICAL ARENA

Over the last decade there has been much controversy concerning the likelihood of age ever being the catalyst for the evolution of a viable political movement. On the one hand, a wide-ranging diversity of opinions has been observed among age groups in various polls. Also, many elderly encounter experiences analogous to those of other minority groups, complete with the stereotyping, prejudice, and discrimination associated with minority status. Therefore, according to the advocates of an age-based political movement, the aged are theoretically opportune candidates for developing an age group consciousness. There is, of course, the alternative reality: the very heterogeneity of the older generation ensures a divergence in the attitudes, expectations, and goals of older people. Even the youth-based political activity of the latter 1960s and early 1970s drew support from other segments of the population and eventually became absorbed by broader based political movements. A clear example of the multifaceted nature of political activity on behalf of the aging is presented by the membership of political organizations whose primary objective is to provide assistance to the elderly. It is not unusual to find division among the ranks on such fundamental issues as income security or health care. An integral part of the conception of the pluralistic nature of American politics concedes that the political arena is not occupied only by concerned citizens, but, more important, by organized interest groups representing various constituencies. No group, however, can wield much power unless its members reach a consensus. These groups then shape public policy through a process of conflict and compromise between and among themselves and governmental agencies. With the continual press of political business, our elected officials tend to rely on interest groups to articulate the desires of their constituents; consequently, the more vocal and powerful the groups, the more responsive the politicians. The role such interest groups play in the political process is sometimes offered as an explanation of the relative powerlessness of the aged, since they have thus far rarely been organized or represented by outspoken advocates. Many studies have previously shown that the political attitudes of the elderly themselves are quite disparate, thereby prohibiting a unified stance. Yet once established, older people do tend to exhibit stable political affiliations. Some data have revealed a greater affinity in their attitudes regarding topics that directly affect them as an age group; nevertheless, that similarity has yet to prove sufficient to transform aged voters into a cohesive political bloc.

According to some analysts, extensive political participation among the elderly will ultimately be founded on the development and use of interest groups or on what was referred to in Chapter 3 as an aged subculture. In formulating the idea of a subcultural model applicable to the elderly, Rose (1965) noted:

> A subculture may be expected to develop within any category of the population of a society when its members interact with each other significantly more than they interact with persons in other categories. This occurs . . . [either where] (1) the members have a positive affinity for each other on some basis or (2) the members are excluded from interaction with other groups in the population to some significant extent.

Among those who argue the opposite, that older people will not become a distinct subculture, the general absence of a sense of group identification among the elderly is often cited. They contend that older people do not develop a lifestyle based on the concrete realities of old age, nor is there much systematic or overt prejudice and discrimination attributable to age itself. Instead, people bring with them to old age an identity forged from experiences in family, occupational, health, and other social realms. These experiences combine variously to direct personal choice. Thus, to expect age alone to be a relevant factor in predicting age group consciousness or political behavior is to invite disappointment. Finally, Streib (1965), one of the more vocal opponents of Rose's position, points out that age is not actually an **ascribed status**, an essential component in his view if a distinct cultural grouping is to evolve. The application of any analysis based on either perceived minority group status or the notion that elderly people are in the midst of formulating a definite interest or political pressure group is still in the theoretical stages. If data on income, employment histories, or educational achievements are examined for the past thirty years, it is evident that today's older generations earn less, work less, and are clustered in relatively lower status occupations when compared to their younger counterparts. Nevertheless, there is little evidence to date that older people will formulate a consciousness based on differential access to resources sufficient to support a cohesive voting bloc (Hudson and Binstock, 1976). At least one example of an age-based interest group recently exerting concerted effort to influence the passage of legislation has been documented in the Adults Only Movement in Arizona (Anderson and Anderson, 1978). A variety of groups and individuals organized a successful political movement that in 1975 secured the enactment of a law enabling communities to restrict their residents to adults only. Given a shared perspective, goals, and similar socioeconomic background, members of this movement were able to act as a unified whole. Some of this group identification has since been threatened by questions of how best to promote and enforce the law that was sponsored.

The potential for a politically involved group of older citizens has yet to be realized, perhaps because of the absence of any generalized age group awareness. Among those older people who exhibit a sharpened degree of age consciousness, there is also a desire expressed for continued or heightened interaction with their peers, more organizations for older people, and increased political participation, through either voting or other collective action (Cutler, 1983). Until recently, however, an overriding sense of age identification among the elderly has not been observed for a variety of reasons. To begin with, an active interest group tends not to focus on a single trait; instead, it usually rallies around a set of interrelated or homogeneous characteristics. Hence it seems that chronological age alone would not be sufficiently binding for any group. To be effective interest groups must also exhibit responsible organizational structures, some financial stability, and, for any national influence, widely dispersed membership. To the extent they manifested political impotence, earlier movements organized by or for older people suffered from their failure to fulfill these criteria, from low levels of age group consciousness, and especially from the competition waged among themselves for members drawn from a limited population (Cottrell, 1960).

## THE ADVENT OF AGE-BASED SOCIAL MOVEMENTS

The first age-based, politically oriented interest groups to take shape in America came about as a result of the economic deprivation and social upheaval of the Depression of the early 1930s, yet few of them managed to outlast the decade. For example, in California alone several age-based social movements amassed sizable followings, flourished briefly, and disappeared just as rapidly. At its peak during the Depression the Utopian Society had attracted around half a million adherents; Upton Sinclair's End Poverty in California (EPIC) movement was equally popular in the years preceding his defeat in the 1934 gubernatorial contest. However, by the waning years of the decade few members of either group could be found. Although EPIC was among the first of the coalitions to propose a pension program, it remained for the McLain and the Townsend movements to speak directly on behalf of the elderly as a disadvantaged segment of the population. Named after the physician who founded it, the Townsend Plan was a spin-off from an earlier group that called itself Old Age Revolving Pensions, Inc. At its apex in 1936 the movement attained a national membership in excess of a million and a half elderly organized into local clubs. Their primary goal, providing a monthly pension of $200 funded through sales taxes, was met to some extent by the implementation of Social Security legislation. As soon as Townsend and his followers were deprived of their mission, the organization went into partial eclipse, though alternative proposals continued to attract some devotees until the group finally disappeared after World War II (Fischer, 1978; Graebner, 1980).

The McLain Movement, which competed with the Townsend Plan for members, did not fare much better. Originally it was part of an association with the homely title of Ham and Eggs that sought to establish financial benefits for older citizens through a referendum in the 1938 California elections. George McLain led a faction more intent on exerting political pressure on local legislatures to improve conditions for the elderly. Eventually, the McLain Movement boasted about 250,000 members spread over thirty-one states and was represented by both a National and a California League of Senior Citizens. It looked for a time as though McLain and his followers had indeed become a force to be reckoned with, but the economic upturn after 1940 spelled doom for them, just as it had for the Townsend group. McLain himself remained politically active until his death, running for public office as late as 1964, but he was never able to appeal to a broad enough segment of the population to advance in either state or national politics. In California his personal charisma continued to attract supporters, but elsewhere the grass-roots organizations he helped found languished and eventually succumbed. McLain's regional branches tended to become isolated, without local involvement beyond the opinions expressed by a small coterie made up of a few concerned elderly partisans. But even they were so heterogeneous a mix that a unified position on their own self-interests was nearly always absent. Despite their popular appeal, neither the McLain nor the Townsend movements are viewed by most social historians as solely responsible for Social Security or any other significant legislation. Many observers instead see the efforts of broad-based labor organizations and the influence of Socialist politics in general during the 1930s as being the prime movers behind the lobbying that led to the enactment of the Social Security Act, although public support for governmental assistance in providing security for old age was certainly rallied by these grass-roots groups (Achenbaum, 1978; Williamson et al., 1982; Carlie, 1969; Fischer, 1978).

The fledgling gray lobby, diffuse as it may have been, helped define categorical assistance programs and the new aged constituency. Inadvertently their activities coupled with the development of the Social Security program circumscribed the standing of those over sixty-five as a social problem. On the positive side, though these movements never approximated anything near a consensus among themselves, they did focus the debate. They marked the emergence of a social movement for the elderly, and for the first time nationwide concern for a targeted group resulted in a fundamental shift in the involvement of the public sector. The elderly had become a "bona fide interest group" whose demands took on a new legitimacy. As members of the Townsend Plan swung a local election their way in Long Beach, California, it looked for a time as if elected officials at all levels would become fully cognizant of the potential leverage of the aged constituency. Unfortunately, the effect of Social Security was to slow the growth of the movement. Now that they were seemingly taken care of, older people evidenced little in the way of a unified force for over two decades (Achenbaum, 1983; Williamson et al., 1982).

## THE SECOND COMING: DEVELOPMENTS SINCE THE 1950s

As financial inadequacies became apparent in the latter 1950s and early 1960s, senior citizens' power once again began to emerge as a viable force. Throughout the 1950s senior citizens' clubs were founded to deal with local issues and culminated in the eventual formation of two national organizations, the National Council on the Aging (NCOA) and the American Association of Retired Persons (AARP). These were quickly followed by the National Association of Retired Federal Employees (NARFE) and various labor union groups. Together they were a catalyst for developing an awareness among the aged, and the general population became aware of the injustices of the Social Security system, the relative deprivation levied on people once they retired, and the potential political repercussions (Williamson et al., 1982). In 1961 the first White House Conference on Aging gave testimony of the Democratic party's effort to court the elderly vote. The decade-long push to establish Medicare also heightened an awareness of the special needs of the country's elderly. Its passage in the mid-1960s may have been a turning point for the political awareness of the so-called senior power movement. The culmination came with the establishment of the Office on Aging (later the Administration on Aging) and the organization of a Senate Special Committee on Aging. Aging had been politicized.

By the time of the second White House Conference on Aging in 1971 the mold was cast. The AARP, the NCOA, the newer National Council of Senior Citizens, and some related groups lobbied hard to broaden the focus of and their share of involvement in the planning process. Assigned a major role, the national organizations signaled the institutionalization of senior power. Should there be any doubt one need only look at the maneuverings surrounding the next White House Conference in 1981. While the exact time probably cannot be pinpointed, it was clear the elderly had arrived on the political scene (Pratt, 1976).

Today numerous national organizations are dedicated to the needs of the elderly. The most significant change is that the majority of these groups do not exist solely for the aged; rather they are groups that have a tangential, though sincere, concern for the elderly and are oriented around labor, professional, fraternal, service, and community action affiliations. According to a recent count, there are, however, at least twenty-six national groups with varying degrees of effectiveness currently involved in aging and political action. The three with the largest memberships are the National Council of Senior Citizens (NCSC), the AARP combined with the National Retired Teachers Association (AARP–NRTA) that acts as a single association, and the NARFE. Together these organizations have an approximate membership of ten million, though it is difficult to say with certainty how much overlap exists. In any event, they do have the potential of wielding substantial power on behalf of older citizens.

No one would contend that all groups are equally political in their orientation; some are service conduits and eschew any avowed political purpose. They have, however, recognized their common concern and banded together to form the Ad Hoc Leadership Council of Aging Organizations to lobby more effectively. Just this step may result in even greater public awareness of the political concerns of older persons and be an exemplar for the elderly themselves that it is permissible to fight for what are perceived to be their rights.

Certainly both major political parties have recognized at least the potential. In the last three presidential elections, beginning in 1976, "seniors desks" have existed as part of the campaign apparatus. These grew out of the earlier "Senior Citizens for Kennedy" wing of the 1960 Democratic campaign. It is far too soon to tell if the Leadership Council will bridge the schism that had precluded the gray lobby from being unified in the past (Achenbaum, 1983), but it definitely has fostered a kind of political age identification not seen in any national elections before 1984.

The NCSC has thus far been more closely involved with partisan politics than have any of the other groups. Born in the 1960s in an effort to lend support to the drive for Medicare legislation, the NCSC was fostered by the labor unions and on many issues has found itself aligned with policies espoused by the Democratic party. In the beginning, financial support was derived almost exclusively from funds provided by the labor unions, but in recent years membership dues have enabled the organization to become financially independent. Although the majority of members and directors still represent unions or are former union members, this is not a prerequisite of membership and anyone may join. Another, and perhaps the best known of the organizations supporting older people, is the successor of what began as the NRTA. The parent organization was founded in 1947 by a retired California teacher, Ethel Percy Andrus, who initially sought legislative reform of pension and tax programs affecting elderly teachers. In the late 1950s Andrus and a New York insurance agent, Leonard Davis, joined forces to offer group life insurance and ultimately health insurance to NRTA members, a plan so popular that the AARP was developed to cover retirants who were interested in participating but who had not been teachers. Today the combined forces of the AARP–NRTA are one organization with a membership in excess of nine million, making it one of the largest organizations of its kind in the country. Beginning in the late 1960s, both groups moved beyond their initial service orientation to become politically and socially active nationally. In contrast to the NCSC, the AARP was formerly nominally identified with Republican political ideologies through its representation of white-collar and professional status retired persons. Following the 1971 White House Conference on Aging, the AARP has deliberately sought to free itself from close identification with either party. Leaders of the two organizations decry such partisan labels, claiming they strive for broad representation to lend credibility to their descriptions of the needs and desires of older Americans (Pratt, 1976). The third organization, the NARFE, draws the majority of its 182,000 plus members from the Washington, D.C., area and only became active nationally after 1970. Since its inception in 1921, the NARFE has focused primarily on pragmatic issues of immediate relevance to retired federal employees, rarely venturing into the broader realms of social and legislative policy questions. Even though overt sponsorship of political candidates would be grounds for forfeiture of their tax-exempt status, several of the groups are nonetheless able to engage in partisan politics through lobbying and informal cooperation with political campaign workers.

Brief mention must also be made of several service-related organizations that have become vocal proponents of the causes of the elderly. Three of the associations are concerned almost exclusively with the long-term institutional care of the aged. They include the American Association of Homes for the Aging, the American Nursing Home Association, and the National Council of Health Care Services. The guiding interest of each of these groups lies in securing federal funding and having some control over the development of regulations with which old age facilities must comply to retain their financial backing. Many of the smaller affiliates that make up these larger associations are commercial enterprises, one example being the chain of nursing homes owned by Holiday Inns. Quite naturally their primary impetus has been on the business aspects of providing goods or services to the elderly. Most of the fiscal support behind these three associations derives from the dues of affiliate members and from voluntary contributions. Other organizations have also become active on behalf of the elderly. A relative newcomer is the National Association of State Units on Aging (NASUA). Membership in this group is comprised of the administrators of the state and territorial agencies serving the elderly, most of which are funded at least in part under the various titles of the Older Americans Act. NASUA's membership is augmented by personnel from technical and advisory positions in governmental agencies whose concerns tend to focus on delivering governmentally supported services. The NCOA is a general service agency that has evolved over the last decade to a relatively strong position as a technical consultant to any organization that addresses itself to problems facing the elderly. The NCOA currently has over 1900 members representing a wide range of health, social work, and community action agencies that devote their energies to the dilemmas facing the elderly in America. The National Caucus on the Black Aged, organized in 1970 by professionals concerned with advancing the position of the black elderly, is one of the more politically active groups in aging. In 1975 a national advocacy organization for Spanish-speaking elderly was founded; while still in its formative stage, the Asociación Nacional Pro Personas Mayores is expected to foster greater political activity among the older Hispanic elderly (Cuellar, 1978; Lacayo, 1980).

Finally, there are the three major organizations of academicians and other professionals who work in the interests of the elderly. Like most professional societies, for years their major thrust has been research and training future professionals. With the budget cuts threatened in the early 1980s, the Gerontological Society of America, the Association for Gerontology in Higher Education, and the American Society on Aging (formerly the Western Gerontological Society) initiated cooperative efforts to lobby Congress to prevent retrenchment in the particular titles of the Older Americans Act under whose aegis research and training are conducted. As members of the Leadership Council these three professional and academic groups have joined the other organizations to present a united front.

Although the early voluntary associations have gradually been replaced by more sophisticated interest groups, the potential for political activism has yet to be realized. Perhaps the most visible are the Gray Panthers. Standing apart from the other organizations, this 50,000 member, grass-roots coalition uses influence and newsworthy techniques to fight age discrimination and threats to the well-being of the elderly. Its leader, Maggie Kuhn, was named one of the twenty-five most influential women in America in the early 1980s, and she has steadfastly challenged age-segregated services and life-styles. Her presence on the national scene, along with that of Claude Pepper and a small collection of other aged advocates, has captured considerable attention from the media, thus highlighting the cause of older persons.

By virtue of their claims to represent the interests of millions of older Americans, concerned professionals and interest groups have often acquired ready access to Congress, as well as to other officials in public and private agencies. Accordingly, the groups have been most vocal up to now in improving benefits within the existing frameworks of Social Security, Medicare, and the Older Americans Act. As the number of elderly continues to expand, it is expected that relevant associations will also grow, thereby enlarging their probable sphere of influence. Older people already account for roughly 20 percent of the voting public, and if the appropriate consciousness raising does take place, they may yet mold themselves into a cohesive political bloc, at least on certain issues. Until that time, changes will continue to be incremental and circuitous at best. Politicians have become more aware of the needs of the aging and in some cases more responsive. Perhaps one ironic indication of the growing visibility of organizations for the elderly in national politics is illustrated by the fate of the NCSC during the heat of the 1972 presidential campaign. Partially as a consequence of its political activities, the NCSC found itself placed on the infamous White House "enemies list," and according to depositions filed in federal court, the Internal Revenue Service was approached in an attempt to acquire the names of important contributors, presumably to head off further political involvement by the group (Butler, 1974). In some quarters, however briefly, certain older people's organizations were apparently perceived to have come of age, meriting a little more attention than otherwise might have been the case (Hudson and Binstock, 1976).

## AGE GROUP IDENTIFICATION

Part of the result of all this collective activity has been an increasing age group consciousness among the elderly (Gurin et al., 1980). If any social or political movement is to continue for long, some recognition of their commonalities must unite the constituency. This is no small task in a heterogeneous elderly population. Greater numbers will not automatically awaken political consciousness; if anything it will only increase heterogeneity. Besides, age is not the only basis of an older person's identity, nor is it the strongest. What is needed, then, if political influence is to be wielded by older cohorts?

Broadening the power base will help, that is, making people of all ages aware that a fair deal for older people is a fair deal for everyone — eventually.

One example is the appeal to middle-aged people who, if they are not now responsible for an older parent, will be old themselves in the near future. Destigmatizing the aging process should also help. As more people are willing to admit their age and identify with their age peers, they will come to recognize their mutual interests. Perhaps the shift to a close identification with age mates will not come until the generation of the 1950s reaches retirement age. They have already been identified throughout their lives as members of a particular category (Jones, 1981). Some, however, claim that age group identification has already arisen among the elderly and that in itself will facilitate political involvement (Cutler, 1981, 1983).

# Political Attitudes and Opinions

Another dimension in which political participation is evaluated concerns basic values, ideologies, and perspectives regarding the role of government and opinions about issues. Intervening factors that must also be taken into account are knowledge and the salience of the issues. For example, an older person who does not own property and has no younger relatives in the local school system does not cast a vote on a question of whether to raise taxes to support public schools. Seemingly, political attitudes can be inferred by this person staying away from the poll. Yet suppose a local referendum was on the ballot in the same district to provide governmental subsidies for transportation or social services for the elderly? Could a different set of attitudes be inferred because the same older person cast a ballot in the second instance?

## AGING AND SOCIOPOLITICAL ATTITUDES

As a consequence of the ubiquitous sociological surveys and opinion polls fielded since the 1930s, many claims have been made about the assumed conservativeness of older people. Reflecting a bias easily dating back to Aristotle, the popular notion is that the elderly, who are miserly, crabby, and overly cautious, are also politically conservative, if not outright reactionaries. Unfortunately, there are some well-intentioned yet ill-conceived studies that reinforce such a view. For example, surveys conducted in the 1950s and early 1960s reported that the older people become, the more rigid and less willing they are to accept change, nonconformity, or even governmental intervention in societal institutions (Stouffer, 1955; Rokeach et al., 1955; Campbell, 1962). While it would make the study of aging infinitely simpler if the relationship between age and attitudes was even half as straightforward as such findings suggest, like everything else we have learned about age changes, it really is not so easy. To begin with, surveys attempting to isolate conservative opinions tend to ask questions about controversial social issues likely to elicit polarized responses from almost any sample. Quite obviously, those people who have little knowledge or experience of the events in question will often express opinions that reflect the nature of the experiences they have had — in short, conservative opinions that affirm the traditional values of the status quo. Nevertheless, in a sense age may still be indicative of what could be called a traditionalist stance on certain political issues. However, as a few researchers have noted, it is not because the majority of older people are especially recalcitrant, but that their attitude changes have not been as rapid or "liberal" as those articulated by the larger proportion of younger citizens (Glenn, 1974; Hudson and Binstock, 1976). This is far from saying that the processes of aging are associated with increasing political conservativeness.

As opinion polls have become more sophisticated, attempts have been made to winnow out the effects of age per se from other factors in the formation of conservative attitudes. We already know that socioeconomic status, education, social mobility, and even sex differentiate opinions held on various issues. Recently it has also been noted the proximity of the question to people's lives influences the opinions they hold. In other words, if an issue actually impinges on an individual's life, affecting his or her family or community as opposed to the country or someplace else in the world, the opinions he or she expresses may vary from those held about issues farther removed. An equally relevant yet often overlooked consideration is what some researchers label the "generational effect." In essence, those who emphasize the need for generational analysis maintain the attitudes individuals hold toward the events taking place around them have been induced in part by the history they have lived through. This is not to say that everyone born of an age will have exactly the same worldview. Sociological differences still count, but those who underwent comparable experiences or were exposed to fairly analogous values as they moved into adulthood will exhibit a marked similarity in the views they express throughout the rest of their lives (Mannheim, 1952; Foner, 1972). The inherent disadvantages of cross-sectional survey research once again emerge in any discussion of political orientation and activity among the aging. It is misleading to look once at a group of individuals of various ages, compare their attitudes and reported behavior, and believe differences based on age alone have been isolated. Researchers are now aware that cohorts or generations must be followed through time before general statements about age changes in political attitudes may be made.

The question of American involvement in foreign wars offers an excellent case in point. Until the late 1960s, the older generations tended to hold less supportive views of international aggressiveness and war than their younger counterparts. In her analysis of opinion polls covering a forty-year period, Erskine (1973) found people over fifty to be generally more opposed to violence than those under thirty. However, with the intensification of American involvement in Indochina, a reversal took place; younger generations began expressing marked opposition to war. Explaining why the negative attitudes of the older people suddenly paled in comparison to the antiwar sentiment expressed by younger people is necessarily post hoc, yet the reversal may reflect the prevailing social attitudes during the formative years of each generation. Following America's involvement in World War II, the postwar generation was more accepting of the need to wage war than the previous generation had been, but as the Cold War became less foreboding, the next generation was not exposed to a similar rationale for maintaining an aggressive posture, and subsequently the protests of the 1960s signaled a further shift away from a militaristic frame of reference. When this happened, one of the dominant themes in the country tended to become crystallized or encapsulated in the attitudes of the people who were just then coming to a political consciousness (Jeffries, 1974).

Still another common misconception about the political consciousness of elderly people is that they become less attuned to the important questions facing society as they become older. To some extent early gerontological studies of opinionation among older people perpetuated this idea by suggesting that the process of disengagement was revealed in part in one's political awareness as demonstrated either by the frequency of neutral or no responses in opinion surveys or by the expression of extremist views calculated to shock the interviewer (Gergen and Back, 1966). Later analyses that took the average educational level of various **cohorts** into account found not only that older people continued to hold strong political beliefs but also that in many cases they actually held stronger opinions than younger people with comparable educations. In his reanalysis of a series of thirty-five public opinion polls, Glenn (1969) found that controlling for education and racial background, as well as for sex — in the past women more often offered neutral responses — eradicated any differences in the propensity toward diminishing opinionation with age. In terms of opinions and, as we shall see later, voting behavior, the most reliable evidence available indicates that political interest not only does not dissipate but in all probability also increases throughout most of adult life. Until gerontologists are able to report the results of their longitudinal panel studies, conclusions about changes in political awareness or involvement must necessarily be based on the less than optimal data gathered in cross-sectional surveys. Despite this, the conflicting evidence does not overwhelmingly support the idea of a decreasing political consciousness among older people (Glenn, 1980).

This is not to say there is no distinction between the opinions expressed by the elderly and by younger adults, merely that they cannot be explained wholly because one group is older than the other. Survey after survey has found that older people express quite liberal attitudes on those issues that directly affect their own self-interest. Figure 10.1 indicates the majority of young adults and nearly an equal proportion of their elderly counterparts think the government should meet the needs of those people who cannot cope because of unemployment, sickness, poverty, or old age. Yet when asked about living standards, the number approving governmental intervention falls equally in each age category. Finally, when asked about the acceptability of social class differentials, once again few significant differences occur between age brackets. Similar patterns can be identified in many other social surveys; age-related differences reflect the proximity of issues.

What is the relationship between age and either liberal or conservative at-

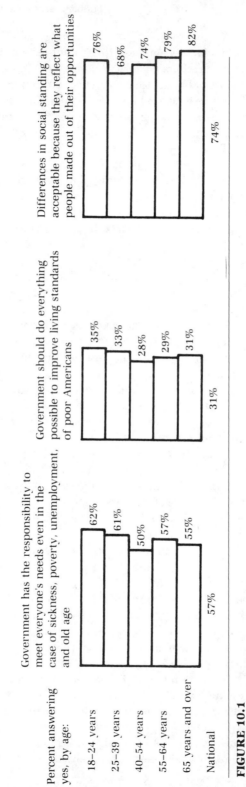

**FIGURE 10.1**

Social attitudes: liberal and conservative by age. (*Source:* "Opinion Roundup." *Public Opinion* 8, 1 [1985]: 36. Data drawn from various National Opinion Research Center General Social Surveys [1983, 1984].)

titudes? What do the labels themselves reflect? Political views deemed liberal at one point in recent history may seem quite the opposite thirty or forty years later. Would it be fair to say a person who had acquired a stance, stuck with it, and aged had really moved either to the right or the left? Figure 10.2 shows two generalized orientations that arguably run in opposite directions. In the first question the percentage of older people willing to bar a person who is against religion from a variety of activities would prompt some observers to conclude people over sixty-five are the most conservative of the age categories shown. Can the same conclusion be drawn from the second question? When all factors are taken into account, older people are neither more nor less conservative, rigid, or reactionary than the rest of the country. In their effort to identify conservativeness among the elderly, Campbell and Strate (1981) were able to identify only two general trends. The elderly respondents exhibited few predictable responses; they saw problems of race, law and order, and civil liberties as more pressing than the middle-aged respondents, but no specific pattern emerged from their concerns. This particular generation of older people may be marginally more conservative, but the differences are not really significant. Furthermore, they probably reflect cohort and period effects; if this is the case, the elderly in the year 2020 may turn out to be more liberal than younger persons (Glenn, 1974; Williamson et al., 1982).

## PARTY AFFILIATION

Another measure of political ideology is often characterized by political affiliation. Belonging to one or the other of the two major political parties in the United States is generally thought to signify ideological leanings. While this is undoubtedly an oversimplification, it is interesting to note a generational difference in an attachment to either party. If the stereotype is correct, more elderly ought to be Republicans; indeed they are. But it is not that simple: cohort effects are present again. Looking at the old-old, the period of socialization to political attitudes was a time when Republican ideologies were more prominent. For those who are just now becoming old, the Democratic party's values were more dominant when they were reaching young adulthood. So where do their loyalties lie? With both (Williamson et al., 1982; Campbell and Strate, 1981). A slightly greater number of the elderly identify with the Republican party, but the elderly also reflect the shifting of liberal and conservative ideologies. As the country moves in one direction or the other, so too do the elderly, which is evidence of a period effect in the sociopolitical attitudes manifested by older persons.

## TAKING A STANCE ON SOCIAL ISSUES

A cohort analysis of trends in attitudes toward legalized abortion between 1965 and 1977 revealed that as attitudes in general became more favorable, a trend that stabilized after 1974, the changing attitudes of the older cohorts exhibited no significant difference from those of the younger. The general public opinion on the topic was similarly reflected among all cohorts sampled.

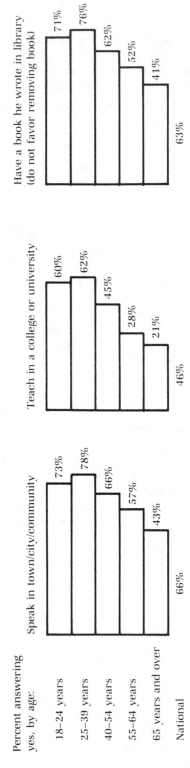

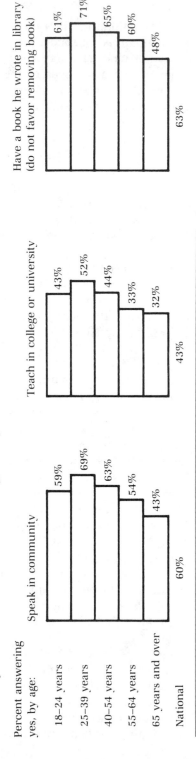

## FIGURE 10.2

Age and sociopolitical attitudes. (*Source:* "Opinion Roundup." *Public Opinion* 8, 1 [1985]: 36. Data drawn from various National Opinion Research Center General Social Surveys [1980, 1982, 1984].)

During a liberalizing social climate the attitudes of the elderly changed in the same direction and at the same rate as those of younger members of the population (Cutler et al., 1980). The results of cross-sectional surveys have usually been the basis for statements that the young and the old differ on a variety of attitudinal dimensions (Tedin, 1978–1979).

Despite the caveats accompanying most cross-sectional attitude surveys, however, a poll commissioned by the U.S. Senate Committee on Government Operations (1973) provides other interesting insights into the association between age and political orientation. When the pollsters asked people how they personally felt about such commonly heard complaints as tax laws being intended to help the rich and special interest groups, or the corruption of governmental officials, nearly three-quarters of each age category from the youngest to the oldest expressed serious feelings of alienation from the political process. Whether these results would have been found a few years earlier is certainly debatable, since Watergate was fresh in the minds of all respondents. It is important to note both the youngest (eighteen to twenty-nine) and the oldest (over fifty) people surveyed expressed strong feelings of discontent, even though neither group was willing to admit they felt powerless to effect changes. Somewhat over half of the respondents on either end of the age continuum continued to believe it was within their power to do something about unjust corrupt officials, while only one-third of them thought there was little possibility of personally doing anything to bring about needed changes.

In terms of actual attempts to make their opinions known, there was a remarkable uniformity between the oldest and the youngest concerning routine activities. Two-thirds of each group had signed petitions, one-third had written their congressional representative, and about one-sixth had written local officials or visited a state legislator. Somewhat fewer had actively campaigned for a presidential candidate, but again both groups were almost equally involved. Although more older people had contributed money to a political cause, it was only when it came to picketing or street demonstrations that any significant disparities between the two groups appeared. While only about a fifth of the younger group had engaged in such activities, this was three times the number of older respondents who had been involved in this particular form of activism. It is worth pointing out that both older and younger respondents were generally somewhat more estranged than those in the middle generation, perhaps reflecting what has been labeled as their peripheral position in society's scheme of things (Cutler and Bengtson, 1974). Despite feelings of political estrangement among older persons, it remains true that political candidates often perceive the elderly as a potentially cohesive voting bloc. Even on the presidential level, prospective officeholders consciously court the favor of older voters, addressing themselves to the basic issues they think most likely to influence the choice among candidates. That perceptions may not coincide with the predictions of social observers is irrelevant once actions are taken to identify issues that will appeal to groups on the basis of age alone (Riemer and Binstock, 1978).

# Political Participation

The evidence on participation rates is far more satisfying than that on attitudes and opinions if only because the figures are firm and the questions clearer. To begin with, in their review of political involvement of the elderly, Hudson and Strate (1985) note that many media studies have indicated that the elderly spend more time attempting to remain abreast of political affairs than their younger counterparts. They are more attentive to campaigning and news shows dealing with attitudes, and when age, education, sex, and the other intervening variables are controlled, political interest appears to increase throughout life with the highest rates reported after sixty. Does this general level of interest, concern, and attention translate into actual involvement? For the most part, yes; only when ill-health or transportation difficulties impede getting to the polls do the overt indicators of participation begin to level off.

## VOTING AND PARTICIPATION IN THE POLITICAL PROCESS

Simply making one's opinions known about various issues is seldom enough to bring about many significant changes. To effect such change, it is generally necessary to be able to wield some form of power over the political process to implement a new direction or to exert control over the behavior of others. There is some truth to the old cliché about a velvet glove veiling an iron fist; raw power in the form of physical force is generally irreconcilable with the philosophies ascribed to by democratic political orders. There are exceptions, of course, when naked force is construed to be legitimate, but under normal circumstances, the only power most people are willing to sanction is power that carries with it authority acquired in the political arena. Aside from the allegedly counterbalancing interest groups that attempt to lobby directly with the nation's lawmakers on behalf of their members, the most widely accepted avenue for exercising our political franchise is through voting.

Among political scientists, the question of participation in the electoral process vs quality of participation is still being contested. Usually, however, most believe that involving the largest number of people possible is the best means of ensuring unbiased results. Taken together, opinions and voting patterns furnish some valuable indicators that the potential for interceding in the political process clearly exists. To begin with, voter turnout rises steadily with age, at least into the retirement years, and even then it does not decline among the better educated, the actively involved, or for those who are not hampered by ill-health or immobility. Already older people are overrepresented in the ranks of the voters, accounting for roughly 20 percent of those who turn out on election day. Future trends point to even greater levels of participation into the later years of life as we witness the aging of the baby boom population. Older people will be better educated, have more time free from work, and more easily overcome such impediments as transportation problems (Jones, 1981; Glenn and Grimes, 1968; Olsen, 1972).

Examining voter turnout in the 1984 election provides information on the trends that have been approximated in nearly all elections in recent years. It must also be pointed out, however, as Table 10.1 indicates, the election of 1984 marked a twenty-year high in the number of people voting, with nearly 60 percent of all eligible people going to the polls. The upswing stemmed in part from a larger turnout among people over sixty-five, as well as a large turnout of women and minority groups. As shown in Figure 10.3, there was a steady increase among age cohorts until a downturn at seventy-four because of inabilities to get to polling places. Even at that, more of the old-old than young adults voted in 1984. As people approach sixty-five a reversal in female-male participation rates occurs. Up to that point, more women than men cast ballots; during their sixties the gender differences reverse, with men of all races voting more frequently. The reason has not been satisfactorily explained thus far, but some contend it has to do with a gender-based, activist stance (U.S. Census, 1985).

Among the elderly population, two-thirds of those who do not vote attribute the reason for not going to the polls as illness. Since similar transitory difficulties might preclude voting in any given election, voter registration might be a better indication of intended political participation. Again, the trend was up-

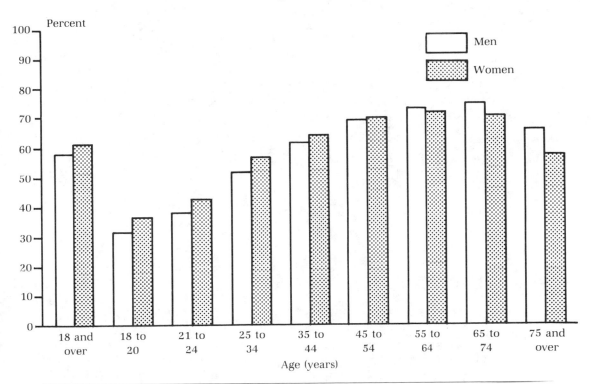

**FIGURE 10.3**
Who voted in the United States, November 1984. (*Source:* U.S. Bureau of the Census. *Population Characteristics*, pp. 5, 7. Current Population Reports, Series P-20, No. 397. Washington, D.C.: U.S. Government Printing Office, 1985.)

**TABLE 10.1**

Voter Turnout and Registration for Recent Elections

*Percent Reported Voting, by Region, Race, Spanish Origin, Sex, and Age, November 1964 to 1984 (Numbers in Thousands. Civilian Noninstitutional Population)*

| Region, Race, Spanish Origin, Sex, and Age | Presidential Elections | | | | | | Congressional Elections | | | | |
|---|---|---|---|---|---|---|---|---|---|---|---|
| | 1984 | 1980 | 1976 | 1972 | 1968 | 1964 | 1982 | 1978 | 1974 | 1970 | 1966 |
| *United States* | | | | | | | | | | | |
| Total, voting age | 169,963 | 157,085 | 146,548 | 136,203 | 116,535 | 110,604 | 165,483 | 151,646 | 141,299 | 120,701 | 112,800 |
| Percent voted | 59.9 | 59.2 | 59.2 | 63.0 | 67.8 | 69.3 | 48.5 | 45.9 | 44.7 | 54.6 | 55.4 |
| White | 61.4 | 60.9 | 60.9 | 64.5 | 69.1 | 70.7 | 49.9 | 47.3 | 46.3 | 56.0 | 57.0 |
| Black | 55.8 | 50.5 | 48.7 | 52.1 | 57.6 | 58.5[a] | 43.0 | 37.2 | 33.8 | 43.5 | 41.7 |
| Spanish origin[a] | 32.6 | 29.9 | 31.8 | 37.5 | (NA) | (NA) | 25.3 | 23.5 | 22.9 | (NA) | (NA) |
| Male | 59.0 | 59.1 | 59.6 | 64.1 | 69.8 | 71.9 | 48.7 | 46.6 | 46.2 | 56.8 | 58.2 |
| Female | 60.8 | 59.4 | 58.8 | 62.0 | 66.0 | 67.0 | 48.4 | 45.3 | 43.4 | 52.7 | 53.0 |
| 18–24 years old | 40.8 | 39.9 | 42.2 | 49.6 | 50.4[c] | 50.9[c] | 24.8 | 23.5 | 23.8 | [3]30.4 | [3]31.1 |
| 25–44 years old | 58.4 | 58.7 | 58.7 | 62.7 | 66.6 | 69.0 | 45.4 | 43.1 | 42.2 | 51.9 | 53.1 |
| 45–64 years old | 69.8 | 69.3 | 68.7 | 70.8 | 74.9 | 75.9 | 62.2 | 58.5 | 56.9 | 64.2 | 64.5 |
| 65 years and over | 67.7 | 65.1 | 62.2 | 63.5 | 65.8 | 66.3 | 59.9 | 55.9 | 51.4 | 57.0 | 56.1 |

*Characteristics of the Voting-Age Population Reported Registered or Voting, November 1984 and 1980 (Numbers in Thousands)*

| Characteristic | 1984 | | 1980 | |
|---|---|---|---|---|
| | Percent Registered | Percent Voted | Percent Registered | Percent Voted |
| Total, 18 years and over | 68.3 | 59.9 | 66.9 | 59.2 |
| Region: | | | | |
| Northeast | 66.6 | 59.7 | 64.8 | 58.5 |
| Midwest[b] | 74.6 | 65.7 | 73.8 | 65.8 |
| South | 66.9 | 56.8 | 64.8 | 55.6 |
| West | 64.7 | 58.5 | 63.3 | 57.2 |
| Years of school completed: | | | | |
| Elementary:  0–8 years | 53.4 | 42.9 | 53.0 | 42.6 |
| High school:  1–3 years | 54.9 | 44.4 | 54.6 | 45.6 |
| 4 years | 67.3 | 58.7 | 66.4 | 58.9 |
| College:  1–3 years | 75.7 | 67.5 | 74.4 | 67.2 |
| 4 years or more | 83.8 | 79.1 | 84.3 | 79.9 |
| Labor force status: | | | | |
| In civilian labor force | 68.4 | 60.5 | 67.4 | 60.4 |
| Employed | 69.4 | 61.6 | 68.7 | 61.8 |
| Not employed | 54.3 | 44.0 | 50.3 | 41.2 |
| Not in labor force | 68.1 | 58.9 | 65.8 | 57.0 |
| Tenure[c]: | | | | |
| Owner occupied | 79.1 | 71.8 | 77.8 | 71.1 |
| Renter occupied | 53.4 | 43.7 | 50.8 | 42.1 |

[a]Persons of Spanish origin may be of any race.
[b]Formerly the North Central region.
[c]Restricted to family householders.
*Source:* U.S. Bureau of the Census. *Voting and Registration in the Election of 1984.* pp. 1, 2. Current Population Reports, P-20, No. 397. Washington, D.C.: U.S. Government Printing Office, 1985 [adapted].

ward from the 1980 statistics; 68 percent of the voting age population was registered. A 2 percent rise in female registrants was noted, while the male rate was essentially unchanged from 1980. The black registration rate climbed by six points to 66 percent and the Hispanic rate rose by 4 percent to 40 percent. Among the black and Hispanic minorities, the spread between the general population and the older voters was approximately the same as among the white population. The reasons for the general pattern of lower participation among Hispanic citizens range from alienation, feelings of inefficacy, language barriers, lower socioeconomic status, threats, and other perceived environmental barriers (Cuellar, 1978; Torres-Gil and Becerra, 1977). Most often, higher educational levels, higher status occupations, more stable employment, higher incomes, homeownership, and length of tenure in a community are all characteristics associated with higher voter participation. In some instances marital status also makes a difference. The proportion of married voters over forty-five is usually greater than the widowed or divorced, who in turn vote in larger numbers than the never married (U.S. Census, 1985, 1984).

A question that cannot now be answered is whether older voters have always exercised their political prerogatives or only do so as they acquire more time and fewer distractions. Depending on which of the two possibilities eventually proves true, the likelihood of the elderly constituting a powerful voting bloc able to deliver votes will vary. In another twenty years the baby boom cohort may have a significant impact on the political process (Rollenhagen, 1984).

It is important to point out that the characteristics of older voters are exactly those that students of social movements have identified as being crucial in the development of political consciousness. For example, political mobilization, at the initial levels involving simply voting attitudes, which apparently grows out of participation in a variety of voluntary groups, is one of the best predictors of voting. Finally, the current attention being focused on the situation of the elderly by the mass media, plus the growing number of people over sixty-five, may also promote an awareness of their own affinity. Not to be forgotten, however, is a major factor already discussed, the emergence of a rudimentary gray power movement that although not yet proven highly effective in attracting a broad membership, may have a definite consciousness-raising function (Pratt, 1976; Ragan and Dowd, 1974; Trela, 1977–1978).

## OTHER POLITICAL BEHAVIOR

Other than voting, what forms of political participation can be found among the elderly? Older people do write their congressional representatives or contact party campaign headquarters to express their opinions. Some even go beyond this to become active campaigners, to attend rallies, or to become totally immersed in politics. Each of these forms of political behavior is found among the elderly, and participation appears to parallel voting, though at a reduced rate. The difference may be that when withdrawal occurs it is more precipitous than with voting. As a consequence, those over sixty-five are some-

what underrepresented among the ranks of the more activist political participants. Yet when the socioeconomic variables affecting voting are controlled,
the gradual decline noted does not take place. Clearly, if educational levels, income security, overall health, and occupational involvement increase among
future generations of old people, so too will their political participation rates
(Nie et al., 1974; Smith et al., 1980; Williamson et al., 1982).

Obviously, one of the more explicit types of political involvement is occupying a position of power. How is political leadership distributed among age
groups? In most industrialized mass societies late middle-aged and older leaders occupy the primary positions of power. On both sides of the Atlantic national leaders are, for the most part, over sixty. Their cabinet-level appointees
are somewhat younger but still middle-aged; their average age has declined
only in the past few decades (Lammers and Nyomarkey, 1980). Supreme Court
justices, Senate and congressional leaders, and ambassadors are even older.
Seemingly, the more important the office the older the holder of that office
will be (Schlesinger, 1966). In the United States, having had a two-term president elected to his second four-year term in the White House at the oldest age
of any president certainly suggests that older people have not been excluded
from positions of leadership. It obviously sensitizes the entire country to the
status of its aged citizens. Even on regional and local levels, older people are
slightly overrepresented in leadership positions. When the focus is broadened
to include more than just elected or appointed officials, when we look at
powerful decision makers in public educational institutions, community agencies, and so on, we again see that middle-aged and older people hold power. It
might even be the case that the challenges of office forestall whatever decrements less stimulated age peers might experience.

Is that not somewhat of a paradox? In a culture that seems to exalt youthful
attributes, our leaders are considerably older. Part of the reason is seniority
and bureaucracy; people accede to powerful positions after having served in
the ranks for some time. Power, once exercised, accrues to those who use it.
Accordingly, they retain it over time. Finally, stability and a proven ability to
handle high-pressure situations are valued alongside youthful characteristics;
in politics the former is emphasized more than the latter. In countries that undergo political turmoil, those who emerge victorious are younger on the
average than the leaders of stable, established political regimes (Hudson and
Strate, 1985). When Mikhail Gorbachev came to power in the Soviet Union in
1985 at fifty-four, it was a newsworthy event and many commentators
wondered if it signaled a changing of the old guard. Since the average age of
members of the Politburo is near seventy, it is probably unlikely.

## The Political Future of the Elderly

Since many studies of political participation focus on time-bound activities, we
must be attuned to the impact of period effects. Just over a decade ago, for instance, there was widespread disaffection. Protests by younger persons were

common occurrences in the early 1970s. The presidential election of 1972, especially the McGovern campaign, drew large numbers of young adults into political activity for the first time. Comparing age groups at that point would cause the elderly to look like they were lagging behind. As the social climate in the country changed, as the young protesters acquired families and career responsibilities, their activities dwindled. Cross-sectional comparisons somewhat later would make one think older people had become more active when their actual involvement may have remained constant.

If the social perspective on political activism is correct, as the protesters themselves begin to age and they perceive a stake in making their voices heard, a cohort effect will emerge. Consequently, political debates in the early decades of the next century could be dominated by a gray power lobby (Jennings and Beck, 1979; Hudson and Strate, 1985).

## A GENERATIONAL ALLIANCE

One possibility for cultivating political consciousness broached quite often is an alliance between the elderly and young adults. As previously mentioned, these two groups often experience similar feelings of alienation and estrangement from the mainstream of society (Agnello, 1973). By virtue of their social location vis-à-vis the rest of the social order, they often find themselves equally bereft of firm social anchors and in subordinate and dependent positions. The elderly are often considered to be beyond whatever contributions they have to make to maintain society's economic and cultural growth, while young adults are usually thought too immature, not yet ready to make a life choice, though it is recognized their contributions will come with the future. Whether any unification ever occurs on a scale sufficiently broad to effectively propose alternatives, there is ample evidence to indicate that in certain respects members of both age categories more nearly resemble one another than either resembles the middle-aged. According to some, their feelings of relative powerlessness and structural marginality may be coalescing to the point where older people are now on the verge of an emerging age group consciousness similar to that which swept through much of the world's youth in the late 1960s (Laufer and Bengtson, 1974; Martin et al., 1974). Some have even forecast, perhaps wistfully, an actual alliance between the old and the young, initiated very probably by the old, although most students of aging predict any intergenerational political movement as unlikely (Cain, 1975; Cameron and Cromer, 1974; Hudson and Binstock, 1976).

The Gray Panthers is an example of one organization drawing its members from both the old and the young that has attempted to meld an intergenerational unity through action. Founded in Philadelphia in the early 1970s, the group first took its cue from the so-called radical activists whose goal was to awaken whites and blacks to the existence of racism in its innumerable guises. Realizing that age biases cut across sex and racial boundaries with equal devastation, the Gray Panthers dedicated themselves to abolishing prejudice on the basis of age wherever it is found. Although federal laws are now in force prohibiting age discrimination in work, they are difficult to enforce and encompass only a relatively small part of the problem. **Ageism**, or what was defined in Chapter 2 as a pejorative evaluation and labeling of older people simply because of their age, seems to be evident in nearly every realm of modern society, especially in America where traditionally youthful vigor has been highly esteemed (Butler, 1974).

The distinction between the individual's feelings of political inefficacy and general disenchantment with the workings of the political system has often been cited. The impact these have on political participation is less readily addressed (Cox, 1980; Cutler, 1977; Rule, 1977). Precisely this kind of issue concerns groups intent on developing power among the aged, but as far as the Gray Panthers and others are concerned, to attack ageism and alienation, it is first necessary to challenge the negative attitudes held toward and by the old. According to Maggie Kuhn, founder of the Gray Panthers, bringing both ends of the age continuum into close association with the avowed purpose of convincing everyone else that older people are indeed valuable members of society will have its effect on the participants and on those for whom their message is intended. Initially, the Gray Panthers were content to advocate alternative life-styles for older people — unions with younger partners, mutual sharing, interaction, and so on — to facilitate a communal consciousness. Of course, we are not yet in an era when militant septuagenarians are about to become common, but it may not be as great a leap as we might suppose from verbal protests over present societal morality to welding a political consciousness among the elderly. Certainly, politicians are sensitive to the possibility of agitated, irate members of the electorate voicing opposition to cutbacks in benefits, programs, and other sources of support. This is not to say that the overall economic pressures will not erode the political legitimacy enjoyed by the elderly in the last half of the 1970s. When issues are framed first in terms of dollars, rather than societal and personal utility, the necessity for political pressure exerted by and on behalf of the elderly becomes even more salient. As national debate over the direction of governmental programs and sponsorship intensifies, the roles to be played in the political arena by the aged beg for increased organization and cohesiveness. The decade of the 1980s may witness the halt of liberal legislation (Bechill, 1979; Estes, 1979; Fritz, 1979; Hudson, 1978).

If the wave of legislative proposals issued by the second-term Reagan administration are indicative of future levels of support afforded older people in the United States, all estimates are that dire times are ahead for the elderly. As we approach the 1990s, competition for finite resources is going to increase. As long as the differences of opinion focus on age-related debates, rather than a more inclusive focus on defense or foreign affairs vs domestic issues, short-term hardships will increase.

## POLITICS OF TOMORROW

The potential for gray power doubtlessly exists. Whether older people, by themselves or in a generational alliance, actually mobilize is another question.

Opinion varies among the experts, but the evidence tends to go against a more activist stance. Like so many other pronouncements, this one too might be a self-fulfilling prophecy (Williamson et al., 1982).

On the other hand, political wisdom suggests that in the future all of that could change. Activists may mellow, but one day they will be old. A dramatic upswing in political awareness, participation, and responsiveness could result. Changes in life expectancy, financial well-being, education, and so on suggest a more informed older electorate in the not too distant future. The presence of age-related lobby groups will help as will experience in the political process. It is not necessary that all old people agree on an issue; it is only essential that they become politically involved for the emergence of gray power.

Militating against this same trend are the structural repositionings that technology *might* bring, the blurring of age borders, identification along lines other than age, and generalized insecurity posed by the threat of the withdrawal of public support. Like everyone else, old people are hesitant to criticize those who are supporting them. Sharp generational conflicts might also polarize political loyalties so that even if they coalesced older people might be blocked from exercising their political will. On the other hand, intergenerational solidarity might make a strictly age-based coalition unnecessary. The future may be gray but it is difficult to predict patterns of political consciousness. The economic dimensions of the changing age structure bring the question of the politics of demography into the general political discussion. Identifying national priorities and the resources available to buttress them raises the prospect of a strain in the altruistic components of our ideology. The way we define the question can either exacerbate or soothe the tensions between generations. One thing is certain: the political process will be affected.

## Summary

In recent years considerable attention has been focused on the potential role of the aged in the political arena. While not a unified or powerful group at present, future developments emphasizing the common predicament of older people may shape them into a powerful political force. During the 1930s the Depression spawned a variety of social movements that looked for a time as though they would indeed serve the needs of older people. With the advent of Social Security, however, most of the groups were deprived of their primary purpose and soon declined. Today there are once again several national organizations dedicated to maintaining the viability of America's elderly. Although there is little consensus among these groups as to the most expedient means of securing a better stake for older people, there is no denying their national political importance. Paradoxically, many of the new interest groups set up on behalf of the elderly have become closely allied with administrative agencies, serving as intermediaries between government and client. Students of organizational growth are quick to point out that in a situation such as this, voluntary associations tend to become bureaucracies that eventually solidify to the extent that those whom they proposed to represent are sometimes left behind, their interests relegated to a secondary position for the sake of the organization's own livelihood.

In addressing the role of age in determining political attitudes we must be cautious in attributing causal significance to any of the factors involved. Differences observed between the political outlook of the old and the young may not reflect age changes but stem instead from a generational bias cast under particular historical circumstances. Popular interpretations of opinion polls often portray the elderly as politically conservative, yet a closer look at the issues in question is needed before any such general conclusions can be drawn. Familiarity, experience, and proximity are in themselves enough to alter the opinions expressed by respondents of various ages. Another misconception about the elderly is that they are less attuned to current events because of the social dislocations they have undergone during retirement or widowhood. However, when important sociological variables are brought into the picture, older people are no less informed or more apathetic than many younger people; just the opposite is true in many cases.

As much as any topic in gerontology, political attitudes reflect both cohort and period effects. Some say they are also a consequence of aging or the maturational process. Having been socialized and become politically aware at a particular time means that attitudes become somewhat crystallized toward certain types of issues. That is not to say they never change; rather the period and the social experiences of a time function as an anchor from which later shifts evolve. Of course, contemporaneous events alter opinions, and the view expressed by the elderly or members of any other age category are influenced by current affairs. Finally, political orientation is also affected by aging, that is, by changes in the life experiences of an individual. To appreciate how attitudes or participation are shaped it is necessary to take all three elements into consideration.

Because their participation rates have been high in mainstream political activities, many questions have been raised about the emergence of older people as a political force. Forecasting trends is a difficult task; forecasting political activities is no different. Increasing age group consciousness, intergenerational alliances, and the aging of a generation already known for being activists suggest the elderly of the future will be more involved than the current generation of old people. On the other hand, the political climate of the past decade and the programs that were once untouchable are now being exposed to close and critical scrutiny. The effect may lead to a further stigmatization of old age and hence a lessening of age group identification. Intergenerational conflict over finite fiscal and social resources will also work against the advent of gray power if only because members of younger cohorts might become equally active in preserving their own stake.

Whether a real or just a potential gray power lobby exists, the implications are that this force will help shape the formulation of social policies affecting the elderly. Denying that the situation of old people constitutes a social

problem also denies the need for and the possibilities of an aged social movement. This presents a paradox, however; by stressing the negative aspects of
aging we affirm the problematic side of the issue but simultaneously do older
people themselves a disservice. It should be clear that there are many positive
aspects of aging we should all look toward. Nonetheless, the situation of old
people and the social policies aimed at relative improvements in their lives are
in the last analysis political questions. Questions must be framed in terms of
problems requiring resolution. In light of the perceived and real crises of the
mid-1980s, the political climate is changing and many programs are facing retrenchment. To date the response, in terms of political mobilization, has been
miniscule. As will be seen in Chapter 11, the political ramifications of social
policy formation extend beyond those discussed in this chapter. It may be that
a new and more pernicious form of ageism is emerging from the political and
economic decisions currently being made. Whether it will work for or against
federal support for the aged cannot be said with certainty (Kearl et al., 1982).
The emphasis on accountability is good and necessary; nevertheless, it also diminishes the legitimacy of the claims of the nation's elderly.

## Discussion Questions

**Nature and
Structure of Politics**

1. Are politics strictly a matter of individual choice? What issues are within the scope of the politics of aging?

**The Elderly as a
Social Movement**

2. How important is age in determining political attitudes?
   Why might members of a particular cohort share a worldview? What other factors might affect their political orientation and lead to variation within the cohort?

3. What were the achievements of the early age-based social
   movements? How did they help to define the situation of
   those over sixty-five as a social problem? What are the
   negative and positive consequences of seeing the situation
   of the elderly as a social problem?

4. What are the potential advantages and disadvantages of
   having the interests of the elderly represented by sophisticated professional groups, as opposed to grass-roots movements? How might the two types of groups complement or
   conflict with each other?

5. How might age group identification among the elderly tend
   to aggravate or ameliorate their political situation?

**Political Attitudes
and Opinions**

6. How do you think the political attitudes of older people
   you know are shaped by the historical circumstances in

which they grew up, by their age group affiliation, and by other factors such as past or present occupation?

7. What do you think it means to be politically liberal or conservative? Do you think the older people you know are more conservative or liberal than young people?

8. How would you measure the strength of a person's political attitudes? By these criteria, are older or younger people more politically committed?

9. What social and political problems might arise if the old and the young each focus only on issues that touch them directly? How might a mutual effort to understand the situation and problems of others lead to a solution of these problems? In your answer focus on some specific areas of concern such as the economy.

**Political Participation**

10. What forms of political participation are open to the elderly? How effective do you think these are in terms of influencing social policies? What factors lead to participation or nonparticipation by the elderly?

11. What are the advantages and disadvantages of having (a) the elderly and (b) the young in positions of political authority? How might the strengths of the two complement each other?

12. Draft a plank in a political platform for the next election focusing on the interests of the elderly.

13. In what ways might demographic changes and the response to these affect the political standing of the elderly in the future? What will the political standing of the elderly be like when your generation is old?

# Pertinent Readings

Achenbaum, W. A. *Old Age in the New Land: The American Experience Since 1790.* Baltimore: The Johns Hopkins University Press, 1978.

———. *Shades of Gray.* Boston: Little, Brown & Company, 1983.

Agnello, T. J. "Aging and the Sense of Political Powerlessness." *Public Opinion Quarterly* 37 (1973): 251–59.

Anderson, W. A., and N. D. Anderson. "The Politics of Age Exclusion: The Adults Only Movement in Arizona." *The Gerontologist* 18, 1 (1978): 6–12.

Bechill, W. "Politics of Aging and Ethnicity." In *Ethnicity and Aging: Theory, Research, and Policy*, eds. D. E. Gelfand and A. J. Kutzik, pp. 137–51. New York: Springer Publishing Company, 1979.

Butler, R. N. *Why Survive? Being Old in America*. New York: Harper & Row, Publishers, 1974.

Cain, L. D. "The Young and the Old: Coalition or Conflict Ahead?" *American Behavioral Scientist* 19, 2 (1975): 166–75.

Cameron, P., and A. Cromer. "Generational Homophyly." *Journal of Gerontology* 29, 2 (1974): 232–36.

Campbell, A. "Social and Psychological Determinants of Voting Behavior." In *Politics of Age*, eds. W. Donohue and C. Tibbitts, pp. 87–100. Ann Arbor: University of Michigan, 1962.

Campbell, J. C., and J. Strate. "Are Old People Conservative?" *The Gerontologist* 21, 6 (1981): 580–91.

Carlie, M. K. "The Politics of Age: Interest Group or Social Movement?" *The Gerontologist* 9, 4, Pt. I (1969): 259–63.

Cottrell, F. "Governmental Functions and the Politics of Age." In *Handbook of Social Gerontology*, ed. C. Tibbitts, pp. 624–65. Chicago: University of Chicago Press, 1960.

Cox, H. "The Motivation and Political Alienation of Older Americans." *International Journal of Aging and Human Development* 11, 1 (1980): 1–12.

Cuellar, J. B. "El Senior Citizens Club: The Older Mexican-American in the Voluntary Association." In *Life's Career — Aging: Cultural Variations on Growing Old*, eds. B. G. Myerhoff and A. Simic, pp. 207–30. Beverly Hills, Calif.: Sage Publications, Inc., 1978.

Cutler, N. E. "Aging and Voluntary Association Participation." *Journal of Gerontology* 32, 4 (1977): 470–79.

———. "Political Characteristics of Elderly Cohorts in the Twenty-first Century." In *Aging: Social Change*, eds. J. N. Morgan, S. B. Kiesler, and V. K. Oppenheimer, pp. 127–57. New York: Academic Press, Inc., 1981.

———. "Political Behavior of the Aged." In *Aging: Scientific Perspectives and Social Issues*, eds. D. S. Woodruff and J. E. Birren, pp. 409–42. Monterey, Calif.: Brooks/Cole Publishing Company, 1983.

———, and V. L. Bengtson. "Age and Political Alienation: Maturation, Generation and Period Effects." *The Annals* 415 (1974): 160–75.

———, et al. "Aging and Conservatism: Cohort Changes in Attitudes About Legalized Abortion." *Journal of Gerontology* 35, 1 (1980): 115–23.

Erskine, H. "The Polls: Pacifism and the Generation Gap." *Public Opinion Quarterly* 36, 4 (1973): 616–27.

Estes, C. L. *The Aging Enterprise*. San Francisco: Jossey-Bass, Inc., Publishers, 1979.

Fischer, D. H. *Growing Old in America*. Oxford, England: Oxford University Press, 1978.

Foner, A. "The Polity." In *Aging and Society*, vol. 3, eds. M. W. Riley, M. Johnson, and A. Foner, pp. 115–59. New York: Russell Sage Foundation, 1972.

Fritz, D. "The Administration on Aging as an Advocate: Progress, Problems, and Prospects." *The Gerontologist* 19, 2 (1979): 141–50.

Gergen, K. J., and K. W. Back. "Cognitive Constriction in Aging and Attitudes toward International Issues." In *Social Aspects of Aging*, eds. I. H. Simpson and J. C. McKinney, pp. 322–34. Durham, N.C.: Duke University Press, 1966.

Glenn, N. D. "Aging, Disengagement, and Opinionation." *Public Opinion Quarterly* 33, 1 (1969): 17–33.

———. "Aging and Conservatism." *The Annals* 415 (1974): 176–86.

———. "Values, Attitudes and Beliefs." In *Constancy and Change in Human Development,* eds. O. G. Brim, Jr., and J. Kagan, pp. 596–640. Cambridge, Mass.: Howard University Press, 1980.

———, and M. Grimes. "Aging, Voting, and Political Interest." *American Sociological Review* 33 (1968): 563–75.

Graebner, W. *A History of Retirement.* New Haven, Conn.: Yale University Press, 1980.

Gurin, P., A. H. Miller, and G. Gurin. "Stratum Identification and Consciousness." *Psychology Quarterly* 43, 1 (1980): 30–47.

Hudson, R. B. "The 'Graying' of the Federal Budget and its Consequences for Old-Age Policy." *The Gerontologist* 18, 5 (1978): 428–50.

———, and R. H. Binstock. "Political Systems and Aging." In *Handbook of Aging and the Social Sciences,* ed. 2, eds. R. H. Binstock and E. Shanas, pp. 369–400. New York: Van Nostrand Reinhold Company, 1976.

———, ed. *The Aging in Politics: Process and Policy.* Springfield, Ill.: Charles C Thomas, Publisher, 1981.

———, and J. Strate. "Aging and Political Systems." In *Handbook of Aging and the Social Sciences,* eds. R. Binstock and E. Shanas, pp. 554–85. New York: Van Nostrand Reinhold Company, 1985.

Jeffries, V. "Political Generations and the Acceptance or Rejection of Nuclear Warfare." *Journal of Social Issues* 30, 3 (1974): 119–36.

Jennings, M. K., and P. A. Beck. "Political Periods and Political Participation." *American Political Science Review* 73, 6 (1979): 737–50.

Jones, L. Y. *Great Expectations: America and the Baby Boom Generation.* New York: Ballantine Books, 1981.

Kearl, M. C., K. Moore, and J. S. Scott. "Political Implications of the 'New Ageism.'" *International Journal of Aging and Human Development* 15, 3 (1982): 167–83.

Lacayo, C. G. "The Asociación Nacional Pro Personas Mayores: Responding to the 'Decade of the Hispanic.'" *Aging* 305–306 (1980): 12–14.

Lammers, W. W., and J. L. Nyomarkey. "The Disappearing Senior Leaders." *Research on Aging* 2, 3 (1980): 329–49.

Laufer, R. S., and V. L. Bengtson. "Generations, Aging, and Social Stratification: On the Development of Generational Units." *Journal of Social Issues* 30, 3 (1974): 181–205.

Mannheim, K. "The Problem of Generations." In *Essays on the Sociology of Knowledge,* ed. K. Mannheim, pp. 276–320. London: Routledge & Kegan Paul Ltd., 1952.

Martin, W., V. Bengtson, and A. Acock. "Alienation and Age: A Context Specific Approach." *Social Forces* LIII, 2 (1974): 266–74.

Nie, N., S. Verba, and J. Kim. "Political Participation and the Life Cycle." *Comparative Politics* 6, 2 (1974): 319–40.

Olsen, M. E. "Social Participation and Voting Turnout: A Multivariate Analysis." *American Sociological Review* 37, 4 (1972): 317–33.

Pratt, H. J. *The Gray Lobby.* Chicago: University of Chicago Press, 1976.

Ragan, P. K., and J. J. Dowd. "The Emerging Political Consciousness of the Aged: A Generational Interpretation." *Journal of Social Issues* 30, 3 (1974): 137–58.

Riemer, Y., and R. H. Binstock. "Campaigning for 'The Senior Vote': A Case Study of Carter's 1976 Campaign." *The Gerontologist* 18, 6 (1978): 517–24.

Rokeach, M., W. C. McGovney, and M. R. Denny. "A Distinction Between Dogmatic and Rigid Thinking." *Journal of Abnormal and Social Psychology* 51, 1 (1955): 87–93.

Rollenhagen, R. E. "Age-Related Changing Levels of Voting Turnout Across Time." *The Gerontologist* 24, 2 (1984): 205–07.

Rose, A. M. "Group Consciousness Among the Aging." In *Older People and Their Social World,* eds. A. M. Rose and W. A. Peterson, pp. 19–36. Philadelphia: F. A. Davis Co., 1965.

Rule, W. L. B. "Political Alienation and Voting Attitudes Among the Elderly Generation." *The Gerontologist* 17, 5 (1977): 400–04.

Schlesinger, J. A. *Ambition and Politics: Political Careers in the United States.* Chicago: Rand McNally & Company, 1966.

Smith, D. H., J. Macaulay, and associates. *Participation in Social and Political Activities.* San Francisco: Jossey-Bass, Inc., Publishers, 1980.

Stouffer, S. A. *Communism, Conformity, and Civil Liberties.* Garden City, N.Y.: Doubleday and Co., 1955.

Streib, G. F. "Are the Aged a Minority Group?" In *Applied Sociology,* eds. A. W. Gouldner and S. M. Miller, pp. 311–28. Glencoe: The Free Press, 1965.

Tedin, K. L. "Age and Social Composition Factors as Explanations for Cleavages in Socio-Political Values." *International Journal of Aging and Human Development* 9, 4 (1978–1979): 295–303.

Torres-Gil, F., and R. M. Becerra. "The Political Behavior of the Mexican-American Elderly." *The Gerontologist* 17, 5 (1977): 392–99.

Trela, J. E. "Social Class and Political Involvement in Age Graded and Non-Age Graded Associations." *International Journal of Aging and Human Development* 8, 4 (1977–1978): 301–10.

U.S. Bureau of the Census. *Voting and Registration in the Election of November, 1984.* Current Population Reports, Series P-20, No. 397. Washington, D.C.: U.S. Government Printing Office, 1985.

———. *Voting and Registration Highlights From the Current Population Survey: 1964 to 1980.* Current Population Reports, Series P-23, No. 131. Washington, D.C.: U.S. Government Printing Office, 1984.

U.S. Senate Committee on Government Operations. "Confidence and Concern: Citizens View American Government." 93d Cong., 1 Sess., Pt. 1, December 1973. Washington, D.C.: U.S. Government Printing Office, 1973.

Williamson, J. B., L. Evans, and L. A. Powell. *The Politics of Aging: Power and Policy.* Springfield, Ill.: Charles C Thomas, Publisher, 1982.

# 11

# SOCIAL POLICY AND AGING

**THE NATURE OF SOCIAL POLICY**
The Multiple Levels of Social Policy
The Relationship between the
  Individual and Society
Unidimensional vs Multidimensional
  Approaches

**SOCIAL POLICY FOR THE
ELDERLY**
Social Policy in Relation to Problems
  of the Elderly
Policy as Social Construction:
  Constituency Concerns
Social Policy as Formative of the
  Lifeworld of the Elderly
Metapolicy and the Elderly
  *The Web of Metapolicy*
  *Setting the Agenda of Public Policy*
  *Choice Opportunities*

**FISCAL POLICIES AND THE
ELDERLY**
Social Security
  *Phase One: Implementation*
  *Phase Two: Expansion*
  *Phase Three: Retrenchment*
The Future of Social Security
Supplemental Security Income
Private Pension Provisions
Individual Retirement Accounts
Age Discrimination and Employment

**HEALTH CARE POLICIES AND
THE ELDERLY**
Development of Health Care for the
  Aged
Medicare and Medicaid
The Issue of Cost
Medicare: A Broken Promise?
Private Health Policy Options
  *Medigap*
  *Long-Term Care*

**ADDITIONAL SOCIAL SERVICE
POLICIES FOR THE ELDERLY**
Death with Dignity
Legal Services
Social Services
Housing

**THE METAPOLICY OF AGING:
ISSUES FOR THE FUTURE**
Intergenerational Equity vs
  Societal Equity
The Issue of Financial Feasibility

**SUMMARY**

**DISCUSSION QUESTIONS**

**PERTINENT READINGS**

In exploring the numerous facets of aging we have alluded to many social policy questions and to the ways in which private troubles are interlinked with public issues (Mills, 1959). We have not, however, dealt directly with social policy itself — the focus of this chapter. We will begin by enumerating various definitions of social policy and their implications. Using these perspectives, we then will examine various areas of social policy and legal statutes relevant to aging and their links with social policy issues that occupy all of society.

## The Nature of Social Policy

Like aging itself, social policy is a complex, socially constructed concept. Its definition may be approached from a number of angles. Three dimensions implicit in the conceptualization of social policy reflect differences in the level of analysis, in the basic approaches to the relationship of social policy and the individual, and in the perspectives informing approaches to social policy. We consider each of these in turn.

### THE MULTIPLE LEVELS OF SOCIAL POLICY

Conceptualizations of social policy embrace different levels of analysis. In defining social policy one may focus on one or several of these. A social policy is sometimes thought of as an expressly articulated approach to a particular — perhaps quite narrowly defined — issue or problem; for instance, a given presidential administration's policy on national defense or a mayor's policy on the development of an inner city area. In this sense social policy may be expressed in legislation or in a declaration of intent by a candidate for office, an elected official, or a political party. While this concept of social strategies is an important part of the political process, an exclusive focus on this level may cloud one's thinking through the distinctions between our societal goals and the practicalities and problems of implementation. This omission may result in two kinds of problems: our issue-oriented policies may be a series of stopgap measures, without any consideration of their wider implications, or they may be grounded in our beliefs about the way things should be without regard to the practical difficulties involved in implementation.

More generally, social policy is a broad approach to the social issues of a person or group, the perspectives influencing their policy decisions on particular issues that may or may not be articulated. It may be as specific as a political platform that states these perspectives, or it may be largely unconscious styles of formulating issues. It may be relatively consistent or fluctuating, and where it is an explicitly formulated perspective, it may or may not correspond to underlying intentions and beliefs. A third level might be called **social metapolicy.** This refers to beliefs about human nature, about social relations, and about the nature of society that underlie general approaches to social problems. It may be grounded in a philosophy of human nature or in a pragmatic desire to manipulate the system to survive, with many gradations in between. It may include a belief in the equality of all persons either in opportunity or in outcome, or it may be based on an assumption that certain people are inferior. Social policy may be based on a tolerance for the perspectives of others or on a crusading desire to spread an absolute truth. It involves the basic dimensions of what we believe life is about and our relations with others. Disagreements regarding social policy may be pragmatic — a matter of the best practical approach to a mutually agreed on problem; they may also frequently be a matter of conflicting metapolicy, which means that even the problem itself is formulated from divergent points of view.

At a fourth level, social policy may be seen as a socially constructed, socially negotiated process of thinking about social issues, formulating social problems, and attempting to resolve them. This implies a fluid, dynamic approach to the state and the political process. Social policy then results from ongoing struggles and compromises between a variety of interest groups, some of which may have more power than others depending on the circumstances.

## THE RELATIONSHIP BETWEEN THE INDIVIDUAL AND SOCIETY

Two basic approaches to the relationship between the individual and society (or the state) affect the formulation and implementation of social policy: a static, instrumental view, sometimes characterized as the social engineering approach, and a more dynamic, dialectical view. The former tends to dichotomize the individual and society — to *reify* social relations and/or the individual. This dichotomy may take various forms. Policymakers may see social institutions as instruments and persons — or more often categories of persons — as objects of social policy. While the designers of such social engineering measures may be motivated by self-interest, they may also be genuinely altruistic. At the other end of the spectrum, individuals may reify the structure: they may see themselves as powerless before the social policy machine, without options for choice or personal initiative. They may also dichotomize the individual and the social and fail to see how their personal troubles are interwoven with public issues.

The dynamic, dialectical approach — toward which we have endeavored to move in this book — sees people both as shaped by and as shapers of social policy. Two primary foci of analysis must be balanced within this approach:

(1) an uncovering of the ways in which social policies shape and characterize people's lives and life chances and (2) a discovery of the ways in which social policies are socially constructed and therefore malleable.

## UNIDIMENSIONAL VS MULTIDIMENSIONAL APPROACHES

Our third major issue in the conceptualization of social policy is the approach one adopts in formulating issues. Depending on the relative weight given to one or another aspect, policy formulation may respond to one or more questions. A desire for social justice vs a specific focus on economic issues to the exclusion of all else is just one example. In considering how policies come to be we need to be aware of a policy's many dimensions and the interactions between them.

We will now analyze social policy and aging with two ends in mind: (1) to uncover the metapolicy informing it and (2) to identify the issues posed. This should open the way for conscious debate of the many dimensions and promote a recognition of its socially constructed nature. To lay the groundwork for the analysis of specific legislative and administrative provisions for the elderly, the next section briefly examines some of the basic approaches underlying the development of social policy for the aged per se and the ways in which policy results from and influences the interplay between various constituencies. We then briefly survey policies concerning income maintenance, health, and legal issues. The final section discusses some of the attitudes underlying these specific policies and the debates surrounding them and point to some of the issues we will face in the future.

# Social Policy for the Elderly

## SOCIAL POLICY IN RELATION TO PROBLEMS OF THE ELDERLY

Many different orientations have been adopted by those who have attempted to formulate general approaches toward social policy for the elderly. Some start with equity and suggest a broad definition of social policy for the elderly, hoping that the procedures, programs, administrative regulations, and laws designed to deal with actual or potential problems are socially just. This, however, leaves us with the question of what social justice is. It is certainly a nebulous concept that varies depending on whom one consults. Generally, it means a fair deal for everyone. Such an approach emphasizes principles drawn from the British social reformer Lord Beveridge. He believed that for the whole of society to function well all of its parts must also function well. He based his ideas on the notion that citizenship carries with it certain rights, and the best way to fulfill those rights is a kind of collective self-help and responsibility.

Another approach, grounded in economic considerations, derives from another British reformer, Lord Keynes. As an economist, Keynes was concerned with macroeconomic processes. He thought that for the entire economy to thrive and grow no portion of the populace could be cut off from an ability to spend. If large segments have no money, the whole economy suffers, so the best policy is to be certain a minimal income is spread across all groups. In short, one can prime the pumps of private enterprise by public spending. In this way Keynes believed fiscal and social stability could be maintained.

So pervasive have the Keynesian fiscal policies become that the term **welfare capitalism** is sometimes used to describe these intimate ties between the public and the private. While providing solutions, however, social policies grounded in Keynesian economics also create problems in funding, entitlement, and fiscal responsibility. As the economy has slowed and we have moved into deficit spending on a large scale, Keynes' theories are increasingly challenged. What has been defended in terms of principles of citizenship and as a way to manage the fluctuations of free market economies is being criticized for diverting funds away from capital development and for encouraging personal short-sightedness or laziness (Gilder, 1981; Murray, 1985). These criticisms are reminiscent of those leveled against proponents of the New Deal. As we move through the second half of the 1980s, a real crisis in social policy has become a crucial political problem.

## POLICY AS SOCIAL CONSTRUCTION: CONSTITUENCY CONCERNS

In the United States public social policy for the elderly has been said to have grown out of the secularization of religious principles of charity toward the less fortunate, the economic hardships of the Depression, and the growing visibility of the elderly. While all of these were important in the development of social strategies for the elderly, actual policy development (as we shall see later) was the result of a dynamic process of conflict and compromise between a variety of ideological concerns. Included among these are the basically philanthropic concerns with the welfare of the poor, the American dream of equal opportunity and access to certain basic necessities for all, and the equally American emphasis on fostering independence, responsibility, and the self-reliance of individuals. The inherent contradictions in these values have segmented both private and governmental income and health maintenance programs based on contributions by participants on the one hand and welfare programs with basic eligibility requirements to ensure that they served only the "deserving" poor on the other. In the course of all this others have focused primarily on what was termed "fiscal responsibility" and viewed the costs likely to arise out of the expansion of social welfare programs and the increasing numbers of eligible recipients with alarm. In the United States throughout this century social welfare has been opposed on the grounds of financial feasibility. This is a legitimate concern because one simply cannot draw on infinite resources. Nonetheless, the availability of resources is mediated by the conflicting claims of various interest groups. Depending on the approach taken — which is to a certain extent influenced by historical circumstances — the same policies may be seen in many different ways. Thus, in the early days those who called for Social Security were called unAmerican by the proponents of rugged individualism. Then, with a greater focus on equal opportunity and an expanding economy to back it up, Social Security became the most "American" of our values. Now, with the current economic crisis and changes in the political climate, Social Security is once again being scrutinized to determine if it is in the best interest of all Americans.

Since the Depression and World War II, both federal and local governments have become increasingly involved in administering all social policy. The welfare state, as the system has come to be called, is supposed to supervise income transfers and social provisions designed to provide some semblance of security, be it economic, health, occupational, or social. This has generated new political demands, both for and against welfare policies, based on social constituencies. The state also has to administer a system of entitlements that are based on the individual's position in the market economy at a time when private enterprise is in turmoil. As a consequence, the contradictions of the **welfare state** are prompting a reexamination of both Keynesian and Beveridgian ideologies (Myles, 1984; Offe, 1984). The agenda for the future is sure to include a number of basic challenges concerning the proper role of the government and whether collective responsibility is a viable principle we wish to retain.

From the point of view of recipients, the primary benefit of social welfare and social insurance policies is obviously the "safety net" such policies promise. For example, Social Security ensures at least a rudimentary income level that is intended to protect the elderly from being entirely dependent on the largess of family, friends, or anyone else. Similarly, Medicare and Medicaid legislation should guarantee access to health care for those who could not otherwise afford it, although, as we shall see, practical problems abound. In both cases the allure of the policies is the promise that they will help reshape the structure of advantage to enhance access to opportunity. Regardless of their adequacy, social policies have a profound influence on people's lives that goes well beyond entitlement. They are the building blocks used to construct the reality of our lives.

## SOCIAL POLICY AS FORMATIVE OF THE LIFEWORLD OF THE ELDERLY

As entitlement policies attempt to provide a measure of security, they also define and delimit the everyday situation of old people. What it means to be old is basically a policy decision; if you draw benefits designated as the province of the old, then you are old. Eligibility for benefits also circumscribes other activities. To request full Social Security benefits between sixty-five and seventy a person must not work full time; if a person works, the benefits are reduced. The choice may rest with the individual, but the control is exercised by the Social Security Administration as an agency of the government. On the one hand, entitlement creates boundaries that define people. On the other hand, without that entitlement their situation could be dire or problematic.

In Chapter 2 we discussed ageism. At that point the definition focused on the social and psychological attitudes of prejudice. Another side to ageism is linked to social policy. By linking entitlements to definitions of social problems we demean recipients. When we characterize any group as objects of charity, we create dependencies that can eventually turn to ill-will. The very policies thought to be helpful for the old define them as less . . . ; here we can include almost anything valued in our culture (Kalish, 1979; Estes, 1979; Kearl et al., 1982). Sometimes the most humane and well-intentioned programs result in a kind of negativity and labeling never originally envisioned. By imposing a definition on people through official constructions of social policy we simultaneously define their status (Mizruchi, 1983). In their attempts to right the wrongs of inequality and neglect policymakers construct categorical age-based realities that may be as constricting as the previous problems. The stereotypical notions of old people feed off of social policies; the result is that individuals are typed in terms of the problems we originally set out to ameliorate. If age is a problem, it does not necessarily arise from increasing longevity, declining birth rates, or physiological involution but from the policies we have forged (Estes, 1979).

The underside of social policies in the welfare state is control over people, resources, and power. Normative expectations are rooted in policy, official regulations, and legal statutes that control even as they emancipate. How much of one or the other actually happens depends on the forces that shape policy formulation. For example, Medicare and Medicaid are proclaimed to be a medical cushion for the elderly. Yet its provisions mostly apply to the types of illnesses characteristic of an earlier phase of life. If we set out to provide medical insurance for old people, why do they now pay twice as much as do younger people and more than they did before Medicare was enacted? The answer to that question will be addressed later; suffice it to say here that the political compromise alluded to before is largely responsible. What is the effect of being treated as medically indigent to receive Medicaid benefits? What happens to people's self-concepts if they have to request (or beg) for treatment and an attending physician demurs saying he or she does not accept Medicare or Medicaid patients? How would it make you feel to be told that nursing visits are no longer possible and your only choice is institutionalization? What about the effect of being set apart (or perhaps aside) as a special group or category of the disadvantaged? All of these and other questions must be considered. It makes little sense to discuss the adjustment and life satisfaction of individuals without looking at the social context in which policies are formulated and implemented. Indeed, the ambivalences of social policy are well captured in the phrase "the philanthropic ogre" (Guillemard, 1983). Social policies legitimize a particular perspective on and an approach to the life situations of the elderly; each then needs to be examined closely.

## METAPOLICY AND THE ELDERLY

When we look at social policies for the aged, we need to remember that it is a mistake to see policies as a series of disjointed and disjunctive service strategies. Instead, they result from negotiated decisions involving a variety of interest groups; policy may be by omission and by intention. If there does not appear to be any overarching integration of the diverse programmatic regulations aimed at older people, we should not be too quick to conclude it is only an oversight. To make sense of policies we must look at their formulation, purpose, function, and place in the context of the larger culture.

Another point to consider is that in the free market economies of the West two general patterns characterize the welfare state. In many European countries a "cradle-to-grave" approach is common — within it social policies are designed to shift the focus slightly with each passing threshold, but intended to provide coverage throughout life for all kinds of difficulties. In the United States we have adhered to what is labeled a "risk-by-risk" strategy. The aim is to deal with one problem at a time by specific entitlement, categorical assistance, and administrative regulations. What is seen as a problem in other countries and covered under the cradle-to-grave formula may not be acknowledged in the risk-by-risk design (Bell, 1983).

**The Web of Metapolicy.** In a recent review of factors affecting conditions underlying the development of age-based social policies — what we here call metapolicy considerations — Hudson and Strate (1985) identify a complex of six interrelated components operating in the policy-making process. First, the impact of industrialization and the economic and ecological changes it brought have generated both resources and displacements that prompted state involvement. Second, the values and ideologies we have already referred to legitimate both a political culture — the proper role of government — and a political structure of administrative bureaus and divisions charged with overseeing particular issues. Third, public input and demands call forth the development of certain types of programs and protections; that is, constituencies develop as a result of earlier efforts in policy and these perpetuate efforts in a given direction. The public may be defined and characterized as age-based groups, individuals, bureaucrats, or professional groups. Fourth, political elites have an effect on policies through their efforts to nurture a favored project or their desire to promote an image of concern for particular groups and issues. These reformers and advocates provide ideas, guidance, and energy to forge policies. They need not, however, be individuals, though they often are. Corporations, collective elite organizations, or professional organizations can also perform the role and they often prompt a more rapid response from policymakers. Fifth, as a consequence of an incrementalist approach to most reform, existing policies, laws, and programs frame the direction subsequent efforts will take. Finally, what Hudson and Strate term "concentrated capital" — the interrelationship between the forces and principles of free market economies and social or state intervention policies — shape the form future policies are likely to take. We earlier referred to such a view under the rubric of political economy, an analysis that attempts to unravel the impact of our capitalist system on our ideology of social policies. We noted that the focus on individualist factors is in keeping with the general thrust of a laissez-faire economic model, although this may actually be merely diverting attention from the structural factors.

**Setting the Agenda of Public Policy.** How is the agenda for social policy established? Who decides which problems we will direct our collective attention to and how? Since government cannot possibly do everything, what factors channel the process of problem selection? In their discussion of agenda building, Elder and Cobb (1984) point out that the decision-making process is highly variable and contextual. They reiterate Cohen and March's (1974) contention that decisions reflect *people*, *problems*, *solutions*, and *choice opportunities*. Who and what are involved are key elements; their time, motivation, resources, and persuasiveness define the nature of the problems, which in turn points the way toward solutions. An agenda does not develop by chance. In a pluralistic society such as the United States the influence of opinion makers reflects the differential access to power and influence. Unfortunately, not all who seek to have an item placed on the agenda are equally powerful. Those who win — at least for the moment — define the problems and limit the solutions. What is commonly termed interest group politics is said by many analysts to shape the social policy agenda. Naturally, those groups will want to protect their own interests while appearing to construct policies favorable to all parties. Hence there will sometimes be a conflict between their stated policy orientations and the metapolicy informing them. To preserve their aims they may try to accommodate other actors in the process and cast programs as an eqalitarian ideology (Ripley and Franklin, 1984).

As new issues emerge the policy agenda may be subdivided, with the forum for discussion allocated to one or another existing administrative unit. The *solutions* offered will be defined in terms of the primary concerns of that unit and may not address the larger question of how the problem originally emerged. Typically, issues or problems not in keeping with the mandate of the agency to which they are sent will face what Elder and Cobb (1984) describe as formidable obstacles to commanding a place on the formal agenda. It is even possible that collective or individual actors may promote an issue on the agenda for proprietary reasons, either out of concern for a constituency or for personal and professional motives. These may work to the advantage of the beneficiaries of the policy; however, the two should not automatically be assumed to be synonymous. Just as proprietary interests work in agenda building, they also function in the solutions offered. Solutions are actually already contained in the definition of the problem; the two are inseparable.

**Choice Opportunities.** By choice opportunities Elder and Cobb (1984) mean the commitments already made and the prospects of the receptivity of new proposals in terms of these commitments. An example of a choice opportunity can be seen in the general political orientation of a given presidential administration. For example, most would agree that it would not have been a good time to bring up the issues of national health insurance during Reagan's presidency, no matter how pressing the issues were. Another choice opportunity might arise from legislation sought by a powerful coalition to piggyback a second program through the bureaucratic labyrinth all policy must negotiate before acceptance.

Obviously, this is not the only model for analyzing how policies are implemented. Policy analysts have advanced many other frameworks for making sense of the process. Nevertheless, it is a useful template for discussion of specific policies and legal mandates for older people. Following an overview of Social Security, pensions, health, and related legal provisions, we will briefly return to our analytic framework to refine its implications for the material we have reviewed.

# Fiscal Policies and the Elderly

## SOCIAL SECURITY

**Phase One: Implementation.** In the United States the advent of publicly supported old age assistance programs occurred later than in most European countries. Although the core values that would ultimately be incorporated in various old age policies were firmly in place by the 1920s, they were not implemented until the country was faced with the economic hardships of the Depression, declines in productivity, and what was viewed as a stagnating labor force (Achenbaum, 1983; Graebner, 1980). Widely hailed as a panacea, the enactment of Social Security can fairly be said to be a critical moment in the accretion of categorical programs for the elderly. Overcoming the opposition of conservatives, the Roosevelt administration sought a collectivist approach to the resolution of a national crisis. The quandary was how to retain the normative values on which the country claimed to be founded — free enterprise and rugged individualism — and yet effect a major restructuring of the government's role in people's lives.

With its passage, Social Security initiated a new and dynamic relationship between public, private, and individual welfare (Achenbaum, 1983). In one legislative act, individuals were provided with a goal toward which they could work throughout their lives. Furthermore, that goal was cast and perceived to be a right or entitlement derived from people's participation in the free enterprise system. To preserve the importance of self-sufficiency the benefits received after retirement were defined as a right for those who had paid their dues and not a form of charity. At the same time employers were relieved of corporate responsibility for the economic well-being of workers released because of age. Corporate interests gained in another way, as the federal government assumed the collection, management, and disbursement responsibilities for the operation of Social Security. At a time when the United States had more workers than jobs, when stagnation had stopped the expansion of production, and private enterprise was in need of development capital and a stable labor force, a better solution could not have been found. In assuming collective responsibility the public sector took on a new role and became altruistic at the same time. A true new deal had been forged, one that enlarged the role of government, tied its policies firmly to private sector economics, and moved the personal hardships of individuals into the public arena. The welfare state and welfare capitalism had been launched in the United States.

Our historical hindsight provides a different perspective on the way in which this national intervention was received. With the 1935 Social Security Act, the United States joined Western Europe in legislating the needs of individuals and in assuring them of minimal public support for their subsistence. As always, however, politics became involved. Not only did a number of political compromises alter the original proposal, but the initial Title I of the act providing for Old Age Assistance (the means-tested income or welfare portion [OAA] was kept distinct from old age insurance [OAI] or what we now think of as Social Security) left it to each of the states to set the amounts and conditions of coverage rather than devising a uniform national code. Even so, it took a court decision before all the states affiliated with the federal government complied with the legislation. Seven states interpreted the federal law as a violation of their state's rights and preferred to retain their own poor law customs in deciding what was appropriate relief among the disadvantaged and the elderly. Interestingly, Roosevelt's Advisory Committee on Economic Security, composed of industrialists, urged a strong federal role. They fought for as much centralized control as possible to keep circumvention, competition, and economic gain among employers from destroying the viability of the program (Quadagno, 1984). They also waged and won a last-minute battle to set up the Social Security trust fund as opposed to the earlier plan to fund benefits out of general revenues. Another interesting stipulation Roosevelt was lobbied to include was the control over old age assistance benefit levels so that they would not be out of step with the minimum wage and thereby create worker unrest. The committee also convinced Roosevelt to add individualized benefits based on previous earnings rather than provide a general retirement wage.

Despite the opposition of states' rights advocates and some conservative groups, the prevailing climate during the Depression was one of interest-group liberalism. The effect was that the federal government appropriated to itself guardianship over the individual's rights and security by means of categorical legislation. The steps taken to protect not only the elderly but also the rest of the labor force — and the two facets of Social Security cannot be separated — were incrementalist; nonetheless, it ushered in a new era. It should not be too surprising that not all workers received the immediate benefits of Social Security coverage; the political infighting behind the public facade was fierce. In the beginning only 60 percent of the work force was employed in occupations and industries included under Social Security. Nor were these sheltered individuals randomly distributed. Marginal occupations not considered essential to macroeconomic well-being were left out. Even today certain categories of workers remain excluded or are insured under alternate federal civil service or state plans. As the economic turmoil surrounding Social Security in the mid-1980s has demonstrated, new groups of workers are now brought in to bolster the trust fund as much as to alleviate inequalities. Then and now, according to Achenbaum (1983) and others, the same people who were subject to racial and other forms of discrimination in social and public life, as well as in the workplace, find themselves on the outside. Seasonal workers, those employed in service occupations, or others whose jobs are characteristically discontinuous were not and are not now covered. The original act was also fairly conservative in other respects. For example, it offered no insurance against occupational disabilities forcing early retirement.

An interesting footnote to the original congressional and administrative debates was the push by many to have sixty set as the official retirement age to deal with the large-scale unemployment problem for workers between sixty and sixty-five. According to Senator Robert Wagner (quoted in Graebner, 1980), this will make "new places for the strong and eager, and will increase the productivity of the young by removing from their shoulders the uneven burden of caring for the old." The Committee on Economic Security objected for labor market reasons, saying it would be too expensive and would do little to alleviate unemployment. Wagner, the consummate liberal, attempted to convince his colleagues in the Senate by pointing out the extent to which old age payments would diffuse purchasing power and thus spur the economy (Graebner, 1980).

By 1939 the insularity of the adequacy of Title I (OAA) and the equity of Title II (OAI) provisions had begun to cause problems. Part of the original compromise had been to leave it to the states to determine what an adequate retirement income was for the indigent elderly — a provision that led to a tenfold disparity in benefits. Other issues had also arisen, such as the political quandary posed by the economics of funding the Social Security trust and the payment of survivors' annuities for spouses and dependents. As amended in 1939, Social Security sought to bring about a closer correspondence between adequacy and equity while assuring dependents of retired workers that coverage would be continued in the event of the wage earner's death. Then Secretary of the Treasury Morgenthau also pushed through the de facto practice of putting Social Security on a pay-as-you-go basis. He implemented higher benefits and expanded the system by "blanketing in" new workers who could claim benefits though they had not previously paid into the system without raising withholding taxes (Achenbaum, 1983; Freeman and Adams, 1982).

During the war years of the early 1940s many of the controversies over Social Security died down as the war economy improved the financial well-being of many workers. A number of amendments were proposed, but with the distractions and the boom times of the war, they were met with little positive reaction. For example, the Wagner-Murry-Dingell bill was introduced and voted down. It was an attempt to acknowledge a debt to agriculture for its part in the war effort and sought to include domestic and farm workers under Social Security and to provide a form of health insurance to all recipients. The political climate at the time maintained that the war economy seemed to be doing the job by providing full employment for everyone; thus, no amendments nor expansions were deemed necessary or appropriate under the circumstances.

**Phase Two: Expansion.** In the twenty-year interval following the end of World War II the Social Security Act was amended five times. With each revision, additional occupations were incorporated, cost-contributing formulas were rewritten, disability benefits were finally added in 1956, and the relative importance of Title I and Title II shifted as more retiring workers began receiving benefits under the insurance provisions. Missing from these revisions was any attempt to include work incentives. The 1960 amendments implemented an earnings test whereby Social Security benefits were reduced by fifty cents for every dollar earned up to $1500 and dollar for dollar beyond that amount. This was actually a disincentive to seek partial employment once Social Security benefits were claimed. Furthermore, under the original Title VIII, such earnings would be subject to the usual array of taxes, including Social Security, but would not be factored into the determination of benefit levels. The early retirement provisions implemented with the 1956 changes, in the face of a recession, allowed women to retire early on reduced benefits between sixty-two and sixty-four; men were given the same option in 1961. In both cases the policy basis for the age reductions sprang from the hope that unemployment levels among older workers would be reduced.

Beginning with the revisions of 1950, benefit levels were increased, and in 1972 the act was rewritten to include automatic adjustments for inflation. With dramatic increases in the number of workers contributing to the system, the modest appreciation in the number claiming benefits and the adjustment of those benefits did not cause alarm. Employers were also content; there was a general acceptance of their claim that their portion of the contribution was actually a fringe benefit accruing to workers. Furthermore, their contribution was used to reduce taxable revenues. By raising Social Security levels corporations that under collective bargaining agreements had promised larger benefits on private pension plans to bring workers up to predetermined levels, could save money by claiming a type of co-insurance and thus pay reduced private benefits. As the economy continued to expand, despite slight modulations, concerns over the adequacy of coverage or the importance of a retirement wage were seldom discussed in public (Myles, 1984; Graebner, 1980).

The situation for the elderly was beginning to look better. Within a seven-year period, two major pieces of legislation moved their concerns to the fore. The 1965 passage of omnibus Older Americans legislation and the 1972 amendments to Social Security wrought a number of significant changes. If there have been any glory years in the recognition of the needs of older citizens, it was during this period. The Older Americans Act and related legislation brought guaranteed medical insurance and a number of other benefits to the elderly for the first time. The 1972 revisions to Social Security not only linked benefit levels to the Consumer Price Index (CPI), thus maintaining stable income replacement rates, but it rewrote the original Title I Old Age Assistance Program to provide a nationalized public assistance plan known as Supplemental Security Income (SSI). SSI was expressly designed to meet the needs of the aged and all blind and disabled individuals unable to work. SSI now has two components: a basic federal payment and an optional state supplement. All those who fall into these categories and have incomes below specified thresholds, have no assets or other sources of support, and meet certain residency requirements, in effect, have a guaranteed annual income.

**Phase Three: Retrenchment.** No sooner were these various reforms implemented than a crisis was declared: in the years since the 1973 publication of long-range deficit projections in the Social Security budget, our national social policies for the elderly have been characterized by brinksmanship politics. The solutions came too little or too late in the view of many and certainly were rarely prospective. Retirement had become too costly. It was time to revise the ideology again: what had been hailed as a right and an opportunity for leisure had to be recast. Because retirement had become mandatory in the public definition of social policy, the reform often rationalized that the changes were made in the interests of personal freedom. In the 1970s there were accelerating retrenchments in federal policies, and even the elderly were blamed either for not having saved for the future or for their overreliance on once mandated services. Short-range or long-range, real or not, the crisis thought to exist in the provision of basic support to older persons in the United States has promulgated an attitude likely to affect all social policies for the elderly (Myles, 1984; Freeman and Adams, 1982; Graebner, 1980).

During the mid-1970s the primary focus of public concern was on adequate financing but within the framework of preserving the Social Security trust fund. Though these monies could be used only to pay benefits, they could not be augmented by general revenues. In keeping with the incrementalist approach and staying within the bounds of policy as precedent, how could the fiscal situation be improved without sacrificing benefits? Benefits had recently been indexed, although in an ill-informed way to the CPI, so it was not politically propitious to revoke these provisions, nor could any of the add-on benefits that had been attached to Social Security over the years be tampered with. The alternative was to raise payroll taxes and the wage ceiling on which the tax rate was based by relatively small amounts. In President Carter's administration there was some talk of using general revenue funds as a stopgap measure during cycles of high unemployment. Despite wide agreement that the payroll tax was actually regressive, affecting the lower paid workers the hardest and actually costing employees when the employers shared increases, the option of increasing the tax was preferred to using general revenues. General revenues were thought likely to increase political demands and prompt even further expansion of the program, thereby causing many associated problems. By avoiding a commingling of monies the deficit problem could be discussed within a closed forum, the existing Social Security trust fund.

Having run into a political impasse, President Carter eventually approved an increase of taxable wages. It was put on a sliding scale from the 1978 rate of 6.05 percent to a 1990 rate of 7.85 percent. The wage base would move up at the same time. By 1981 it was to be $29,700, and by 1990 it is scheduled to be even higher. Exactly how high taxable income would rise was to be determined on the basis of average wages. Obviously, the political climate had changed as a result of the funding shortfalls and the wrangling over resolution. In Reagan's administration there was an even greater shift toward issues of cost containment at the expense of adequacy for recipients. In Congress and in committee meetings it was noted that nationwide economic difficulties, unemployment, the shrinking of the export market, and the relative slowing in the gross national product (GNP) were all serious and were implicated in the shrinking public benefits. The public rhetoric, however, continued to focus on those who received benefits. By 1983 the inviolable status of benefit levels had been breached and the amendments of that year were designed to ensure solvency over the next seventy-five years by reducing benefits, raising the taxable ceiling and the rate of taxation, and enlarging the number of covered occupations still further. In addition, after the year 2000 the retirement age will officially become sixty-seven.

Social Security obviously did not disappear from the political agenda. In every session of Congress new amendments have been introduced. In between sessions the administration has also suggested additional cutbacks and directed much of its political rhetoric to the need to further reduce not only benefits, but the government's involvement in the economic well-being of older citizens. Currently the debate is over eliminating minimum benefit levels, dependent student benefits, certain disability allowances, changes in the monthly formula for benefits, and so on. Perhaps most important the autonomy of Social Security was abolished and it is now considered as part of the total national budget.

Actually, the lower birth rates of the late 1920s and the 1930s will mean fewer retirees during the 1990s; thus, work-to-retiree ratios will stabilize and adequate monies should be available. None of these changes has apparently considered the reductions in the current birth rate, which means fewer dependents will be on the younger end of the age continuum. The real crunch will come only when the baby boom generation begins to retire. As yet unrealized birth rates and changes in the GNP will also affect what happens then (Munnell, 1984; Freeman and Adams, 1982).

The latest figures and regulations available are shown in Tables 11.1 and 11.2. As a result of frequent congressional action, the actual dollar amounts and taxation components may change annually. On reaching sixty-five, workers who have been employed for the requisite number of quarters in covered occupations — at last count some 95 percent of all occupations were included — may begin drawing full Social Security benefits. No one is required to earn more than forty quarters to be entitled to full benefits. Since benefit rates, however, are based on the indexed amount of earnings, those with longer employment histories and higher earnings receive higher benefits. Those who continue working after sixty-five are eligible for still higher benefits when they retire. Those who retire early must take a lifelong reduction in benefit rates. The effects of

**TABLE 11.1**

Social Security at a Glance, 1985

Number of Recipients: 35.2 million, including nearly 11.0 million spouse, children, and survivor beneficiaries

Withholding Rate:

| | **Of Employee Wages Employers and Employees Will Each Pay** |
|---|---|
| 1985 | 7.05% |
| 1986–1987 | 7.15% |
| 1988–1989 | 7.51% |
| 1990 and later | 7.65% |

- The "wage base" (maximum amount of earnings on which Social Security taxes are paid) is $39,600 in 1985. Figure is adjusted annually as earnings levels rise.
- The rate for self-employed persons in 1985 is 14.10%. But self-employed persons get a tax credit of 2.3%, so the effective rate is 11.8%. The credit will be 2.0% for 1986–1989. After 1989, these credits will be replaced with deductions designed to treat the self-employed much like employees and employers are treated for Social Security and income tax purposes.

Projected Payments: $171.1 billion in retirement
$ 18.1 billion in disability

| Maximum Benefits: 1985 | | Average Benefits: 1985 | |
|---|---|---|---|
| Retired worker, sixty-five | $ 718/mo | Single worker | $449/mo |
| Retired worker, sixty-two | $ 574/mo ($718 less 20%) | Couple | $776/mo |
| Couple and spouse, sixty-five | $1077/mo ($718 plus 50%) | Widow | $415/mo |
| Couple, worker, and spouse, sixty-two | $ 843/mo ($718 less 20% plus $359 less 25%) | Men | $495/mo |
| | | Women | $379/mo |

**Effects of Retirement Time on Benefit Rates**

- If workers work past the full benefit retirement age, monthly benefits are increased by 3 percent for each year that the worker does not draw benefits. Starting in 1990, the credit will be gradually increased until it reaches 8 percent in 2008.
- If workers draw benefits prior to 65, benefit rates are permanently reduced according to the following schedule (reduction months = number of months worker receives benefit before reaching sixty-five):

| Reduction Months | Reduction Factor | Reduction Months | Reduction Factor | Reduction Months | Reduction Factor |
|---|---|---|---|---|---|
| 1 | .994 | 13 | .928 | 25 | .861 |
| 2 | .989 | 14 | .922 | 26 | .856 |
| 3 | .983 | 15 | .917 | 27 | .850 |
| 4 | .978 | 16 | .911 | 28 | .844 |
| 5 | .972 | 17 | .906 | 29 | .839 |
| 6 | .967 | 18 | .900 | 30 | .833 |
| 7 | .961 | 19 | .894 | 31 | .828 |
| 8 | .956 | 20 | .889 | 32 | .822 |
| 9 | .950 | 21 | .883 | 33 | .817 |
| 10 | .944 | 22 | .878 | 34 | .811 |
| 11 | .939 | 23 | .872 | 35 | .806 |
| 12 | .933 | 24 | .867 | 36 | .800 |

**TABLE 11.1, cont'd**
Social Security at a Glance, 1985

**Effect Of Work and Other Income and Taxes on Social Security Benefits**

- If a person receiving Social Security Benefits works . . .
  *In 1985*, full benefits will be received if:

| Age | Amount of Earnings |
|---|---|
| Under 65 | $5400 or less |
| 65–70 | $7320 or less |
| Over 70 | No limit |

$1 will be deducted for every $2 above the exempt amount.

*Starting in 1990*, $1 in benefits will be withheld for each $3 in earnings above the annual limit for persons sixty-five and over.

- Taxes: Effective as of 1984 (paid in 1985) up to one-half of Social Security benefits may be subject to federal income tax for any year in which a person's adjusted gross income plus nontaxable interest income and one-half of Social Security benefits exceeds a base amount of $25,000 for individuals and $32,000 for couples.

additional earnings and new taxes on Social Security benefits are summarized in Tables 11.1 and 11.2.

## THE FUTURE OF SOCIAL SECURITY

To date much of the discussion emanating out of Washington, D.C., and from critics of Social Security has focused on the economic crisis of the system. The political volatility of the issue has brought a new set of actors into the debate, often as surrogates during the close infighting. In the past decade not only has the Department of Treasury issued its own technical documents, but the Office of Management and Budget (OMB) has entered the fray, often circulating its own financial projections that are beyond the grasp of all but the most expert. When Social Security is discussed on the evening news, it is frequently within the context of congressional testimony and shows OMB personnel presenting dire predictions of the impending fiscal instability. Interestingly, no one ever asks why other federal expenditures are not held to the same solvency requirements as are Social Security and Medicare. Yet, other than talking about social justice, the countervailing opinion has not yet been well presented (Freeman and Adams, 1982).

The terms of the debate have so far been set by pessimists, but are there other issues that ought to be considered? In an insightful review of the Social Security issues the Gerontological Society of America (in press) has attempted to broaden the focus. In combating the concept of intergenerational conflict the report goes to great length to point out that funds allocated to the elderly benefit all segments of the population and the economy. It also reiterates the point we have stressed — we will all be old before long. We may criticize benefit levels now, but when it is our turn, will we want to live under the strictures that present reductions will impose? Furthermore, if collective funds are not

**TABLE 11.2**

Supplemental Security Income at a Glance

Number of recipients: January, 1985

> 3.9 million receiving SSI
> 1.34 million age 65+
> 940,000 age 65+ receiving both SS and SSI
> 580,000 age 65+ receiving state supplement to SSI (16 states and District of Columbia supplement SSI payments)

**Eligibility**

*Basic eligibility under aged category*

> Sixty-five or older
> Residents of United States or possessions
> U.S. citizen or immigrant lawfully admitted for permanent residence

*Income eligibility 1985 (adjusted annually)*

| | | |
|---|---|---|
| Single | Below $325/mo* | First $20 of income not counted |
| Couple | Below $488/mo | |

*Resource eligibility 1985*

| | | |
|---|---|---|
| Single | $1600 | (Will increase each year through 1989 by $100 and $150 |
| Couple | $2400 | for single and couple, respectively) |

Gifts and inheritance must be counted as income and reported.

Major exclusions: (1) One's primary residence
(2) $4500 fair market value of auto
(3) In-kind assistance (through 1987)
(4) $2000 of equity value for household goods and personal effects

*Income eligibility figure for a single person is only 75 percent that of the poverty limit for an older person living alone ($5234).

used to support those elderly in need, from where will such support come? The answer is obvious to every person who has older relatives, or most of us. For those who have no younger family on which they can rely, the potential is a life beset by hardship. True, some of the elderly are solvent and could live without their Social Security, but it is a false assumption to suggest that as a group the elderly can absorb cutbacks without ill-effects.

In keeping with the tendency to treat the elderly as a unified category there has been little, if any, talk of limiting public benefits for persons whose incomes are three or four times higher than the poverty level. Instead, the cutbacks are aimed at the general population of the elderly, including those minorities, women, and others who reach old age already economically disadvantaged and who must rely heavily on the Social Security benefits they receive. For the old-old group of the elderly, regardless of their social and historical diversity, such reductions would be particularly devastating. Despite much talk to the contrary, even the cutbacks are regressive, especially affecting those who have the most limited incomes. At present nearly one-sixth of the older population lives below the poverty level. Apart from whether that figure is acceptable, one question remains: do we want to plunge another one-half or three-quarters of a million old people into poverty by freezing cost of living adjustments? Additional recessions would be even more detrimental; up to one-half of the elderly could end up in poverty if the worst possible scenario, the total abolition of the system, came to pass.

Critics have responded by saying that true as these figures may be, it is not any more fair either to shortchange high-income persons by making them pay more or children by concentrating public expenditures on the old (Preston, 1984). As far as it goes, the argument sounds reasonable; it makes no mention, however, of the tax benefits that accrue to the rich. Neither does it discuss the benefits bestowed on the young by those who preceded them in the nation's development. Similarly ignored is that some estimates have placed the cost of raising a child to independence at twenty some 25 to 33 percent higher than supporting a person from sixty until he or she dies (Myles, 1984; GSA, in press).

Because the debate has concentrated on direct expenditures, such as Social Security and Medicare, the impact of tax preference and relief programs has been neglected. Yet these are also a form of social welfare policy designed for certain interest groups to achieve some defined objective. In his review of tax expenditures Nelson (1983) cites exclusions, exemptions, deductions, preferential rates, tax credits, and deferrals as examples of public policies contained in the Tax Code. He found that the combined effect of these policies annually targeted tens of billions of dollars in benefits for the wealthiest old. Before we begin to chip away at direct expenditures, perhaps this aspect of our fiscal policy deserves more attention — especially considering that the tax expenditures allocated to the wealthy elderly have and will continue to rise, if present trends are not altered, at an annual rate of $23.2 billion in 1986. The bulk of the increases will come from subsidies to employer and self-employed private pension schemes. From the evidence the U.S. Senate Committee on the Budget (1982) has presented, it would be fair to say that the affluent elderly are doing well financially. If it were possible to redistribute their tax advantages among all of the elderly, poverty would be eliminated (Nelson, 1983). It is apparent that despite the growth in public sector spending and federal revenue policies, the market-based income distribution in the United States has been relatively unaltered in the years since World War II (Devine, 1983).

Difficult as it might be to measure the intangibles of societal development from which younger people profit, if only in terms of productivity and life expectancy, neither should they be ignored. Underpinning not only the economic argument but also the benefits received by different cohorts of people is the issue of fairness — that most central of American values. If we move the discussion into values and beyond the scope of what has already been introduced, the issues become even more problematic. We end up having to ask just what is it that the country supposedly stands for and if we are willing to change that. The difficulty with categorical age-based policies is that they do not incorporate the varieties of need levels within each category. Just as we pride ourselves on our compassion, so, too, should we pride ourselves on our ability to discriminate needs (Binstock, 1985).

## SUPPLEMENTAL SECURITY INCOME

Up to the mid-1980s SSI had avoided being the subject of major political controversies at the national level. All that began to change in 1984 when SSI was the subject of considerable congressional attention. Its 3.9 million recipients were faced with new requirements, stricter limits on earnings in the means test, and many other restrictions imposed by the Deficit Reduction Act of that year. Among the individual states, reductions in SSI, like Medicaid, are frequently seen as a way to hedge against the inflationary spiral eroding the state budget. Since its inception in 1972 as Title XVI of the Social Security Act, it has functioned as a catch-all welfare provision for aged, blind, and disabled persons who either do not receive Social Security or who fall below minimal income thresholds. In 1984 slightly over one-half of all eligible low-income elderly (3.9 million) participated in the program, and funds allocated for their welfare amounted to $9 billion drawn from general revenues (U.S. Senate, 1985). From the outset both federal and state monies were pooled to make payments in a given locale, but in the past few years the proportion that the states contribute has been shrinking. Though the federal contribution is established by law, local discretion is permitted in setting state supplements. In 1980 eight states provided no supplement. Among the other states there was a threefold discrepancy in the amounts distributed in 1983. The obvious result is state-determined inequalities even when the cost of living is controlled.

The payment mechanism can either be administered by the state or left to the federal government. Exactly half of the states have chosen to administer it themselves to have closer control of recipient eligibility. The way the law is written older people are forced to live on their own, not with friends or relatives, or face losing up to one-third of their benefits. Even with full benefits, the payment does not rise above poverty level subsistence for many elderly, as pointed out earlier. It is ironic that in sixteen states the eligibility requirements for Medicaid are more stringent than for SSI (Harrington, 1983). In an effort to control costs Congress has considered the option of canceling cost of living allowances (COLA) and in 1985 is seriously discussing freezes in 1986. If this occurs, individual benefits will be reduced 3 or 4 percent or an amount equal to the increase in the 1985 CPI. It would also decrease the base on which subsequent COLAs are calculated (U.S. Senate Special Committee on Aging, 1985a). Seemingly, the burden of balancing the federal budget is being levied on the segment of the population that has the least to contribute.

## PRIVATE PENSION PROVISIONS

In the more than 100 years since the American Express company offered the first private pension plan, pensions have had a checkered history. Until the Employee Retirement Income Security Act (ERISA) of 1974 and the establishment of a federally insured Pension Benefit Guarantee Corporation to guarantee payments, the rate of return on funds invested in private pension plans was abysmal. In 1973 then Secretary of Labor James Schulz testified before the Senate that the vagaries of pension coverage made for rather long odds of anybody ever actually receiving any return on their contributions (U.S. Senate Special Committee on Aging, 1973). To improve the situation and the financial situation for the elderly the government stepped in to regulate private pensions.

Private pensions are a big business. There are over 50,000 individual plans, and by 1984 they amounted to the single largest pool of capital in the United States, having reached over $900 billion. These monies are invested in market enterprises and capital development under guidelines of "prudent" fiduciary responsibility written into the 1974 ERISA legislation. So important have they become for business that Drucker (1976) refers to "pension fund socialism" to describe their role in the marketplace. Yet how funds are invested and what interest rates are returned to the pension are hotly debated issues and many problems remain. Management is another troublesome area; between 1980 and 1982 private pension funds were abandoned at a record rate, placing an inordinate burden on federal insurance protection. Yet, with less than half of all workers covered by private pensions, the federal government has been reluctant to set policing and monitoring requirements too stringently to avoid discouraging new plans. For funds that perform well, a loophole in the law permits windfall profits to go to the sponsoring company and not to individual beneficiaries. At present such surpluses total over $1.1 billion; clearly, a share of this needs to find its way to those who draw benefits (Hendricks and Calasanti, in press; Keller, 1984).

For the employee who is covered and receives an annuity in addition to Social Security payments, replacement levels are between 60 and 75 percent of prior earnings. Despite federal regulations, half of the workers covered are not vested and are thus at risk either because of changing jobs or from the poor performance of their pension plans. ERISA now mandates that an employee's pension be fully vested after ten years, even if employment is later severed. Nearly 70 percent of workers over fifty are now protected by federal legislation. State and local governmental pensions, however, are not protected under the law.

Another gap in pension income adequacy affects women particularly strongly, since their work histories have traditionally been discontinuous. They are also concentrated in the service and retail sectors of the economy where private pensions are not widespread and salaries are relatively low. The Retirement Equity Act (REA) of 1984 was designed to remedy these inadequacies by improving survivor protection, to ensure a liberalizing of ERISA standards taking into account discontinuous work patterns by providing new break-in service rules and by clarifying the treatment of pension benefits after a divorce. Despite these efforts it is difficult, as the U.S. Senate Special Committee on Aging (1985) itself notes, to avoid the conclusion that these and related concerns remain a relatively low priority among policymakers and political representatives.

## INDIVIDUAL RETIREMENT ACCOUNTS

The Individual Retirement Account (IRA) program was established originally in 1975 as a tax-favored saving procedure to permit workers who were not otherwise covered by private pension plans to save for their retirement. In 1981, as part of a policy to stimulate national economic growth by expanding savings to finance business purchases of plants and equipment (U.S. Senate Special Committee on Aging, 1982), the law was changed to encourage all workers and their nonworking spouses to institute their own tax sheltered annuities through savings or investment portfolios. President Nixon, in transmitting the original bill, described IRAs as a well-crafted way to reward and reinforce the finest elements of the American character — self-reliance, prudence, and independence. For those who have sufficient discretionary income to open an IRA the amounts invested are deducted from current earnings with taxes on both principal and interest deferred until the time of withdrawal after fifty-nine and before seventy. In 1985 individuals were permitted to invest up to $2000 with $4000 allowed to couples. At the end of 1984 less than 17 percent of the work force had started an IRA. As might be expected, IRA holders are primarily the higher paid: over 58 percent of those earning over $50,000 a year had established IRAs, but only 11 percent with incomes below $20,000 were participating. Nonetheless, the total pooled monies in various IRAs had reached $132 billion at the beginning of 1985, and Congress will probably enlarge the permitted amounts up to perhaps as much as $7000 for couples in the near future, since they have proved so popular with the middle class (Plutchok, 1985). Funds deposited or invested under IRAs are also being used to promote capital development by vendors directly or via loans to other private enterprises. An earlier sister program known as Keogh Plans provides coverage for the self-employed. Those who work for themselves may set aside tax deductible amounts of up to $15,000, or 15 percent of their incomes — whichever is less — and then withdraw monies under the same regulations that apply to IRAs.

## AGE DISCRIMINATION AND EMPLOYMENT

Economic adequacy in later life is closely tied to the question of age biases in the workplace. As the U.S. Senate Special Committee on Aging (1985) points out, beginning with the passage of Social Security, federal policies on employment have been directed at easing older workers out of the labor force. Private pensions entail a similar logic, with 90 percent offering incentives for early retirement. As pointed out in Chapter 8, employment rates begin to drop by middle age: only 70 percent of men between fifty-five and sixty-four are still active in the work force. Though penalties are imposed for drawing early benefits under Social Security, and incentives are geared to working past sixty-five, three-quarters of new claimants are younger than sixty-five. Inducements in some private sector industries brings the retirement age even lower.

Other factors besides voluntary withdrawal influence labor force participation. When forced out by discrimination, workers may have little choice but to retire and begin to draw public or private pensions. The quandary is how to forestall retirement with the heavy drain on Social Security monies and yet maximize employment opportunities for workers of all ages — including those in the earliest phase of their working lives. Though a number of value dimensions are involved, we will concentrate our attention here on policies against age discrimination.

The Age Discrimination in Employment Act (ADEA) took effect in 1968 with the avowed goal of promoting employment opportunities for older workers. From the time of Taylorism and the advent of efficiency studies in the workplace shortly before World War I, older workers have been discriminated against. Most researchers agree that no good evidence supports the belief that older workers are less productive or less able to do their jobs. They may have to be trained in new routines to retain their former skill levels, which costs money, but they can and do learn. Whether because of negative attitudes, industry-imposed job scheduling demands, or mandatory retirement justified by proclaimed mismatches between older workers' skills and job requirements, age bias in employment was deemed serious enough to require a national policy statement. The legislation, in effect, required employers to formulate ability protocols and to prohibit arbitrary age limits against workers between forty and seventy. There are certain exemptions, of course, but under the law cause has to be demonstrated for such a discharge. Amendments incorporated in 1978 brought coverage to state and local government employees and removed the upper age limit on federal workers. In 1982 the ADEA required employers to maintain fringe benefit packages for their workers over sixty-five rather than shift them to Medicare as had previously been done. This has been controversial, because it is a disincentive for the private sector in its attempt to preserve Medicare funds.

Mandatory retirement policies continue to exist outside of federal employment and are constantly being challenged in court. In 1984 over 13,000 charges were filed with the ADEA enforcement agency. In 1985 the Supreme Court struck down the use of chronological age as a criterion in hazardous occupations (firefighting) and may have allowed for even wider ranging challenges. The arguments for and against mandatory retirement continue to rage. Proponents argue about the predictability of timing, the preservation of personal dignity via categorical treatment, and opening job opportunities for younger workers, minorities, and women. Opponents suggest that retirement is associated with loss of status, loss of skills and experience for employers and employees, loss of income, and increased claims on Social Security or private pension programs (U.S. Senate Special Committee on Aging, 1985a).

As the Senate summary points out, the political dimensions of the debate are little concerned with the merits of the issue. Rather they focus on pragmatic issues centering on enforcement and awarding damages when discrimination is determined: costs for employers in the retention of older employees and questions of public safety. Another issue is whether pension benefits insured under ERISA should continue to accrue under the ADEA. Since 1978 the law says they are not, and only about half the ERISA protected plans do. Estimates suggest that if pensions continue to grow between sixty-five and seventy, another 50,000 workers would continue to work. Abolishing seventy as the mandatory retirement age would bring the total to 68,000 who stay on the job. The effect is to deprive individuals of additional benefits (albeit in exchange for salaries) and to protect employers and Social Security. Continuing to provide health insurance for employees between sixty-five and sixty-nine may cost up to $500 million, and smaller businesses might have difficulties finding insurance carriers. As the retirement age moves to sixty-seven and over after the year 2000, this argument will be irrelevant. In 1984 the enforcement of the ADEA was shifted from the Department of Labor to the Equal Opportunity Commission, which reversed the policy, began drafting clarifications, and in 1985 found its budget and mandate eroded under budgetary cuts and court challenges, although only sixty-three lawsuits were filed.

Despite the changes scheduled to take place at the end of the century concerning the official length of the work period, no slowing of the trend of full retirement is expected. Pressures emanating from private sector employers and changes in the nature of the work experience do not provide any reassurance that older workers will become any more active in the labor force. There are definite disincentives operating on the level of governmental policy voluntarily to delay retirement, but some labor analysts suggest the primary choice may not rest with the individual worker. The 1983 amendments to the Social Security Act may only prove that the same people will still be out of the work force but will have lower incomes and less recourse (U.S. Senate Special Committee on Aging, 1985).

# Health Care Policies and the Elderly

## DEVELOPMENT OF HEALTH CARE FOR THE AGED

The United States is unique in a number of respects, one being that it is the only industrialized country in the world without some form of national health insurance. While there is considerable heterogeneity in provisions among countries, in other industrialized nations it is generally true that health care provisions for the elderly are part of a cradle-to-grave system designed to provide health care for the entire population. In the United States we have constructed a hybrid system composed of various strategies that segments health care provisions for various sectors of the population. Enacted in 1965 as Title XVIII of the Social Security Act, Medicare is based on a social insurance model designed partially to offset the cost of health care for the elderly and some of the disabled. It was carefully designed to keep the fee-for-service principle intact and to permit the medical profession to retain control over the distribution and access to medical care. Medicaid, a public assistance program, is aimed at the indigent. Health care for the remainder of the population is based on private third-party insurance. Most private third-party payments plans draw heavily on market models of fee-for-service. There is, however, some overlap between payment systems for the elderly, notably in the case of Medi-gap insurance programs — a new sector of the insurance industry — and recent market-based approaches to Medicare cost control.

The passage of Medicare and Medicaid legislation came about only after a long struggle. The American Medical Association and a number of affiliated groups spent over $50 million lobbying against a bill that underwent more than eighty revisions from the time the initial proposal was introduced in 1957 to its final approval in 1965. The divisive political and social debate took its toll on the bill's provisions and has occupied the time and attention of all who have been concerned with health care in the intervening two decades. In large measure the conflict has focused on superficial accusations of "socialized medicine" by those who are concerned with proprietary medical care and new social demands vs those who are concerned with equal access. Actually, the struggle goes back over fifty years to when the idea was first broached in Congress. At every turn the course of the debate has been affected by changing historical and economic circumstances and the prevailing opinion of successive administrations.

By the turn of the century national health plans had already been instituted in Europe. As early as 1883 the Sickness Insurance Act had been enacted in Germany to stem the rising tide of support for socialism among the German working classes. The National Health Insurance Act in Great Britain was passed by Lloyd George and the Liberal party in 1911. Pressures for some kind of public insurance system in the United States soon followed with the 1915–1918 campaign of the American Association for Labor legislation (Brown, 1984). The first serious legislative attempt by the administration to move toward national health insurance, however, came with the Social Security Act of 1935, which is generally regarded as the most important antecedent of Medicare and Medicaid. As passed into law, the act included minimal provisions for federal matching payments to states for medical expenses incurred by welfare recipients for whom assistance had hitherto been left to the states and localities (Estes et al., 1984). Initially, President Roosevelt had intended that the bill should include a suggestion that the new Social Security Board study the need for a government health insurance, but this provision was withdrawn in the face of strong opposition from the powerful medical profession. Since Roosevelt feared they might stop the entire bill, he declined to push for including medical protection.

Throughout the 1940s repeated attempts were made to establish a compulsory national health insurance program only to be defeated by the campaigns of the American Medical Association. The 1949 version of the Wagner-Murray-Dingell bill was personally endorsed by President Truman and backed by his advisers, the labor movement, and public opinion, if the polls are correct. The metapolicy underpinnings of this bill were based on a concern with equal access: the view that an individual's access to health care should not be determined by financial resources. As drafted the bill advocated a national insurance plan financed by a payroll tax and administered by a federal agency and would have covered all medical, dental, hospital, and nursing services for contributors and their dependents. It would have included subsidized protection of the poor and allowed freedom of participation by physicians and hospitals and free choice for patients and physicians. As a result of the strident opposition of the American Medical Association and fears of socialism, the proposal was defeated. Any serious hopes of getting national health legislation through Congress in the short run were also defeated. Bills were introduced through 1952, but with the rise of McCarthyism and the Korean War, public support had changed and the broad base of popular support for liberal political measures that had gathered force during the 1940s was dissipated (Brown, 1984).

A major factor in the ebb of popular support for national health insurance plans was the development of alternative provisions for health care that segmented the health care delivery interests of the population. The first hospital insurance plan — the pioneer for Blue Cross insurance — was introduced in 1929 by Baylor University Hospital in Dallas, Texas, in response to hospitals' needs for greater financial stability. During the same time the 1928–1931 study by the Committee on Costs of Medical Care reported that persons in upper-income families averaged one and a half times as many hospital admissions and twice as many physician visits each year as members of low- and moderate-income families. In response to the push toward compulsory national insurance that resulted from studies of this type, the American Medical Association and the American Hospital Association advocated expanding voluntary private insurance plans, such as the Blue Cross hospital plan and the Blue Shield plans primarily covering physicians' fees, as alternatives more representative of the American values of the freedom and self-reliance. Yet by 1940 less than 10 percent of the population was covered by private hospital insurance and far fewer for surgeons' and other physicians' fees. By 1950, however, 51 percent of the population had some form of private hospital insurance, and the spread of private insurance to unionized workers had undermined the support of labor for a national health plan (Brown, 1984).

Furthermore, there was an expanding tradition of separate categorical aid for the poor that would provide some relief to those who were unable to afford medical care without presenting a threat to the free enterprise system within medicine. The 1950 Social Security Amendments made limited federal matching funds available to the states to cover hospital, physician, and other medical care for public assistance recipients through vendor payments made directly by welfare agencies (Brown, 1984; Estes et al., 1984).

Given the growing visibility of the health care needs of the elderly in the late 1950s, there was a confrontation between those who, like Representative Aime Forand, favored a social insurance approach (limited hospital and surgical insurance for all of the aged financed by Social Security) and those like Representative Wilbur Mills and Senator Robert Kerr who favored a social welfare approach (public assistance for the indigent elderly financed by federal tax revenues). With the passage of the Kerr-Mills Act in 1960, the public assistance model won out at least for the moment. This act increased federal matching grants to states for vendor payments for medical care under Title I (OAA) of Social Security. It created a new category, the "medically needy" or "medically indigent" among the elderly who, while they might not meet eligibility requirements for cash assistance, were nonetheless too poor to pay their medical bills. Since participation by the states was voluntary and each state was free to set its own eligibility levels for financial and medical assistance, the segment of the population that benefited from the act varied widely from state to state. Furthermore, it carried with it the stigma that had come to be attached to the receipt of public assistance (Brown, 1984; Estes et al., 1984).

As noted earlier, the Medicare and Medicaid programs enacted into law in 1965 have continued to preserve the dichotomy between social insurance and public assistance. They are the result of a compromise, mediated by Wilbur Mills, Chairman of the Ways and Means Committee, between a number of competing proposals, including the King-Anderson bill that proposed to provide limited hospital insurance to all of the elderly and the welfare type Eldercare proposal of the American Medical Association that suggested providing a wide range of services administered by the states under a public assistance model. This compromise, as Mills explained, was deliberately designed to "build a fence around the Medicare program" by preempting future demands for liberalization and wider coverage by including the voluntary premium-supported physicians' insurance program under Medicare Part B (Brown, 1984). Actually, the legislative changes of 1984–1985 can be seen as an attempt to placate those who advocate tighter control and who are generally critical of the way the system operates.

## MEDICARE AND MEDICAID

The 1965 Social Security Amendments were signed into law by President Johnson in the presence of Harry Truman who, so many years before, had worked for compulsory health insurance for the entire population. Together Medicare (Title XVIII) and Medicaid (XIX) were designed to ensure health care for all the elderly, including the nonpoor. As we shall see, it was not long before the problems and the gaps in the implementation of this ideal became apparent.

Medicare is designed primarily as a federal social insurance program with benefits earned as a right by entitled persons under Social Security. It consists of two parts: Part A (Hospital Insurance or HI) and Part B (Medical Insurance or SMI), both of which contain deductibles, copayments, and exclusions. The current benefit structure under Medicare Parts A and B is shown in Table 11.3. There have been considerable alterations in benefits since the inception of Medicare in the mid-1960s, most notably in increasing deductibles and copayments for services. On the positive side, in response to increasing pressures for providing alternatives to institutionalization, there has been a liberalization of home health care benefits, with the elimination of the prior hospitalization re-

**TABLE 11.3**

Medicare Part A: Summary of Covered Services, 1985

**MEDICARE (PART A): HOSPITAL INSURANCE — COVERED SERVICES PER BENEFIT PERIOD (1)**

| Service | Benefit | Medicare Pays[a] | You Pay[b] |
|---|---|---|---|
| Hospitalization | First 60 days | All but $400 | $400 |
| Semiprivate room and | 61st to 90th day | All but $100 a day | $100 a day |
| board, general nursing and | 91st to 150th day[a] | All but $200 a day | $200 a day |
| miscellaneous hospital ser- | Beyond 150 days | Nothing | All costs |
| vices and supplies | | | |
| Posthospital skilled nurs- | First 20 days | 100% of approved | Nothing |
| ing facility care — in a | | amount | |
| facility approved by Medi- | Additional 80 days | All but $50 a day | $50 a day |
| care. You must have been | Beyond 100 days | Nothing | All costs |
| in a hospital for at least 3 | | | |
| days and enter the facility | | | |
| within 30 days after hos- | | | |
| pital discharge. (2) | | | |
| Home health care | Unlimited visits as medically neces- sary | Full cost | Nothing |
| Hospice care | Two 90-day periods and one 30-day period | All but limited costs for outpa- tient drugs and inpatient respite care | Limited cost sharing for out- patient drugs and inpatient respite care |
| Blood | Blood | All but first 3 pints | For first 3 pints |

[a]60 reserve days may be used only once; days used are not renewable.
[b]These figures are for 1985 and are subject to change each year.
(1) A benefit period begins on the first day you receive service as an inpatient in a hospital and ends after you have been out of the hospital or skilled nursing facility for 60 days in a row.
(2) Medicare and private insurance will not pay for most nursing home care. You pay for custodial care and most care in a nursing home.

quirement and of the one hundred-visit limit. Beginning in late 1983 Part A was expanded to cover hospice care for terminally ill Medicare participants (Gibson et al., 1984). In 1984 there were some 28 million elderly enrolled in Medicare Parts A and/or B, representing 96.5 percent of the population sixty-five and older. At a 1984 estimated cost of $63 billion, Medicare is second only to Social Security among domestic program expenditures.

As may be seen from Table 11.3, Part A (HI) provides limited coverage for hospital and posthospital nursing home expenditures and medically necessary home health care. It is financed by an increase in Social Security taxes that is paid into a special trust fund. Anyone who is eligible for Social Security (OAI) benefits is automatically covered by Medicare Part A. A number of exceptions are made for disabled persons over fifty, for those with chronic renal disease, and for those who do not qualify for OAI. Because it is financed by all working persons out of mandatory Social Security taxes, it may be considered compul-

**TABLE 11.3, cont'd**

Medicare Part B: Summary of Covered Services, 1985

**MEDICARE (PART B): MEDICAL INSURANCE — COVERED SERVICES PER CALENDAR YEAR**

| Service | Benefit | Medicare Pays | You Pay |
|---|---|---|---|
| Medical expense<br>Physician's services, inpatient and outpatient medical services and supplies, physical and speech therapy, ambulance, etc. | Medicare pays for medical services in or out of the hospital; some insurance policies pay less (or nothing) for hospital outpatient medical services or services in a doctor's office | 80% approved amount (after $75 deductible | $75 deductible[a] plus 20% of balance of approved amount (plus any charge above approved amount)[b] |
| Home health care | Unlimited visits as medically necessary | Full cost | Nothing |
| Outpatient hospital treatment | Unlimited as medically necessary | 80% of approved amount (after $75 deductible) | Subject to deductible plus 20% of balance of approved amount |
| Blood | Blood | 80% of approved amount (after first 3 pints) | For first 3 pints plus 20% of balance of approved amount |

[a]Once you have had $75 of expense for covered services in 1985, the Part B deductible does not apply to any further covered services you receive the rest of the year.

[b]You pay for charges higher than the amount approved by Medicare unless the doctor or supplier agrees to accept Medicare's approved amount as the total charge for services rendered.

*Source:* U.S. Department of Health and Human Services. *Guide To Health Insurance for People with Medicare.* Washington, D.C.: U.S. Government Printing Office, 1985. [NOTE: As of January 1, 1985, new deductibles (up to $492) and other dollar amounts will be in effect.]

sory. Those aged persons who are not eligible are permitted to enroll voluntarily by paying a monthly premium, set at $174 per month in 1985. A relatively small number of the elderly take advantage of this opportunity because of the cost of premiums. In addition to those who qualify under Social Security, or who voluntarily purchase Medicare Part A, there are some 3.5 million elderly for whom their state Medicaid program elects to purchase Medicare benefits in partial fulfillment of their medical care needs.

Medicare Part B (SMI) is a voluntary program into which anyone eligible for Part A may enroll after paying a monthly premium of $15.50 in 1985. The best time to enroll is three months prior to or four months following the sixty-fifth birthday. Enrollment at any other time means a lifetime increased premium, but otherwise enrollment is open during the first quarter of each year. It is supported by monthly premiums paid by enrollees into another trust fund and matched by general federal tax revenues. Benefits and copayments under

Medicare Part B are outlined in Table 11.3. Generally, these include physicians' fees, x-ray examinations, ambulance and emergency room treatment, and other services at 80% of approved charges rate less the annual deductible. Because of the definition of approved charges, Part B actually paid only 55 percent of the total cost of these services prior to the 1984 revisions. It is too soon to calculate exactly the current payment percentages, but they will be even lower because of new restrictions. Not covered are prescription drugs, dental care, eyeglasses, hearing aids, and many other services that must be paid for by elderly patients either by themselves or indirectly through private health insurance (Davis, 1985).

Medicaid is a public needs–determined assistance program that, following the well-established procedures for such programs, is financed by federal matching grants from general revenues to the states; the federal government retains only limited controls over program development or implementation. Designed as medical welfare, Medicaid may also in some instances be used to make copayments under Medicare, but in most cases it functions independently. It also may come into force when Medicare benefits are expended and all other assets are exhausted. It is the primary source of public funding for nursing home care for the elderly. Federal contributions to the states' approved Medicaid programs vary by state, ranging from 50 percent for states with higher per capita incomes to 83 percent for poorer states. Because participation in Medicaid by the states was voluntary, some states were slow to initiate programs. Alaska and Arizona in particular were reluctant to develop Medicaid programs because of their large Eskimo and Indian populations, most of which they claimed would be eligible for coverage. Alaska finally implemented a Medicaid program in 1972, while Arizona adopted a very conservative plan only in 1982 (Brown, 1984). In other states restrictive amendments have been enacted regularly since the program's inception and justified under the promise of maximum flexibility. The outcome has been a uniform tightening of the benefits offered and the population covered, a reduction in the types of expenses used to cover eligibility, and a move to require prior approval before treatment can be rendered and reimbursed. Some states have also imposed enrollment fees as the federal government has retreated from its position of no-expense assistance for the needy.

Under Title XIX state Medicaid programs are required to cover certain basic medical services, including inpatient and outpatient hospital care, physicians' services, laboratory and x-ray studies, and care in a skilled nursing facility or home health care. Optional services, which states may choose to cover with matching federal assistance, include drugs, eyeglasses, private duty nursing, intermediate care facility services, inpatient psychiatric care, physical therapy, dental care, and other services. Clinic services, prescribed drugs, prosthetic devices, emergency hospital services, and intermediate care facility services are added by over forty-one states. Limitations on services, including types of services covered, number of covered days, or copayment on drugs, may also be imposed by states. All of this means wide variations in the comprehensiveness of coverage by states and a great variation in setting income thresholds, spend down requirements, or income-to-medical care ratios. In 1981 the Supreme Court upheld the rights of states to evaluate the eligibility of applicants by imposing tighter restrictions on the acceptability of the transfer of assets to qualify for Medicaid coverage. Since that decision the right of states to extend such conditional eligibility requirements from SSI to Medicaid has been recognized in legislation and judicial interpretation.

Title XIX requires state Medicaid programs to cover all "categorically needy": those receiving cash benefits under Old Age Assistance, Aid to the Blind, Aid to Families with Dependent Children (AFDC), Aid to the Permanently and Totally Disabled, and other persons not receiving cash benefits because of particular eligibility restrictions imposed by the states. State programs may also cover additional "categorically-related needy" groups and "categorically-related medically needy" (such as the aged, blind, disabled, and children, who would be eligible for public assistance but whose incomes are above the state's standards for cash assistance) on an optional basis. Because of the current latitude in setting eligibility requirements that allows states to determine the income levels for public assistance cash grants — and therefore Medicaid eligibility — well below the federal poverty level, many people are not eligible for Medicaid yet cannot afford to purchase adequate medical care. It has been estimated that somewhere between 40 and 67 percent of all poor persons in the United States do not meet the eligibility requirements for Medicaid (Brown, 1984) and that only one out of every four poor, aged Medicare enrollees — those with incomes below the federal poverty level — is also covered by Medicaid (U.S. Senate Special Committee on Aging, 1984a).

## THE ISSUE OF COST

From the start the Medicare and Medicaid programs were much more costly than anyone had anticipated. Within a year of their implementation, the increasing concerns with cost containment competed with considerations of the adequacy of benefits both in Congress and in state legislatures. Amendments to Social Security in the last two decades have been designed to afford the states and the federal government more options to regulate and to control both eligibility requirements and rising costs. Among the strategies implemented have been the imposition of cost-sharing as a disincentive for eligible recipients to use services, programs to control provider fraud and abuse, restrictive reimbursement practices, review of hospital and nursing home use, and the regulation of capital investment in health care facilities. Cost-sharing refers to the requirement of additional contributions by beneficiaries in the form of increased premiums for Medicare Part B and similarly rising deductibles and copayments. Until 1981, however, the major funding cutbacks were confined to Medicaid. As a public assistance program, with revenues drawn mainly from a regressive tax, the major burden of which was borne by the working and lower-middle classes and the major benefits of which accrued primarily to the poor and relatively powerless, it was an easier target for political opponents than Medicare, whose beneficiaries were spread across all classes. In 1981, however, the attempt to control Medicare costs began in earnest with a vote by Congress to eliminate or reduce certain Medicare benefits, increase Medicare copayments and deductibles, and reduce reimbursement rates to hospitals (Brown, 1984).

In Chapter 5 we discussed the escalating costs that gave rise to fears regarding the solvency of the Medicare trust fund. Those concerns contributed to the move toward Medicare cost-cutting and culminated in the passage of the Tax Equity and Fiscal Responsibility Act (TEFRA) of 1982 that mandated the development of a prospective payment system for Medicare hospital costs. Factors accounting for escalating health care costs include economy-wide inflation (allegedly the cause of 44 percent of the increase between 1982 and 1983), higher rates of inflation in the health care industry than in the economy at large (26 percent), overall population growth (11 percent), and other factors, including the aging of the population, increased consumption per capita, and changes in the types of medical services provided (19 percent) (Gibson et al., 1984). As noted in Chapter 5, high health care or industry-specific rates of inflation are in part attributable to incentives to spend that result from liberal retrospective third-party reimbursement systems: hence the move toward prospective payment was no surprise. While cost-containment measures seem to have slowed the rate of growth of medical expenditures, in 1984 the Board of Trustees still estimated that the Medicare trust fund would no longer be able to meet its obligations by 1991 (Gibson et al., 1984).

Rising costs, however, were not the only issue. In a different political climate an alternative solution might have been sought. The Reagan administration, however, wished to increase defense spending and reduce taxes in the face of an escalating budget deficit. Its solution was to control the costs of domestic service programs. In the early 1980s many cost-containment measures were directed against Medicaid. The Omnibus Reconciliation Act of 1980 changed the Medicaid nursing home reimbursement system to allow more flexibility by the states in determining reasonable reimbursement rates for such care. Under this new strategy many states went to partially or fully prospective payment systems that resulted in lower rates and appeared to translate into lower expenditures per recipient (Harrington and Swan, 1984). There has also been a reduction in nursing home use by Medicaid patients, believed to result from selective admission policies that discriminate against Medicaid recipients for whom reimbursement rates are lower than for private-pay patients — an option that nursing homes are able to exercise because of the limitations imposed by the states on the construction of nursing home beds (Gibson et al., 1984). The Omnibus Reconciliation Act of 1981 reduced federal Medicaid matching funds granted to the states by 3 percent in fiscal 1982 and 4 percent in fiscal 1983. An extension of the legislation authorized a 4.5 percent reduction for 1984. States were also allowed to offset at least some of these decreases by a variety of fiscal and policy programs directed toward cost-cutting. Included among these measures were reducing the growth of program expenditures to a targeted rate and defining as acceptable an unemployment rate 50 percent greater than the national average. The act also again broadened the discretion allowed states in reducing benefits and tightening eligibility requirements (Gibson et al., 1984; Brown, 1984).

In Chapter 5 we discussed the 1984 implementation of the DRG prospective payment system for hospital expenses. A number of other measures have also been considered and in some cases implemented. The rationale behind the logic for cost-sharing is that, as well as saving money in the form of revenue, copayments are disincentives to health care use since people are less likely to use services when they pay a significant proportion of the bill themselves (Congressional Budget Office, 1983). Proponents of this strategy argue that it discourages the unnecessary use of health services; critics argue that it hinders access to care for the needy. While Congress enacted some cost-sharing measures in 1981, in recent years cost-sharing measures have been vigorously opposed on the grounds that they will impose hardships on the most needy. It may turn out that Medicare recipients will be subject to a lower quality of care than at anytime during the last twenty years (U.S. Senate Special Committee on Aging, 1984a).

The responsiveness of the political system to budgetary pressures and constraints can be clearly seen in both the changes enacted and the weighing of acceptable alternatives. In 1982 Congress authorized prospective per capita payments to health maintenance organizations and other medical programs that contracted to provide comprehensive medical service to Medicare beneficiaries. There has also been an attempt to solve the problem of mounting costs by increasing the base of persons covered by, and therefore paying into, the Medicare trust fund. In January 1983 coverage of federal employees by Medicare became effective, and in 1984 participation in Medicare by employees in nonprofit organizations was made mandatory. Self-employed persons were required to pay both the employee's and the employer's share of the Medicare tax, thus doubling their contribution to the Medicare trust fund. Furthermore, in 1984 legislation was passed prohibiting employers from eliminating health care coverage for employees sixty-five to sixty-nine. In effect, this makes it possible for these people to choose between coverage by an existing employer plan or Medicare, with the idea of reducing the number of those dependent on Medicare for their medical assistance and reimbursements (Gibson et al., 1984). An option considered but not yet adopted was to offer Medicare vouchers to beneficiaries that would allow them to enroll in private health insurance plans or health maintenance organizations at a specified cost. Beneficiaries would be responsible for premium costs over and above the value of the voucher and would receive a cash differential if they found a lower premium elsewhere. This proposal was criticized on the grounds that it could lead to a decreased quality of care because of exploitation by unscrupulous insurance companies and a sacrifice of benefits in the interests of short-term economy on the part of the elderly. Some critics strongly argued that it was unlikely to lead to significant savings for the Medicare program (Congressional Budget Office, 1982; Harrington, 1983).

Particular attention has also been addressed to rising expenses for physician services under Medicare Part B. It was estimated that in 1985 Medicare's supplementary medical insurance program (SMI) would be the third largest federal domestic program, with expenditures of $25 billion, following Social Security and Medicare Part A. With a 16.1 percent increase from 1984 to 1985, it was the fastest growing of the domestic programs. Of the $25 billion paid out under Medicare Part B, 75 percent would go for physician services. Physician reimbursement under Medicare Part B traditionally has been based on a combination of the individual physician's customary charges and the prevailing rates in the geographic area of practice with indexing procedures gradually factored in to restrain costs. Since 1970 the rate of increase for Medicare expenditures for physicians has been significantly greater than the national average. For example, from 1980 to 1982 the average annual increase for physician fees covered by Medicare was 20.9 percent; the national rate was 14.9 percent (U.S. Senate Special Committee on Aging, 1984b). According to the Senate Special Committee on Aging, increases in expenditures for physician services were attributed to an increased supply of physicians, the availability of funding from third-party payers, rapid technological changes resulting in a decrease in the number of primary care physicians, and a corresponding increase in the number of medical specialists. Despite rising costs, there appears to have been little change in the per capita use of physician services over the past decade.

As well as contributing to rising Medicare expenditures, increases in physicians' fees have also imposed a financial burden on the elderly themselves. Only slightly over half of the physicians accept Medicare payment assignment. If a physician agrees to the assignment, he or she bills the Medicare program directly and accepts the program's reasonable charge determination — together with the deductible and copayment due from the patient — as payment in full. If the physician does not accept the assignment, he or she bills the patient directly. The patient then seeks reimbursement from the Medicare program and is responsible for any difference between the Medicare program's reasonable charge determination and the total bill, in addition to copayments and the deductible (U.S. Senate Special Committee on Aging, 1984b).

Key questions with regard to physician reimbursements posed by the Senate Special Committee on Aging included the advisibility and probability of developing competitive market forces and incentives to restrain the costs of health care, including physician fees. Also, the debate continues over the propriety of Medicare protecting the elderly and the disabled against rising physicians' fees vs shifting such burdens to the consumer to encourage more cost-conscious behavior. Finally, there is no consensus about ways in which assignment rates can be improved to provide greater financial protection for the recipients. Possible options for dealing with the issue of rising expenses include competitive purchasing for physicians' services based on bids as opposed to fees, reimbursement on the basis of preestablished government fee schedules, and integrating hospital and physician payments for inpatient services to provide an incentive to the hospitals to hold down costs and thereby attract physicians to their staffs. It was feared, however, that stricter Medicare reimbursement policies for physicians might result in unrecovered costs being passed on to the consumer that would then place an increased financial burden on those who were unable to afford it. In view of this the committee recommended developing incentives to encourage physicians to accept Medicare assignment or to extending mandatory assignment to include nonhospital physicians (U.S. Senate Special Committee on Aging, 1984b). Mandatory assignment still carries with it the danger that more physicians would refuse to treat Medicare patients because of lower remuneration schedules. A fifteen-month legally mandated freeze on physician fees was imposed in July 1984. The number of physicians who complied with the freeze is the subject of continuing controversy. Depending on the source of information, it appears that between 42 and 90 percent cooperated, not overwhelming evidence of professional concern for the plight of Medicare and Medicaid recipients. To put real "teeth" into the freeze the Congress passed Public Law 98–369 mandating an across the board freeze for fifteen months beginning July 1, 1984. At the same time the laboratory fee schedule was adjusted down to reimburse independent laboratories and physicians for only 60 percent of prevailing charges — a combination of measures expected to save Medicare $105 million during the last three months of fiscal 1984 and $485 million in 1985 (Gibson et al., 1984). Measures have also been instituted to encourage the acceptance of the assignment, including publication of a list of accepting physicians, and fee schedule updating procedures that favor physicians accepting the assignment. The AMA, which had proposed a voluntary self-regulated freeze on fees as an alternative to a mandatory program, responded to these incentives by filing suit in federal court claiming such cost-containment measures are a violation of the Constitution (U.S. Senate Special Committee on Aging, 1985a).

## MEDICARE: A BROKEN PROMISE?

Binstock (1985) notes that there are competing interpretations of the importance of Medicare. The legislation has been variously described as health insurance for persons no longer eligible for employee group plans, as a mechanism for income redistribution, or as an intentional first step toward national health insurance. Certainly, the intent underlying Medicare and Medicaid legislation was ambivalent: it was a negotiated compromise among those who wished to extend medical care to all, those who feared the undermining of individual responsibility, and those who were concerned with financial feasibility. At every juncture the interests of the health care industry were openly pronounced. There was a basic concern for the adequacy of the coverage, however, on the part of some who pushed for the legislation, and the hope was that Medicare and Medicaid would ensure access to basic medical protection for the elderly and the indigent (Stein, 1985). From the beginning, as we have seen, there has been a concern with cost containment, and in the 1970s and 1980s this concern has overridden the preoccupation with adequacy in congressional deliberations. The basic question was rephrased; no longer was it whether the elderly were receiving adequate care but was too much being spent on the health care of the elderly as opposed to other age groups. Ideological critiques of the inadequacy of Medicare and Medicaid have proliferated, and Estes et al. (1984) refer to the program not so much as a system of care as a financing mechanism. While acknowledging considerable improvements in access to health care as a result of Medicare and Medicaid, these critiques center on the programs' failure to adequately relieve the elderly of the burden of health care costs, the failure to provide certain services (particularly comprehensive long-term care and preventive measures), the tendency to segment the health care interests of the elderly and the poor from those of the general population, and the use of a market model of health care by those involved in both the original legislation and in the attempts at reform (Brown, 1984; Estes et al., 1984).

Despite high Medicare-Medicaid expenditures and that Medicare pays 74 percent of covered hospital and 55 percent of covered physician fees, the elderly are left with sizable expenses that amount to 29 percent of total health care expenditures. These patient expenditures are composed of deductibles, copayments, the balance due on unassigned physician fees, payment for services not covered by Medicare, and premiums for private insurance to fill the gaps left by Medicare. While on the average the elderly actually paid less than 6 percent of their hospital costs from their personal resources, an average of 41.6 percent of nursing home costs and 31.3 percent of other services were paid directly by patients or their families (U.S. Senate Special Committee on Aging, 1985a; Waldo and Lazenby, 1984). The shift toward services outside the hospital encouraged by the DRG system tends to further increase expenses for the elderly. Indeed, uninsured expenses are growing at a faster rate than the income of the elderly. In 1984 health care expenditures averaged 15 percent of the per capita income for the elderly — the same percentage as in 1966 before Medicare was fully implemented (U.S. Senate Special Committee on Aging, 1984a). Brown (1984) comments that the Medicare and Medicaid programs have not so much reduced expenses for health care as they have increased the total amount spent on health care per elderly person. The poor fare worst in all this. If we consider the noninstitutionalized elderly alone, health care expenditures amount to over 14 percent of the income of the poor and near poor but only 1 percent of that of high-income groups, even though they spend more in dollar amounts on health care. The burden of cost-sharing tends to fall heaviest on those who are sick and poor. Only one in four of the poor or near poor elderly today are covered by Medicaid; those who are covered by Medicare alone have the highest expenses and the lowest use of physicians' services when health status is taken into account (U.S. Senate Special Committee on Aging, 1984a).

As we noted earlier, the gaps in Medicare coverage are numerous: there is no payment for outpatient drugs, eyeglasses, basic dental care, or preventive measures, and there are limits to the amount of hospital coverage offered. Nursing home and home health protection is limited to skilled care: there is no reimbursement for those who require custodial care rather than skilled medical attention. Nor does Medigap insurance generally cover long-term care. Long-term care under Medicaid is generally limited to an inadequate coverage of nursing home care for the indigent. Relatives of the patient whose nursing home bill is paid by Medicaid may be forced to "spend down" assets to reach poverty levels before their benefits begin. Also, reimbursement rates and procedures are such that many nursing homes selectively avoid admitting Medicare and Medicaid patients. It has been suggested by some that states perpetuate nursing home bed shortages by keeping a close watch on certificates of need for additional beds as an indirect means of controlling Medicaid expenditures (Gibson et al., 1985; Stein, 1985; U.S. Senate Special Committee on Aging, 1984a, 1985a). There has been some expansion of skilled nursing home health services under Medicare, notably with hospice benefits for terminally ill patients. Nevertheless, the lack of significant support for preventive home health care or other types of services designed to maximize the independence of the elderly has been counted as a factor in the continued maintenance of system-sponsored dependency (Estes et al., 1984). Others have lamented the failure of the system to finance preventive care for young and middle-aged people who might then exhibit reduced demand for chronic care when they become elderly (Davis, 1985).

Medicare and Medicaid have also been criticized for segmenting the health care interests of the elderly from those of the rest of the population and the interests of the poor from those of the nonpoor. Binstock (1985) decries the tendency of advocates of intergenerational equity to focus their criticisms on high levels of health care spending for the elderly as unfair to other generations, while ignoring the actual disparities of need and use within generations. The health care interests of all generations are linked if one takes a long-range view. Also, the rationing of health care is far more likely to take place along the lines of financial status than of age. There is an undeniable tendency for practitioners to avoid treating patients who are eligible for Medicaid. Consequently, those recipients are treated as second-class citizens deserving only second-class care (Davis, 1985).

Cost-sharing and prospective plans as means of containing federally underwritten expenditures are quite consciously based on market models of service (Congressional Budget Office, 1982). This metapolicy has been criticized by those who define health care more in the nature of a right (Estes et al., 1984) or a public service (Brown, 1984) than a market commodity. Health care delivery differs from the market situation in that consumers do not have full or unlimited access to information; they are thus unable to form an adequate basis for evaluating one form of treatment against another. Furthermore, competition within the health care industry is limited (Gibson et al., 1984; Davis, 1985). Unlike the market, health care is dominated by third-party payors. Consumers do not on the whole directly pay for services (goods) at the time of receipt. Critics argue that this means people consume more health care because they perceive it as not costing anything — a consequence that Medicare seeks to forestall by its system of copayments. Third-party payment may, however, also cut the other way. Because the third parties who are paying for the commodity are not the people receiving the services, they may be more interested in keeping costs down than in maximizing the quality of care. Furthermore, the market theory that assumes such devices as cost-sharing lead directly to people being more discriminating in their use of services and in avoiding unnecessary care presumes the consumers have the means to pay for care. A recent House of Representatives investigation into the quality of health among the poor in West Virginia since the initiation of the cost-cutting measures cites a report by the American Hospital Association noting that patients are coming to hospitals with more serious diseases that result in part from the delays in seeking care for financial reasons (U.S. House of Representatives, 1984). Similarly, a recent Government Accounting Office study notes that patients are being discharged earlier and are in a poorer state of health since the initiation of DRGs, creating a need for increased health care in the community (U.S. Senate, 1985b). On the institutional level those hospitals with a large share of low income patients, particularly public and inner-city hospitals and large rural hospitals in areas where the rates are unfavorable, are the most likely to feel the effect of DRGs. Davis (1985) suggests the importance of other goals, such as sustaining a humane and just society that may moderate the drive toward the production and consumption of services and promote health care designed to be sensitive to the needs of consumers and to market forces.

## PRIVATE HEALTH POLICY OPTIONS

As federal policies on health have received greater media attention and public criticism, a range of private options has been created. These proprietary plans are largely marketed as means to circumvent the exclusions in Medicare. Clearly, privately held health insurance is a traditional option in the United States. How well it affects the health concerns of the elderly merits careful examination.

**Medigap.** As an increasingly visible sector of the health care industry, medigap policies are growing in popularity. Unfortunately, such supplemental policies, though they do offer hospital indemnity protection, seldom provide the kind of long-term care protection not offered by Medicare. In other words, like Medicare itself, they primarily cover the types of health care costs older people have the least need for — acute care costs. Generally, medigap plans pay roughly 15 percent of the health care costs of the 67 percent of the Medicare recipients who purchased the coverage.

Under Section 507 of Public Law 96–265, procedures now exist for "Voluntary Certification of Medicare Supplemental Health Insurance Policies." As implied in the title, however, such approval is not compulsory. For the older consumer the question is whether the policies they purchase have an equitable return for their premiums and adequate coverage. Beyond the marketing rhetoric we need to look closely at the actual reimbursement stipulations. Other issues are duplication of provisions, lack of disclosure, informed choice, exemptions for preexisting conditions, and high-pressure marketing. Few medigap policies cover custodial care, home health care, or other forms of long-term institutionalization outside of a skilled nursing facility.

**Long-Term Care.** Estimates are that some 50,000 older people were covered by at least twelve companies writing insurance in 1985 for long-term care. Some provide up to three or four years of coverage in licensed nursing facilities after skilled nursing care is no longer necessary. Generally, the policies offer a preset indemnity of between $10 and $50 daily rather than complete coverage. Most include a deductible or reduced benefit period. The effect is that repeated short-term custodial periods are not usually covered completely. Underwriters also carefully define insurable events that mandate consumers must screen each policy carefully for exclusions.

# Additional Social Service Policies for the Elderly

In addition to these pervasive programmatic issues are policy questions that are more focused and affect small subsegments of the population. Often these concerns are less articulated and appear in normative procedures. They may, however, also be global policies that affect the lives of the elderly by virtue of special or unusual circumstances.

## DEATH WITH DIGNITY

Death with dignity concerns have accompanied the rapid advances in medical technology. A number of complex questions have emerged about every person's decision-making powers over life and death, as well as the right of others to decide if an individual is no longer competent. Furthermore, the question of the legal definitions of death has become more problematic.

How these questions are answered affects all medical practitioners concerned with organ transplants and the cessation of life supports, and their own malpractice. Formerly a person was considered dead when unassisted breathing and heartbeat stopped. To avoid the proliferation of lawsuits the AMA and the American Bar Association proposed a Uniform Determination of Death Act in 1980 that included the concept of brain death, the cessation of electrical impulses. The AMA has also advocated policies regarding refusal of treatment and the termination of life support. As might be expected, the most troublesome question for all concerned is the course of action when the patient is incompetent. Prior to her death in June 1985, Karen Ann Quinlan's plight attracted considerable attention and established a precedent. The Quinlan case made clear that the courts will stay actively involved in determining the legitimacy of terminating life supports. Patients themselves have been allowed the right to participate in the decisions if they have prepared a *living will*. Over one-fifth of the states have enacted laws that recognize living wills, with the intent to prohibit extraordinary efforts to preserve life. Such legislation usually grants legal immunity to physicians who follow the terms of the living will.

## LEGAL SERVICES

Legal services have been provided to low-income persons, the elderly included, through a federal program since 1966. Under President Nixon the Legal Services Corporation was constituted as an independent, nonprofit corporation to insulate it from political pressures. By 1985 funds had been so drastically reduced that the 325 legal services programs fell well below the number stipulated as minimally necessary under the original enabling legislation. President Reagan justified the budget reductions in part by stating they would prompt more pro bono work by private attorneys and spur private participation in service delivery. Supporters of legal services respond by asserting it is far more likely to mean more older people among the 8.7 million eligible elderly will go without legal representation. Competent legal services are of vital importance in helping the elderly to obtain basic access to and protection for benefits and services to which they are entitled. Typical legal problems of older persons relate to securing government benefits, consumer fraud, property tax exemptions and assessments, guardianships, involuntary commitment to an institution, nursing homes, and probate matters (U.S. Senate Special Committee on Aging, 1985a). A central theme of the American value system is the right to legal protection, yet the retrenchment of funding for the legal protection of the elderly means there may be no justice for some and less justice for all.

## SOCIAL SERVICES

A wide range of other social provisions and policies are incorporated under the policy objectives of the Older Americans Act. Policies regarding nutrition, housing, community services, senior employment, and so on are all designed to help maintain independent life-styles. Since most coverage under the Older Americans Act is coordinated by State and Area Agencies on Aging, there is an intervening, administrative level channeling the OAA's intent. The over $1 billion appropriated in 1984 to the OAA was filtered through fifty-seven State Units on Aging, 660 Area Agencies on Aging, and 15,000 community organizations.

Under Title III, which covers a comprehensive coterie of nutrition, multipurpose senior centers, and so on, President Reagan proposed a consolidation of the various funding plans into single awards to states to permit greater local flexibility and discretion. In 1986 29 percent of the monies can be transferred without approval by federal officials; in 1987 this will rise to 30 percent. Other revisions made in 1984 permit states to "target" services more closely to those elderly with the greatest economic and social needs. As part of the 1984 revisions (Title III-B), families of Alzheimer's disease victims, the abused elderly, and nutrition education programs all received greater attention. Despite the expansion of such social services, the budgetary proposal for Title III for 1984 was 5 percent less than the previous fiscal year. Proposals to reduce other titles were also made, with losses in some cases (Title IV — training, research, and discretionary grants and programs) projected to be up to 77 percent. Though funding levels were maintained in 1985, future proposed cuts are realistically anticipated.

Title XX of the Social Security Act provided 75 percent federal financing for most social services. Initially, the law required that at least half of the state's federal allotment be used for services to recipients of Aid to Families with Dependent Children (AFDC), SSI, or Medicaid. The remaining funds could be used to provide services to persons whose income fell below a specified poverty level. As part of the 1981 Omnibus Reconciliation Act, Congress created the Social Services Block Grant (SSBG) program that eliminated most of the restrictions in Title XX, thus allowing more freedom to states in allocating funds. While some advocates of the elderly have supported the SSBG program on the grounds that the simplication of the federal requirements could lead to greater administrative efficiency and effectiveness in the delivery of services, others have criticized it on the grounds that removing the categorical requirements would lead to the elderly losing out in the competition for scarce social services funding. Although some states, including Florida, have shifted their SSBG funds away from the elderly, not all have done so. In 1984 the Reagan administration moved to terminate the Community Services Block Grant (CSBG) program, which had its origin in the 1960s War on Poverty. The community services funds have been used to develop programs that assured access for older persons to existing health, welfare, employment, housing, legal, consumer, education, and other services. At last count, however, the move to eliminate CSBGs was rejected by both houses (U.S. Senate Special Committee on Aging, 1985a).

The Older American Volunteer Programs (OAVP) administered under ACTION are viewed as cost effective and, as such, have not been challenged. According to the Reagan administration, the OAVP relieve demands on public sector support programs through volunteer involvement. In 1984 OAVP funding constituted over two-thirds of the budget of ACTION programs and included the Retired Senior Volunteer Program (RSVP), the Foster Grandparents Program (FGP), and the Senior Companion Program (SCP). Each provides opportunities to people over sixty to contribute services to their communities or to be reimbursed at an hourly rate of $2.20 for those services where some payment is included in a remuneration program.

## HOUSING

In the years since the original Housing Act of 1937 federally sponsored housing and its utilization by the elderly have grown significantly. By 1984 older persons occupied 46 percent of all public housing. Since 1959 Section 202 programs have targeted the elderly as deserving special consideration. Since housing costs are a major expenditure in the budgets of most elderly — over half for older women living alone — financial support policies are particularly important. As taxes and repair and replacement costs continue to escalate, and as the number of the old-old grows, the demand for housing support will increase for larger proportions of the population than at present. Despite such predictions, the federal government has not considered housing a legitimate entitlement and needs outstrip supply by a margin of three to one in all age groups.

In 1983, in response to the administration's concern over deficits, the Housing Act was subjected to significant cuts in federally assisted public housing. Under the revised statutes less than 10 percent of newly constructed units are designated for the elderly. Other cost-containment measures have also been implemented, such as increasing the renter's share to 30 percent from 25 percent of the total cost. While these amendments may not seem significant, they must be evaluated from the standpoint of a person who is seventy-eight — the average age of the elderly living in Section 202 housing. Other types of housing assistance are available, but these, too, have been trimmed in recent years. The outcome is clear: despite an avowed desire to help older persons retain their independence, adequate housing and shelter in the community are becoming ever more difficult to obtain. With fixed incomes averaging well below the rest of the population, additional hardships are imposed as a result of the changing funding priorities of federal policy.

## The Metapolicy of Aging: Issues for the Future

In our study of the various dimensions of aging and the implications of these for social policy, we have alluded to many underlying dilemmas at metapolicy level. These are the orientations that link age-related issues to those of vital concern to us as members of society. Although somewhat complex in their ramifications, these dilemmas center on several basic questions:

- Does posing the difficulties of the allocation of resources in terms of equity of distribution between generations mask more fundamental differences in value orientations?
- Are the questions of the financial feasibility in providing services to the elderly necessarily politically constrained?
- How do the relationships between structural factors and social policies affect the thinking, acting, aging individual and the character of his or her life?
- Do social policies and their creation and revision encourage dependencies we then attribute to individuals?

### INTERGENERATIONAL EQUITY VS SOCIETAL EQUITY

In giving primacy to the question of intergenerational equity — whether more resources are being allocated to programs for the elderly than to programs for other generations — we may lose sight of other ways of approaching issues of equity (Binstock, 1985; GSA, in press). Inequities exist within and between generations. There is tremendous variation in every generation spanning from the wealthy to those well below the poverty level. In old age those who had been discriminated against, disadvantaged, or on the lowest rung of the societal ladder throughout the earlier years of their lives remain in the same situation. Why not consider the allocation of resources within generations on the basis of need? Why cut direct financial aid to those below the poverty level while leaving indirect aid to those who have room for discretion untouched?

If we take a broader view, the interests of people in different generations may be interrelated rather than irrevocably pitted against one another. Every person in society, if he or she lives long enough, passes through old age. Today's young and middle-aged have a vested interest in developing policies that will improve the lives of the elderly, since these will affect their own lives later. Risk-by-risk policies often obscure the underlying questions by creating pressures among generations and interest groups to compete against one another for scarce resources. As a result, many of the issues we have discussed as dimensions of aging that affect people throughout their life course are often ignored. Relevant to each generation are issues of the maintenance and restoration of health, income maintenance for the old, middle-aged, and young, long-term care, housing, and legal services. For example, all of society benefits by ensuring the optimal health of all its members. It makes little sense to assert that individuals are entirely responsible for maintaining all aspects of their own health. The President's Commission on Ethical Problems in Medicine itself recognized the communal nature of physical well-being:

> The Commission concludes that society has an ethical obligation to ensure equitable access to health care for all. This obligation rests on the special importance of health care: its role in relieving suffering, preventing premature death, restoring functioning, increasing opportunity, providing information about an individual's condition and giving evidence of mutual empathy and compassion. Furthermore, although lifestyle and the environment can affect health status, differences in the need for health care for the most part are undeserved and not within an individual's control (1983).

The point the commission makes is clear: while policy provisions may be targeted for those at risk, they benefit everyone. Health care for the elderly is no more confined to their own interests as elders than polio vaccine is confined to the interests of children alone.

## THE ISSUE OF FINANCIAL FEASIBILITY

But what about paying for all this? Is not the problem precisely that services for the elderly now cost too much according to the contributors? Surely, we would be in even worse shape if such services were extended to the general population. The question is obviously vital. Methods of funding need careful consideration. It is not possible in the present American value system to advocate providing an unlimited range and quantity of services for all. The availability of funds, as we have repeatedly emphasized, is socially constructed. We need to consider where our priorities as a society lie in determining how financing mechanisms are constructed and what alternatives exist. As Myles (1984) and others have pointed out, many countries with lower GNPs and lower average incomes than the United States offer what appears to be a nearly universal provision of socially valued services. Then, too, we need to remember that youth dependency ratios are decreasing and that the apparent dependency of the elderly is in part socially constructed. While some older people may need and welcome retirement, many could continue to be contributing members of society if policy imperatives were not disincentives.

Finally, we must recognize the political economic values inherent in the ways in which we construct the questions we ask about such things as financing. While we do not mean to allude to a good vs bad value orientation, the different societal goals reflected in posing such issues is intimately tied to underlying decisions about the nature and direction of national economies and interest groups. The recent debates about Medicare in the United States, for example, have focused on issues of cost effectiveness and competition, values that are important in a capitalist economy. We might expect similar debates in countries with different modes of production to focus on other topics and to then be reflected in different types of social policy. We need to be conscious of these underlying values not only to scrutinize their viability but also, if we agree these concerns deserve top priority, to see if policy decisions match these issues.

## Summary

What is too frequently construed as intergenerational conflict over finite resources might better be phrased in terms of the interdependence among generations. All people, regardless of age, are equally valuable. Unless we are now willing to publicly claim certain categories of people are incompetent or without worth to society, we must be cautious about treating people merely as the objects of policy. In reality they are coparticipants in its formulation, as well as the subjects of its eventual protection and restriction. The policy agenda is determined by many factors: pluralist concerns, elite actors, organizations and agencies, class interests, and societal history. We must not forget the prospect that policy positions taken now will be precedents for the future. As the Gerontological Society of America (in press) report on emerging issues maintains, we all have a common stake in policies formulated for any particular subgroup. The more we divide into subgroups the smaller the stake will seem.

When looking at social policy issues, a number of levels of analysis are possible. Depending on the level examined and the metapolicy assumptions made, vastly different conclusions are possible. Because so many of our entitlement policies are based on categorical classifications, it is easy to ignore the great dissimilarities within categories. Social Security, as a categorical entitlement, has roots deep in the mainstream values and traditions of the United States. While apparently ensuring financial well-being in old age, it is closely tied to private sector economic arrangements. Benefits received under Social

Security are proportionate to presumed contributions as evidenced by lifetime earnings profiles. It does not matter that factors other than human capital may enter into reward structures in the workplace. As we move toward the end of the 1980s, Social Security has been the subject of a great deal of criticism. Unfortunately, the main thrust of such challenges has focused on direct benefits while ignoring the indirect advantages accruing to select categories of the elderly.

Health care policies are also receiving close scrutiny. Again the focus has been on direct benefits and their cost. Many of the proposed revisions are little more than a shifting of financial responsibility without any concern for the prevention of need or the adequacy of protection. As important as health is in the determination of nearly all facets of life and well-being, it is surprising that the debate to date has concentrated on intergenerational inequities. The healthy elderly were healthy youths. As the federal government retreats from its central role in guaranteed health security, private options have come into existence. For the most part these preserve the traditional fee-for-service principles long established as the norm for providing health care in the United States. They also tend to concentrate on protection against short-term acute illnesses characteristic of the earlier decades of life. It may be that the time for reexamining societal goals is overdue. Redefining the basic tenets of society's contribution to the quality of life would refocus political priorities from funding constraints to creating and revising programs designed to foster independence and security.

Besides national legislative policies, other policies also shape the life situations of the elderly. Each of these in its own way characterizes and limits the range of possible options open to an older person. Not surprisingly, each also reflects the factors of shifting priorities that in recent years seem to be moving away from adequacy toward stopgap restraints.

## Discussion Questions

**What Social Policy Is**

1. Select a policy taken by federal or state government to resolve a problem related to aging. What is the general approach to social issues implied in this policy? What are the beliefs about society and about human nature underlying it? How might this policy reflect negotiations between groups?

2. How does the policy selected in question 1 shape the lives of those it affects? What latitude do people have to modify it or the way in which it is applied?

3. Do you think this policy is socially just? What political or practical difficulties might arise in implementing it?

**Social Policy for the Elderly**

4. What are the positive and negative consequences of social welfare policies for the elderly? How might the negative consequences be ameliorated?

5. Why do you think we have adopted a risk-by-risk strategy of social policy in the United States? How might the mechanisms for setting an agenda and the political organization of the United States contribute to such a choice? What are the advantages and disadvantages of a risk-by-risk approach as opposed to a cradle-to-grave approach?

**Fiscal Policies and the Elderly**

6. What are the strengths and the problems of the Social Security system? What measures would you use to resolve the fiscal issues of the Social Security trust fund?

7. What are the advantages and problems of SSI? What would you do to solve the problems?

8. What role do you think private plans, such as pensions and individual retirement accounts, should play in providing financial security for retirement?

9. Design your own income maintenance plan for the elderly. Be sure to consider (a) issues of inclusiveness and social justice, (b) economic feasibility, (c) political feasibility, and (d) the use of a variety of means of income maintenance.

**Health Care Policies and the Elderly**

10. What are the strengths and weaknesses of Medicare and Medicaid?

11. Do you favor the continuation of a mixed system, a national insurance plan, a national health system, a totally private system, or some other system for providing health care for the population? Why? How would you integrate providing health care for the elderly and for the rest of the population under the plan you chose? What features would you build in to ensure the maximization of health and cost effectiveness?

**Legal and Social Service Policies**

12. Do you have or wish to have a living will for yourself? If so, what provisions would it contain? How would you feel about your parents or grandparents having living wills? What are the potential advantages and problems of living wills?

**13.** Do you think the elderly are more or less likely than the general population to be in need of legal services? What special kinds of services might the elderly need?

**14.** What are the advantages and disadvantages of the federal regulation and supervision of social service programs as opposed to allowing flexibility to the states? Propose a plan for funding and delivering social services that might overcome the problems of each of these approaches and would ensure proportionate attention to the problems of the elderly.

**15.** What provisions would you make for housing for the elderly?

**The Metapolicy of Aging**

**16.** Do you think it is more fruitful to pose the development of policies and services for the elderly in terms of intergenerational equity or of social justice?

**17.** Outline a public education program for making people more aware of social policy issues related to aging and the impact of these on their lives.

# Pertinent Readings

Achenbaum, W. A. *Shades of Gray: Old Age, American Values, and Federal Policies Since 1920.* Boston: Little, Brown & Company, 1983.

Bell, W. *Contemporary Social Welfare.* New York: Macmillan Inc., 1983.

Binstock, R. H. "The Oldest Old: A Fresh Perspective or Compassionate Ageism Revisited." *Milbank Memorial Fund Quarterly/Health and Society* 63, 2 (1985): 420–51.

Brown, E. R. "Medicare and Medicaid: The Process, Value, and Limits of Health Care Reform." In *Readings in the Political Economy of Aging*, eds. M. Minkler and C. Estes, pp. 117–43. Farmingdale, N.Y.: Baywood Publishing Company, Inc., 1984.

Cohen, M., and J. March. *Leadership and Ambiguity.* New York: McGraw-Hill Book Company, 1974.

Congressional Budget Office. *Containing Medical Care Costs Through Market Forces.* Washington, D.C.: U.S. Government Printing Office, 1982.

———. *Changing the Structure of Medicare Benefits: Issues and Options.* Washington, D.C.: U.S. Government Printing Office, 1983.

Davis, K. "Health Care Policies and the Aged: Observations from the United States." In *Handbook of Aging and the Social Sciences*, eds. R. H. Binstock and E. Shanas, pp. 727–44. New York: Van Nostrand Reinhold Company, 1985.

DeVine, J. A. "Fiscal Policy and Class Income Inequality: The Distributional Consequences of Governmental Revenues and Expenditures in the United States, 1949–1976." *American Sociological Review* 48, 5 (1983): 606–22.

Drucker, P. *The Unseen Revolution: How Pension Fund Socialism Came to America.* New York: Harper & Row, Publishers, 1976.

Elder, C. D., and R. W. Cobb. "Agenda-Building and the Politics of Aging." *Policy Studies Journal* 13, 1 (1984): 115–29.

Estes, C. *The Aging Enterprise.* San Francisco: Jossey-Bass, Inc., Publishers, 1979.

Estes, C. L., L. E. Gerard, J. S. Zones, and J. H. Swan. *Political Economy, Health and Aging.* Boston: Little, Brown & Company, 1984.

———, R. J. Newcomer, and Associates. *Fiscal Austerity and Aging: Shifting Government Responsibility for the Elderly.* Beverly Hills, Calif.: Sage Publications, Inc., 1984.

Freeman, G., and P. Adams. "The Politics of Social Security: Expansion, Retrenchment, and Rationalization." In *The Political Economy of Public Policy*, eds. A. Stone and E. J. Harpham, pp. 241–61. Beverly Hills, Calif.: Sage Publications, Inc., 1982.

Gibson, R. M., K. R. Levit, H. Lazenby, and D. R. Waldo. "National Health Expenditures, 1983." *Health Care Financing Review* 6, 2 (1984): 1–31.

Gilder, G. *Wealth and Poverty.* New York: Basic Books, 1981.

Graebner, W. *A History of Retirement: The Meanings and Function of an American Institution 1885–1978.* New Haven: Yale University Press, 1980.

Gerontological Society of America. *Emerging Issues in Aging.* Washington, D.C.: Gerontological Society of America (in press).

Guillemard, A-M. "Introduction." In *Old Age and the Welfare State*, ed. A-M. Guillemard, pp. 3–15. Beverly Hills, Calif.: Sage Publications, Inc., 1983.

Harrington, C. "Social Security and Medicare: Policy Shifts in the 1980s." In *Fiscal Austerity and Aging*, eds. C. L. Estes, R. J. Newcomer, and Associates, pp. 83–111. Beverly Hills, Calif.: Sage Publications, Inc., 1983.

———, and J. H. Swan. "Medicaid Nursing Home Reimbursement Policies, Rates and Expenditures." *Health Care Financing Review* 6, 1 (1984): 39–49.

Hendricks, J., and T. M. Calasanti. "Social Policy on Ageing in North America." In *Ageing and Social Policy: A Critical Assessment*, eds. C. Phillipson and A. Walker. London: Heinemann Educational Books (in press).

Hudson, R. B., and J. Strate. "Aging and Political Systems." In *Handbook of Aging and the Social Sciences*, eds. R. Binstock and E. Shanas, pp. 554–85. New York: Van Nostrand Reinhold Company, 1985.

Kalish, R. A. "The New Ageism and the Failure Model: A Polemic." *The Gerontologist* 19, 4 (1979): 398–402.

Kearl, M., K. Moore, and J. S. Osberg. "Political Implications of the New Ageism." *International Journal of Aging and Human Development* 15, 3 (1982): 167–83.

Keller, B. "Another Stab at Pension Reform." *The New York Times* (July 15, 1984).

Menefee, J., B. Edwards, and S. Schieber. "Analysis of Non-Participation in the SSI Program." *Social Security Bulletin* (June 1981): 3–21.

Mills, C. W. *The Sociological Imagination.* New York: Oxford University Press, 1959.

Mizruchi, E. "Abeyance Processes, Social Policy and Aging." In *Old Age and the Welfare State*, ed. A-M. Guillemard, pp. 45–52. Beverly Hills, Calif.: Sage Publications, Inc., 1983.

Munnell, A. H. "Navigating a Few Rough Spots Ahead: The Social Security Solution — Cont." *The New York Times* (August 12, 1984): F-2.

Murray, C. *Losing Ground: American Social Policy, 1950–1980.* New York: Basic Books, 1985.

Myles, J. *Old Age in the Welfare State: The Political Economy of Public Pensions.* Boston: Little, Brown & Company, 1984.

Nelson, G. M. "Tax Expenditures for the Elderly." *The Gerontologist* 23, 5 (1983): 471–78.

Offe, C. *Contradictions of the Welfare State.* Cambridge, Mass.: The MIT Press, 1984.

Plutchok, J. "IRA — Where to Put the Money." *The New York Times* (March 10, 1985): F-11.

Preston, S. H. "Children and the Elderly in the U.S." *Scientific American* 251, 6 (1984): 44–49.

Quadagno, J. S. "Welfare Capitalism and the Social Security Act of 1935." *American Sociological Review* 49, 5 (1984): 632–47.

Ripley, R., and G. Franklin. *Congress, the Bureaucracy and Public Policy.* Homewood, Ill.: Dorsey Press, 1984.

Shanas, E., and G. L. Maddox. "Health, Health Resources and the Utilization of Care." In *Handbook of Aging and the Social Sciences,* eds. R. H. Binstock and E. Shanas, pp. 696–726. New York: Van Nostrand Reinhold Company, 1985.

Social Security Administration. *The Supplemental Security Income Program for the Aged, Blind and Disabled: Selected Characteristics of State Supplementation Programs as of October, 1979.* Washington, D.C.: U.S. Government Printing Office, 1980.

Stein, A. "Medicare's Broken Promise." *New York Times Magazine* (February 17, 1985): 44 ff.

U.S. Department of Health and Human Services. *Medicare and Medicaid Date Book, 1981.* Health Care Financing Administration. Washington, D.C.: U.S. Government Printing Office, 1981.

———. *Guide to Health Insurance for People with Medicare.* Washington, D.C.: U.S. Government Printing Office, 1985.

U.S. House of Representatives. *Rising Health Care Costs and the Elderly.* Washington, D.C.: U.S. Government Printing Office, 1984.

U.S. President's Commission for the Study of Ethical Problems in Medicine and Biomedical and Behavioral Research. *Securing Access to Health Care: A Report on the Ethical Implications of Differences in the Availability of Health Services,* vol. 1. Washington, D.C.: U.S. Government Printing Office, 1983.

U.S. Senate Committee on the Budget. *Tax Expenditures: Relationship to Spending Programs and Background Material on Individual Provisions.* Washington, D.C.: U.S. Government Printing Office, 1982.

U.S. Senate Special Committee on Aging. *Future Directions in Social Security.* Washington, D.C.: U.S. Government Printing Office, 1973.

———. *Developments in Aging: 1981,* vol. I. Washington, D.C.: U.S. Government Printing Office, 1982.

———. *Medicare and the Health Costs of Older Americans: The Extent and Effects of Cost Sharing.* Washington, D.C.: U.S. Government Printing Office, 1984a.

———. *Medicare: Paying the Physician — History, Issues and Options.* Washington, D.C.: U.S. Government Printing Office, 1984b.

———. *Developments in Aging: 1984,* vol. I. Washington, D.C.: U.S. Government Printing Office, 1985.

———. *News.* Washington, D.C.: U.S. Government Printing Office, February 26, 1985.

Waldo, D. R., and H. C. Lazenby. "Demographic Characteristics and Health Care Use and Expenditures by the Aged in the United States: 1977–1984." *Health Care Financing Review* 6, 1 (1984): 1–29.

# PART FOUR

# LOOKING AHEAD

# 12

# THE PROSPECTS
# OF AGING

**THE FUTURE OF AGING: THE
ISSUES**

**THE ELDERLY OF
TOMORROW**
General Projections
Interpersonal Relations and the
  Prospect of Aging
  *Reflections from Inside*
  *Men, Women, and Aging*
  *The Social Contextuality of the Self*

**PREPARING THE WAY — SOCIAL
POLICY ISSUES**
Social Security
Working Ahead
Making Room for The Future: The
  Prognosis on Health
  *The Issues*
  *The Biomedical Dimension: Scientific
    Medicine and the Health of the
    Elderly*
  *Sociocultural and Political Dimensions*
  *The Issue of Cost*
  *Developing Appropriate Levels of Care*

**THE RESPONSE**
Gerontology as a Vocation
Careers in Aging
  *Counseling*
  *Academic Researchers and Teachers*
  *Nurses*
  *Other Nursing Home Personnel*
  *Physicians*
  *Other Health Professionals*
  *Social Workers*
Training and Course Work
The Challenge

**SUMMARY**

**DISCUSSION QUESTIONS**

**PERTINENT READINGS**

# The Future of Aging: The Issues

It should be apparent that aging is not an issue that can be neatly isolated. Although grounded in biological realities, aging is socially constructed and interpreted. Its contours are intimately intertwined with other central issues in our society and in our world today. What is the purpose of a pluralistic society and for whose benefit does it exist? How do we balance needs and available resources? What relative priorities do we place on budget items such as defense spending, as opposed to programs directed toward income maintenance, social services, and health? How are social values embodied in social policy? Why are women at particular risk for economic hardship throughout their lives, especially during old age? Why are some ethnic minorities at greater risk for economic hardship, ill-health, and shortened life expectancies? What is the effect of the structure of international relations on people of Third World countries and on their elderly in particular? What do we want for ourselves at different times in our lives? The old of today are people like ourselves who have aged through the years, as we too shall unless death intervenes.

We all have a stake in today's public policy choices regarding aging. One generation follows another's footsteps and the transition from one to the other is the substance of social progress (GSA, in press). Policies affect the young of today through the ways in which the tax burden is allocated and by influencing their opportunities for saving for retirement. These policies also structure their worldview and shape their responsibilities for older relatives and their own economic security when they reach advanced ages in the twenty-first century (Estes et al., 1984). Social policies formulated now will help determine what the baby boom generation and those who follow will encounter along the way.

As we stated at the outset and have illustrated throughout the text, aging involves a complex interplay of physiological, economic, social structural, cultural, and material factors. Within the constraints woven by these factors is at least some room for conscious personal choice between alternatives and for interactive, communal efforts to shape social policy. As individual agents, we are not free to do as we will: our lives and the very patterns of our consciousness are shaped by the society we live in, its power structures, and its interpretive systems. But neither is the current shape of aging nor the social problems now associated with it inevitable. We may, for instance, continue to have increasing numbers of the elderly on Social Security, presenting a growing financial responsibility on a diminishing work force — or we may restructure the working life cycle so that fewer hours of work are spread throughout the life stages and provide flexible retirement programs. Or we may create cooperative communities in which people provide services for each other, as has been done in some Third World countries (Hampson, 1985). The aging themselves should not be treated as the objects of social services but as co-creators of social policy. Basic to our whole conception of social policy for aging is the notion of reciprocity: the elderly of today helped build what we see around us.

In the next section we will look at some of the givens of today and their implications for projections for tomorrow: population structures, changing dependency ratios, and the interplay between individual and social factors. In the following section we will look at the social policy decisions that the future will pose for us in terms of finances, work, and health. Finally, we will consider the need for a response to this challenge in terms of careers in aging and in the response required of us all as members of society.

# The Elderly of Tomorrow

## GENERAL PROJECTIONS

Despite the slowing rate of expansion among industrialized populations, if zero population growth were attained immediately, the effects would not be observed for fifty to seventy-five years. Those people who will be the aged at the turn of the century have already established secure life-styles, while the large group of post-World War II boom babies will only be entering the so-called empty nest phase in the year 2000. The numerical size of these cohorts is not in question except to the extent that mortality rates will reduce their numbers.

If low growth projects hold true, the aggregate of Americans over sixty-five in the year 2000 will exceed 33.6 million, nearly one-quarter higher than is presently the case. High series projections, which are based on low death rates and high fertility, approach 36.6 million elderly, or roughly one-third more than projections for 1985. For 2080 projections range between 49 and 108.9 million people over sixty-five — meaning the number of the elderly will have increased between two- and five-fold in the century since 1980. The lower death rates, if they indeed occur, would indicate significant improvements in personal and societal health, coupled with more favorable environmental inputs, ranging from pollution control to better educational programs aimed at nutritional, safety, and medical advances. Reflections of the possible refinements in health maintenance would be most dramatic among those over seventy-five. While contemporary mortality rates will result in increasing that portion of the elderly population by 60 percent, only a small reduction in mortality would double the size of the very old group. If a slight decline in death rates is observed, the average life expectancy would be five years longer for people aged sixty-five in 2000 than for those who are sixty-five today.

Physiologists and other biological scientists do not yet agree on whether the natural processes of aging will be arrested during future decades. Speculations about diminishing mortality rates rely primarily on health breakthroughs that would check the known diseases now limiting the life span, such as atherosclerosis and various forms of cancer. Research on cancer may spawn important spin-offs, for many of the factors associated with malignancies seem to be particularly common among the aged. Extensive research is already under way to investigate basic immunological systems perhaps involved in aging and the disruption of the body's internal communication processes that enable it to discriminate between inherent and foreign elements. Additional studies are being carried out on DNA encoding, enzyme synthesis, inhibitory agents for lipofuscin and collagen accumulations, as well as long-term nutritional requirements and drug effects. The answers to life's questions are still somewhere beyond the horizon, but the search will impart valuable new evidence to help fill out the mosaic that is today still a mystery. There is less hope among scientists that physiological functions themselves will be unraveled to the extent that intervention will mean prolonging the life span. Although a more healthy old age appears certainly related to greater longevity, there is not a clear or simple causal link between the two. Innumerable factors mediate, and there is a growing awareness of the role of social variables affecting life expectancy, from housing, nutrition, and sanitation to smoking, alcoholism, and relative affluence. It should not be expected, however, that the experience of disability in very old age will be substantially altered or removed; at best, this time of life will continue to be constrained by physical and in some cases mental problems. The crucial question is whether we really want to add years to life without significant changes in the quality of life available to old people.

Our most telling charge for the future is to compress the period of declining vigor in the later years. The health sciences, having largely conquered the acute causes of death, must now turn to the chronic debilitating conditions that creep up over the years. Age-specific life expectancy for those in their middle or later years has not improved much in recent decades. At seventy, between eleven and fifteen years remain, depending on sex, race, and socioeconomic background. This is essentially the same as for seventy-year-olds four or even five decades ago. Recall Figure 5.1 for a moment. While the survival curves have been improving, a few more changes are required to bring the average age at death close to the early eighties. Looking at the 1970–1980 line, we see that since the early part of the century we have moved almost 80 percent of the way toward an "ideal" rectangular curve (Fries, 1980). What is left?

If the decline in heart diseases noted in Chapter 5 continues, many of the debilities of later life can be postponed. According to Fries (1980), the "plasticity" of aging is evident by changes in such problems as heart disease. Slight modifications in life-style, exercise, smoking, and so on have already been shown to decrease the incidence of chronic ailments. Most of the chronic conditions identified as the cause of death are a long time coming for each individual. They are silent for many years, going unnoticed until some threshold is passed when physicians are called. Slow down the asymptomatic development and the boundaries of ill-health may be pushed back far enough so premature deaths will no longer be a concern. That is to say, not until the late seventies or early eighties need chronic disability or death be much of a reality. As long as a few individuals do not age according to the averages, as long as some among us show individual variation above the norm, then there is hope we can all slow the physical processes to fit our own schedules.

Just as overall health status is likely to shift gradually in the next two decades, so too will the proportion of people who live in or who are associated with multigenerational families. Individuals are becoming parents and grandparents at ever younger ages, thereby creating a considerable probability of four- and even five-generational families in the near future. Women whose children were born during the postwar baby boom will be sixty-five or older around the year 2000. They will have more adult children than women in previous generations as a result of their higher survival rates. The obvious implications arise in part from previous findings that 80 percent of all elderly today live close to their children and are generally able to see them more than once a week. The majority of old people do not *live* in extended families, preferring to maintain an independent status as long as feasible. Nonetheless, all families turn to their own members when they are in need of assistance — a trend not likely to change in the coming years unless there are dramatic alterations in the delivery of social services. Although existing patterns and types of mutual aid differ by social class and subcultural background, there is a definite tendency for those parents who do live with adult children to be more often women, sick, or over seventy-five. This will remain the case in the future as the numbers of the old-old slowly expand. A quite plausible forecast is an increase in the proportion of very old adults who share accommodations with their young-old children. Despite that twice as many elderly currently live with adult children or other relatives as live in nursing homes, it would be unreasonable to expect institutions to care for an ever larger clientele without thoroughgoing changes. The present standards of care are already under attack for permitting profits at the expense of human integrity. The criticisms aimed at the nursing home industry in the early 1970s brought many changes, yet each time congressional committees call for testimony the elderly stand in line to tell of even more problems. The likely outcome will be greater policing of the nation's nursing homes by either the federal Health Care Financing Administration or state agencies. As long as the risk of hospital-prompted illness remains significantly higher among the elderly than among young people, watchful scrutiny will be necessary (National Institute on Aging, 1980).

Other facets of life will also change for those who will become old in the twenty-first century. One change will be the increased presence of the elderly in the labor force. The extent of these changes is contingent on changing dependency ratios and the ways in which these ratios are conceptualized and interpreted. There are of course increasing numbers of people over sixty-five in the population, which means that the old age–dependency ratio is rising — but there are also decreasing numbers under eighteen, and some resources could be diverted from the needs of youth to the needs of the elderly. As we saw in Chapter 2, age–dependency ratios give only an approximate estimate of the number of workers to those not in the work force. Since up to 20 percent of those over sixty-five may be in the work force, while many younger people may not be, and because age–dependency ratios do not take account of the changes in economic-dependency ratios resulting from increased participation of women in the work force, they are highly speculative. Yet, as shown by Figure 12.1, government projections indicate that the number of those paying Social Security payroll taxes for each beneficiary sixty-five and over will decrease. Still, Marshall (1981) contends that because of political considerations and the different levels of government administration involved, it is difficult to transfer resources from the young to the old, and there is still a potential for intergenerational conflict, either because of the increasing investment of the

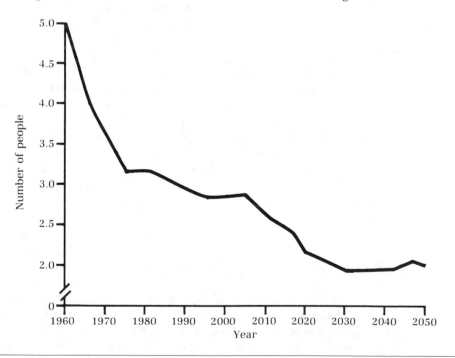

**FIGURE 12.1**
Projected number of people paying Social Security payroll taxes per beneficiary sixty-five and over. United States, 1960–2050. (*Source:* U.S. House of Representatives, Select Committee on Population. *Domestic Consequences of United States Population Change,* Figure 13, p. 73, 95th Cong., 2nd Sess., 1978.)

work force in supporting the elderly or because of competition between the generations for jobs.

Earlier retirement, greater experimentation with second careers, and perhaps more equitable pension plans will have a profound impact on the complexion of the retirement years. It is possible that fifty-five will be the new age for official retirement from the first career in which a specified number of years have been *vested*. Alternatively, two or more careers may be pursued by those who wish to work well into later life. By the turn of the century the majority of older people will have a high school diploma; many more will have additional continuing educational experience. One effect of this extension of the educational process will be to diminish some portion of the differences currently observed between young adults and the elderly. Another development may be more active and vocal involvement in the political and social arenas, an outgrowth of the increase in average educational levels and rising expectations during times of social affluence. Moreover, with increasing numbers, the elderly might even become a formidable political force in the twenty-first century. A great many changes will have to be implemented for that to take place, however (Binstock, 1984, 1985).

As we look back over the magnitude of change that has taken place during the last twenty-five to fifty years, it is not difficult to appreciate why our grandparents sometimes express awe at the world they see around them. Projecting at least the same magnitude of change into the future (there are few who envision any possibility for slowing the rate of technological growth), we can acquire a better grasp of the way life may appear to those who will become elderly early in the twenty-first century. A closer look at some of the areas of change and the challenges that may arise for the old of tomorrow is warranted.

## INTERPERSONAL RELATIONS AND THE PROSPECT OF AGING

**Reflections from Inside.** What do we mean when we ask how old a person is? Will age mean the same thing for future generations of the elderly as for those who are old today? We ordinarily answer the question of how old someone is by giving the chronological age, but this simple response is likely to mask wide variations. Physiologically, separate components of the body age at different rates; thus, it is entirely possible to have the eyes of a young adult, the lungs of an older person, yet show middle age on the calendar. Asking people how old they feel might not provide any better information, since their answers will likely be phrased in relative terms. "Do you mean compared to my children? To others who have lived the same length of time? Or to what?" Usually they will offer two or three responses. "Last birthday I was . . . , but I feel . . . years younger. No different than I did when I was. . . . I've still got my health, so I'm in better shape than Joe, who is . . . years younger than I am." It is quite common for adults over twenty-five to report they actually feel younger than their birth certificates indicate. In fact, most of us often hold a more youthful self-concept than our years might predict. Even those in their seventh and eighth decades frequently express their contempt for "old folks" — meaning individuals either older or less healthy than themselves. As many researchers have discovered, the elderly consistently exempt themselves from the reprehensible qualities attributed to others who are at a comparable point in life (Bultena and Powers, 1978; Ward, 1977; Rosow, 1974).

Personal conceptions of age are always subjective, though they may include a complex interweaving of objective criteria such as stage of family life cycle, career and employment patterns, health, or socioeconomic background. Self-concepts are never in themselves singular; people have as many facets or selves as they have social roles and none ever remain static. At the same time nearly all see themselves as original and exceptional; indeed, no two people have the same biography. But the sense of uniqueness goes beyond individuality to encompass a belief that although our age mates are obviously becoming older, we alone have a particular youthfulness. The person we appear to be to someone else is not necessarily the one we are for ourselves. The real "me" is the one inside. Externally age may show, but these signs are generally dismissed as merely superficial. Compared to the inner person, outward appearances are hardly proof of anything. No amount of reality testing will bring about a complete congruence between our own and others' conceptions of us, primarily because it is impossible to climb out of our bodies for an objective look. In a sense the process of *psychological distancing* implied by self-perceived youthfulness is a protective device, insulating us from negative attacks on self-image. As DeBeauvoir (1973) observes, this may be part of the reason behind the unwillingness to use medical facilities or the failure to follow a physician's orders that others find so irksome about many older people. They cannot understand why an older person would act in what would seem to be counter to his or her best interests.

Percentages vary from one study to another, but somewhere between one-half to two-thirds of those over sixty-five continue to think of themselves as no more than middle-aged, a perception actually well-established by the third decade (Kastenbaum et al., 1980; Bultena and Powers, 1978; Ward, 1977). Approximately the same factors operate in terms of personal age as influence subjective evaluations of health or estimated chances of survival. Just as social involvements, social class, sex, and so on play pivotal roles in shaping ideas of survival, so do they offset personal images of age. In constructing and maintaining self-concepts men adjust their self-images more to external events; women more to their personal feelings or abilities (Back, 1974). Internally most have an intuitive sense of sameness about themselves. In any event those who perceive themselves to be younger have higher morale, greater satisfaction, better health, fewer somatic concerns, increased mobility, and more optimistic frames of mind than their age peers who feel somehow older. On the opposite side, only one-fifth or less of the elderly regard themselves as being older than their chronological age. Usually these people are recovering from a serious illness or some other displacing event and have not regained their equilibrium. The impact of ill-health on other aspects of one's self-concept is complex and not to be underestimated (Palmore et al., 1979; Garrity and Marx, 1979). Among additional phenomena contributing to older self-images, researchers have also counted the sudden removal of social props, the absence of friendly reinforcers, or institutionalization and its corresponding stigma and devaluation. The consequences for the group who view themselves as old beyond their years are predominantly negative — resulting in lower morale, increased dependency, ill-health, and even earlier deaths. Practically, it makes a great deal of difference whether individuals consider themselves to be old or not so old.

**Men, Women, and Aging.** How will the experience of future generations of elderly men and women differ from that of the elderly today, both in sex roles and in relations between the sexes? Will women's greater participation in the labor force mean that they are likely to suffer role losses similar to men at retirement? Or do women tend to bring different attitudes to both work and retirement? And if future generations of the elderly are more involved in home life and leisure activities when young, will they have greater psychological resources to draw on during their later years? How will the relations between the sexes during retirement be affected by women's changing roles in society and family? While we recognize the very real structural injustices under which women, and particularly elderly women, suffer, we would hope that future generations will go beyond a bitter battle between militant feminism and an equally intransigent male chauvinism. More fruitful would be a dialogue between people of both sexes based on a mutual respect; men and women can learn from each others' perspectives to develop a more rounded view.

**The Social Contextuality of the Self.** What is it that shapes our self-image as younger or older than our years, or as masculine or feminine according to a particular model? Do our self-conceptions come from the inside? Or are they imposed on us by social roles or the judgments of those around us? Are we independent beings who shape our own destiny or are we puppets whose strings are pulled by the structure of society? Do we shape social structure or are we molded by it?

As implied at the beginning of this text, we subscribe to a view between these two extremes. People both shape and are shaped by social structure and social policy and their consequences. Circumstances and events have a major impact on us, but the mindset with which we perceive them will influence both our perception of and our response to them. Zautra and Reich (1983), for example, point to the ways in which small undesired events or annoyances in the daily lives of the elderly may contribute to depression or demoralization, while desired events contribute to feelings of well-being. These events influence affective states by diminishing or enhancing feelings of personal competence or personal control over events and consequences. If a person has sufficient psychosocial resources, or can acquire coping techniques for dealing with the annoyances, he or she will suffer less demoralization. It seems successfully overcoming minor difficulties can lead to increased feelings of competence and further successes in the future. Thus, demoralization among the elderly is seen by Zautra and Reich as resulting from a combination of external and internal factors: the occurrence of difficulties that may be beyond the person's control because of economic or other factors and the development of psychosocial resources that enable some measure of coping. This would suggest the need for a two-pronged intervention: implementing social policies to lessen the degree elderly persons are subjected to circumstances beyond their control and the possibility of acquiring appropriate personal resources to exert a measure of economic control. In a similar vein Marshall (in press) views the individual as participating actively in fashioning a life course, as capable of exercising choice. He points out, however, that this can only be done with a knowledge of the available alternatives. Clearly, the question of social structure is involved — and social structure for Marshall (1981) is both created by and creates the individual. He sees a constant tension between the stability that follows from structural constraints and social consensus and the instability that follows from human intentionality.

Perhaps one of the major contributions of social gerontological theory, as Marshall (in press) also implies, can be to help us make the connection among personal, individual, and structural levels, to realize the ways in which the "personal troubles" of the elderly actually stem from "public issues" (Mills, 1959). By taking such a view we see how valuable personal resources are in carving out an older person's social life space. Making the connection between the life of the elderly individual and the structural context in which he or she lives is useful in a number of ways: it enables us to go beyond seeing the victim as a scapegoat and it removes the sense of personal guilt for things beyond a person's control. It can also provide a clearer idea of the options and limitations imposed by current circumstances. Being aware of this balance may make for a more intelligent and informed choice of realistic options; it can also make people aware of the ways in which social policy is shaped by people and by interest groups. Knowing that policy is socially constructed, we also realize there are possibilities for change.

## Preparing the Way — Social Policy Issues

Successful aging is a nebulous concept incorporating diverse attitudes and behaviors. There are as many maxims for adequate preparedness for the retirement years as there are advisors, though obviously practical antidotes for poor planning are rather scarce. Coupling what is known about the present aged population with predictions about future social conditions increases the urgency for altered or new programming. The integration of facts and hypotheses is laden with uncertainty, yet it remains one of the most important goals of any study involving such a broad range of problems. Several areas have been consistently identified as crucial for ensuring a successful old age.

Improved income, housing, health, nutrition, and more recently, transportation have claimed the attention of the elderly and their advocates. While interrelationships are multiple and complex, the proposed universal remedy often comes close to a blanket economic determinism. Without sufficient income, even if it is not the ultimate panacea, all other well-intentioned programs are jeopardized.

## SOCIAL SECURITY

In 1985 two-thirds of the 36.6 million people receiving Social Security depended on benefits for over half their income. Not only will any freeze on cost-of-living adjustments put an additional half million persons into poverty but such a recession will actually do nothing to improve the federal deficit. By law Social Security taxes can be used for no other purpose than income security programs. Furthermore, of the $200 billion earmarked for the elderly in the 1981 federal budget, 92 percent was set aside to fund entitlement programs underwritten by lifetime earnings conditions. Long-run differentials in the Social Security trust fund would be affected, but the slight drop in new beneficiaries in the 1990s (Depression era babies) will do that anyway. Doing away with minimum floors for new beneficiaries might also help the trust fund, but it will specially affect minorities and women. At present about 14 percent of Social Security recipients face life below the poverty level, and another 9 percent are very near that level. Eliminating thresholds and cutting back on food stamp eligibility at the same time — over 2.3 million older persons are on food stamps — mean dire times ahead (Storey, 1983).

Recommendations for reform emanating from the National Commission on Social Security Reform are reported to have been hammered out in secret bargaining meetings held outside of the mandated legislative process by what one commentator called the Gang of Nine — five members of the commission and four White House aides. The result was that the principles of distributive justice have been subjected to political and partisan budgetary considerations (Light, 1985).

One of the long-run implications of the various proposed reductions in Social Security is an impending crisis in legitimacy in which the guarantees of the program look to future recipients for present revenues. Rather than consider using general revenues or abolishing the taxation ceilings on withholdings, the focus is on reducing benefits and withholding more taxes for low- and middle-income workers. Seemingly, the new fiscal austerity will be implemented at the expense of the majority of wage earners. The standard response when benefit pay out exceeds income in nearly all insurance or transfer programs is to limit the provisions. Some have referred to the type of retrenchments recommended for Social Security as a form of age discrimination under the guise of cost control (Selby et al., 1982). The amount spent on Social Security is small compared with other pension programs — 60 percent of all military pensions go to the richest one-fifth of the population. Actually, the annual cost of military pensions exceeds the combined cost of the food stamp program,

AFDC, and SSI for the elderly. Then, too, congressional pensions that averaged $35,387 in 1984, a figure comparable to what corporate executives received in retirement, make the average pension benefit of $12,988 for Social Security recipients seem unfair.

Altogether, the 1983 amendments eliminated two-thirds of the deficit projected over the next seventy-five years by raising taxes, cutting benefits, and bringing new occupations into coverage. When the retirement age is raised to sixty-seven in the year 2000, the remainder of the deficit will be resolved. After 1988, when the trust fund begins to be replenished, the number of new claimants will begin to fall and withholding taxes will be raised, so surpluses should accumulate until about the year 2015 when the boom babies begin to retire. For some time thereafter deficits will return and another tax increase will be probable. After 2057, claims will start dropping again but future fertility rates will determine the well-being of the Social Security system at that point (Munnell, 1984).

For those who retire some years from now at least one leg of the so-called three-legged stool of income security (Social Security, private pensions, and individual savings) may not be as bad as the current controversy makes it seem. Nonetheless, most workers heading toward retirement may face some restrictions in their budgets. Individual savings seldom amount to a very significant amount of retirement income (Schulz, 1985).

As Schulz (1985) makes clear and as we pointed out in the previous chapter, the collective deferred assets of private pension annuities make a major difference for those who are able to participate. With private annuities to augment Social Security payments, replacement income levels run between 60 and 75 percent of previous earnings. The accumulated monies in private pension plans amount to the single largest pool of capital in the United States.

Individual Retirement Accounts (IRAs) come closest to providing the third leg of the stool. As pointed out earlier, the $2000 limit will probably be raised in 1986; some estimates are that the ceiling could go as high as $7000 for couples and perhaps 60 percent of that amount for individual workers. By deferring allowable amounts now and paying taxes on them after sixty-five benefits accrue to individuals as savings and tax differentials. At the end of 1984 IRAs totaled some $132 billion. These funds are also available to private enterprise as loans (Plutchok, 1985).

For individuals able to participate in all three retirement plans the retirement years will probably not hold any grave difficulties. But for those who must depend on Social Security for most of their income the economic circumstances will not be nearly so rosy. This group will probably have to depend on family contributions to augment their income.

Of course, inflation, a constant specter for those on fixed incomes, will continue. Indexing federal tax brackets to inflation helps at the individual level but creates revenue problems for the federal government and by extension for many domestic support programs as well. At present other possible difficulties on the horizon are the heavier tax burden on single individuals, the abolition of double deductions after sixty-five, and taxes on some employee benefits such as life and health insurance. A freeze on cost-of-living adjustments (COLAs) will also hurt the old-old, especially older women living alone. On the other hand, certain proposed pension rights for women may counterbalance some of the negative forces. At present only about 10 percent of older women receive monies from private pension plans. The proposed changes would aid a substantial number by protecting their rights to survivor's annuities from deceased spouses who died before reaching retirement age and by requiring both spouses to agree in writing to waive the survivor annuity options if they so desired.

Whether the so-called Social Security crisis of the mid-1980s is real, it has affected the view people have of their own financial prospects. As can be seen in Figure 12.2, as late as 1984 (before the budgetary crisis of 1985) respondents of all ages expressed some real concerns about the future of Social Security. While it is highly unlikely the system will fail, the perception of doubt will erode morale and the sense of well-being among current and potential recipients. The political acceptability of one option over any other possibility is at the real heart of the matter. Concerted and cooperative federal intervention seems to many to be the only viable means of dealing with long-term guarantees of income security. Above all, it should be remembered, as we noted in the previous chapter, Social Security benefits not just the elderly but also the rest of the population.

It is unlikely that retirement programs will soon alter the basic assumptions of the present system or offer innovative changes. New data must be collected to measure the impact of lengthening years in retirement and of shorter work expectancy, as well as new economic and employment demands. These should also include the possible costs and incentives for encouraging workers to remain in the labor force. The variables that enter into determining an adequate retirement income must be delineated. An adequate income will probably require multiple projects coupling basic income maintenance with a contributory scheme related to occupational experiences. Finally, the very foundation of the current system must be restructured to reduce and eliminate areas of discrimination between sex and racial groups or occupational or marital status. Direct income transfers will continue to be complemented with service programs, such as health care and housing subsidies, although such delivery systems must be carefully evaluated to appraise their success in creating satisfying environments for aged recipients.

## WORKING AHEAD

As we have seen, Social Security and nearly all other social policies pertaining to older people are predicated on the socioeconomic consequences of free market economies. In Chapter 8 we made clear that financial status in retirement mirrors the structure and status dimensions of a person's work history. There is no reason to assume factors presently influencing participation in the labor market will undergo any dramatic change in the near future. But what will work be like?

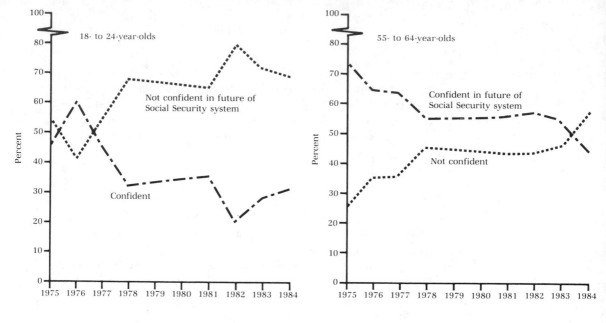

| | National | | 18–24 years | | 25–29 years | | 30–34 years | | 35–44 years | | 45–54 years | | 55–64 years | | 65 and over | |
|---|---|---|---|---|---|---|---|---|---|---|---|---|---|---|---|---|
| | Conf. | Non-conf. | Conf. | Non-conf. | Conf. | Non-conf. | Conf. | Non-conf. | Conf. | Non-conf. | Conf. | Non-conf. | Conf. | Non-conf. | Conf. | Non-conf. |
| 1975 | 63% | 37% | 45% | 55% | 59% | 41% | 51% | 49% | 62% | 38% | 66% | 34% | 74% | 25% | 82% | 18% |
| 1976 | 58 | 43 | 60 | 41 | 46 | 54 | 41 | 60 | 51 | 50 | 55 | 45 | 65 | 35 | 78 | 22 |
| 1977 | 50 | 50 | 45 | 55 | 35 | 64 | 37 | 62 | 45 | 54 | 49 | 51 | 64 | 36 | 75 | 25 |
| 1978 | 39 | 60 | 32 | 68 | 27 | 73 | 35 | 65 | 24 | 76 | 41 | 60 | 55 | 45 | 62 | 37 |
| 1981 | 42 | 57 | 35 | 65 | 24 | 75 | 26 | 75 | 34 | 66 | 40 | 59 | 56 | 43 | 73 | 26 |
| 1982 | 32 | 67 | 20 | 80 | 15 | 85 | 15 | 84 | 18 | 82 | 31 | 70 | 57 | 43 | 66 | 34 |
| 1983 | 35 | 66 | 28 | 72 | 21 | 79 | 20 | 80 | 25 | 75 | 30 | 69 | 54 | 46 | 67 | 33 |
| 1984 | 32 | 68 | 31 | 69 | 19 | 81 | 30 | 70 | 21 | 79 | 26 | 74 | 43 | 57 | 48 | 51 |

**Note:** Confident = "Very confident" + "Somewhat confident"; Non-confident = "Not too confident" + "Not at all confident."
**Source:** Survey by Yankelovich, Skelly and White for the American Council of Life Insurance, latest that of September 1984.

**Question:** There has been a lot of discussion about the financial condition of the Social Security system. Do you think Social Security will exist or not when it is time for you or your spouse to retire?

☐ Yes, Social Security will exist when it is time for me to retire   ▦ No, it will not exist   ‖ Already retired, voluntary

**By age:**

| | | |
|---|---|---|
| 18–30 years | 33% | 67% |
| 31–44 years | 43% | 57% |
| 45–59 years | 64% | 32% / 4% |
| 60 and over | 41% | 12% / 46% |
| National | 44% | 46% |

**Source:** Survey by ABC News/Washington Post, January 11–16, 1985.

**Question:** How confident are you that your income after your retirement will be enough for you to live on adequately—very confident, somewhat confident, not too confident, or not at all confident? (Asked of respondents who were not retired)

☐ Confident that income after retirement will be adequate   ‖ Non-confident

**By age:**

| | | |
|---|---|---|
| 18–29 years | 35% | 64% |
| 30–44 years | 41% | 58% |
| 45–64 years | 40% | 60% |
| 65 and over | 56% | 43% |
| National | 39% | 62% |

**Note:** Confident = "Very confident" + "Somewhat confident"; Non-confident = "Not too confident" + "Not at all confident."
**Source:** Survey by CBS News/New York Times, April 7–11, 1983.

**FIGURE 12.2**
Confidence in the future of the Social Security system. (*Source:* "Opinion Roundup." *Public Opinion* 8, 2 [1985]: 22.)

For middle-aged and older male workers we suspect that continuing participation in the labor market will become even more problematic. The decline in middle-aged men who are employed is unlikely to change in the near future. Similarly, labor force participation for men over sixty-five has been cut in half in the past three decades. There is every reason to expect this downward spiral to last into the early decades of the next century. Recalling Figure 8.1, we can ascertain what the magnitude of the changes over the next fifteen years will be. Part of the decline is caused by the availability of pension benefits. These enable men to retire when they want to or need to rather than waiting for sixty-five. Counterbalancing this, however, is the increase in mandatory retirement age to seventy, although this increase is unlikely to change the direction of the general trend.

As observed earlier, women's labor force participation rates have been on the rise. In the ten years leading up to sixty-five the rate of increase has leveled off in recent years, and for those even older it has dropped a few points. Better pension rights may affect the number who want or have to keep working, but there are unlikely to be any significant shifts over the remainder of the century.

What will probably be the case is that older workers will permeate the borders of retirement far more successfully than they have in the past decade. We may also see greater flexibility in lifelong patterns of work and leisure. Once people retire the first time they may return to the labor force either part time in their former occupations or reenter as members of the service sector. In either case there will be a blurring of what we have traditionally thought of as retirement. Age and job discrimination will remain factors in their decisions, and the shifts of the economy will affect how readily they pass back and forth, but we suspect that upwards of 20 percent of workers over retirement age will at least seek to remain in the work force.

One question we have not yet addressed centers on the nature of the work experience in the years ahead. In all probability automation and technological developments will change the nature of that experience. It has already made significant inroads and will accelerate in the next ten years. Growth will occur primarily in service industries, which have been outstripping all others for several years. Accordingly, while lifelong career trajectories bring upward mobility, greater autonomy and responsibility are probably somewhat diminished. Traditionally, employee fringe benefits have been less prominent in the service sector than elsewhere and we have seen little to suggest that situation will be altered. Furthermore, the continued growth of the service sector will alter the composition of the labor force. The rate of entry for women, especially minority women, into the labor force will continue to increase with the development of the service sector. Unfortunately, movement upward from entry level positions may be limited for both sexes and all ethnic groups, though the rate for women and minorities will lag behind the male mobility rate. None of this is to say the professions, technical occupations, or salaried managers will cease to grow, only that their importance as career possibilities will shrink in comparison with openings in the service occupations.

The future of old age income security will be tied firmly to events in the private sector. As the economy goes, so goes old age security. There is little that can be done about that no matter how much one might wish to change the basis on which income policies are formulated. Contrary to the popular stereotype, the elderly of today are not homogeneous, and old people in the future will remain heterogeneous. Some will have solid work histories and will have affluent retirements. Others will have grown old on the lower end of the economic continuum and their retirement incomes will be far from adequate. Generally, however, we would maintain that the status of the elderly relative to the rest of the population will continue to improve as it has for the past two decades. Part of that improvement will be from the flexibility the elderly demonstrate in their labor force participation, in their leisure activities, and in their retirement (Chen, 1985; Robinson et al., 1985).

## MAKING ROOM FOR THE FUTURE: THE PROGNOSIS ON HEALTH

**The Issues.** While health is a biological concept, it is also very definitely a socially constructed phenomenon. Social structural factors have a profound effect both on health and on the incidence and severity of illness. Social factors also determine the ways people think about health and illness. The creation of approaches to the management of illness and the extent to which the promotion of health involves social policy choices are also part of this constitutive process. Thus the health of the elderly in the future is not simply a matter of scientific and medical breakthroughs — or the lack of them — but is also a matter of social policy, the structure of social relations, and, to a certain degree within these constraints, of personal choice. Accordingly, we will briefly address the questions raised by the various dimensions of health: the biomedical dimension, the broad sociocultural dimension including life-style factors, the issue of costs, and the question of developing appropriate levels of care for those who will become old in the future.

**The Biomedical Dimension: Scientific Medicine and the Health of the Elderly.** What are the promises and the challenges for scientific medicine with regard to the health of the elderly? We have increased life expectancy but have we benefited from the extensions? Much of the gain is largely because we have controlled infant mortality: age-specific life expectancy in the later years is little changed. But is the quality of those years improved? Are people healthier in the years after sixty-five or seventy? That is where real needs currently lie. Again, as pointed out in Chapter 5, the major advances of medical science have been in the area of acute, infectious diseases; the current challenge lies with the chronic degenerative conditions where there has been relatively little progress made. We also noted in Chapter 5 that how health is conceptualized is an important issue in deciding what is the picture of health. In terms of future prospects the rectangularization of the life curve that has already taken place effectively sets the outside parameters of optimum survival: the task is to maximize health and well-being within the life space circumscribed by the curve. To do so we must address the chronic multiple causative conditions that exist for so many years in the second half of life. Acute conditions are within our control for the most part.

While this statement is broadly true, it requires some qualification. Enormous advances have indeed been made against the infectious diseases, and some former killers such as smallpox have been virtually eliminated, but infectious disease continues to be a problem, and mortality information compiled by the National Center for Health Statistics shows that deaths from septicemia (infection involving the bloodstream) have been rising for nearly three decades and went up 3 percent in 1981 (Feinlieb, 1985). The fight against infectious diseases therefore goes on with the development of ever new generations of antibiotics. There are a number of reasons for continued problems with infectious diseases; for example, as new antibiotics are developed and used, new antibiotic-resistant strains of bacteria tend to develop, thus requiring yet newer antibiotics to combat them. Increasing numbers of people have immune defense mechanisms against infectious disease that are impaired as a result of such factors as the increasing incidence of cancer coupled with the development of drugs to prolong survival, as well as the rising numbers of the old-old. Furthermore, as we saw in Chapter 9, some people, such as Puerto Ricans and Native Americans, are at a high risk for infectious diseases because of chronic poverty and inadequate living conditions.

On the other hand, while medicine is far from having found a cure for the chronic degenerative diseases, considerable advances have been made. Recent work on **oncogenes** — small, discrete fragments of genetic material (DNA) that can transform at least some types of cells into malignant tumor cells — and **proto-oncogenes** — normal genes in human and animal cells that can be activated into cancer-causing oncogenes — holds considerable promise for understanding the causes of cancer. While this work is still confined to the research laboratory and has no clinical application yet, it might be a crucial key in the search for the causes and cures for certain types of cancer (Weinberg, 1983; Hunter, 1984).

Considerable advances have been made in the medical management of some of the consequences of the degenerative conditions. Ophthalmology is a rapidly advancing field of medicine. The advances in the surgical treatment of cataracts and of retinal disease over the past few years have been phenomenal. Today corneal transplants are relatively common. The development of the operating microscope and the laser have opened new vistas, and the advances in contact lenses have made their use easier for the elderly.

The management of cardiovascular disease is another rapidly developing field with the advent of both surgical and noninvasive techniques for relieving vascular blockages. So, too, does the refinement of arterial grafts. Percutaneous transluminal coronary angioplasty is another procedure becoming common. With new technology a small balloonlike sack can be maneuvered through the vascular tree to the site of a narrowing, where it is inflated to compress plaque buildup. Another area currently under investigation is the use of new experimental drugs (streptokinase and tissue plasminogen activator) to dissolve clots in the blood vessels leading to the heart in the few hours following a heart attack, thus minimizing tissue damage to the heart. Streptokinase is also beginning to be used in community hospitals to manage clots that block major blood vessels to the legs. Dilation of blocked blood vessels leading to the brain and the surgical removal of the blockage from the carotid arteries are also being attempted to minimize the damage after strokes. Their use had been confined to patients at risk because of narrowing of the arteries. But not all research efforts are concentrating on secondary treatment. With the discovery of a biochemical agent referred to as CSA (chondroitin-4 sulfate A), a naturally occurring hormone found in connective tissue, some researchers are hopeful they will soon be able to reverse or even prevent the accumulation of fatty deposits along the walls of the vascular system.

Human insulin, manufactured in the genetic engineering process that uses DNA to induce bacteria to manufacture the necessary proteins, is now becoming generally available. While there is a great deal of controversy whether human insulin is indeed less likely to cause the type of allergic reaction that sometimes occurs from pork or beef insulin, this new process at least has the advantage of ensuring an inexhaustible supply of insulin. So long as manufacturers were dependent on the meat market for their supply, there was the threat of an impending shortage of insulin by the end of the century because of dramatic increases in the incidence of diabetes and of population growth. Human insulin is faster acting and of shorter duration than the pork or beef variety, facts that some have seen as promoting more careful attention to diabetes control by physicians and patients (Bonnheim, 1982; Skyler, 1982). The use of an implantable insulin pump that would monitor and respond to changes in metabolism is also under investigation. The positive side of such a device for all users, including the elderly, is that it enables precise and minute doses to be released as necessary.

Orthopedists have made considerable refinements in joint replacement to repair damage caused by degenerative arthritis. Here and in other areas of medical research electronic technology promises amazing results. Electrotherapy is being used to stimulate bone healing and to help the growth of new bone and bone mass. A similar procedure also shows promise in treating nerve damage. Recent blood cleaning procedures, such as plasmapheresis, are helping filter the blood of arthritic patients and thus relieve some of their discomfort. One of the newer developments is a total hip replacement covered with porcelain. The ceramic prosthesis is carefully applied so that over time bone grows into the porcelain, thereby avoiding dislodgement and other problems related to the use of glue in anchoring. Arthroscopic surgery, which allows the insertion of an instrument into a joint through a small incision, has been of considerable assistance in managing early arthritis of the joints. The use of a combined regimen of estrogens and progesterones, together with calcium supplements and exercise programs, are being shown to be helpful in retarding osteoporosis among postmenopausal women. In terms of human suffering this is surely an important advance considering that 80 percent of all hip fractures are associated with osteoporosis, that some 17 percent of hip fracture patients die within three months, and that one-quarter of white women over sixty suffer compression fractures of the spine caused by osteoporosis (Machol, 1982).

A particularly tragic disablement of old age, and one that has so far yielded little to medical research, is Alzheimer's disease. Recently, however, there have been some crucial initial advances with the development of imaging scanning techniques. Positron emission tomography (PET) scans, for example, can pinpoint minute regions where abnormal growth or lesions may have barely started. One of the most exciting uses of PET is its ability to reveal the chemical metabolism of the brain, its actual working, thus making it possible to identify the chemical components of thinking and to diagnose Alzheimer's disease at a much earlier stage. The most important consequence is that it opens up the possibility of intervention techniques and the ability to distinguish among Alzheimer's disease, multiple infarct dementia, and treatable pseudodementia. Computerized axial tomography (CAT) scanners can provide electronically reconstructed views of the brain in amazing detail and can help surgeons lay out operating techniques before actual surgery begins to save time and to minimize risks. The newer magnetic resonance imaging (MRI) machine even goes beyond CAT scans to provide clear images of plaques and other irregular changes in brain anatomy. Two experimental drugs, physostigmine and bethanecol, which increase levels of the brain chemical acetylcholine, have been found to delay deterioration in patients with Alzheimer's disease by up to three years.

In summary we must highlight some points about the ways in which medical technology meshes with the social construction and the experienced reality of health. It is important to remember that while basic research is essential for gaining an increased understanding of biological processes and that this research may be useful in the future, the ultimate goal of medical care is improving the quality of life. Older people (and people in general) are likely to derive more benefit from primary medical interventions that improve or maintain the quality of life rather than from the secondary techniques that keep them alive at all costs. This distinction must remain an important consideration in determining the direction of medical research. While advanced life support techniques are valuable and have made it possible for both the young and the old to survive acute life-threatening episodes, we face serious problems in cost containment and ethical issues that will have to be addressed over the next twenty years. Medical advances are not only success stories, they are also challenges.

The development and availability of medical techniques to assuage the impact of chronic disease presents dangers and temptations in the medicalization of the social. While those who are already suffering from chronic disease deserve access to relief, this should not divert attention for the social changes necessary to prevent the occurrence of similar suffering in future generations of the elderly. Aging is a multifaceted phenomenon; to concentrate merely on its medical aspects is tantamount to ensuring the perpetuation of hardship and social psychological difficulties in the future. All other things being equal, life satisfaction is a causative factor in nearly every other dimension we have discussed; it would be a poor use of resources to concentrate on health without looking at the underlying causes.

Finally, we need to consider the costs and benefits involved in the use of medical technology. Is what we are getting worth the effort? Costs of the brain imaging machines range between $800,000 and $4 million, and their application costs about $1000 for each use. Between 1977 and 1982, according to the Congressional Office of Technology Assessment, high-powered medical technology accounted for almost 30 percent of the rise in Medicare payments. Are we making the best uses of the available resources? In assessing the costs and the benefits of health care we need to look not only at absolute dollar figures but also at the benefits derived, the alternative possibilities, and what type and amount of health care people would consider appropriate for various stages in their own lives. Another dimension of the same issue centers on who primarily benefits from the new technology: the manufacturers or the handful of patients who are able to purchase access. Artificial hearts, for example, are wonderful provided the many thousands of indigent elderly who cannot now afford basic health care are ensured of equal access. We cannot ignore the impact of technology in directing future efforts.

**Sociocultural and Political Dimensions.** Often our lives are circumscribed by our physical dimension. As we saw earlier, on occasion our health problems are primarily a matter of physiology and are best managed by medical techniques. It is toward this type of problem that the search for medical breakthroughs is best directed. However, as Sigerist (1941) pointed out, what a physician does is "determined primarily by the social and economic structure of society and by the technical and scientific means available to medicine at that time." In short, medicine reflects values, traditions, and the definitions of problems. Our health policies therefore cannot derive from our technological models (Fein, 1981).

Within the realm of the physiological there is great flexibility, depending on factors such as life-style and environment. Furthermore, as we suggested in Chapter 5, health is more than a matter of the absence of physical illness. It includes dimensions such as the maximization of function and a sense of well-being. Looking at Table 4.2, we see that it shows many ways in which personal life-style can retard various dimensions of functional aging from cardiac reserve, physical endurance, performance on intelligence tests, and reaction time to social ability (Fries and Crapo, 1981). Some, however, contend that to focus on the physiological or individual life-style aspects of health alone is to depoliticize the social (Kuhn, 1984; Walker, 1984; Minkler and Estes, 1984). While physiology and individual life-style factors have a vital impact on the health of the elderly, so, too, do social structural factors. This is true in a variety of ways; for instance, the distribution of opportunity is structured so that certain groups, such as blacks, Native Americans, and Puerto Ricans particularly, are more likely to suffer from economic deprivation and the health hazards this implies. Then, as we saw in Chapter 5, there are health hazards in the workplace that carry over into old age: black lung, brown lung, chronic tension, and stress. And in our leisure time we share a culture and face an advertising industry and an economy that encourages people to seek solace in the very products research has shown to be detrimental.

Although it would be difficult to accomplish for sociopolitical reasons, in terms of what we know today one of the more immediate ways to improve health among tomorrow's elderly would be the widespread cessation of smoking, the elimination of alcohol abuse, the enforcement of safety standards, and the elimination of risks from the workplace. Another way to improve health patterns would be a redistribution of resources so that all were able to attain an acceptable standard of living. Prevention and restructuring social and economic relations are perhaps less dramatic and less popular than esoteric medical breakthroughs, but would be more likely to improve the quality of life among tomorrow's elderly and would certainly be more cost effective.

In working toward measures of this type we must remember the economic factors. If both smoking and alcohol consumption were dramatically reduced nationally, it would be necessary to find alternative sources of employment and income for those who are currently working in the tobacco and alcohol industries. It might also be necessary to provide economic incentives to enforce safety standards in industry. Care would also have to be taken that a focus on preventive medicine did not perpetuate today's inequities by offering cheap, ameliorative medicine to the poor when they were in need of expert medical care, while reserving sophisticated technological medicine for those who have the resources to pay.

**The Issue of Cost.** One of the most frequently alluded to challenges of the future is the issue of the cost of health care, particularly for the elderly. More people are living well into old age at the same time that worldwide economic shortfalls have become pressing. Some would see it simply in terms of using any means to keep expenses within manageable bounds in view of escalating costs: who can look at the $47 million increase in Medicare in the twenty-year period ending in 1985 and not wonder how costs could be contained? The issue, however, is not as simple as that: the question of health care expenditures for the elderly is not merely a question of cost efficiency, it is one of cost effectiveness — and that implies not only keeping costs down but also quality of care and questions of equal access. We need to look not only at what we are spending but also at how healthy the elderly are as a result of those expenditures and whether care is denied to certain classes or categories of people. While the traditional fee for service reimbursement system for Medicare was criticized on the grounds that it led to escalating costs by encouraging physicians and hospitals to spend money, the new cost-cutting measures have been criticized on the grounds that they tend to prejudice quality and access to care. Among the most widely voiced criticisms of the DRG prospective payment system reviewed in Chapter 5 is that it tends to lead to a bottom-line mentality on the part of health care administrators, which may result in substituting less costly but also less effective forms of therapy, cutting unprofitable services from health care, and denying access to hospitalization to patients who are likely to cost the institution money. The attempt to contain costs by raising premiums on Medicare Part B and copayments has been criticized on the grounds that it is likely to limit access to care for the low-income elderly who will not be able to afford the increased expenses (Estes et al., 1984). This is not to say that health policies should not be changed — problems are rampant. It is just to suggest that shortsighted changes now will be magnified in the future, let alone how it affects those who are at its mercy today. As pointed out in referring to Social Security, the benefits of a health care policy will ensure equal access, and quality care extends far beyond the mere users of the system.

Rather than aiming simply to keep costs down it might make more sense to aim toward cost effectiveness in the sense of using the available health care resources to maximize the health of the elderly as widely as possible. If all people are healthy, so is the nation. This task, however, involves a number of rather complex issues.

To begin with, what are the available resources? People sometimes speak as though there were a fixed amount of money available to be spent on the health of the elderly. The amount is socially defined through appropriations. Determining how much should be spent on health involves a number of questions, including the total amount of income available for all phases of the budget, the effects of inflation, the impact of increasing numbers of people needing care (which may mean that although dollar costs are rapidly increasing, the effective amount spent on each person may not be increasing at anything near the same rate), and the priority we place on health over and against other aspects of the budget such as defense, space research, education, and income maintenance. Having decided on how much is to be spent, the next problem is to allocate health care expenses between the age groups. On a number of occasions we have taken up Clark's (1985) suggestion that this should be thought of in terms of how much would one wish to have spent on health care at different times of life rather than in terms of competition between age groups. Some have suggested that the solution lies in a broadly based national health or national insurance system to which all would contribute and from which all would benefit (Brown, 1984). Others have also suggested there is a reluctance to spend money on health care for the elderly in capitalist societies because of the tendency to define health in functional terms based on economic productivity defined as participation in the labor market (Kelman, 1975; Estes et al., 1984). That the elderly are seen as unproductive in these terms is, like so much else, a social construction: nonparticipation of the elderly in the work force is socially enforced. No one seems to consider there are also other forms of productiveness that may or may not contribute to the gross national product (Walker, 1984).

Just what is the best health care available for the money is far from clear. Not only does this involve philosophical differences about what is meant by good health and good health care, but there are also problems of assessing cost effectiveness piecemeal on the basis of a price tag. A particular technique may be costly and yield little in terms of quality of life. It might, however, have a higher price tag than a different technique but yield better results in terms of quality of life and ultimately be more cost effective in total expenditures for a patient during a particular illness. For instance, CT scanning is much more expensive than an x-ray test, and to get a CT scan when an x-ray will do is a waste of money. CT scans can, however, obviate unnecessary surgery, thus sparing the patient suffering and thus actually cost less than the alternative. Similarly, while DRGs cut the cost of individual hospitalizations, they may not affect the cost of a particular illness but merely transfer such costs elsewhere.

There is thus the need to develop a clearer overview of what we want from health care that includes health maintenance, prevention, and restorative medicine. We need a mechanism for evaluating and maximizing cost effectiveness in terms of total patient care rather than a simple comparison of two types of isolated encounters with health professionals or institutions. Establishing health maintenance organizations and developing a national health or national insurance system have been suggested as approaches to the problem of costs and patient care, but these too have had their share of criticisms.

**Developing Appropriate Levels of Care.** The development of social policies to ensure appropriate levels of care for the elderly presents an important and difficult challenge for the future. Clearly, we need a vehicle to create an overall health policy that will look at cost effectiveness and the contribution of health measures to the quality of life in a wider context. Rather than focusing on isolated episodes of care, such a view must take account of the overall costs and benefits and the ways in which health issues mesh with other concerns. Some policy analysts favor creating a national health service or at least a national health insurance system. In some cases health planning agencies have been tried, although they have been criticized for a lack of attention to the needs of the elderly; other possibilities might include creating mechanisms to stimulate dialogue and an interdisciplinary approach among health care providers and social service agencies.

It is, however, also clear that providing appropriate levels of health care for the elderly involves working through — and living with — a series of important dilemmas.

- How do we provide access to care for the severely ill who are in need of high levels of technology without committing an undue portion of the budget to secondary or tertiary care? To do so would surely contribute to a spiral of rising hospital costs.

- How do we focus on preventive medicine and health maintenance without constraining those who are in need of curative medicine?
- How do we maximize independence and avoid stereotyping the elderly as frail and ill without depriving people of support when they need it?
- How do we provide support in the form of long-term care, when necessary, without actually creating dependence?
- How do we give due attention to the impact of structural factors on health without ignoring the role of physiological and life-style factors?
- Can we encourage people to take responsibility for their health and to make informed choices without blaming them for ill-health resulting from structural and physiological factors beyond their control? Can we ensure an equitable distribution of access for the elderly from all social classes?
- How do we remember that old people should be involved in the development of health policy rather than remain just a dependent group that needs to be taken care of?

One of the major criticisms of the health care system for the elderly in the United States is its tendency to focus on medical intervention, hospital treatment, and nursing home care at the expense of prevention, health maintenance, and support for independent living in the community. Because of patterns of financing and the interests of the nursing home industry, institutional care has become the de facto long-term care policy in the United States (Estes et al., 1984). The growth of the nursing home industry over recent decades has been phenomenal. Between 1969 and 1980 there was a 27.1 increase in the number of nursing homes, a 73 percent increase in the number of nursing home beds, and a 97.8 percent increase in the number of full-time employees working in nursing homes. By 1980 there had been a 75 percent increase since 1969 in the number of people residing in nursing homes (U.S. Department of Health and Human Services, 1984). Nationwide about 80 percent of nursing homes are privately owned and about 70 percent of all nursing home beds are in these homes. Interestingly, Florida, one of the states with the highest proportion of elderly residents, has the lowest average number of nursing home beds per 1000 persons sixty-five and over: a mere 21.4 per 1000 as compared to a high of 95.0 per 1000 in South Dakota (U.S. Department of Health and Human Services, 1983). What are the factors that account for the differences? Could it be that because of the greater concentration of elderly people better community support facilities have been developed for them in the Sunshine State? It may also be that those who move south to retire belong to a relatively affluent group whose greater resources are liable to be reflected in fewer health problems during retirement.

According to recent projections presented by the U.S. Senate Special Committee on Aging (1985), when actual nursing home residents (about 1.4 million in 1985) are added to the 5.2 million community dwelling elderly who are unable to perform daily routine maintenance chores without assistance, the total impaired elderly population reaches some 6.6 million persons. These figures, as shown in Figure 12.3, are predicted to grow at an even faster rate than they have over the past few years. Changing mortality rates among the elderly, the aging of the baby boom generation, and the prospective payment system imposed by revisions to Medicare provisions are thought to be the driving forces. Despite the evidence, relative appropriations for home health services have not kept up with funds for long-term institutionalization. In future years, as more patients are discharged from hospitals under DRG stipulations, the committee reports that current extended care patterns will be obsolete. As a consequence, there will be a range of serious but unmet needs among the elderly attempting to remain in their communities (U.S. Senate Special Committee on Aging, 1985).

What this adds up to is a tremendous commitment of resources to long-term institutional care. Expenditures for nursing home care more than doubled between 1975 and 1984, reaching $33 billion or 8.5 percent of national health care expenditures. Estimates in 1984 implied an expenditure of $880 per person, though costs increased by age, and by 1990, if present trends continue, it is predicted that expenditures on all aspects of nursing home care in

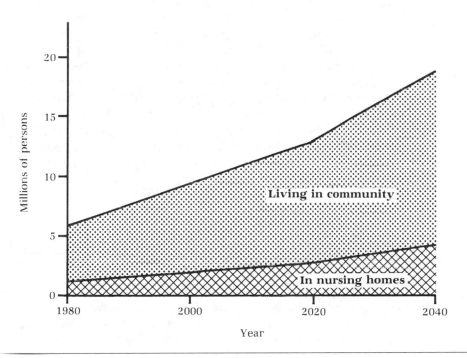

**FIGURE 12.3**
Older persons in need of long-term care. (*Source:* U.S. Senate Special Committee on Aging. *Developments in Aging: 1984*, vol. I, p. 129. Washington, D.C.: U.S. Government Printing Office, 1985.)

the United States will be more than $60 billion (Waldo and Lazenby, 1984; Freeland and Schendler, 1984).

In addition to being a very expensive way of caring for people, nursing homes tend to foster dependency. In the face of the lack of alternatives old people who might be able to remain relatively independent in the community with a little more social and economic support are placed in nursing homes. Estimates of inappropriate placements, in institutionalizing people who could function equally well or better outside an institution, range from 5 to an amazing 75 percent, depending on the criteria used. National surveys had implied that only approximately one-third of nursing home residents are extremely dependent, which lends credibility to the high figure (Harrington, 1984).

Since the point of entry to nursing homes is traditionally through the hospital, with which many nursing homes are closely allied, patterns of nursing home care tend to follow the institutional model of the hospital, rather than more participatory models designed to maximize the independence of residents and prepare them to return to the community where possible. Little (1982) identifies three main types of setting for the care of the elderly: closed institutional settings, including nursing homes, psychiatric hospitals, and acute care hospitals; open community settings, such as community health and social services, and residential homes; and informal, unorganized home settings in which the individual may be self-sufficient or may receive care largely from family or friends. Which way will be predominant in the future?

While there have been some moves toward providing care in open community settings, the United States tends to concentrate its resources on closed institutional settings. In Europe in general and in Great Britain in particular there has long been a commitment to providing care in the community. Walker (1984), however, criticizes the British system for focusing on open community settings in the sense of care by professionals as opposed to supporting the independence of the elderly. He also notes that in Britain relatively few resources are earmarked for care in the community. Like care in the United States, care in Great Britain tends to reinforce a situation in which women bear the major burden of supporting the dependent elderly in terms of loss of career opportunities. Challenges for the future in both the quality of life and cost effectiveness include providing community structures to enable the elderly to retain the relative independence of informal or open community settings as long as possible. When institutionalization is necessary, the challenge is to create settings that foster maximum participation and independence by the elderly and, when desirable, return to the community. As Keith (1982) points out in her work on retirement communities in France, resident participation, even when it leads to dissonance, has a remarkably positive effect.

Beginning with Title III of the Older Americans Act as amended in 1978, a mandate for governmental assistance for independent living has been issued. With Title XX of the Social Security Act, the call has been for articulating local program expenditures for integrated outreach programs for the elderly and low-income families. In every revision since its inception the Older Americans

Act has sought more consideration of the long-term care needs of the elderly and strategies designed to help them retain their place in the community. It will take more than legislation, however, to implement a move away from institutional care. Nor should funding be withdrawn from nursing homes until viable alternatives have been provided: nursing homes will continue to flourish and the size of the institutionalized population will increase. What is called for, as a part of an integrated policy, are economic and service structures to support the independence of the elderly in the community and to use the contributions they have to offer for as long as possible.

# The Response

## GERONTOLOGY AS A VOCATION

Taking into consideration the increasing size of the elderly population, changing health patterns, emergent governmental policies, and the political realities of the situation, the facts add up to more attention being focused on tomorrow's old people. To respond to their needs gerontology as a vocation offers career opportunities that are not likely to be diminished in the foreseeable future. In accordance with the 1978 amendments to the Older Americans Act, a continuing effort to evaluate current and future personnel needs in aging was initiated. Subsequently, several estimates have been made of blanket personnel requirements, as well as what specific areas of need will exist in 1990. Projections just for the decade of the 1980s have brought to light urgent and immediate shortages in selected areas. Estimates made during the mid-1970s were for a doubling or even tripling of some types of trained specialists to work with the elderly. Overall deficiencies existed, so much so in fact that the Administration on Aging in commenting on the critical deficit of qualified personnel was able to declare: "The gap between the need for trained personnel and the capacities of present training programs is so great that there is no danger of overtraining for several decades" (Birren, 1971). A similar statement was issued by delegates to the United Nations as part of their survey of the national and international manpower picture. In both cases it was reported that unmet needs can only be surmounted if the supply of skilled administrative and managerial personnel is greatly expanded. Yet few advances were made; in 1973 and again in 1975 members of the U.S. Senate Special Committee on Aging were able to note that hundreds of thousands of workers had to be trained in the next five years if the growing requirements of aging were to be satisfied (United Nations, 1973; U.S. Senate, 1973, 1975).

Now, over a decade later, how do employment prospects look for students seeking career opportunities in aging? Inquiries made in mid-1985 to the Administration on Aging, Department of Labor, Gerontological Society of America, and some experts in personnel failed to uncover any recent systematic fieldwide projections. In all cases budget cuts were identified as at least partially responsible for not having the latest data. Some statistics are available for selected areas, nursing homes, for example, but for others what information is available dates from 1984 or earlier. A new inventory is under way under the aegis of the Association for Gerontology in Higher Education and the Administration on Aging, but it is only just beginning. Nonetheless, we will attempt to provide a candid appraisal based on what we believe to be the trends.

For a college graduate looking for work in gerontology during the second half of the 1980s are the job prospects any better or worse than for other college graduates? Depending on the specialization and the willingness to relocate, the situation still looks favorable. Though the promise of immense growth in all areas of gerontology is not as great as it had been, partly because of shifting policies and political decisions, many unmet needs remain. Expert opinion offered in conjunction with revisions to the Older Americans Act in the early 1980s suggests that in 1985 some 200,000 positions will be available. Most of these positions will be in areas of direct service delivery — both social and health related — and in administrative and paraprofessional positions. The Ad Hoc Committee on Enhancement of Training in Geriatrics and Gerontology of the Department of Health and Human Services noted personnel shortages in many health and social fields but an oversupply in others. No conclusive projections were made, however, since nearly every branch of the federal government, as well as a diffuse group of professional and service occupations, potentially need trained gerontologists. Furthermore, since the National Center for Educational Statistics does not list gerontology as an academic discipline, there is no sure way to tell how many students are currently in training or have recently entered the job market. What we do know is that courses on aging have been spreading rapidly. We also know that when all training and career preparation monies are added together they totaled some $35 million in 1984 (National Institute on Aging, 1984).

A related issue in medicine is the absence of geriatrics as a specialty in most of the country's 126 medical schools. Over two-thirds of the medical schools offer courses, but these are mostly electives with small enrollments. These courses are taught by an average full-time equivalent faculty in geriatrics of only 2.5 faculty positions. A 1981 Rand Corporation projection of faculty needs for optimum geriatric training noted that at least 1350 physician faculty members were necessary to meet the educational responsibilities in aging. Estimates are that some 8000 to 10,000 teaching geriatricians should be hired by 1990 if appropriately equal emphasis is to be given to the elderly population of the United States. How many physicians currently claim geriatrics as a primary interest in which they have expertise? According to a 1982 AMA survey, there are fewer than 700, and there is no reason to assume that number has increased appreciably (National Institute on Aging, 1984).

## CAREERS IN AGING

Having offered these disclaimers, what information can be provided? To service the needs of the 36 million or more people who will be sixty-five or older in the year 2000 a variety of trained professionals will be needed. We will review a selected number of professions and offer the latest predictions available. Remember two things, however: first, projections become out of date quickly and they generally respond to political dictates; second, probably few if any openings exist within a fifty-mile radius of any of the 1300 schools offering specializations in aging. College graduates like to remain where they think the best career potential is — this is not where most jobs are waiting. To work in aging a person must be willing to relocate. There are exceptions, of course.

The time for justifying the study of aging is long past. The needs are imperative: without skilled resource people, aging programs of all stripes will remain underdeveloped or, worse yet, mismanaged, perhaps furnishing little more than custodial care. Education and training must be implemented on all levels — in institutions of higher learning, high schools, and in-service programs — to ready young adults, the middle-aged, and even the retired to meet the challenges of a substantial need for more workers. During the 1980s projections call for recruiting extensive numbers of people to fill newly created jobs, not to mention those who will be required to offset attrition. The number of positions to be filled will of course vary by level. A limited cadre of teachers, researchers, and scientific technicians responsible for professional leadership, for producing new knowledge, and for providing advanced training must be recruited. Further, a larger core of people capable of translating knowledge into practical terms is required. These will be primarily managerial, administrative, and supervisory personnel or technical experts affiliated with community colleges or vocational institutes. Finally, the greatest growth must take place among those who are in daily contact with older people, those who will make the actual application of what is learned to deal effectively with immediate problems and situations.

**Counseling.** With the realization that older individuals benefit as much from psychological counseling as anyone else, counselor education has been increasing rapidly. Division 20 of the American Psychological Association has increased in size, as has the Association for Counseling and Human Development. New professional journals and a burgeoning number of textbooks all suggest that gerontological counseling is a growth specialty. The only areas developing more courses are marriage and family counseling.

Graduates of the various counseling programs find employment in traditional counseling settings and wherever an older clientele is served. In their attempt to identify employment prospects for gerontological counselors, Myers and Blake (1984) found only 5 percent of their admittedly small sample had not found employment in their specialty within two years of entering the job market. Nonetheless, mental health centers and long-term care facilities are not staffing positions with gerontological counselors to the extent these researchers expected. Even less is known about employment prospects for clinical psychologists specializing in gerontology, but with the numbers of the elderly growing and the prevalence of stress, there is clearly a need.

**Academic Researchers and Teachers.** Two basic personnel categories can be used to characterize personnel needs in the nation's colleges and universities: basic biomedical scientists and the broad category of social gerontology. With enrollments declining it is not likely that many new faculty or research positions will materialize in the next few years, but there are possibilities for redefining existing positions. In 1981 Kane et al. (1981) forecast that between 1700 and 2600 biomedical and behavioral scientists were needed to provide basic research data in gerontology. While graduate level training has continued apace, a need still remains in a wide range of academic specialties for experts capable of addressing the problems facing the elderly in our society. One target suggested in the 1981 report was to have between 1300 and 2000 trained researchers with doctorates. Social gerontology is not a clearly defined specialty, but it does lie at the core of aging issues. Social gerontologists customarily do research and teach in higher education institutions and are consultants to government and industry. Their basic orientation is influenced by the traditional academic disciplines. To be quite honest the growth potential here appears to be less than in many other areas.

**Nurses.** Direct service delivery in all health care settings is focused on nursing. The need for nurses with formal specialized training is great. Depending on the exigencies of health care financing, nursing will continue to play an important role — or even a more important one. About one-sixth of the 1400 professional education programs in nursing offer a gerontology nursing specialization. Many of the others offer at least some courses (Knowles, 1982). Affecting the growth of nurse practitioner programs in gerontology is the paucity of trained faculty members. In recent years, however, there has been a tremendous growth in the number of such programs. Of the 140 graduate degree programs, over twenty-five provide a specialization in gerontologic nursing for the clinical situation.

According to the 1984 National Institute on Aging report, if current staffing patterns continue, roughly twice as many nurses (150,000) will be needed in nursing homes by 1990 as are presently employed. By the year 2000 a further addition of 100,000 more will be required. Interestingly, registered nurses account for only about one-seventh of all nursing personnel in nursing homes; LPNs are about equal in number and nurses' aides constitute three quarters of the total nursing staff in long-term care facilities.

**Other Nursing Home Personnel.** A growth rate of 73 percent in the decade leading up to 1985 was expected to bring total nursing home employment to 1,431,000 people (Administration on Aging, 1980). Approximately half of these will be service workers, LPNs, aides, attendants, and so on. While it is too soon to say what the recent implementation of cost-cutting measures will be, they have put somewhat of a chill on the expansion of jobs in the health industry across the board. With labor costs accounting for up to two-thirds of the budgets of hospitals and long-term care facilities, a real move is afoot to curtail the growth of new jobs.

While the demand for less skilled staff positions has declined as a result, discharge planners, home health workers, rehabilitation personnel, and financial managers knowledgeable in the application of prospective payment systems (DRG coordinators) are in short supply (Kahl and Clark, 1985). Some positions, especially in the clerical and maintenance lines are projected to nearly double by 1995. Others will experience a more modest growth curve. Though they will continue to increase somewhat, entry-level positions will be slow to open up (Bureau of Labor Statistics, 1984).

**Physicians.** One area in which the supply is running far behind demand is in medicine. Looking as far ahead as 2030, a recent report recommends increased training programs and support for a variety of health care personnel. Estimates of between 8000 and 10,000 geriatricians in 1990 require a substantial influx of students now. Personnel configurations vary, depending on which future model is chosen, but approximately 900 academic geriatricians will be needed to staff existing training programs. At least 1500 must be trained to comply with the demand. Up to 16,000 primary care physicians are needed to give care to the elderly even if the majority of care provision still rests on other medical specialties. Geropsychiatrists will also be required — a total of at least 1778 by 1990. A cadre of geriatric nurse practitioners and physician's assistants is also essential if personnel needs are to be met (Kane, 1980).

As pointed out earlier, while two-thirds of the medical schools have courses in geriatrics, they are understaffed and undersubscribed. Geriatric training is also offered in about fifteen schools of osteopathic medicine, but these too require additional trained faculty, fifty to one hundred according to some estimates. If the figures given earlier (up to 10,000 geriatricians) are correct, the future supply will not catch up to demand for several decades. Since admissions have stabilized and overall growth has leveled out, it is unlikely that larger numbers of medical students will elect to specialize in geriatrics. Given the strictures imposed by prospective payment plans, it is also unrealistic that a career track in aging will be appealing economically. Nonetheless, there is a real need for those who might opt to specialize in aging. The American Medical Student Association has identified training opportunities and can provide guidance in that direction.

**Other Health Professionals.** Occupational therapists, dentists, physicians' assistants, optometrists, speech therapists, audiologists, nutritionists, pharmacists, and other public health professionals and health care administrators also are invaluable to the elderly. Forecasts made before the recent revisions to Medicare and prospective payment plans suggested these professions had a bright future in serving the elderly's needs. It is too soon to sound the alarm, but the kinds of ancillary services they provide are under seige at present.

In 1980 it was thought that over 16,000 health services administrators, 2800 dietitians, 1300 occupational therapists, 2100 physical therapists, and 2900 speech pathologists or audiologists were needed (Administration on Aging, 1980). Though it is not possible to provide a mid-decade update, if we were to hazard a guess it would be that cost containment and political decisions have limited growth in these areas. Thus, while the need remains, opportunities in the field have been constrained.

**Social Workers.** The Bureau of Labor Statistics has recently identified geriatric social workers as one of the twelve most rapidly growing occupational titles. Both BSWs and MSWs have fared well in employment in recent years, but projections for the future suggest those with an MSW will be in greater demand. Prediction of staffing needs is risky, since personnel with other professional degrees are often substituted. In 1979 the AOA predicted a growth of about 12,000 annually to nearly 700,000 geriatric social workers by 1990, but recent funding recessions will probably reduce that number. The National Association of Social Workers (1983) recently reported that only about 2 percent of those trained were actually working in nursing homes, though a great many more were employed in the general category of hospital social worker. The National Committee for Gerontology in Social Work Education should have more current figures available and can indicate which of the 343 accredited BSW programs, eighty-eight MSW programs, or forty-six doctoral degree programs have outstanding gerontology education opportunities.

As important as social work is in all prosthetic environments where older persons receive services, geriatric social workers have a unique contribution to make to the health and well-being of the elderly. Whether as advocates or in helping with preventive, supportive, or restorative services, social workers are an indispensible link between the older client and the formal networks of care providers.

## TRAINING AND COURSE WORK

No matter how attractive the career opportunities, formal training is essential if the quality of services for the nation's elderly is to improve. The country as a whole has a choice to make regarding education and training. Those who are not content with the glacial pace of universities prefer to have funding for their service programs now. In turn the academic community argues that to ignore education is to short change tomorrow. Without a sound background and a holistic grasp of the issues, the effectiveness of stopgap approaches begins to fade even as they are applied. The debate will go on and interested parties will be at odds over their share of the finite resources. In the meantime how might those who want to pursue a career in aging best prepare to meet the challenges?

Throughout this text we have continually pressed for an interdisciplinary approach. By this we have meant to suggest that experts in any given specialty should have at least a slight acquaintance with other specialties. A concomitant of this interdisciplinary view is that specialists show a willingness to adopt an integrated approach to various issues, to solicit input from gerontologists who are professionally prepared to take a slightly different view. Another point we have attempted to make clear is that aging is a transactional process. It is not predetermined but shapes itself as it moves along. Human beings are seldom passive; they take a hand in their own fates — too frequently gerontologists lose sight of that simple fact (Gergen, 1980). A third aspect of our approach throughout this text has been that aging should not, indeed cannot, be looked at in isolation. The course of human affairs reflects the basic organization of the productive process and the consequences of the political realm. As was pointed out in the previous chapter, sixty-five did not become the demarcation point by chance or for scientific reasons — it was a political decision.

With all of this in mind, we urge the prospective gerontologist to engage in an interdisciplinary, multifaceted training process. Stage one is presumably under way for the student reader who has reached this point in the text. Regardless of the academic title of this course, we hope the content has been interdisciplinary and that this will be the focus all the way through training. This text has been designed to speak to the primary issues identified as central by the Foundations of Gerontological Education Project (Foundations Project, 1980). In addition to interdisciplinary survey courses, a social policy course should round out the first stage of gerontological education.

The second level should be devoted to more intensive study of specified topical areas. Specialization within academic disciplines can then take place at the third stage. It is here that concentration on core issues can occupy courses in any of a variety of social science, social work, allied health, and biomedical disciplines. Depending on the career focus, practical experience in the subject in the form of direct contact with the elderly can be undertaken at either the second or third level. For those more interested in a research agenda this type of experience may be substituted for the field work or practicum (Tibbitts et al., 1980). After pursuing a program designed to provide for a well-rounded and interdisciplinary approach to the issues of aging, we hope the gerontologist will emerge from his or her educational experience fully appreciative of the flexibility of the aging process.

Within the last few years a great deal has been accomplished toward establishing career-oriented training programs. For the prospective student of gerontology, opportunities for undergraduate majors and basic or applied graduate level degrees are more readily available. From coast to coast numerous colleges and universities have inaugurated or broadened their instruction in aging. While support for training in gerontology is currently in flux, opportunities for assistance with educational expenses do and will continue to exist. An emphasis on the interdisciplinary focus necessary adequately to address the problems and needs of old people is far from universal; however, those centers most intimately involved in the study of aging processes are structured so they can draw on the resources of multiple vantage points. The sometimes fragmented perspectives of the various disciplines focusing on aging must be brought to bear on the totality of the experience of growing old in and for society. There is no disagreement among those familiar with the field that gerontology is indeed a challenging and rewarding endeavor.

## THE CHALLENGE

What about those of us who are not interested in careers in gerontology? What relevance do the issues of aging have for us? A great deal, for we are growing older every minute. Aging, as we saw at the outset of this text, is not a kind of static alien state populated by other beings: the old. Rather it is a process that each of us must live within a particular culture, under a particular set of historical circumstances, and under specific, changing structural constraints. In some ways aging is a shared human experience; in others, because of the precise circumstances in which we find ourselves, it presents new challenges for each of us. The elderly of today are our fellow participants in society. Like us, they lived through childhood, youth, and middle life. The ways in which they lived helped create the world as we know it today. Like them, we too will grow old, and the quality and texture of our old age tomorrow will in part be determined by the social policies that we help influence today, as well as by our personal life-styles and health practices. Surely, the elderly, as people who have worked throughout their lives to shape the face of society deserve a voice in the social policies affecting them. And surely, they have something to teach us about what it means to grow old that will make our own old age a more meaningful experience.

By now it should be apparent to the student that much can be done to improve the quality of old age. On the personal level there are issues of planning for retirement, both economic and in terms of developing interests to give meaning and purpose to our later years. Further, the style of life engaged in during youth and middle age (smoking, drinking, exercising) can influence the chances of our later years being an experience of chronic illness or of reasonably functional ability. Our personal options, however, are limited by social policy and structural factors. Imagine what it would be like to be excluded from the labor force and to be obliged to live on a fixed, inadequate income. Imagine how you would manage on between $80 and $90 a week, with no extras, to cover housing, food, clothing, and medical care, particularly if you were in any way impaired and had high medical expenses. It is in our own interests as the elderly of tomorrow, as well as in the interests of generational fairness toward today's elderly, to work for policies that view the elderly as persons rather than as "social problems." Policies should be implemented that afford them the opportunity to participate in and contribute to society as long as they are willing and able to do so. While physiology, culture, and social structure shape our lives, we are not totally powerless. There is much we can do to ensure that the years of added life expectancy of those who will be old tomorrow will be of high quality, and not merely meaningless or painful.

## Summary

Anticipating what the coming decades will hold for the elderly is unquestionably a task fraught with ambiguity. While demographic projections may suggest the shape of future events, they hardly tell the whole story. The proportion of older people in the population will continue to increase — it is unlikely to even begin to stabilize until the middle of the next century. Medical science may extend the period of physical well-being until late in the seventh decade, allowing people to lead full and active lives free from nagging chronic disabilities. Current estimates are for people in the near future to live about as long as now. However, dramatic breakthroughs can never be ruled out. If, for example, mortality resulting from cardiovascular and related heart diseases were to be brought under control, average life expectancies might approach the century mark. There is no denying the enactment of Medicare and the initial Older Americans Act in 1965 were historic milestones helping to extend the promise of health care to all older people. Unfortunately, many of the improvements envisioned in the delivery of health services have been whittled away in the political process of establishing priorities. Nonetheless, there is a growing awareness of the need to focus on what it means to become old in the mass societies of an advanced industrial age.

To accommodate the expanded numbers of elderly, certain basic institutional and societal patterns will have to undergo changes. At present, Social Security constitutes the financial mainstay for the majority of the elderly; yet it is common in the United States that whenever economic stability is threatened, cutbacks in the payments to older people occur. Although observers think it is unlikely that tomorrow's elderly will be worse off than at present, a substantial minority will continue to be forced to exist below nationally established poverty levels. Additional sources of income, revised pension programs, and even individual retirement annuities will undoubtedly become more widespread; at the same time the structure of the Social Security system will need a major overhaul.

Retirement benefits for women are probably destined for drastic revision in the years to come. As more women participate in the labor force, demands for more equitable retirement schemes will increase. Women who select childcare and homemaking responsibilities as their primary careers may eventually be covered by Social Security, receiving retirement credits for performing necessary roles. Judging from the best contemporary evidence, our whole conception of retirement may be altered, as work life, careers, and leisure are redefined to encompass greater flexibility.

In large measure the fate of the elderly in the twenty-first century rests on adequate preparation today. The usefulness and the promise of basic research will be obviated if it is not supplemented by a corps of trained experts who stand prepared to offer a broad spectrum of essential services. Not only will future generations of older people be better educated (high school graduation will be the norm by the year 2000), but they will have had experience seeking professional help in time of need. The demand for personnel to work with the elderly will easily outstrip the supply at least through 1990 and, many predict, beyond as well. Occupational opportunities exist on all levels, and while the challenge is great, the rewards are even greater. Specialists are required of course, but they, as all professionals in the field, must also have a general overview of the aging process if they are to contribute to the well-being of the nation's elderly. Gerontology is a field of study in which innovation and new perspectives are necessary for finding solutions to problems that ultimately confront us all.

# Discussion Questions

**The Future of Aging**

1. Go back to the list of things that you think should be changed about the living conditions of old people in this country, which you made in response to Chapter 1, Question 2. Are there any ways in which you would change your list given what you have learned in this course? If so, what changes would you make and why?

2. How are the problems on your list and your proposed solutions to them relevant not only to the elderly but to all members of society?

**The Elderly of Tomorrow**

3. As you see it, how is the nature of dependency ratios changing and what are the implications of these changes? How would you solve any problems that might result from them?

4. What are the implications of multigenerational families for the lives of the old-old, young-old, and young?

5. What do you think the sex roles and the relationship between men and women in their sixties, seventies, and eighties will be like in the year 2000?

6. Make a list of the problems encountered by a particular old person you know. To what extent are these problems personal troubles or public issues or a combination of both? How might changes in social policy and structure alleviate these problems? How could people from different disciplines contribute to solving them? What could the person do given the particular situational constraints involved?

**Social Policy Issues**

7. Suggest as many ways as possible in which income levels affect the lives of elderly persons. What social policy and personal measures would you advocate to ensure adequate income levels among the elderly?

8. How do the interests of young and older workers coincide and conflict? Do you think a labor market policy that medi-

ated the interests of younger workers, older workers, and employers could be developed? Why or why not?

9. How are the health interests of the young and the old linked? Where do you think the greatest potential for improving the health of the elderly lies? How do biomedical, life-style, and social structural levels fit?

10. Would you favor adopting national insurance, a national health service, health maintenance organizations, or some other plan for ensuring cost effectiveness, access, and quality of care in meeting the health needs of the population? What are the potential advantages or disadvantages of each of these plans?

11. If you had to live in a nursing home as a resident, what would you want out of life there? How could the independence of future generations of the elderly be maximized both in the community and in institutions?

**The Response**

12. Outline an integrated policy for meeting the needs for workers in gerontology over the next few decades. Consider projected needs, training, and ways of encouraging an interdisciplinary approach.

13. Is there anything you plan to do, as a result of this course, to improve the life chances for your own old age?

# Pertinent Readings

Administration on Aging. Occasional Papers in Gerontology. *Human Resource Issues in the Field of Aging: The Nursing Home Industry.* Washington, D.C.: U.S. Government Printing Office, 1980.

Back, K. W. "Transition to Aging and the Self-Image." In *Normal Aging II,* ed. E. Palmore, pp. 207–16. Durham, N.C.: Duke University Press, 1974.

Binstock, R. "Reframing the Agenda of Policies of Aging." In *Readings in the Political Economy of Aging,* eds. M. Minkler and C. L. Estes, pp. 157–67. Farmingdale, N.Y.: Baywood Publishing Company, Inc., 1984.

———. "The Oldest Old: A Fresh Perspective on Compassionate Ageism Revisited." *Milbank Memorial Fund Quarterly* 63, 2 (1985): entire issue.

Birren, J. E. "Background and Issues in Training." 1971 White House Conference on Aging. Washington, D.C.: U.S. Government Printing Office, 1971.

Bonnheim, R. "Human Insulin." *Diabetes Forecast* (1982).

Brown, E. R. "Medicare and Medicaid: The Process, Value and Limits of Health Care Reforms." In *Readings in the Political Economy of Aging,* eds. M. Minkler and C. L. Estes, pp. 117–43. Farmingdale, N.Y.: Baywood Publishing Company, 1984.

Bureau of Labor Statistics. *Industry-Occupational Matrix.* Washington, D.C.: U.S. Government Printing Office, 1984.

Bultena, G. L., and E. A. Powers. "Denial of Aging: Age Identification and Reference Group Orientation." *Journal of Gerontology* 33, 5 (1978): 748–54.

Chen, Y. P. "Economic Status of the Aging." In *Handbook of Aging and the Social Sciences,* eds. R. Binstock and E. Shanas, pp. 641–65. New York: Van Nostrand Reinhold Company, 1985.

Clark, P. G. "The Social Allocation of Health Care Resources: Ethical Dilemmas in Age-Group Competition." *The Gerontologist* 25, 2 (1985): 119–25.

DeBeauvoir, S. *The Coming of Age.* Trans. P. O'Brian. New York: Warner Paperback Library, 1973.

Estes, C. L., L. E. Gerard, and M. Minkler. "Reassessing the Future of Aging Policy and Politics." In *Readings in the Political Economy of Aging,* eds. M. Minkler and C. L. Estes, pp. 270–74. Farmingdale, N.Y.: Baywood Publishing Company, Inc., 1984.

———, et al. *Political Economy, Health and Aging.* Boston: Little, Brown & Company, 1984.

Fein, R. "Social and Economic Attitudes Shaping American Health Policy." In *Economics and Health Care,* ed. J. B. McKinlay, pp. 51–57. Cambridge, Mass.: The MIT Press, 1981.

Feinlieb, M. "Gaps Close, But Not All the Way." *New York Times* (February 17, 1985): E-5.

Foundations Project. "Foundations for Gerontological Education." *The Gerontologist* 20, 3, Pt. II (1980): entire issue.

Freeland, M. S., and C. E. Schendler. "Health Spending in the 1980s: Integration of Clinical Practice Patterns with Management." *Health Care Financing Administration Review* 5, 3 (1984): 1–68.

Fries, J. F. "Aging, Natural Death, and the Compression of Morbidity." *The New England Journal of Medicine* 303, 3 (1980): 13–135.

———, and L. M. Crapo. *Vitality and Aging: Implications of the Rectangular Curve.* San Francisco: W. H. Freeman & Company, 1981.

Garrity, T. F., and M. B. Marx. "The Relationship of Recent Life Events to Health in the Elderly." In *Dimensions of Aging,* eds. J. Hendricks and C. D. Hendricks, pp. 98–113. Cambridge, Mass.: Winthrop Publishers, Inc., 1979.

Gergen, K. J. "The Emerging Crisis in Life-Span Developmental Theory." In *Life-Span Development and Behavior,* eds. P. B. Baltes and O. G. Brim, Jr., pp. 31–63. New York: Academic Press, Inc. 1980.

Gerontological Society of America. *Emerging Issues in Aging.* Washington, D.C.: Gerontological Society of America (in press).

Hampson, J. "Elderly People and Social Welfare in Zimbabwe." *Ageing and Society* 5, 1 (1985): 39–67.

Harrington, C. "Public Policy and the Nursing Home Industry." In *Readings in the Political Economy of Aging,* eds. M. Minkler and C. L. Estes, pp. 144–54. Farmingdale, N.Y.: Baywood Publishing Company, Inc., 1984.

Hunter, T. "The Proteins of Oncogenes." *Scientific American* 251, 2 (1984): 70–79.

Kahl, A., and D. E. Clark. "Health: Crossroads Over the Horizon?" *Occupational Outlook Quarterly* 29, 2 (1985): 4–11.

Kane, R. L., et al. *Geriatrics in the United States: Manpower Projections and Training Considerations.* Santa Monica: The Rand Corporation, 1980.

Kastenbaum, R., et al. "The Ages of Me: Toward Personal and Interpersonal Definitions of Functional Aging." In *Being and Becoming Old*, ed. J. Hendricks, pp. 71–85. Farmingdale, N.Y.: Baywood Publishing Company, Inc., 1980.

Kelman, S. "The Social Nature of the Definition of Health." In *Health and Medical Care in the U.S.: A Critical Analysis*, ed. V. Navarro, pp. 3–20. Farmingdale, N.Y.: Baywood Publishing Company, Inc., 1975.

Keith, J. *Old People as People*. Boston: Little, Brown & Company, 1982.

Knowles, L. "Gerontological Nursing." *International Journal of Nursing Studies* 20, 1, (1982): 45–54.

Kuhn, M. "Challenge to a New Age." In *Readings in the Political Economy of Aging*, eds. M. Minkler and C. L. Estes, pp. 10–22. Farmingdale, N.Y.: Baywood Publishing Company, Inc., 1984.

Light, P. *The Politics of Social Security Reform*. New York: Random House, 1985.

Little, V. *Open Care for the Aging*. New York: Springer Publishing Company, 1982.

Machol, L. "Postmenopausal Osteoporosis: New Approaches to Prevention." *Contemporary Obstetrics and Gynecology*, 20, 2 (1982): 153–61.

Marshall, V. "Societal Toleration of Aging: Sociological Theory and Social Response to Population." In *Adaptability and Aging 1*. Paris: International Center of Social Gerontology, 85–104, 1981.

———. "Dominant and Emerging Perspectives in the Social Psychology of Aging." In *Later Life: The Social Psychology of Aging*, ed. V. Marshall. Beverly Hills, Calif.: Sage Publications, Inc. (in press).

Mills, C. Wright. *The Sociological Imagination*. New York: Oxford University Press, 1959.

Minkler, M., and C. L. Estes, eds. *Readings in the Political Economy of Aging*. Farmingdale, N.Y.: Baywood Publishing Company, Inc., 1984.

Munnell, A. H. "The Social Security Solution, Cont.: Navigating a Few Rough Spots Ahead." *New York Times* (August 12, 1984): F-3.

Myers, J. E., and Blake, R. H. "Employment of Gerontological Counseling Graduates: A Follow-up Study." *The Personnel and Guidance Journal* 62, 6 (1984): 333–35.

National Association of Social Workers. *News* 28, 10 (1983): 6–7.

National Institute on Aging. "Senility Reconsidered: Treatment Possibilities for Mental Impairment in the Elderly." *Journal of the American Medical Association* 244, 3 (1980): 259–63.

———. *Report on Education and Training in Geriatrics and Gerontology*. Washington, D.C.: National Institute on Aging, 1984.

Palmore, E., et al. "Stress and Adaptation in Later Life." *Journal of Gerontology* 34, 6 (1979): 841–51.

Plutchok, J. "IRAs — Where To Put the Money." *New York Times* (March 10, 1985): F-11.

Reich, J. W., and A. Zautra. "Daily Event Causation: An Approach to Elderly Life Quality." *Journal of Community Psychology* 12, 4 (1984): 312–22.

Robinson, P. K., S. Coberly, and C. E. Paul. "Work and Retirement." In *Handbook of Aging and the Social Sciences*, eds. R. Binstock and E. Shanas, pp. 503–27. New York: Van Nostrand Reinhold Company, 1985.

Rosow, I. *Socialization to Old Age*. Berkeley: University of California Press, 1974.

Schulz, J. H. *The Economics of Aging*. Belmont, Calif.: Wadsworth Publishing Company, 1985.

Selby, P., et al. *Aging 2000: A Challenge for Society*. Boston: The MIT Press, 1982.

Sigerist, H. *Medicine and Human Welfare*. New Haven, Conn.: Yale University Press, 1941.

Skyler, J. S. "Human Insulin of Recombinant DNA Origin: Clinical Potential." *Diabetes Care* 5, Suppl. 2 (1982): 181–86.

Storey, J. R. *Older Americans in the Reagan Era: Impacts of Federal Policy Changes*. Washington, D.C.: The Urban Institute Press, 1983.

Tibbitts, C., H. Friedsam, P. Kerschner, G. Maddox, and H. McClusky. *Academic Gerontology: Dilemmas of the 1980s*. Ann Arbor: Institute of Gerontology, University of Michigan, 1980.

Tolley, G. S., and R. V. Burkhauser. "Federal Economic Policy Toward the Elderly." In *Social Policy, Social Ethics and the Aging Society*, eds. B. L. Neugarten and R. J. Havighurst, pp. 45–53. Washington, D.C.: National Science Foundation, 1977.

United Nations. *Questions of the Elderly and the Aged: Conditions, Needs and Services, and Suggested Guidelines for National and International Action*. No. A/9126. New York: United Nations, 1973.

U.S. Bureau of the Census. *Projections of the Population of the United States by Age, Sex, and Race: 1983–2080*. Current Population Reports, Series P-25, No. 952. Washington, D.C.: U.S. Government Printing Office, 1984.

U.S. Department of Health and Human Services. *Nursing and Related Care Homes*. Series 14, No. 29. Washington, D.C.: U.S. Government Printing Office, 1983.

———. *Trends in Nursing and Related Care Homes and Hospitals, United States, Selected Years, 1969–80*. Series 14, No. 30. Washington, D.C.: U.S. Government Printing Office, 1984.

U.S. Senate. "Training Needs in Gerontology." 93d Cong., 1st Sess. Washington, D.C.: U.S. Government Printing Office, 1973.

———. "Developments in Aging: 1974 and January–April, 1975." 94th Cong., 1st Sess. Washington, D.C.: U.S. Government Printing Office, 1975.

U.S. Senate Special Committee on Aging. *Developments in Aging: 1984*, vol. 1. Washington, D.C.: U.S. Government Printing Office, 1985.

Waldo, D. R., and H. C. Lazenby. "Demographic Characteristics and Health Care Use and Expenditures by the Aged in the United States: 1977–1984." *Health Care Financing Review* 6, 1 (1984): 1–29.

Walker, A. "Community Care and the Elderly in Great Britain: Theory and Practice." In *Readings in the Political Economy of Aging*, eds. M. Minkler and C. L. Estes, pp. 73–93. Farmingdale, N.Y.: Baywood Publishing Company, Inc., 1984.

Ward, R. A. "The Impact of Subjective Age and Stigma on Older Persons." *Journal of Gerontology* 32, 2 (1977): 227–32.

Weinberg, R. A. "Oncogenes." *Ca—A Cancer Journal for Clinicians* 33, 5 (1983).

Zautra, A. J., and J. W. Reich. "Life Events and Perceptions of Life-Quality: Developments in a Two-Factor Approach." *Journal of Community Psychology* 11, 1 (1983): 121–32.

# GLOSSARY

**Achieved status** An achieved social position attained as a result of one's efforts, as opposed to an *ascribed status*, which is attributed to one as part of some aspect of an individual's identity that is beyond his or her control (e.g., sex, familial relations).

**Acute conditions** Those illnesses marked by rapid onset, definite crisis, and self-limiting aftermath. Usually brought on by exogenous factors that result in a traumatic course. Acute illnesses most frequently afflict individuals in the first half of life.

**Age changes** Age-related change occurring over time as a result of intrinsic factors.

**Age cycle effect** The general age-based patterning of events for members of a cohort as they grow older; for instance, education, entry into the labor force, labor force participation, and exit from the labor force.

**Age differences** Differences between people of diverse ages often attributed to the effects of the aging process but which may in fact result from non-age factors.

**Age distribution** Descriptive statistical measure of the proportionate age mix in a population.

**Ageism** Negative or pejorative image of and attitudes toward an individual simply because he or she is old. The extent to which the public in general holds a negative view toward the elderly is questionable, though in the past it may have been more extensive.

**Age grading** The assignment of a series of successive statuses, with varying degrees of prestige, on the basis of age. For example, age grades in a tribal society might include warriors and elders.

**Age norms** Guidelines of age-appropriate behavior within a given complex of roles. Age norms provide a general definition of acceptable behavior but do not supply detailed stipulations for each and every possible performance.

**Age-specific life expectancy** The number of years that, based on statistical probability, one might expect to live at a given age. For instance, the life expectancy for a black woman of fifty-nine in 1981 was twenty-one years. Age-specific life expectancies change as social and environmental conditions change.

**Age-status asynchronization** An inconsistency that develops when relative criteria employed in different social spheres do not reflect similar standing in terms of age. Asynchronization results in role conflict and ambiguous definitions of appropriate behavior.

**Aging effects** Consequences of aging per se, in contrast to cohort or period effects.

**Anticipatory socialization** Learning the obligations, expectations, and rights associated with a new role preparatory to actually assuming it. Throughout most of life an implicit component of most roles is preparation for subsequent roles. Such ongoing preparation makes adjustment much easier.

**Ascriptive status** or **ascribed status** A social position that accrues to one as part of one's identity and is beyond one's control, for instance, woman or uncle, as opposed to *achieved* status, which one attains as a result of one's efforts.

**Atherosclerosis** Thickening of interior walls of arteries (intima) from deposits containing cholesterol and other fatty substances.

**Birth cohorts** Aggregation of people born in any given time period and thus passing through the same historical events at roughly the same age.

**Carotid arteries** The major blood vessels on each side of the neck that carry the oxygen-rich blood on its route from the heart to the brain.

**Cell necrosis** Death of a cell.

**Chronic conditions** Lacking in specifiable etiology, chronic diseases involve endogenous systemic disruptions that do not run a short-term course. Because they involve a number of body functions, the chronic diseases that older people suffer from most frequently are usually resistant to cure.

**Chronological age** Age as measured by calendar time since birth.

**Cohort** As used by demographers, cohort refers to all those persons born during some specified period or passing through age-related changes at approximately the same historical time (for instance, the class of 1987).

**Cohort analysis** Study of age-related changes based on data obtained by following a particular cohort or cohorts of people over a number of years, for instance, an analysis of age-related changes in physical fitness based on a comparison of physical examinations of the same group of people at different ages.

**Cohort effects** Effects resulting from the properties of specific birth cohorts under consideration, such as relative size and structure, for instance, the influence of the large size of the baby boom cohort on the experience of its members.

**Consensual validation** Affirmation of personal characteristics reflected back to the actor in the course of social interaction.

**Cross-sectional or period analysis** Study of age-related changes based on a comparison of two or more age groups of people at the same period in time.

**Dementia** A state of mental deterioration caused by organic impairment and characterized by extreme forgetfulness and inability to reason.

**Dependency ratios Societal-dependency ratios** consist of the ratio of those who are not economically productive to those who are, and thus are a way of quantifying the number of those dependent on workers. **Age-dependency ratios** count all those below the legal age for labor force entry (fifteen or sixteen years; child dependency) and all those past the usual age for retirement (sixty-five years; aged dependency) as dependent and all those in the middle years as productive. **Economic-dependency ratios** are based on labor force participation (or nonparticipation) rather than age, and thus reflect the fact that many of the elderly work while many of the middle-aged do not.

**Domiciliary care** Outreach services, such as nursing, physical therapy, or home help, provided to individuals in their own homes.

**Ecological fallacy** The mistaken belief that statistical norms derived from the study of a population actually describe the characteristics of the individuals in that population.

**Endothelial lining** The layer of cells lining the arteries, heart, and lymphatic vessels.

**Entropy** A concept based on the second law of thermodynamics, which contends energy becomes increasingly unavailable over time.

**Environmental press** Challenges or demands made by the ecosystem that activate behavioral responses.

**Etiology** The study of the causes of disease.

**Extended care facility** Originally designated by Medicare legislation as requiring more extensive professional-level staff than a skilled nursing facility.

**Extended families** Families including three or more generations, generally in the same household or residential complex. Some researchers characterize family units composed of two separate nuclear families as extended.

**Fertility rate** Number of births per 1000 women of childbearing age in a given period.

**Filial responsibility** Care and respect of older family members, especially parents.

**Functional age** An indicator of age based on performance capacities rather than simply chronological age.

**Genome** Complete set of chromosomes found in higher orders of life.

**Gerontocracy** A political system in which the elders, by virtue of their age and wisdom, constitute the ruling group.

**Homeostasis** A state of maintaining equilibrium.

**Human capital** Store of individual attributes, such as education, that are commonly used to explain achieved status.

**Index of aging** A demographic measure of changing age composition in a particular population. Often calculated by comparing those persons over sixty-five with those under fifteen to reveal the extent to which the population is aging.

**Individual fallacy** Unwarranted generalization about the population on the basis of one's own individual experience.

**Infarction** Tissue death from obstruction of the blood supply to the area. A myocardial infarction refers to the death of heart muscle; a cerebral infarction to the death of brain tissue. May occur in any organ of the body.

**Institutional neurosis** Referred to as a form of psychological railroading, marked by such symptoms as an erosion of unique personality traits, increasing dependency, psychological distancing, and a decreasing attentiveness to external events. Some researchers attribute this neurosis to institutionalization and misplaced priorities of staff who fail to treat the elderly with appropriate respect and humane concern.

**In vitro** In an artificial environment — outside a living organism.

**Life expectancies** The average length of time individuals born at a particular point in history can reasonably expect to live.

**Life span** Maximum length of life possible for members of a species.

**Lipofuscin** Any one of a class of inert fatty pigments formed by the solution of pigment in fat; accumulates in old body cells (sometimes referred to as age or liver spots when appearing on back of hands, chest area, or temple region of the head).

**Lumen** Cavity or channel within a tube or tubular organ — interior of an artery.

**Morbidity** Any departure from complete physical well-being; the incidence of illnesses.

**Neurotransmission receptors** Chemical agent released, upon excitation, that crosses the synapse.

**Nuclear family** The conjugal family composed of parents and children living under one roof. The predominant form of family life today, as compared to the extended family *assumed* to be more common in the past in which the conjugal family as well as blood relatives from two or more generations lived under one roof. Modified extended families are still very much in evidence where two or more generations live in close proximity and maintain close contact, but do not live under one roof.

**Occlusion** Blockage of an artery.

**Oncogenes** Discrete bits of viral genetic material (DNA) that in themselves can transform some types of host cells into cancer cells.

**Ontogenetic** Relating to the intrinsic course of development of the individual organism, as opposed to *phylogenetic*, relating to the evolution of a group or race of organisms.

**Period effects** The changing historical and sociocultural conditions to which various cohorts are exposed as they move through the life cycle, for instance, the level of technology, state of the economy, wars, and political events.

**Personal care facility** A protected environment for persons who are generally independent in their daily activities but require some support or supervision.

**Pleiotropism** Genes that have a dual function, expressing more than one inherited characteristic.

**Post-fixed mitotic cells** Nondividing cell lines of the central nervous system, liver, and other organs.

**Presbyopia** Age-related changes in the elasticity of the crystalline lens of the eye resulting in farsightedness; an inability to change focal length.

**Proprioceptive** or **kinesthetic system** Somesthetic senses with receptors located throughout the body (soma) that send messages concerning touch, balance, and body position directly to the brain.

**Proto-oncogene** A normal gene that may be activated into becoming an oncogene.

**Rites of passage** Originally, the ceremonial rites marking transition from one social status to another. Presently used to refer to both explicit and implicit status passage that is denoted by some type of occasion.

**Scleral buckle procedure** An operative technique used to repair detachment of the retina (the sensory membrane that lines the eye and receives the images formed by the lens) from the sclera that forms the eyeball. A rubber band or "buckle" is anchored in such a way that the sclera is compressed against the retina and reattachment occurs.

**Senescence** The aging process, particularly in the second half of life, which results in increased vulnerability to displacing stimuli of any type.

**Senile dementia** *See* Dementia.

**Skilled nursing facility** Skilled nursing and/or skilled rehabilitative services furnished under the direction of a physician and requiring the skills of technical or professional personnel, such as an RN, LPN, licensed physical therapist, and speech therapist, who may either give direct care or supervise care by other personnel. An *intermediate care facility* is for persons with stable, chronic medical conditions requiring intermittent skilled services along with continuous supervision of activities of daily living.

**Social epidemiology (environmental) approach** Approach to the study of disease in which the role of environmental and life-style factors, such as smoking, diet, and obesity, in causing and perpetuating disease are examined.

**Social metapolicy** The general belief system and worldview underlying approaches to social policy, for instance, beliefs about human nature, the nature and purpose of society, and an individual's primary goals in life, that shape construction of social policy.

**Status displacement** Reduction in standing in occupational or social activities. Often results from age biases toward older workers.

**Symbolic interactionism** A sociological theory incorporating interpretative or symbolic meanings among individuals as they shape use and perception of objects or people.

**Systolic hypertension** High blood pressure from the contraction phase of the cardiac cycle. Indicated by the first sound heard on auscultation and by arterial pressure.

**Terminal drop** A decline in cognitive abilities thought by some researchers to occur just prior to death. Perhaps as a result of disruptions within the central nervous system, various investigators have noted a marked drop in intellectual functioning as death draws near.

**Thrombosis** Development of a thrombus or clot in a blood vessel or in one of the cavities of the heart caused by coagulation of the blood, which then remains at its point of formation.

**Welfare capitalism** Welfare administered by the state predicated on principles of private enterprise but also essential for the maintenance of the economic viability of the private sector. Based on programs of British social and economic reformers.

**Welfare state** Programs, expenditures, and subsidies administered by institutions of the government designed to achieve economic or social objectives for designated segments of the population.

# INDEX

*No Author Index*

Activity theory of aging, 89–90
Acute conditions, 158
Affective disorders, 231–233
Age-appropriate behavior, 31–33
Age cycle effect, 43
Age-dependency ratios, 43–44, 65–67, 510
Age differences, 8
Age discrimination, 329–332, 474–476
Age Discrimination in Employment Act, 329–330, 475
Age grading, 30–31
Age norms, 31
Age-status asynchronization, 32–33
Age stratification theory of aging, 95–100
Age structure of population, 14, 17, 38–44, 57–65, 70
Ageism, 34–38
Aging
  in advanced industrial society, 57–70
  attitudes toward, history of, 53–57
  functional capacity and, 141–147
  in historical periods, 44–53
  interpersonal relations and, 511–514
  levels of, 4–5
  metapolicy of, 494–496
  nature of, 5–6, 29–30
  physiology of (*see* Biological theories of aging)
  projections, 507–511
  prospect of, 511–514
  psychology of, 202–203
  in Third World, 70–72, 407–413
Alcohol abuse, 180–181, 236

Alzheimer's disease, 137, 239–240, 523
American Association of Retired Persons, 427, 428
American Indians (*see* Native Americans)
Anticipatory socialization, 35, 84, 333
Arthritis, 174
Asian Americans, 397–400
  Chinese, 401–403
  Filipino, 405–407
  immigration of, 400–401
  Japanese, 403–405
Atherosclerosis, 127, 166–169
Audition, 205–206

Baby boom, 11, 19, 67
Biological theories of aging
  cellular theories, 132–135
  cross-linkage theory, 140
  free radical theory, 138–140
  immunological theory, 137
  molecular theories
    error theory, 136
    program theory, 136–137
    somatic mutation, 135–136
  neuroendocrine theory, 137
  rate of living theory, 130
  stress theory, 131
  waste product theory, 138–140
Birth cohorts, 17
Black Americans
  demographic characteristics, 380–381
  experience of aging, 382–384
  health, 384–385
  social situation, 385–386

Cancer, 172–174
Cardiovascular accidents, 171–172
Cardiovascular diseases
  atherosclerosis, 166–169
  cardiovascular accidents, 171–172
  heart disease, 169–171
  hypertension, 172
Career development
  psychologically oriented, 324
  sociologically oriented, 323–324
Career patterns, 322–323, 324–326,
    511, 513
Cellular theories of aging, 132–135
Cerebrovascular accidents, 171–172
Chinese Americans, 401–403
Chronic conditions, 158
Chronological age, 30, 40
Cognitive functioning
  creativity, 219–221
  and death, 217–219
  learning, 209–213
  metamemory, 209–213
  psychomotor response, 208–209
  reaction time, 208–209
  sensory memory, 209–213
Cohort, 8, 17, 19, 30, 97–100, 433
Cohort analysis, 42–43
Cohort effect, 43
Collagen, 140
Congregate living facilities, 280–288
Continuing education, 289–291
Continuity theory of aging, 92–94
Creativity, 219–221
Criminal victimization of elderly,
    294–297
Cross-linkage theory of aging, 140
Cross-sectional analysis, 42–43

Data, interpretation of (*see* Statistics)
Death, anticipation of, 299–300
Death with dignity, 491–492
Dementia, multi-infarct, 30, 156–157,
    237–238, 240
Dental problems, 175–176
Deoxyribonucleic acid, 135–136
Dependency ratios, 43–44, 62–63
Dependency theory, 109–110
Development in adulthood, 221–224
Diabetes mellitus, 174–175, 395

Diagnosis related groups, 188–192, 526
Discrimination, age, 329–332, 474–476
Diseases of elderly
  Alzheimer's disease, 137, 239–240,
    523
  arthritis, 174
  cancer, 172–174
  cardiovascular diseases
    atherosclerosis, 127, 166–169
    cerebrovascular accidents, 171–172
    heart disease, 169–171
    hypertension, 172
  dental, 175–176
  diabetes mellitus, 174–175
  rheumatism, 174
Disengagement theory of aging, 87–89
Domiciliary care homes, 283
Dual economy models, 111–114

Ecological fallacy, 8–9
Economic-dependency ratios, 43–44,
    510
Economy, changing, and labor
    patterns, 318–320
Ecosystem, 177
Education, 290
  of minorities, 379
Employment, 474–476 (*see also* Work)
Entropy, 126, 129
Environment and health, 181–183
Epidemiology, social, 153–154
Error theory of aging, 136
Exercise, 185
Expenses of elderly, 359–360
Extended care facilities, 283, 286
Extended family, 255

Family relations
  abuse, 269–270
  conflict, 269–270
  interaction, 259–261, 267–276
  modernization, 266–267
  patterns, 255–259
  separation, 263–265
  sexual functioning, 271–276
  widowhood, 257–258, 263–265
Filial responsibility, 254
Filipino Americans, 405–407
Finances (*see* Income)

Fiscal policies and elderly
employment, 474–476
Individual Retirement Accounts, 474,
516
private pension provisions, 472–473
Social Security, 462–472, 510,
515–518
Supplemental Security Income, 472
Free radical theory of aging, 138–140
Friendships, 291–292
Functional age, 30
Functional capacity, 141–146

Gerontocracy, 401
Gerontological Society, 22, 23
Gerontology, social
activity theory, 89–90
advancement of, 21–22
age stratification theory, 95–100
careers in
academic, 534
counseling, 533
health professions, 535–536
nursing, 534
nursing home personnel, 534–535
physicians, 535
social work, 536
continuity theory, 92–94
Depression and, 15–17, 19
development, 17, 20–23, 514
disengagement theory, 87–89
focus, 22–23
historical foundations, 20–21
incentives, 14–15
modernization theory, 100–103
political economy, 108–114
scope, 17, 20–23
social environmental theories,
103–108
subcultural theory, 90–93
theory, role in, 81–86
training, 536–538
Gray Panthers, 430, 444–445

Health
conceptualization of, 154–156
definition of, 157–158
factors affecting
alcohol, 180–181

Health (cont.)
factors affecting (cont.)
emotions, 186
environment, 181–183
exercise, 185
longevity, 178–179
nutrition, 183–185
tobacco, 179–180
levels of analysis, 156
mental, 225–229 (see also Mental
disorders)
of minorities, 374–375
perspectives on, 153–154
problems (see Diseases of elderly)
and rectangularization of life curve,
159–160
social factors affecting, 157
sociocultural conceptualizations,
156–157
sociocultural context, 176–178
Health care
cost effectiveness, 187–188
cost containment, 188–192,
483–487, 525–527
policies
development of, 476–479, 527–531
Medicaid, 482–483, 487–490
Medicare, 187–193, 479–482,
487–490
private options, 490–491
Hearing, 205–206
Heart disease, 169–171
Hispanic Americans
demographic characteristics, 387–390
experience of aging, 390–392
profile of, 387–390
Housing, 493–494
Hypertension, 172

Immunological theory of aging, 137
Income
expenditures of elderly, 359–360
indicators of, 351–354
of minorities, 375, 376, 378
patterns of, 354–357
satisfaction and, 357–359
Index of aging, 44, 62
Indians (see Native Americans)
Individual fallacy, 9

Individual Retirement Accounts, 474, 516

Industrial Revolution, 53

Industrialized societies, aging in, 57–70
 labor patterns, 318–320, 330, 338–341
 morbidity and mortality patterns, 160–165

Infarction, 168

Institutionalization, 283–285

Institutional neurosis, 284

Intelligence
 death and, 217–219
 multidimensionality of, 214
 testing, 214–217

Internal colonialism, 111

Japanese Americans, 403–405

Kinesthetic sensitivity, 204–205

Learning, 209–213

Legal services, 492

Leisure
 education, 289–291
 friendships, 291–292
 pursuits, 289
 volunteer work, 292–294

Life expectancy, 38–40, 41–53, 58, 73, 159
 increases in, 67–69, 179
 and life-style factors, 179–186

Life satisfaction
 and health, 186
 and retirement, 321–322

Life span, 42

Life-style
 alcohol abuse, 180–181
 emotions, 186
 environmental factors, 181–183
 exercise, 185
 and functional variability, 144–146
 and longevity, 178–179
 nutrition, 183–185
 sociocultural context, 176–178
 tobacco abuse, 179–180

Lipofuchin, 138–139

Longevity, 178–179 (*see also* Life expectancy)

Medicaid, 482–483, 487–490

Medicare, 187–193, 479–482, 487–490

Medication and mental functioning, 242–243

Memory, 209–213

Mental disorders
 affective, 230–233
 Alzheimer's disease, 137, 239–240, 523
 multi-infarct dementia, 30, 156–157, 237–238, 240
 neurotic, 233–235
 psychotic, 235
 self-destructive behaviors, 235–237
 treatment
  medication, 242–243
  psychotherapy, 243–244

Metamemory, 209

Minorities, 370–372 (*see also* specific minority groups)
 economic disadvantages, 359–360, 375
 health of, 374–375
 and labor market, 347–350, 375–379

Modernization theory of aging, 100–103

Molecular theories of aging
 error theory, 136
 program theory, 136–137
 somatic mutation, 135–136

Morbidity and mortality, patterns of, 160–165
 of Native Americans, 394

Multi-infarct dementia, 30, 156–157, 237–238, 240

National Association of Retired Federal Employees, 427, 428

National Council on Aging, 427, 428, 429

National Council on Senior Citizens, 427, 428

Native Americans
 experience of aging, 393–395
 profile of, 392–393
 social issues, 393–397

Neuroendocrine theory of aging, 137

Neurotic disorders, 233–235

Nursing homes, 281–283, 528–530

Nutrition and diet, 183–185

Old Age Assistance Act, 463, 464, 492
Organic brain syndromes
    Alzheimer's disease, 137, 239–240,
      523
    multi-infarct dementia, 30, 156–157,
      237–238, 240

Pensions, private, 472–473
Period analysis, 42–43, 100
Period effect, 43
Personal care homes, 283
Philippines (*see* Filipino Americans)
Physiological function and age,
    141–147
Physiological theories of aging (*see*
    Biological theories of aging)
Physiology
    and social context, 128
    and sociological factors, 126–128
Political arena, age groups in, 423–425
Political attitudes, aging and, 431–435
    party affiliation, 435
    social issues and, 435–437
Political economy
    dependency theory, 109–110
    dual economy models, 111–114
    internal colonialism, 111
Political future of elderly, 443–446
Political participation, 438–443
Politics
    nature of, 421
    structure of, 421–422
Population
    age-dependent, 65–67
    age structures, 14, 17, 38–44, 41–42,
      57–65, 70
    distribution of elderly by family
      status, 262
    elderly families, 261–262
    expansion of elderly, 69–70
    future trends, 507–511
    historical trends
      classical antiquity, 46–49
      colonial America, 51–52
      Middle Ages, 49–51
      modern era, 52–53
      prehistoric period, 45–46
      Renaissance, 49–51

Population (*cont.*)
    male-female ratio, 258
    minority elderly, percentage of,
      372–374
Poverty levels, 352–353
    of minorities, 375–378
Program theory of aging, 136–137
Psychogenic mental disorders
    affective, 230–233
    neurotic, 233–235
    psychotic, 235
    self-destructive behaviors, 235–237
    treatment, 241–244
Psychological development
    alternative models, 223–224
    sex roles, 224–225
    stage theories, 221–223
Psychological disorders (*see* Mental
    disorders)
Psychomotor response, 208–209
Psychosis, 235
Psychotherapy, 243–244

Rate of living theory of aging, 130
Reaction time, 208–209
Rectangularization of life curve, 40,
    141, 158–160
Religion, role of, 297–299
Relocation, 278–280
Retirement
    compulsory, 319, 475–476
    individual approach, 320–321,
      335–337
    structural approach, 321–322, 337
Retirement communities, 280–281
Rheumatism, 174
Rites of passage, 33–34
Role allocation, 98

Self-image, 332–335, 513
Senescence, 29, 147
Senile dementia, 30, 137
Sensory functioning
    audition, 205–206
    kinesthetic sensitivity, 204–205
    smell, 203–204
    taste, 203–204
    threshold, 204
    visual acuity, 206–207
Sensory memory, 211–213

Separation, 263–265
Sex roles, 224–225, 229, 513
Sexuality
    incidence, 272–273
    interest, 272–273
    response cycles, 273–276
Skilled nursing facilities, 283
Smoking, 179–180
Social environmental theories, 103–108
Social metapolicy, 455
Social movements and elderly, 422–431
Social policy and elderly
    approaches to, 456
    constituency concerns, 457–458
    death with dignity, 491–492
    housing, 493–494
    issues, 514–531
    legal services, 492
    and lifeworld, 458–459
    metapolicy, 459–462
    multiple levels, 454–455
    problems, 456–457
    relationship between individual and
        society, 455–456
    social services, 492–493
Social Security
    expansion, 465–466
    future of 469–472, 515–518
    implementation, 462–464
    payroll taxes, 510
    retrenchment, 466–469
Social Security Act, 15, 22, 24
Social Security Amendments, 479, 516
Social services, 492–493
Socialization, 98
Somatic mutation theory of aging,
    135–136
Spanish Americans (see Hispanic
    Americans)
Stage theories of development,
    221–223
Statistics
    adequacy of, 10
    generalizability of, 13–14
    interpretation of, 7–13
Status
    achieved, 6, 100
    ascriptive, 100, 424
    displacement, 100

Stereotypes of elderly, 4, 13, 24,
    35–37, 326–328
Stress theory of aging, 131
Subcultural theory of aging, 90–93
Suicide rates, 235–236
Supplemental Security Income, 470,
    472
Symbolic interactionism, 90
Theory, 81–86
Temporal orientation, 300–302
Terminal drop in cognitive abilities,
    217–219
Third World
    aging in, 70–72, 407–413
    morbidity and mortality patterns in,
        161
    population structure in, 70
Thrombosis, 168
Tobacco, 179–180

Unemployment rates, 328–332,
    343–345

Visual acuity, 206–208
Volunteer work, 292–294
Voting patterns, 438–443

Waste product theory of aging,
    138–140
Welfare capitalism, 457
Welfare state, 458
Widowhood, 257–258, 263–265

Work
    age discrimination, 329–332,
        474–476
    future, 517–520
    individual approach, 320–321
    in Japan, 341–342
    minorities and, 347–350, 375–379
    self-image and, 332–335
    in Soviet Union, 342
    status displacement, 328–329
    stereotypes of older workers,
        326–328
    structural approach, 321–322
    in Western countries, 338–341
Working women, 321, 343–347, 513,
    519